The Death of Jesus

Tradition and Interpretation in the
Passion Narrative

by

Joel B. Green

WIPF & STOCK · Eugene, Oregon

Wipf and Stock Publishers
199 W 8th Ave, Suite 3
Eugene, OR 97401

The Death of Jesus
Tradition and Interpretation in the Passion Narrative
By Green, Joel B.
Copyright©1988 Mohr Siebeck
ISBN 13: 978-1-61097-128-7
Publication date 5/1/2011
Previously published by Mohr Siebeck, 1988

"This edition reprinted 2011 by Wipf and Stock through special arrangement with J.C.B. Mohr (Paul Siebeck). Copyright J.C.B. Mohr (Paul Siebeck) 1987".

To Pamela

Preface

Proclamation of the crucified Messiah is always close at hand when one attempts even the most cursory articulation of the Christian faith. Viewed simultaneously as scandal and eschatological turning-point the cross of Christ is the cornerstone of Christian faith and praxis. This is not to say that the crucifixion of Jesus has at all times and in all places been subjected to a single interpretation by Christian believers. Already in the dawning years of the Christian movement Jesus' disciples understood his death in numerous ways, utilizing a variety of images. This study takes as its primary points of departure the prominence of the cross-event for Christians and the variety of its interpretations. Here we seek a partial answer to the question how earliest Christianity understood the death of Jesus. A full resolution of this problem would greatly swell what is already a lengthy essay, so we have restricted ourselves to only one aspect of the larger question – namely, the significance of Jesus' death as witnessed in the narrative of Jesus' passion. It is hoped that this investigation will be followed by others which together may treat this whole issue more comprehensively.

Originally this study took the form of a 1985 University of Aberdeen dissertation, and the years of study thus represented accrued a rather sizeable debt I can only begin to repay through this vote of thanks: above all, to Pam, my wife, and Aaron and Allison, our two children – whose many sacrifices constitute no mean gift of love: to Professor I. Howard Marshall – my doctoral supervisor and Christian brother; to Dr. Paul Ellingworth – who turned his critical eye to the whole of part one and made a number of beneficial comments; to Greg Cootsona – who interacted with me at some length on the contents of chapter four; and to Allister and Jane Strachan and Diane Clarke – who provided invaluable services in the preparation of this project. A large number of individuals, groups, and churches contributed to a scholarship fund set up by the Pleasant Mound United Methodist Church, Dallas, Texas. For their support, the administrative work of Pat Culver, and the oversight of Chuck Cox, Richard Dunagin, Mike Harms, and Mike Walker, I am most grateful. To the trustees of A Foundation for Theological Education, who awarded me a John Wesley Fellowship, and to the trustees of the John H. Moore Fellowship, I owe this final word of appreciation for their encouragement and financial assistance. While they must not be held responsible for what is written herein I am conscious that the undertaking and completion of this project would have remained no more than a dream without the encouragement received from these many persons.

June 1988
Joel B. Green

Contents

Preface v
Contents vii
Abbreviations xi
Introduction: The Cross: Historical Event and Interpretive Problem 1

Part One:

The Existence and Shape of an Early Passion Narrative

Chapter One: The Problem of a Pre-Canonical Passion
   Narrative: *Forschungsbericht* and Methodology 9
     I. *Forschungsbericht* 9
     II. Methodology 14

Chapter Two: The Relationship between the Canonical Passion
   Narratives: 1. The Gospel of Matthew 20
     I. Introduction 20
     II. Redaction in the Matthean Passion Narrative 20
     III. Conclusion 23

Chapter Three: The Relationship between the Canonical Passion
   Narratives: 2. The Gospel of Luke 24
     I. Introduction 24
     II. Luke 22:1–2 (Mark 14:1–2) 25
     III. Luke 22:3–6 (Mark 14:10–11) 26
     IV. Luke 22:7–13 (Mark 14:12–16) 27
     V. Luke 22:14–20 (Mark 14:17, 22–25) 28
     VI. Luke 22:21–23 (Mark 14:18–21) 43
     VII. Luke 22:24–27 (Mark 10:41–45) 44
     VIII. Luke 22:28–30 (Matt 19:28) 46
     IX. Luke 22:31–34 (Mark 14:26–31) 48
     X. Luke 22:35–38 50
     XI. Luke 22:39–46 (Mark 14:26, 32–42) 53
     XII. Luke 22:47–54a (Mark 14:43–53) 58
     XIII. Luke 22:54b–62 (Mark 14:53–64, 66–72) 61

viii   *Contents*

     XIV. Luke 22:63–65 (Mark 14:65)......................66
      XV. Luke 22:66–71 (Mark 14:53b, 55–64; 15:1)...........68
     XVI. Luke 23:1–5 (Mark 15:1b–5).......................77
    XVII. Luke 23:6–12..................................80
  XVIII. Luke 23:13–25 (Mark 15:6–15)...................82
     XIX. Luke 23:26–32 (Mark 15:20b–21)..................86
      XX. Luke 23:33–38 (Mark 15:22–32a, 36) 90
     XXI. Luke 23:39–43 (Mark 15:32b) ·94
    XXII. Luke 23:44–46 (Mark 15:33–38) 95
  XXIII. Luke 23:47–49 (Mark 15:39–41) 99
  XXIV. Luke 23:50–56a (Mark 15:42–16:1).................101
   XXV. Conclusion 102

Chapter Four: The Relationship between the Canonical Passion
Narratives: 3. The Gospel of John............................105
       I. Introduction 105
     II. Three "Test Cases" for a Johannine-Synoptic Literary
          Relationship within the Passion Narrative.............106
    III. The Shape of the Johannine Passion Narrative 128
    IV. Conclusion 133
     V. The Relationship between the Canonical Passion
         Narratives: Summary.............................134

Chapter Five: Mark and His Gospel: Redactional Procedure and
Literary Plan..136
       I. Introduction 136
     II. Mark the Evangelist – A Conservative Redactor? 137
   III. The Relationship between Mark 1–13 and 14–16 148

Chapter Six: The Passion in the Early Church: Form-Criticism
Revisited..157
       I. Introduction 157
     II. W. H. Kelber and the Markan Passion Narrative..........158
   III. The Implicatins of Narrative Coherence 160
   IV. Jesus' Death in Earliest Christianity 164
     V. The "Suffering/Vindication" Genre and a Pre-Canonical
         Passion Narrative................................169
   VI. Summary 173

Chapter Seven: The *Sitz im Leben* for the Early Passion
Narrative..175
       I. Introduction 175
     II. Early Christian Instruction 176

III.	Early Christian Missinary Preaching	182
IV.	Early Christian Worship	187
V.	Concluding Remarks	214
Summary		216

Part Two:

The Significance of Jesus' Death in the Passion Narrative

Chapter Eight: Jesus' Suffering and Death in the Passion
Narrative..221
      I. Introduction..221
     II. Conspiracy and Anointing...........................223
    III. The Supper Scene..................................234
    IV. Three Prophecies..................................244
     V. Prayer in Gethsemane..............................253
    VI. The Arrest..263
   VII. Peter's Denial and Jesus before the Sanhedrin........271
  VIII. Jesus before Pilate................................283
    IX. Jesus' Crucifixion and Death.......................292
     X. Final Matters......................................311

Chapter Nine: Jesus' Death in the Passion Narrative:
Thematic Overview..314
      I. Jesus' Death Interpreted in the Passion Narrative.........314
     II. The Passion Narrative and Atonement-Theology..........320

Appendix..324

Index of Passages..331

Abbreviations

I. General

Whenever applicable abbreviations of primary and secondary materials follow those listed in *JBL* 95 (1976) 331–346; and Joseph A. Fitzmyer, *The Dead Sea Scrolls: Major Publications and Tools for Study; with an Addendum (January 1977)* (Missoula, Montana: Scholars, 1977) 1–8. Otherwise, the following are employed:

MHT	Moulton, James Hope; Howard, Wilbert Francis; and Turner, Nigel. *A Grammar of New Testament Greek.* 4 vols. Edinburgh: T. & T. Clark, 1906–76.
NIDNTT	Brown, Colin, ed. *The New International Dictionary of New Testament Theology.* 3 vols. Grand Rapids, Michigan: Zondervan, 1975–78.
RefTRev	*Reformed Theological Review.*
TDOT	Botterweck, G. Johannes, and Ringgren, Helmer, eds. *Theological Dictionary of the Old Testament.* 4 vols. Grand Rapids, Michigan: Wm. B. Eerdmans, 1974–80.
TWOT	Harris, R. Laird; Archer, Gleason L.; and Waltke, Bruce K., eds. *Theological Wordbook of the Old Testament.* 2 vols. Chicago: Moody, 1980.
TynB	*Tyndale Bulletin.*

II. Symposia, Essay Collections, and *Festschriften*

Abba	Jeremias, Joachim, *Abba: Studien zur neutestamentlichen Theologie und Zeitgeschichte.* Göttingen: Vandenhoeck & Ruprecht, 1966.
Advance	Fitzmyer, Joseph A. *To Advance the Gospel: New Testament Essays.* New York: Crossroad, 1981.

Abbreviations

Apocalypse — Collins, John J., ed. *Apocalypse: The Morphology of a Genre.* Chico, California: Scholars, 1979.

Apostolic History — Gasque, W. Ward, and Martin, Ralph P., eds. *Apostolic History and the Gospel: Biblical and Historical Essays Presented to F. F. Bruce on His 60th Birthday.* Exeter: Paternoster, 1970.

Authoritative Word — McKim, Donald, ed. *The Authoritative Word: Essays on the Nature of Scripture.* Grand Rapids, Michigan: Wm. B. Eerdmans, 1983.

Botschaft — Dibelius, Martin. *Botschaft und Geschichte.* Vol. 1. Edited by Günther Bornkamm. Tübingen: J. C. B. Mohr (Paul Siebeck), 1953.

Christ the Lord — Rowdon, Harold H., ed. *Christ the Lord: Studies in Christology Presented to Donald Guthrie.* Downers Grove, Illinois: InterVarsity, 1982.

Christological Perspectives — Berkey, Robert F., and Edwards, Sarah A., eds. *Christological Perspectives: Essays in Honor of Harvey K. McArthur.* New York: Pilgrim, 1982.

Crucified Messiah — Dahl, Nils Alstrup. *The Crucified Messiah and Other Essays.* Minneapolis, Minnesota: Augsburg, 1974.

Das Evangelium — Stuhlmacher, Peter, ed. *Das Evangelium und die Evangelien: Vorträge vom Tübingen Symposium 1982.* Tübingen: J. C. B. Mohr (Paul Siebeck), 1983.

Einheit — Lohse, Eduard. *Die Einheit des Neuen Testaments.* Göttingen: Vandenhoeck & Ruprecht, 1973.

Essays — Moule, C. F. D. *Essays in New Testament Interpretation.* Cambridge: Cambridge University, 1982.

Évangelica — Neirynck, Frans. *Évangelica. Gospel Studies – Études D'Évangile: Collected Essays.* Edited by F. van Segbroeck. Leuven: Leuven University, 1982.

Évangile de Jean — de Jonge, M., ed. *L'Évangile de Jean: Sources,*

	Rédaction, Théologie. Leuven: Leuven University, 1977.
Évangile selon Marc	Sabbe, M., ed. L'Évangile selon Marc: Tradition et Rédaction. Leuven: Leuven University, 1974.
Experience	Bornkamm, Günther. Early Christian Experience. London: SCM, 1963.
Gospel Perspectives	France, R. T., and Wenham, David, eds. Gospel Perspectives. Sheffield: JSOT. Vol. 1: Studies of History and Tradition in the Four Gospels, 1980. Vol. 2: Studies of History and Tradition in the Four Gospels, 1981. Vol. 3: Studies in Midrash and Historiography, 1983.
God's Christ	Jervell, Jacob, and Meeks, Wayne, eds. God's Christ and His People: Studies in Honour of Nils Alstrup Dahl. Oslo: Universitetsforlaget, 1977.
Griesbach	Orchard, Bernard, and Longstaff, Thomas R. W., eds. J. J. Griesbach: Synoptic and Text-Critical Studies 1776–1976. Cambridge: Cambridge University, 1978.
Ideal Figures	Collins, John J., and Nickelsburg, George W., eds. Ideal Figures in Ancient Judaism: Profiles and Paradigms. Chico, California: Scholars, 1980.
Interpretation of Matthew	Stanton, Graham, ed. The Interpretation of Matthew. Philadelphia: Fortress, 1983.
Jesus	Dahl, Nils Alstrup. Jesus in the Memory of the Early Church. Minneapolis, Minnesota: Augsburg, 1976.
Jesus and Gospel	Benoit Pierre. Jesus and the Gospel. Vol. 1. London: Darton, Longman and Todd, 1973.
Jesus and Hope	Jesus and Man's Hope. Vol. 1. Pittsburgh: Pittsburgh Theological Seminary, 1970.
Jesus and Paul	Hengel, Martin. Between Jesus and Paul: Studies in the Earliest History of Christianity. Philadelphia: Fortress, 1983.
Jesus and Politics	Bammel, Ernst, and Moule, C. F. D., eds. Jesus and the Politics of His Day. Cambridge: Cambridge University, 1984.
Jesus und Paulus	Ellis, E. Earle, and Grässer, Erich, eds. Jesus und Paulus: Festschrift für Werner Georg

	Kümmel zum 70. Geburtstag. 2d ed. Göttingen: Vandenhoeck & Ruprecht, 1978.
John	Charlesworth, James H., ed. *John and Qumran.* London: Geoffrey Chapman, 1972.
Lukas	Schneider, Gerhard. *Lukas, Theologe der Heilsgeschichte: Aufsätze zum lukanische Doppelwerk.* Bonn: Peter Hanstein, 1985.
Luke-Acts	Talbert, Charles H., ed. *Luke-Acts: New Perspectives from the Society of Biblical Literature Seminar.* New York: Crossroad, 1984.
Messianic Secret	Tuckett, Christopher, ed. *The Messianic Secret.* Philadelphia: Fortress, 1983.
More Studies	Dodd, C. H. *More New Testament Studies.* Manchester: Manchester University, 1968.
Neotestamentica et Semitica	Ellis, E. Earle, and Wilcox, Max, eds. *Neotestamentica et Semitica: Studies in Honour of Matthew Black.* Edinburgh: T. & T. Clark, 1969.
New Light	Burkhill, T. A. *New Light on the Earliest Gospel.* London: Cornell University, 1972.
New Synoptic Studies	Farmer, William R., ed. *New Synoptic Studies: The Cambridge Gospel Conference and Beyond.* Macon, Georgia: Mercer University, 1983.
NT Age	Weinrich, William C., ed. *The New Testament Age: Essays in Honor of Bo Reicke.* 2 vols. Macon, Georgia: Mercer University, 1984.
NT Apocrypha	Hennecke, Edgar. *New Testament Apocrypha.* 2 vols. Edited by Wilhelm Schneemelcher. Philadelphia: Westminster, 1963/65.
NT Essays	Higgins, A. J. B., ed. *New Testament Essays: Studies in Memory of Thomas Walter Manson.* Manchester: Manchester University, 1959.
NT Interpretation	Marshall, I. Howard, ed. *New Testament Interpretation: Essays on Principles and Methods.* Grand Rapids, Michigan: Wm. B. Eerdmans, 1977.
NT Language	Elliott, J. K., ed. *Studies in New Testament Language and Text: Essays in Honour of George D. Kilpatrick on the Occasion of His Sixty-fifth Birthday.* Leiden: E. J. Brill, 1976.

NT Themes	Käsemann, Ernst. *Essays on New Testament Themes*. London: SCM, 1964.
NT und Kirche	Gnilka, Joachim, ed. *Neues Testament und Kirche: Für Rudolf Schnackenburg*. Freiburg: Herder, 1974.
Orientierung	Hoffmann, Paul, ed. *Orientierung an Jesus. Zur Theologie der Synoptiker: Für Josef Schmid*. Freiburg: Herder, 1973.
Oxford Studies	Sanday, William, ed. *Oxford Studies in the Synoptic Problem*. Oxford: Clarendon, 1911.
Passion in Mark	Kelber, Werner H., ed. *The Passion in Mark: Studies on Mark 14–16*. Philadelphia: Fortress, 1976.
Perspectives – Luke-Acts	Talbert, Charles H., ed. *Perspectives on Luke-Acts*. Edinburgh: T. & T. Clark, 1978.
Perspectives – Mark	Petersen, Norman R., ed. *Perspectives on Mark's Gospel*. Missoula, Montana: Scholars, 1980.
Redaktion und Theologie	Limbeck, Meinrad, ed. *Redaktion und Theologie des Passionsberichtes nach den Synoptikern*. Darmstadt: Wissenschaftliche, 1981.
Political Issues	Cassidy, Richard J., and Scharper, Philip J., eds. *Political Issues in Luke-Acts*. Maryknoll, New York: Orbis, 1983.
Prophecy and Hermeneutic	Ellis, E. Earle. *Prophecy and Hermeneutic in Early Christianity: New Testament Essays*. Tübingen: J. C. B. Mohr (Paul Siebeck), 1978.
Rechtfertigung	Friedrich, Johannes; Pöhlmann, Wolfgang; and Stuhlmacher, Peter, eds. *Rechtfertigung: Festschrift für Ernst Käsemann zum 70. Geburtstag*. Tübingen: J. C. B. Mohr (Paul Siebeck), 1976.
Reconciliation and Hope	Banks, Robert, ed. *Reconciliation and Hope: Essays on Atonement and Eschatology Presented to L. L. Morris on His 60th Birthday*. Grand Rapids, Michigan: Wm. B. Eerdmans, 1974.
Rückfrage	Kertelge, Karl, ed. *Rückfrage nach Jesus: Zur Methodik und Bedeutung der Frage nach den historischen Jesus*. Freiburg: Herder, 1974.
Ruf Jesu	Lohse, Eduard, ed. *Der Ruf Jesu und die Antwort der Gemeinde: Exegetische Untersuchungen Joachim Jeremias zum 70. Geburtstage*

	gewidmet von seinen Schülern. Göttingen: Vandenhoeck & Ruprecht, 1970.
Sabbath	Carson, D. A., ed. *From Sabbath to Lord's Day*. Grand Rapids, Michigan: Zondervan, 1982.
Studien	Richter, Georg. *Studien zum Johannesevangelium*. Edited by Josef Hainz. Regensburg: Friedrich Pustet, 1977.
Studies	Morris, Leon. *Studies in the Fourth Gospel*. Exeter: Paternoster, 1969.
Suffering and Martyrdom	Horbury, William, and McNeil, Brian, eds. *Suffering and Martyrdom in the New Testament: Studies Presented to G. M. Styler by the Cambridge New Testament Seminar*. Cambridge: Cambridge University, 1981.
Tod Jesu	Kertelge, Karl. ed. *Der Tod Jesu: Deutungen im Neuen Testament*. Freiburg: Herder, 1976.
Trial of Jesus	Bammel, Ernst, ed. *The Trial of Jesus: Cambridge Studies in Honour of C. F. D. Moule*. London: SCM, 1970.
Werder und Wirken	Albertz, Rainer; Müller, Hans-Peter; Wolff, Hans Walter; and Zimmerli, Walther, eds. *Werder und Wirken des Alten Testaments: Festschrift für Claus Westermann zum 70. Geburtstag*. Göttingen: Vandenhoeck & Ruprecht, 1980.

Introduction

The Cross: Historical Event and Interpretive Problem

Jesus of Nazareth was crucified under Pontius Pilate — concerning the facticity of this event there can be little question. On this point five lines of evidence converge. Not only is it (1) recounted in remarkable detail in the four canonical Gospels[1], and (2) referred to as an historical event at numerous points by the various authors of the NT materials, but (3) it is also unmistakably attested in *The Annals* of the Latin historian Tacitus[2]. Additionally, (4) it is apparent from Christian and non-Christian sources of the apostolic and post-apostolic eras that it was precisely the offense of the shameful nature of Jesus' death, by crucifixion as a common criminal, that Christianity's opponents seized upon by way of discrediting the claims made by Christians on behalf of their Lord, and that those Christians had to overcome if their faith was to be credible and their mission successful[3]. Finally, (5) as A. E. Harvey has emphasized, inasmuch as the statement *crucifixus est sub Pontio Pilato* was incorporated into the ancient creeds of the church, by including an historical event in their confession, early Christians, living little more than a century after the cross-event, gave testimony to their conviction that the crucifixion of Jesus was an historical fact no one could possibly deny[4]. For these reasons the death of Jesus on the cross can be looked upon as an historical occurrence with virtual certainty[5].

---

1 Martin Hengel (*Crucifixion in the Ancient World and the Folly of the Message of the Cross* [Philadelphia: Fortress, 1977] 25) notes that the passion narratives in the Gospels are the most detailed crucifixion accounts available to us from the ancient world.
2 Tacitus, *Ann.* 15.44. Jesus' sentencing by Pilate and his crucifixion are also mentioned in Josephus, *Ant.* 18.64, but this reference is found in a paragraph that speaks so positively of Jesus Christ in his life, death, and resurrection that it is under suspicion as a Christian interpolation — see Hans-Ruedi Weber, *The Cross: Tradition and Interpretation* (London: S.P.C.K., 1979) 14–15; Louis H. Feldman, "The *Testimonium Flavianum*: The State of the Question", in *Christological Perspectives*, 179–199.
3 Cf. Hengel, *Crucifixion*, esp. pp. 1–21, 84–85. See further below, chapter 6.
4 A. E. Harvey, *Jesus and the Constraints of History* (Philadelphia: Fortress, 1982) 11.
5 G. A. Wells (e.g. *The Historical Evidence for Jesus* [Buffalo, New York: Prometheus, 1982]) is practically alone in denying this conclusion, along with his denial of the very existence of the man Jesus. He argues that Christian testimonies to the existence of Jesus are worthless in that they are faith-statements, and that non-Christian historians only reported what Christians believed to have been the case. In effect, he dismisses as tendentious the sum total of evidence

However, "not every event possesses an immediately clear and unavoidable meaning within its own context"[6]. The crucifixion of Jesus surely fits into this category, for to claim for it historical *certitude* hardly begins to answer the question concerning its historical *significance*. Indeed, only to treat Jesus' death as an historical incident is to be left, with Cleopas and his companion on the Emmaus-road, in puzzlement.

For early Christianity, as viewed through the pages of the NT, the cross of Jesus was capable of a variety of interpretations[7]. Of these, the most central to the NT materials is the interpretation of the crucifixion as the decisive saving event[8]. Indeed, in his recent monograph, *The Atonement*, Martin Hengel has argued that the soteriological interpretation of Jesus' death as a vicarious, atoning sacrifice belongs to the earliest stratum of Christian thought and, ultimately, is to be traced back to Jesus' own understanding of his death. By way of introducing and setting the agenda for our own contribution to understanding how Jesus' death was interpreted in earliest Christianity it will be helpful to review Hengel's seminal work.

Hengel's study is divided into two major sections — the first of which is concerned to demonstrate the points of conceptual contact between the message of the atoning death of Jesus and categories of thought and expression current in the Greco-Roman world of the first century A.D. Part two,

---

supporting the existence of Jesus. Ultra-skepticism of this kind would disallow any knowledge of antiquity. However, Wells has failed to give an adequate alternative account for the rise of Christianity and the rise of an opposition to Christianity — both of which took seriously the existence of an earthly Jesus — in history. For a more positive reading of the evidence, see Gary R. Habermans, *Ancient Evidence for the Life of Jesus: Historical Records of His Death and Resurrection* (Nashville: Thomas Nelson, 1984).

6 Wolfhart Pannenberg, *Jesus – God and Man* (London: SCM, 1968) 246.
7 See the variety of emphases noted in, e.g., Gerhard Delling, *Der Kreuzestod in der urchristlichen Verkündigung* (Göttingen: Vandenhoeck & Ruprecht, 1972); Gerhard Friedrich, *Die Verkündigung des Todes Jesu im Neuen Testament* (Neukirchen-Vluyn: Neukirchener, 1982); Karl Kertelge, ed., *Der Tod Jesu: Deutungen im Neuen Testament* (Freiburg: Herder, 1976); Hans Kessler, *Die theologische Bedeutung des Todes Jesu: Eine traditionsgeschichtliche Untersuchung* (Düsseldorf: Patmos, 1970); Jürgen Roloff, "Anfänge der soteriologischen Deutung des Todes Jesu", *NTS* 19 (1972–73) 38–64; Peter Stuhlmacher, *Versöhnung, Gesetz und Gerichtigkeit: Aufsätze zur biblischen Theologie* (Göttingen: Vandenhoeck & Ruprecht, 1981); Weber, *Cross*.
8 See esp. Robert J. Daly, *The Origins of the Christian Doctrine of Sacrifice* (Philadelphia: Fortress, 1978); Martin Hengel, *The Atonement: The Origins of the Doctrine in the New Testament* (Philadelphia: Fortress, 1981) — an expansion of his earlier article, "The Expiatory Sacrifice of Christ", *BJRL* (1979–80) 454–475; Eduard Lohse, *Märtyrer und Gottesknecht: Untersuchungen zur urchristlichen Verkündigung vom Sühntod Jesu Christi*, 2d ed. (Göttingen: Vandenhoeck & Ruprecht, 1963); I. Howard Marshall, "The Development of the Concept of Redemption in the New Testament", in *Reconciliation and Hope*, 153–169; Leon Morris, *The Apostolic Preaching of the Cross*, 3d ed. (Leicester: Inter-Varsity, 1965); *idem, The Cross in the New Testament* (Grand Rapids, Michigan: Wm. B. Eerdmans, 1965); Rudolf Pesch, *Das Abendmahl und Jesu Todesverständnis* (Freiburg: Herder, 1978); Vincent Taylor, *The Atonement in New Testament Teaching*, 2d ed. (London: Epworth, 1945); Frances Young, *Sacrifice and the Death of Christ* (London: S.P.C.K., 1975; reprint ed., London: SCM, 1983).

The Cross

with which we are more directly concerned, is constructed as an inquiry into the origin of the soteriological interpretation of Jesus' death. As point of departure Hengel turns to the Pauline formulae and pre-Pauline traditions, for "[these materials] bring us closest in time and content to the earliest preaching of the primitive community to which we have access"[9]. Among the relevant data he discerns two basic forms of expression, each with its own tradition-history. On the one hand is the "surrender formula" (e.g. Rom 4:25; 8:32; Gal 1:4; 2:20; et al.). On the other, Hengel refers to a "dying formula", best known for its expression in 1 Cor 15:3b: Χριστὸς ἀπέθανεν ὑπὲρ τῶν ἁμαρτιῶν ἡμῶν (cf. Rom 5:6, 8; Gal 2:21; 1 Thess 5:9–10; et al.). These traditions, being pre-Pauline in origin, assure us that the soteriological interpretation of Jesus' death ("for us") can be traced back at least as far as the earliest Greek-speaking Christian community.

Rejecting the views that the "righteous sufferer" and the "martyr prophet" are adequate categories for explicating the fundamental meaning of Jesus' passion, and the view that the resurrection/exaltation was justification for holding Jesus to be God's Messiah, Hengel goes further to underscore the importance for his inquiry of the fact that it was *the Christ* who had died, according to the ancient formulae and the Markan passion narrative. He argues that the ancient theme, the crucifixion of Jesus *as the Messiah*, would have required that atoning and sacrificial significance be accorded Jesus' death in the earliest community in order for the expression "the cross of Christ" to be acceptable to Jewish Christians. Thus, Christians in Jerusalem rejected the temple cult and replaced the cycle of atoning sacrifices associated with the temple with the universal, once-for-all, atoning death of Jesus. This interpretation of Jesus' death is traced back through the ransom-logion and Last Supper-sayings (Mark 10:45 and 14:24, respectively) to Isa 52:13–53:12. From whence did this message arise in earliest Christianity? Hengel does not regard this as an alien intrusion into Christianity from the Hellenistic world, but traces its roots to Jesus himself: "It was not primarily their own theological reflections, but above all the interpretative sayings of Jesus at the Last Supper which showed them how to understand his death properly"[10].

While our brief survey of *The Atonement* is inadequate to lay out in full the complexity of Hengel's argument, it is sufficient as a basis for raising a number of programmatic observations. In the first instance, the brevity of Hengel's study does not allow for a full defense of his position. Some of his conclusions — particularly those having to do with the backgrounds of Mark 10:45 and 14:24 in Isa 53 — unpopular in certain contem-

---

9 Hengel, *Atonement*, 34.
10 Hengel, *Atonement*, 73.

porary, critical circles, will require further substantiation. Second, one wonders if the hiatus between parts one and two of *The Atonement* is historically justified. That is, must a study of the origins of the soteriological interpretation of Jesus' death circumvent possible Hellenistic influence to the degree Hengel implies? Third, we must ask whether Hengel's choice of the Pauline material as point of departure is sufficient to the task at hand. A query of this nature is especially apropos at those points at which Hengel asserts one, uniform, earliest interpretation of the relation between Jesus' death and the Christian understanding of salvation[11]. Do other texts outside the Pauline corpus have a claim to represent the thought of earliest Christianity and bear on our understanding of the significance attributed to Jesus' death in earliest Christian times?

In investigating the significance attached to Jesus' death in the primitive church — the wider agenda Hengel has set for himself in *The Atonement* — all of the relevant evidence must be given its full weight. It is precisely here, at the point of drawing too tightly the boundaries around what constitutes relevant evidence, that Hengel's monograph raises important questions for the student of early Christian thought. How do materials that seem to exhibit a variant understanding of the relation of Jesus' death and early soteriology fit into Hengel's schema? In fact, two substantial deposits of NT material deserve more attention in this regard than has been given hitherto.

On the one hand, whereas Hengel himself allows that the Petrine speeches of Acts contain "'archaic' material", he disallows the possibility that the soteriology of Acts, which emphasizes not the cross but the exaltation of Jesus as the decisive salvific event, rests on old tradition[12]. Indeed, elsewhere Hengel can only comment: "It is without doubt a serious failing that Luke does not take up the Pauline theology of the cross and that justification by faith alone without the works of the law takes very much a back place with him . . ."[13].

Of course, Hengel is not alone in his failure to come to terms adequately with the place of the Lukan soteriology within the development of early Christian thought. Modern students of Luke-Acts have been much more interested in the *content* of Luke's understanding of salvation — an interest that has resulted in a focus on the "Lukan soteriology" as though it were peculiar to Luke[14]. In fact, a complete investigation of the Lukan soterio-

---

11 Cf. Hengel, *Atonement*, 70–71.
12 Hengel, *Atonement*, 34. On his basically positive evaluation of Luke as an historian, see *idem, Acts and the History of Earliest Christianity* (London: SCM, 1979).
13 Hengel, *Acts*, 67.
14 See, e.g., Dom Jacques Dupont, *The Salvation of the Gentiles: Essays on the Acts of the Apostles* (New York: Paulist, 1979); James D. G. Dunn, *Unity and Diversity in the New Testament*

logy – its content, background, and place in the development of Christian thought – is lacking; nevertheless, enough evidence is at hand in the NT to suggest that the Lukan understanding of salvation is not unique to Luke and that it may date back to the dawning years of the Christian church and, perhaps, even to Jesus himself[15]. In short, anyone wishing to reconstruct the early Christian understanding of salvation must not overlook or dispense too readily with the testimony of Luke-Acts.

On the other hand, in view of long-standing opinions regarding the generally primitive character of the passion narrative it is surprising that Hengel has not dealt more fully with its understanding of Christ's death. Can it be integrated into the schema defended in *The Atonement*? Hengel himself believes that ". . . [Mark] took over a much earlier account in his passion narrative"[16]; presumably, however, he is convinced that the theology of Mark 14–15 is nonetheless that of the Second Evangelist. Is such a conclusion justified? Is it possible to get to an earlier (i.e. pre-canonical) understanding of Jesus' passion via an investigation of the passion stories passed down to us? Hengel denies that the categories of "righteous sufferer" and "martyr prophet" are adequate for interpreting Jesus' death, but what if these are precisely the categories employed in an ancient, pre-canonical passion narrative, as some have argued?

In point of fact, the passion narratives, because of the nature of their portrayal of Jesus' death, confront us with an intriguing problem which, itself, can be divided into three interrelated questions: *(1) Was there an*

(Philadelphia: Westminster, 1977) 16–21; J. Massyngbaerde Ford, "Reconciliation and Forgiveness in Luke's Gospel", in *Political Issues*, 80–98; Richard Glöckner, *Die Verkündigung des Heils beim Evangelisten Lukas* (Mainz: Matthias-Grünewald, 1975); Michael Dömer, *Das Heil Gottes: Studien zur Theologie des lukanische Doppelwerkes* (Köln: Peter Hanstein, 1978); Kevin Giles, "Salvation in Lukan Theology", *RefTRev* 42 (1983) 10–16, 45–49; I. Howard Marshall, *Luke: Historian and Theologian* (Grand Rapids, Michigan: Zondervan, 1971) [hereinafter cited as *Luke*]; Ralph P. Martin, "Salvation and Discipleship in Luke's Gospel", *Int* 30 (4, 1976) 366–380; Robert F. O'Toole, *The Unity of Luke's Theology: An Analysis of Luke-Acts* (Wilmington, Delaware: Michael Glazier, 1984); Richard Zehnle, "The Salvific Character of Jesus' Death in Lucan Soteriology", *TS* 30 (1969) 420–444.

A similar note to that sounded here is registered with regard to recent redaction-critical work on the Gospel of Matthew in Graham Staton, "Introduction – Matthew's Gospel: A New Storm Centre", in *Interpretation of Matthew*, 10–11.

The debate concerning the authorship of Luke-Acts – and that of the other canonical Gospels – need not be entered into for the purposes of this study. Rather, our use of "Luke" as the author of the Third Gospel and the Acts of the Apostles, and of "Matthew", "Mark", and "John" as the authors of the First, Second, and Fourth Gospels, respectively, is a matter of expediency.

15 See the programmatic remarks in I. Howard Marshall, "The Resurrection in the Acts of the Apostles", in *Apostolic History*, 92–107; *idem, Luke*, 174–175; Joel B. Green, "The Death of Jesus, God's Servant," in *The Suffering and Death of the Lukan Jesus*, ed. Dennis Sylva (Bonn: Peter Hanstein, forthcoming).

16 Hengel, *Atonement*, 43.

early, pre-canonical passion narrative? (2) If so, how did it interpret Jesus' death? (3) Why is the atoning significance of Jesus' death not more prominent and pervasive in the passion story, if Hengel's reconstruction is even broadly correct?

In summary, then, two kinds of evidence may be set forth as having the potential to complicate Hengel's straightforward thesis concerning the earliest interpretation of Jesus' death as the saving event *par excellence* — namely, the soteriology of Luke-Acts and the understanding of Jesus' death in the passion narrative. In this study we propose to focus on only one of these areas of discussion, that concerning the narrative of Jesus' suffering and death. At the end of the day our results will not be as comprehensive as we might otherwise desire; however, the state of scholarship with respect to the problem of a pre-canonical passion narrative and the understanding of Jesus' death contained therein requires detailed analysis that precludes our embracing a further topic of debate, but which will itself constitute an important contribution to our understanding of the interpretation of Jesus' death in earliest Christian times.

Our study of the passion narrative will be undertaken under two major headings. The first will take up the initial question posed above — that dealing with the question of the existence and shape of an early passion narrative. The latter two questions noted earlier, having to do with the significance of the death of Jesus in the passion story, will be treated in part two.

Part One

The Existence and Shape of an Early Passion Narrative

Chapter One

The Problem of a Pre-Canonical Passion Narrative: *Forschungsbericht* and Methodology

I. *Forschungsbericht*

The last two decades have seen a growing body of literature debating the extent to which the evangelists, especially Mark, wielded their redactional pens in providing for their Gospels a passion narrative[1]. This new interest in the passion story follows on the heels of the advent of redaction-critical inquiry in the study of the Gospels, but its roots go deeper, into the work of the form-critics. Early in this century the trail-blazers of the form-critical method observed that the passion narrative was fundamentally distinct from the other Gospel materials, primarily due to its topographical and chronological coherence. Karl L. Schmidt, Martin Dibelius, and Rudolf Bultmann found agreement on the existence of a connected story of Jesus' suffering and death prior to the composition of the Gospels, even if they were at variance with one another on the questions of the exact content and boundaries of the early account, and of its *Sitz im Leben*. As for the latter issue Schmidt saw the story primarily in terms of its value as a martyr-tale, while Dibelius and Bultmann were both inclined to attribute its *Sitz im Leben* to the demands of early Christian preaching[2].

---

1 For surveys of the research, see Gerhard Schneider, "Das Problem einer vorkanonische Passionserzählung", *BZ* 2 (1972) 222–244; John R. Donahue, "From Passion Traditions to Passion Narrative", in *Passion in Mark*, 1–20; Detlev Dormeyer, *Die Passion Jesu als Verhaltensmodell* (Münster: Aschendorff, 1974) 1–23; Rudolf Pesch, *Das Markusevangelium*, vol. 2, 3d ed. (Freiburg: Herder, 1984) 7–10; Till Arend Mohr, *Markus- und Johannespassion: Redaktions- und traditionsgeschichtliche Untersuchungen der Markinische und Johanneischen Passionstradition* (Zürich: Theologischer, 1982) 11–44.

2 Karl L. Schmidt, *Der Rahmen der Geschichte Jesu: Literarkritische Untersuchungen zur Aeltesten Jesusüberlieferung* (Berlin: Trowitsche und Sohn, 1919; reprint ed., Darmstadt: Wissenschaftliche, 1964) 303–309. Martin Dibelius, *From Tradition to Gospel* (Cambridge: James Clarke, 1971) 22–23, 178–180; Rudolf Bultmann, *The History of the Synoptic Tradition* (Oxford: Basil Blackwell, 1963) 275. In addition, see Vincent Taylor, *The Formation of the Gospel Tradition* (London: Macmillan, 1949) 44–62. A number of commentators on Mark have taken over with little amendment the earlier, form-critical opinion that a continuous narrative of the passion must have already taken shape at an early date – e.g. C. E. B. Cranfield, *The Gospel according to Saint Mark* (Cambridge: Cambridge University, 1959) 412–462; Eduard Schweizer,

As early as 1922 one aspect of that early research was being questioned — namely, the *Sitz im Leben* of the narrative. Georg Bertram, later followed by Gottfried Schille, emphasized the role of worship in the development of the passion story[3]. However, the most basic premise of the form-critics — the early existence of a pre-canonical passion narrative — remained virtually unchallenged until the 1960s.

In the meantime study of the passion tradition did not lie dormant. In the early 1950s Wilfred L. Knox observed in the Markan story the alternation between the "disciples" and the "Twelve" and on this basis postulated a conflation of two sources in Mark[4]. An evolutionary, four-stage development was suggested by Joachim Jeremias. In his study of *The Eucharistic Words of Jesus* he argued that a *short account* of the passion narrative, beginning with Jesus' arrest, arose from an *early kerygmatic outline* (such as in 1 Cor 15:3—5). There followed a *long account*, narrating in close succession the triumphal entry, the temple cleansing, the questioning of Jesus' authority, the betrayal announcement, the Last Supper, Gethsemane, the arrest, and so on. Finally, the tradition was expanded to the *form found in the four Gospels*[5]. Vincent Taylor claimed to have uncovered two principal sources behind the Markan narrative: Source A — a straightforward, non-Semitic, summarizing complex such as might have been useful in a Roman Christian community; and Source B — a Semitic, vivid, self-contained narrative with supplementary details from Peter's reminiscences[6]. Inasmuch as Bultmann had already theorized about a developmental process behind the passion tradition, however, these subsequent attempts to account for the passion narrative constituted no radical departure from earlier form-critical study.

Even the dawn of redaction-critical research in Markan studies with the publication of Willi Marxsen's *Mark the Evangelist* marked no change. Marxsen observed:

The Good News according to Mark (Atlanta: John Knox, 1970) 284—363; D. E. Nineham, *The Gospel of Mark* (Harmondsworth: Penguin, 1963) 365—435; William L. Lane, *The Gospel according to Mark* (Grand Rapids, Michigan: Wm. B. Eerdmans, 1974) 485—581.

3 Georg Bertram, *Die Leidensgeschichte Jesu und der Christuskult: Eine formgeschichtliche Untersuchung* (Göttingen: Vandenhoeck & Ruprecht, 1922); Gottfried Schille, "Das Leiden des Herrn: Die evangelische Passionstradition und ihr 'Sitz im Leben' ", *ZTK* 52 (1955) 161—205.

4 Wilfred L. Knox, *The Sources of the Synoptic Gospels*, vol. 1: *St. Mark*, ed. H. Chadwick (Cambridge: Cambridge University, 1953) 115—147.

5 Joachim Jeremias, *The Eucharistic Words of Jesus* (Philadelphia: Fortress, 1966) 89—96. Similarly, see Eduard Lohse, *Die Geschichte des Leidens und Sterbens Jesu Christi* (Gütersloh: Gerd Mohn, 1964) 9—25.

6 Vincent Taylor, *The Gospel according to St. Mark*, 2d ed. (London: Macmillan, 1966; reprint ed., Grand Rapids, Michigan: Baker, 1981) 653—664; esp. p. 658. Taylor's theory was slightly revised by Sydney Temple, "The Two Traditions of the Last Supper, Betrayal, and Arrest", *NTS* 7 (1960—61) 77—85.

> The passion narrative admittedly represents the first stereotyped written unit in the tradition of Jesus. The tradition then developed backwards ... Mark thus prefixes the passion story with the tradition of Jesus, and prefixes that tradition with the tradition about the Baptist[7].

As we shall see, however, as a redaction critic Marxsen has hardly had the last word on the Markan passion account.

In 1963 Etienne Trocmé published his study of the formation of Mark's Gospel. Therein, and in his more recent analysis of the four canonical passion stories, he argued that chapters 1–13 and 14–16 of Mark so differed from one another that the "first edition" of Mark must have circulated without the last three chapters – i.e. the original edition lacked a passion and resurrection narrative. He also argued for a pre-canonical passion report originating in community worship, to which Mark 14–16 closely adheres[8].

To Johannes Schreiber belongs the distinction of being the first to develop the relationship of the passion story to the remainder of the Gospel as a unified whole. In his study of the crucifixion account Schreiber claimed he discerned two pre-Markan traditions – one historical, the other heavily influenced by Jewish apocalyptic. Schreiber attempted to show that it was Mark who first wove these two traditions into a single narrative[9]. A few years later, following up on Schreiber's thesis, Wolfgang Schenk extended these two traditions into the whole passion narrative. Schenk argued that in providing for his Gospel a passion narrative Mark brought together two existing traditions – the one with an apologetic purpose proving Jesus' innocence, the other an apocalyptic tradition[10].

In the meantime Eta Linnemann had concluded that there was *no* pre-canonical, connected narrative of Jesus' passion. In her *Studien zur Passionsgeschichte* she presented her case against the form-critical arguments for an earlier narrative, and, after studying selected pericopae in the Markan narrative, she argued that from beginning to end Mark's passion account was the composition of the evangelist. She did allow, however, that in constructing his passion story Mark had made use of a number of independent reports. Thus, Linnemann was of the opinion that the whole of the Gospel

---

7 Willi Marxsen, *Mark the Evangelist* (Nashville: Abingdon, 1969) 31. It is not surprising, then, that Marxsen quotes with approval (*Mark*, 30) the provocative statement of Martin Kähler (*The So-Called Historical Jesus and the Historic, Biblical Christ* [Philadelphia: Fortress, 1964] 80, n.11) that one could call the Gospels passion narratives with extended introductions.
8 Etienne Trocmé, *The Formation of the Gospel according to Mark* (London: S.P.C.K., 1975) 215–259; idem, *The Passion as Liturgy: A Study in the Origin of the Passion Narratives in the Four Gospels* (London: SCM, 1983).
9 Johannes Schreiber, *Theologie des Vertrauens: Eine redaktionsgeschichtliche Untersuchung des Markusevangeliums* (Hamburg: Rennebach, 1967) 22–82.
10 Wolfgang Schenk, *Der Passionsbericht nach Markus* (Leipzig: Gerd Mohn, 1974). For a summary of the two traditions, see Schenk, *Passionsbericht*, 272–274.

of Mark was the work of one redactor whose purpose was to show that the Crucified One was the Son of God[11]. A similar thesis — that the redactional work of Mark must have been the same throughout the Second Gospel — is presupposed in the collection of essays on *The Passion in Mark* edited by Werner H. Kelber[12].

Additional, minutely-detailed contributions to the problem of a pre-Markan passion story were published in the 1970s, first by Ludger Schenke, then by Detlev Dormeyer[13]. In 1971 Schenke authored a study of tradition and redaction in Mark 14:1–42 — a work that was followed in 1974 by a less extensive examination of the remainder of the Markan passion account. Utilizing literary-critical and tradition-historical tools Schenke concluded that the primitive passion story began with the Gethsemane scene and focused above all on the OT motif of the Suffering Righteous One by way of explaining the offense of a crucified Messiah. The present form of the passion narrative is the result of Mark's redaction of that pre-canonical account, together with his redaction and composition in the earlier section of his story for which there was no pre-Markan, connected narrative. Like Schenke, Dormeyer analyzed the Markan passion narrative with the aid of word statistics, while also bringing into the discussion points of style, form, genre, and theology. His study claims to have isolated the hand of three redactors: T — the oldest redactor whose narrative created a new genre, the "Christian Acts of Martyrs"; Rs — a secondary redactor who divided the work of T into separate scenes with independent dialogue, thus paving the way for the "Gospel" genre; and Rmk — the final redactor (Mark) who solidified the loose-fitting Rs into a self-autonomous narrative.

Most striking about this brief survey so far is the abundance of contradictions, the almost complete lack of consensus among the scholars, on a wide variety of issues: the age, scope, authorship, *Sitz im Leben*, and the nature of the passion tradition. Had a verse-by-verse comparison of the scholarly work been given the disagreement would have been even more pronounced. In the words of John Donahue, "the suggested divisions of the text of the Passion Narrative . . . encourage a fragmentation of the text which rivals

---

11 Eta Linnemann, *Studien zur Passionsgeschichte* (Göttingen: Vandenhoeck & Ruprecht, 1970).

12 This volume (*Passion in Mark*) *assumes* more than *proves* that Mark 14–16 is from beginning to end the handiwork of the evangelist who composed the earlier chapters. The dissertation of Frank J. Matera (*The Kingship of Jesus: Composition and Theology in Mark 15* [Chico, California: Scholars, 1982] credits the Second Evangelist with the composition of Mark 15.

13 Ludger Schenke, *Studien zur Passionsgeschichte des Markus: Tradition und Redaktion in Markus 14, 1–42* (Würzburg: Echter, 1971); idem, *Der gekreuzigte Christus: Versuch einer literarkritischen und traditionsgeschichtlichen Bestimmung der vormarkinische Passionsgeschichte* (Stuttgart: Katholisches, 1974); Dormeyer, *Passion Jesu: idem, Der Sinn des Leidens Jesu* (Stuttgart: Katholisches, 1979).

attempts early in this century to divide the Pentateuchal narrative into a multitude of J's, E's, and P's"[14]. The most recent scholarship on the subject appears less apt to engage the text in such minute, word-by-word decomposition and reconstruction, but diversity of opinion continues, as exemplified by three recent commentators on Mark.

Rudolf Pesch claims that current attempts to analyze Mark's passion story on literary-critical grounds have led down a cul-de-sac. Hence, he calls for a new methodological starting point that takes into account the character of Mark as a conservative redactor. Pesch's study underscores the theological and literary coherence of the passion narrative — which, he contends, embraces 8:27–33; 9:2–13, 30–35; 10:1, 32–34, 46–52; 11:1–23, 27–33; 12:1–17, 34c–37, 41–44; 13:1–2; 14–16. The whole is traditional, dating back to within the first decade of Christianity[15].

Walther Schmithals, however, regards Pesch's approach as "wissenschaftlich unhaltbar"[16]. According to the argument of his commentary, the present shape of the Markan passion narrative is primarily due to the redaction of the evangelist, though Schmithals lists a substantial number of verses as having derived from a *Grundschrift* (an asterisk [*] indicates a redactional intrusion into a traditional verse): 14:13–16, 22–25, 26–27, 29b–31, 32ab, 34b–36, 37*, 38–40, 41*, 43*, 46, 48–50, 53a, 54*, 66b–72; 15:1*, 3–11, 15, 22–24, 27, 29a, 31*, 32b, 34–37, 40–41, 42*, 43–47.

For his part, Joachim Gnilka is skeptical about the possibility of reconstructing a reliable pre-history of the passion story. He is nonetheless confident that a pre-canonical tradition underlies the Markan story, and he suggests that an early source embraced the contents of Mark 14:32–16:8[17].

Most recently, against the backdrop of confusion involved in the search for a text behind the text, Werner H. Kelber has argued that the evidence is best accounted for if Mark is credited with the composition of the bulk of the passion narrative. While agreeing with Pesch that the passion account is a literary unit not given to decomposition, Kelber asserts that form-critical presuppositions favoring a pre-canonical story are groundless. More-

---

14 Donahue, "From Passion Traditions", 15. Similarly, Werner H. Kelber (*The Oral and the Written Gospel* [Philadelphia: Fortress, 1983] 189) observes: "Without exaggeration, the stylistic, literary-critical decomposition of the passion text has led to a vast divergence of opinions on almost every single verse."

15 Pesch, *Mark*, 2:1–27. See also, *idem*, "Die Ueberlieferung der Passion Jesu", in *Rückfrage*, 148–173. Pesch has recently defended his view in his essay "Das Evangelium im Jerusalem: Mk 14, 12–26 als Aelteste Ueberlieferungsgut der Urgemeinde", in *Das Evangelium*, 83–156.

16 Walter Schmithals, *Das Evangelium nach Markus*, 2 vols. (Gütersloh: Gerd Mohn, 1979) 2:589; see 2:586–706.

17 Joachim Gnilka, *Das Evangelium nach Markus*, 2 vols. (Neukirchen-Vluyn: Neukirchener, 1978–79) 2:348–350.

over, he claims that an evolutionary development of the passion narrative is improbable in light of what we know about the development of the synoptic tradition. Hence, he concludes that Mark is the probable author of the first written passion narrative[18].

Our brief survey of works having to do with the possibility of a pre-canonical passion narrative has focused above all on attempts to get behind the Markan passion story to an earlier layer of tradition. As we will see, the passion narratives of Matthew, Luke, and John have also come under scrutiny in this respect, though not to the extent we have noted with the passion story of the Second Gospel[19]. Even so, it is now clear that the issues involved in the problem of a pre-canonical passion account are complex. No consensus of opinion exists from which we might proceed with our own interpretive agenda; hence, it will be necessary to consider anew the evidence and offer our own solution to the problem. In doing so we will adopt an approach readily distinguished from that pursued by such exegetes as Schenke and Dormeyer. The fact that this procedure, focusing above all on the Second Gospel, has led to such varying and, at times, even contradictory results may well be taken as an indicator that an alternative approach is better suited to the quest. At least in this respect there is wisdom in Pesch's (and Kelber's) argumentation.

II. Methodology

A. Introduction

The sort of agreement between the first three Gospels that gave rise to their being described as "synoptic" extends as well to the Fourth Gospel with the beginning of the passion narrative. It has been observed that with respect to the passion story the accounts of the four Gospels are in closer agreement than with any other portion of their contents. As Dibelius justifiably remarked:

> The Passion story is narrated by all four evangelists with a striking agreement never attained elsewhere. Even John, who deals freely enough with the facts reported by tradition, binds himself to this tradition in the highest degree when describing the Passion[20].

---

18 Kelber, *Gospel*, 185–199; esp. pp. 195–196. For stylistic reasons, Howard Clark Kee (*Community of the New Age: Studies in Mark's Gospel* [London: SCM, 1977]32) opts for a Markan-constructed passion story. See *idem*, "The Function of the Scriptural Quotations and Allusions in Mark 11–16", in *Jesus und Paulus*, 165–188; here he argues that chapters 11–13 and 14–16 use the OT in virtually the same way.
19 Studies more specifically focused on the Matthean, Lukan, and Johannine narratives will be noted in the respective chapters below.
20 Dibelius, *Tradition*, 179. Similarly, see Jeremias, *Eucharistic Words*, 89–90; Schwiezer, *Mark*, 284; Lohse, *Geschichte*, 11, 23–24; Nineham, *Mark*, 365; et al.

Methodology

After even a superficial perusal of a four-Gospel synopsis one might well be surprised if there were no literary relationship embracing all four passion accounts. Indeed, the question ought not be, Is there a relationship?, but, How is the relationship best explained? Does the evidence point directly to the conclusion, voiced by Lohse, ". . . dass es schon in sehr früher Zeit einen Bericht vom Leiden Jesu gebeben haben muss, der die einzelnen Stationen des Passionsweges anführte und das Geschehen beschrieb"[21]? Or is the evidence better explained with recourse to the hypothesis that one of the evangelists produced the first passion account, with the other three somehow dependent on that one, seminal work[22]?

The possibility of direct literary dependence by each Gospel on another (or others), on a pre-canonical narrative source, or on both, can be decided only in the context of a detailed comparison of the canonical accounts. Only then can we say, for example, whether John's passion story is a theological rewriting of Mark's, or whether Luke's passion narrative is a conflation of Mark 14–15 and a non-canonical, pre-Lukan *Quelle*.

B. The Work of Etienne Trocmé

A comparison of this kind has been attempted by Etienne Trocmé[23]. Beginning with Mark Trocmé restates in abridged form his conviction that chapters 1–13 enjoyed a separate existence from 14–16, the latter appended to the former by a later editor. In support of this thesis he insists that chapters 1–13 have no relationship with 14–16; in fact, there are a number of contraditions between these two parts of the Gospel. Further, one cannot appeal to the uniformity in style and vocabulary between chapters 1–13 and 14–16 since Mark had no distinctive literary style. Trocmé holds that there never occurred any real theological or literary fusion between the two sections of the Second Gospel.

Turning to the other Gospels Trocmé first shows that Matthew had at his disposal a copy of Mark with the appended passion narrative, along with a few midrashic traditions. Luke, on the other hand, possessed a copy of Mark without the appendix; thus, his passion narrative is not at all based on Mark's. However, parallels between the two narratives as we now read them indicate that there existed a common archetype behind Mark and Luke. In John one finds a greatly edited form of a continuous passion story built along the same lines as, but not based on, the Synoptic narratives.

---

21 Lohse, *Geschichte*, 11.
22 Cf. Linnemann, *Studien*, 54–69; Schneider, "Problem", 222, 229–231.
23 Trocmé, *Passion*, 7–46. On what follows, see Joel B. Green, review of *The Passion as Liturgy: A Study in the Origins of the Passion Narratives in the Four Gospels*, by Etienne Trocmé, in *EvQ* 56 (3, 1984) 185–188.

Trocmé concludes that the passion narratives of Mark, Luke, and John are each based on a common archetype, but do not share direct literary dependence.

Trocmé is certainly to be commended for his fresh and surprisingly detailed arguments. Nevertheless, at a few points his study is less than convincing, two of which deserve brief comment here. First, there is little to commend his theory that Mark 1–13 had an independent existence. Significantly, one finds no supportive textual evidence, nor are we told how Matthew, but not Luke, obtained a copy of the "revised edition" of the Second Gospel. Moreover, as will be shown below, Trocmé has largely overstated the evidence in completely denying a Markan redactional style and in his list of alleged contradictions between chapters 1–13 and 14–16[24]. Nor has he dealt adequately with the allusions to and predictions of the passion and resurrection in chapters 1–13 as they find their fulfillment in chapters 14–16 – to name only one important way in which the whole of Mark 1–16 has the appearance of a single, integrated work[25].

Second, Trocmé is not convincing in his attempt to show that Luke did not depend on Mark while composing his passion narrative. This is due not only to his inability to demonstrate that Luke made use of a copy of Mark without a passion-addendum, but also to his questionable reliance on statistical analysis. By comparing Markan and Lukan word usage pericope by pericope he fails to account for occasional word-for-word agreement wherein a direct literary relationship seems certain[26]. Additionally, his procedure leaves no room for the recognition of literary dependence without slavish copying – i.e. where Luke may have made extensive use of his own style and vocabulary while following Mark.

In fact, it is not too much to say that Trocmé's methodology, which relies heavily on dubious statistical analyses, constitutes the Achilles' heel of his study. His basic conclusion – that there was a pre-canonical, connected narrative underlying the passion accounts of Mark, Luke, and John – may be right; however, if that conclusion is to be upheld it must be given a more substantial underfooting. There is need, therefore, for a further comparative examination of the canonical passion narratives based on a more sound methodology.

---

24 See below, chapter 5; also the extended critique of Trocmé's book by T. A. Burkill, "The Formation of St. Mark's Gospel", in *New Light*, 180–264; esp. pp. 241–264. Trocmé is surely right to call into question certain exaggerated claims regarding Markan style. See now, however, Hubert Cancik, ed., *Markus-Philologie* (Tübingen: J. C. B. Mohr [Paul Siebeck],1984); Marius Reiser, *Syntax und Stil des Markusevangeliums* (Tübingen: J. C. B. Mohr [Paul Siebeck]; 1984).
25 See below, chapter 5.
26 See below, chapter 3.

Methodology is particularly important when comparing the Gospels of Mark and Luke, and we shall see that a combination of tools will provide the most secure results.

C. Assumptions

A comparative study of the nature we propose necessarily builds on judgments regarding the literary relationships of the Gospels. The question of the possible use of the Synoptic Gospels by John will be taken up when we consider the passion narrative of the Fourth Gospel, for it is in the context of the passion story that the Fourth Gospel is closest to the other three. As for the Synoptic Gospels, this study will presuppose the two-document hypothesis[27].

The focus of this study will be the passion stories of the four canonical Gospels. As we have shown elsewhere, the *Gospel of Peter*, while paralleling some of this material, does not give us direct access to a primitive passion account; its presentation of Jesus' suffering and death is largely dependent on the canonical Gospels[28]. Hence, we will not devote a full study to the *Gospel of Peter*, but will only refer to it occassionally by way of indicating how a certain theme has been further developed, or when it seems possible that it represents a primitive stratum of the passion material.

D. Word Statistics

We have already noted the methodological importance of word statistics in Trocmé's examination of the passion stories. By breaking the individual narratives into their constitutive pericopae he was able to formulate a percentage of Markan words used by Matthew and Luke in each subunit. Trocmé reasoned that dependence on Mark would be indicated by a relatively high percentage of word-for-word borrowing. That there is some validity to this approach to source criticism was suggested at the close of the nineteenth century when John C. Hawkins provided indications of the Gospels' sources based on statistical observations[29].

The weakness of this approach when turning to a study of the passion narratives, however, has been noted already in the examination of the

---

27 See Christopher M. Tuckett, *The Revival of the Griesbach Hypothesis: An Analysis and Appraisal* (Cambridge: Cambridge University, 1983); and my own defense of this position in "The Death of Jesus: Tradition and Interpretation in the Passion Narrative." (Ph.D. dissertation, University of Aberdeen, 1985) 43–59.
28 See my "The Gospel of Peter: Source for a Pre-Canonical Passion Narrative?"*ZNW* 78 (1987) 293–301.
29 John C. Hawkins, *Horae Synopticae: Contributions to the Study of the Synoptic Problem* (Oxford: Clarendon, 1899).

Lukan passion story by Vincent Taylor[30]. He observed that, when working pericope by pericope, or when dealing with the narrative as one unit, one will often be impressed by the low percentage of Markan words used by Luke, particularly as compared with the earlier parts of the Third Gospel. However, one might easily overlook the clusters of Markan words in such Lukan texts as 22:7—13, 50, 52; 23:3, 44—45. This certainly is an important observation, but there is a further issue both Taylor and Trocmé failed to detect, to the detriment of their respective studies — namely, the use of word statistics fails to acknowledge Luke's borrowing from Mark where Luke may be more freely editing his Gospel source. That is, one must allow fully for Luke's redactional interests — both stylistic and theological — in treating the question of Luke's sources. Before one may have recourse to a non-Markan source for the passion account one must deal with the possibility — at each point in the canonical narrative in question — that another canonical narrative has been rewritten, even extensively.

A third problem with the use of word statistics exists — the possibility that agreements in wording may stem from the use of a common source by two or more evangelists. So, for example, one might argue that the agreements in language between Mark and Luke in the passion narrative are due to their independent usage of a further source.

For these reasons, while we will not neglect the information provided by word statistics, especially where agreement or lack of agreement is overwhelming, our study will not be slavishly bound to this tool, and we will balance observations of this kind with additional findings.

E. Redaction Criticism

In mentioning the possibility of extensive rewriting we brought to the fore a second tool, redaction criticism. Under this heading we include literary- and style-criticism, as well as attention to the evangelist's theological interests. When an evangelist does not appear to have followed his canonical source(s) we must ask if that source has been rewritten only, or if a second tradition has been borrowed. By focusing on redactional style and vocabulary this tool can help direct such judgments. Moreover, if we suspect redactional work at a given point we may legitimately inquire whether this amendment serves the theological goals of the evangelist being studied.

One important proviso should be entered here, though we shall have occasion to mention it again in what follows: We will not assume that redaction and creation are necessarily synonymous. That is, we regard it

---

[30] Vincent Taylor, *The Passion Narrative of St. Luke: A Critical and Historical Examination* (Cambridge: Cambridge University, 1972) 31—33.

as methodologically suspect to jump from a decision that, say, Luke's redactional hand is evident in a given pericope, to the conclusion that Luke has created a story or some part of a story "from nothing".

F. Narrative Source or Independent Traditions?

Other methodological tools — such as form- and tradition-criticism—will be employed along the way, though none with the regularity of the two aforementioned. Before moving on to the study itself, however, a further decisive point must be stated explicitly. To decide for a separate *narrative source* the evidence must point to more than a simple re-working of a canonical account with the addition of a few, independent, unconnected traditions. That is, we must recognize the distinction between pre-canonical passion *materials* and a pre-canonical passion *narrative*. This issue raises its head in a most vexing way with respect to the Lukan passion narrative for there portions of the passion narrative are best explained with reference to non-Markan source material. But what kind of source(s)? Guidelines for making this decision are best discerned in the decision-making process itself, so, having raised this critical concern, we shall table further consideration of it until we begin drawing together the results of our exploration of the Lukan passion story.

G. The Contours of This Study

In view of the current state of affairs with regard to the study of a pre-canonical passion narrative our investigation must cast the net somewhat wider than has been the case heretofore, and draw our conclusions from a larger pool of evidence. We will make particular use of source-, redaction-, form-, and tradition-criticism, and have formulated our line of pursuit in view of the shape of the currect debate on the subject. Three primary issues will be taken up: (1) Do the First, Third, and Fourth Evangelists give evidence of a pre-canonical passion narrative (chapters 2–4); (2) Do the redactional procedure and literary plan of Mark provide any evidence for a pre-Markan passion narrative (chapter 5); and (3) Do form-critical arguments provide any conclusive testimony pertaining to a pre-canonical passion narrative (chapters 6–7)? Finally, a summary of our investigation of a pre-canonical passion narrative will be given. By following this outline we hope to offer a fresh argumentation that takes into account the full body of evidence relevant to our question.

Chapter Two

The Relationship between the Canonical Passion Narratives

1. The Gospel of Matthew

I. Introduction

Both with regard to content and structure the Matthean passion narrative is very closely modeled after the Markan. As to *vocabulary* and *content* it has been observed that four-fifths of the Matthean narrative is a recast of its Markan counterpart[1]. As to *structure* the only departure from Mark is Matthew's clearer definition of the termination of the Jewish "consultation" in Matt 27:1. This verse appears as an immediate continuation of the proceedings in 26:59–68, thus eliminating the vagueness of the Markan parallel[2]. Of course, if Matthew has closely followed Mark, there is also ample evidence that he has amended his Gospel source.

II. Redaction in the Matthean Passion Narrative

The editorial work of Matthew can be seen primarily in the following ways.

A. A Preference for Direct Discourse

Narrative sentences in Mark sometimes reappear as direct discourse in Matthew. The first example of this editorial device in the passion story comes at the very outset, where the chronological data of Mark 14:1 are recast as Jesus' words to his disciples in Matt 26:2: οἴδατε ὅτι.... A more

---

[1] So Nils Alstrup Dahl, "The Passion Narrative in Matthew", in *Jesus*, 39; Donald P. Senior, *The Passion Narrative according to Matthew: A Redactional Study* (Leuven: Leuven University, 1975) 1.

[2] Cf. Senior, *Passion*, 210–217, 340; Eduard Schweizer, *The Good News according to Matthew* (Atlanta: John Knox, 1975) 501.

formal illustration is found in the context of the Lord's Supper. There, Mark's narrative statement, καὶ ἔπιον ἐξ αὐτοῦ πάντες (14:23c), becomes in Matthew a command of Jesus: πίετε ἐξ αὐτοῦ πάντες (26:27c). Further examples include 14:10–11/Matt 26:14–15; 14:39/26:42; 14:64/26:66. These changes may simply be the consequence of the evangelist's innovation, but in some cases could reflect a preference for direct discourse in the oral tradition. Particularly in the case of the eucharistic pericope the amendment may be due to liturgical influence[3].

B. Characteristic Terminology

Into the Markan narrative, the First Evangelist has inserted his own characteristic redactional words and phrases. As before, this tendency raises its head already at the very beginning of the passion narrative, with the addition of the phrase καὶ ἐγένετο ὅτε ἐτέλεσεν ὁ Ἰησοῦς πάντας τοὺς λόγους τούτους (26:1). With this formula (cf. 7:28; 11:1; 13:53; 19:1), the Second Evangelist regularly closes Jesus' major discourses. The introduction of πᾶς into the expression here draws attention at the outset of the passion narrative to the conclusion of Jesus' time of teaching. A further example of this phenomenon is the insertion of καὶ ἰδοὺ in 26:51; this amendment places special emphasis on the sword episode.

C. Stylistic Improvements

In the Matthean narrative, as in the whole of the first Gospel, one finds indications of the evangelist's having "cleaned up" the Markan style. So, for example, in Matt 26:16, Mark's awkward πῶς αὐτὸν εὐκαίρως παραδοῖ (14:11) is recast as εὐκαιρίαν ἵνα αὐτὸν παραδῷ. One may also note the Matthean form of the account of Peter's denial, with its clear evidence of Matthew's stylistic editing (26:69–75). Of course, to speak of his having made stylistic improvements is not to say that in every case Matthew has employed better Greek[4].

D. Omission of Unnecessary Information

Apparently, Matthew regarded certain details in the Markan story as verbose or otherwise superfluous, and he made corresponding deletions.

---

[3] So Hermann Patsch, *Abendmahl und historische Jesus* (Stuttgart: Calwer, 1972) 69–70; Schweizer, *Matthew*, 490–491; David Hill, *The Gospel of Matthew* (Grand Rapids, Michigan: Wm B. Eerdmans, 1972) 332. *Contra* Pesch, *Abendmahl*, 25; Robert H. Gundry, *Matthew: A Commentary on His Literary and Theological Art* (Grand Rapids, Michigan: Wm. B. Eerdmans, 1982) 528. On Matthew's preference for direct discourse, see E. P. Sanders, *The Tendencies of the Synoptic Tradition* (Cambridge: Cambridge University, 1969) 259–262.

[4] For Semitic Greek in Matthew's passion narrative, see Dahl, "Passion", 43; Matthew Black, *An Aramaic Approach to the Gospels and Acts*, 3d ed. (Oxford:Clarendon,1967)*passim*.

Most obvious is Matthew's decision to leave out the account of the fleeing young man (Mark 14:51–52) — an episode which apparently served no purpose for him. A second major deletion comes in the story of the Passover preparation (26:17–20), where Matthew retains the skeleton of the account while reducing Mark's version by some 40 per cent. As a result, the Markan emphasis on Jesus' foreknowledge gives way to a concentration on Jesus' words and the disciples' obedience.

E. Minor Additions

Matthew makes minor additions for the purpose of clarifying the story structure, making clear a theological point, or adding additional information. Examples under this heading include intrusions at 26:3, 15, 25, 28, 31, 55, 65; 27:1, 11, 21, 34, 36, 37. Particular attention may be drawn to three of these incidents: 26:25 — where Judas is named as the betrayer; 26:28 — where Jesus' death is said to be εἰς ἄφεσιν ἁμαρτιῶν; and 26:65 — where the charge of blasphemy made against Jesus by the Jewish Council is more clearly expressed.

F. The Use of Old Testament Language

Some Markan verses are mildly amended to render them as allusions to OT texts. In describing Jesus' agony, Matthew weakens Mark's ἤρξατο ἐκθαμβεῖσθαι καὶ ἀδημονεῖν (14:33) to ἤρξατο λυπεῖσθαι καὶ ἀδημονεῖν (26:37) — an allusion to Ps 42:5 (Matt 26:38). See also the allusion to Ps 69:21 in Matt 27:34 and to Ps 22:8 in Matt 27:43[5].

G. Major Additions

A few Matthean insertions, however, are of more substance — namely, the Jesus-saying in 26:52–54, the account of Judas's death in 27:3–10, the report of the dream of Pilate's wife in 27:19, the account of Pilate's hand-washing in 27:24–25, the apocalyptic details at the crucifixion in 27:51b–53, and the report of the guard at the tomb in 27:62–66. What is remarkable about these insertions is that, with the possible exception of 27:3–10, each of them is tightly woven into the fabric provided by the Markan account. In fact, Donald P. Senior insists, again with the possible exception of 27:3–10, that they "... find their ultimate inspiration within the framework and content of the source material provided by Mark"[6]. As will become clear below, we are not as inclined as Senior to credit Matthean *creation* with certain of these amendments. Comparison among the various

---

[5] Additional verses wherein Matthew relates the passion more closely to the OT are listed in Dahl, "Passion", 43–44.
[6] Senior, *Passion*, 343–344; see also pp. 336, 340.

passion accounts strongly suggests Matthew's knowledge of *other (i.e. non-Markan) traditional materials*[7]. In any case, there does seem to be a direct relationship between the Markan framework and the special material. As for 27:3–10, Senior has successfully argued that the account of the fate of the betrayer, far from being a glaring excursus into an otherwise smooth narrative structure, serves to confirm Jesus' prophetic knowledge of his betrayer (cf. 26:24–25) in the same way that the account of Peter's denial (26:69–75) is a fulfillment of Jesus' prediction (cf. 26:31–35)[8].

III. Conclusion

The vast majority of differences between the Matthean and Markan passion accounts may be explained with reference to Matthew's redaction of his Gospel source. It is true, as we shall see in chapter 8, that one may uncover minor instances where Matthew appears to have been influenced by non-Markan material, but these are far from providing a basis for theorizing about a lengthy *Sonderquelle* behind Matthew's story of Jesus' suffering and death. As for the more substantial appearances of Matthean *Sonderqut*, these are so firmly embedded in the Markan context and content that one may justifiably hypothesize a close intermingling of the written and oral traditions prior to the composition of Matthew's Gospel[9]. No reason exists, however, to postulate a second, non-Markan, written, narrative source for Matthew's passion narrative[10].

---

[7] See below, chapter 8. See also Dale C. Allison, Jr., *The End of the Ages Has Come: An Early Interpretation of the Passion and Resurrection of Jesus* (Philadelphia: Fortress, 1985) 40–50.
[8] Senior, *Passion*, 343–397 (=*ETL* 48 [1972] 372–426).
[9] Cf. Schweizer, *Matthew*, 483: "In the Passion narrative, too, Matthew basically follows Mark. But we can observe an oral tradition, in the main running parallel to Mark but occasionally diverging and supplanting the Markan account." See also Dahl, "Passion", 38, 45.
[10] This is true regardless of one's decision as to the source(s) for Matthew's special material — whether Matthean creativity (Gundry), pre-Matthean midrashic notes (Trocmé), or some other. Of course, one could argue that Matthew and Mark utilize a common source, "but within the passion story such a hypothesis would mean only a superfluous complication of the picture; such an Ur-Markus would only be a pallid double for our Mark" (Dahl, "Passion", 37). Further, it would be hard to explain why Matthew, having followed Mark 1–13, would then switch to a second, almost identical, source for the passion narrative. If, as Trocmé argued, Mark's Gospel first circulated without chapters 14–16, one might suggest such a source, but we have already dismissed this aspect of his thesis as untenable.

Chapter Three:

The Relationship between the Canonical Passion Narratives

2. The Gospel of Luke

I. Introduction

When compared with the source-critical problem in Matt 26–27, the situation with regard to the Lukan passion story is infinitely more complex. The relationship between Luke's narrative and the Markan parallel is much less straightforward, as evidenced by numerous differences in detail, structural variations, and the overall low percentage of common vocabulary. Concerning the last means of comparison, Taylor reports that with respect to the passion narrative only 27 per cent of Luke's words are taken from Mark — a significant decrease from the figure of 53 per cent in earlier sections of the Third Gospel which parallel the Second[1]. So vexing is this state of affairs that at least one modern interpreter has concluded that Luke's passion narrative shares no literary relationship with Mark 14–15 at all[2]. Most scholars, however, would concede that Luke has borrowed at least some material from his Markan source in the process of redacting his own account of Jesus' passion, and many would agree that the Third Evangelist had access to additional traditional material. Without a doubt, the largest degree of disparity among exegetes centers on the character of that "additional traditional material": Was it a second *narrative source*? Or, has Luke only incorporated into the Markan narrative a number of *independent traditional fragments*? In view of the lack of any consensus on this issue, our treatment of the relationship between the Lukan and Markan passion stories must be carried out with greater attention to detail than was necessary in our discussion of the Matthean account. We propose to deal with the source-problem in Luke 22–23 pericope by pericope, then draw

---

1 Taylor, *Passion*, 32 (citing John C. Hawkins, "Three Limitations to St. Luke's Use of St Mark's Gospel", in *Oxford Studies*, 78).
2 Trocmé, *Passion*, 27–37.

together our conclusions regarding the possibility of a non-Markan, pre-Lukan narrative tradition of Jesus' suffering and death.

II. Luke 22:1−2 (Mark 14:1−2)

In the introduction to his passion narrative, Luke sets the scene chronologically and reports the plot against Jesus while closely following his Markan source. Verbal agreement is high, and, in spite of one or two peculiarities, the variations from Mark may be explained in terms of Lukan redaction without recourse to a second source[3].

V 1: Ἐγγίζω is less precise than Mark's ἦν . . . μετὰ δύο ἡμέρας, but appears to be a favorite word for Luke (Matt − 7x; Mark − 3x; Luke-Acts − 24x). His description of the festival, ἡ ἑορτὴ τῶν ἀζύμων, conforms to the wording of the LXX (e.g. Exod 23:15; 34:18; Deut 16:16; 2 Chr 8:13; 30:13, 21, 22; 35:17; et al.)[4]. Interestingly, the explanatory phrase ἡ λεγομένη appears in the Third Gospel only in the passion narrative − here and in 22:47, though it is present 3 times in Acts (3:2; 6:9; 9:36); for communicating this idea, Luke is much more fond of ὁ καλούμενος[5].

---

[3] So Taylor, *Passion*, 42; I. Howard Marshall, *The Gospel of Luke: A Commentary on the Greek Text* (Grand Rapids, Michigan: Wm. B. Eerdmans, 1978) 786−787; Joachim Jeremias, *Die Sprache des Lukasevangeliums: Redaktion und Tradition im Nicht-Markusstoff des Dritten Evangeliums* (Göttingen: Vandenhoeck & Ruprecht, 1980) 285; Gerhard Schneider, *Das Evangelium nach Lukas*, 2 vols. (Gütersloh: Gerd Mohn, 1977) 2:439−440.

[4] On Luke's use of words and phrases of Septuagintal origin, see the convenient treatment in Joseph A. Fitzmyer, *The Gospel according to Luke*, 2 vols. (Garden City, New York: Doubleday, 1981/85) 1:114−115. Also Nigel Turner, "The Quality of the Greek in Luke-Acts", in *NT Language*, 387−400.

[5] Fitzmyer, *Luke*, 1:110. In this study of the Lukan passion narrative we will have occasion from time to time to refer to the linguistic data collected by other scholars − esp. Lloyd Gaston, *Horae Synopticae Electronicae: Word Statistics of the Synoptic Gospels* (Missoula, Montana: Society of Biblical Literature, 1973); Jeremias, *Sprache*; Fitzmyer, *Luke*, 1:109−113; Anton Büchele, *Der Tod Jesu im Lukasevangelium: Eine redaktionsgeschichtliche Untersuchung zu Lk 23* (Frankfurt am Main: Josef Knecht, 1978). The attractiveness of Gaston's lists over those of Hawkins (*Synopticae*) consists in Gaston's close attention to the question of *sources* in compiling his lists − that is, he has not simply given us another list of word-occurrences in each Gospel (though, admittedly, his *source-critical* decisions may be open to question). Jeremias bases his decisions on similar criteria while also paying attention to the use of phrases and to the data from Acts. Of course, when using word statistics one must exercise caution against deciding prematurely that Luke's source L and a possible non-Markan passion narrative formed an integrated whole with its own standard *Vorzugsvokabeln* prior to the writing of the Third Gospel. It is on this score that Jeremias's insights must be treated cautiously − and on which many of the linguistic judgments made by Taylor (*Passion*), following Friedrich Rehkopt (*Die lukanische Sonderquelle* [Tübingen: J. C. B. Mohr (Paul Siebeck), 1959]), go amiss. Unfortunately, the lists of "Luke's characteristic words" set forth by Fitzmyer are merely taken over from Hawkins's work, and so indicate the characteristic vocabulary of the Third Gospel, but not the vocabulary of the Luke *the redactor*. Similarly, Büchele's employment of word statistics makes no allowance for the influence on Luke of his sources. The information Fitzmyer provides on Lukan stylistic preferences (*Luke*, 1:107−108) is more helpful.
Where the above analyses appear to flounder, or where they provide no assistance on specific words or phrases, we must undertake our own study of Luke's redactional preferences.

Luke's apparent identification of the Feast of Unleavened Bread and the Passover is indicative of the virtual inseparability of the two in current practice[6].

V 2: Luke's description of the Jewish leaders is identical to Mark's. The addition of τό, to introduce an indirect question, is typically Lukan[7]. He abbreviates Mark's account, omitting the reference to stealth and introducing ἀνέλωσιν (ἀναιρέω – "to do away with", as in Septuagintal and Classical Greek[8]) in place of Mark's more detailed "arrest . . . and kill." Avoiding an unnecessary redundancy, Luke deletes μὴ ἐν τῇ ἑορτῇ. His ἐφοβοῦντο γὰρ τὸν λαόν may be nothing more than a paraphrastic rendering of Mark's μήποτε ἔσται θόρυβος τοῦ λαοῦ, which serves to underscore the distinction between the people and the Jewish leaders. This motif will reappear again and again in the Lukan passion narrative and is also prevalent in the missionary sermons in Acts: in Luke's view, from a human standpoint the Jewish officials must bear primary responsibility for Jesus' death[9].

Hence, for these introductory verses, it seems highly probable that Luke has only redacted his Gospel source.

III. Luke 22:3-6 (Mark 14:10−11)

Omitting the story of Jesus' anointing at Bethany (Mark 14:3−9; cf. Luke 7:36−50)[10], Luke moves directly to his account of Judas's betrayal. Trocmé is correct in his observation of the clumsiness of style in this story — particularly as evidenced by the excessive use of καί — and in his notation of the low percentage of Markan words found in Luke's record (45.5%)[11]; nevertheless, it should not be overlooked that nothing of consequence in Mark's account is found missing in Luke's. The variations between the two are primarily due to Lukan additions. Later, we will argue that the affinities between Luke and John are due to shared traditions and not direct literary dependence[12]. Verse 3 includes an example of such affinity.

---

6 Alfred Plummer, *A Critical and Exegetical Commentary on the Gospel of S. Luke*, 5th ed. (Edinburgh: T. & T. Clark, 1901) 490; Samuel Sandmel, *Judaism and Christian Beginnings* (New York: Oxford University, 1961) 213.

7 Heinz Schürmann, *Jesu Abschiedsrede* (Münster: Aschendorffsche, 1957) 11−12; Fitzmyer, *Luke, 1:108.*

8 Plummer, *Luke*, 490.

9 On this *Tendenz*, see esp. Richard J. Cassidy, *Jesus, Politics, and Society: A Study of Luke's Gospel* (Maryknoll, New York: Orbis, 1978). Also *idem*, "Luke's Audience, the Chief Priests, and the Motive for Jesus' Death", in *Political Issues*, 146−147; Robert F. O'Toole, *The Unity of Luke's Theology: An Analysis of Luke-Acts* (Wilmington, Delaware: Michael Glazier, 1984) 19; Eduard Schweizer, *The Good News according to Luke* (Atlanta: John Knox, 1984) 302. As we will see, E. Jane Via ("According to Luke, Who Put Jesus to Death?", in *Political Issues*, 122−145) is right to suggest that Cassidy has overstated his case in giving the chief priests and their allies responsibility for Jesus' death in the Lukan schema (cf., esp., 23:13, 18, 21, 23). However, Via herself may be guilty of overstating her case in the opposite direction (above all, see 23:48).

10 On which see below, chapter 4.

11 Trocmé, *Passion*, 28−29. His computations render a percentage of 42.2.

12 See below, chapters 4 and 8.

V 3: Εἰσῆλθεν δὲ σατανᾶς εἰς is clearly non-Markan, but does have a parallel in John 13:27: εἰσῆλθεν εἰς ἐκεῖνον ὁ σατανᾶς (cf. 13:2). Elsewhere, Luke avoids the use of σατανᾶς in his Markan source, much preferring διάβολος[13]. Ἰσκαριώτην, used of Judas, differs from Mark (Ἰσκαριώθ) and earlier Lukan usage (6:16 – Ἰσκαριώθ), but agrees with the parallels in John 13:2, 26. Καλούμενος is Lukan[14]. Ὄντα ἐκ τοῦ ἀριθμοῦ is unparalleled in the Gospels as an expression for a disciple, but ἀριθμός is used to describe a Christian convert in Acts[15]; here it replaces Mark's Semitic ὁ εἷς[16].

V 4: Συνελάλησεν makes explicit what is already implied in Mark. Luke has a general preference for συν- words[17]. The services of the στρατηγοί (temple police[18]) would be needed in the event of an arrest (cf. 22:52). On τὸ πῶς, see above on 22:2.

V 5: Mark's οἱ δὲ ἀκούσαντες is deleted as superfluous. Συντίθημι (again, a συν- word – cf. above on 22:4), meaning "to agree" in the middle case, comes from Classical usage; here it replaces Mark's ἐπαγγέλλομαι.

V 6: Underscoring Judas's responsibility in the betrayal, Luke adds that he agreed (ἐξομολογέω) to the offer of the money. Two additional changes reflect Luke's stylistic preferences[19]: εὐκαιρίαν replaces Mark's adverbial εὐκαίρως; and Luke's τοῦ + infinitive (denoting purpose) is a rewriting of Mark's πῶς- clause. Ἄτερ appears in biblical Greek only here and in 22:35 (cf. 2 Macc 12:15). Ἄτερ ὄχλου αὐτοῖς is a throwback to the thought of 22:2 (cf. Mark 14:2) and is probably Lukan.

Apart from v 3, Luke's narration of Judas's conspiracy with the Jewish officials appears to rest solely on the Markan account. The peculiarities we noted in v 3, particularly when the Johannine parallels are noted, strongly suggest Luke's knowledge of additional material, however. Had this tradition been oral, it would be difficult to explain why Luke would have felt so bound to it that he would depart from his characteristic language. Hence, we conclude that Luke had a written note about the satanic influence at work through Judas; it may be that Luke's alternative tradition embraced a full conspiracy scene – from which Luke has only extracted this detail.

IV. Luke 22:7–13 (Mark 14:12–16)

The form of the story of the preparation for the Passover in Luke is not identical to the Markan version, but the percentage of words taken

---

13 Marshall, *Gospel of Luke*, 788; Helmut Koester, *Introduction to the New Testament* (Philadelphia: Fortress, 1982) 1:108 (who notes Luke's tendency to replace Aramaic and Latin loan-words in Mark with appropriate Greek terms).
14 See above on 22:1.
15 In view of Luke's use of the term elsewhere (e.g. Acts 6:7; 11:21; 16:5), Marshall's suggestion *(Gospel of Luke*, 788) that Luke's wording implies that Judas was not one with the other disciples may be discounted.
16 On Mark's ὁ εἷς as a Semitism, see Black, *Aramaic Approach*, 93, 105; Pesch, *Mark*, 2:337. Sanders (*Tendencies*, 190–255) demonstrates that among the Synoptic Gospels Semitic constructions are least common in Luke.
17 Taylor, *Passion*, 43.
18 See Joachim Jeremias, *Jerusalem in the Time of Jesus* (Philadelphia: Fortress, 1969) 165–166.
19 On Luke's aversion to Mark's adverbs and adverbial phrases, see Taylor, *Passion*, 43. On the τοῦ + infinitive construction, see Fitzmyer, *Luke*, 1:108.

from Mark is very high (60.4%) and the variations are mostly stylistic. Luke's redaction emphasizes Jesus' initiative in having preparations made for the meal, and names Mark's "two disciples" as Peter and John. No other significant variations occur, and there is general unanimity that this pericope was based solely on its counterpart in the Second Gospel[20]. Hence, a detailed examination is unnecessary.

V. Luke 22:14–20 (Mark 14:17, 22–25)

Luke's version of the Last Supper, on the other hand, bristles with difficulties, and it will be best to break our discussion of it into four parts – dealing first with v 14, then the Lukan transposition of Markan material, followed by treatments of vv 15–18 and vv 19–20.

A. Verse 14

What was Luke's source for v 14? After seven pages of detailed analysis, Schürmann concludes that it is a "moralische Gewissheit" that this verse merely represents Luke's editing of Mark 14:17–18a[21]. His argument is based especially on Luke's editorial preferences – for example: Luke avoided some terms (e.g. ὀψία, Luke – φ; Mark – 6x; Matt – 7x), and he has substituted his own vocabulary for Mark's (e.g. οἱ ἀπόστολοι σὺν αὐτῷ for μετὰ τῶν δώδεκα). Jeremias is unconvinced by this line of reasoning, noting that "... Luke 22.14 and Mark 14.17 have actually only one word in common, the word 'and' "[22]. While the two versions obviously intend to say much the same thing, there is in fact little to tie the Lukan text to the Markan. Taking 22:14 as the introduction to the meal-episode[23], we might anticipate that it was already a part of Luke's source for vv 15–18 (or vv 15–20). That is, we tentatively suggest that to answer the source-question for vv 15–18 is to answer the same question for v 14. Additional comments will follow our discussion of the larger passage in question.

---

20 See Joel B. Green, "Preparation for Passover (Luke 22:7–13): A Question of Redactional Technique", *NovT* 29 (4, 1987) 305–319. See also Taylor, *Passion*, 44–46; Heinz Schürmann, *Der Paschamahlbericht* (Münster: Aschendorffsche, 1953) 75–104; Marshall, *Gospel of Luke*, 789–792; Schneider, *Luke*, 2:441–443; Jeremias, *Sprache*, 285. Contra Trocmé, *Passion*, 29–30.
21 Schürmann, *Paschamahlbericht*, 104–110. See also, Schneider, *Luke*, 2:444; and, tentatively, Marshall, *Gospel of Luke*, 794–795.
22 Jeremias, *Eucharistic Words*, 99 n.1. But, cf. Mark's γενομένης and Luke's ἐγένετο. See also, idem, *Sprache*, 286; Taylor, *Passion*, 48–49; Plummer, *Luke*, 494; Rehkopf, *Sonderquelle*, 90 n.4.
23 So Kurt Aland, et al., eds., *The Greek New Testament*, 2d ed. (London: United Bible Societies, 1966); Eberhard Nestle, et al., eds., *Novum Testamentum Graece*, 26th ed. (Stuttgart: Deutsche Bibelstiftung, 1979); Albert Huck, *Synopsis of the First Three Gospels with the Addition of the Johannine Parallels*, 13th ed., revised by Heinrich Greeven (Tübingen: J. C. B. Mohr [Paul Sie-

B. The Lukan Transposition

Second, we may note that Luke has transposed the order of events as given by Mark, placing the Supper-tradition prior to the betrayal announcement. On the basis of this observation, Jeremias has argued that Luke has deliberately set aside his Markan source in favor of a *Sonderquelle*. Luke, he says, is "an enemy of rearrangement" who painstakingly reproduces the Markan order when following the Markan narrative. On the basis of Luke's deviations from the sequence of the Markan passion account, Jeremias posits for Luke an alternative tradition underlying Luke 22:14–24:53[24]. Similarly, Schürmann is convinced that Lukan transpositions signal the evangelist's use of another source. Unlike Jeremias, however, he allows that these deviations in order are the end product of Luke's attempt to collate Markan and non-Markan pericopae[25]. More recently, Neirynck has taken issue with the supposition that Luke's dislocations of Markan sections suggest his indebtedness to non-Markan sources. His dissenting opinion is grounded in his detailed treatment of Schürmann's exegesis of two important passages where Markan material has been utilized out of sequence – Luke 6:17–21 and 8:19–21. First, Neirynck insists that Schürmann was wrong to argue that the basis of Luke 6:12–16 is non-Markan tradition and that 6:17 exhibits traces of the Q-source. Then he notes that Schürmann's explanation of Luke 8:19–21 as a *Nachtrag* is dependent on his judgment that 8:1–3 is a non-Markan passage. In fact, Neirynck urges, 8:1–3 is not based on a *Sonderquelle*, but is a Lukan redactional composition worked up from Markan motifs[26].

As recent commentators have pointed out, Luke 6:12–16 is under Marken influence but the use of a further source cannot be categorically dismissed[27]. On the other hand, if additional material was employed by

---

beck), 1981). *Contra* Kurt Aland, ed., *Synopsis of the Four Gospels: Greek-English Edition of the Synopsis Quattuor Evangeliorum* (London: United Bible Societies, 1976); John Bernard Orchard, ed., *A Synopsis of the Four Gospels in Greek. Arranged according to the Two Gospel Hypothesis* (Edinburgh: T. & T. Clark, 1983).

24 Jeremias, *Eucharistic Words*, 97–99. On the problem posed by the Lukan transpositions, see also, idem, "Perikopenumstellungen bei Lukas?", *NTS* 4 (1958) 115–119; Rehkopf, *Sonderquelle*, esp. pp. 1–2. Gerhard Schneider, *Verleugnung, Verspottung und Verhor Jesu nach Lukas 22,54–71: Studien zur lukanische Darstellung der Passion* (Münster: Kosel, 1969) esp. pp. 144–151; Frans Neirynck, "The Argument from Order and St. Luke's Transpositions", in *Evangelica*, 757–768; Schürmann, *Paschamahlbericht*, 2 n.9; Fitzmyer, *Luke*, 1:71–72.

25 Schürmann, *Abschiedsrede*, 3–35. See also his *Das Lukasevangelium*, vol 1, 3d ed. (Freiburg: Herder, 1984) esp. pp. 323, 471; Schneider, *Verleugnung*, 144–151.

26 Neirynck, "Argument from Order", 761–767. Fitzmyer (*Luke*, 1:72) declares himself to be in basic agreement with Neirynck.

27 See Marshall, *Gospel of Luke*, 237; Fitzmyer, *Luke*, 1:613–614; Schneider, *Luke*, 1:145. See further, Schürmann, *Luke*, 1:318–319, 323; Tim Schramm, *Der Markus-stoff bei Lukas: Eine literarkritische und redaktionsgeschichtliche Untersuchung* (Cambridge: Cambridge University, 1971) 113–114.

Luke (or both by Matthew and Luke) — say, for the list of disciples — this is still no compelling argument either that this material resembled that Lukan text or that it was taken from Q (cf. Acts 1:13). More important than the sort of linguistic evidence dominating Neirynck's discussion, however, is a point effectively communicated by Schramm:

> Die literarkritische Beurteilung von Lk 6,12–19 darf nicht vorübergehen an dem erstaunlichen Phänomen, dass Mt (4,25; 5,1) *und* Lk (6,17ff.) die gleiche Mk-Stelle (3,7ff.) für die Rahmung der Bergpredigt/Feldrede verwenden, dabei sogar die gleichen Elemente aus Mk 3 für die Einleitung der Predigt in Anspruch nehmen. Das kann schwerlich Zufall sein[28].

Thus, both in Matthew and Luke, Mark's "healing summary" is taken out of its "proper" sequence in order to associate it directly with the Sermon on the Mount/Plain — which Mark does not record. Coincidence of this degree is difficult to attribute to chance.

As for Neirynck's thesis regarding the Markan character of Luke 8:1–3, again it must be recognized that the evidence is ambiguous enough to place any certainty on the source-critical question outside our grasp[29]. However, even if we adopt Neirynck's *analysis* there is no compelling reason to also embrace his *conclusion*, for it is one thing to say that Luke has, in 8:1, returned to Markan *themes* (so his analysis), but quite another to assert that Luke has begun to borrow Markan *material* (so his conclusion). Using material from non-Markan sources or highlighting Markan motifs — in either case Luke could be constructing a summary passage that serves a transitory function, before which he relies on non-Markan material, after which he depends on Mark.

In short, Neirynck's essay has not dealt the death-blow to the "argument from transposition" that he (and Fitzmyer) might have us think, and there is some justification for taking this phenomenon as an argument favoring the non-Markan character of 22:14–20.

In this context it should not be overlooked that Luke and John (13:1–30) are in agreement in recounting the betrayal announcement after the Supper. This coincidence supports the thesis that Luke's sequence is not of his own invention but is drawn from pre-Lukan, non-Markan tradition.

C. Verses 15–18

Next, we turn to the problem of the source behind vv 15–18 — considered apart from vv 19–20 due to the appearance that the former verses

---

28 Schramm, *Markus-stoff*, 113. Cf. Fitzmyer, *Luke*, 1:613–614.
29 Jeremias, (*Sprache*, 174–178) and Schneider (*Luke*, 1:179–180) regard the whole (apart from the names) as Lukan. Marshall (*Gospel of Luke*, 315–316) suggests a combination of material from L and Q. Fitzmyer (*Luke*, 1:695–696) regards the whole as Lukan but allows the possibility of minor intrusions from L.

constitute a self-contained unit³⁰. The origin of these verses – whether they represent a Lukan editing of a pre-Lukan, non-Markan account or a Lukan creation based on Mark 14:22–25 – has been hotly contested, with detailed arguments presented on both sides. Among these studies, Schürmann's is particularly remarkable for its exhaustive attention to minutiae³¹. Schürmann undertook both literary- and form-critical analyses of these four verses, concluding that Luke had only slightly revised a pre-Lukan, non-Markan source, independent of Mark. Similar conclusions were reached by Jeremias³². On the other hand, Pesch has sought to demonstrate on redaction-critical grounds that vv 15–18 are the product of Luke's own hand, whereby Luke drew on his own *Vorzugswendung* and Markan material to construct the account³³. In this case, it is not easy to square one scholar against another; therefore, while taking into account the significant work of these exegetes, we shall attempt our own appraisal of the evidence.

We may begin our investigation by setting out the parallels between the Markan *Vorlage* and the Lukan text. Our presentation of the verses will be adjusted to reveal the parallels between vv 16 and 18 of Luke 22.

Luke 22:15:   καὶ εἶπεν πρὸς αὐτούς· ἐπιθυμίᾳ ἐπεθύμησα τοῦτο

Luke 22:15:   τὸ πάσχα φαγεῖν μεθ' ὑμῶν
Mark 14:12: φάγῃς τὸ πάσχα
Mark 14:14:   τὸ πάσχα   μετὰ τῶν μαθητῶν μου φάγω

Luke 22:15:   πρὸ τοῦ με παθεῖν·

Luke 22:16:   λέγω γὰρ ὑμῖν ὅτι   οὐ μὴ φάγω
Mark 14:25: ἀμὴν ʼλέγω   ὑμῖν ὅτι οὐκέτι οὐ μὴ πίω
Luke 22:18:   λέγω γὰρ ὑμῖν   οὐ μὴ πίω ἀπὸ τοῦ νῦν

Luke 22:16:   αὐτοῦ   ἕως
Mark 14:25: ἐκ τοῦ γενήματος τῆς ἀμπέλου ἕως τῆς ἡμέρας ἐκείνης
Luke 22:18: ἀπὸ τοῦ γενήματος τῆς ἀμπέλου ἕως

Luke 22:16: ὅτου πληρωθῇ   ἐν τῇ βασιλείᾳ τοῦ θεοῦ.
Mark 14:25: ὅταν αὐτὸ πίνω καινὸν ἐν τῇ βασιλείᾳ τοῦ θεοῦ.
Luke 22:18:   οὗ   ἡ βασιλεία τοῦ θεοῦ ἔλθῃ.

Luke 22:17: καὶ δεξάμενος ποτήριον εὐχαριστήσας εἶπεν·
Mark 14:23: καὶ λαβὼν   ποτήριον εὐχαριστήσας

Luke 22:17: λάβετε τοῦτο καὶ διαμερίσατε εἰς ἑαυτούς.
Mark 14:23: ἔδωκεν αὐτοῖς καὶ ἔπιον ἐξ αὐτοῦ πάντες.

---

30 Cf. Schürmann, *Paschamahlbericht*, 50–52; Jeremias, *Eucharistic Words*, 160–164, Taylor *Passion*, 49–50.
31 Schürmann, *Paschamahlbericht*, 1–74.
32 Jeremias, *Eucharistic Words*, 160–164.
33 Pesch, *Abendmahl*, 26–31. Similarly, G. D. Kilpatrick, *The Eucharist in Bible and Liturgy* (Cambridge: Cambridge University, 1983) 38–39.

As can be readily seen, v 15 has no parallel in the Markan eucharistic words, but Luke may have drawn some of his terminology from the earlier account of the preparation for the Passover. The parallel consists only in four words, however, and in all probability these words would have been used in any source describing the event.

V 15a: Jeremias identifies καὶ εἶπεν as a phrase characteristic of Luke's special source – and so it may be (e.g. 11:5; 17:5; et al.); however, even where it is absent in Luke's sources he is capable of using the expression (e.g. 8:45; 9:3; 20:34)[34]. The construction verb of speaking + πρός + accusative, a Septuagintalism, is a favorite of Luke's (e.g. 1:13, 18, 34; 4:4, 21, 36; 5:22; et al.) which cuts across all of Luke's sources[35]. As for εἶπον, it is also used regularly, without respect for Luke's sources[36]. Hence, the vocabulary of v 15a provides no decisive indication of a non-Markan origin.

V 15b: Functioning in the same way as an infinitive absolute in Hebrew (and Aramaic – cf. 1QapGen 20.10–11), the dative ἐπιθυμίᾳ strengthens the force of ἐπεθύμησα[37]. This construction, quite rare in the NT, is not uncommon in the LXX, and this phrase is close to Gen 31:30: ἐπιθυμίᾳ γὰρ ἐπεθύμησας ἐπελθεῖν (cf. Num 11:4; Ps 105 [106]:14). Comparable idioms in Acts 5:28 (παραγγελίᾳ παρηγγείλαμεν ὑμῖν) and 23:14 (ἀναθέματι ἀνεθεματίσαμεν ἑαυτούς) suggest that Luke may be intentionally copying Septuagintal style here (cf. also Luke 22:29; Acts 4:17; 7:17 [p45 D E p vg^mss mae]). It has been claimed that ἐπιθυμέω is a characteristic Lukan word[38]. Putting aside for the moment the present verse, the verb is found in the Synoptics only in material taken from Q and Luke's special source L[39]. Hence, while it is true that it appears most often in Luke, it is not necessarily due to Luke's editorial preferences. In fact, the opposite claim may have the better case. Nothing additional can be made of the combination ἐπιθυμέω + infinitive, as it is also found in Matt 5:28 and in the LXX (e.g. Gen 31:30, cited above). Regarding the presence of τοῦτο, if Luke was not following a source other than Mark, why would he have added this pronoun? Luke's preferred preposition for expressing "with" is σύν[40], not μετά; this suggests that Luke is not composing freely, but it is not a decisive argument against his having borrowed from the earlier Markan text. Prepositions with the genitive of the articular infinitive (πρὸ τοῦ με παθεῖν) are not novel in the NT[41], but πρὸ τοῦ may well betray Luke's hand (cf. 2:21; 11:38). Παθεῖν is used in Luke-Acts in an absolute sense for Jesus' death (Luke 22:15; 24:46; Acts 1:3; 3:18; 17:3), but this

---

34 Jeremias, *Eucharistic Words*, 161 n.3; idem, *Sprache*, 286.
35 Turner, "Quality", 395; Fitzmyer, *Luke*, 1:116.
36 Gaston, *Electronicae*, 31, 64.
37 BDF, para. 198.6; C. F. D. Moule, *An Idiom Book of New Testament Greek*, 2d ed. (Cambridge: Cambridge University, 1959) 177–178; MHT, 2:443.
38 E. g. Pesh, *Abendmahl*, 28; Fitzmyer, *Luke*, 1:110.
39 Matt – 2x; Mark – ∅; Luke-Acts – 5x. The occurrence of ἐπιθυμέω may be Lukan; however, the verse may have been taken from Luke's source – cf. Marshall, *Gospel of Luke*, 657–659; Jeremias, *Sprache*, 267. Barnabas Lindars (*Jesus Son of Man: A Fresh Examination of the Son of Man Sayings in the Light of Recent Research* [London: S.P.C.K., 1983] 93–94, 133, 136, 168) seems to waver between attributing 17:22 to Luke and leaving open the possibility of its place in Luke's source material. Part of his basis for regarding it as Lukan, however, is his premature judgment that ἐπιθυμέω is a characteristic Lukan word (210 n.10). The verb is used once in Acts (20:33), in Paul's address to the Ephesian elders. Here, Luke may be drawing on a tradition about, or an acquaintance with, what was known to be characteristic of Paul's fulfillment of his apostolic ministry (Charles K. Barrett, "Paul's Address to the Ephesian Elders", in *God's Christ*, 107–121). Inasmuch as the Lukan context and this usage in Acts associates the term with "farewell discourses", we may raise the possibility that this accounts for the presence of the term here.
40 Fitzmyer, *Luke*, 1:111.
41 BDF, para. 403. Jeremias (*Sprache*, 286) regards this constructon as Lukan.

nuance certainly predates his redaction[42]. All in all, the evidence does not lend itself to support a Lukan editing of Mark, and we conclude that v 15b is likely a Lukan version of a pre-Lukan, non-Markan source.

Without a doubt, the parallelism between vv 16, 18 and Mark 14:25 is striking. A number of variations are worthy of note, however: Luke's substitution of γάρ for ἀμήν; the absence of ὅτι in v 18[43]; the omission of οὐκέτι by Luke[44]; the addition of ἀπό τοῦ νῦν in v 18; the substitution of ἀπό for ἐκ in v 18; the omission of τῆς ἡμέρας ἐκείνης by Luke; the substitution of ὅτου for ὅταν in v 16 and the lack of any corresponding word in v 18; and the varying ways of referring to the consummation of the kingdom of God in the three verses. Three remarks stem from these observations. First, the correspondence between Luke's version and Mark's is not so great as might at first appear. While the differences may be the result of Luke's redactional preferences, this is not self-evident. Second, if Luke had constructed vv 16 and 18 from Mark 14:25, we might well be surprised that the correspondence between vv 16 and 18 is not much more pervasive. As Patsch has observed:

> Was aber am stärksten gegen eine Abhängigkeit von Mk spricht, is die Tatsache, dass V. 16 und V. 18 nicht so parallel gebaut sind, wie man sie bei historisierender Konstruktion erwartet hätte[45].

Third, many of the parallels — e.g. preposition + τοῦ γενήματος τῆς ἀμπέλου, and the reference to the consummation of ἡ βασιλεία τοῦ θεοῦ — might be expected in an eschatological text reflecting Jewish anticipation of the banquet in the kingdom[46]. For these reasons, the so-called "parallels" do not point unambiguously to Lukan dependence on Mark 14:25 for his vv 16 and 18.

V 16: Λέγω γάρ ὑμῖν is also found in 3:8; 10:24; 14:24; 22:18, 37. Unless one presupposes an answer to the source question for 22:15–18, 37, no occurrence of this phrase appears outside material taken from pre-Lukan sources. It cannot be argued directly on the basis of earlier usage that Luke brought this phrase forward from Mark 14:25, substituting γάρ for ἀμήν. Luke apparently has an aversion to ἀμήν (cf. the deletion in Luke 10:24/Matt 3:17) and often substitutes for it alternative words (e.g. ἀληθῶς in 9:27; ναί in 11:51). But unless one assumes 22:15–18 is based on Mark, never does Luke's γάρ replace an ἀμήν. Arguing indirectly, however, the sheer quantity of ways in which Luke avoids ἀμήν leaves open the possibility that he has only amended Mark here. Οὐ μή appears 12 times in Luke prior to the passion narrative. Of these occurrences, 10 are in material taken from pre-Lukan sources. The combination occurs in Acts only in quotations from

---

42 Wilhelm Michaelis, "Πάσχω", in *TDNT*, 5:913.
43 A minority of witnesses (C* D N pc) omit ὅτι in Luke 22:16, a probable assimilation to v 18.
44 Οὐκέτι οὐ μή φάγω is read by a number of mss. in Luke 22:16, though not in the most reliable witnesses. Bruce M. Metzger (*A Textual Commentary on the Greek New Testament* [London: United Bible Society, 1971] 173) judges that the copyists inserted οὐκέτι so as to alleviate an otherwise abrupt saying.
45 Patsch, *Abendmahl*, 94.
46 Cf. Isa 25:6–9; 32:12; 55:1–2; 65:13; *1 Enoch* 62:14; *2 Bar.* 29:5–8; Rev 19:17; Friedrich Büchsel, "Γένημα", in *TDNT*, 1:685; Marshall, *Gospel of Luke*, 799; Geoffrey Wainwright, *Eucharist and Eschatology* (London: Epworth, 1971) 18–25.

the LXX. Aside from 22:16, Luke uses ἕως ὅτου twice (12:50; 13:8). Both verses are peculiar to Luke. Ἕως appears alone in a third text where Matthew and Mark have no parallel (17:8), and Matthew and Luke agree against Mark in using ἕως ἄν at Matt 24:34/Luke 21:32 (Mark 13:30 reads μέχρις). There is no consistency in Luke's use of ἕως ὅτου, so Pesch inaccurately labels this combination as a "lk Vorzugswendung"[47]. Πληρόω, appearing in the passive form as a circumlocution for divine activity, reflects Semitic usage[48].

V 18: On λέγω γὰρ ὑμῖν and οὐ μή, see above on v 16. Luke uses ἀπὸ τοῦ νῦν in his Gospel 5 times – 1:48; 5:10; 12:52; 22:18; and 22:69 (Acts – 1x: 18:6). It appears to be a Lukan addition in 5:10, and in 22:69 it corresponds to ἀπ' ἄρτι in Matt 26:64. Thus, it may be a Lukan addition here. Luke has a preference for ἀπό[49]. As noted above on v 16, Luke's use of ἕως is too ambiguous for a firm source-critical decision. As for the "coming" of the kingdom, a form of ἔρχομαι appears in references to the kingdom of God also in Luke 11:2 and 17:20 (cf. 10:9, 11; 11:20; 19:11). In 11:2, the context is the "Lord's prayer", and the form is paralleled in Matt 6:10. While 17:20a (ἐπερωτηθεὶς δὲ ὑπὸ τῶν Φαρισαίων πότε ἔρχεται ἡ βασιλεία τοῦ θεοῦ ἀπεκρίθη αὐτοῖς καὶ εἶπεν) may be a Lukan composition, v 20b (οὐκ ἔρχεται ἡ βασιλεία τοῦ θεοῦ μετὰ παρατηρήσεως) is probably pre-Lukan[50]; that is, Luke has likely composed the kingdom-reference in v 20a from that in v 20b. In light of these two earlier texts, 22:18c may justifiably be thought to rest on non-Markan tradition.

Hence, the weight of the evidence tips the balance in favor of a pre-Lukan, non-Markan source for 22:16 and 18.

Luke 22:17 is paralleled in the cup-word of Mark 14:23. The correspondence between the two texts is noteworthy – the differences appearing in Luke's use of δεξάμενος rather than λαβών, and in the move to direct address in v 17b as opposed to Mark's narrative description. Nevertheless, the similarity is no more than might be expected if these texts were developed within the matrix of Jewish distribution terminology[51].

V 17: In a liturgical context, δέχομαι (rather than λαμβάνω) is puzzling. Kilpatrick has drawn attention to the frequent use of λαμβάνω in the LXX in sacrificial contexts, where the term signifies the act which initiates the "holy action"[52]. In view of this background, the disparity here is all the more troubling. Of course, one finds in this no reason for postulating that δέχομαι (with this nuance) was preferred by Luke. There is no easy way from Mark's narrative (14:23c) to Luke's direct discourse (22:17c) as the wording is quite dissimilar. Διαμερίζω appears in Luke 6 times, compared with only once each in Matthew and Mark (and that in the parallels to Luke 23:34). The compound verb replaces μερίζω in 11:17–18 (Mark 3:25–26; Matt 12:25–26) and so may replace μερίζω here. Pesch describes the phrase εἰς ἑαυτούς as a hapaxlegomenon[53], but it is also read in 7:30 (cf. 15:17). If he means it is hapax *in this sense* (i.e. in reading ἐν for εἰς), then he is correct.

---

47 Pesch, *Abendmahl*, 29. According to Jeremias (*Sprache*, 286–287) it is non-Lukan!
48 Cf. Black, *Aramaic Approach*, 229–236; esp. pp. 235–236; Jeremias, *Eucharistic Words*, 162. Contra Pesch (*Abendmahl*, 29), there is no conceptual parallel between ἕως ὅτου τελεσθῇ (12:50) and ἕως ὅτου πληρωθῇ (22:16). In the former text, Jesus' death is to be "perfected"; in the latter, not Jesus' death but the Passover is to be "fulfilled".
49 Gaston, *Electronicae*, 65; Pesch, *Abendmahl*, 29.
50 Cf. Robert Maddox, *The Purpose of Luke-Acts* (Edinburgh: T. & T. Clark, 1982) 135–136; Marshall, *Gospel of Luke*, 652–654; Jeremias, *Sprache*, 266; Schneider, *Luke*, 2:354; Schweizer, *Luke*, 271.
51 Patsch, *Abendmahl*, 92–93.
52 Kilpatrick, *Eucharist*, 85.
53 Pesch, *Abendmahl*, 29.

In all likelihood, then, v 17 rests on a pre-Lukan, non-Markan source.

Before moving on to an analysis of vv 19–20 we should take note of Kilpatrick's attempt to explain vv 15–18 as based on Mark with some phrases from the Third Evangelist. In his view these "other features" that have been conflated with the Markan text originate in Luke's intention to paint the Last Supper as a Passover. He observes four parallels:

> First, these verses correspond to the Haggada; they give a kind of interpretation of the elements of the observance. Secondly, there is the reference to the Passover, with an eschatological exposition of it. Thirdly, there is a taking of the cup with thanksgiving, without an immediate participation. Finally, there is an eschatological interpretation of the cup[54].

Regarding this hypothesis we may outline three points of response. First, Kilpatrick assumes rather than argues that early Christianity had to wait for Luke to write his Gospel in order to "positively and explicitly" associate the Last Supper and the Passover. (a) Too easily does he slip away from identifying the Last Supper (historically) as a Passover. By adopting Johannine chronology he thinks he has circumvented the whole debate, but what of the Passover features in the Johannine context[55]? (b) It is obvious that Christianity at the time of Paul was making explicit use of Passover imagery to explicate the significance of Christ's death (1 Cor 5:7). From whence did this association come? If not from the Last Supper, would not such an identification have led to explaining the Last Supper in Passover terms? (c) Already in Mark's passion story there is a quite explicit identification of the Last Supper as a Passover meal (Mark 14:12–16).

Second, our literary analysis has already demonstrated both the probable traditional character of Luke 22:15–18 and its probable independence from Mark 14:22–25. Third, where else does Luke demonstrate the sort of interest in the Passover required by this theory? *Contra* Kilpatrick, then, it would seem contrary to the evidence to argue that Luke 22:15–18 is *Luke's* attempt to cast the Last Supper as a Passover celebration.

We conclude that 22:15–18 is neither a Lukan creation nor a reworking of Markan material: it represents with some editing a pre-Lukan, non-Markan tradition. Further conclusions as to the nature of this tradition and its present literary context must await a consideration of additional evidence.

D. Verses 19–20

The fourth issue to be taken up in our treatment of 22:14–20 concerns the Lukan version of the eucharistic words (vv 19–20). Two interrelated problems come into focus here — the problematic textual tradition of vv

---

54 Kilpartrick, *Eucharist*, 42; cf. pp. 38–42.
55 See below, chapter 4.

19b–20[56] and the relation of the Lukan text to Mark 14:22–24. We will deal with the latter problem while discussing the former.

The long form of the text, retaining vv 19b–20, is supported by all Greek manuscripts except D and by most ancient versions and the Fathers. The short text omits vv 19b–20 and is read by D it. A long history stands behind efforts to establish the original text and until relatively recent times the shorter text enjoyed wide acceptance. Judgments in its favor have primarily rested on five arguments[57]. (A) It is a maxim of textual criticism that one should choose as the more original reading that which best explains the origin of the other(s)[58]. In this case, it is easier to account for the long text as an assimilation of the Lukan text to Mark 14:24 and 1 Cor 11:24 than to explain the omission of vv 19b–20. (B) In general, the textual critic is advised to favor the shorter reading[59]. (C) Luke systematically avoids references to the sacrificial character of the death of Jesus. (D) Verses 19b–20 retain a number of non-Lukan elements. (E) If the longer text is accepted, one must then account for the presence of two cups in the Lukan account of the meal (vv 17, 20).

In more recent years, these arguments have been disputed and the longer text has received a growing number of adherents. Chief among its champions has been Schürmann and Jeremias[60]. We may outline the arguments supporting the longer text as follows. (A¹) Only part of the Western tradition supports the shorter text; the remaining Western mss. and representa-

---

56 Six textual forms affecting our reading of Luke 22:17–20 have survived and are conveniently set forth in parallel columns in Metzger, *Textual Commentary*, 175.
57 Cf. Plummer, *Luke*, 496–497; Norval Geldenhuys, *Commentary on the Gospel of Luke* (Grand Rapids, Michigan: Wm. B. Eerdmans, 1951) 58–59; Kevin Giles, "Is Luke an Exponent of 'Early Protestantism'? Church Order in the Lukan Writings", *EvQ* 54 (4, 1982) 202; Walter Edward Pilgrim, "The Death of Christ in Lukan Soteriology", (Th.D. thesis, Princeton Theological Seminary, 1971) 167ff.; Hans Lietzmann, *Mass and Lord's Supper* (Leiden: E. J. Brill, 1979) 175–177; M. Kiddle, "The Passion Narrative in St. Luke's Gospel," *JTS* 36 (1935) 277; Kilpatrick, *Eucharist*, 28–34; B. P. Robinson, "The Place of the Emmaus Story in Luke-Acts", *NTS* 30 (1984) 488–489. Arthur Vööbus ("A New Approach to the Problem of the Shorter and Longer Text in Luke", *NTS* 15 [1968–69] 457–463) has defended the originality of the shorter text from the novel perspective of "motif history" and "cult tradition". In doing so, he completely ignores the accepted criteria for textual criticism. Moreover, he builds his case on the dubious assumption that Luke 22:24–27 was borrowed from Mark 10:41–45 (on which see below, chapter 3.VII).
58 Bruce M. Metzger, *The Text of the New Testament: Its Transmission, Corruption, and Restoration* (Oxford: Oxford University, 1968) 207.
59 Metzger, *Text*, 209.
60 Heinz Schürmann, "LK 22,19b–20 als ursprüngliche Textüberlieferung", *Bib* 32 (1951) 364–392, 522–541 = *Traditionsgeschichtliche Untersuchungen zu den Synoptischen Evangelien* (Düsseldorf: Patmos, 1968) 159–197; idem, *Der Einsetzungsbericht* (Münster: Aschendorffsche, 1955); Jeremias, *Eucharistic Words*, 139–159. See also, Taylor, *Passion*, 50–58; Marshall, *Gospel of Luke*, 799–801; idem, *Last Supper and Lord's Supper* (Grand Rapids, Michigan: Wm. B. Eerdmans, 1980) 36–38; E. Earle Ellis, *The Gospel of Luke* (London: Thomas Nelson, 1966)

tives from all other textual groups support the longer reading. Hence, the external evidence for the long text is overwhelming. Moreover, Jeremias has demonstrated that in the majority of instances where D it (vet-syr) alone support an abbreviated text in Luke the longer text is the original[61]. (B[1]) Verbal peculiarities make it highly improbable that Luke 22:19b–20 is drawn from the parallel texts in 1 Cor 11 and Mark 14[62]. In addition, because we are dealing here with liturgical traditions some verbal similarity is to be expected even in the absence of direct literary dependence (C[1]) Non-Lukan stylistic features in 22:19b–20 indicate only that the text was a primitive, liturgical tradition incorporated without revision by Luke. (D[1]) Without vv 19b–20, the short form manifests an untenable structure. Verses 19 and 21 are incongruous. Verse 19a can hardly stand on its own. (E[1]) The claim that Luke deliberately and categorically avoided sacrificial themes in association with Jesus' death is unfounded. (F[1]) If the Last Supper was a Passover, the double reference to the cup (vv 17, 20) is easily explained. (G[1]) On the other hand, if a later scribe inserted vv 19b–20 as an interpolation from Paul and/or Mark, then why did the scribe leave the two cup-references? (H[1]) Several hypotheses have been offered to explain why the long text would have been shortened: (a) to preserve a secret formula from pagans; (b) to reflect liturgical practice in the second century; (c) due to confusion over the two cups (i.e. to harmonize Luke's account with the other institution-narratives) a scribe dropped the second reference; and (d) due to scribal peculiarities.

Regarding these arguments a few preliminary remarks are in order. First, arguments A, D, B[1], and C[1] are closely related and call for a comparative analysis of the eucharistic pericopae (see below). Second, concerning C and E[1], one has only to refer to Acts 20:28 to pull the rug from under the assertion that Luke systematically avoided sacrificial themes associated with Jesus' death. Moreover, it will not do to assume too quickly that Luke has edited the ransom-saying from Mark 10:45 out of his parallel account of Jesus' lesson to his disciples on servanthood (22:24–27)[63]. Third, argument E is nullified by F[1] and G[1]. Fourth, with reference to A[1], it is surely a major obstacle for supporters of the short text that this text is read by only one Greek manuscript – and that by one whose idiosyncratic alterations are legend. Fifth, the force of D[1] is somewhat diminished by the abruptness of 22:21, regardless of which text is accepted as original. Last,

---

233–235; Metzger, *Textual Commentary*, 173–177; Schweizer, *Luke*, 332; J. H. Petzer, "Luke 22:19b–20 and the Structure of the Passage", *NovT* 26 (3, 1984) 249–252.
61 Jeremias, *Eucharistic Words*, 145–152.
62 See Schürmann, *Einsetzungsbericht*, 17–81; Dibelius, *Tradition*, 209–210.
63 See further below, chapter 3.VII.

supporters of the long text certainly must account for the abbreviation of the text (arguments A and H¹), and not all of the possibilities mentioned are satisfying. In particular, while Jeremias (followed by Taylor and Metzger) has valiantly argued for (a), he does not account for the fact that the "secret and sacred" sayings are left standing in the parallel texts, nor for the fact that even the shorter form in Luke reads τοῦτό ἐστιν τὸ σῶμά μου — which, by his theory, should also have been omitted. It is with the remaining options — (b), (c), and (d) — that the long form enters the realm of probability.

At this juncture it is convenient to note the observations by J. H. Petzer on the structure of the narrative in question. In his recent essay on this passage he demonstrates the necessity of vv 19b–20 for maintaining the sign-explanation structural pattern of both this and the parallel accounts in Matthew, Mark, and Paul. He pictures the structure of Luke's institution-narrative thus[64]:

A	a	τὸ πάσχα φαγεῖν	sign:	eating (bread)	(15, 16a)	a	
	b	τῇ Βασιλείᾳ	explanation:	Kingdom	(16b)	b	
B	a'	το ποτήριον, πίω	sign:	drinking(cup)	(17, 18a)	a'	
	b'	ἡ Βασιλεία	explanation:	Kingdom	(18b)	b'	
A'	a''	ἄρτον	sign:	bread	(19a)	a''	
	b''	τὸ σῶμά μου	explanation:	body	(19b)	b''	
B'	a+	ποτήριον	sign:	cup	(20a)	a+	
	b+	τὸ αἷμά μου	explanation:	blood	(20b)	b+	

As can be readily seen, the omission of vv 19b–20 would change drastically the balance of the structure of the whole, and this is corroborative evidence for the originality of these verses.

Before a final judgment on the textual issue is handed down, however, a detailed comparison of Mark 14:22–24; Luke 22:19b–20; and 1 Cor 11:23–25 is in order. It will be helpful first to set out the pertinent texts in parallel.

Mark:	καὶ ἐσθιόντων αὐτῶν λαβὼν ἄρτον	εὐλογησὰς	ἔκλασεν
Luke:	καὶ λαβὼν ἄρτον	εὐχαριστήσας	ἔκλασεν
Paul:	ἔλαβεν ἄρτον καὶ	εὐχαριστήσας	ἔκλασεν

Mark:	καὶ ἔδωκεν αὐτοῖς καὶ εἶπεν· λάβετε·	τοῦτό ἐστιν τὸ σῶμά
Luke:	καὶ ἔδωκεν αὐτοῖς λέγων·	τοῦτό ἐστιν τὸ σῶμά
Paul:	καὶ εἶπεν·	τοῦτό μού εστιν τὸ

---

64 Petzer, "Luke 22:19b–22", 251.

Mark:	μου.
Luke:	μου τὸ ὑπὲρ ὑμῶν διδόμενον· τοῦτο ποιεῖτε εἰς τὴν ἐμὴν
Paul:	σῶμα τὸ ὑπὲρ ὑμῶν· τοῦτο ποιεῖτε εἰς τὴν ἐμὴν

Mark	καὶ λαβὼν ποτήριον
Luke:	ἀνάμνησιν. καὶ τὸ ποτήριον ὡσαύτως μετὰ
Paul:	ἀνάμνησιν. ὡσαύτως καὶ τὸ ποτήριον μετὰ

Mark:	εὐχαριστήσας ἔδωκεν αὐτοῖς, καὶ ἔπιον ἐξ
Luke:	τὸ δειπνῆσαι,
Paul:	τὸ δειπνῆσαι

Mark:	αὐτοῦ πάντες. καὶ εἶπεν αὐτοῖς· τοῦτό
Luke:	λεγών· τοῦτο τὸ ποτήριον ἡ
Paul:	λεγών· τοῦτο τὸ ποτήριον ἡ

Mark:	ἐστιν τὸ αἷμά μου τῆς διαθήκης τὸ ἐκχυννόμενον
Luke:	καινὴ διαθήκη ἐν τῷ αἵματί μου τὸ ὑπὲρ ὑμῶν
Paul:	καινὴ διαθήκη ἐστὶν ἐν τῷ ἐμῷ αἵματι·

Mark:	ὑπὲρ πολλῶν.
Luke:	ἐκχυννόμενον.
Paul:	τοῦτο ποιεῖτε, ὁσάκις ἐὰν πίνητε, εἰς τὴν ἐμὴν ἀνάμνησιν.

A careful scrutiny of this "synposis" sugests, first, there is indeed a strong case for insisting that Luke 22:19–20 is a "Mischtext", based on the traditions found in Mark and Paul. Every phrase and almost every word in the Lukan passage is either identical to or finds a close correspondence in either the Markan or the Pauline parallel. There are three possible explanations for this phenomenon. One could argue that Luke 22:19b–20 is a later addition to the Third Gospel, based on the other two traditions. Alternatively, one could claim that the long text is original, but that Luke joined the Pauline and Markan traditions to produce his own version[65]. Finally, one could hypothesize that Luke's text was associated with the others at an earlier point in the development of the eucharistic tradition.

Second, a remarkable piling-up of non-Lukan features appears in these two verses. Jeremias notes the following: ὑπέρ, ἀνάμνησις, ἐμός used attributively in v 19, the word order of καὶ τὸ ποτήριον ὡσαύτως (cf. 5:10, 33; 10:32; 20:31), the omission of the copula in v 20b, and τὸ ... ἐκχυννόμενον in the nominative in v 20b even though it qualifies αἵματι[66].

Third, vv 19–20 contain no characteristic Lukan words[67]. These latter two observations, when taken together, indicate the absence of Lukan redaction in vv 19–20, and render highly unlikely the hypothesis that Luke is responsible for constructing these verses.

---

65 On this view, see Pesch, *Abendmahl*, 31–34.
66 Jeremias, *Eucharistic Words*, 154–155; Cf. Kilpatrick, *Eucharist*, 31–32; Taylor, *Passion*, 55.
67 As listed by Fitzmyer, *Luke*, 1:110–111; Gaston, *Electronicae*. Cf. Taylor, *Passion*, 55.

In his Moorhouse Lectures (1975) on *The Eucharist in Bible and Liturgy*, Kilpatrick sets forth an important case against the originality of vv 19b—20, and regards the non-Lukan nature of the language and style of these verses as pivotal for this determination. He notes that some interpreters explain away this phenomenon by arguing that Luke would have been hesitant to change the language of this material because of its liturgical-traditional character (see point C^1 above). He counters that ample evidence exists in early Christianity that the liturgy was altered, and draws attention to the variations in the NT accounts and the later accounts in Justin, Hippolytus, and so on. He then suggests that Luke deliberately omitted the Markan words of institution because he found Mark's reference to "drinking blood" unacceptable.

As compelling as this reasoning may at first appear, it is not without its problems. First, Kilpatrick himself provides evidence in the case of Paul — to whom he credits knowledge of two separate eucharistic traditions, one each in 1 Cor 10 and 11 — that a NT author might retain a eucharistic tradition without revision — or, in the case of Paul, without harmonization. More importantly, he has not dealt with *Luke's* attitude toward such traditions, and the problematic language of Acts 20:28 is suggestive that Luke was capable of taking over liturgical-type material without revision[68]. Second, if Mark's language regarding "drinking blood" was so offensive, why is it found in Mark's Gospel in the first place? And in Matthew's? Did Luke understand the use of such language so woodenly that he could not have been aware of its metaphorical referent? Did Luke not himself celebrate the eucharist and so have no understanding of the meaning of such language nor have any alternative language to offer if indeed he found Mark's wording problematic? We conclude that Kilpatrick's thesis founders on close inspection.

Returning, then, to our list of observations regarding the eucharistic "synopsis", we note fourthly that in liturgical texts describing the Supper we naturally expect some correspondence in wording and phrasing. Points of contact in such cases suggest familiarity among the writers with common tradition, whether oral or written, but not necessarily direct literary dependence.

Fifth, we must ask, What sort of editor would the author of 22:19b—20 have had to have been in order to formulate such a hodge-podge collection from Mark and Paul? What would have motivated such an enterprise?

---

[68] See Eduard Schweizer, *Luke: A Challenge to Present Theology* (London: S.P.C.K., 1982) 44—45; Marshall, *Luke*, 171—174.

Last, we may outline a number of differences between Luke's version of the eucharistic tradition and the other two. In 22:19, εἶπεν, read by Mark and Paul, becomes λεγών. This shift could possibly be explained with recourse to Lukan redaction. Also in 22:19, Luke, for no apparent reason, adds διδόμενον to the σῶμα-word. It could be argued that the addition was Luke's attempt to gain better symmetry with the cup-word, which employs ἐκχυννόμενον. However, as we shall see momentarily, if Luke or some other writer were editing for parallelism then that editorial principle was not applied consistently. In 22:20, ὡσαύτως μετὰ τὸ δειπνῆσαι represents a word order that is both non-Lukan and non-Pauline (cf. 1 Cor 11:25). Contra both Mark and Paul, Luke has no ἔστιν in the cup-word — an omission which is contrary to Luke's normal style. This omission also has a negative impact on the symmetry of the two interpretive sayings in Luke. Ἐν τῷ αἵματί μου appears in a different word sequence than the similar expression in 1 Cor 11:25, and Luke has the first person pronoun in the genitive case, Paul in the dative. Τὸ ὑπὲρ ὑμῶν ἐκχυννόμενον, in 22:20, is parallel to the phrase in Mark 14:24, but in a different word order. Moreover, Mark has πολλῶν whereas Luke uses ὑμῶν. Finally, again working against the symmetry of the Jesus-logia, Luke has no τοῦτο ποιεῖτε (. . .) εἰς τὴν ἐμὴν ἀνάμνησιν in 22:20, contra 1 Cor 11:25. Why would Luke borrow the phrase for v 19 and not for v 20? Schürmann provides an extremely detailed anslysis of the relation of the Lukan text with that of Mark and Paul, from which he claims that Luke's wording cannot be explained as an editing of Paul's and Mark's eucharistic pericopae[69]. Without going into the details of his exhaustive inquiry we have already begun to see the difficulty confronting the hypothesis that Luke 22:19b–20 is merely an interpolation from Mark 14:22–24 and 1 Cor 11:23–25.

We conclude that Luke 22:19–20 is dependent neither on the Markan tradition nor on the Pauline. While the points of intersection between Paul's tradition and Luke's are sufficient to suggest Luke's debt to a tradition very much like Paul's, there is still adequate reason to deny a direct literary relationship between Luke 22:19–20 and 1 Cor 11:23–25. More probably, Luke and Paul are each dependent on a common, earlier form of the same tradition. We can go on to say that, as to the textual problem of 22:19b–20, the external and internal evidence points to the originality of the longer text. It was the Third Evangelist himself who incorporated this tradition into his Gospel. Due to the apparent lack of connectives between

---

69 Schürmann, Einsetzungsbericht, 17–81.

vv 14 and 15, and 18 and 19, it will be necessary to say a word about the literary unity of Luke 22:14—20 before departing from this section.

There can be little doubt that the eucharistic words of Jesus circulated as independent tradition in primitive Christianity (1 Cor 11:23—25). It follows, then, that the tradition employed in Luke 22:19—20 may have existed apart from its immediate context in Luke. A similar assumption can be made regarding vv 15—18. This is evident first from our literary analysis of the passage. Moreover, while these verses are not repeated elsewhere in the NT, the eschatological motif to which they witness is present in Mark 14:25 and 1 Cor 11:26. Importantly, in both of these non-Lukan versions, the eschatological motif, while apparently inherent to the eucharistic tradition[70], is loosely connected. As for the Markan text, Taylor has offered a reasonable hypothesis that v 25 is the residue of a narrative tradition[71]. As for the Pauline text, v 26 is probably a Pauline formulation based on a Synoptic-like tradition. Still further, as previously observed, Luke 22:15—18 exhibits a degree of (liturgical?) parallelism between vv 15 and 17, 16 and 18 — though the correspondence is neither extensive nor formal. On the basis of these considerations we may theorize that vv 15—18 enjoyed circulation independent of the eucharistic tradition within the context of early Christian fellowship meals — meals characterized above all by eschatological hope. Unlike vv 19—20, vv 15—18 retain no eucharistic interpretation of the Last Supper (cf. John 13:1—17 and the fellowship meals in Acts) and no explicit emphasis on the soteriological significance of Jesus' death (though, perhaps there is an implicit emphasis on the role of Jesus' death as precursor to the coming of the kingdom). The emphasis of vv 15—18 is primarily prophetic and eschatological.

How, then, did vv 15—18 and 19—20 come to be joined? Early Christianity saw an obvious connection between the effects of the death of Jesus and the sacrificial character of the paschal lamb (cf. 1 Cor 5:6—8; 1 Pet 1:13—19). This link may have provided the early impetus for joining together the two independent strands of material, vv 15—18 and vv 19—20. The effect thus achieved was to place the Last Supper squarely within the historical and conceptual context of the Passover. Verse 14 was then added as a needed introduction to the whole. As evidence for Lukan redaction is minimal overall, and altogether lacking in the connective seams, it is reasonable to further suppose that vv 14—20 (at least) constituted a literary unit prior to Luke's writing. It may even have been a part of a larger account, but this remains to be seen.

---

70 Cf. Wainwright, *Eucharist*, 18—59.
71 Taylor, *Mark*, 543.

VI. Luke 22:21–23 (Mark 14:18–21)

As noted previously, Luke's narrative transposes the sequence of events found in Mark 14:18–25. Thus, in a sequence corresponding to that in John 13:1–17, 18–30, the prediction of the betrayal follows the Last Supper in Luke. Relative to Mark's account, Luke's is brief. Only 39.1 per cent of Luke's wording is Markan, but this statistic should not be allowed to disguise the close verbal agreement between Luke 22:22 and Mark 14:21ab.

V 21: Much of the material in Mark 14:18b, 20 is distilled here. Consequently, the betrayal announcement follows abruptly from v 20. Luke has only πλήν in place of Mark's ἀμὴν λέγω ὑμῖν. Luke is capable of using πλήν as an adversative conjunction apart from his sources[72], but he never substitutes it for an introductory ἀμήν in Mark. In fact, it would have been quite out of character for Luke to have edited out this whole Markan phrase here. Ἰδού, however, may be Lukan[73]. Ὁ παραδιδούς με parallels Mark's εἷς ἐξ ὑμῶν παραδώσει με (cf. ἰδοὺ ὁ παραδιδούς με in Mark 14:42). On this abbreviation, see above on 22:3. The use of χείρ to denote a person is consistent with usage in the LXX and is not peculiar to Lukan style[74]. Luke's fondness for Septuagintalisms may be responsible for the use of this idiom in this instance, or it would explain his taking it over from a non-Markan source if he read it there. Both Mark and Luke have μετ' ἐμοῦ, but whereas in Mark the betrayer is identified as the "one who is dipping bread into the dish with me", in Luke he is simply "at the table". It is arguable that this shift reflects the literary positon of the scene after the meal in Luke; however, John, whose order is akin to Luke's, includes the Markan idea of "dipping the morsel", albeit in a variant form.

V 22: Except for the middle clause expressing divine purpose and the use of πλήν, the wording of this verse corresponds precisely with that in Mark 14:21ab. Mark's central phrase, ὑπάγει καθὼς γέγραπται περὶ αὐτοῦ, corresponds to Luke's κατὰ τὸ ὡρισμένον πορεύεται. Ὁρίζω appears only here in the Synoptics, but carries the idea of "divine appointment" in Acts 2:23; 10:42; 17:31. God's foreknowledge, purpose, and determination are important concepts for Luke – he uses this verb along with other terms to convey these related ideas[75]. This word, then, may be credited to Lukan redaction of Mark. Πορεύομαι appears some 88 times in Luke-Acts. Luke substitutes it for Mark's ὑπάγω at 5:24; 8:48; 22:8, 22; and for ἀπέρχομαι at 4:42; 9:12. He apparently borrows it from Q at 7:6, 22; 11:26; 15:4. Of the 49 occurrences of the word in the Third Gospel, however, most are in contexts wherein the evangelist is following neither Mark or Q, so the source-question here remains ambiguous. Gaston omits πορεύομαι from his list of characteristic Lukan vocabulary, but notes that Luke does use the term editorially from time to time[76]. Marshall suggests that the verb may have been used already in Luke's source(s) to denote the "way of Jesus" (cf. 9:51; 13:22; 22:33)[77]. Luke has no aversion to γέγραπται, however (cf. 2:23; 3:4; 4:4, 8; et al.), nor apparently to καθὼς γέγραπται (cf. 2:23). Apart from Mark 14:21, where Mark uses the verb to refer to the Scriptures either directly or indirectly, Luke has only one parallel passage (Mark 11:17/Luke 19:46),

---

[72] Luke 6:35; 10:11(?); 11:41; 12:31(?); 19:27(?); 22:22. Contra Taylor, *Passion*, 60; Jeremias, *Sprache*, 288.
[73] But, cf. Rehkopf, *Sonderquelle*, 10–11.
[74] Cf. Eduard Lohse, "Χείρ", in *TDNT*, 9:424–437.
[75] See Marshall, *Luke*, 103–115, 188–192; David L. Tiede, *Prophecy and History in Luke-Acts* (Philadelphia: Fortress, 1980) 97–102; O'Toole, *Unity*, 23–28.
[76] Gaston, *Electronicae*, 66; Schürmann, *Paschamahlbericht*, 90.
[77] Marshall, *Gospel of Luke*, 809; cf. Rehkopf, *Sonderquelle*, 15–17.

and there Luke borrows γέγραπται. Hence, it is not clear why Luke would have wanted to edit Mark so extensively here.

Already read in v 21, πλήν substitutes for Mark's δέ. The strengthened adversative also appears in the close conceptual and structural parallel to this verse in 17:1 (Matt 18:7): ἀνένδεκτόν ἐστιν τοῦ τὰ σκάνδαλα μὴ ἐλθεῖν, πλὴν οὐαὶ δι' οὗ ἔρχεται. Luke may have employed πλήν in 22:22 with this earlier logion in mind. Alternatively, the similarity in shape between 17:1 and 22:22 raises the possibility that this kind of woe-saying had already achieved a fairly fixed form. Hence, Luke 22:22 need not rest on Mark[78]. If he were following Mark here, Luke may have omitted as redundant Mark's second reference to the Son of Man, but it is difficult to understand why he would also have omitted the whole of Mark 14:21c – especially since he includes the parallel clause in 17:1–2.

V 23: Luke's record of the disciples' reaction to Jesus' announcement differs from Mark's (14:19) in terms of language, content, and context. In Luke's version, the disciples are not "sorrowful", nor do they ask, "Is it I?" Moreover, one reads nowhere in this pericope of a move among the disciples or by the evangelist to identify the betrayer. Both Mark and Luke employ ἤρξαντο, and Luke's συζητεῖν πρὸς ἑαυτούς corresponds roughly with Mark's λεγεῖν αὐτῷ εἷς κατὰ εἷς. Συζητέω is not characteristically Lukan, but may lead the way for the dispute of v 24; this association would be expected if the verses were connected in a pre-Lukan tradition. Conversely, Luke may be responsible for constructing this bridge. As in 22:2, the construction τό + indirect question is Lukan. The use of the optative εἴη also suggests Lukan redaction[79]. Μέλλω is Lukan, and so may be πράσσω – which never appears in Mark or Matthew[80]. Contacts with Mark in this verse are minimal.

At some points in this brief pericope Lukan redaction is quite evident, though difficult to explain if Luke's only source were the Second Gospel. In addition to the linguistic evidence we have considered, we may add a *traditionsgeschichtliche* observation that speaks for the non-Markan, pre-Lukan character of the Lukan report. Luke's account is conspicuous for the absence of any attempt to identify specifically the betrayer or otherwise point the finger of blame (cf. Matt 26:22, 23, 25; Mark 14:19–20; John 13:23–30). This speaks not only for the non-Markan nature of Luke's foundation-source here, but also for the relative antiquity of the Lukan tradition on the point[81]. Hence, it is more likely that Luke knew a parallel account of this story (which he has conflated with Mark's) than that this account rests solely on that of the Second Gospel.

VII. Luke 22:24–27 (Mark 10:41–45)

The Lukan account of the dispute over precedence among the disciples finds no parallel in the Markan passion narrative. However, a pericope

---

78 Rehkopf (*Sonderquelle*, 13–21) argues that Luke 22:22 and Mark 14:21 are independent Greek versions of an Aramaic Jesus-logion.
79 Fitzmyer, *Luke*, 1:110; Jeremias, *Sprache*, 289.
80 Gaston, *Electronicae*, 66; Jeremias, *Sprache*, 289.
81 See Sanders, *Tendencies*, 292; Taylor, *Passion*, 60; Bultmann, *History*, 264–265.

with unmistakeable similarities in content is present earlier in the Second Gospel (10:41 –45). Luke has not incorporated this earlier material into a pericope corresponding to the Markan context and this may speak in favor of the notion that Luke has simply held the Markan material back for inclusion here. Be that as it may, a number of reasons exist for doubting that these verses are a Lukan editing of Mark, and for theorizing that Mark and Luke have each given independent versions of the same tradition[82].

First, the Lukan context is confirmed by the parallel account in John 13:1-17 where, in a version independent of Luke, the same theme is communicated by Jesus[83]. More generally, the presence of any discourse at all following the Last Supper is supported by the Johannine narrative.

Second, the Lukan context is confirmed by the language of 22:24–27 and, to a lesser extent, by that of Mark 10:41–45. In particular, the sharp accent on $\delta\iota\alpha\kappa o\nu\acute{e}\omega$ ("to serve at table") and the double antithesis $\acute{o}$ $\acute{a}\nu\alpha\kappa\epsilon\acute{\iota}\mu\epsilon\nu o\varsigma - \acute{o}$ $\delta\iota\alpha\kappa o\nu\tilde{\omega}\nu$ place this paragraph squarely within the confines of the meal episode[84].

Third, and closely related, the saying in 22:27, unlike the more general logion of Mark 10:45, is marked off by its peculiarity, its specific reference to a concrete situation — that of a meal in which Jesus is $\acute{o}$ $\delta\iota\alpha\kappa o\nu\tilde{\omega}\nu$[85].

Fourth, Luke's tendency to avoid duplication in his sources[86] might explain his omission of Mark 10:41–45.

Fifth, historically, a dispute of this kind is not inconceivable at this point in the order of events. It might have arisen because of the seating arrangement at the meal, or in the context of Peter and John's having "served" the others by making preparations for the meal (22:7–13)[87]. On the other hand, the argument ($\sigma v\zeta\eta\tau\acute{e}\omega$) about who would betray Jesus (22:23) could have given rise to declarations of who was the greatest. In this case, the $\kappa\alpha\acute{\iota}$ of v 24 would recall the dispute of v 23.

Sixth, as has been well-documented already by Schürmann and Taylor, the language of Luke's account is quite dissimilar to that in Mark's[88]. In general, Luke presents a more Graecized form than does Mark — note esp-

---

82 Of course, it is possible that Jesus gave a similar teaching on two separate occasions — cf. Morris, *Apostolic Preaching*, 30; Sydney T. Page, "The Authenticity of the Ransom Logion (Mark 10: 45b)", in *Gospel Perspectives*, 1:150, 152. Nevertheless, the similarity of these two pericopae favors some sort of literary relationship.
83 See below, chapter 4; Lindars, *Jesus*, 77; Raymond E. Brown, *The Gospel according to John*, 2 vols. (London: Geoffrey Chapman, 1966/71) 2:557–558; Page, "Authenticity", 151–152.
84 Cf. Hermann W. Beyer, "Διακονέω", in *TDNT*, 2:81–87; Roloff, "Anfänge", 55–56.
85 Roloff, "Anfänge", 56; Edward Schillebeeckx, *Jesus: An Experiment in Christology* (London: William Collins, 1974) 304.
86 Fitzmyer, *Luke*, 1:81–82.
87 See Green, "Preparation for Passover".
88 Schürmann, *Abschiedsrede*, 63–99; Taylor, *Passion*, 61–64.

ecially the presence in Luke of φιλονεικία, εὐεργέτης, μείζων, νεώτερος, κυριεύω, and ἡγούμενος[89]. This fact does not point to the relative lateness of the Lukan version, however, for the two evangelists may simply have incorporated into their Gospels a different Greek translation of a common Aramaic source[90].

Finally, it will not do to conjecture that Luke has edited Mark 10:41– 45 to produce the present text, for his version cannot be accounted for as a mere redaction of Mark.

V 24: 'Εγένετο, δὲ καί, and τὸ τίς are characteristic of Lukan redaction[91]. Apart from this verse, φιλονεικία appears nowhere in the NT and is absent from the LXX. Luke is not found of μείζων as a comparative but uses μέγας (cf. Mark 10:43) as a superlative in 9:48.

V 25: Luke prefers εἶπεν πρός + accusative. When εἶπεν + dative appears in Luke, it is almost always borrowed from Luke's sources (e.g. 3:14; 4:3; 5:27; 6:39; 7:13, 22; 8:25, 48; et al.). Nevertheless, Luke's editorial practice does permit the use of εἶπεν + dative even when he changes his sources (e.g. 6:10; 9:20)[92]. This is the sole occurrence of κυριεύω in the Synoptic Gospels. Because Luke prefers compound verbs, his replacement of Mark's κατακυριεύω with the simplex form would be hard to explain. 'Εξουσιάζω is found only here in the Synoptics, and εὐεργέτης appears in the NT only here (cf. Acts 4:9; 10:38, where other members of the word group appear). Marshall suggests that this motif – the reputation of those in authority – may be Luke's addition to the tradition[93]. This proposal finds support in the use of καλέω in its typically Lukan sense of "to call" or "to name".

V 26: Mark's very descriptive words are all reformulated in the Lukan version, but not with words from Luke's characteristic vocabulary. Nevertheless, the antithetical form read in Mark reappears in Luke, and there is thus good reason for supporting the hypothesis that Mark and Luke give variant forms of a common tradition.

V 27: The two-fold question of v 27a is missing in Mark, but v 27b is similar to Mark 10:45a. 'Ανακεῖμαι appears in Luke only here; elsewhere he apparently prefers κατακεῖμαι. Luke has no parallel for Mark 10:45b.

The cumulative weight of these various lines of argumentation leaves little doubt that Luke has used a non-Markan, pre-Lukan source for 22: 24–27. Moreover, we noted the closeness with which the pericope is welded to its context. Taken together, these facts suggest that we are dealing here with no Lukan insertion but with an earlier narrative.

VIII. Luke 22:28–30 (Matt 19:28)

As with the preceding section on service, Jesus' continued discourse on the future role of the disciples is without parallel in the Markan passion

---

89 Cf. Lohse, *Märtyrer*, 119; Joachim Jeremias, *New Testament Theology*, vol. 1: *The Proclamation of Jesus* (New York: Charles Scribner's Sons, 1971) 293.
90 So Black, *Aramaic Approach*, 222. Among the relevant evidence he notes: Mark's μέγας = Luke's μείζων (*rabba*); πρῶτος = ἡγούμενος (*rish*); δοῦλος = διακονῶν ('*abhda*); and διάκονος = νεώτερος (*talya*).
91 Cf. 9:46; Fitzmyer, *Luke*, 1:100–111; Jeremias, *Sprache*, 290.
92 *Contra* Jeremias, *Sprache*, 290.
93 Marshall, *Gospel of Luke*, 812.

narrative. Indeed, no parallel exists in the whole of the Gospel of Mark, but a similar text is found in the First Gospel. Verbal agreement between the Markan and Lukan versions in the last clause of the pericope and conceptual agreement elsewhere make it certain that the two are somehow related.

V 28: Matthew and Luke agree only in the use of ὑμεῖς in reference to the disciples. Διαμένω appears in the Synoptics only here and in 1:22. Matthew's ἀκολουθέω occurs more often in Luke with reference to the disciples' following Jesus. Had the latter term been original it is difficult to see why Luke would have altered it; on the other hand, Matthew may have assimilated the text to concur with 19:27. At two earlier points (4:13; 8:13), Luke appears to have added πειρασμός. He employs the noun to refer to "trials and tribulations" in 8:13 (cf. Mark 4:17; Matt 13:21). Both in 8:13 and in 4:13 the thought of satanic opposition is clear. Elsewhere, the word is taken from his sources (11:4; cf. below on 22:40, 46). We conclude that the phrase ἐν τοῖς πειρασμοῖς μου may be a Lukan insertion.

V 29: Only here in the Synoptics does διατίθεμαι appear (cf. Acts 3:25). Ὁ πατήρ μου is not characteristic of Lukan redaction[94]. Matthew has no real parallel to this verse.

V 30: Nor is v 30a paralleled by Matthew. The thought of eating and drinking in the kingdom has a long history prior to Luke[95]. In v 30b, Luke lacks Matthew's redundant ὑμεῖς and his reference to *twelve* thrones. Otherwise the wording is the same even if the word order is different. As this statement follows the prediction of the betrayal in Luke, it is likely that Luke deleted the first δώδεκα so as not to include the betrayer among those who sit on thrones.

In addition to the difficulties in wording between the versions of Matthew and Luke, one should consider the evidence linking this pericope with its context in Luke. (A) It is cast in the form of a farewell speech, which is wholly appropriate to the "table-talk" following the Last Supper[96]. (B) The kingdom-reference in vv 29–30 recalls that same emphasis in vv 16 and 18. (C) Διατίθεμαι, διαθήκη, and the pervasive idea of the βασιλεία all function together in revealing the effect of Christ's work[97]. (D) Eating and drinking in the kingdom corresponds to the meal context of vv 15–20. (E) The whole section, vv 15–30, is set apart by its eschatological outlook.

---

94 The expression appears in 2:49 and 24:49 in texts with no Synoptic parallel, and in 10:22 where it is also read in Matt 11:27. Other places where it is found in Matthew, but not in the Lukan parallel, include Matt 10:32/Luke 12:8; 10:33/12:9; 12:50/8:21; 26:29/22:18; 26:39/22:42. Of these instances, the last is especially telling, for Mark's αββα ὁ πάτηρ is replaced both by Matthew and Luke: πάτηρ μου in Matthew, πάτηρ in Luke. If Luke had a preference for the expression or for any other, similarly personal address, surely it would have been exhibited here. Cf. Jeremias, *Sprache*, 291.
95 See above, chapter 3 n.46; Wainwright, *Eucharist*, 105–106; Edward J. Kilmartin, *The Eucharist in the Primitive Church* (Englewood Cliffs, New Jersey: Prentice-Hall, 1965) 1–16.
96 William S. Kurz ("Luke 22:14–38 and Greco-Roman and Biblical Farewell Addressess", *JBL* 104 [2, 1985] 251–268) states that Luke gathered unrelated sayings into the farewell speech form for his Last Supper narrative. However, he assumes this point rather than argues it, nor does he deal with the possibility that Luke found this "farewell address" in his source, nor with the possibility that the account is largely historical. As Barrett ("Paul's Address", 109) has observed, "... real farewell speeches are apt to take the same form as fictitious ones".
97 Cf. Ernst Käsemann, "The Pauline Doctrine of the Lord's Supper", in *NT Themes*, 128.

It thus appears that Luke and Matthew have presented variant forms of the same tradition[98].

We have seen that the material underlying 22:14–30 is, on the whole, non-Markan and pre-Lukan, and that throughout this section editorial amendment is minimal. Moreover, we have observed the close verbal and conceptual ties binding together these pericopae. These points constitute significant evidence that Luke possessed a connected narrative, embracing this material at least.

IX. Luke 22:31–34 (Mark 14:26–31)

The setting for the prediction of Peter's denial in Luke agrees with that in John 13:36–38, but differs from that in Mark[99]. For this reason, Mark's reference to the departure to the Mount of Olives (14:26; cf. Luke 22:39) is premature for Luke. Additionally, Luke does not record the scriptural quotation in Mark 14:27 or the passing note about the post-resurrection appearance in Galilee (Mark 14:28). Indeed, for Luke those appearances center in and around Jerusalem (24:13–53), not Galilee. Mark, on the other hand, has no parallel to 22:31–32. Mark 14:29 and 31 correspond to 22:33, and 14:30 is similar to 22:34. Overall, the percentage of words in Luke found also in Mark is low (17.7%), though for v 34 that figure is considerably higher (53.3%).

VV 31–32: With no transitional clause from v 30 to v 31 the narrative shift is abrupt. There is no Markan parallel and it is generally agreed that these verses constitute a pre-Lukan tradition[100]. The parallel text in Matt 16:17–19 demonstrates even further than the linguistic evidence that with vv 31–32 we are dealing with old tradition. In the Matthean text Peter's confession of the Christ is followed by Jesus' blessing, his statement that knowledge of this kind has its source with "my heavenly Father", and his promises regarding Peter's future, prominent role in the church and the church's capacity to stand strong against Hades. The coincidence of these two texts is astonishing in light of their very different contexts and the striking differences in content. Both name Peter as Simon, identify an other-worldly opponent, guarantee that this opponent will not have the role of conquerer, give Peter a place of prominence among the believers, and indicate Peter's future

---

98 So also Taylor, *Passion*, 64; Marshall, *Gospel of Luke*, 814–818; T. W. Manson, *The Sayings of Jesus* (London: SCM, 1949) 216–217, 339; Schneider, *Luke*, 2:451. Gundry (*Matthew*, 392) writes that Matthew has imported the tradition lying behind Luke. *Contra* Maddox, *Luke-Acts*, 151 n.100; Lindars, *Jesus*, 124–125.

99 For this reason, Günter Klein, ("Die Verleugnung des Petrus: Eine traditionsgeschichtliche Untersuchung", *ZTK* 58 [1961] 294) regards this pericope as pre-Lukan. But Luke may be responsible for this new setting (so Linneman, *Studien*, 93–94), so we must not let this point prejudge the issue at hand.

100 Cf. Linnemann, *Studien*, 72; Taylor, *Passion*, 65–66; Marshall, *Gospel of Luke*, 818–819; Schürmann, *Abschiedsrede*, 99–112; Manson, *Sayings*, 339–340; Schneider, *Luke*, 2:452; idem, "'Stärke deine Brüder!' (Lk 22, 32): Die Aufgabe des Petrus nach Lukas", in *Lukas*, 147–148; Schweizer, *Luke*, 334; Jeremias, *Sprache*, 291–292.

"pastoral" role. While much about Matt 16:17–19 may be Matthean, these points of intersection are too significant and pervasive to be set aside lightly[101]. Instead, we seem to have here two versions of an old logion which, because of its appropriateness to the post-resurrection setting, was subjected to emendation in the pre-Gospel epoch. Because of the artificiality of its ties to the Matthean context (Matthew's introduction of this material overturns the passion announcement/rebuke cycle of his Markan source – 8:31–33) and its explicit use of ἐκκλησία we may question the relative age of the Matthean account *vis-à-vis* the Lukan – the setting of which is supported by the emphasis on Peter in the passion narrative in the four Gospels, by parallels in other farewell speeches of antiquity, and indirectly by the further parallel in John 21: 15–19[102].

V 33: This verse finds some correspondence in the thought and wording of Mark 14:29, 31. Luke does not identify the speaker as Peter (Mark 14:29). The reader will understand that Simon (v 31) is replying to Jesus, but Πέτρος is a characteristic word in Lukan redaction[103], so we would not have been surprised if Luke had borrowed the name from Mark here – if indeed he was following Mark at this point. The vocative κύριε is not read in Mark, but is attested in John 13:37; hence it may be pre-Lukan. Rehkopf asserts that Luke's "Todesbereitschaft" is an indication that he could not have been following Mark[104], but μετά ... εἰς θάνατον πορεύεσθαι does have a parallel in Mark's συναποθανεῖν (14:31). Given Luke's preference for compound verbs in general, and συν- words in particular, however, this alteration would be odd if Luke was redacting only Mark. Mark's ἐὰν δέῃ (14:31) parallels Luke's ἔτοιμος. This noun appears 2 additional times in the Third Gospel, drawn from Q (Luke 12:40/Matt 24:44; 14:17/22:4, 8). He changes Mark's ἔτοιμος (14:15) into a verb in 22:12. Mark has nothing corresponding to εἰς φυλακήν, nor, strictly speaking, to πορεύομαι. Luke, on the other hand, has no parallel for ὡσαύτως δὲ καὶ πάντες ἔλεγον (Mark 14:31).

The greatest difference, however, comes in the *focus* of Luke's passage when compared with Mark's. In the latter, Peter is already saying he will not deny Jesus – a motif not yet present in Luke. Furthermore, by his response in Mark, Peter sets himself apart from and above the other disciples. No such note of comparison is sounded in the Lukan text. Rather, Peter is concerned only with verbalizing *his* faithfulness; he makes no allusion to what the others might do. The sum of these considerations casts doubt on the possibility of constructing a convincing case for taking this verse as a Lukan redaction of Mark. Moreover, its contacts with John both in the use of the vocative and the general focus of the text suggest a traditional, non-Markan foundation.

V 34: As in v 33, the speaker is only implied, in contrast to Mark 14:30. Εἶπον is preferred by Luke[105]. Luke characteristically drops Mark's ἀμήν (see above on 22:16). The vocative Πέτρε is not in Mark, but could be an assimilation to Mark 14:29; in view of Luke's preference for Πέτρος (see above on 22:33) its presence here is not surprising. Luke's οὐ ... ἕως parallels Mark's πρίν (cf. John 13:38). In the parallel to this verse in 22:61, Luke borrows Mark's πρίν; why not here? Mark's emphatic but verbose σήμερον ταύτῃ τῇ νυκτί is shortened to σήμερον. Mark is alone in referring to the cock's crowing twice. Otherwise, the wording regarding the cock is identical, though it appears in a different order. At the close of the verse Luke adds εἰδέναι, perhaps in view of the actual event (22:57). It would not be unreasonable to theorize that this tradition had achieved a relatively firm shape and was well known from early times – a theory encouraged by John 13:38b. If that was the case, such verbal agreement as is found in this verse would not be remarkable.

We may bring our discussion of this pericope to an end by summarizing our conclusions: vv 31–32 are Luke's redaction of a pre-Lukan, non-Markan source; v 33 also rests on pre-Lukan, non-Markan material; and

---

101 Gundry (*Matthew*, 330–335) argues for the Matthean composition of vv 17–19, but he neglects these parallels and introduces linguistic evidence that stretches our credulity too far.
102 Schneider, "'Stärke deine Brüder'!".
103 Gaston, *Electronicae*, 65; Schweizer, *Luke*, 102.
104 Cf. Rehkopf, *Sonderquelle*, 84 n.1; Jeremias, *Sprache*, 135–136, 292.
105 Gaston, *Electronicae*, 64.

v 34 is probably taken from Mark, though we have allowed for a similar, non-Markan source for this prophecy.

X. Luke 22:35–38

Luke's pericope about the two swords is without parallel in the canonical Gospels. There is general unanimity that at least part of this passage rests on tradition[106]. In what follows we propose to outline a series of arguments which together demonstrate not only that this pericope is substantially pre-Lukan but also that it is well-suited to its immediate context in the passion narrative – and thus not likely to have been a late insertion[107].

First, a comparison of the relevant texts demonstrates that the citation of Isa 53:12 in v 37 is unlikely to have originated with Luke.

Luke 22:37: καὶ μετὰ ἀνόμων ἐλογίσθη.
Isa 53:12 MT: ואת־פשעים נמנה
Isa 53:12 LXX: καὶ ἐν τοῖς ἀνόμοις ἐλογίσθη.
1 Clem 16:13: καὶ ἐν τοῖς ἀνόμοις ἐλογίσθη.

A comparison of these phrases reveals that the text of the Lukan citation diverges from the LXX in employing a different preposition and in not reading the article. Lampe argues that Luke's citation may rest on an alternative Greek textual tradition of the LXX: "1 Clement, for example, gives it as τοῖς ἀνόμοις without a preposition (16:13)"[108]; for this reason we have also cited the text from 1 Clement, which *does* employ the preposition and, indeed, follows the LXX text without alteration. Moo argues that Septuagintal influence is clear and draws attention to the coincidence of ἐλογίσθη and a form of ἄνομος in both the Lukan and LXX texts[109]. However, this is not certain since λογίζομαι does translate נמנה in 2 Chr 5:6; Isa 53:12[110] – and in any case the *sense* of these terms overlap; and since ἄνομος translates פשע 3 times in the LXX of Isaiah[111]. In fact, as

---

106 E.g., H. -W. Bartsch, "Jesu Schwertwort, Lukas XXII.35–38: Ueberlieferungsgeschichtliche Studie", *NTS* 20 (1974) 190–203; G. W. H. Lampe, "The Two Swords (Luke 22:35–38)", in *Jesus and Politics*, 335–351; Schneider, *Luke*, 2:454; Schweizer, *Luke*, 334; Marshall, *Gospel of Luke*, 823–827; Trocmé, *Passion*, 31; Taylor, *Passion*, 66–68; Schürmann, *Abschiedsrede*, 116–139.
107 *Contra*, e.g., Trocmé, *Passion*, 31; Linnemann, *Studien*, 93–94.
108 Lampe, "Two Swords", 339.
109 Douglas J. Moo, *The Old Testament in the Gospel Passion Narratives* (Sheffield: Almond, 1983) 133–134.
110 See H. W. Heidland, "Λογίζομαι, λογισμός", in *TDNT*, 4:284 n.2.
111 Moo, *OT – Passion*, 134. Moo makes too much of his observation that ἄνομος is relatively scarce in the NT, especially in the sense of "one who is unrighteous". The force of this line of reasoning is reduced when it is realized that פשע can signify "to transgress against God" (cf. BDB, 833) – a rendering which would be close semantically to a more literal rendering of ἄνομος as "paying no heed to the law" (cf. W. Gutbrod, "Άνομος", in *TDNT*, 4:1086).

numerous interpreters have observed, the citation in 22:37 is explicable as a literal translation of the MT[112]. Characteristically, Luke quotes from the LXX, so this citation should not be credited to him[113].

Second, Zimmermann and Black have demonstrated the high probability that the rather enigmatic Greek text of the sword-logion may be traced back to an Aramaic original[114]. Zimmermann goes on to indicate that in its Aramaic form the saying contained a word-play in which the meaning of the saying would have been quite clear — focusing on the disciples' lack of understanding. This suggests a pre-history in the developing tradition, not a Lukan origin.

Third, apart from the lengthy introduction to the OT citation — λέγω γὰρ ὑμῖν ὅτι τοῦτο τὸ γεγραμμένον δεῖ τελεσθῆναι ἐν ἐμοί — which probably represents Luke's desire to emphasize the *heilsgeschichtliche* purpose and necessity of Jesus' fate[115], there is actually little evidence of a linguistic nature to indicate that Luke is responsible for the formulation of this passage[116].

Fourth, as Lampe has seen, this pericope is one of a group of Jesus' sayings in the Gospels which have to do with the general theme of eschatological warnings of impending trials and distress. In thus pointing to the future, this text is intimately related with the four preceding pericopae — which, together with this one, comprise Jesus' *Tischgespräche*. The eschatological orientation of this passage is made clear by the time designations that indicate that the present time (i.e. Jesus' passion) is the turning-point: ὅτε . . . ἀλλὰ νῦν. The change in missionary instructions should not be

---

112 E.g., BDF, para. 145.2; R. T. France, *Jesus and the Old Testament* (London: Tyndale, 1971; reprint ed., Grand Rapids, Michigan: Baker, 1982) 244; Gleason L. Archer and Gregory Chirichigno, *Old Testament Quotations in the New Testament* (Chicago: Moody, 1983) 123; Martin Rese, *Alttestamentlichen Motive in der Christologie des Lukas* (Gütersloh: Gerd Mohn, 1969) 154.
113 "There is no evidence that Luke knew any Hebrew . . . " (Fitzmyer, *Luke*, 1:118). See also Schweizer, *Luke*, 334; Marshall, *Gospel of Luke*, 824, 826.
114 Frank Zimmermann, *The Aramaic Origin of the Four Gospels* (New York: Ktav, 1979) 136–137; Black, *Aramaic Approach*, 179.
115 On this motif in Luke, see, e.g., Eduard Lohse, "Lukas als Theologe der Heilsgeschichte", in *Einheit*, esp. pp. 150–153; Tiede, *Prophecy*, 97–125; Marshall, *Luke*, 104–107; Büchele, *Tod Jesu*, e.g., pp. 175–176; O'Toole, *Unity*, 26–28. That v 37 may betray Lukan redaction, cf. Tiede, *Prophecy*, 124; Marshall, *Gospel of Luke*, 826.
116 Cf. Taylor, *Passion*, 67–68; Schürmann, *Abscheidsrede*, 116–134; Jeremias, *Sprache*, 292–293. Morna D. Hooker (*Jesus and the Servant* [London: S.P.C.K., 1959] 86) suggests that the obscurity of the passage casts doubt on its genuineness. However, Schleiermacher appeals to the same canon as evidence for its genuineness and originality (quoted in Plummer, *Luke*, 506–507). Other arguments have been offered in support of the saying's authenticity — e.g. " . . . it is naturally related to the context . . . " (Vincent Taylor, *Jesus and His Sacrifice* [London: Macmillan, 1929] 193; Joachim Jeremias and Walther Zimmerli, "Παῖς θεοῦ", in *TDNT*, 5:716), and " . . . it has every appearance of being a spontaneous utterance" (Taylor *Jesus*, 193) — but these judgments are less objective.

taken woodenly as a literal command, for it is meant to signify the hostility with which Jesus' disciples will now be confronted – cf. Mark 13:13; John 15:18–21; 16:1–4, 33; and, especially, Matt 10:34–36/Luke 12:51–53 (peace-sword/peace-division).

> The violent language is intended to convey one clear picture: whereas the disciples of Jesus had once been made welcome everywhere, now each must be prepared for a lonely struggle to survive in a bitterly hostile world; no one henceforth will provide him [sic] with food or shelter, and he [sic] will be in constant danger of attack[117].

This understanding of the text leads to four observations.

(A) Verses 35–38 are tied to vv 21–34 by a common emphasis on "what will happen". We are not dealing with a string of unrelated sayings.

(B) The location of these sayings at Jesus' last meal is not in any way artificial. "Farewell discourses" with warnings or revelations about the future are common in the literature of the OT (e.g. Gen 47:29–50:14; Josh 23:1–24:32; 1 Sam 12; 1 Kgs 2:1–9; 1 Chr 28:1–29:28), ancient Judaism (e.g. *T. 12 Patr.*; *As. Mos.*; *Jub.*), and early Christianity (e.g. Acts 20:17–38; 1 Tim 1:12–17; 6:20; 2 Tim 3:1–9; 2 Pet 1:12–15; 3:3–12)[118].

(C) In particular, vv 35–38 are related to vv 28–30 and 31–34, for all three pericopae anticipate the distress associated with *this* eschatological moment. Verses 28–30 speak directly of πειρασμός, vv 31–34 introduce the idea of Peter's being tested by Satan, and these verses predict the upcoming eschatological trial to face the disciples.

(D) This will happen in accordance with the will of God (so v 37). When will it happen? In the next section (XI) we will see that these forward-looking sayings anticipate Jesus' passion, with its eschatologically decisive moment during the time of "distress" while Jesus and the disciples are on the Mount of Olives. Hence, the reference to Isa 53:12 is a general allusion to Jesus' passion – at which time he takes on the role of the Suffering Servant, performing the will of God in his death.

We conclude, then, that 22:35–38 is based on pre-Lukan material. This material has significant points of contact with preceding sections and may well have been associated with them in Luke's *Sondergut*.

---

117 Lampe, "Two Swords", 338; cf. pp. 337–338. See also Hans Conzelmann, *The Theology of St. Luke* (London: Faber and Faber, 1960; reprint ed., London: SCM, 1982) 80–81; Cassidy, *Jesus*, 45–46.

118 See further, Ethelbert Stauffer, *New Testament Theology* (London: SCM, 1955) 344–347; James I. H. McDonald, *Kerygma and Didache: The Articulation of the Earliest Christian Message* (Cambridge: Cambridge University, 1980) 73, 79, 86–87, 98–99; Lampe, "Two Swords", 338; Kurz, "Luke 22:14–38".

XI. Luke 22:39–46 (Mark 14:26, 32–42)

In constructing this story, was Luke dependent only on Mark's parallel account, or did he have access to another tradition? In recent years, the two main studies to have taken up this question are those of Linnemann and Taylor, and they come to opposite conclusions. According to Linnemann, Luke's account can be explained solely in terms of his redaction of the Markan version, albeit with considerable editorial license[119]. Taylor, on the other hand, regards these verses as non-Markan in origin, though he allows for the possibility that Luke 22:46b is an addition to the narrative from Mark[120]. Relative to Mark's version of Jesus' prayer, the Lukan rendition records a number of variations. On the most superficial level we may note the obvious brevity of the Lukan story, and, momentarily excluding vv 43–44 for comparative purposes, that only 33 per cent of Luke's vocabularly is also found in Mark. Nevertheless, the accounts are broadly similar and close verbal agreement between the two appears in vv 39, 42, and 46.

V 39: Unlike the parallel in Mark 14:26, Luke records no reference to the singing of a hymn prior to departing the meal; apparently this was considered by Luke an unnecessary detail. Otherwise, Mark's wording is closely followed, though Luke adds ἐπορεύθη κατὰ τὸ ἔθος. Πορεύομαι, in the third person singular (cf. Mark's third person plural verbs – ἐξῆλθον and ἔρχονται), emphasizes Jesus' action apart from the disciples, thus drawing attention to his "going" as a fulfillment of his mission. While Luke does use πορεύομαι in his redactional activity, it is not characteristic of his redactional vocabulary, and this quasi-technical use of the term may be pre-Lukan (see above on 22:22). The disciples are not thereby excluded from Jesus' mission and fate, however: they follow him (ἠκολούθησαν δὲ αὐτῷ καὶ οἱ μαθηταί). Ἀκολουθέω is a relatively common word among the Synoptic writers, used in Matthew 26 times, Mark – 20, Luke – 17, Acts – 3. On 9 occasions of its use in Mark (1:18; 2:15; 3:7; 5:24; 6:1; 8:34; 10:32; 11:9; 15:41), Luke does not take over the word. As for the occurrences in the Third Gospel, with the exception of 23:27 where the source is not readily evident, Luke always takes the verb from his sources (from Q – 7:9; 9:57, 59, 61; from L – 5:11; from Mark – 5:27, 28; 9:23, 49; 18:22, 28, 43; 22:10, 54; from oral tradition –9: 11[121]). There is, then, a good case against its having been introduced by Luke here. Κατὰ τὸ ἔθος is a Lukan phrase (cf. 1:9; 2:42; 21:37); however, as a comparable idea is present in the Johannine narrative (18:2), it may have been inspired by a non-Markan tradition.

V 40: Luke omits the Gethsemane-reference in Mark, replacing εἰς χωρίον οὗ τὸ ὄνομα Γεθσημανί (Mark 14:32) with γενόμενος δὲ ἐπὶ τοῦ τόπου. Ὁ τόπος is also read in John 18:2, but Luke's

---

119 Linnemann, *Studien*, 34–40. Linnemann's literary- and tradition-critical conclusions are accepted by Glöckner, *Verkündigung*, 174–176. See also, John Martin Creed, *The Gospel according to St. Luke* (London: Macmillan, 1953) 271–272; Schneider, *Luke*, 2:457.
120 Taylor, *Passion*, 69–72. Other scholars who appeal to a non-Markan, pre-Lukan tradition behind 22:39–46 include Rehkopf, *Sonderquelle*, 84; Trocmé, *Passion*, 32; Marshall, *Gospel of Luke*, 828–833; Schramm, *Markus-stoff*, 50–51; R. S. Barbour, "Gethsemane in the Tradition of the Passion", *NTS* 16 (1969–70) 241; Karl Georg Kuhn, "Jesus in Gethsemane", in *Redaktion und Theologie*, 90–93; Schweizer, *Luke*, 342.
121 An appeal to oral tradition seems the best way to account for the fact that Matt 14:13; Luke 9:11; and John 6:2 all agree against Mark 6:33 in the use of ἀκολουθέω at this point in the story – cf. Schweizer, *Matthew*, 319; Marshall, *Gospel of Luke*, 864.

omission of "Gethsemane" is not unusual given his apparent aversion to Aramaic place-names (cf. 23:33). Luke has already introduced οἱ μαθηταί (v 39) and so omits Mark's reference here. Εἶπεν αὐτοῖς, which replaces Mark's καὶ λέγει τοῖς . . . , is possibly Lukan (see above on 22:25). Luke omits the command to the disciples at this point in Mark (καθίσατε ὧδε ἕως προσεύξομαι). In its place Luke has προσεύχεσθε μὴ εἰσελθεῖν εἰς πειρασμόν. Similar counsel appears in 22:46. With this imperative, then, Luke brackets the whole story. As in 22:28, so here πειρασμός suggests satanic opposition. As Luke has clearly introduced the term in 4:13 and 8:13, he has probably added it here as well. That this concept comes in for special emphasis at this juncture calls to mind earlier references to satanic activity in the passion narrative – with Judas (22:3) and with Simon Peter (22:31) – and alerts the reader to the significance of the developing scenario. An important struggle of cosmic proportions is about to take place, and, as suggested by the position of the command at the outset, the disciples are to have a part in it (cf. also ἀκολουθέω in v 39). They must do more than sit (Mark 14:32); they must also be praying.

The command here and in 22:46 could have had its origin in Mark 14:38: γρηγορεῖτε καὶ προσεύχεσθε, ἵνα μὴ ἔλθητε εἰς πειρασμόν. Linguistic evidence suggests that γρηγορέω is not an important term for Luke in this sort of context (though it is for Mark – see esp. 13:37), but a similar concept appears in 21:36: "Be on the watch (ἀγρυπνεῖτε) at all times, and pray that you may be able to escape all that is about to happen . . . ". Moreover, in 22:46, Luke does replace the verb (and not simply omit it as in v 40): like Jesus (v 45), the disciples are to "arise". Hence, a similar thought would not have been out of place here if Luke had been following Mark at this point. Additionally, Luke's προσεύχομαι + infinitive is an unusual construction (v 40)[122], made all the more puzzling in that both v 46 and Mark 14:38 read προσεύχομαι + ἵνα-clause. These differences are difficult to explain under the hypothesis that Luke was merely redacting Mark. The change from ἔρχομαι in Mark to εἰσέρχομαι can be credited to Luke's fondness for compound verbs.

More enigmatic is the deletion of Mark 14:33–34 from the Lukan account – the separation by Jesus of Peter, James, and John; the note concerning his distress; his expression of the same to his disciples; and his admonition to watch. Apparently, Luke has no aversion to this kind of segregation of the disciples (9:28); therefore, the only plausible reasons for his purposely deleting this text (assuming Luke was following Mark here) would have been either to de-emphasize Jesus' agony or to replace the Markan version with the tradition reflected in Luke 22:43–44. Concerning the first possibility, Linnemann has stated:

> Die Absonderung der drei Jünger dürfte weggefallen sein, weil Lukas an der Klage Jesu Mk. 14, 34 und der Mitteilung seines Zitterns und Zagens Anstoss nahm und mit Wegfall die Aussonderung funktionslos wurde[123].

On the face of it, this explanation comes to grief if (1) vv 43–44 are genuine and (2) vv 43–44 accentuate Jesus' distress. It is worthy of note that Linnemann herself accepts the text as original to Luke[124]. On a general note, we should mention that throughout Luke-Acts one finds a heavy emphasis on Christ's suffering, and the Markan text would have added a poignant witness to that important motif.

However, Jerome H. Neyrey has argued that the term περίλυπος (and the simple λύπη), found in Mark 14:34, embraced negative connotations from popular Hellenistic philosophy that Luke would not have wanted to associate with Jesus[125]. Neyrey theorizes that, according to Luke, Jesus' time of prayer on the Mount of Olives is actually a time of struggle (rendering ἀγωνία as "combat") against λύπη (i.e. "irrational passion"). Jesus remains emotionally restrained and in control throughout the struggle; his strength never wavers. So, concludes Neyrey,

---

122 BDF, para. 392.1c.
123 Linnemann, *Studien*, 37. See also the remarks in Werner H. Kelber, "Mark 14:32–42: Gethsemane. Passion Christology and Discipleship Failure", *ZNW* 63 (1972) 177.
124 She regards these verses as "eine lukanische Bildung" (Linnemann, *Studien*, 38–39).
125 Jerome H. Neyrey, "The Absence of Jesus' Emotions – the Lucan Redaction of Lk. 22, 39–46", *Bib* 61 (1980) 153–171.

Jesus ... is not a victim, out of control, subject to irrational passion; on the contrary, he is portrayed as practicing virtue, singleheartedly searching for God's will and being manfully [sic] obedient to God[126].

Unlike Jesus, the disciples fail in their struggle and so become the victims of λύπη (22:45).

If this non-emotional interpretation of vv 43–44 could be upheld, Linnemann's case would gain support. However, it is not without its problems. First, the stress on πειρασμός (vv 28, 40, 46) must surely be taken to mean that Jesus' (and the disciples') struggle is not against "irrational passion", but against Satanic opposition. Despite his arguments to the contrary, there really is no room for this satanic element in Neyrey's interpretation of Jesus' ἀγωνία against λύπη. Second, it is doubtful that Neyrey's interpretation takes seriously enough the details of vv 43–44. The impression one gains is that Jesus *needed* the strengthening (ἐνισχύων) of the angel; and, that Jesus' sweat was like drops of blood falling to the ground suggests he was experiencing no little distress. Third, it is περίλυπος, not λύπη, which is read in Mark; hence, it is περίλυπος to which Luke is alleged to have taken offence. Yet, it is not at all clear that περίλυπος would have carried the negative connotations for Luke that Neyrey attributes to λύπη. The noun in question appears to signify no more than "deep sorrow" in Luke 18:23. Fourth, even Neyrey's examination of the background of λύπη is unnecessarily limited and potentially misleading. Not only does he neglect to mention the evolving possibility of a more positive interpretation of the term than that given by Stoicism, but he also neglects the relatively neutral use of the term (neutral in the sense of making judgments about one's moral or spiritual condition) as an antonym for "happiness", or as a general term for "pain"[127]. Fifth, "combat" is not the only, nor even the more common, rendering of ἀγωνία. Indeed, in view of the other indications of Jesus' distress in vv 43–44, we have ample reason for adopting Brian Beck's translation for Luke's γενόμενος ἐν ἀγωνίᾳ as "becoming profoundly disturbed"[128]. Thus, assuming for the moment the originality of vv 43–44 to the Lukan text, neither Linnemann's nor Neyrey's theories adequately account for Luke's redactional activity in deleting Mark 14:33–34.

Some fifty years ago, L. Brun postulated that Luke 22:43–44 is Luke's substitute for Mark 14:33–34[129]. His essay has recently been criticized by Bart D. Ehrman and Mark A. Plunkett on the grounds that Luke has already made other amendments to the Markan material that put his own theological stamp on the story and, thus, this substitution was unnecessary on Brun's thesis[130]. In point of fact, a simpler version of Brun's argument would have been more convincing as a way of explaining why Luke omitted the Markan text, though this hypothesis should by no means be regarded as a "proof" that vv 43–44 are original to Luke. It is commonly recognized that Luke has an aversion to doublets[131]. If Luke had access to Mark 14:33–34 *and* a tradition on which his vv 43–44 are based, then his tendency to avoid duplication in his sources could explain his omission of the Markan material.

V 41: Here Luke's narrative corresponds to Mark 14:35a, though the two versions share only the opening καί. Luke has αὐτός and ἀπ' αὐτῶν – words for which Mark offers no parallel. The occurrence of these words is surprising, for they are unnecessary – the sort of redundancy Luke often avoids. For προέρχομαι in Mark, Luke has ἀποσπάω. The latter verb is rare in the NT, appearing elsewhere only in Matt 26:51; Acts 20:30; and 21:1. It may be Lukan, but this would not explain why the evangelist would have wanted to replace Mark's word, which is employed in Luke-Acts 6 times, as compared with only once in Matthew and twice in Mark. Ὡσεί belongs to Luke's

---

126 Neyrey, "Absence", 171.
127 Cf., e.g., Tob 2:5; 7:18; Isa 35:10; 40:29; 51:11; 1 Macc 6:4; Rom 9:2; 2 Cor 2:1, 3; Phil 2:27; Heb 12:11; 1 Pet 2:19; Rudolf Bultmann, "Λύπη, λυπέω", in *TDNT*, 4:312–322; Hermann Haarbeck and Hans-Georg Link, "Λυπέω", in *NIDNTT*, 2:419–421.
128 So Brian E. Beck, "*Imitatio Christi'* and the Lucan Passion Narrative", in *Suffering and Martyrdom*, 37–40. Cf. Ethelbert Stauffer, "Ἀγωνία", in *TDNT*, 1:140.
129 L. Brun, "Engel und Blutschweiss: Lc 22,43–44", *ZNW* 32 (1933) 265–276.
130 Bart D. Ehrman and Mark A. Plunkett, "The Angel and the Agony: The Textual Problem of Luke 22:43–44", *CBQ* 45 (1983) 412.
131 See, e.g., Fitzmyer, *Luke*, 1:81–82.

redactional vocabulary[132]. Λίθου βολήν replaces μικρόν; Luke's reference is thus more specific and provides an unexpected detail if Luke was merely redacting Mark. Θεὶς τὰ γόνατα, repeated in Acts 7:60; 9:40; 20:36; and 21:5, is Lukan. This posture for prayer is occasionally used in the OT and may connote one's humility in praying or the urgency of the prayer itself[133].

In Luke's account, Jesus prays only once, as opposed to the three-fold repetition described by Mark. The effect thus achieved is a special emphasis on the decisiveness, the deep resolve, characterizing Jesus' acceptance of the "cup". Luke deletes Jesus' first prayer in the Markan version — that reported in indirect discourse (14:35b), and moves directly to that given in direct speech (see below on v 42). The metaphorical use of ὥρα (i.e. "the hour appointed by God"[134]), is not unknown to Luke and, in fact, is employed in the story of the arrest (22:53; cf. Mark 14:41). Hence its absence here requires explanation. Certainly the omission of Mark's εἰ δυνατόν ἐστιν ... πάντα δυνατά σοι (14:35–36) and the substitution of εἰ βούλει (22:42) focus attention more clearly on God's will and Jesus' obedience to it. Perhaps Luke excised ἀπ' αὐτοῦ ἡ ὥρα while removing the rest, by way of abbreviating the Markan story for clarity and sharpness of focus. In any case, the concept to which the hour-motif points — i.e. the necessary fate of Jesus — is present in the cup-metaphor of v 42.

V 42: Mark's καὶ ἔλεγεν (14:36) becomes λέγων in Luke. Πατήρ is read without αββα; thus, Luke avoids another Aramaism. The Attic spelling of βούλομαι (βούλει, rather than βούλῃ) is rare, and reflects literary usage[135]. The phrase παρένεγκε ... ἐμοῦ is read both in Mark and Luke, though the position of τοῦτο shifts. Πλήν replaces Mark's ἀλλά. Mark's οὐ τί ἐγὼ θέλω ἀλλὰ τί σύ appears in Luke as μὴ τὸ θέλημά μου ἀλλὰ τὸ σὸν γινέσθω. The Lukan text thus corresponds more favorably with the petition in the "Lord's Prayer": γενηθήτω τὸ θέλημά σου (Matt 6:10; no parallel in the Lukan version!); and with the Matthean parallel to Luke 22:42: γενηθήτω τὸ θέλημά σου (26:42). While it could be that Luke is simply editing his Markan source, this correspondence with an alternative (Matthean!) tradition not found elsewhere in Luke should warn us against dismissing the possibility of a further source. The effect of these two revisions *vis-à-vis* the Markan text — the choice of βούλομαι and the use of "Lord's Prayer" terminology — is to make central (even more so than is the case with Mark) to Jesus' prayer God's will concerning Jesus' fate and Jesus' corresponding obedience.

VV 43–44: The textual evidence for these two verses is so ambiguous that the problem of reconstructing Luke's original text is rendered a knotty one[136]. It is common for practitioners of textual criticism to place great import on the absence of these verses in such ancient and widespread witness as p69vid.75 ℵ1 A B T W and others[137]. However, due consideration should also be allowed the ancient, widespread witnesses favoring the genuineness of the text: ℵ*.2 D 0171 f1 bopt Justin and others. The textual evidence is divided, though it is clear that such an omission in so many and diverse traditions cannot be accidental. Much more probable is that the verses were omitted for doctrinal reasons — as illustrated by the ancient scholium quoted by Strauss: ὅτι τῆς ἰσχύος τοῦ ἀγγέλου οὐκ ἐπεδέετο ὁ ὑπὸ πάσης ἐπουρανίου δυνάμεως φόβῳ καὶ τρόμῳ προσκυνούμενος καὶ δοξαζόμενος[138]. This solution will prove more convincing if it can be shown that vv 43–44 are with Lukan redaction[139].

---

132 Gaston, *Electronicae*, 65; Jeremias, *Sprache*, 114, 294.
133 Cf. Hans Schönweiss, "Προσέρχομαι", in *NIDITT*, 2: 862.
134 Cf. Gerhard Delling, "Ὥρα", in *TDNT*, 9: 678.
135 Cf. BDF, para. 27.
136 Ehrman and Plunkett, ("Angel and Agony", 401) regard this as "a classical problem for textual criticism"; they have catalogued a fairly exhaustive list of witnesses to the text (402).
137 E.g. Metzger, *Textual Commentary*, 177; Ehrman and Plunkett, "Angel and Agony", 402–403, 416.
138 The marginal note thus interprets the ἐνισχύω ascribed to the angel as "declaring strength" — i.e. as the offering of a doxology (David Friedrich Strauss, *The Life of Jesus Critically Examined*, ed. Peter C. Hodgson [Philadelphia: Fortress, 1972] 638). See the similar texts cited in Ehrman and Plunkett, "Angel and Agony", 404–405. See also Creed, *Luke*, 273; G. B. Caird, *The Gospel of St. Luke* (London: Black, 1963) 243; Geldenhuys, *Luke*, 577; Schweizer, *Luke*, 343.
139 Ehrman and Plunkett ("Angel and Agony", 412–415) argue that vv 39–46, without vv 43–44,

Luke 22:39–46 (Mark 14:26, 32–42)

Three words in this text appear only here in the NT: ἀγωνία, ἱδρώς, and θρόμβως. Similarly, ἐνισχύω appears in the NT only here and in Acts 9:19, and the comparative form of ἐκτενῶς is read only here (cf. Acts 12:5; 26:7; 1 Pet 1:22; ἐκτενῶς is found in Joel 1:14 and Jonah 3:8, but the comparative form is absent from the LXX as well). The use of these five terms does not point unambiguously to Luke's hand. Nevertheless, given the breadth of Luke's vocabulary as evidenced in his two-volume work, we would be foolish not to count these as corroborative testimony.

Προσεύχομαι is often used in Lukan redaction and καὶ ἐγένετο is often found in the Third Gospel, but of the vocabulary in vv 43–44 only ὡσεί belongs to Luke's characteristic redactional vocabulary[140]. While not peculiar to Luke, the aorist passive of ὁράω occurs quite frequently in Luke-Acts, relative to other NT books[141]. Ὤφθη ἄγγελος has close parallels in 1:11 and Acts 7:30. Angels play a significant role in Luke-Acts, though ordinarily they are described as "of God" (12:8, 9; 15:10; Acts 10:3; 27:23) or "of the Lord" (2:9; Acts 5:19; 8:26; 12:7, 23), and not "from heaven". Angels are, however, sent from God (1:26) or from the Lord (12:11), and in 2:15 an angel returns to heaven (cf. 2:13). Further ἀπό + οὐρανοῦ does appear in Luke (9:54; 17:29; 21:11), and οὐρανός is used as a circumlocution for God in 15:18, 21. Hence, the usage here can be accounted for in terms of Lukan redaction. The phrase ὡσεὶ θρόμβοι αἵματος καταβαίνοντες ἐπὶ τὴν γῆν also conforms to Lukan style, which makes good use of simile (cf. 3:22; 10:18; 11:44; 22:31; et al.). Moreover, as with the note about Jesus' sweat, it is characteristic of Luke to indicate physical manifestations at extramundane events (cf. 1:20; 3:22; Acts 2:2–3; 9:18; et al.)[142].

These various lines of evidence cannot be used to argue that Luke is responsible for creating vv 43–44, as Ehrman and Plunkett have rightly observed[143]. However, the evidence is certainly compatible with Lukan redaction of an already existing tradition, and there is thus good reason for taking these verses as original to the Lukan text. As Schneider has observed, here is an example of *Redaktionsgeschichte im Dienste der Textkritik*[144]. Additionally, as will be seen, the inclusion of these verses helps us understand v 45.

V 45: This verse follows closely its counterpart in Mark 14:37a, but the first phrase is unique to Luke. Ἀναστάς, a Septuagintalism (e.g. Gen 19:15; 22:3; 23:7; 24:10; et al.), is found elsewhere in Luke (e.g. 1:68; 6:8; 15:20) For καὶ ἔρχονται in Mark, Luke has the participial form ἐλθών. This revision is consonant with Luke's tendency to eliminate parataxis in Mark in favor of a subordinate clause.

The disciples are again explicitly mentioned (cf. v 39) due to the extended interlude in the Lukan story line; the reference is assumed in Mark. Luke has not taken over Mark's three-fold return of Jesus to the sleeping disciples, just as he edited out the three-fold pattern of Jesus' prayer. In consequence, the failure of the disciples, prominent in Mark, fades into the background as Jesus' submissive prayer is spotlighted. Luke's εὗρεν κοιμωμένους αὐτούς corresponds to Mark's καὶ εὑρίσκει αὐτοὺς καθεύδοντας. Luke otherwise uses both κοιμάομαι (Acts 7:60; 12:6; 13:36) and καθεύδω (8:52; 22:46). As he follows Mark in using καθεύδω in v 46, it is likely that the present revision only reflects his desire for variation.

Luke is alone in explaining the cause of the disciples' sleeping as ἀπὸ τῆς λύπης (for ἀπό to denote cause[145], cf. 19:3; 21:26; 24:41). Λύπη appears only here in the Synoptics. In this narrative, Luke has persistently associated the disciples with Jesus' fate (see above on vv 39, 40; cf. Mark 14:

---

exhibit a clear chiastic structure; thus, in their view, vv 43–44 constitute an intrusion into Luke's final redaction. However, as they themselves are forced to admit, this reasoning is not in itself conclusive. If it can be shown that vv 43–44 are consistent with Lukan redaction on other grounds, the objections of these two exegetes to the originality of the verses in the Lukan text will fall to the ground.

140 Gaston, *Electronicae*, 65–66; Fitzmyer, *Luke*, 1:110.
141 Matt – 1x; Mark – 1x; Luke-Acts – 13x; 1 Cor – 4x; 1 Tim – 1x; Heb – 1x; Rev – 2x.
142 Cf. Neyrey, "Absence", 167.
143 Ehrman and Plunkett, "Angel and Agony", 408–409.
144 Gerhard Schneider, "Engel und Blutschweiss (Lk 22, 43–44): 'Redaktionsgeschichte' im Dienste der Textkritik", in *Lukas*, 153–157.
145 BDF, para. 210.1.

50, for which there is no Lukan parallel; Luke 23:49); thus, the λύπη of the disciples should be understood in relation to the ἀγωνία of Jesus (v 44).

If Luke represents the disciples as trying, within their limits, to be obedient to Jesus, and carrying out the command to pray, he may have considered that, if the demands of prayer were such that even Jesus sustained them only with difficulty and by angelic help, the disciples would have been totally exhausted by them[146].

V 46: Luke's wording is largely that of Mark (14:37b, 38a). However, in Luke, Jesus' question extends to all the disciples, and not to Peter alone. Moreover, Jesus' monologue is drastically abbreviated in Luke, though the Lukan redaction retains the essentials of the Markan version. On ἀναστάντες . . . , see above on vv 40, 45. As in v 40, Luke has replaced Mark's simplex ἔρχομαι with a compound.

In conclusion, there can be little doubt that in constructing this story Luke was dependent on the Markan narrative. Nevertheless, vv 40–44, and possibly v 45, raise insurmountable obstacles against a theory that Luke depended *solely* on Mark, for then his redactional procedure becomes inexplicable. It may be that Luke has supplemented the Markan story with a few independent pieces of tradition, along with recasting the whole to suit his own style and theological agenda. On the other hand, the possibility of a parallel tradition recounting this episode, in the main agreeing with, but occasionally diverging from, the Markan story, cannot be ruled out on the evidence we have assembled.

XII. Luke 22:47–54a (Mark 14:43–53)

We include v 54a in Luke's story of Jesus' arrest for otherwise any reference to the arrest itself is found lacking. By omitting Mark's mention of the approaching betrayer, Luke ties this pericope all the more closely to Jesus' words in 22:46. We should therefore understand that the πειρασμός of 22:28, 40, and 46 continues – a view supported by the language of v 53: αὕτη ἐστὶν ὑμῶν ἡ ὥρα καὶ ἡ ἐξουσία τοῦ σκότους. Σκότος, in particular, implies the persistence of this motif, for darkness signifies the realm of Satan[147]. The pericope itself exhibits a number of structural variations *vis-à-vis* Mark's version, and the percentage of Lukan words also found in Mark is not particularly high (38.8%). Nonetheless, a large measure of verbal correspondence with Mark is found in 22:50, 52, 53, and many of

---

146 Beck, "*Imitatio Christi*", 40; see pp. 38–40.
147 Cf. Acts 26:18: . . . τοῦ ἐπιστρέψαι
   ἀπὸ   σκότους   εἰς   φῶς
καὶ   τῆς ἐξουσίας τοῦ σατανᾶ ἐπὶ τὸν θεόν . . . . This parallelism clearly indicates the equation of "darkness" with "satanic rule", the opposite of "light" and "God". In the Lukan passion narrative, σκότος is to be understood in relation to the implicit and explicit references to satanic activity – 22:3, 28, 31, 40, 46. Cf. Col 1:13; Hans Conzelmann, "Σκότος", in *TDNT*, 7:439; Schweizer, *Luke*, 345.

the differences between the two accounts can be credited to Luke's redaction of the Markan text.

V 47: Luke roughly parallels Mark 14:43a, 45 here. As so often happens, Mark's καὶ εὐθὺς is dropped[148]. Both Matthew (26:47) and Luke add ἰδού by way of introducing a new element into the narrative. By bringing forward Mark's ὄχλος and delaying his description of the composition of the arresting party, Luke situates Judas and his act of betrayal at center stage in this whole section. Ὁ λεγόμενος is unusual, both in that Luke prefers ὁ καλούμενος for this idea and because here the participle does not modify or further describe an already-mentioned person or thing (see above on 22:1, 3). With εἷς τῶν δώδεκα, Luke parallels Mark's wording precisely — which is surprising in view of our earlier comments on 22:3. For Mark's παραγίνομαι, Luke has προέρχομαι; this change is also enigmatic in that Luke substitutes for προέρχομαι in Mark 14:35 his own ἀποσπάω (22:41). Moreover, whereas Mark uses παραγίνομαι only here, it is read in Luke-Acts 28 times. However, it may be that Luke wanted to stress the prominent role of Judas; furthermore, Luke does use παραγίνομαι in his description of the crowd in 22:52. Omitting the explanation of Judas's action (Mark 14:44) and mention of his verbal greeting (14:45), Luke moves directly to Judas's act of betrayal. With the use of ἐγγίζω, a favorite word for Luke[149], Mark's account of the preliminaries of Judas's identification of Jesus is greatly abbreviated. These two amendments are consistent with Luke's apparent interest in highlighting Judas's treachery. As for the kiss, Luke's version reads φιλέω whereas Mark has καταφιλέω; perhaps Luke understood the latter term to signify a decided nuance of affection (cf. 7:38, 45) and avoided its use in this context.

V 48: Mark has no parallel to Luke here, and it is possible that Jesus' response to Judas here and in Matt 26:50 both stem from a similar stream of tradition not incorporated by Mark[150]. Interestingly, except for the omission of the definite article before "Jesus" in Luke, Matthew and Luke are in precise agreement in the introduction to their respective sayings. This possible indirect relationship between Matthew and Luke speaks against the view that Jesus' response to Judas is a Lukan creation[151].

V 49: Rather than follow Judas's act of betrayal with the arrest, Luke transposes Mark's narrative sequence (Mark 14:46, 47), thus again emphasizing the role of the disciples alongside Jesus. One finds in Mark no real parallel to this verse, though it may be based on Mark 14:47. Ἰδόντες δέ is a typical Lukan introduction (cf. 2:17; 5:8, 12; 7:39; 8:28, 34, 47; 9:54; 13:12; 18:15; et al). Οἱ περὶ αὐτόν is a recast of Mark's equally vague τῶν παρεστηκότων. Ἐσόμενον is Lukan[152]. As in Matt 26:51, πατάσσω replaces Mark's παίω; πατάσσω + "sword" is more common in the LXX.

V 50: Here, Mark 14:47 is followed very closely indeed. For καί, Mark reads δέ, and Luke's εἷς τις ἐξ αὐτῶν is very much like Mark's parallel. Πατάσσω is again employed by Luke (see above

---

148 Mark uses εὐθύς or καὶ εὐθύς 43x, Luke – 3x (E. J. Pryke, *Redactional Style in the Marcan Gospel: A Study of Syntax and Vocabulary as Guides to Redaction in Mark* [Cambridge: Cambridge University, 1978] 87). Cf. Paul Ellingworth, "How Soon Is 'Immediately' in Mark?", *BT* 29 (1978) 414–419.
149 Gaston, *Electronicae*, 65; Jeremias, *Sprache*, 295.
150 This depends on how one translates Matthew's ἑταῖρε, ἐφ' ὃ πάρει. On the possibility of Matthew and Luke having drawn from a similar tradition, see the relevant comments in Schweizer, *Matthew*, 495; Gustav Stählin, "Φιλέω", in *TDNT*, 9:140 n.241; Gundry, *Matthew*, 537.
151 It is difficult to understand why a "Son of Man" reference would have had a more emotive effect at this juncture than a simple first person pronoun; thus, we must table Lindars's conjecture that Luke has for this reason substituted the title for an original "I" (Lindars, *Jesus*, 133–134, 143, 166–168). While in the present context "Son of Man" is certainly titular (James D. G. Dunn, *Christology in the Making* [Philadelphia: Westminster, 1980] 66), Marshall (*Gospel of Luke*, 837) is correct in asserting that here, if anywhere, "Son of Man" could originally have been a circumlocution for "I".
152 Marshall, *Gospel of Luke*, 836; Jeremias, *Sprache*, 295.

on v 49). Mark's mention of the drawing of the sword is dramatic but unnecessary to the story line, and Luke omits it accordingly. He also substitutes οὖς for ὠτίον in Mark, but takes up Mark's word in 22:51; hence, the change here is probably due to Luke's desire for linguistic variation. Luke and John (18:10) agree in specifying the *right* ear as the one amputated. Otherwise, except for word order, Luke and Mark are in verbal agreement here.

V 51: There is no parallel to this verse in Mark, but Matt 26:52a; Luke 22:51a; and John 18:11a all record a reaction by Jesus to the incident. Ἀποκριθεὶς δὲ ὁ Ἰησοῦς εἶπεν is a Septuagintalism, but may be drawn from Mark 14:48. Ἐάω is found in the NT only 11 times, 9 of which are in Luke-Acts. This suggests its Lukan derivation here. Luke is unique in recording the healing of the ear. This detail serves to underscore the lack of resistance offered by Jesus, as verbalized in v 51a; the implication is that "all is going according to God's plan" (cf. Matt 26:52–54; John 18:11). Also, that Jesus heals the slave points to Jesus' innocence: he cannot be blamed even for the brash conduct of one of his followers. Ἅπτω is normally associated with healing in the Synoptics and is not peculiar to Luke[153]. Ἰάομαι, on the other hand, is characteristic of Lukan redaction[154].

V 52: Εἶπον δὲ Ἰησοῦς πρός conforms to Lukan style and suggests Lukan redaction (see above on 22:15). In place of Mark's ambiguous αὐτοῖς (14:48), Luke spells out the persons to whom Jesus is speaking. In doing so, he draws on language similar to that in Mark 14:43. However, whereas in Mark's account the crowd has been sent out by the Jewish leaders (chief priests, scribes, and elders), here the chief priests and elders themselves form part of the crowd. In addition, Luke's mention of the στρατηγοὺς τοῦ ἱεροῦ (cf. 22:4) is without correspondence in Mark. Given its parallels in John 18:12 (οἱ ὑπηρέται τῶν Ἰουδαίων)[155], there is reason for supposing that Luke is constructing his narrative from a non-Markan source[156]. This hypothesis is given additional support from the fact that Luke 9:22 follows the passion prediction of Mark 8:31 in listing the elders, chief priests, and scribes – but here the latter party does not come in for mention. All of these persons are now described by Jesus in Luke as τοὺς παραγενομένους ἐπ᾽ ἐμέ. In this way, Luke makes use of Mark's παραγίνομαι (14:43). As for Jesus' question to the arresting party, Mark and Luke are in agreement, except Luke omits συλλαβεῖν με.

V 53: The Markan parallel is 14:49, and at the outset there is some agreement. Luke's version has Jesus μεθ᾽ ὑμῶν while Mark reads πρὸς ὑμᾶς, but this constitutes no distinction in nuance. Luke regularly avoids Mark's κρατέω (cf. Mark 1:31/Luke 4:39; 6:17/3:19–20; 9:27/9:42; 12:12/20:19; 14:1/22:2; et al.). Verse 53b corresponds to Mark 14:49b in point – i.e. both assert that the sequence of events is proceeding according to a preordained plan. However, the *heilsgeschichtliche* necessity of Jesus' passion, so important for Luke, is actually more explicit in Mark's version; for this reason, little basis exists for supposing that Luke has created the phrase to replace Mark's.

V 54a: Luke omits Mark 14:50–52 – the reference to the fleeing of Jesus' followers and to the young man who ran away naked. With this amendment, Luke again brings to the fore the place of the disciples *with* Jesus. Συλλαμβάνω, used for Jesus' arrest, may be borrowed from Mark 14:48 (cf. however John 18:12); we may recall that in Luke's parallel to the Markan text the verb was omitted. However, if Luke had wanted to borrow this *detail* from Mark, why did he not use the "more Lukan" *language* of Mark 14:46: οἱ δὲ ἐπέβαλον τὰς χεῖρας αὐτῷ (cf. Luke 20:19; 21:12)? Luke's αὐτόν substitutes for Mark's τὸν Ἰησοῦν (14:53); the personal reference was required by Mark due to the long interlude of vv 50–52. The combination ἤγαγον καὶ εἰσήγαγον εἰς is awkward (see the textual variants!), especially in view of Mark's parallel ἀπήγαγον ... πρός (14:53). The reference to "the house of the high priest" may be based on Mark 14:53–54, where Jesus is said to

---

153 Cf. Matt 8:3, 15; 9:20, 21, 29; 14:36; 20:34; Mark 1:41; 3:10; 5:27, 28, 30, 31; 6:56; 7:33; 8:22; Luke 5:13; 6:19; (7:14); 8:44, 45, 46, 47; Gerd Theissen, *The Miracle Stories of the Early Christian Tradition* (Philadelphia: Fortress, 1983) 62, 92–93.
154 Gaston, *Electronicae*, 64; Jeremias, *Sprache*, 295.
155 David R. Catchpole (*The Trial of Jesus: A Study in the Gospels and Jewish Historiography from 1770 to the Present Day* [Leiden: E. J. Brill, 1971] 151 n.1.) argues that the χιλίαρχος of John 18:12 is identical with the στρατηγός of Luke 22:52.
156 Cf. Paul Winter, *On the Trial of Jesus*, 2d ed., ed. T. A. Burkill and Geza Vermes (Berlin: Walter de Gruyter, 1974) 66–67.

have been taken to the high priest, followed to the courtyard by Peter. Unlike Mark, Luke does not mention at this point the assembly of the members of the Sanhedrin. The placing of the arrest only here at the close of the story, and not sooner as in the other Synoptics (Luke and John are again in agreement), portrays Jesus as the one in control of the events now unfolding.

The evidence through which we have now sifted does not point unambiguously to Luke's employment of a non-Markan source for his account of Jesus' arrest. Quite the contrary, a large portion of the pericope can be explained in terms of a rather free editing of Mark's version of the story. Luke's redactional interests, however, cannot explain all of these differences. Additionally, one must somehow account for the correspondences in this story (against Mark) between Luke and Matthew; Luke and John; and Luke, Matthew, and John. To be sure, such agreements are not extensive, but remarkable nonetheless given the absence of any direct literary relationship between these three Gospels[157]. Mutual dependence on common (but not identical) non-Markan material by these three evangelists is almost certain. Even more certain is that Luke's narrative of the arrest rests on Mark's account *and* on additional source-material; that is, the probability is high that the Third Evangelist knew a second account of the arrest of Jesus.

XIII. Luke 22:54b–62 (Mark 14:53–64, 66–72)

Mark's intercalation of the accounts of Jesus' trial before the Jewish leaders and Peter's denial is not reproduced in Luke. In fact, the chronology of the trial is at variance with that of the Markan version. As for the narrative of Peter's denial, the two versions are materially the same, and the percentage of words in Luke common to the Markan vocabulary is relatively high (44.3%). However, a comparison of the stories reveals some far-reaching dissimilarities in chronological detail, the identity of characters, and the geographical schema[158]. Moreover, the dramatic progression attached to the triple denial read in Mark has been nullified in Luke's narrative of the event[159], though this is not to say that Luke has left the reader without his own dramatic emphasis (cf. esp. 22:61). Not surprisingly, these facts have given rise to various, even conflicting explanations of the source-question for Luke's account. Thus, Linnemann, Taylor, and Schneider all agree that here Luke has only reworked the Markan *Bericht*, while Catchpole has argued at great length that Luke has employed a second, non-Markan *Quelle*[160].

---

157 See below, chapter 4.
158 See the comparative chart of the four canonical accounts in Brown, *John*, 2:838–839.
159 Cf. Trocmé, *Passion*, 92.
160 Linnemann, *Studien*, 97–101; Taylor, *Passion*, 77–78; Schneider, *Verleugnung*, 73–96; *idem*,

V 54b: Luke's introduction of Peter closely follows that of Mark 14:54. As is frequently the case, he substitutes δέ for καί, and drops Mark's superfluous pronoun (αὐτῷ)[161]. Luke also deletes Mark's ἀπό. There is a sense in which ἀπό before μακρόθεν is redundant, though it is also true that the adverb is often used with the preposition since by this time -θεν had already all but lost its earlier separative force[162].

V 55: Here Luke provides details unknown to, but not inconsistent with, Mark 14:54c. Mark's parataxis is eliminated in favor of the genitive absolute − a characteristic substitution in Luke's editing of Mark[163]. Περιαψάντων δέ πῦρ finds no parallel in the Synoptic parallels, but relates favorably with John 18:18. Περιάπτω occus only here in the NT. Likewise, there is no Synoptic parallel for Luke's ἐν μέσῳ. The combination is a product of Lukan redaction in 8:7 (Mark 4:7), but is present in Q at Luke 10:3/Matt 10:16. It also appears in 24:36 and 5 times in Acts. Μέσος is a favorite word for Luke[164], and the construction with ἐν may be his handiwork. Τῆς αὐλῆς is present already in Mark 14:54. Luke's καί συγκαθισάντων . . . αὐτῶν roughly agrees with καί ἦν συγκαθήμενος μετὰ τῶν ὑπηρετῶν in Mark 14:54. Συνκαθίζω appears in the NT only here and in Eph 2:6; συνκάθημαι is also found in the NT only twice − here in Mark and Acts 26:30. If Luke was editing Mark at this point he would have had to add the detail about the people (unidentified) sitting together (around the fire?), then joined by Peter; moreover, he would have had to avoid Mark's periphrastic construction − ἦν συγκαθήμενος. However, Catchpole has argued that Luke prefers periphrastic constructions[165]. It is odd that Peter's name is mentioned again (cf. 22:54b), especially since the persons sitting together remain anonymous (cf. Mark 14:54: ὑπηρέται). Additionally, *contra* Mark's version, the fire in Luke is needed only for light (22:56), and not for heat (Mark 14:54). The combination μέσος + genitive is unusual, found only here in Luke[166].

Under the theory that Luke is merely editing Mark, what purpose would all of these revisions serve? The added detail about "lighting the fire", the omission of the guards' identity, the redundant naming of Peter, and the absence of the warming effect of the fire − all of these amendments could be Luke's way of drawing attention more pointedly to Peter's presence in the courtyard by the light of the fire. He is there not to warm himself but as a follower of Jesus. The double-reference to "sitting" serves to disassociate Peter from the guards: he is in their midst but he is not one with them. In addition, locating Peter "among them" stresses the pressure he would have felt when confronted with his relation to Jesus. On the other hand, it is true that this motif would have been better served by an explicit identification of the "αὐτῶν" as persons antagonistic to Jesus and his cause. Thus, the language of this verse can be roughly accounted for as the editorial product of Luke's hand if he had only Mark before him, but we cannot yet rule out the possibility of his having possessed and employed a further source.

Luke, 2:464−465; Catchpole, *Trial*, 160−174. Catchpole's presentation is remarkable for its attention to matters of detail and to the overall structure of the narrative, but is marred by two faulty methodological presuppositions: (A) In dealing with Luke's linguistic usage, he fails to account for the relevant data in Acts (cf., e.g., p. 173, for his treatment of φημί). For studies of Lukan redactional interests NT scholarship cannot afford to separate the two parts of this double-work. (B) He assumes that if Luke used a non-Markan source in the present pericope it must be the same source (and reflect the same vocabulary and style) as that employed by the evangelist earlier in his Gospel (i.e. L).

As for Schneider's detailed analysis, we agree time and time again with his statements regarding word-usage, but insist that he has paid insufficient attention to the differences in structure between the two accounts. In addition, he does not always indicate why Luke would have introduced the amendments he must have if he followed only Mark here.

161 On these two Lukan stylistic features, see Fitzmyer, *Luke*, 1:108.
162 BAG, 487−488; BDF, para. 104; MHT, 2:164.
163 Fitzmyer, *Luke*, 1:108; Schneider, *Verleugnung*, 161.
164 Gaston, *Electronicae*, 66.
165 See the argument with examples in Catchpole, *Trial*, 172; and the discussion in Fitzmyer, *Luke*, 1:122−123.
166 Cf. Catchpole, *Trial*, 171. There is weighty support for the variant reading ἐν μεσῷ, but it should probably be regarded as a later assimilation to the same construction in the verse.

Luke 22:54b–62 (Mark 14:53–64, 66–72)

V 56: This verse is an abbreviated parallel to Mark 14:66–67. Luke has no καὶ ὄντος ... ἔρχεται, but this introductory phrase could have been edited out as an unnecessary, if vivid, detail. Nor does Luke identify the maid as τοῦ ἀρχιερέως, though this may be understood. (Luke has already indicated that this episode takes place at the high priest's home.) Ἰδοῦσα δὲ αὐτόν is Luke's equivalent to Mark's καὶ ἰδοῦσα τὸν Πέτρον. Peter's name has just been given in 22:55, so the personal pronoun would not be surprising except that Peter is also named in 22:54 and Luke still gives his name again in the subsequent verse. Again, Luke substitutes δέ for καί. Mark's μία τῶν παιδισκῶν has become παιδίσκη τις in Luke. Τις + noun is typically Lukan[167]. Again avoiding Mark's portrayal of Peter "warming himself by the fire", Luke substitutes for θερμαινόμενον his καθήμενον πρὸς τὸ φῶς. Here we see the purpose of Luke's fire: it provides the light whereby Peter is recognized. The language here may be borrowed from Mark 14:54. For Mark's ἐμβλέψασα αὐτῷ λέγει, Luke's version reads ἀτενίσασα αὐτῷ εἶπεν. In both versions of the story, therefore, the maid gets a closer look at Peter. Of its 14 occurrences in the NT, ἀτενίζω is found 12 times in Luke-Acts, 2 in 2 Corinthians. Hence, its Lukan derivation is likely in this instance. As for the accusation itself, Luke has καὶ οὗτος σὺν αὐτῷ ἦν, whereas Mark reads καὶ σὺ μετὰ τοῦ Ναζαρηνοῦ ἦσθα τοῦ Ἰησοῦ. Luke's accusation is thus given in the third person, with no audience specified, while in Mark the accusation is narrated in the second person. Σύν is preferred over μετά in Lukan redaction, but he has no aversion to identifying Jesus as a Nazarene or as from Nazareth (11x in Luke-Acts). What, then, could have motivated this revision? Incidentally, to whom does the καί refer?

V 57: Here, Luke's introduction agrees exactly with that in Mark 14:68a: ὁ δὲ ἠρνήσατο λέγων; however, the content of the denial is given in two different forms. In Mark, Peter asserts that οὔτε οἶδα οὔτε ἐπίσταμαι σὺ τί λέγεις; in Luke we read οὐκ οἶδα αὐτόν, γύναι. Actually, Peter's denial here in Luke corresponds more closely to that in Mark 14:71: οὐκ οἶδα τὸν ἄνθρωπον τοῦτον ὃν λέγετε. Luke's wording (and that in Mark 14:71) is reminiscent of the Jewish ban-formula; this suggests the primitive character of the Lukan rendition[168]. Ἐπίσταμαι, used in Mark 14:68, appears only there in the Synoptics, but is present 9 times in Acts. Luke's αὐτόν may have arisen from Mark's σὺ τί λέγεις, but this hardly seems likely. The vocative γύναι is in an abnormal position[169]. However, a similar word order is given in Luke 5:8 (L?); Acts 2:37; 26:7, so it is not necessarily pre-Lukan. Luke has nothing corresponding to Mark's καὶ ἐξῆλθεν ἔξω εἰς τὸ προαύλιον, hence his version is in geographical agreement with John's account. Luke's deletion of the Markan phrase was a necessity, however, for Peter was required in the courtyard at the end of this pericope. Hence, this could have been an editorial elimination, regardless of how the source-question is ultimately decided[170].

V 58: Mark 14:69 has nothing to compare with Luke's time designation, μετὰ βραχύ. Βραχύς is found only 7 times in the NT, 3 of which are in Luke-Acts. Compared to Mark, Luke offers a character revision in designating the second accuser, from Mark's ἡ παιδίσκη (as in Mark 14:66–67) to ἕτερος. Ἕτερος is a Lukan favorite, and its presence here may be due to Luke[171]; however, the thought of a second person, distinct from the first maid, may be pre-Lukan (cf. Matt 26:71; John 18:25). Ἰδὼν αὐτὸν ἔφη is Luke's abbreviation of ἰδοῦσα αὐτὸν ἤρξαντο πάλιν λέγειν in Mark 14:69. Φημί, found in Luke-Acts 33 times, may be Lukan. Both ἤρξαντο and πάλιν are unneces-

---

167 Cf. Marshall, *Gospel of Luke*, 841; Fitzmyer, *Luke*, 1:111; Jeremias, *Sprache*, 165.
168 Cf. Helmut Merkel, "Peter's Curse", in *Trial of Jesus*, 69; Marshall, *Gospel of Luke*, 842; Catchpole, *Trial*, 273.
169 Cf. BDF, para. 474.6.
170 This is true regardless of how one judges Catchpole's discussion (*Trial*, 168–169) of the pre-Lukan character of 22:61a.
171 That ἕτερος is present in Lukan redaction, see Gaston, *Electronicae*, 65; Jeremias, *Sprache*, 297. Catchpole (*Trial*, 173) argues that Luke could not be responsible for introducing the term here for " ... when ἕτερος is introduced redactionally [by Luke] there is never lacking in the source the idea of otherness/distinctiveness from something mentioned previously". Catchpole's dictum is often true – cf. 4:43; 8:6, 7; 16:18; 17:34, 35; 19:20; 20:11. However, it is on slim ground indeed, and is likely negated, in the case of 6:6; 9:29.

sary[172], and Luke omits them accordingly. The charge with which Peter is confronted is broadly similar in Luke and Mark: καὶ σὺ ἐξ αὐτῶν εἶ (Luke); οὗτος ἐξ αὐτῶν ἐστιν (Mark). Luke, however, has switched to the second person, while Mark now narrates in the third. Moreover, Luke identifies no audience for the accusation, while Mark mentions τοῖς παρεστῶσιν. Again, the purpose of the καί is puzzling. When turning to compare the two versions of the denial, one finds that Mark has given his rendition in indirect discourse, Luke in direct. It is not like Luke to introduce direct speech where there was none in his source; indeed, his tendency is to move away from direct discourse[173]. Luke's version of the denial is simple, corresponding with the οὐκ εἰμι of John 18:25, though Luke also has the vocative ἄνθρωπε. Unlike Mark, Luke adds ὁ Πέτρος.

V 59: Mark's parallel is 14:70. For μετὰ μικρόν, Luke has διαστάσης ὡσεὶ ὥρας μιᾶς; Luke's clause is thus more specific than the vague chronological reference in Mark. Διίστημι is used only 3 times in the NT – all in Luke-Acts (22:59; 24:51; Acts 27:28), and ὡσεί belongs to Luke's redactional vocabulary[174]. Hence, the language of this phrase is compatible with Lukan redaction. This does not explain why Luke would have wanted to add such detail here, or in 22:58, however. Luke drops Mark's superfluous πάλιν again, and reads ἄλλος τις for Mark's οἱ παρεστῶτες. Τις, used thus, is Lukan (see above on 22:56). For Mark's simple ἔλεγον, Luke has διϊσχυρίζετο λέγων. Διϊσχυρίζομαι is likely a Lukan addition, for it appears in the NT only here and in Acts 12:15. Luke omits Mark's τῷ Πέτρῳ as self-evident. As for the content of the charge itself, Luke substitutes for ἀληθῶς (which he reserves as an equivalent for ἀμήν[175]) his own ἐπ' ἀληθείας. Καὶ οὗτος μετ' αὐτοῦ ἦν is Luke's parallel for Mark's ἐξ αὐτῶν εἶ. Again, one observes a shift in person: now Luke has the third, Mark the second! Μετά is not Luke's preferred term for denoting "with". Moreover, in view of 22:56 (καὶ αὐτὸς σὺν αὐτῷ ἦν) and the use of ἐκ in Mark 14:70, its use here is all the more unexpected. Finally, with the shift from second person to third in the predicate excepted, the final designation of Peter as a Galilean is identical in both accounts.

V 60: Luke's story at this juncture is roughly parallel to Mark 14:71–72. However, Luke has nothing to correspond with the harshness of Mark's opening ὁ δὲ ἤρξατο . . . ὅτι; rather, Mark's portrait of Peter has been softened with Luke's simple εἶπεν δὲ ὁ Πέτρος. For the third denial, Luke has ἄνθρωπε, οὐκ οἶδα ὃ λέγεις whereas Mark's version reads οὐκ οἶδα τὸν ἄνθρωπον τοῦτον ὃν λέγετε. For a third time, then, Luke employs the vocative – and that under no influence from the Markan text. In actuality, this statement of denial in Luke is closer to that in Mark 14:68, while the present denial in Mark is closer to that in Luke 22:57. As in 22:57, Luke's form here recalls the Jewish ban-formula. For Mark's καὶ εὐθύς, Luke has καὶ παραχρῆμα. Παραχρῆμα is a Lukan favorite[176] which replaces Mark's εὐθύς at Luke 5:25; 8:44, 55; 18:43. With ἔτι λαλοῦντος αὐτοῦ (absent from Mark), Luke stresses the literal fulfillment of Jesus' prediction (cf. 22:34). As in 22:34, the order of "cock" and "crow" has been transposed *vis-à-vis* the Markan account. As before, Luke knows nothing of a "second crowing"; this suggests Luke's knowledge of a different tradition than that incorporated in Mark.

V 61: There is no parallel for Luke's καὶ στραφεὶς ὁ κύριος ἐνέβλεψεν τῷ Πέτρῳ, and it is under suspicion as a Lukan creation[177]. Στρέφω occurs in Luke 7 times, 3 of which can probably be credited to Lukan redaction (7:9; 10:23; 14:25); the other 4 are found in texts with no Synoptic parallel (7:44; 9:55; 22:61; 23:28), so a judgment as to source is not certain. The verb is frequently employed in Luke to introduce a dominical saying[178], especially when that saying brings home a certain point, almost as an aside, in view of a present event, often in a person-to-person context. This use of στρέφω is not unique to Luke – cf. Matt 9:22; 16:23. Among the texts using the term in Luke, 22:61 is novel in that no saying is thus introduced, strictly speaking; however, the verb does

---

172 Cf. Pryke, *Redactional Style*, 96.
173 Sanders, *Tendencies*, 261–262; Catchpole, *Trial*, 273–274.
174 Gaston, *Electronicae*, 65; Jeremias, *Sprache*, 297.
175 Marshall, *Gospel of Luke*, 843. *Contra* Catchpole, *Trial*, 173–174.
176 Gaston, *Electronicae*, 64; Jeremias, *Sprache*, 297.
177 Bultmann, *History*, 282–283; Lindars, *Jesus*, 133–134.
178 Cf. George Bertram, "Στρέφω", in *TDNT*, 7:715.

serve this same general purpose, for Jesus' action brings to mind his earlier word to Peter – and in this indirect way introduces a logion of Jesus. These observations do not prove that Luke has created this whole statement, but indicate only that στρέφω is used in a way consistent both with Lukan redaction and the introductory function of the verb attested in Matthew and Luke.

On the other hand, the addition of ὁ κύριος is not characteristic of Luke's editing of Mark[179]; we would expect "Jesus" here. Moreover, the presence of the title here (twice in 22:61) recalls Κύριε in 22:33 – a verse which, we have argued, rests on pre-Lukan, non-Markan tradition. It is not inconceivable that this whole story about Peter circulated on its own at one time, so the vocative in 22:33 may be viewed in relation to the title in 22:61 – both coming to Luke from non-Markan material[180]. Luke omits ἐμβλέπω in 18:22/Mark 10:21; 18:27/10:27; 22:56/14:67, but introduces it into a Markan section at 20:17 (Mark 12:10). As we have previously observed, Luke frequently changes his vocabulary to avoid repetition; if ἐμβλέπω was present in his source here, this might account for his choice of another term in 22:56. The verb can signify "to look" or "to be able to see" (Matt 6:26; Mark 8:25; Acts 22:11), "to look intently" (Mark 14:67), or "to look with discernment or reproof" (Matt 19:26; Mark 10:21, 27; Luke 20:17). It probably carries the third nuance here.

In place of Mark's καὶ ἀνεμνήσθη ὁ Πέτρος (14:72), Luke's version reads καὶ ὑπεμνήσθη ὁ Πέτρος. Ὑπομιμνῄσκω occurs only here in the Synoptic Gospels and never in Acts. Ἀναμιμνῄσκω is almost as rare in the Synoptics, appearing only in Mark 11:21 (for which there is no Lukan parallel) and 14:72. Jeremias has noted an interesting parallel between Luke 22:61 and Acts 11:16[181]:

Luke: καὶ ὑπεμνήσθη ὁ Πέτρος τοῦ ῥήματος τοῦ κυρίου ὡς εἶπεν.
Acts: ἐμνήσθην δὲ   τοῦ ῥήματος τοῦ κυρίου ὡς ἐλεγεν.

As impressive as this correspondence appears, it should not be overlooked that the presence of ῥήματος in the Lukan text is suspect and may be due to a later attempt to assimilate the Lukan text to the Matthean and Markan parallels. The other reading, τοῦ λογοῦ, is also well-attested and has the advantage of being by far the more difficult reading since its presence here differs from Lukan usage elsewhere. Even so, the case for Lukan redaction in this phrase is well-founded. As for the repetition of the logion itself, Mark and Luke are in precise agreement except that Mark's δίς is replaced with σήμερον (as in 22:34).

V 62: This verse parallels Mark 14:72c, but is an exact replica of Matt 26:75c. The whole verse is absent in a minority of witnesses, and this has caused some critics to consider it a later assimilation to the Matthean text. In support of this is the Matthean character of the language[182], and the fact that 22:61 could serve as a finale to this whole scene in Luke (cf. a similar format in John 18:27). On the other hand, it has been urged that it is more probable that the verse was accidently omitted from such few witnesses than that it was added without substantial revision in so overwhelming a majority of witnesses[183]. It is hardly believable that Luke and Matthew independently edited Mark's text to achieve this degree of commonality; so, regardless of how one judges the text-critical question, one may still safely assume that in 22:62 Luke is not following Mark.

Thus, the evidence pertinent to evaluating the literary relationship of the Markan and Lukan renditions of the narrative of Peter's denial of Jesus has shown itself to be highly ambiguous. While much of the language em-

---

179 Cf. Caird, *Luke*, 165; Catchpole, *Trial*, 165; Marshall, *Gospel of Luke*, 844.
180 That 22:33 and 22:61 should be read together for interpretive purposes, see Eric Franklin, *Christ the Lord: A Study in the Purpose and Theology of Luke-Acts* (London: S.P.C.K., 1975) 52. On the possibility of a Petrine tradition on this nature, see the summarizing remarks in Kim E. Dewey, "Peter's Curse and Cursed Peter (Mark 14:53–54, 66–72)", in *Passion in Mark*, 113–114; Koester, *NT Introduction*, 2:160–164, 324–328. Cf. *Acts Pet.* 2.3.7.
181 Jeremias, *Sprache*, 297–298.
182 Gundry, *Matthew*, 551. C. M. Tuckett, ("On the Relationship between Matthew and Luke", *NTS* 30 [1, 1984] 137–138) argues against the originality of this verse on internal grounds.
183 Metzger, *Textual Commentary*, 178.

ployed by Luke can be explained in terms of a redaction of Mark (as Schneider has also seen), shifts in the identity of Peter's challengers, the content of the accusations, and the language of the denials, as well as the introduction of non-Markan chronological details remain inexplicable if Luke was following only Mark (as Catchpole also saw). Further, the shift in person within the three accusations as recorded by the evangelists is puzzling. Still further, we have noted several specific instances where variations from Mark are not conducive to a solution explicated solely in terms of Lukan redactional interests, style, and vocabulary — where additional source material is very likely. Hence, we cannot conclude with Catchpole that Luke represents an account of Peter's denial independent of Mark, but neither can we side with those who regard the Lukan text as a mere editing of the Markan story. A hypothesis of a pre-Lukan, non-Markan parallel tradition used by Mark alongside the Markan material best accounts for the evidence at hand.

XIV. Luke 22:63−65 (Mark 14:65)

Far-reaching discrepancies characterize the Lukan account of the mockery of Jesus in relation to its counterpart in Mark. Most obvious are the differences in setting and timing: in Luke the mockery is situated after Peter's denial but before the hearing before the Sanhedrin, while in Mark the mockery occurs in front of the Sanhedrin following the trial, preceding the denial by Peter. Dissimilarity extends further, into matters of detail. The identity of the mockers in Luke is given as "the men who were holding him in custody", while in Mark the mockery is carried out first by τινές — presumably members of the council, then by the "guards". The actions taken against Jesus are delineated in Luke as ἐμπαίζω, δέρω, περικαλύπτω, and ἐπερωτάω + λέγω; but in Mark as ἐμπτύω, κολαφίζω, λέγω, and λαμβάνω + ῥάπισμα. In fact, of the 27 words used by Luke in this pericope, only 4 (i.e. 14.8%) are also used in Mark — and the 4 common words are hardly noteworthy: καί, αὐτός, λέγω, and προφητεύω. Moreover, Luke, who elsewhere has amply demonstrated his interest in the *heilsgeschichtliche* aim of Jesus' passion, often tying it to OT prophecy[184], here fails to integrate the allusions to the Servant of Yahweh found in the Markan text[185]. This alone is a strong hint that Luke is indebted to a non-

---

184 See above, chapter 3.X.
185 In particular, Isa 50:6 has been seen in the background of Mark 14:65. Verbal agreement is found in the use of ῥάπισμα, τό ... πρόσωπον, and ἐμπτύω. Cf. Nineham, *Mark*, 408−409; Kee, "Function", 170; Hooker, *Jesus*, 90−91; Ernest Best, *The Temptation and the Passion:*

Markan source[186]. With the combined weight of these factors it is little wonder that a number of interpreters have theorized that in this pericope Luke is dependent on a non-Markan source[187].

V 63: Mark's καὶ . . . τινὲς is replaced in Luke by καὶ οἱ ἄνδρες οἱ συνέρχοντες αὐτόν. Following, as it does, the reference to Peter in 22:60–62, αὐτός ought to refer to Peter. On the other hand, it is Jesus who has been arrested, not Peter, so the antecedent of the pronoun is obviously "Jesus". The tradition employed by Luke, then, has not been combined smoothly with the Markan material he has borrowed in 22:61. Ἀνηρ belongs to Luke's redactional vocabulary[188], and he uses "οἱ . . . οἱ" constructions in Acts 9:7; 19:17. Συνέχω appears in the NT 12 times, 9 of which come in Luke-Acts. Three times in the Gospel it is due to Lukan redaction (4:38; 8:37, 45), 3 times it is found in texts without Synoptic parallels (12:50; 19:43; 22:63), and 3 times it is read in Acts (7:57; 18:5; 28:8). The verb is capable of a variety of nuances[189], and its usage in Luke-Acts reflects this breadth. It can denote "suffering", as with sickness (Luke 4:38; Acts 28:8; cf. Matt 4:24), "seized", as with fear (Luke 8:37), "surrounded" or "pressed hard upon", as by a crowd (Luke 8:45; 19:43), "to devote oneself" or "to be constrained" (Luke 12:50; Acts 18:5; cf. 2 Cor 5:14), "to close" or "to shut" (Acts 7:57), and, as in 22:63, "to hold in custody". This last nuance is unparalleled in Lukan usage; hence, despite the verb's relatively high number of appearances in Luke-Acts we cannot be sure of its Lukan derivation in this case[190]. Contra Mark, Luke mentions only one group engaged in mockery.

As a parallel for Mark's ἤρξαντο . . . ἐμπτύειν τῷ προσώπῳ[191] καὶ κολαφίζειν αὐτόν, Luke's version reads ἐνεπαίζον αὐτῷ δέροντες. Taylor allows that in editing Mark Luke may have purposely deleted ἄρχομαι as an unnecessary auxiliary verb[192], but the verb may best be understood literally in this instance. In this case Luke's redactional procedure is not so easily explained. Given the fact that Mark's infinitives do not reappear in any form in Luke (with the later, ambiguous exception of λέγω), it is more probable that Luke is following his own source here.

Ἐμπαίζω is found in the NT only in the Synoptics (Matt – 5x; Mark – 3x; Luke – 5x). In 18:32 Luke borrows the word from the passion prediction in Mark 10:34, but as to his usage elsewhere (14:29; 22:63; 23:11,36) there are no strict Synoptic parallels. It would appear that Luke borrows the verb from tradition, but not slavishly. In 23:35 he avoids the term as a description of the action of the high priests (Mark 15:31). When Jesus is the object of the verb, Gentiles are the subject. Δέρω appears only 14 times in the NT (Matt – 1x; Mark – 3x; Luke-Acts – 5x; Paul – 2x). Of the occasions of its use in the Third Gospel, twice it is found in material reported only by Luke (12: 47–48), twice in the parable of the wicked husbandmen where it is taken from Mark (Luke 20: 10–11/Mark 12:3, 5), and finally in the present text. Luke omits the term in Mark 3:9/Luke 21:12.

The Markan Soteriology (Cambridge: Cambridge University, 1965) 149; Schweizer, Mark, 327: idem, Luke, 347.
186 Cf. Catchpole, Trial, 180–182; Marshall, Gospel of Luke, 845.
187 Bultmann, History, 271; Winter, Trial, 27–28; Trocmé, Passion, 32–33; Catchpole, Trial, 174–183; Taylor, Passion, 79–80; Plummer, Luke, 517; Schneider, Verleugnung, 96–104; Marshall, Gospel of Luke, 845–846.
188 Gaston, Electronicae, 65; Jeremias, Sprache, 298.
189 Cf. Helmut Koester, "Συνέχω", in TDNT, 7:882–885.
190 Contra Jeremias, Sprache, 298.
191 The phrase καὶ περικαλύπτειν αὐτοῦ τὸ πρόσωπον is omitted from Mark 14:65 in D a sys^p bo^mss and is also absent from the Matthean parallel (26:67) where its inclusion would have made much better sense. Moreover, τῷ προσώπῳ αὐτοῦ (or αὐτοῦ τῷ πρόσωπῳ) is read after ἐμπτύειν in D Θ 565 700 a f sy^p. Presumably, then, καὶ περικαλύπτειν is a later addition to the Marken text, suggested by the phrase in Luke 22:64. Cf. Taylor, Mark, 571; Catchpole, Trial, 175.
192 Taylor, Passion, 80. Cf. Pryke, Redactional Style, 79.

It is not likely to be redactional, therefore, and Schneider has drawn attention to the formal parallelism between vv 63 and 64 –

καὶ ... συνέχοντες αὐτὸν ἐνέπαιζον ... δέροντες ...
καὶ περικαλύψαντες αὐτὸν ἐπηρώτων λέγοντες –

as a further indication of its primitiveness[193]. As noted previously, Luke's failure to employ Mark's ἐμπτύω (and ῥάπισμα, below) marks his puzzling omission of Mark's allusion to Isa 50:6.

V 64: For καὶ περικαλύψαντες αὐτὸν ἐπηρώτων λέγοντες Mark has only καὶ λέγειν αὐτῷ. For προφήτευσον, τίς ἐστιν ὁ παίσας, Mark has only προφήτευσον[194]. If this form of mocking is understood in analogy to that in Mark 15:16–20 and Luke 23:11, it is fair to say that in both Mark and Luke Jesus is thought to be a prophet, albeit a false one, by his enemies[195]. However, the respective pictures given by the two evangelists diverge from this common base. In Mark the idea is "Play the prophet now!" – i.e. "Deliver a prophetic oracle!" Contrariwise, in Luke the blindfolded Jesus is to declare who it was that hit him: "Exercise the prophetic gift of second sight!"[196] (cf. 7:39). It is most likely that Matt 26:68 and the present text, both of which record the question after the imperative of προφητεύω, are ultimately dependent on a common source[197].

V 65: Mark has nothing with which to compare this verse in Luke, nor does Luke have anything corresponding to Mark's καὶ οἱ ὑπηρέται ... ἔλαβον. Luke's concluding statement has the appearance of the summarizing statements he uses elsewhere – e.g. Luke 3:18; 8:3; 21:37–38; Acts 2:40; 15:35; et al. – and may be understood on this basis as the handiwork of the Third Evangelist.

Our survey of the relevant data has indicated that in 22:63–65 Luke is not dependent on the Markan material. Verses 63–64 rest on pre-Lukan, non-Markan tradition, with Matthew and Luke probably sharing a common tradition to which can be traced back the question of Matt 26:68/Luke 22:64; and v 65 is a Lukan creation.

XV. Luke 22:66–71 (Mark 14:53b, 55–64; 15:1)

In relating the story of Jesus' hearing before the Sanhedrin Luke follows a path that diverges markedly from the parallel account in Mark's Gospel. Not only does the Lukan pericope appear in a dissimilar narrative sequence and incorporate a variant chronology and christology relative to the Markan account, but the character of the enquiry is different as well. While the report as it stands in Mark may not for the most part read like a formal

---

193 Schneider, *Verleugnung*, 99–100.
194 A number of witnesses (N W X Δ Θ f^{13} 33 565 892 1424 *pc* vg^{mss} syh sa^{mss}) add the question χριστέ, τίς ἐστιν ὁ παίσας σε. The omission, however, is well-attested (ℵ A B C D L 067 *M* lat sy) and the longer text probably arose as a later assimilation to Matt 26:68 or Luke 22:64.
195 Cf., e.g., Ben F. Meyer, *The Aims of Jesus* (London: SCM, 1979) 238; Jeremias, *NT Theology*, 77–78; David Hill, *New Testament Prophecy* (Atlanta: John Knox, 1979) 51–52; Pesch, *Mark*, 2:441; Martin Hengel, *The Charismatic Leader and His Followers* (Edinburgh: T. & T. Clark, 1981) 42. This does not mean, however, that Jesus was condemned precisely for his being a false prophet (as Hengel seems to imply). Jesus was also mocked as messiah, king, and healer.
196 See Taylor, *Mark*, 571; Catchpole, *Trial*, 175–176. Even if one rejects our text-critical decision on Mark 14:65, it must be admitted that Mark's intended meaning may still diverge from Luke's, and that the coincidence in meaning between Matthew and Luke here is remarkable.
197 Schneider, *Verleugnung*, 102; Marshall, *Gospel of Luke*, 846. Cf. Tuckett, "On the Relationship between Matthew and Luke", 136–137.

trial[198], it does include a number of elements — e.g. the testimony of witnesses and the explicit pronouncements of both charge (blasphemy) and verdict (death) — that set the Markan episode apart from the much more informal hearing described by Luke. In fact, a large number of particulars read in the Markan account are found lacking in the Lukan, most of which are of major importance either for their contribution to the story line or for their allusion to the Jewish Scriptures[199]. There is, nevertheless, a remarkably high percentage of words in Luke common to the parallel accounts (42.6%).

V 66: Luke's version opens with a temporal note — καὶ ὡς ἐγένετο ἡμέρα; Mark's parallel is in 15:1: καὶ εὐθὺς πρωΐ. Catchpole has argued against the view that Luke has only edited Mark at this point[200], but from the standpoint of linguistic considerations his reasoning is not compelling. Luke's Gospel never reads πρωΐ (Matt – 3x; Mark – 5x; Acts – 1x), and in 4:42 Luke replaces Mark's καὶ πρωΐ (1:35) with γενομένης δὲ ἡμέρας. Ἡμέρα + γίνομαι also appears in 6:13; Acts 12:18; 16:35; 23:12; 27:29, 33, 39. Moreover, ὡς, as a temporal conjunction, is characteristic of Luke-Acts[201]. Therefore, it cannot be denied that Luke may have freely rewritten Mark at this introductory point, though linguistically it is possible for Luke to have redacted an independent source as well. Indeed, inasmuch as Luke locates *this* hearing in the morning (*contra* Mark), he very well could be witnessing to an alternative tradition.

For συνέρχομαι in Mark 14:53, Luke has συνάγω. Neither verb is especially Lukan: συνέρχομαι is found in Luke twice, Acts 17 times; συνάγω is read in Luke 6 times and in Acts 11 times. When it is used in the Third Gospel, συνάγω seems to have originated in pre-Lukan material — from Q in 3:17; 11:23; and from L in 12:17–18; 15:13.

Does τὸ πρεσβυτέριον τοῦ λαοῦ correspond to Mark's οἱ πρεσβύτεροι (15:1)? In favor of this identification we may note the following. (A) "The elders" clearly made up a third group within the Sanhedrin (to which reference is here being made), alongside the ἀρχιερεῖς and γραμματεῖς[202] — who are also mentioned in this verse. (B) Elsewhere, Luke numbers the "elders" as a group with the chief priests and scribes (e.g. 9:22; 20:1). (C) "The elders" are named with the arresting party in 22:52, and one would expect their presence at the subsequent hearing. (D) In 19:47 τοῦ λαοῦ qualifies οἱ πρῶτοι — designating a group alongside but separate from the chief priests and scribes, and is thus a probable reference to οἱ πρεσβύτεροι[203] — but no other similar expression employing τοῦ λαοῦ is found in Lukan redaction. On the other hand, the other two usages of the noun in the NT — Acts 22:5 and 1 Tim 4:14 — more clearly refer to τὸ πρεσβυτέριον as a designation of the whole Jewish council. As for τοῦ λαοῦ, a parallel is found in Acts 5:21, where Luke parenthetically designates τὸ συνέδριον as πᾶσαν τὴν γερουσίαν τῶν υἱῶν Ἰσραήλ (cf. Exod 12:21 LXX). Mark and Luke agree on naming (οἱ) ἀρχιερεῖς and γραμματεῖς as members of the council, but in

---

198 So Harvey, *Jesus*, 31.
199 Joseph B. Tyson ("The Lucan Version of the Trial of Jesus", *NovT* 3 [1959] 252–253) observes that a number of these changes actually work *against* Luke's more general apologetic *Tendenz*.
200 Catchpole, *Trial*, 186–190. *Contra* Schneider, *Verleugnung*, 106; Taylor, *Passion*, 81; Marshall, *Gospel of Luke*, 848; Jeremias, *Sprache*, 299.
201 BDF, para. 455.2. On the other hand, Jeremias (*Sprache*, 299) asserts that the construction καὶ ὡς + aorist infinitive is pre-Lukan. His evidence is not decisive, however.
202 Cf. Emil Schürer, *The History of the Jewish People in the Age of Jesus Christ (175 B.C. – A.D. 135)*, rev ed., vol. 2, ed. Geza Vermes, Fergus Millar, and Matthew Black (Edinburgh: T. & T. Clark, 1979) 212–213; Jeremias, *Jerusalem*, 222–226.
203 So Jeremias, *Jerusalem*, 223; Cassidy, "Audience", 148; Marshall, *Gospel of Luke*, 722.

Luke's version the two groups are joined with the close connective τε καί²⁰⁴. Τὸ πρεσβυτέριον is not joined in this manner to the chief priests and scribes, and this shift serves to distinguish the nature of this reference. Hence, we should render τὸ πρεσβυτέριον as "the council" and not identify Luke's language with Mark's²⁰⁵. This speaks against Luke's dependency on Mark here.

Τέ may easily be attributed to Luke's hand (Matt – 3x; Mark – 0; Luke – 9x; Acts – *passim*). Καὶ ἀπήγαγον αὐτόν corresponds to Mark's καὶ ἀπήγαγον τὸν Ἰησοῦν (14:53). Ἀπάγω is something of a technical term with respect to leading prisoners to justice²⁰⁶, so it is expected here regardless of the source.

In Mark 14:53 Jesus is led πρὸς τὸν ἀρχιερέα, after which Mark records the gathering of the chief priests, elders, and scribes. In effect, then, Jesus is led before the Sanhedrin. In Luke Jesus is led εἰς τὸ συνέδριον αὐτῶν. For "their Sanhedrin", see Acts 23:28. The meaning in Luke does not depart substantially from that of Mark's account. How closely the two versions agree depends to a large degree on how one renders Luke's τὸ συνέδριον. Is it "the council chamber" or "the council itself"? Most often in Acts it designates the council as a body of persons and not as a meeting place – cf. 4:5; 5:21, 27; 22:30; 23:1, 15, 20, 28; 24:20. A minority of cases exist where the sense is at least ambiguous, however, and one may justifiably take it as a designation of place – cf. 4:15; 5:34, 41; 6:12, 15; 23:6. Had Luke intended his readers to understand Jesus was taken "before the council" he would have retained Mark's πρός – a favorite preposition for Luke²⁰⁷. In addition, ἀπάγω suggests a change of setting and, with εἰς, denotes movement "into a place" rather than "before an assembly". The weight of probability supports the rendering "council chamber"²⁰⁸. This variation from Mark is yet another indication that Luke may be drawing on additional source material.

V 67: Luke deletes a large section of the Jewish trial as reported by Mark – including the idea that witnesses against Jesus were sought by the chief priests and the whole council, the many false witnesses whose testimonies were contradictory, the specific allegation regarding the temple-saying, the question of the high priest directed at Jesus' silence, and the double reference to Jesus' silence (Mark 14:55–61a). A number of observations deserve brief mention regarding this lengthy omission. (A) It may be argued that Luke knew this section, as evidenced by certain linguistic reminiscences – e.g. μαρτυρία in 22:71 and in Mark 14:55, 56, and 59²⁰⁹. Such argumentation has little basis for support, however, as possible reminiscences are very few and all are capable of alternative explanations. As for μαρτυρία, this term would be expected in a trial-like scene, so the agreement can easily be explained more in terms of coincidence than of dependence. (B) Moreover, Luke has no hint that others were called upon or given opportunity to testify for or against Jesus; indeed, the exclamation of the council in 22:71a – "What further evidence do we need?" – renders all additional evidence superfluous. (C) But why would Luke miss the opportunity to further demonstrate the aggressive role of the chief priests in having Jesus put away? Elsewhere, we see that this is an important theme for Luke²¹⁰. (D) Why would Luke side-step this opportunity to further demonstrate Jesus' innocence – the witnesses cannot even agree on his guilt²¹¹?

---

204 "Τέ ... καί provides a closer connection than simple καί" (BDF, para. 444.2).
205 See Schürer, *History*, 2:206; Günther Bornkamm, "Πρέσβυς", in *TDNT*, 6:654; Ernst Haenchen, *The Acts of the Apostles* (Oxford: Basil Blackwell, 1971) 625; LSJ, 1462.
206 Schneider, *Verleugnung*, 109–110; BAG, 79.
207 Gaston, *Electronicae*, 65.
208 So Catchpole, *Trial*, 191–192; Eduard Lohse, "Συνέδριον", in *TDNT*, 7:780; Marshall, *Gospel of Luke*, 848; Schneider, *Verleugnung*, 110.
209 See the note in Schneider, *Verleugnung*, 129–130. It is not insignificant that William R. Farmer (*Synopticon: The Verbal Agreement between the Greek Texts of Matthew, Mark, and Luke Contextually Exhibited* [Cambridge: Cambridge University, 1969] 130) lists only ἀρχιερεῖς and τὸ συνέδριον as providing verbal linkage between Mark and Luke here.
210 For this tendency in Luke, cf. Cassidy, "Audience", 148–150, 153–162; *idem, Jesus*, 52–54.
211 For the import of this theme in Luke, cf. 23:4, 14–15, 22, 41; Büchele, *Tod Jesu*, 76–96; Weber, *Cross*, 117–124; Beck "*Imitatio Christi*", 31; David Schmidt, "Luke's 'Innocent' Jesus: A Scriptural Apologetic", in *Political Issues*, 111–121.

(E) Franklin has asserted that for Luke the destruction of the temple in Jerusalem no longer belongs within the sphere of eschatological happenings, so Luke does not portray Jesus as hostile to the temple. In line with this perspective, reasons Franklin, Luke omits the temple accusation in Mark 14:57–58[212]. Franklin is correct in his observation of the essentially positive attitude of Jesus toward the temple in Luke, as is indicated by Luke's redaction of such Markan texts as 11:11–17 (Luke 19:45–46) and the positive role given the temple in Luke 1–2 and Acts 1–5. Must we, therefore, agree with Franklin that Luke has omitted the accusation about the temple by way of maintaining a consistent theology of the temple? This is doubtful, for elsewhere Luke has incorporated traditional material at variance with his generally positive stance regarding the temple – e.g. Luke 13:35[213]; 23:45; Acts 6:11–14[214]; 7:44–50.

(F) Finally, in omitting Mark's reference to Jesus' silence (14:61) Luke fails to take up an allusion to Isa 53:7[215], by which Jesus is further identified with the Servant of Yahweh. As Morna Hooker has been quick to point out, the language of this text does not correspond to that of Isa 53:7 LXX, but one need not on this basis conclude with Hooker that it is incredible that the Markan text nonetheless employs an allusion to the Isaianic passage[216]. On this matter Goppelt's insight is still instructive:

> Much of the NT abounds with allusions to the OT that have little resemblance to the exact wording. These allusions make up the larger portion of the NT use of Scripture and form the heart of its view of Scripture. The typology of the Synoptic Gospels is usually a simple reminder of the OT parallels by means of names that are given to NT phenomena or by allusions that are included in the narrative. These allusions may be simply the use of figurative language or the author's unintentional imitation of familiar narratives. Most of them, however, are intended to evoke comparison with the OT passages that they bring to mind[217].

The lack of precise verbal agreement in the Markan narrative should not blind us to the conceptual correspondence, but may be used as an indicator that the narrator was not concerned to mold the story around the OT text. (In Luke 23:9 Jesus does maintain his silence.) Of course, in removing

---

212 Franklin, *Christ the Lord*, 90–92.
213 Ὁ οἶκος likely refers to the temple, but this is a disputed rendering. Cf. Otto Michel, "Οἶκος", in *TDNT*, 5:119–125; Joachim Jeremias, *The Parables of Jesus*, 3d ed. (London: SCM, 1972) 168; Marshall, *Gospel of Luke*, 576; Ellis, *Luke*, 191.
214 Haenchen (*Acts*, 274) has argued that Luke has transported the charge against Jesus in Mark 14:57–58 to this context. This would not negate the point made here – namely, that Luke does include negative mention about the temple. In any case it should not be overlooked that there is good reason to suspect that Jesus himself criticized the temple and taught that it would be superseded (cf. Leonhard Goppelt, *Theology of the New Testament*, 2 vols. [Grand Rapids, Michigan: Wm. B. Eerdmans, 1981/82] 1:95–97; E. P. Sanders, *Jesus and Judaism* [London: SCM, 1985] 61–76, 296–306; Harvey, *Jesus*, 129–134; see further below, chapter 8), and early Hellenists, of whom Stephen is a representative figure in Acts, carried forth and developed this motif. Hence, the Acts text may well rest on good tradition apart from the Markan passage – cf. Martin Hengel, "Between Jesus and Paul", in *Jesus and Paul*, 21–23; idem, "The Origins of the Christian Mission", in *Jesus and Paul*, 55–57; Maddox, *Luke-Acts*, 52–53; Leonhard Goppelt, *Apostolic and Post-Apostolic Times* (London: Adam and Charles Black, 1970; reprint ed., Grand Rapids, Michigan: Baker, 1977) 54, 57–58.
215 Cf. Henry Barclay Swete, *Commentary on Mark* (London: Macmillan, 1913; reprint ed., Grand Rapids, Michigan: Kregel, 1977) 358; Nineham, *Mark*, 407; Schweizer, *Mark*, 564; Moo, *OT – Passion*, 148–151.
216 Hooker, *Jesus*, 89. Also Hans Walter Wolff, *Jesaja 53 im Urchristentum* (Berlin: Evangelische, 1950) 75–76.
217 Leonhard Goppelt, *Typos: The Typological Interpretation of the Old Testament in the New* (Grand Rapids, Michigan: Wm. B. Eerdmans, 1982) 198–199. See also, Kee, "Function", 165 n.2. Hooker's methodology has come under critical fire from R. T. France, "The Servant of the Lord in the Teaching of Jesus", *TynB* 19 (1968) 28–29.

the additional witnesses from the trial scene Luke has no need for Jesus to maintain his silence in the present text. This may be, but we have still seen that the removal of this whole section from Mark appears to work against Luke's redactional design and activity as we know it elsewhere, and no ready explanation for his present procedure has been forthcoming if he was dependent solely on the Markan account.

As one may postulate good reasons for Luke to have retained the various individual motifs in Mark 14:55–61a, then, it will be necessary to ask whether we can posit a reasonable explanation for Luke's omission of the whole. With this omission Luke's trial narrative is remarkable for its brevity and lack of details integral to an actual trial. Indeed, Luke can hardly be said to have narrated a *trial* at all. The hearing before the Sanhedrin, the purpose of which was to establish the charge against Jesus, signals a travesty of justice and serves to underscore the guilt of the Jewish leaders. It is this guilt which one finds as a recurring theme in the kerygma of the *Actareden*. One cannot help but observe, however, that certain elements in the Markan version would have furthered this more general apologetic *Tendenz*, so we must conclude this part of our investigation by insisting that Luke's omission of the Markan material is explicable only if he was guided by a further source which reported a hearing of a different character than that narrated in Mark. It remains to be seen whether the linguistic data of v 67 support this initial observation.

Luke records that the Sanhedrin addressed Jesus, whereas Mark has it that the high priest spoke on their behalf. It is characteristic of Luke to omit parataxis in Mark (ἐπηρώτα ... καὶ λέγει) in favor of a genitive absolute or, as in this instance, a subordinate participial construction (λέγοντες)[218]. However, it is unclear why Luke would have completely done away with Mark's ἐπερωτάω since the verb is a favorite for Luke[219]. As president of the Sanhedrin, the high priest was its spokesperson[220]. Luke is aware of this fact (cf., e.g., Acts 5:27); why, then, would he have deleted this detail if he was following Mark? Ordinarily, Lukan redaction favors greater specificity; it is not like him to make specific references like this one more general[221]. Moreover, the connection of this verse with v 66, with λέγοντες qualifying the unspecified subject of ἀπήγαγον, is difficult[222]. The imperative addressed to Jesus is this: εἰ σὺ εἶ ὁ χριστός, εἰπὸν ἡμῖν. Mark's parallel appears as an interrogative: σὺ εἶ ὁ χριστὸς ὁ υἱὸς τοῦ εὐλογητοῦ. Underlying both is the notion that Jesus was under suspicion as a messianic pretender (cf. 23:35–39). It is not coincidental that the Matthean and Johannine forms of this tradition agree with Luke against Mark in the command to "tell us": ἡμῖν εἴπῃς (Matt 26:63); εἰπὲ ἡμῖν παρρησίᾳ (John 10:24). This strongly suggests a similar, but non-Markan, source underlying the Lukan narrative[223].

The separation of the titles "Messiah" and "Son of God" in Luke – in the form of two questions as opposed to the one in Mark – has been the basis for a great deal of speculation among NT critics[224]. Rather than attempt to interact with each here we may follow the more expedient route of listing a number of telling observations. (A) In Mark one observes the identification of the two titles by the way the question is phrased (see also Mark 1:1). (B) In the view of the Third Evangelist, "Messiah" and "Son of God" are equated (cf. esp. 1:31–32; 4:41; Acts 9:20–22). (C) While the titles were related in post-biblical Judaism, any claim to an equality or interchangeability of the

---

218 Cf. Fitzmyer, *Luke*, 1:108; Schneider, *Verleugnung*, 112.
219 Gaston, *Electronicae*, 65.
220 Cf. Schürer, *History*, 2:202, 215–218.
221 Cf. Catchpole, *Trial*, 193–194; Marshall, *Gospel of Luke*, 849.
222 Marshall, *Gospel of Luke*, 849.
223 Cf. Catchpole, *Trial*, 195–196; John Amedee Bailey, *The Traditions Common to the Gospels of Luke and John* (Leiden: E. J. Brill, 1963) 60–61; Schneider, *Verleugnung*, 113.
224 Cf., e.g., Conzelmann, *Luke*, 84, 171; Helmut Flender, *St. Luke: Theologian of Redemptive History* (London: S.P.C.K., 1967) 44–46; Oscar Cullmann, *The Christology of the New Testament* (Philadelphia: Westminster, 1959) 279–280; Catchpole, *Trial*, 193–200; David M. Hay, *Glory at the Right Hand: Psalm 110 in Early Christianity* (Nashville: Abingdon, 1973) 69–70; Franklin, *Christ the Lord*, 56; Paul W. Walaskay, 'And so we came to Rome': *The Political Perspective of St. Luke* (Cambridge: Cambridge University, 1983) 39.

two, even at Qumran, exceeds the available evidence[225]. (D) In the present text the titles, while related, are not equated[226]. Therefore, against Luke's own christology, the separation of the titles in the Lukan version reflects a more primitive view, not based on the Markan account. Mark's rendition thus shows signs of secondary theological development.

For the crisp, direct reply of Jesus in Mark 14:62 — ἐγώ εἰμι — Luke records a lengthy, obscure, noncommittal answer the effect of which was to expose the unbelief of the Jewish leaders. Both Mark and Luke employ δέ and εἶπον, but there the similarity ends. Ἐάν is present in Luke 24 times, but almost without exception appears to be taken from pre-Lukan material. Significantly, of the 28 times it is found in Mark, Luke avoids ἐάν on all but 5 occasions (Mark 1:40/Luke 5:12; 9:50/14:34; 11:3/19:31; 11:31/20:5; 12:19/20:28). At times he uses ἄν as a substitute (Mark 6:10/ Luke 9:4; 8:35/9:24; 8:38/9:26), but in most cases Luke either rewrites Mark's text so that no such word is necessary (Mark 3:24–25/Luke 11:17; 5:28/8:44; 9:18/9:39; 10:12/16:18; 13:11/12:12; 13:21/17:23; 14:14/22:10) or offers no parallel text (Mark 3:28; 6:22–23; 7:11; 8:3; 9:43, 45, 47; 14:9, 31). The double negative οὐ μή ("for making categorical and emphatic denials"[227]) + the aorist subjunctive or future indicative of a verb is virtually limited to quotations of the LXX or sayings of Jesus and should not be regarded as Lukan[228]. Πιστεύω is used with great reserve in Luke's Gospel when compared with the usage in Acts, so it may be questioned whether its presence here should be attributed to Lukan creativity[229]. These factors, together with the similar response in John 10:25a, point to the non-Markan, pre-Lukan character of Jesus' answer in v 67b.

V 68: The second half of Jesus' answer to the council's first question is given here, in a verse with no Markan parallel. As in 22:67b, the presence of ἐάν and οὐ μή may be taken as initial evidence against Lukan creation. Schneider has made too much of the parallel reply in 20:1–8, as Catchpole has shown, but it is nevertheless true that this reluctance to speak directly on Jesus' part should not be seen in isolation from 20:1–8, 20–26, 27–40[230].

V 69: Both Luke and Mark (14:62b) now allude to the Son of Man, but the form of Luke's reference departs from Mark's. The variations can be listed as follows. (A) Mark has nothing corresponding to Luke's initial ἀπὸ τοῦ νῦν. Matthew 26:64, on the other hand, has a similar phrase: ἀπ᾽ ἄρτι. (B) In place of Mark's ὄψεσθε, Luke has ἔσται. (C) Following Mark's circumlocutional δύναμις (=God), Luke has the appendage τοῦ θεοῦ. (D) Finally, Luke has no verbal connection with Dan 7:13 (apart from the title itself).

The source-critical picture provided by these dissimilarities has been variously assessed. In his article on "ὁ υἱὸς τοῦ ἀνθρώπου", Carsten Colpe argues that Luke 22:69 is independent of Mark[231].

---

225 On this problem, see Eduard Lohse, "Υἱός, II. Palestinian Judaism", in *TDNT*, 8:360–362; Geza Vermes, *Jesus the Jew: A Historian's Reading of the Gospels* (Philadelphia: Fortress, 1973) 197–199; Martin Hengel, *The Son of God: The Origin of Christology and the History of Jewish-Hellenistic Religion* (Philadelphia: Fortress, 1976) 43–45; Joseph A. Fitzmyer, *A Wandering Aramean: Collected Aramaic Essays* (Chico, California: Scholars, 1979) 90–93, 105–106; Seyoon Kim,*"The 'Son of Man' " as the Son of God* (Tübingen: J. C. B. Mohr [Paul Siebeck], 1983) 22 n.33.
226 Cf. Catchpole, *Trial*, 197. *Contra* Conzelmann, *Luke*, 84, 171. Both Walaskay (*Political Perspective*, 39) and Franklin (*Christ the Lord*, 56) observe that the titles are not equated, but try, unsuccessfully, to explain this phenomenon in terms of Lukan redaction. Walaskay distinguishes, with no background support, the one title as "religious" and the other as "political". Franklin asserts that "Messiah", unlike "Son of God", was inadequate for Luke since it failed to do justice to Luke's exaltation motif. But see Acts 2:33–36!
227 Dana-Mantey, *Grammar*, 266–267.
228 See BDF, para. 365; Schneider, *Verleugnung*, 115; Jeremias, *Sprache*, 299.
229 Cf. Marshall, *Gospel of Luke*, 849.
230 Schneider, *Verleugnung*, 117; Catchpole, *Trial*, 276–278. On the possibility of interpreting this "dialog" within the matrix of the conversations of Luke 20, see Cassidy, *Jesus*, 64, 166 n.5. Without delving into the source-question, Cassidy treats the trial strictly on the level of Lukan theology. The conceptual relation, however, is pre-Lukan.
231 Carston Colpe, " Ὁ υἱὸς τοῦ ἀνθρώπου", in *TDNT*, 8:435–436.

He discusses the following points. (A) Luke's form contains the minimal statement and has no reference to Dan 7:13. (B) Luke's portrayal of Jesus as appointed judge coheres well with the overall picture of the Son of Man material. (C) Luke's version of Jesus' response is more primitive than Mark's, for here Jesus' reply is veiled. (D) Luke's version lacks the apocalyptic element given in Mark with the visionary ὄψεσθε. (E) Lastly, Colpe allows that the elucidation of the periphrastic δύναμις with τοῦ θεοῦ may be Lukan. Catchpole is not convinced by Colpe's discussion[232]. As for (A), Catchpole argues first that this omission by Luke is characteristic of Luke's redactional compression, and offers Mark 9:1/Luke 9:27 as an analogous example. Putting aside the fact that this one example is hardly foundation enough to posit a "Lukan characteristic", and that its analogous status is questionable in any case, Catchpole's explanation does not overcome the fact that in 21:27 Luke does make reference to Dan 7:13, drawing on the Markan parallel. Secondly, he asserts that ἔσται in Luke requires the absence of the allusion to Dan 7:13. According to Catchpole, Luke's use of this verb avoids the unfulfilled prediction in Mark; additionally, it reveals Luke's *Tendenz* to correct the Son of Man's present humiliation by an immediate exaltation.

Catchpole's overall thought here is reminiscent of Conzelmann's study of Lukan theology[233]. He argued that Luke, in deleting the Danielic phrase, deliberately omits a reference to a future parousia; in this way, Mark's future-oriented eschatology is avoided. However, subsequent study has demonstrated that Luke's thought does have a "not yet" emphasis[234]. Moreover, while it is true that Luke accentuates the humiliation-vindication motif, as Catchpole has argued, Luke was hardly the first to do so[235], so its presence here need not be credited to Lukan creativity. Finally, a growing body of literature is pointing to the relative antiquity of Son of Man texts devoid of direct allusions to Dan 7:13 over against those with direct or indirect references to the OT text[236]. While we are skeptical of any *a priori* assumption that a Son of Man saying alluding to Dan 7 *cannot* be authentic[237], should a general tendency of this kind prove to be the case, then this line of evidence would be an additional indication of the primitiveness of the Lukan passage *vis-à-vis* the Markan.

Hence, Catchpole's arguments against Colpe's (A) have not proven convincing. He does not deal with (B), but argues in the case of (C) that Luke could have superimposed the Markan material on the additional tradition, thus introducing v 69 into material taken from his other source. In fact, he regards v 69 as an intrusion from Mark, interrupting the otherwise smooth connection between vv 67–68 and 70. As with (B), (D) is skipped over, but Catchpole agrees with Colpe on (E). He lists 4:43; 5:26; 6:12; 8:11, 39; 9:20; and 18:43 as illustrative of this "typical Lukan editorial emphasis", then goes on to argue that the presence of τῆς δυνάμεως is too strong an overlap to be regarded as coincidental. Catchpole's "examples" are largely irrelevant to the present text, however, for in none of these texts does Luke amplify a periphrastic reference, and only in 9:20 does τοῦ θεοῦ appear as the sole addition to the Markan text. Δύναμις, appearing in both texts, does indeed point to literary dependence. On the other hand, the conceptual agreement between Luke and Matthew against Mark (see above) is a strong indication of a common, non-Markan tradition. Further, we need not regard v 69 as an intrusion into the thought of the pericope. As in 19:41–44, so here,

---

232 Catchpole, *Trial*, 157–159. Catchpole's argumentation is framed, in part, as a response to Colpe.
233 Cf. Conzelmann, *Luke*, 56–57, 84–85 n.3, 109, 116. Also, Hay, *Glory at the Right Hand*, 69–70; Lindars, *Jesus*, 141.
234 Cf., e.g., Maddox, *Luke-Acts*, esp. chapter 5; Stephen G. Wilson, *The Gentiles and the Gentile Mission in Luke-Acts* (Cambridge: Cambridge University, 1973) chapter 3; I. Howard Marshall, "Luke and His 'Gospel'", in *Das Evangelium*, 301; E. Earle Ellis, *Eschatology in Luke* (Philadelphia: Fortress, 1972); A. J. Mattill, Jr., *Luke and the Last Things* (Dillsboro, North Carolina: Western North Carolina, 1979).
235 See below, chapter 6.
236 E.g. Vermes, *Jesus*, 177–186; Norman Perrin, "Son of Man", in *IDBSup*, 833–836; William O. Walker, Jr., "The Son of Man and the Synoptic Problem", in *New Synoptic Studies*, 261–301.
237 Cf. George B. Caird, "Jesus and Israel: The Starting Point for New Testament Christology", in *Christological Perspectives*, 67; idem, *The Language and Imagery of the Bible* (London: Gerald Duckworth, 1982) 138–139.

failure to acknowledge who Jesus is becomes the basis for judgment. Here, the members of the council fail to acknowledge who Jesus is – though, ironically, they call upon him to acknowledge his true identity – and hand him over to Pilate, but (and this is the point) *he* is vindicated while *they* bring upon themselves heavenly judgment for rejecting him[238]. We conclude, then, that the evidence for deciding the source-critical question does not point unequivocally to either view, but does slightly favor the positing of a pre-Lukan, non-Markan tradition for v 69.

V 70: Now Luke's version takes up the second half of the Markan question (14:61). As in 22:67, the subject of the verb "to speak" is plural, as opposed to the singular reference to the high priest in Mark 14:61. Here, Luke recalls the members of the council with πᾶς. The word is often used in Lukan redaction[239], but is not peculiar to him; here it may have been suggested by Mark 14:64: οἱ δὲ πάντες. With respect to the Markan form of the question, Luke's version adds οὖν and substitutes θεός for the periphrastic εὐλογητός. If we take the οὖν as a logical connective[240], the question of the council becomes an attempt to have Jesus clarify the Son of Man reference. Apparently, the members of the council infer his claim to divine sonship on the basis of his allusion to Ps 110:1. Again, avoiding Mark's straightforward "I am" (14:62), Luke has ὁ δὲ πρὸς αὐτοὺς ἔφη · ὑμεῖς λέγετε ὅτι ἐγώ εἰμι. Obliquely, then, Jesus consents to this inference[241]. Πρός + accusative following a verb of speaking is a construction regularly found in the Third Gospel; it may be Lukan here (see above on 22:15).

Vermes has asserted that the form of Luke's answer is more primitive than Mark's since it possesses no advantage which would justify its substitution for Mark's "I am"[242]. Two observations add weighty support to this thesis. First, as Kim has already noted, the connection between the Son of Man and Son of God titles must be *inferred* – that is, the identification is of an indirect nature. Had the early church produced the identification out of its post-Easter faith we would have expected a more direct association[243]. Second, elsewhere Luke relates the exaltation of Jesus not with Jesus' status as *Son of God*, but with his *Messiahship* and *Lordship* (cf., e.g., Acts 2:34–36). Finally, we may refer to the arguments given above on 22:67 regarding the two-question format of the Lukan text as additional evidence that here we are dealing with a non-Markan, pre-Lukan tradition taken over by Luke.

V 71: Luke omits Mark's dramatic picture of the high priest tearing his garments (14:63) and moves directly to the verbal response of the council. Again, whereas Mark has the high priest speaking, Luke records that "they said". As for the initial exclamatory reply, Mark's version reads τί ἔτι χρείαν ἔχομεν μαρτύρων;, while Luke's reads τί ἔτι ἔχομεν μαρτυρίας χρείαν;. The shift from "testimonies" or "witnesses" to the singular "testimony" is concomitant with the actual narrated events in Luke: additional testimony had neither been sought or allowed. The language is very close to Mark's account, and one may readily suggest that here Luke has redacted his Gospel source; of course, the possibility exists that the variation stems from Luke's other source. Luke reads αὐτοὶ γὰρ ἠκούσαμεν ἀπὸ τοῦ στόματος αὐτοῦ for Mark's ἠκούσατε τῆς βλασφημίας. In both versions Jesus' own testimony is judged adequate for taking the case to Pilate. Ἀπὸ τοῦ στόματος αὐτοῦ could be Luke's own contribution to the narrative[244]. Luke omits the details of Jesus' condemnation by the Sanhedrin, found in Mark.

---

238 Cf. Paul Christoph Böttger, *Der König der Juden – Das Heil für die Völker* (Neukirchen-Vluyn: Neukirchener, 1981) 85–87; Jack Dean Kingsbury, *The Christology of Mark's Gospel* (Philadelphia: Fortress, 1983) 122–124.
239 Gaston, *Electronicae*, 66.
240 *Contra* Catchpole, *Trial*, 197. Catchpole is obliged to render the particle as a simple connective since he regards 22:69 as an intrusion from Mark. Cf. Flender, *Luke*, 415; Cassidy, *Jesus*, 166 n.6; Kim, *Son of Man*, 4–6.
241 BDF, para. 441.3; Franklin, *Christ the Lord*, 92; Vermes, *Jesus*, 148; Schneider, *Verleugnung*, 126.
242 Vermes, *Jesus*, 148.
243 Kim, *Son of Man*, 5–6.
244 Cf. 4:22; 11:54; 19:22; Schneider, *Verleugnung*, 131–132.

In Luke, then, Jesus is not said to have been guilty of blasphemy, nor is he condemned as deserving death by the Jewish leaders. This omission should be seen in relation to Acts 13:27–28:

οἱ γὰρ κατοικοῦντες ἐν Ἰερουσαλὴμ καὶ οἱ ἄρχοντες αὐτῶν τοῦτον ἀγνοήσαντες καὶ τὰς φωνὰς τῶν προφητῶν τὰς κατὰ πᾶν σάββατον ἀναγινωσκομένας κρίναντες ἐπλήρωσαν, καὶ μηδεμίαν αἰτίαν θανάτου εὑρόντες ᾐτήσαντο Πιλᾶτον ἀναιρεθῆναι αὐτόν.

Many exegetes render κρίνω as "to pass judgment", and thus must take the sense of the text as "in my opinion (Paul's or Luke's), there were no real grounds for condemning Jesus to death, but the Jewish leaders did it anyway". So Wilckens writes: "Die Juden haben also in Wahrheit keine sachlich zutreffende Begründung für ihren Antrag auf das Todesurteil"[245]. However, this interpretation raises a tension between "having condemned" and "they found no cause of death in him". Having recognized this problem, Harvey goes on to set forth a convincing case for the view that Luke offers evidence in 22:71 and Acts 13:27 for an alternative tradition according to which Jesus was not found guilty by any Jewish court[246]. We may set forth the more cogent of his points as follows. (A) In Acts 13:27–28 κρίνω can signify "to make a decision" as in the close parallel in Acts 25:25. (B) Luke omits the Markan words which may be taken as a verdict against Jesus by the Jews. (C) Luke omits κατακρινοῦσιν from the third passion prediction (18:32; cf. Mark 10:33). (D) Apart from the account of the trial in Matthew and Mark and the three passages related to it (Matt 20:18; 27:3; Mark 10:33), the treatment of Jesus by the Jews is nowhere in the NT referred to as "a judgment", but always as "a handing over". (E) Jesus' burial in a private tomb, emphasized in Acts 13:29, contradicts Jewish law (*Sanh.* 6.5) if Jesus was condemned to death by a Jewish court.

To these points we may further add that from the viewpoint of Jewish and Roman juridical history, Harvey's thesis is quite plausible, even appealing. According to Josephus (*Ant.* 18.117–118), John the Baptist became suspect because of his eloquence which might possibly have led to some form of sedition; so, as a preventative measure, Herod had him put away. More to the point, Jesus-bar-Ananias was regarded as a potential source of a serious disturbance and was therefore handed over by the Jewish authorities to the Roman government (*B.J.* 6.300–305). Thus,

> violent reactions by Jewish religious authorities towards one of their subjects, and their handing over of him [sic] to the jurisdiction of the Romans, do not necessarily imply that in their judgment a religious or political crime has *actually* been committed[247].

The sum of this evidence suggests that Luke's omissions with respect to Mark 14:64 are not to be explained purely in terms of Lukan redaction, for in all likelihood Luke was following an alternative tradition.

Aspects of 22:66–71 obviously betray Luke's redactional pen, but we have noted several points along the way at which, if Luke were constructing his account solely on the basis of the Markan episode, he has wandered far afield from his usual redactional pattern and introduced a christology at variance with what we would normally associate with the Third Evangelist. Additionally, some amendments in detail, especially in v 66, are difficult to explain in terms of Luke's redacting Mark. Finally, at some points we found good reason for judging Luke's version of the hearing as more primitive than Mark's, and in at least one point (i.e. the absence of an explicit Jewish condemnation of Jesus) he appears to have reproduced a variant tradition altogether. The positing of additional traditional material seems an inescapable conclusion for coming to terms with the source-critical question for this section.

---

245 Wilckens, *Missionsreden*, 135. Cf. Catchpole, *Trial*, 184–185.
246 Harvey, *Jesus*, 20–21, 174–175. See also Winter, *Trial*, 40–41.
247 Geza Vermes, *Jesus and the World of Judaism* (London: SCM, 1983) viii. Cf. Sanders, *Jesus*, 296–305.

XVI. Luke 23:1–5 (Mark 15:1b–5)

While the charge against Jesus is not explicitly made in the hearing before the Jewish leaders, the members of the Sanhedrin apparently believe sufficient evidence exists to warrant a hearing before the Roman procurator. Thus we come to the first phase of the ensuing trial process. Apart from v 3, Luke's account corresponds only broadly to Mark's. In fact, putting aside v 3 for the moment, only 6 words are shared by Luke and Mark: ὁ, δέ, Πιλᾶτος (2x), κατηγορέω, and αὐτός. Mark has no real parallel to Luke's vv 2, 4, 5; and Luke omits Mark's vv 3–5. Not surprisingly, some scholars have postulated that in v 3 Luke has inserted material from Mark into his *Sondergut*[248].

V 1: In contrast to the Markan account, Luke does not mention that Jesus was bound prior to being taken before Pilate. His text reads: καὶ ἀναστὰν ἅπαν τὸ πλῆθος αὐτῶν. Ἀνίστημι is not especially Lukan though he does use it in his redactional activity[249]. Ἅπας, on the other hand, is characteristic of Luke[250]. Elsewhere, πλῆθος can designate the membership of the Sanhedrin (cf. Acts 23:7). The addition of ἅπας (cf. 8:37; 19:37; Acts 25:24) emphasizes πλῆθος, underscoring the collective responsibility of all the membership in the subsequent fate of Jesus[251]. For ἀπήνεγκαν καὶ παρέδωκαν Πιλάτῳ (Mark 15:1), Luke has ἤγαγον αὐτὸν ἐπὶ τὸν Πιλᾶτον. Ἀπάγω is the expected verb to communicate the idea of "being brought before the authorities" (see above on 22:26), but Luke has ἄγω in 12:58 and 22:54. If Luke has been following Mark we cannot easily account for his failure to take over Mark's παραδίδωμι – a word Luke uses in passion predictions and allusions (9:44; 18:32; 20:20; 22:21–22; 24:7; cf. 12:58; 21:12, 16), in the passion narrative itself (22:4, 6, 21–22, 48), and in subsequent reports of, and retrospective allusions to, the passion of Jesus (24:20; Acts 3:13; cf. Acts 21:11; 27:11; 28:17).

V 2: At this point, Luke's narrative sequence represents a transposition of the Markan order, for Luke reports Pilate's question to Jesus following the accusations of the Jewish leaders. Luke introduces the explicit charges with ἤρξαντο δὲ κατηγορεῖν αὐτοῦ λέγοντες. This finds its counterpart in Mark 15:3: καὶ κατηγόρουν αὐτοῦ οἱ ἀρχιερεῖς πολλά. There are two obstacles to crediting Luke's phrase to his redaction of Mark, the common use of κατηγορέω + αὐτός notwithstanding. First, ἄρχομαι + infinitive is characteristic of Markan style, not Lukan[252]. Second, it is questionable whether Luke, who is eager to demonstrate the guilt of the chief priests in Jesus' death, would bypass this opportunity to name them as the accusers before Pilate if he were following Mark (15:3). As for the accusations themselves, Luke is unique among the Synoptic evangelists in specifying the charges given to Pilate against Jesus by the Jewish leaders. The charges, of which there are three, are emphatically political in nature, and it is worth noting that John 19:12–15 agrees with Luke in ascribing to Jesus' trial a distinct political agenda.

Along with the summary in 23:5, the present charges resemble those against Paul in Acts 17:6–7 (cf. 21:28; 24:2–5)[253].

---

248 E.g., Taylor, *Passion*, 86–87; Marshall, *Gospel of Luke*, 851–854; Büchele, *Tod Jesu*, 27–28; Schweizer, *Luke*, 351.
249 Gaston, *Electronicae*, 65; Jeremais, *Sprache*, 300.
250 Gaston, *Electronicae*, 64; Jeremias, *Sprache*, 300.
251 Cf. Gerhard Delling, "Πλῆθος", in *TDNT*, 6:279; Büchele, *Tod Jesu*, 27.
252 Cf. Pryke, *Redactional Style*, 79–87; Trocmé, *Passion*, 16–17; Jeremias, *Sprache*, 300. Contra Gerhard Schneider, "The Political Charge against Jesus (Luke 23:2)", in *Jesus and Politics*, 409.
253 See the additonal points of contact between Luke 23:1–25 and Acts 25–26 as charted by O'Toole, *Unity*, 68–71.

23:2: τοῦτον . . . διαστρέφοντα τὸ ἔθνος ἡμῶν
23:5: ἀνασείει τὸν λαὸν διδάσκων καθ' ὅλης τῆς Ἰουδαίας καὶ ἀρξάμενος ἀπὸ τῆς Γαλιλαίας ἕως ὧδε.
17:6: οἱ τὴν οἰκουμένην ἀναστατώσαντες οὗτοι καὶ ἐνθάδε πάρεισιν

23:2: καὶ κωλύοντα φόρους Καίσαρι διδόναι
17:7: καὶ οὗτοι πάντες ἀπέναντι τῶν δογμάτων Καίσαρος πράσσουσιν

23:2: καὶ λέγοντα ἑαυτὸν χριστὸν βασιλέα εἶναι.
17:7: βασιλέα ἕτερον λέγοντες εἶναι Ἰησοῦν.

Among the several points of intersection we may draw special attention to four. (A) Jesus' ministry had widespread influence in Judea, while Paul's was influential throughout the Empire (οἰκουμένη is thus used in an exaggerated way). (B) Both Jesus and Paul were allegedly stirring up sedition among the people. (C) Jesus and Paul were accused of disloyalty to Caesar. (D) With an ironic play on a word with religious and political connotations, βασιλεύς, both charges name Jesus as a rival king. Agreements of this kind have led at least one interpreter to voice the opinion that here in chapter 23 Luke has conformed his Gospel to Acts[254]. That v 2 is the fruit of Lukan redaction is also suggested by the oft-mentioned fact that earlier in the Third Gospel Luke has dismissed the validity of each of these charges as, at best, misrepresentations of Jesus' mission and stance[255]. What of the language of v 2; does it suggest Lukan redaction?

Διαστρέφω is not common in the NT, appearing only 7 times. It is read once in Matthew, in a text taken from Q (17:7; Luke 9:41). Apart from the Q passage and 23:2, Luke uses the verb in Acts 13:8, 10 of the work of Elymas the sorcerer and in Acts 20:30 of "those who distort the truth". The usage in Phil 2:15 is similar to that in Q where it is descriptive of a "wicked and perverse generation". Τὸ ἔθνος normally refers to "the Gentiles" or "the nations" in Luke-Acts (48x), but does designate the Jews in 7:5; Acts 10:22; 24:2, 10; 26:4; 28:19. A close parallel to this accusation is found in Exod 5:4 – where Moses and Aaron are accused of turning the people (διαστρέφετε τὸν λαόν) from their work for Pharoah – and Luke may have been influenced by it in his effort to portray Jesus as the "prophet like Moses"[256]. However, why would Luke use τὸ ἔθνος instead of ὁ λαός – an important description for the Jewish people in his writing? Κωλύω is found in the NT 22 times, 12 in Luke-Acts. On 4 occasions Luke draws the verb from his sources (18:16/Mark 10:4; 9:49–50/9:38–39; 11:52[?]). It is clearly redactional in 6:29, and with the additional 6 uses of the term in Acts, we cannot help but conclude that Luke could have introduced the verb here. Φόρος is used in the Synoptics only in Luke 20:22; 23:2, and the relation between these two texts is obvious. On the basis of this linguistic survey we can conclude little except that the language employed here is consistent with Lukan redaction regardless of the source question[257].

The one bit of decisive evidence here, then, is the parallel political emphasis found in John's Gospel, and this points to a non-Markan tradition underlying the Johannine and Lukan texts. Nevertheless it is not beyond reason that Luke has greatly embellished this tradition and woven the motif of Jesus' innocence into the fabric of these charges throughout the Gospel.

V 3: Luke is alone in preparing the reader for Pilate's question. His introduction to the query – ὁ δὲ Πιλᾶτος ἠρώτησεν (ἐπηρώτησεν in A D L W Θ Ψ 063 f¹·¹³ M) αὐτὸν λέγων – is very close to that in Mark 15:2: καὶ ἐπηρώτησεν αὐτὸν ὁ Πιλᾶτος; and the question is identical in both accounts: σὺ εἶ ὁ βασιλεὺς τῶν Ἰουδαίων;. With these words Pilate follows up only on the third charge leveled against Jesus; hence, it is obvious that he understood (and Luke's readers are to under-

---

254 Schmidt, "Luke's 'Innocent' Jesus", 118–119.
255 Cf., e.g., Walaskay, *Political Perspective*, 40, 88–89 n.8; Cassidy, *Jesus*, 65; Schmidt, "Luke's 'Innocent' Jesus", 112–116; Tiede, *Prophecy*, 112; Maddox, *Luke-Acts*, 94.
256 So Schmidt, "Luke's 'Innocent' Jesus", 119.
257 Schneider ("Political Charge", 409–412) concludes from similar evidence that v 2 is the product of Lukan creativity, drawing some material from Mark. But on those points where Mark has no strict parallel Schneider moves too easily from "redaction" to "creation".

Luke 23:1–5 (Mark 15:1b–5)

stand) the political nature of the accusations. Luke's preference for εἶπον comes to light in the introduction of Jesus' response, where Mark's λέγω in ὁ δὲ ἀποκριθεὶς αὐτῷ λέγει is replaced with εἶπον in Luke's version. Otherwise, the clause is identical in Luke. As in Mark's account, so in Luke's Jesus answers σύ λέγεις. As impressive as these points of correspondence seem, they lose their force when it is realized that in all four Gospel accounts the question and answer are identical[258].

V 4: Luke has already reported the accusations of the Jewish leaders and so does not follow the order of Mark 15:2–3. Also missing in Luke are Mark's vv 4–5, where Pilate questions Jesus about his silence, Jesus maintains his silence, and Pilate "wonders". Again, then, Luke passes over an opportunity to set the trial scene within the general context of the Servant of Yahweh (who did not open his mouth [Isa 53:7]).

Pilate's pronouncement to the chief priests and the multitudes is rather abrupt, for: (A) we might expect his questioning to have extended beyond the straightforward query and ambiguous reply given; (B) the Sanhedrin has made the accusations, but Pilate's announcement is given to the chief priests (only) and the crowds; and (C) the latter group has not been introduced previously. The impression one gains is that Luke (or perhaps the source he employed) has not found it necessary to provide the intervening details. The singling out of the chief priests is evidence of Luke's particular emphasis on their guilt, but since Luke has bypassed at least two opportunities to accentuate this motif even more by drawing from Mark's narrative we may safely assume that this motif was evident to some degree in Luke's non-Markan material, and that Luke was interested in demonstrating the guilt of all the Jewish leaders and not only one select group.

On the construction verb of speaking + πρός + accusative, see above on 22:15; it is probably Lukan. As for the actual pronouncement of Jesus' innocence, Mark offers no parallel. This is the first of three such declarations in Luke (cf. 23:14, 22) and it is significant that John also records a threefold pronouncement of Jesus' innocence (18:38; 19:4, 6). For the present declaration, Luke reads οὐδὲν εὑρίσκω αἴτιον ἐν τῷ ἀνθρώπῳ τούτῳ, while John has ἐγὼ οὐδεμίαν εὑρίσκω ἐν αὐτῷ αἰτίαν. These correspondences strongly suggest a common, non-Markan source behind the Lukan and Johannine accounts[259].

V 5: Pilate's pronouncement elicits even more urgent testimony against Jesus. This verse has some agreement with Mark 15:3, for in both verses the chief priests are named as the accusers (οἱ δέ refers both to the chief priests and crowds of v 4 in Luke). This is the only appearance in the NT of ἐπισχύω, and ἀνασείω occurs elsewhere only in Mark 15:11. Here it is Jesus' teaching which "stirs up the people". For καθ' ὅλης τῆς 'Ιουδαίας, see Acts 9:31; 10:37; the phrase is probably Lukan[260]. Ἄρχομαι + ἀπό reflects Semitic influence, but is probably Lukan[261]. The reference to Galilee provides a point of contact for phase two of the trial, where Jesus is sent to Herod Antipas[262]. This verse is predominantly Lukan, and it may belong in the list of capsulized summaries for which the Third Evangelist has a particular fondness (see above on 22:65).

We conclude, then, that Luke knew a narrative tradition other than Mark for this phase of Jesus' trial. Verses 2, 4, and 5 are based on that non-Markan source, but are very much Lukan in style and thought in their present form. Verse 3 may have been taken from Mark, but we have seen that an alternative source even here cannot be dismissed out of hand; and v 1 may be explained as Lukan redaction of Mark or of another source. The latter seems the more likely option.

---

258 See further below, chapter 8.VIII.B.
259 Cf. Bailey, *Traditions*, 69–72; Maddox, *Luke-Acts*, 164; Marshall, *Gospel of Luke*, 853.
260 Cf. BDF, para. 225; Jeremias, *Sprache*, 301.
261 Cf. 14:18; 24:27, 47; Acts 1:22; 8:35; 10:37; Black, *Aramaic Approach*, 299; Moule, *Idiom Book*, 181; Jeremias, *Sprache*, 301.
262 Harold W. Hoehner (*Herod Antipas* [Cambridge: Cambridge University, 1972] 233–234 n.7, see also, idem, "Why Did Pilate Hand Jesus over to Antipas?", in *Trial of Jesus*, 85 n.10) regards this as historical.

XVII. Luke 23:6—12

Taking his cue from Jesus' Galilee roots, Pilate sends Jesus to Herod Antipas. This pericope has no parallel in the other Gospels; consequently, some have suspected its Lukan derivation. Three primary arguments have been voiced against its traditional character and we shall consider each in turn.

(A) It is alleged that the language and style of the pericope is Lukan, and that these two measures do not betray the existence of a pre-Lukan source[263]. Before dealing with this point in some detail, three preliminary observations are in order. First, as we have noted throughout this investigation, the presence of Lukan vocabulary and style does not unambiguously indicate Lukan creativity. Second, as we have maintained, students interested in Lukan vocabulary cannot restrict their investigations to the construction of statistical lists of word occurrences. Rather, they must distinguish between those cases where a redactor has taken over the word in question from a source and where the word has been introduced into source material[264]. In their treatments of this passage (as elsewhere) Taylor and Büchele are both guilty of counting only appearances of words, and not considering the source question. Third, Taylor's conclusion that the vocabulary of 23:6—12 does not suggest the use of a source rests on his assumption that if there were a source its vocabulary would be that of L — a fallacious premise since Luke could be employing a passion source independent of L.

In any case, the vocabulary of the pericope does not turn out to be *peculiarly* Lukan after all[265]. The following words found in this paragraph are sometimes used by Luke in his editing but do not belong to his characteristic redactional vocabulary: ἀκούω (2x), ἐπερωτάω (2x), ἱκανός (2x), γίνομαι (2x), γραμματεύς, and ἀλλήλων. Words belonging to Luke's editorial vocabulary that are found in this section include πρός (2x), περί, and λόγος. In addition, we may mention other words or expressions bearing on this problem. Ἐν ταύταις ταῖς ἡμέραις is undoubtedly Lukan, for it is found in the NT only in Luke-Acts (see also the similar ἐν ἐκείναις ταῖς ἡμέραις). Χαίρω is used in Matthew 6 times, Mark — 2, Luke — 11, and Acts — 7. In the Third Gospel the verb is taken from Q in 6:23 (cf. Matt 5:12); 15:5 (cf. Matt 18:13); from Mark in 22:5 (Mark 14:11);

---

263 Cf. Taylor, *Passion*, 87; Büchele, *Tod Jesu*, 32.
264 See also Gaston, *Electronicae*, 1; Frans Neirynck, "The Redactional Text of Mark", in *Evangelica*, 618—619.
265 See Gaston, *Electronicae*, 64—66; Jeremias, *Sprache*, 301—303; Fitzmyer, *Luke*, 1:110; Büchele, *Tod Jesu*, 32.

and is read in L texts at 1:14, 28; 10:20; 13:17; 15:32; 19:6. It is clearly redactional only in 19:7 (cf. Mark 11:9), where it takes the same nuance as "joy in salvation" or "joy in Christ" as in Acts 5:41; 8:39; 11:23; 13:48; 15:31. Otherwise, the verb takes the standard form of a salutatory greeting (Acts 15:23; 23:26). It is not certain, therefore, whether we should simply attribute the term to Lukan redaction in 23:8. Χρόνος is used in Lukan redaction at 4:5(?); 8:27, 29; 20:9, and is read in texts with no Synoptic parallel in 1:57; 18:4. Thus, one should lean towards regarding it as redactional here — a decision rendered all the more plausible by the fact that the combination χρόνος + ἱκανός is never read in Matthew or Mark, but is found in Luke 8:27; 20:9; Acts 8:11; 14:3; 27:9. Little can be decided from the use of ἀναπέμπω. It apears 4 times in Luke-Acts and only one other time in the NT (Phlm 11), but 3 of the occurrences in Luke-Acts come in this immediate context (23:7, 11, 15). *Luke's redactional hand is therefore evident in this pericope, but there is insufficient basis here for insisting that the whole is a Lukan creation.*

(B) Many have noted the connection of this text with Acts 4:24–28, regarding it as a "fulfillment" of Ps 2:1–2[266]. Dibelius, for one, has gone further, conjecturing that Luke developed the present story from Ps 2, for in Acts 4:25–27 the psalm is quoted and its characters interpreted so as to refer to Herod, Pontius Pilate, the Gentiles, and the people of Israel in Jerusalem[267]. Walaskay has labeled this "a most convincing theory about the genesis of the tradition"[268], but it is not without its drawbacks[269]. First, this psalm is not cited either directly or indirectly in the trial narrative. If Luke saw this occurrence in relation to Ps 2, why did he not make it clear at this point? Second, Acts 4:27 reflects knowledge of a tradition in which Herod conspires with Pilate against Jesus. Tertullian (*Adv. Marc.* 4.42.2) seems to have known a similar (but not identical) tradition, as does the author of the *Gospel of Peter* (1:1). Yet, Herod's responsibility for Jesus' death is actually circumvented by Luke 23:15. Indeed, the Acts portrayal stands in tension not only with Luke 23, but with Luke's larger tendency to exonerate Rome. Third: nevertheless, a tradition like Luke 23:6–12 is presupposed by the text in Acts, for it is doubtful that the psalm could have given rise to this interpretation if Herod

---

266 E.g., Dibelius, *Tradition*, 199; Bultmann, *History*, 273; Creed, *Luke*, 279–280; Büchele, *Tod Jesu*, 32; Archibald M. Hunter, *The Work and Words of Jesus*, rev. ed. (London: SCM, 1973) 150 n.2.
267 Dibelius, *Traditon*, 199. Cf. Creed, *Luke*, 279–280.
268 Walaskay, *Political Perspective*, 43.
269 This hypothesis has been challenged by Matthew Black, "The Arrest and Trial of Jesus and the Date of the Last Supper", in *NT Essays*, 24; Hoehner, *Herod*, 228–230; Winter, *Trial*, 191 n.1.

had no place in the story of Jesus' death. Dibelius's hypothesis, then, does not stand up to close scrutiny.

(C) Walaskay proposes that Luke created the scene by way of filling out the Jesus-Paul parallel:

> Perhaps Luke has styled the account in the Gospel *after* the lavish and full account that he has included in Acts 26. Here Paul gives his last, grand apology before Herod Agrippa, Festus, Bernice, and all the great men of Caesarea. Luke would not allow Jesus to be treated less fairly than his apostle, so he is also made to appear before a Herodian[270].

This theory meets its Armageddon in the way Walaskay has presented it, for it is doubtful that Luke would have deliberately drawn a parallel in which Paul, portrayed as so accomplished a rhetorician, is juxtaposed with the silent and ridiculed Jesus! Moreover, as we have already seen, there is good reason for believing that a tradition about the hearing before Herod Antipas existed prior to Luke.

Arguments against the pre-Lukan character of this story have not been found convincing, and we may justifiably conclude that Luke has not created the tradition *ex nihilo* or from pieces of the Markan trial narrative. Additionally, we may draw attention to how well connected this account is with the surrounding material. This suggests Luke had knowledge of an *alternative continuous narrative tradition*, at least at this point. This hypothesis will receive support if the following verses are also shown to be both non-Markan and pre-Lukan.

XVIII. Luke 23:13—25 (Mark 15:6—15)

With this pericope we enter the third and final stage of Jesus' trial before governmental authorities. Just as we found no Synoptic parallel for the previous scene before Herod, so we read no parallel for vv 13—16, where the hearing before Pilate is resumed. This may be cause for suspecting vv 6—16 as a Lukan insertion into a Markan context[271]. If true, vv 13—16 would be seen as the conclusion of the tradition about the hearing before Herod. Below, we will note important literary reasons for rejecting this view. Here it is sufficient to observe that vv 13—16 have very little to do with Herod for he is only mentioned by Pilate in v 15; additionally, in our discussion of v 4 we found reason for holding that Luke's schema whereby Jesus is declared innocent three times (the second of which comes in vv 14—15) was pre-Lukan. As for the relationship of vv 17—25

---

[270] Walaskay, *Political Perspective*, 43. O'Toole (*Unity*, 70), however, upon noting this parallel, writes: "Whatever be the case, this does not say that the Lucan compositions do not contain earlier tradition".

[271] So Bultmann, *History*, 276.

to the Markan text, this is not easy to assess. The number of common words in Luke amounts to a mere 30.1%, and Luke's account transposes much of the Markan narrative sequence. Moreover, the emphases of the two accounts vary. Nevertheless, a broad similarity exists between the two stories and Luke's dependence on Mark seems certain at some junctures.

V 13: Συνκαλέω is read only 8 times in the NT, 7 in Luke-Acts. The odd occurrence is Mark 15:16, a usage not taken over by Luke. Its addition to the Lukan text is clearly redactional in 9:1 (cf. Mark 6:7), but the source is not easily determined for 15:6 (Q?) or 15:9 (L?). With the 3 additional uses of the term in Acts (5:21; 10:24; 28:17), along with the relative sparsity of the verb in the vocabulary of the NT, we may legitimately suppose it is Lukan here. Ἄρχοντες, used for Jewish leaders, is also Lukan (cf. 14:1; 23:35; 24:20; Acts 3:17; 4:5, 8; 13:27), as is λαός[272]. It is remarkable that at each phase of the trial a different list of audience-participants is given.

V 14: For the construction verb of speaking + πρός + accusative, see above on 22:15; it is probably Lukan. Προσφέρω is found in Matthew 15 times, Mark – 3, Luke – 4, and Acts – 3. Twice, Luke borrows the verb from Mark (Luke 5:14/Mark 1:44; 18:15/10:13), but he edits it out of Mark 2:4 (Luke 5:19). The other two occurrences of the word in the Third Gospel come in the present verse and in 23:36. In Acts it is found in 7:42 – in a citation from Amos 5:25-27 LXX, and in 8:18; 21:26. Hence, in the present text it may be Lukan, but this is far from certain[273]. Ἀποστρέφω occurs 9 times in the NT – twice in Matthew and once each in Luke and Acts. Here it refers back to vv 2, 5 – which we regarded as traditionally based, if heavily Lukan in their present form. Had this word been found in Luke's source at this point we can easily imagine his employing different, but complementary language in the earlier pericope; we have seen that where Luke uses other terminology for the sake of variety he often employs the traditional term last. It is not unreasonable, however, that Luke is responsible for the introduction of all these words used in charging Jesus, though the political concept to which they all give witness is pre-Lukan. Λαός belongs to Luke's characteristic vocabulary (see above on v 13). Ἐνώπιον may also be Lukan. In the NT, only in Luke-Acts is ἀνακρίνω used with its forensic nuance of judicial investigation[274]. Pilate's declaration of Jesus' innocence (with οὐθέν; the textual variant οὐδέν is an assimilation to v 15) has its parallel in John 18:4. This is the second pronouncement of this kind, and Marshall suggests Luke has thus employed standard legal terminology[275].

V 15: Here only does one find reference to Herod in this pericope. His verdict of Jesus' innocence is used to support Pilate's. The language of v 15a does not suggest Lukan invention, and the statement is straightforward and colorless. Ἀναπέμπω, used earlier, need not point to Luke's hand (see above on 23:7, 11). Πράσσω, found at the close of this verse, is probably Lukan, for it is used in Luke-Acts 18 times, but never in Matthew or Mark. On the other hand, its use in the Third Gospel does not point unambiguously to Lukan redaction, for in no instance of its use is the source question clearly answered (L? – 3:13; Q? – 19:23; ? – 22:23; 23:41). Πεπραγμένον αὐτῷ is perhaps the only genuine example of the dative of agent in the NT[276].

V 16: Elsewhere in Luke-Acts, παιδεύω appears in 23:22, where it has the same sense of "to chastise" or "to whip" as here; and in Acts 7:22; 22:3, where it requires its more usual rendering of "to train" or "to educate"[277]. The word is not found in Matthew or Mark, and is read only 9

---

272 Fitzmyer, *Luke*, 1:110; Büchele, *Tod Jesu*, 35; Gaston, *Electronicae*, 64; Jeremias, *Sprache*, 303.
273 Jeremias (*Sprache*, 303) regards its use here as non-Lukan.
274 For ἐνώπιον, see Fitzmyer, *Luke*, 1:110; Büchele, *Tod Jesu*, 35; Jeremias, *Sprache*, 303. For ἀνακρίνω, see Plummer, *Luke*, 524; Büchele, *Tod Jesu*, 34; Jeremias, *Sprache*, 303.
275 Marshall, *Gospel of Luke*, 859. Cf. MHT, 2:341.
276 BDF, para. 191. Cf. Moule, *Idiom Book*, 47, 204.
277 Cf. Georg Bertram, "Παιδεύω", in *TDNT*, 5:621. He notes that outside the NT there is no concrete instance in which the verb signifies "to strike" or "to scourge". Nevertheless, he argues, the

other times in the NT. Despite Walaskay's attempt to attribute this word to Lukan redaction on the grounds that παιδεύω does not suggest the conclusion of a real criminal trial[278], there is little basis for attributing the word to Luke. It is noteworthy that in John 19:1–12 Pilate has Jesus scourged as a proposed compromise with Jesus' accusers – a repetition of the motif found in Luke, though absent from the other Synoptic accounts. This suggests the pre-Lukan character of the idea, if not necessarily the vocabulary. The remaining terminology of this verse offers no help for pointing to Luke's possible source(s).

V 17: This verse is omitted by a large number of early witnesses, and in others it is found after v 19. This instability emphatically points to its secondary character. Moreover, it is much easier to explain its addition as an assimilation to the Markan and/or Matthean text than to account for its omission[279]. Conzelmann regards the absence of this detail as due to Luke's redactional interests: it is the Jews who bring up this whole matter of releasing Barabbas and thus they declare their solidarity with rebels[280]. This explanation is not convincing, however, for Luke could have informed his readers of this custom as an editorial note without having Pilate initiate the transaction. As it stands in Luke, the request of the Jews is inexplicable. This suggest Luke's use of an alternative source.

V 18: The transition from v 16 to v 18 is smoothly accomplished without v 17. As in vv 4–5, Pilate's pronouncement of Jesus' innocence elicits the aggressive response of his accusers. Interestingly, Matt 27:21 and John 18:40 agree with Luke against Mark in having the demand to release Barabbas in direct speech. As we have previously noted (see above on 22:58), it is out of character for Luke to introduce direct speech where there was none in his source. Ἀνακράζω is not found in Matthew or Acts, but is read twice in Mark and 3 times in Luke. At 4:33 Luke borrows the word from Mark 1:23, but he offers no parallel for Mark 4:69. In 8:28 the verb is added by Luke to material taken from Mark 5:6–7. Thus, the word can be used redactionally by the Third Evangelist, but it is not particularly Lukan. With reference to Cassidy's thesis that Luke focuses especially on the chief priests as bearers of the guilt for Jesus' death, it should be mentioned that, *contra* Mark 15:11, Luke does not credit the chief priests with stirring up the crowds to have Barabbas released in Jesus' stead. Rather, in Luke, "they all cried out" – presumably referring to the chief priests, the rulers, and the people (v 13). Παμπληθεί is a rare adverbial compound found only here in the NT; it is probably Lukan[281]. For αἶρε τοῦτον, compare John 19:15; Acts 8:33 (Isa 53:8); 21:36; 22:22. Ἀπόλυσον δὲ ἡμῖν τὸν Βαραββᾶν, while cast in direct speech (on which see above), is similar to, and may be based on, Mark's τὸν Βαραββᾶν ἀπολύσῃ αὐτοῖς.

V 19: Now Luke goes back to identify Barabbas (cf. Mark 15:7). Two words sometimes used in, but not characteristic of, Lukan redaction are employed: γίνομαι and πόλις[282]. In both versions of the description, Barabbas is said to have been held in prison for involvement in an uprising (στάσις) and for murder. Luke adds that the revolt took place "in the city", but deletes the association of Barabbas with other imprisoned rebels found in Mark. Luke has probably only rephrased the Markan account here[283].

V 20: Luke's text reads πάλιν δὲ ὁ Πιλᾶτος προσεφώνησεν αὐτοῖς θέλων ἀπολῦσαι τὸν Ἰησοῦν. This has some agreement with Mark 15:12: ὁ δὲ Πιλᾶτος πάλιν ἀποκριθεὶς ἔλεγεν αὐτοῖς· τί οὖν [θέλετε] ποιήσω [ὃν λέγετε] τὸν βασιλέα τῶν Ἰουδαίων. There are, however, some obvious dissimilarities. It is possible that Luke revised Mark's direct speech into indirect, but if he did he has drastically changed the sense of Mark's address. Luke gives no indication that Pilate asked the Jews for their advice concerning Jesus' fate, nor does Mark have anything with which to compare Luke's concern over Pilate's motive in addressing the Jews. Additionally, in Luke the focus of attention is

---

term does carry the idea "to treat as a child", and dealing with a child included whipping; hence, this usage "is not a special biblical usage".
278 Walaskay, *Political Perspective*, 44.
279 Cf. Metzger, *Textual Commentary*, 179–180.
280 Conzelmann, *Luke*, 87.
281 BDF, para. 122.
282 Gaston, *Electronicae*, 65–66.
283 Likewise, Winter, *Trial*, 139–140. Cf. Jeremias, *Sprache*, 304.

Luke 23:13–25 (Mark 15:6–15)

"Jesus"; in Mark, "the King of the Jews". Luke will later use this nomenclature for Jesus (23:28); why not here? Προσφωνέω is rare in the NT, found only once in Matthew, 4 times in Luke, and twice in Acts. The verb may be introduced by Luke into the pericope about choosing the Twelve (6:13; cf. Mark 3:13), but elsewhere appears to have been taken from his sources (Q – 7:32/Matt 11:26: L – 13:12). The evidence, then, is not overwhelming, and we can only guess that it is Lukan here[284]. The remaining vocabulary offers little by way of suggesting an answer to the question of Luke's source(s), so the differences in content must be allowed decisive weight.

V 21: With this verse and the next we find a close parallel with Mark, though even here we note interesting deviations. Luke's introductory clause is οἱ δὲ ἐπεφώνουν λέγοντες, whereas Mark has οἱ δὲ πάλιν ἔκραξαν. Luke may have removed πάλιν since, strictly speaking, this is the first time the Jews have called for Jesus' crucifixion. However, αἴρω (v 18) certainly carried this nuance. He apparently has no fondness for κράζω. Where the verb is read in Mark (10x), Luke borrows it only twice: Mark 3:11/Luke 4:41(?); 10:48/18:39. However, it is found in Luke-Acts 15 times, whereas ἐπεφωνέω appears only 4 times. Nevertheless, inasmuch as the use of the latter verb is restricted to Luke-Acts in the NT, it is difficult to avoid the conclusion that Luke has redacted Mark here. As for the shout of the crowds, Luke has σταύρου σταύρου αὐτόν for Mark's σταύρωσον αὐτόν. Only Luke has the present imperative, but John 19:6 agrees in doubling the verb σταυρόω. These observations are difficult to explain if Mark was the sole Lukan source.

V 22: For ὁ δὲ Πιλᾶτος ἔλεγον αὐτοῖς in Mark 15:14, Luke has ὁ δὲ τρίτον εἶπεν πρὸς αὐτούς. Earlier we argued for the traditional quality of the three-fold declaration of Jesus' innocence, accented here with ὁ τρίτον. Εἶπεν πρὸς αὐτούς is probably Lukan (see above on 22:15). As for the declaration itself, Luke has a two-pronged statement of innocence, the first of which closely resembles Mark's. The two renditions differ only in that οὗτος is added in the Lukan version, and it is reasonable to suppose that Luke has here borrowed from Mark. The second part of the announcement reads οὐδὲν αἴτιον θανάτου εὗρον ἐν αὐτῷ. Mark has no parallel, but John 19:6 is comparable: οὐχ εὑρίσκω ἐν αὐτῷ αἰτίαν. Luke's third pronouncement has points of contact with the first and second (vv 4, 14–15), but this is not surprising and does not automatically point to Lukan creation. It is worth noting that it is only after the scene with Herod that Pilate adds the qualifier θανάτου to Jesus' guiltlessness in Luke. With this third announcement, "the innocence of Jesus could not be more firmly underlined"[285]. The final clause of v 22 is a doublet, expressing the same intention of v 16. No decisive argument for or against its redactional character can be tendered. The points of contact with vv 15–16 speak against vv 6–16 being an independent traditional fragment.

V 23: Again we read of the people's response after Pilate's announcement of Jesus' innocence. Ἐπίκειμαι is used 7 times in the NT, never in Matthew or Mark, but twice in Luke and once in Acts (27:20). In Luke 5:1 the word may be pre-Lukan. Here it could be Lukan and in v 23a Luke may well be redacting Mark. This is also true of v 23b, where Mark's ἔκραξαν· σταύρωσον αὐτόν would then have been recast as αἰτούμενοι αὐτὸν σταυρωθῆναι. It would be consistent with normal Lukan editorial activity for him to have replaced direct discourse with indirect (see above on 22:58). Further, we have already seen that Luke has no fondness for κράζω. On the other hand, αἰτέω is not particularly Lukan either. In every instance of its occurrence in the Third Gospel outside this pericope its use can be explained easily enough as having stemmed from one of Luke's sources (Q – 6:30; 11:9, 10, 11, 12, 13; L – 1:63; 12:20, 48; Mark – 23:52). The final clause of this verse is unparalleled and, coming as it does at the end of a verse exhibiting heavy Lukan redaction, it should probably be credited to Lukan creativity. Κατισχύω is rare in the NT, appearing only in Matt 16:18; Luke 21:36; 23:23. Little of a positive nature can be drawn from this fact, but at least it does not speak against a Lukan composition of v 23c.

V 24: Verses 24 and 25 conclude this pericope with a narrative of Pilate's subsequent action. Luke's version, if drawn from Mark, has been greatly expanded. For καὶ Πιλᾶτον ἐπέκρινεν γενεσ-

---

284 So Jeremias, *Sprache*, 304.
285 Marshall, *Gospel of Luke*, 861. Cf. Robert F. O'Toole, "Luke's Position on Politics and Society in Luke-Acts", in *Political Issues*, 6; Cassidy, *Jesus*, 68; Conzelmann, *Luke*, 87–88; Bultmann, *History*, 282; Büchele, *Tod Jesu*, 40.

θαι τὸ αἴτημα αὐτῶν, the Markan parallel reads ὁ δὲ Πιλᾶτος βουλόμενος τῷ ὄχλῳ τὸ ἱκανὸν ποιῆσαι (15:15). Luke has nothing to correspond with the Markan emphasis on Pilate's motivation. Ἐπικρίνω appears nowhere else in the NT and only twice in the LXX (2 Macc 4:47; 3 Macc 4:2). In both instances of its use in the Jewish-Hellenistic texts the verb is indicative of a miscarriage of justice, and, given the travesty of the court proceedings as reported by Luke, this may be the intended nuance here. It is difficult not to credit Luke with this change from the Markan κατακρίνω[286]. Αἴτημα is found only here in the Synoptics, and only 2 additional times in the NT (Phil 4:6; 1 John 5:15). Γίνομαι is sometimes used in Lukan redaction, but so is ἱκανός – which is found in the Markan version but missing from Luke's[287]. On the basis of this and the following verse it is impossible to argue accurately that Luke's Pilate is without blemish in his treatment of the whole Jesus-affair[288]. Nevertheless, there remains a certain tension between this text and Acts 4:24–28.

V 25: For Mark's simple ἀπέλυσεν αὐτοῖς τὸν Βαραββᾶν (15:15b), Luke has ἀπέλυσεν δὲ τὸν διὰ στάσιν καὶ φόνον βεβλημένον εἰς φυλακὴν ὃν ᾐτοῦντο. The description of Barabbas is reminiscent of Mark 15:7 and Luke 23:19, and the ὃν ᾐτοῦντο recalls the ὃν παρῃτοῦντο of Mark 15:6. There is little reason to doubt that Luke is redacting Mark here, placing special emphasis on the guilt of the one who was released, as opposed to the innocence of the one who was delivered up to the cross. Finally, Luke narrates: τὸν δὲ Ἰησοῦν παρέδωκεν τῷ θελήματι αὐτῶν. Mark 15:15c reads: καὶ παρέδωκεν τὸν Ἰησοῦν φραγελλώσας ἵνα σταυρωθῇ. Luke often replaces Mark's καί with δέ[289]; here, however, the revision is more than stylistic for it underscores the aforementioned contrast. Luke omits the reference to the flogging and the direct mention of the crucifixion. Instead, in a phrase we should probably credit to Luke's own hand[290], Pilate has Jesus delivered up "to their will". Αὐτῶν should be taken as a reference to the Jews, and especially to the Jewish leaders. Thus it is they, and not Pilate, who bear primary responsibility for Jesus' death.

Verses 13–25 present a mixed picture as regards Luke's redactional activity. The three-fold pronouncement of contact with the Johannine tradition, the unparalleled vv 13–16, the absence of v 17 – these factors are among the more prominent pointing to a non-Markan, pre-Lukan source. At other points, however, there is no need to posit an alternative source, for Luke's text can be explained easily enough with appeal to his editing of the Markan trial narrative and to his own creative hand. We conclude on the basis of this inquiry that Luke did know another account of the Roman trial of Jesus which overlapped with the Markan, and that in relating this phase of Jesus' trial he has conflated his two sources while including a few phrases of his own invention.

XIX. Luke 23:26–32 (Mark 15:20b–21)

By way of accenting the agency of the Jewish leaders in having Jesus executed, and at the same time playing down the responsibility of the Romans, Luke omits the scene in which Jesus is mocked by the Roman

---

286 See G. D. Kilpatrick, "Ἐπιθύειν and ἐπικρίνειν in the Greek Bible", *ZNW* 74 (1983) 152–153. Cf. Plummer, *Luke,* 527; Marshall, *Gospel of Luke,* 861.
287 Gaston, *Electronicae,* 65.
288 Cf. Maddox, *Luke-Acts,* 95; Tiede, *Prophecy,* 108–109, 113; Cassidy, *Jesus,* 69–70.
289 Fitzmyer, *Luke,* 1:108.
290 Likewise, Taylor, *Passion,* 89.

soldiers (Mark 15:16–20a) and moves directly to his account of the *Via Dolorosa*[291]. Relative to Mark's account, which extends over one verse only, Luke's is quite lengthy. In addition to borrowing material from Mark, the Third Evangelist records a tradition (vv 27–31) not found in Mark, and brings forward a reference to the two evil-doers with whom Jesus was crucified (v 32). Discounting vv 27–31, 46.4 percent of Luke's vocabulary is common to Mark's narrative.

V 26: Luke's text is very close to Mark 15:20b–21, and there can be little doubt that he has simply rewritten the Second Gospel here. Characteristically, he has revised Mark's parataxis, substituting his own ὡς + dependent participial clause for Mark's καί[292]. For καὶ ἐξάγουσιν αὐτόν in Mark, then, Luke has καὶ ὡς ἀπήγαγον αὐτόν. Given the technical nature of ἀπάγω (see above on 22:66) it is not a surprising addition here. Following this phrase, Luke again omits a direct reference to Jesus' crucifixion (cf. Mark 15:15; Luke 23:25), this one given in Mark's ἵνα-clause. Mark's καὶ ἀγγαρεύουσιν παράγοντά τινα Σίμωνα Κυρηναῖον is recast as ἐπιλαβόμενοι Σίμωνά τινα Κυρηναῖον. Ἀγγαρεύω is obscure, appearing in the NT only in Matt 5:41; 7:32; Mark 15:21. Luke is fond of ἐπιλαμβάνομαι, using it often in his redactional activity[293]. For this reason, we need not follow Ford in explaining this amendment as Luke's way of avoiding "the provocative reference to pressing into service"[294]. Luke's ἐρχόμενον ἀπ' ἀγροῦ duplicates the Markan text, but he leaves out the names of Simon's sons as irrelevant details. For Mark's simple ἵνα ἄρῃ τὸν σταυρὸν αὐτοῦ, Luke has ἐπέθηκαν αὐτῷ τὸν σταυρὸν φέρειν ὄπισθεν τοῦ Ἰησοῦ. For this use of ἐπιτίθημι, compare 15:15 (cf. Acts 15:10, 28)[295]. Φέρω is not particularly Lukan. It occurs in Matthew 6 times, Mark – 15, Luke – 4, Acts – 11. In Luke 5:18 the verb stems from Mark 2:3; however, in every other appearance of the word in Mark Luke either uses a substitution (Mark 1:32/Luke 4:40; 9:19/9:41; 9:20/9:42; 11:2/19:30; 11:7/19:35; 12:15/20:24; 15:22/23:33), edits the Markan material so that no such verb is needed (Mark 4:8/Luke 8:8; 9:17/9:38–40; 12:16/20:24), or offers no parallel text (Mark 6:27–28; 7:32; 8:22). Moreover, ὄπισθεν is used only twice in Luke – here and in a text taken from Mark 5:27 (8:44). In 8:44 the word has no connection with "discipleship" or "following Jesus". Luke apparently prefers ὀπίσω over ὄπισθεν to denote "discipleship" (see 9:23; 14:27; 21:8; Acts 20:30) and never employs φέρω in the sense of "taking up (the cross)" (see 9:23 – αἴρω; 14:27 – βαστάζω). While it may be that the discipleship theme is present here (see also ἀκολουθέω in v 27)[296], it is not clear why Luke would have altered Mark's wording, especially in order to use φέρω + ὄπισθεν! Could it be that this motif and accompanying language were present in, or suggested by, the pre-Lukan tradition of vv 27–31?

VV 27–31: This passage is one of several warnings to Jerusalem given by Jesus in Luke's Gospel (cf. 11:49–51; 13:1–5, 34–35; 19:41–44; 21:20–24). Walaskay holds that the present passage

---

291 Cf. Franklin, *Christ the Lord*, 93; Trocmé, *Passion*, 33–34. Of course, historically, the Romans and not the Jews would have carried out the crucifixion, but by omitting the Markan pericope and by leaving ambiguous the subject of ἀπάγω in v 26, Luke spares the Romans and implicates the Jews. See further below; Büchele, *Tod Jesu*, 42.
292 Fitzmyer, *Luke*, 1:108. But, cf. Jeremias, *Sprache*, 305.
293 Gaston, *Electronicae*, 64; Jeremias, *Sprache*, 304.
294 J. Massyngbaerde Ford, "Reconciliation and Forgiveness in Luke's Gospel", in *Political Issues*, 94; *idem, My Enemy Is My Guest: Jesus and Violence in Luke* (Maryknoll, New York: Orbis, 1984) 128. Redaction criticism is used wrongly when it is pressed into service to explain every amendment theologically. In this case, Luke's mere preference for one word over another begs for no additional explication.
295 Cf. also Christian Maurer, "Ἐπιτίθημι", in *TDNT*, 8:160.
296 Cf. Weber, *Cross*, 123; Flender, *Luke*, 74, 158; Marshall, *Gospel of Luke*, 863; Büchele, *Tod Jesu*, 43; Ford, *Enemy*, 128; Schweizer, *Luke*, 357; Schneider, *Luke*, 2:481.

is "Luke's own material" – presumably, then, he believes it has its origin in Lukan redaction[297]. Similarly, Büchele argues, "Die konzentration vom relativ vielem typisch lk Vokabular könnte nahelegen, an eine Eigenkompositon des Lk zu denken"[298]. We can conveniently break down a possible argument for this being a Lukan creation into four parts. (A) Verse 27 was invented by Luke to indicate a fulfillment of Zech 12:10–14. (B) The passage was built around Hos 10:8. (C) The passage is based on similar texts found earlier in Luke's Gospel. (D) The vocabulary is Lukan. A convincing argument might combine two or more of these points.

(A) It might be supposed that the mourning and lamenting of the people on the way to the cross point to the mourning over the "one whom they have pierced" in the text from Zechariah. If Luke did see such a connection, however, it is unlikely that he would have drawn the parallel so early in his narrative: a "fulfillment" properly belongs *following* the crucifixion (e.g. 23:48).

(B) The relevant section of Hos 10:8 LXX reads: ἐροῦσιν τοῖς ὅρεσιν· Καλύψατε ἡμᾶς, καὶ τοῖς βουνοῖς· Πέσατε ἐφ' ὑμᾶς. Luke, however, has reversed the order of the requests, καλύψατε and πέσατε (πέσετε in Luke), and for ἐροῦσιν he has (τότε ἄρξονται) λέγειν. Luke's order, also found in Rev 6:16, is supported by LXX^A, but France notes the possibility that this recension of the Greek OT represents an assimilation to the NT[299]. Of course, this does not rule out the possibility that Luke used a LXX text similar to LXX^A. In any case, this citation could not have given rise to the whole passage (vv 27–31) for it accounts for only one of four allusions to coming judgment. It plays a subordinate role, and the motif of weeping and mourning, central to the Lukan passage, is completely absent from it.

(C) Is it, then, possible to account for these verses as dependent on the earlier warnings to Jerusalem in Luke's Gospel? We can note the following parallels. (1) Θυγατέρες Ἰερουσαλήμ (23:28) might be seen as comparable to τὰ τέκνα σου (i.e. Jerusalem's) in 13:34, for both refer symbolically to Jerusalem's inhabitants. (2) Κλαίω + ἐπί (23:28) is read in 19:41. (3) The emphasis on ἐαυτάς . . . καὶ τὰ τέκνα ὑμῶν (23:28) is found in 19:44: σὲ καὶ τὰ τέκνα σου. (4) Ὅτι . . . ἔρχονται ἡμέραι (23:29) is similar to ὅτι ἥξουσιν ἡμέραι in 19:44; (5) Μακάριαι αἱ στεῖραι καὶ αἱ κοιλίαι αἱ οὐκ ἐγέννησαν καὶ μαστοὶ οἳ οὐκ ἔθρεψαν (23:29) states positively what 21:23 states negatively: οὐαὶ ταῖς ἐν γαστρὶ ἐχούσαις καὶ ταῖς θηλαζούσαις. These "parallels" account for most of vv 28–29, but they are not all equally convincing. Θυγατέρες Ἰερουσαλήμ (1) is a firm expression from the LXX (e.g. Cant 2:7; 3:5, 10; 5:8, 9, 16, 17; 8:4; Mic 4:8; Zeph 3:14; Zech 9:9; Jer 52:1), and it is highly unlikely that it has evolved from the language of 13:34. Κλαίω + ἐπί is found in the NT only in Luke and it may be a feature of Lukan style. This points to Lukan redaction, but not necessarily to literary dependence on the earlier text. Moreover, nowhere other than in this text are Jerusalem's inhabitants told to mourn; indeed, only in 13:1–5 are they told to do anything, and there they are to repent.

As for (4), ἥκω and ἔρχομαι are close in meaning, but this whole phrase is used often in Luke and so its appearance here is not particularly noteworthy. What is worthy of mention is that τότε, and not ἐν ἐκείναις ταῖς ἡμέραις, begins 23:29. Not only is this latter phrase read in 21:23 but, as we have mentioned earlier (see above on 23:7), it is a favorite in Lukan redaction. Finally (5), we must admit the possibility that the blessing-formula in 23:29 represents a recasting of the woe-formula in 21:23, but it should not go unnoticed that the vocabulary is dissimilar; the two could easily independently reflect the same orbit of thought[300]. Thus, we do not find this argument convincing, though we cannot deny on the ground covered to this point that it has some merit. However, when one turns to consider possible parallels for vv 30–31 this hypothesis unravels, for

---

297 Walaskay, *Political Perspective*, 45–48, 92 n.36. Similarly, Jerome H. Neyrey, "Jesus' Address to the Women of Jerusalem (Lk. 23.27–31) – A Prophetic Judgment Oracle", *NTS* 29 (1, 1983) 74–86. Lloyd Gaston (*No Stone on Another: Studies in the Significance of the Fall of Jerusalem in the Synoptic Gospels* [Leiden: E. J. Brill, 1970] 244–365), on the other hand, regards the whole series of warnings against Jerusalem, including this one, as belonging to proto-Luke.
298 Büchele, *Tod Jesu*, 43. Additional arguments for Lukan creativity are noted in Marshall, *Gospel of Luke*, 862–863. He regards this text as pre-Lukan.
299 France, *Jesus*, 241.
300 A possibility not adequately reckoned with by Neyrey ("Jesus' Address").

there is nothing in the earlier warnings that would suggest the citation of Hos 10:8 or the proverbial logion of v 31.

(D) We may begin our consideration of the terminology of vv 27–31 by observing that this passage contains only one word which is characteristic of Lukan redaction: λαός[301]. A number of additional terms merit detailed consideration. In our discussion of 22:39, we found that ἀκολουθέω is not a Lukan word. Here we may add that Luke appears to prefer other verbs to communicate the idea of "discipleship" (cf. Mark 8:34/Luke 9:23; Matt 10:38/Luke 14:27; 21:8; Acts 20:30). Πλῆθος, on the other hand, may well be Lukan, for of the 32 instances of its use in the NT, 25 come in Luke-Acts. Πλῆθος +τοῦ λαοῦ is a combination peculiar to Luke-Acts in the NT. Luke's emphasis on women is well-known[302]; perhaps he is responsible for their mention here. Κόπτω is relatively rare in the NT, used only 3 times in Matthew, Mark – 1, Luke – 2, Revelation – 2. In the two occurrences in Luke, 8:52 and 23:27, the verb denotes "to mourn". Θρηνέω is used only 4 times in the NT (Matt – 1x; Luke – 2x; John – 1x). Matthew 11:17 and Luke 7:32 both stem from Q, so we have no previous instance of Luke's redactional use of the verb. Apart from 23:27, κόπτω and θρηνέω are not used in tandem, though it may be significant that κλαίω (cf. 23:28) and κόπτω are found together in 8:52. On στρέφω, see above on 22:61; it may be Lukan here. Θυγάτηρ Ἱερουσαλήμ appears only here in the NT (but cf. Matt 21:5; John 12:15), but Luke does employ comparable constructions with θυγάτηρ in 1:5 and 13:16. Κλαίω is read twice in Matthew, Mark – 3, Luke – 9, and Acts – 3. In the majority of instances in Luke it is pre-Lukan, but we have already noted that κλαίω + ἐπί may be Lukan. For πλήν, see above on 22:21; it could have been introduced by Luke.

The remaining terminology is either of a specialized nature or appears in OT or proverbial quotations, and so offers nothing to our discussion. We have already noted the surprising use of τότε if Luke was freely composing here. Finally, we may note the presence of the Aramaic-like plural ποιοῦσιν in 23:31, and that some exegetes have found reason to believe that other aspects of the passage reflect an Aramaic substructure[303].

On the basis of these considerations we conclude that vv 27–31 came to Luke in a non-Markan source, but shows signs of Luke's editing.

V 32: This verse, strictly speaking, has no parallel in Mark, though it corresponds to the idea present in Mark 15:27; here in Luke it serves a transitional purpose. Κακοῦργος replaces Mark's λῃστής and is also read in vv 33 and 39. In this way Luke consistently refers to those crucified with Jesus, and this speaks against the view of Büchele that this verse is a Lukan creation to indicate a specific fulfillment of Jesus' prophecy in 22:37 (where ἄνομος is used)[304]. The term is used in the NT only in Luke's passion narrative and in 2 Tim 2:9. Elsewhere, Luke borrows λῃστής from Mark (Mark 11:17/Luke 19:46; 14:48/22:52), so the change here must be intentional. If the noun appeared in a pre-Lukan tradition in v 39, the present revision is easily explained as an assimilation to that subsequent usage. In any case, it disassociates Jesus from the political-revolutionary connotations of the Markan word, while retaining the association of Jesus with criminals. Ἕτερος is often used in Lukan redaction[305], and ἀναιρέω, found in Luke-Acts 21 times but only 3 additional times in the NT, is also likely to be Lukan here. There is therefore every reason to suspect that v 32 is a free Lukan composition suggested by Mark 15:27. With this verse, Luke's readers are given an early hint that in what follows Jesus, like the Servant of the Lord, will be treated as a criminal, an evil-doer.

As for the relationship of Luke's pericope to its counterpart in Mark the evidence has been straightforward, and we have been able to conclude

---

301 Gaston, *Electronicae*, 64.
302 Cf. Plummer, *Luke*, 528; Quentin Quesnell, "The Women at Luke's Supper", in *Political Issues*, 66–71; Cassidy, *Jesus*, 21–24; Marshall, *Luke*, 139–140; O'Toole, *Unity*, 118–126.
303 Cf. Black, *Aramaic Approach*, 126–127; Bultmann, *History*, 37, 115–116; Marshall, *Gospel of Luke*, 862–865.
304 Büchele, *Tod Jesu*, 44. Cf. Moo, *OT – Passion*, 133–137.
305 Gaston, *Electronicae*, 65; Jeremias, *Sprache*, 305.

that v 26 is Luke's redaction of Mark, and that vv 27–32 are non-Markan. For v 32 Luke probably owes his initial inspiration to Mark, however. Finally, we have found evidence to support the pre-Lukan character of vv 27–31. Luke, then, was cognizant of a non-Markan tradition of the *Via Dolorosa*.

XX. Luke 23:33–38 (Mark 15:22–32a, 36)

When we turn to consider the Lukan account of the crucifixion we are immediately struck with the number of differences in detail between it and the Markan parallel. Luke has deleted certain features of the Markan narrative, and his recounting of the episode is marked by its own distinctive ingredients. Among the variations from Mark's story in Luke's account are the following omissions from Mark:
  (A) the name "Golgotha";
  (B) the initial offer of wine and Jesus' rejection of it;
  (C) the chronological reference to the "third hour";
  (D) the (explicit) – mocking of the passers-by, including the allusion to Ps 22:7b and the reference to the temple-saying;
  (E) the assertion by the chief priests and scribes that "seeing is believing"; and
  (F) the allusion to Elijah's coming;
and the following components peculiar to the Lukan portrayal:
  (A) the prayer of Jesus from the cross on behalf of his executioners;
  (B) the allusion to Ps 22:7a;
  (C) the designation "the Chosen One"; and
  (D) the interpretation of the offering of the wine as an act of mockery, together with the verbal mockery by the soldiers.
Additionally, the sequence of events in Luke's pericope represents a modification of the Markan scene, and several less extensive variations in wording and emphasis are apparent. Can all of these differences be explained in terms of Luke's editing of one source, Mark?

V 33: Since 23:26, readers of the Lukan narrative have been kept in suspense as to the identity of the subject intended by the series of verbs cast in the third-person: ἀπήγαγον, ἐπέθηκαν, ἤγοντο, and now, ἦλθον and ἐσταύρωσαν. The mystery embraces v 34 as well (ἄφες αὐτοῖς, οἴδασιν, ποιοῦσιν, and ἔλαβον). Who are "they"? We would naturally conclude "they" are the Romans, as in Mark's account, and, historically speaking, this is undoubtedly true, but "[Lukas] lässt die Frage anfänglich – wohl bewusst – in der Schwebe"[306]. Luke, nonetheless, leaves hints that it was, in fact, the Romans who executed Jesus[307], but in such a way that responsibility is never deferred from the chief priests and other Jewish leaders.

---

306 Büchele, *Tod Jesu*, 42.
307 We may note the following: Pilate gives the verdict; Jesus is executed by crucifixion (a Roman,

For καὶ φέρουσιν αὐτὸν ἐπὶ τὸν Γολγοθᾶν τόπον in Mark 15:22, Luke has καὶ ὅτε ἦλθον ἐπὶ τὸν τόπον. Luke is not fond of φέρω (see above on 23:26) or of Aramaic place-names (see above on 22:39), so his version is easily explained as a revision of the Markan scene. For ὅ ἐστιν μεθερμηνευόμενον Κρανίου Τόπος, Luke has the simple τὸν καλούμενον Κρανίον. Because he has edited out Γολγοθᾶ, there is no need to "translate" the expression, and τόπος has already been used. Καλέω, in the participial sense of "which is called", is Lukan (see above on 22:1). At this juncture Luke omits Mark's first reference to Jesus' having been offered wine (οἶνος) and his rejection of the offer (15:23). Presumably, the purpose of the wine was to dull the senses of the one to be executed[308], and Jesus' refusal would have been consistent with, and indeed a contribution to, the martyrological theme a number of investigators have associated with the Lukan passion account[309]. Might Luke have omitted this Markan detail as a doublet (cf. Mark 15:36)?

Luke's ἐκεῖ ἐσταύρωσαν αὐτόν follows the simplicity of Mark 15:24: καὶ σταυροῦσιν αὐτόν. It is not like Luke to introduce ἐκεῖ into his sources, and he edits it out of Mark about as often as he takes it over (edited out: Mark 1:38; 2:6; 6:5, 33; 11:5; 16:7; borrowed: Mark 3:1/Luke 6:6; 5:11/8:31; 6:10/9:4; 13:21/17:21, 23; 14:15/22:12). The adverb stems from Q in 10:26(?); 11:26; 12:34; 17:37; 21:2(?), and is found in L-texts in 2:6; 12:18; 15:13. There is enough ambiguity in the question of Luke's sources to leave open the possibility that he has added the term here, however. Characteristically, Mark's use of the historic present (found 3x in the Markan parallel to this verse, and relatively often in the whole Markan crucifixion story) has been revised to the aorist tense.

Luke has transposed Mark's statement (15:27) about the two persons crucified on either side of Jesus, thus associating the three more intimately, even to the point of using the one verb to describe the action taken against them all. Even more closely than in the Markan text, then, where Mark's description of the event suggested the later application of Isa 53:12 to Jesus' fate (read by a minority of witnesses at Mark 15:28), an allusion to the fate of the Servant of the Lord is drawn. For κακοῦργος, see above on 23:32. In describing the crucifixion scene, Mark places the two rebels thus: ἕνα ἐκ δεξιῶν καὶ ἕνα ἐξ εὐωνύμων; whereas Luke's account reads: ὃν μὲν ἐκ δεξιῶν ὃν δὲ ἐξ ἀριστερῶν. It is characteristic of Luke to introduce μέν ... δέ for the sake of balance, and to omit superfluous pronouns[310]. As for the changes in terminology little can be said. Luke has no aversion to εἷς (used 66x in Luke-Acts); also ἀριστερός and εὐώνυμος are each used only once in Luke and Acts. Luke may be following Mark here, but the parallel thought in John 19:18b should warn us against viewing this possibility as a certainty.

V 34: There can be little doubt that v 34a represents an authentic prayer of Jesus, but it is heavily disputed whether it is original to Luke's Gospel[311]. The textual evidence is evenly divided, so inter-

---

not a Jewish, death penalty – cf. Hengel, *Crucifixion*; Winter, *Trial*, 90–96; Joseph A. Fitzmyer, "Crucifixion in Ancient Palestine, Qumran Literature, and the New Testament", in *Advance,* 125–146; but cf. 135); the political nature of the charges, especially as evidenced by the inscription on the cross; and Pilate's jurisdiction over Jesus' body. These factors indicate the efficacious role of the Romans in Jesus' death. Both Walaskay (*Political Perspective*, 44–45) and Via ("According to Luke", 131) go too far in having Luke exonerate the Romans and place full responsibility for Jesus' crucifixion at the feet of the Jewish leaders.

308 Cf. Prov 31:6; *Sanh.* 43a; Cranfield, *Mark*, 455; Taylor, *Mark*, 589.
309 Luke's martyrological portrayal of Jesus' death has been emphasized by Dibelius, *Tradition,* 201; Conzelmann, *Luke,* 81, 83–90; Charles H. Talbert, "Martyrdom in Luke-Acts and the Lukan Social Ethic", in *Political Issues*, 99–110; *idem, Reading Luke: A Literary and Theological Commentary on the Third Gospel* (New York: Crossroad, 1982) 212–214; Barbour, "Gethsemane", 238–241; Ford, *Enemy*, 118–120. These attempts to see in Luke's passion narrative a portrait of Jesus' death as that of a martyr are overstated, however – cf. Beck, "*Imitatio Christi*"; David Seccombe, "Luke and Isaiah", *NTS* 27 (1981) 252–259; Joel B. Green, "Jesus on the Mount of Olives (Luke 22:39–46): Tradition and Theology", *JSNT* 26 (1986) 38–43.
310 Fitzmyer, *Luke*, 1:108.
311 Cf. Metzger, *Textual Commentary*, 180: " ... the logion ... bears self-evident tokens of its dominical origin ...." Some, however, have argued that the prayer was created for Jesus on the

nal evidence must be given weighty consideration, and it points emphatically to the originality of the prayer. The motif of forgiveness is important to Luke, as suggested by the relatively abundant use of ἀφίημι and ἄφεσις in Luke–Acts (cf. esp. 1:77; 7:47–50; Acts 2:38; 5:31; 10:43; 13:38; 26:18) and the clear occurrence of the concept in such important texts as 15:11–32 and Acts 3:19[312]. Likewise, the ignorance of those responsible for Jesus' death (e.g. Acts 3:17; 13:27; 14:16; 17:30; 26:9; cf. Luke 12:47–48) is integral to Luke's understanding of the kerygma[313]. Furthermore, as Marshall has observed, the structure of the passion narrative, in which a saying of Jesus is found in each major section, suggests the originality of v 34a[314]. Of course, it can still be argued that the deletion of a saying of such importance is hardly conceivable[315], but then we must ask, important to whom? – for what may be of the utmost significance to modern critics may have been of relatively little consequence to early copyists. In fact, anti-Semitism could easily have provided the impetus for omitting this text in some manuscripts[316]. In any case, the force of the internal evidence is inescapable.

In v 34b, Luke, as in the Markan parallel, draws upon Ps 22:18 (21:19 LXX; 22:19 MT). Taylor regards this as a Markan insertion into Luke's *Sonderquelle*[317], but the presence of a similar OT reference in John 19:24 suggests that this idea was firmly fixed in the tradition, so it may have been in Luke's other material as well. For the second time Luke makes a puzzling omission from the Markan story, this time omitting the reference to the time of the crucifixion (Mark 15:25). The enigmatic nature of this deletion is heightened by the inclusion of Mark's second and third chronological statements (the sixth and ninth hours) in 23:44. Moreover, Matthew's redaction of Mark agrees with Luke's. Matera has tried to justify Luke's and Matthew's elimination with reference to Mark's conception of a "crucifixion day", but his argument still does not explain why *Luke* might have found this reference problematic[318]. Following this, Mark records the inscription on the cross (15:26), a detail Luke postpones until v 38.

V 35: Mark 15:29–30 provides an extensive record of how Jesus was mocked by the passers-by. His portrayal and terminology betray the influence of Ps 21:8b LXX: ἐλάλησαν ἐν χείλεσιν, ἐκίνησαν κεφαλήν (cf. ἐβλασφήμουν αὐτὸν κινοῦντες τὰς κεφελὰς αὐτῶν καὶ λέγοντες – Mark 15:29). Luke also draws on Ps 21:8 LXX, but unlike Mark he uses the *first half* of the verse: πάντες οἱ θεωροῦντες με ἐξεμυκτήρισαν με (cf. Luke's καὶ εἱστήκει ὁ λαὸς θεωρῶν. ἐξεμυκτήριζον . . .). Also distinguishing Luke's account from Mark's is that in Luke "the people" appear basically benign, even though the δὲ καί may relate them indirectly to the mockery being carried out by the ἄρχοντες[319]. The passive nature of their "looking on" is further suggested by v 48. Luke omits Mark's reference to the temple-saying as well, but picks up the challenge to "save yourself" below. All of these variations may be due to Luke's use of an alternative source, but it is not impossible that he has only redacted Mark here, albeit extensively.

---

basis of the similar prayer of Stephen in Acts 7:60. This is highly unlikely as Lohse (*Märtyrer*, 129–130) has correctly argued. For the originality of the text to Luke's Gospel, see Büchele, *Tod Jesu*, 45–46; Plummer, *Luke*, 544–545; Marshall, *Gospel of Luke*, 867–868; Lohse, *Märtyrer*, 129–130; Taylor, *Jesus*, 198–199; Talbert, "Martyrdom", 109 n.4; Schweizer, *Luke*, 359; Schneider, *Luke*, 2:483. *Contra* Metzger, *Textual Commentary*, 180; Jeremias, *NT Theology*, 298; Creed, *Luke*, 286.

312 Cf. also Marshall, *Luke*, 138–139; Ford, "Reconciliation", 80–98; *idem*, *Enemy*, 131–133.
313 Cf. also Tiede, *Prophecy*, 111; D. Daube, " 'For they know not what they do': Luke 23,34," *TU* 79 (1961) 59; Ford, *Enemy*, 131–133.
314 Marshall, *Gospel of Luke*, 868. Cf. also Talbert, "Martyrdom", 109 n.4.
315 Jeremias, *NT Theology*, 298.
316 Cf., e.g., Taylor, *Jesus*, 198–199; Marshall, *Gospel of Luke*, 867–868; Schweizer, *Luke*, 359.
317 Taylor, *Passion*, 93.
318 Matera, *Kingship*, 25–26.
319 A number of interpreters see Luke as disassociating completely "the people" from the action of mockery – so, e.g., Franklin, *Christ the Lord*, 94; Via, "According to Luke", 143 n.36; Büchele, *Tod Jesus*, 47. It cannot be denied that Luke gives "the people" no such role explicitly, but the force of the δὲ καί must not be overlooked.

"Ιστημι is Lukan (Matt – 20x; Mark – 11x; Luke-Acts – 60x), and the emphasis gained through its employment fits well with Lukan thought. Regardless of how one judges the participation of "the people" in the mockery, the "Jewish leaders" certainly occupy pride of place in the scene (on this rendering of ἄρχοντες and its Lukan derivation, see above on 23:13). This is accomplished by naming them as the subject of ἐκμυκτηρίζω and λέγω, and by omitting Mark's ὁμοίως.

For the content of their verbal abuse in Luke we read: ἄλλους ἔσωσεν, σωσάτω ἑαυτόν, εἰ οὗτος ἐστιν ὁ χριστὸς τοῦ θεοῦ ὁ ἐκλεκτός. The comparable text in Mark reads ἄλλους ἔσωσεν, ἑαυτὸν οὐ δύναται σῶσαι. ὁ χριστὸς ὁ βασιλεὺς Ἰσραὴλ καταβάτω νῦν ἀπὸ τοῦ σταυροῦ, ἵνα ἴδωμεν καὶ πιστεύσωμεν (15:31–32). Luke's account compares favorably with Mark's but a few points should be noted. Σωσάτω ἑαυτόν is reminiscent of the word of Jesus in 4:23, where he predicts that they will say to him: ἰατρέ, θεράπευσον σεαυτόν. In the present text the imperative is cast in the third preson, reflecting ἑαυτόν in Mark 15:31. Luke adds the conditional εἰ, thus removing some of the irony of the Markan account. The addition of τοῦ θεοῦ recalls the Lukan editing of Mark in 9:20. Ὁ ἐκλεκτός is peculiar to Luke (cf. 9:35) and may be an allusion to Isa 42:1[320]. Jewish apocalyptic knew the expression as a messianic designation[321], and, while Luke is likely responsible for its insertion here, the title itself is pre-Lukan.

V 36: With this verse Luke's narrative takes up the second phase of the mockery of Jesus, this time by the soldiers. Unlike Mark, Luke reports that the soldiers mock Jesus by what they do and

---

320 Cf. Beck, *"Imitatio Christi"*, 43 n.46; Marshall, *Luke*, 113; Jeremias and Zimmerli, "Παῖς θεοῦ", 689. On the other hand, Moo (*OT – Passion*, 156) argues that "the chosen one" was simply an appropriately paradoxical ascription for deriding one who was apparently abandoned so completely by the Father with whom so intimate a relationship had been claimed. There is no literary support for the meaning suggested by Moo, however, and it describes a rather vague situation as providing the motivation for the use of so specific and religiously important a nomenclature as this.

321 Cf., e.g., *1 Enoch* 39:6–8; 45; 48:6–10 (cf. Ps 2:2); 49 (cf. Isa 42:1); 51:52; 62–63 (cf. Isa 52:13–53:12); *Apoc Abr.* 30–31; G. Schrenk, "'Ἐκλεκτός", in *TDNT*, 4:184–185, 189; George W. E. Nickelsburg, *Jewish Literature between the Bible and the Mishnah* (Philadelphia: Fortress, 1981) 215, 217, 218, 220. The concept of "the Elect One" thus had ties with the Davidic Messiah and the Servant of Yahweh.

Of course, the dating of these apocalyptic texts may cast doubt on their relevance here. The *Apocalypse of Abraham* was certainly written after A.D. 70. The dating of the Similitudes of Enoch remains a matter of controversy. J. T. Milik (ed., *The Books of Enoch: Aramaic Fragments of Qumran Cave 4* [Oxford: Clarendon, 1976]; esp. pp. 91–98) credits the word to Christian Greek composition in the second half of the second century, but this thesis has drawn fire at several points. It is highly unlikely that a Christian writer would have identified Enoch with the Son of Man (71:14) and not have mentioned Jesus at any point in the text. Moreover, its absence from the Qumran text, a point exploited by Milik, is not proof that the work was a later composition (cf. Richard N. Longenecker, *The Christology of Early Jewish Christianity* [London: SCM, 1970; reprint ed., Grand Rapids, Michigan: Baker, 1981] 83–84; Dunn, *Christology*, 77). Further, possible historical references found in the text are so ambiguous that they offer little help – cf. the remarks in Milik, *Enoch*, 95–96; John J. Collins, "The Jewish Apocalypses", in *Apocalypse*, 39; M. A. Knibb, "The Date of the Parables of Enoch: A Critical Review", *NTS* 25 (1979) 345–359; Christopher L. Mearns, "Dating the Similitudes of Enoch", *NTS* 25 (1979) 360–369; Matthew Black, "The 'Parables' of Enoch (1 En 37–71) and the Son of Man", *ExpTim* 88 (1, 1976) 6–7; Nickelsburg, *Jewish Literature*, 221–222. In any case, it appears most likely that the texts in question were completed in the first century A.D.

However, as Nickelsburg (*Jewish Literature*, 219–220, 222; *idem, Resurrection, Immortality, and Eternal Life in Intertestamental Judaism* [Cambridge: Harvard University, 1972] 70–74) has pointed out, in chapters 62–63 the author has employed a traditional judgment scene, also attested in Wis 2, 4–5, which expanded Isa 52–53 with material from Isa 13–14. This speaks for the early provenance of the idea.

say. Ἐμπαίζω is not Lukan, but has been taken from Mark 15:31[322]. Προσέρχομαι is characteristic of Lukan redaction[323], and προσφέρω may also be Lukan (see above on 23:14). So, v 36 may be regarded as an extensive revision of Mark 15:36 (cf. 15:30). It is possible to see here an allusion to Ps 69:21[324].

V 37: Luke omits the allusion to Elijah's coming, but instead provides a verbal mockery of Jesus by the soldiers, employing words from Mark 15:31–32 and Luke 23:35. "King of Israel" in Mark has been replaced by "King of the Jews", the latter agreeing with the inscription on the cross in 23:38. Mark's use of πιστεύω is contrary to Lukan thought and he avoids it accordingly. Given Luke's bias toward the Romans it is not easy to understand why he would have introduced on his own this mockery scene. The language he employs could well have come from Mark, but this does not explain why he would have introduced this detail into his narrative. For this reason, an hypothesis of a pre-Lukan narrative of the crucifixion, recording three consecutive mockeries (cf. v 39) finds support.

V 38: The statement about the inscription on the cross is very close to Mark 15:26. Δὲ καί has been introduced by Luke, but this is not unusual in Lukan usage. Also, Luke adds οὗτος at the close of the inscription itself. Apart from the fact that the inscription was firmly fixed in the tradition[325], there is no reason for suspecting that Luke has taken this sentence from any source other than Mark.

Thus, we have found that the variations from Mark, extensive though they be, are not as supportive of a non-Markan passion narrative as we might have assumed at first, for many can be accounted for with recourse to Luke's terminological preferences and theological interests. Be that as it may, some details – e.g. the deletion of Jesus' rejection of the wine and Luke's omission of Mark's time-reference – remain puzzling, while others – e.g. Jesus' prayer from the cross and the soldiers' mockery – point strongly to Luke's use of additional material. Moreover, the three-fold structure of the mockery – Jewish leaders, soldiers, criminal – indicates Luke's use of a connected narrative tradition which paralleled the Markan material.

XXI. Luke 23:39–43 (Mark 15:32b)

With the mention of the criminals crucified with Jesus Luke radically departs from the simple, summarizing note given by Mark. Indeed, the two versions agree only in the use of αὐτός for Jesus as the object of this further verbal abuse. The theology of the pericope is very much Lukan – especially in its declaration of Jesus' innocence and in its universal offer (even to a crucified criminal) of a present (σήμερον) salvation. Some of the language, too, is Lukan: ἕτερος; φοβέω + θεός (cf. 1:50; 18:2; Acts 10:2; 13:26); κρίμα, in a forensic sense (cf. ἀνακρίμα in 23:14); the balancing μέν . . .

---

322 See Jeremias, *Sprache*, 306.
323 Gaston, *Electronicae*, 65.
324 Cf. Goppelt, *Typos*, 101; Moo *OT – Passion*, 278–279; Büchele, *Tod Jesu*, 48; U. P. McCaffrey, "Psalm Quotations in the Passion Narratives of the Gospels", *Neot* 14 (1981) 86.
325 See below, chapter, 8.IX.C.

δέ; and πράσσω (see above on 23:15). Not surprisingly, some exegetes have concluded that these verses are of Lukan origin[326].

On the other hand, a number of observations reveal how unlikely it is that this story is completely a Lukan creation. First, nothing in Mark suggests the criminals were not both involved in mocking Jesus, nor is there any suggestion in any of the mockery scenes that anyone was seeking salvation from Jesus. Hence, the εἷς . . . ἕτερος and the καὶ ἡμᾶς are without parallel. Second, κρεμάννυμι, for "to crucify", is pre-Lukan[327]. There is no perceivable reason for Luke to have substituted this term for σταυρόω or συσταυρόω. He has used the more common term in 23:32–33, and in order to revise Mark's text here he would have had to bypass a συν- compound for which he has a special liking. Third, there is no basis for presupposing that Luke has deliberately chosen κακοῦργος over, say, ἄνομος (see above on 22:37; 23:32). We have previously suggested that the word was present in Luke's source here. Fourth, the attitude expressed by the second criminal is consonant with the Jewish sentiment that to accept one's punishment as justified is an expression of penitence[328]. Finally, as we have observed earlier, Luke is hardly to be credited with introducing on his own accord the introductory ἀμήν σοι λέγω in v 43 (see above on 22:17).

These factors are best understood as suggesting that in this pericope we find a heavily edited version of a pre-Lukan story.

XXII. Luke 23:44–46 (Mark 15:33–38)

In narrating the death of Jesus, Luke has followed Mark's version for the most part. A comparatively large percentage of Luke's vocabulary is common to Mark (48.9%), but there are differences in the progress of the story.

---

326 Cf., e.g., Bultmann, *History*, 282–283; Schenk, *Passionsbericht*, 102–109. Büchele (*Tod Jesu*, 51) writes: "Die Quellenfrage soll und braucht hier nicht entschieden zu werden".

327 This use of κρεμμάνυμι is restricted in the NT to Luke 23:39; Acts 5:30; 10:39; Gal 3:13 (cf. Acts 13:29; 1 Pet 2:24). Presumably, this sense of the verb takes as its point of reference Deut 21:22–23 (LXX: κρεμάσητε αὐτὸν ἐπὶ ξύλου . . . κρεμάμενος ἐπὶ ξύλου) – a text applied to crucifixion already in pre-Christian times (cf. Philo, *Spec. Leg.* 3.152; idem, *Post C.* 61; idem, *Somn.* 2.213; 4QpNah 3–4.1.7–8; 11QTemple 64.6–13; Johannes Schreiber, "Ξύλον", in *TDNT*, 5:37–41; Hengel, *Crucifixion*, 84–85; Fitzmyer, "Crucifixion", 138–139). Inasmuch as Deut 21:22–23 renders absurb any confession of a *crucified Messiah* (for such an one would be cursed of God), it is reasonable to suspect that the phrase "hung on a tree" stems from early Christian apologetic (cf. William Horbury, "Suffering and Messianism in Yose ben Yose", in *Suffering and Martyrdom*, 154; Lindars, *NT Apologetic*, 232–235). In Gal 3:13 and 1 Pet 2:24, Jesus' substitutionary death is closely associated with this phrase.

328 Cf. Lohse, *Märtyrer*, 38; Marshall, *Gospel of Luke*, 872.

V 44: Luke takes over Mark's time note, καὶ γενομένης ὥρας ἕκτης (15:33), recasting it as καὶ ἦν ἤδη ὡσεὶ ὥρα ἕκτη. The addition of ἤδη is surprising, but not unparalleled (cf. 7:6; 14:17; 19:37; 21:30). Ὡσεί is a characteristic addition in Lukan redaction[329]. As for the detail regarding darkness covering the whole land, Luke has added a καί and transposed the order of σκότος and ἐγένετο in Mark, but otherwise the statements are identical.

V 45: Luke introduces an explanation for the darkness not found in Mark: τοῦ ἡλίου ἐκλιπόντος. A genitive absolute is not surprising in Lukan editorializing[330]. Luke omits Mark 15:34–35 (see below on v 46) and transposes the detail about the tearing of the temple curtain from Mark 15:38. He renders καὶ τὸ καταπέτασμα τοῦ ναοῦ ἐσχίσθη εἰς δύο ἀπ' ἄνωθεν ἕως κάτω (Mark) as ἐσχίσθη δὲ καταπέτασμα τοῦ ναοῦ μέσον. Luke often revises Mark's καί in favor of δέ. The substitution of μέσος for Mark's more lengthy description corresponds to classical usage and is consistent with Luke's terminological preferences[331].

In a recent essay[332] Frank Matera has argued that the sole source underlying Luke 23:44–48 is Mark 15:33–39, and that the differences between the two stories of Jesus' death should be attributed to Luke's editorial activity and theological *programme*. Regarding the transposition of the account of the rending of the temple veil in Luke he writes:

First, [Luke] wishes to avoid the impression that the death of Jesus is the end of the temple and its cult. The temple will still have a positive role to play in Acts and Luke's attitude toward it is basically benevolent. Therefore, he has altered Mark's account lest his narrative give the impression of the temple's final destruction. Second, Luke has altered Mark's order in order to align the torn curtain with the sun's failure and the three hours of darkness ... The tearing of the temple curtain, alongside the sun's failure, becomes a portent that the "last days" have been set in motion by Jesus' death[333].

As we have seen, Matera is basically right in his observation that Luke's attitude toward the temple is essentially more positive than Mark's. Likewise we have seen that Luke is capable of including negative mention of the temple, but these references are in the minority. Hence, in order to explain the present text as having stemmed from Lukan redactional efforts it is important to explain why Luke would have included this material, and it is precisely here that Matera's thesis falls short.

If, as Matera insists, Luke wanted to avoid the impression that Jesus' death is the end of the temple, then why include this detail at all? In his story of the trial of Jesus before the Jewish leaders Luke has shown us that he was quite capable of leaving out Markan material regarding the temple; why not do so here? As it now stands, the tearing of the temple veil simply cannot be disassociated from the death of Jesus. Moreover, Matera's argument that the torn curtain becomes a portent that the "last days" have come seems to rest on the notion that the destruction of the temple in Jerusalem is of importance for Luke as a major eschatological event. But this is open to serious question. In this respect the key text is Luke 21:5–7, wherein Jesus prophecies the destructon of the temple, followed by the query, "Teacher, when will this be, and what will be the sign when this is about to take place?" This way of phrasing the question does not appear to embrace the larger issue regarding the time of the eschaton (as in Mark 13:4; Matt 24:3), but only the concern about the historical destruction of the temple[334]. That is, the destruction of the temple is, in this context, drained of its eschatological import[335] and Matera's thesis is left high and dry.

---

329 Gaston, *Electronicae*, 65; Jeremias, *Sprache*, 307.
330 Cf. Fitzmyer, *Luke*, 1:108.
331 Plummer, *Luke*, 538; Gaston, *Electronicae*, 66.
332 Frank J. Matera, "The Death of Jesus according to Luke: A Question of Sources", *CBQ* 47 (1985) 469–485.
333 Matera, "Death of Jesus", 475.
334 Some exegetes, however, argue that Luke's retention of ταῦτα suggests the eschatological scope of the anonymous question – cf. Marshall, *Gospel of Luke*, 760–761; J. Zmijewski, *Die Eschatologiereden des Lukas-Evangeliums: Eine traditions- und redaktionsgeschichtliche Untersuchung zu Lk 21,5–36 und Lk 17, 20–37* (Bonn: Hanstein, 1972) 93–95. But this view does not appear to do justice to Luke's redaction in Luke 21.
335 So Fitzmyer, *Luke*, 2:1335; Maddox, *Luke-Acts*, 51; Franklin, *Christ the Lord*, 87–91.

In this context we should also be aware of the fact that, *contra* Matera's assumption, the time of darkness has apparently lost its eschatological cutting-edge in Luke's account. By providing a purely natural explanation for this phenomenon (23:45 — τοῦ ἡλίου ἐκλιπόντος) Luke's version severely weakens this notion when compared with the Markan parallel (cf. the heightening of this motif in Matt 27:45, 51–53!). This also speaks against Matera's explanation.

Of course, it is not enough simply to reject Matera's thesis on this point. Luke *has* retained this reference to the temple veil and we must ask why. The point of departure for resolving this issue lies in the temple-theology which is set in place already in the Lukan birth narrative. According to this view, the temple is not harshly rejected, but its role is akin to that of a servant: the temple leads to Christ and finds its fulfillment in him. Its validity extends only so far as to point toward and give way to Christ[336]. In the context of this overarching scheme, the retention of the temple-reference in Luke's death scene suggests that at the climactic point of Jesus' passion the temple gives way to or is displaced by Jesus[337].

V 46: For Mark's two references to Jesus' crying out from the cross, Luke has only one, and the introduction to it corresponds roughly to the second in Mark's account. Mark has ὁ δὲ Ἰησοῦς ἀφεὶς φωνὴν μεγάλην (15:37) where Luke has καὶ φωνήσας φωνῇ μεγάλῃ ὁ Ἰησοῦς εἶπεν. Luke's εἶπεν is a necessary addition since he, unlike Mark, actually records a saying here. Φωνήσας φωνῇ μεγάλῃ is Lukan (cf. Acts 16:28) and reflects his fondness for cognate words[338]. As for the saying itself, here Jesus quotes Ps 31:5.

From whence did Luke derive the citation of Ps 31:5 which he reads in its place? Is it pre-Lukan? In actuality, a number of testimonies converge to indicate the good probability that Luke is not independently responsible for placing this citation in this context.

First, we must recognize that the citation of Ps 22:1 would have been offensive not only to the Third Evangelist, but also to the *Urgemeinde*. Indeed, it is precisely this point which suggested to an earlier generation of NT scholars the authenticity of the Markan version of the death cry[339]. In addition to the Lukan evidence there is the substitution from ἐγκατέλιπές με in Mark 15:34 (which duplicates the LXX) to ὠνείδισάς με in D (and certain Old Latin mss.). Undoubtedly secondary, this variant reading weakens the sense of the original text, robbing it of its scandalous character. Further, if the Fourth Evangelist had before him material containing the "cry of dereliction" (whether in Mark's Gospel or another source), there is no question that he too would have omitted it, substituting in its place a logion more suited to his particular passion theology[340]. For this reason we have little *prima facie* reason to suspect that Luke is playing the part of the innovator in neglecting to pass on the citation of Ps 22:1; indeed, there is every reason to suspect that the substitution (if it is a substitution) was made prior to the time of the writing of Luke's Gospel.

Second, there is the interesting coincidence between Luke's citation of Ps 31 and the way in which both Matthew and John report Jesus' death. Matthew 27:50 records that Jesus "yielded up [his] spirit" (ἀφῆκεν τὸ πνεῦμα) and John 19:30 reports that he "delivered up [his] spirit" (παρέδωκεν τὸ πνεῦμα); thus, both texts are much closer to Luke's version of Jesus' last words (...παρατίθεμαι τὸ πνεῦμά μου) than to Mark's simple "he expired". This collusion may very well stem from common material which predates these three Gospels[341].

---

336 See Franklin, *Christ the Lord*, 87–92.
337 See O'Toole, *Unity*, 184.
338 Cf. Plummer, *Luke*, 538; Marshall, *Gospel of Luke*, 875; Jeremias, *Sprache*, 307; Taylor, *Passion*, 95.
339 See, e.g., Goppelt, *Typos*, 104; Taylor, *Jesus*, 157–159.
340 See Barnabas Lindars, *The Gospel of John* (Grand Rapids, Michigan: Wm. B. Eerdmans, 1972) 582; C. K. Barrett, *The Gospel according to St. John*, 2d ed. (Philadelphia: Westminster, 1978) 647; et al.
341 The coincidence between John's text and Luke's quotation was noted by Barrett (*John*, 554; cf. already F. Godet, *A Commentary on the Gospel of St. Luke*, 2 vols., 5th ed. [Edinburgh: T. & T. Clark, n.d.] 2:338), who postulates that John's text may be based on and explained by the Lukan. This hypothesis is based on Barrett's conviction that the Fourth Evangelist knew the

Third, we may draw attention to the text form of the Lukan citation.
Luke: πάτερ, εἰς χεῖράς σου παρατίθεμαι τὸ πνεῦμά μου.
MT: בְּיָדְךָ אַפְקִיד רוּחִי.
LXX: εἰς χεῖράς σου παραθήσομαι τὸ πνεῦμά μου.
It is immediately clear that the Lukan text is very close to both the MT and the LXX – the only distinction being in the introduction of the vocative of πατήρ (over against both the LXX and MT), the use of the plural form of χείρ (over against the MT), and the tense of παρατίθημι (over against the LXX). With respect to the first, we may recall that πατήρ is the normal address for God by Jesus in the Third Gospel. On the other hand, the possibility that beneath this vocative lies an instance of Jesus' use of the familiar "Abba" should not be discounted too easily[342]. The use of χεῖρας is not surprising, even if the underlying OT text is the MT, for the number is not consistently translated from the MT in the LXX and, in any case, is largely irrelevant in this figurative sense of "hand". Singular or plural, both refer to the power of God (cf., e.g., Pss 89:13; 92:4; 102:25; 111:7; 119: 73; et al.). As for the third difference, while it may be that Luke has changed the tense of the verb (as Matera suggests[343]), it should not be overlooked that the Hebrew imperfect can be represented in Greek either by the present or the future. Moreover, *contra* Moo's assertion that influence from the LXX is certain here in that παρατίθημι renders פקד only twice in the LXX[344], we should remember that פקד, used *in this sense* (i.e. "to commit or entrust") is relatively rare in the MT[345]. Hence, the Lukan citation (apart from the addition of πατήρ) is explicable *solely* in terms of a translation from the MT, and this is consistent with the notion that Luke is following a *Sonderquelle*.

Finally, with reference to Acts 7:59 and 1 Pet 4:19, Barnabas Lindars has theorized that Ps 31:5 was taken up by early Christians as a helpful text appropriate in contexts where there was an imminent danger of death[346]. Similarly, the parallel usage of the psalm by Jews as an evening benediction has long been noted – though it is true that there is uncertainty regarding how far back this practice can be dated[347]. The existence of both "parallels", however, demonstrates the appropriateness of this psalm in this context, supports the hypothesis that it stems from early tradition, and, in fact, leaves open the possibility of the saying's authenticity.

For all of these reasons, we argue for the likelihood that Luke found this citation in an alternative source and inserted it here where Mark had failed to include any particular saying. That is, Luke both omitted reference to the offensive Ps 22:1 of Jesus' "first outcry" in Mark, and used material from his *Sonderquelle* to fill in the content of what in Mark's account would have been the second, "great" cry. After the transitional τοῦτο δὲ εἰπών, Luke gives the same final observation as is found in Mark: ἐξέπνευσεν.

With the exception of the quotation in v 46, therefore, Luke's version of the account of Jesus' death probably represents a light editing of his

---

Synoptic Gospels (an hypothesis we deny – see below, chapter 4), but this would not explain the Matthean parallel.

342 See Joachim Jeremias (*Abba: Studien zur neutestamentlichen Theologie und Zeitgeschichte* [Göttingen: Vandenhoeck & Ruprecht, 1966]56–58; *idem, NT Theology*, 62–64; James D. G. Dunn, *Jesus and the Spirit: A Study of the Religious and Charismatic Experience of Jesus and the First Christians as Reflected in the New Testament* (Philadelphia: Westminster, 1975) 21, 23. Moo (*OT – Passion*, 281–282 n.4) points out that if Luke has introduced this vocative in imitation of Jesus' regular usage then it must be asked why he has not added it more often. See also Barnabas Lindars, *NT Apologetic*, 95; he leaves open the possibility of its genuineness here while noting the parallels in Luke 10:21; 11:2; 22:42.

343 Matera, "Death of Jesus", 477. See also Traugott Holtz, *Untersuchungen über die alttestamentlichen Zitate bei Lukas* (Berlin: Akademie, 1968) 58.

344 Moo, *OT – Passion*, 280.

345 *BDB* (824) lists only three texts where the verb is used in this sense – 1 Kgs 14:27; 2 Chr 12:10; Ps 31:6 (31:5).

346 Lindars, *NT Apologetic*, 95; *idem, John*, 582. Cf. Rese, *Alttestamentliche Motive*, 200–201.

347 Str-B, 2:269; Büchele, *Tod Jesu*, 53.

Markan source. The citation of Ps 31:5 has been taken from an alternative source. The evidence for a non-Markan, pre-Lukan account here is indeed weak, but the presence of an alternative, old "last word" may itself be indicative that Luke knew a crucifixion account other than Mark's, but which was built along much the same lines as that in Mark.

XXIII. Luke 23:47–49 (Mark 15:39–41)

Following Jesus' death both Mark and Luke record the presence and reaction of witnesses to the crucifixion. Mark lists two such parties, whereas Luke has expanded the story to include three. Thirty per cent of the words found in Luke are also present in Mark, with a large degree of verbal agreement centered in v 49.

V 47: For ἰδὼν δὲ ὁ κεντυρίων (Mark 15:39), Luke has an identical phrase, only substituting his ἑκατοντάρχης for Mark's κεντυρίων, a Latin loan-word. In the NT, Mark is alone in employing the Latinism, but ἑκατοντάρχης is used 21 times, 17 in Luke-Acts. Luke omits as unnecessary Mark's ὁ παρεστηκὼς ἐξ ἐναντίας αὐτοῦ, moving directly to what the centurion saw. For this, Mark has ὅτι οὕτως ἐξέπνευσεν, thus recalling Jesus' "expiration" in 15:37. Luke, however, has τὸ γενόμενον. With this revision, which may reflect Luke's terminological preferences[348], the Third Evangelist widens the scope of the centurion's vision. In the Markan account, the centurion presumably responds only to Jesus' dying breath, but in Luke's recounting the whole crucifixion episode is in view.

What was the centurion's reaction? Mark records: εἶπεν· ἀληθῶς οὗτος ὁ ἄνθρωπος υἱὸς θεοῦ ἦν. Luke's version reads: ἐδόξαζεν τὸν θεὸν λέγων· ὄντως ὁ ἄνθρωπος οὗτος δίκαιος ἦν. The introductory clause, "he glorified God", reflects a Lukan interest found throughout his writings (cf. 2:20; 5:25–26; 7:16; 13:13; 17:15; 18:43; Acts 4:21; 11:18; 13:48; 21:20). Luke avoids ἀληθῶς except as an equivalent for ἀμήν (see above on 22:59). Ὄντως is not particularly Lukan, but is also found in 24:34. As for Luke's δίκαιος as a substitute for Mark's υἱὸς θεοῦ, this revision has been the subject of some controversy and Taylor, for one, is unwilling to see the Lukan term as a purposeful modification of the Markan text unless Luke was following another source[349]. To be sure, the amending of so positive a confession would be surprising unless by the use of δίκαιος Luke had intended something equally positive[350]. This he has done. Δίκαιος continues the theme of Jesus' innocence, points to Jesus' death as the fate of the Suffering Righteous, and alludes to his fate as the Suffering Servant of Yahweh (as in Acts 3:13–14)[351]. Thus, there is no reason to suspect that Luke was dependent on an alternative source at this point.

V 48: No parallel exists in the Markan passion narrative to Luke's description of the repentance of the multitudes following Jesus' death. In a very brief treatment, Matera asserts that this detail should be credited to Lukan creative activity – and that for two reasons. First, he notes the linguistic similarity between 23:48 (τύπτοντες τὰ στήθη) and 8:13 (ἔτυπτεν τὸ στῆθος). This agreement, he argues, is difficult to explain if Luke was following a special source at this point. Second, Matera regards Luke as having good motivation for creating this response since the theme of repentance as the proper response to Jesus' death is an important one in Luke-Acts[352].

---

348 Cf. Taylor, *Passion*, 95; Gaston, *Electronicae*, 65; Jeremias, *Sprache*, 308.
349 Taylor, *Passion*, 96. Cf. Jeremias, *Sprache*, 308.
350 Cf. Beck, "*Imitatio Christi*", 41; Schmidt, "Luke's 'Innocent' Jesus", 117; Franklin, *Christ the Lord*, 62–63.
351 On the Isaianic background of Acts 3:13–14, see below, chapter 8.
352 Matera, "Death of Jesus", 484.

In fact, the linguistic evidence favoring Luke's redaction is much stronger than Matera noted. Thus, for example, πᾶς and γίνομαι are sometimes used in Lukan redaction, and ὄχλος belongs to Luke's editorial vocabulary[353]. Συνπαραγίνομαι appears only here in the NT; however, given Luke's fondness for compound verbs, and especially those with the συν- prefix, it very well could be Lukan. In this context ὑποστρέφω apparently has a double meaning: "to return home" and "to repent". It may also be Lukan in origin, for it is found in Luke-Acts 33 of its 37 appearances in the NT. The issue, then, is not whether Luke's hand is present in the text, for this is self-evident, but the presence of "Lukanisms" in this text is not in itself proof that Luke was not following a non-Markan source. Before such a verdict can be returned, we must ask if additional, supportive evidence can be found.

Presumably, Matera regards such evidence as forthcoming from the presence of the repentance-motif in this verse. In his view this is most fitting for, in Lukan thought, "the death of Jesus should and does lead to repentance"[354]. Of course, repentance is a major soteriological theme in Luke-Acts — see, e.g., Luke 19:9; Acts 2:38; 3:19; 5:30–31; 17:30; 20:21; et al. However, *contra* Matera's assertion, repentance is not tied especially to the death of Jesus. In the three texts where the call to repentance is most explicit (Acts 2:38; 3:19; 5:30–31), Jesus' passion is in view, but *the call to repentance receives its chief impetus from God's having exalted the crucified Jesus*. In Acts 2:38 the call to repent comes immediately following the acme of the Pentecost address — in a verse which is itself a kind of summary of the sermon: "God has made this Jesus, whom you crucified, both Lord and Christ". This form of the *Kontrastschema*[355] places the emphasis not on the death of Jesus but on what God has done by way of overturning that death. A similar argument is present in Acts 3: 13–26, a Petrine speech which is framed by the reference to God's having "glorified/raised up his servant" (vv 13, 26). And in Acts 5:30–31, Israel's capacity to repent and receive forgiveness is directly linked in a cause-effect relationship to Jesus' exaltation. Clearly, then, Matera has run past the evidence in insisting that the repentance theme in Luke 23:48 is bound up with the cross in Lukan theology. In fact, the opposite claim has the better case, and this speaks for the pre-Lukan character of this text.

In addition to this point, we may draw attention to the fact that the reaction of the crowd brings to the fore once again the traditional innocence-motif found in Luke's passion account. That this idea is traditional is certified by the already-noted criterion of multiple attestation, applied to the parallels in Luke 23:4, 14, 22 and John 18:38; 19:4, 6[356].

Interestingly, both the *Gospel of Peter* and the Old Syriac have parallels to the Lukan note of sorrow, though both are far more dramatic in content:

Gos. Pet. 7:25: Then the Jews and the elders and the priests, perceiving what great evil they had done to themselves, began to lament and to say, "Woe on our sins, the judgment and the end of Israel is drawn high"[357].

Old Syriac: And all they that happened to be there and saw what happened were beating on their breasts and saying, "Woe to us! What hath befallen us? Woe to us for our sins"[358]!

The collusion of these more dramatic accounts is remarkable, and provides good support for the idea that a more general response, such as Luke records, may be pre-Lukan in character[359].

V 49: This verse and Mark 15:40 share the same content and purpose, and some of the same vocabulary; however, Luke's rendition has been so drastically rewritten that we will not compare the two versions phrase by phrase, but will note verbal agreements as they occur. Ἵστημι is probably

---

353 See Jeremias, *Sprache*, 308–309; Gaston, *Electronicae*, 64–66.
354 Matera, "Death of Jesus", 484.
355 See Roloff, "Anfänge", 38–64.
356 See further, Rudolf Schnackenburg, *The Gospel according to St. John*, vol. 3 (New York: Crossroad, 1982) 251, 258; Marshall, *Gospel of Luke*, 853.
357 Christian Maurer, "The Gospel of Peter", in *NT Apocrypha*, 1:185.
358 Black, *Aramaic Approach*, 269.
359 See the discussion of the possibility that the Old Syriac has been directly influenced by early, non-canonical materials in Black, *Aramaic Approach*, 262–269.

Lukan, as are πᾶς (see above on 23:48) and γνωστός. This last term is read in the NT only 3 times apart from its 14 occurrences in Luke-Acts. Ἀπὸ μακρόθεν and καὶ γυναῖκες both appear in the Markan parallel. It is remarkable that δὲ καί is read in Mark but not in Luke here (see above on 23:35). Συνακολουθέω appears only here in Luke-Acts (and elsewhere in the NT in Mark 5:37; 14:51), but has presumably been inspired by ἀκολουθέω in Mark's parallel. The technical sense of the verb, along with the geographical reference and Luke's οἱ γνωστοὶ αὐτῷ, suggest that the verb may have a double significance here: "they" both followed him and were his disciples[360]. Hence, the witnesses to the crucifixion in Luke include the Roman centurion, the "crowd", and Jesus' followers. In the end, all three parties (but not the Jewish leaders) have acknowledged his messiahship. Τῆς Γαλιλαίας comes from the parallel text in Mark. Luke does not record the list of names given by Mark (but cf. Luke 8:2–3). For ὁράω in Luke, Mark has θεωρέω. It is likely that this revision can be credited to Luke's desire for terminological variety, for he employs θεωρία and θεωρέω in v 48. This piling up of "sight words" – ἰδών θεωρία, θεωρέω, and ὁράω – in vv 47–49 suggests that Luke is interested in establishing the validity of these events through the testimony of eyewitnesses (cf. 1:2).

We conclude that vv 47 and 49 represent Luke's redaction of Mark. Verse 48 is less easy to explain in terms of source, but as it continues the traditional motif found earlier in Luke's narrative, and as it is paralleled conceptually in other testimonies, we are inclined to regard it as having been based on a non-Markan source, if heavily Lukan in its present redaction.

XXIV. Luke 23:50–56a (Mark 15:42–16:1)

Despite Trocmé's assertion to the contrary, Luke's account of the burial of Jesus is best explained as a redaction of his Markan source[361]. This is most evident in the case of vv 50–54, but is highly probable for vv 55–56a, too.

In regard to vv 50–54, 43.1 per cent of the Lukan vocabulary is also found in Mark. Luke deletes a few Markan details: that Joseph "took courage", Pilate's enquiry into Jesus' death, the purchasing of the linen shroud, and the rolling of the stone against the door of the tomb. He transposes Mark's chronological reference from the beginning of the narrative to a later position (Mark 15:42; Luke 23:54). His description of Joseph is more extensive (23:50–51); he underscores Joseph's piety. (Such "character references" are common in Luke – e.g. 2:25; Acts 6:3, 5, 8; 10:2; 11:24). A further, more significant addition is in 23:53c, where the tomb is qualified thus: οὗ οὐκ ἦν οὐδεὶς οὔπω κείμενος. Similar expressions are found in Matt 27:60 and John 19:41b. A linguistic comparison between the three texts does not suggest any sort of literary dependence; a common oral tradition is therefore most likely.

---

360 See Büchele, *Tod Jesu*, 56.
361 Trocmé, *Passion*, 34. Cf. Taylor, *Passion*, 99–103. Taylor agrees that vv 50–54 stem from Mark, but argues that vv 55–56a belong to an alternative tradition.

As for vv 55–56a, it may be argued that this passage is non-Markan, but the evidence is not persuasive. As in v 49, Luke does not repeat the names of the women provided in the Markan account, and the terminology here is reminiscent of the earlier text. Συνέρχομαι is not a surprising addition in Lukan redaction, for not only is it a συν- compound, but the verb is found in Luke-Acts 19 of the 32 times it occurs in the NT (Matt – 1x; Mark 3x). Verse 56 describes the women's actions as having taken place just before the Sabbath, whereas Mark has the preparation for the anointing following the Sabbath. This variance may be taken as an indication that Luke is using an alternative source, but the change may be due to nothing more than Luke's editing of Mark. Linguistic evidence may be taken to support either conclusion.

With certainty, then, we may regard vv 50–54 as having been based on the Markan text. Verses 55–56a may also have originated with Mark, but this is less sure.

XXV. Conclusions

With this, we come to the end of our analysis of Luke 22–23, the Lukan narrative of Jesus' suffering and death. Our investigation has demonstrated the virtual certainty that the Third Evangelist made use of the Markan passion account in addition to certain non-Markan source material. For the sake of convenience, we have provided a visual summary of our findings for each pericope, charting Luke's use of his sources, as an appendix.

The difficult but highly consequential question facing us now is this: What form or forms did Luke's additional source material have? Did Luke have access to a string of independent traditions, whether oral and/or written? Did Luke have before him a continuous, non-Markan narrative? By way of seeking to respond to this problem we outline the following observations based on our inquiry.

(A) First, there is no real basis for arguing that Luke has used Matthew's passion narrative as a source for his own. There is no agreement between the First and Third Evangelists in the material peculiar to Matthew[362], and what few minor agreements against Mark exist are insufficient to support a theory of direct literary dependence.

(B) There can be no doubt that Mark's passion narrative has served as source material for Luke.

(C) Likewise, it is virtually certain that our evangelist has employed non-

---

362 Matt 27:3–10 and Acts 1:16–20 provide variant traditions about Judas's death, but literary dependence is highly improbable given the degree of divergence from one version to another.

Conclusions

Markan, pre-Lukan material in the process of constructing his own account of Jesus' passion.

(D) This additional material, we have seen, has numerous points of contact with the Johannine passion narrative — with respect to language, structure, and emphases. As we will show, the Fourth Evangelist had no direct knowledge of any of the Synoptic Gospels and yet has provided in his own Gospel a passion narrative that closely models that of the Synoptics. This suggests that the Lukan material was not a collection of isolated fragments but was a part of a developing narrative.

(E) In fact, points in the Lukan narrative at which non-Markan, pre-Lukan elements are absent are very rare. The recounting of only two episodes derives from the Gospel of Mark only: the preparation for the Passover (22:7–13) and the burial scene (23:50–55b). One may well question the probability that Luke would have had access to so many independent, fragmented traditions.

(F) Pre-Lukan, non-Markan material used in the passion story does not have the appearance of having come to Luke in the form of independent fragments. For example, in our study of 22:39–46 we argued that vv 43–44, for which there was no Markan counterpart, were probably contained in a variant *story* of Jesus' prayer on the Mount of Olives. Similarly, if on a larger scale, we argued for the pre-Lukan character of the *narrative* of the Last Supper and saw the appropriateness of an extended "table-talk" in that context. Likewise, we argued that Luke had access to alternative stories of Jesus' hearing before the Jews and of Peter's denial, and that the Herod-account was not merely a fragment which Luke allowed to be sandwiched into the story of Jesus' trial before Pilate.

While our enquiry has not yet directly touched on this, it is also worth asking about the probability of a pre-canonical account of, say, Jesus' arrest, circulating on its own. What purpose might this have served in isolation from the story of Jesus' prayer of submission or the subsequent trial or both? Trocmé is surely on the right track when he takes up the question whether the various episodes of the passion account had an independent existence[363]. What *Sitz im Leben*, he asks, could account for the formation and circulation of the various pericopae, considered *in isolation*? If we are convinced that Luke has used non-Markan material throughout his passion narrative, as our analysis has demonstrated, this reasoning takes on great importance. However, here we are touching on form-critical issues which must be held in reserve for the present[364].

---

363 Trocmé, *Passion*, 49–51. His conclusion that "... none of the episodes that precede Jesus' arrest in the Passion narrative is likely to have been a separate unit of tradition ... " (51) fails to take seriously enough the obvious early isolation of the eucharistic words (1 Cor 11:23–25).
364 See below, chapters 6–7.

To summarize, our most basic point is simply this: With only two exceptions, at every turn we have found reason to believe that Luke had access to stories that paralleled the stories of the Markan account. On the one hand, due to the extent of Lukan redaction we cannot hope to reconstruct with any precision the scope of those stories nor determine with complete certainty that these stories formed a continuous narrative — any more than we could construct *Mark's* continuous narrative or determine that Luke used *Mark's* continuous narrative as a source, or even determine that there was a continuous story like *Mark's*, without a copy of *Mark's Gospel* in hand. On the other hand, because there are parallel stories at each point along the way (save two) we can reasonably propose that Luke knew a second, unified narrative *like Mark's*[365].

If we find form-critical grounds for asserting the plausibility of a pre-canonical passion narrative, then our proposal concerning a Lukan *Sonderquelle* for the passion account will be significantly enhanced. We have here already, though, an important section in the wall of evidence that there was a pre-canonical story of Jesus' passion. The stability of this edifice will increase as other sections are added.

---

365 See the programmatic statement by Schramm (*Markus-Stoff*, 50–51) to the effect that from 22: 14 onwards Luke follows a special, written source which he embellishes with the Markan material.

Chapter Four:

The Relationship between the Canonical Passion Narratives

3. The Gospel of John

I. Introduction

"The question whether John used one or more of the Synoptic Gospels continues to be hotly debated"[1]. Clearly, however, how one answers this question is of great consequence for how one views the tradition-history of the passion narrative. Earlier, we observed the degree to which the Johannine *Vorlage* coincided with that of the Synoptic Gospels once one entered the realm of the account of Jesus' suffering and death[2]. At that point we posed the question, How is this relationship to be explained? If the author of the Fourth Gospel was dependent only on a canonical passion story (or stories) in providing his own Gospel with a passion account, then the Gospel of John offers us no independent evidence for our investigation. On the other hand, if John was not dependent on one or more Synoptic Gospels, or if there is evidence he has used further source material for his passion narrative, this fact will have far-reaching significance for our inquiry. In this chapter we will focus the more general question of the relationship between John and the Synoptic Gospels by concentrating on the passion story. Not only is this material central to our overall argument, but, as Brown has observed, "the Passion Narrative supplies the best material for a study of the relationship of the Fourth Gospel to the Synoptic Gospels . . ."[3]. This is true in the first instance because it is the longest narrative of

---

1 Barnabas Lindars, "John and the Synoptic Gospels: A Test Case", *NTS* 27 (1981) 287. For the debate, see Josef Blinzler, *Johannes und die Synoptiker: Eine Forschungsbericht* (Stuttgart: Katholisches, 1965) 16–60. See also C. K. Barrett, "John and the Synoptic Gospels", *ExpTim* 85 (1974) 228–233; Howard M. Teeple, *The Literary Origin of the Gospel of John* (Evanston, Illinois: Religion and Ethics Institute, 1974) 59–70; Frans Neirynck, "John and the Synoptics", in *Évangelica*, 365–387.
2 See further below, chapter 4.III.
3 Brown, *John*, 2:787. See also Peder Borgen, "John and the Synoptics in the Passion Narrative", *NTS* 5 (1958–59) 246–259; Anton Dauer, *Die Passionsgeschichte im Johannesevangelium: Eine*

the same action shared by the "quadruple tradition", but more precisely because of the relatively high degree of convergence in matters of detail between the canonical traditions here. Thus, in what follows, we shall undertake analyses of three texts from John's narrative, all of which have been cited as proof of Johannine dependence on one or more of the Synoptic Gospels.

II. Three "Test Cases" for a Johannine-Synoptic Literary Relationship within the Passion Narrative

A. John 12:1–8 (Matt 26:6–13; Mark 14:3–9; Luke 7:36–50)

This pericope constitutes John's version of the anointing of Jesus. All four canonical Gospels record comparable stories, and it will be best to initiate our investigation of possible literary relationships by first charting the points of convergence and divergence in the unfolding scenario.

A. Setting (Matt 26:6–7; Mark 14:3; Luke 7:36; John 12:1–2).
  1. Matthew, Mark, John – in Bethany (Judaea!).
     Luke – in Galilee.
  2. Matthew, Mark – in the home of Simon the Leper.
     Luke – in the home of Simon the Pharisee. "Simon" was a relatively common name[4], and attempts at harmonization must move beyond the mere intersection of the accounts on this name.
     John – in an undesignated place, perhaps the home of Lazarus. In any case, John is alone in mentioning the presence of Lazarus, Martha, and Mary[5].
  3. Matthew, Mark – within the passion narrative, after the triumphal entry into Jerusalem, perhaps two days before the Passover[6].
     Luke – relatively early in Jesus' ministry. Luke has no pericope in his passion narrative with which to compare the Markan anointing scene. Cribbs tries to explain Luke's chronology as an attempt to iron out the differences between the Markan/Matthean and Johannine renditions of this episode[7]. This view, however, (1) overemphasizes the similarities of Luke's account with John's and the dissimilarities between John's and the Markan/Matthean form, (2) credits the developing Johannine tradition allegedly known by Luke with too finalized a form and too authoritative a position, (3) fails to explain why only Luke has no anointing scene in the context of the passion narrative, and (4) fails to account for

---

traditionsgeschichtliche und theologische Untersuchung zu John 18. 1–19, 30 (München: Kösel, 1972); Hans Klein, "Die lukanische-johanneishe Passionstradition", *ZNW* 67 (1976) 155–186; M. Sabbe, "The Arrest of Jesus in Jn 18, 1–11 and Its Relation to the Synoptic Gospels", in *Évangile de Jean*, 203–234; idem, "The Footwashing in Jn 13 and Its Relation to the Synoptic Gospels", *ETL* 58 (4, 1982) 279–308.

4 BAG, 751.
5 That Lazarus sits at the table and that Martha serves may suggest but does not prove that he is host and she hostess. Cf. Barrett, *John*, 411; Leon Morris, "The Relationship of the Fourth Gospel to the Synoptics", in *Studies*, 33.
6 It is not certain how we are to relate the time references in Matt 26:1 and Mark 14:1 to this episode.
7 F. Lamar Cribbs, "St. Luke and the Johannine Tradition", *JBL* 90 (1971) 437–441.

the several distinctive details and emphases of the Lukan version (not taken up by Cribbs) over against the other three. Much more plausible is that Luke has taken his account from his *Sonderquelle,* employed it relatively early in the narrative sequence of his Gospel, and avoided the Markan parallel as a doublet[8].

John — prior to the triumphal entry, perhaps six days before the Passover.

4. Matthew — Jesus reclined at the table (ἀνάκειμαι).

Mark, Luke — Jesus reclined at the table (κατάκειμαι; Luke also uses κατακλίνω).

John — Lazarus (and others) reclined at the table (ἀνάκειμαι) with Jesus.

B. The Woman and the Ointment (Matt 26:7; Mark 14:3; Luke 7:37—39; John 12:3).

1. Matthew, Mark — an unspecified woman.
   Luke — a "sinner".
   John — Mary.
2. Matthew, Mark — ἔχουσα ἀλάβαστρον μύρου.
   Luke — κομίσασα ἀλάβαστρον μύρου.
   John — λαβοῦσα λίτραν.
3. Matthew — βαρυτίμου.
   Mark — νάρδου πιστικῆς πολυτελοῦς.
   Luke — ∅.
   John — νάρδου πιστικῆς πολυτίμου. The verbal agreement between Mark and John here is all the more striking on account of the relative scarceness of the word πιστηκός — never found among Greek writers before the NT era. It may derive from פִּסְתָּקָא, in which case the ointment would be *myrobalanum*[9].
4. Matthew, Luke, John — ∅.
   Mark — she broke the alabastron.
5. Matthew, Mark — she anointed (καταχέω) his head.
   Luke — weeping, she wet his feet with her tears, wiped them with the hair of her head, kissed his feet, and anointed (ἀλείφω) his feet with the ointment.
   John — she anointed (ἀλείφω) his feet, then wiped his feet with her hair.
6. Matthew, Mark, Luke — ∅.
   John — the house was filled with the fragrance of the ointment.

C. The Reaction (Matt 26:8—9; Mark 14:4—5; Luke 7:39; John 12:4—6).

1. Matthew — the disciples reacted.
   Mark — some persons reacted.
   Luke — the Pharisee-host reacted.
   John — Judas reacted. Judas is described as one of his disciples, the one who would betray him.
2. Matthew, Mark — emphasis first on waste, then on money for the poor.
   Luke — emphasis on the woman's status as a sinner and Jesus' lack of prophetic insight.
   John — emphasis on money for the poor. Mark and John agree in naming the value of the ointment as δηναρίων τριακοσίων, though Mark qualifies this amount with ἐπάνω.
3. Matthew, Luke — ∅.
   Mark — a summarizing statement: "And they were scolding her".
   John — an explanation of Judas's tainted motivation.

D. Jesus' Response (Matt 26:10—13; Mark 14:6—9; Luke 7:40—50; John 12:7—8).

1. Matthew, Mark, John — ∅.
   Luke — parable of two debtors. While this mixture of parable and pronouncement-story may well represent a conflation, we need not think Luke is responsible for the combination[10].

---

8 Cf. Fitzmyer, *Luke,* 1:684; Marshall, *Gospel of Luke,* 306; Schürmann, *Luke,* 1:429—443; Schweizer, *Luke,* 137—141; Schneider, *Luke,* 1:175—179.
9 Black, *Aramaic Approach,* 223—225; cf. BAG, 662.
10 Cf. Jeremias, *Parables,* 87; Fitzmyer, *Luke,* 1:684; Marshall, *Gospel of Luke,* 306—307, 310; Schweizer, *Luke,* 138.

2. Nevertheless, though in different ways, Mark/Matthew and Luke each focus on the woman's ministration on Jesus' behalf.
3. Matthew, Luke – ∅.
   Mark – ἄφετε αὐτήν.
   John – ἄφες αὐτήν[11].
4. Matthew, Mark – "Why do you trouble her/the woman?" "She has done a beautiful thing to me".
   Luke, John – ∅.
5. Matthew, Mark, John – "For you will always have the poor with you . . . ."
   Luke – ∅.
6. Matthew, Luke, John – ∅.
   Mark – "And you can help them whenever you wish".
7. Matthew, Mark, John – ἐμὲ δὲ οὐ πάντοτε ἔχετε.
   Luke – ∅.
8. Matthew, Luke, John – ∅.
   Mark – summarizing statement: "She has done what she could".
9. Matthew, Mark, John – ∅.
   Luke – Jesus compares the action of the woman with the inaction of Simon, using the woman as an example of one who served with gratitude.
10. Matthew, Mark, John – reference to Jesus' anointing for burial.
    Luke – ∅.
11. Matthew, Mark – reference to the ongoing significance of the woman's act. This verse in Mark (14:9) is widely regarded as the handiwork of the Second Evangelist[12].
    Luke – Jesus announces that the woman's sins are forgiven.
    John – ∅.

From this comparison of the four versions of the story it is obvious that Matthew has used only his Markan source in constructing his version. Luke's version, on the other hand, contains discrepancies from Mark that make it highly improbable that his account rests on Mark's. Matthew and John agree with one another against the other accounts only in the abbreviation of the saying about the poor (D.6, above), and so it unnecessary to suggest for them a literary relationship. Luke and John agree significantly against the Markan/Matthean tradition in the act of anointing (B.5), but otherwise are quite dissimilar. In fact, even within the context of this point of correspondence it is not easy to understand John's redactional activity if he were following Luke, for his version introduces an inexplicable action on the part of the woman[13]. The most remarkable agreements are verbal in nature, and exist between Mark and John in B.3., C.2, D.3, D.5, and D.7. Again, however, the large quantity of points at which the

---

11 John 12:7 is difficult to understand due to its obscure construction – cf. MHT, 1:175; Barrett, *John*, 414.
12 See the discussion below, chapter 8.III.B.
13 That a woman would wipe a man's feet with her hair as recorded by John and Luke would be regarded as a disgraceful act, explicable only in view of the woman's shock and overwhelming gratitude – a detail not included in John's version. See Jeremias, *Parables*, 126. Also, a quite unexpected, novel feature is added: the woman in John's account wipes away the ointment. In Luke it is the wetness from her tears that she wipes away.

Markan and Johannine texts diverge demands a plausible explanation before we can accept the hypothesis that John is directly dependent on the Markan *Vorlage*.

In his treatment of the traditions, Bailey insists on linguistic grounds that we can be absolutely certain that John knew the Gospels of Mark and Luke. In conflating the two traditions, however, John introduced into his own text two problems: (A) it is inexplicable that Mary would wipe the ointment from Jesus' feet; and (B) Mary does not come as a repentant sinner in John, so the use of her hair in place of a towel is enigmatic.

> The only explanation of these difficulties is that they stem from John's having purposely and carefully combined the two accounts of the anointing as they appear in the present gospels of Mark and Luke, though the combination brought with it a striking unevenness[14].

What would motivate John to progress in this way? According to Bailey, because John is now approaching the account of Jesus' passion, an area where the traditions were "unusually early crystallized", he is more dependent on the Synoptics here than in earlier portions of his Gospel. Bailey's explanation is hardly convincing, for we might expect that an evangelist who molded his traditions to his own interests and style throughout his Gospel, as John has done, can hardly be credited with "purposely and carefully" combining these two traditions *in order to create problems*. Moreover, Bailey has overlooked the fact that Luke's account of the anointing is not within his passion narrative, so John would not have been under the compulsion Bailey describes. Still further, if John had felt the need to stick more closely to the Synoptic Gospels in the passion narrative, how can we explain his account of the Last Supper — a scene so radically different from that in the Synoptics?

Like Bailey, Barrett believes John's account is drawn from Mark's and Luke's, but he suggests that John was also dependent on a third, non-canonical source. He is of the opinion that the names of Lazarus, Martha, and Mary may have been added by the Fourth Evangelist. According to Barrett, John opts for the anointing of Jesus' head in order to avoid the crude messianic connotations of the Markan text, in spite of the unintelligibility of the "wiping" thus introduced. The omission of the reference to the act of the woman being remembered wherever the gospel is proclaimed may be due to its having been replaced by the metaphoric use of the scent that filled the room. Barrett draws attention to a further confusing note — that regarding the anointing for burial of Jesus' body. John provides his own narrative of the anointing of the corpse (19:38—42), and thus does

---

14 Bailey, *Traditions*, 3; cf. pp. 1—5.

not need Mark's anticipatory anointing. That it is mentioned, albeit in abbreviated form, is due to his continuing to follow his Markan source[15].

Barrett's hypothesis, while an advancement over Bailey's, is not without its problems. First, Jesus' messiahship is not unimportant to the Fourth Evangelist (cf. 1:41; 4:25–26; 9:22; 11:27; 20:31[!]), so it is unclear what Barrett has in mind when he declares that John is unwilling to take over Mark's "crude reference" to the anointing of Jesus as Messiah. Closely related, it is not altogether clear why we should think Mark 14:3–9 would have been understood by John as a messianic anointing[16], if indeed John knew the Markan account. Second, if John deliberately followed Luke in the anointing of Jesus' feet, thus omitting significant details from his Markan and Lukan sources (e.g. the kissing of Jesus' feet and the wetting of his feet with the woman's hair — both in Luke), why did he not also omit the problematic wiping of his feet with her hair?

Again, if John is capable of omitting some parts of Luke's and Mark's stories, why include the reference to Jesus' burial at all, since it is inconsistent with his own story line? This problem is heightened since, according to Barrett's source hypothesis, the reference to burial has been transposed from the Markan sequence by the Fourth Evangelist. Obviously, then, John was not slavishly following his Markan source. Fourth, the theory whereby the metaphoric spreading of the scent replaces the remembrance of the woman's deed wherever the gospel is preached throughout the world is weakened by the fact that the Rabbinic parallels cited by Barrett are all late (as Barrett admits). On the other hand, if John had a pre-Markan tradition before him, and if Mark was the originator of his 14:9, this would explain his omission of this detail. Fifth, and most important, since Barrett recognizes that John uses material *in addition to* the Synoptics in this pericope, no real reason exists to postulate John's use of the Synoptics at all! The points of correspondence could be explained in terms of common tradition.

Finally, we may note the attempt of Sabbe to explain John's pericope as a rewriting of the Markan and Lukan accounts[17]. His discussion is set in the midst of his treatment of the relationship between John 13 and the Synoptic accounts of the Last Supper. He observes "an obvious parallelism" between the stories of the anointing and of the footwashing:

---

15 Barrett, *John*, 410–415.
16 See below, chapter 8.II.B.
17 Sabbe, "Footwashing", 298–302.

12:2	δεῖπνον	13:2, 4
12:3	λαβών, λαβοῦσα	13:4
12:3 (11:2)	τοὺς πόδας	13:5,6,8,10,12,14
12:3 (11:2)	ἐκμάσσω	13:5
12:5, 6, 8	Judas's "interest" in the poor	13:29
12:6	Judas's possession of τὸ γλωσσόκομον	13:29

The parallelism of the actions of the washing and anointing leads Sabbe to regard them as two components of the one symbolic action (cf. Matt 6:17; Ruth 3:3; 2 Kgs 12:20). He then suggests that the Johannine redaction of the anointing in 12:3 can be explained only as an abbreviation of Luke 7:38, where the two actions — anointing and washing — occur in tandem. In the two scenes — John 12 and 13 — we see (1) an analogous reaction from, and similar role played by, Judas, (2) an analogous perspective on Jesus' death, and (3) analogous chronological introductions.

Sabbe then asserts that Luke's version of the anointing is only a reworking of the Markan, and that the Johannine is a redactional elaboration dependent on the Markan and Lukan stories. What we find missing in Sabbe's essay is any explanation of *why* Luke and John would have redacted their source(s) as they must have under his thesis. While Sabbe has put forth an interesting case for the parallelism of the stories of the anointing and footwashing, his further arguments do no more than indicate that Mark, Luke, and John shared a common basis for their individual accounts. Nowhere does he offer suggestions for why Luke would have so drastically altered the Markan tradition; moreover, his assumption that John's version "implies" the washing (wetting) of Jesus' feet read in Luke finds no support whatsoever in the Johannine text. This detail must be imported from Luke by Sabbe, for John has not done so. Hence, Sabbe's case fails to convince.

Any hypothesis that posits Mark and/or Luke as the source(s) for John's portrayal of Jesus' anointing must account for John's redactional activity under that hypothesis — his conflation of his sources, his omission of numerous details, and his unnecessary introduction of inconsistencies within the story itself and within the Gospel read as a whole. This has not been done. Admittedly, the verbal correspondences between Mark and John are significant. Nevertheless, the variations, of which there are many, must also be allowed their due weight. Hence, it seems most probable that in constructing his account of Jesus' anointing John drew on a source which itself reflected cross-fertilization between the traditions represented by the Gospels of Luke and Mark.

B. John 13:1–30 (Matt 26:14–35; Mark 14:10–31; Luke 22:3–30)

Undoubtedly, these four texts are intended to describe the same meal, Jesus' Last Supper. Superficially, this is evident not only in the position the scene holds in the narrative sequence of the four Gospels, but also from its immediate relation to the pronouncement of the betrayal of Judas. Additional mention must be made of the following points of agreement: the presence of chronological introductions; the service-motif, shared by Luke and John; the prediction of Peter's denial; the table-talk, found in Luke and, more extensively, in John; and a common perspective on the divine purpose behind Jesus' passion. There are, however, important points of divergence. To name the most obvious, John is alone in reporting the scene of the washing of the disciples' feet by Jesus, and in omitting the reports of the preparation of the Passover and the eucharistic words of Jesus.

Johannine stylistic features are found throughout 13:1—30[18], so we can speak confidently of characteristic Johannine redaction here, but of what sort of redaction? Has John built this passage from a Synoptic foundation, from other source material, or perhaps through some combination of both?

We may observe at the outset that John 13:1—30 consists of two stories set in the context of the Last Supper: vv 1—20 report the washing of the disciples' feet, while vv 21—30 record the betrayal announcement. The latter story is intimately related with the former both by the meal references in 13:2, 23, 26, and by the anticipatory and transitional elements in 13:10—11, 18—20. Of course, properly speaking, the Johannine meal scene stretches through the end of chapter 17; these 30 verses have been selected for comparative purposes only.

Alleging that two, conflicting interpretations are given the footwashing, a number of scholars have regarded vv 1—20 as a composite of traditions or a combination of a traditional interpretation with that of the evangelist[19]. Indeed, Bailey regards this as proof that John did not freely compose the story out of Luke 22:27 (as some scholars have held[20]), but drew from pre-Johannine tradition[21]. It may be granted that the text provides two interpretations of the action — the one symbolic and efficacious and the other exemplary, but these two are not mutually exclusive. As Dunn has rightly observed:

> The union of the two interpretations in the complete presentation is neither artificial nor unexpected, but is entirely of a piece with one particular strand of imitatio Christi which appears both elsewhere in John's writing and in other New Testament books[22].

---

18 Cf. Sabbe, "Footwashing", esp. pp. 283—287, 292; Max Wilcox, "The Composition of John 13:21—30", in *Neotestamentica et Semitica*, 143—156.
19 See the surveys in Sabbe, "Footwashing", 279—283; Georg Richter, "Die Fusswaschung John 13, 1—20", in *Studien*, 48—55.
20 So, e.g., Strauss, *Jesus*, 625; Barrett, *John*, 436.
21 Bailey, *Traditions*, 36—37.
22 James D. G. Dunn, "The Washing of the Disciples' Feet in John 13:1—20". *ZNW* 61 (1970) 249. Cf. Barrett, *John*, 443.

Examples of this phenomenon may be found in John 12:23—26 and, to a lesser degree, in 15:12—13. Of course, this is not to belittle the literary-critical problems in the Johannine version of the Last Supper[23], but only to point out that the presence of two interpretations of the footwashing is not a clear indication of the use of a source or sources by the evangelist.

There is therefore at least a *prima facie* chance that along with this whole scene both interpretations are the literary creation of John, based perhaps on the Synoptic Gospels. In order to support or deny this possibility, a point-by-point consideration of the evidence is imperative.

Sabbe, whose apparent purpose is to maximize every possible point of contact between the Synoptic and Johannine Gospels, first draws attention to the chronological introduction to the Johannine Supper as suggestive of his dependence on the Synoptic form of the narrative[24]. To be sure, the mere fact that John records a chronological reference has its Synoptic counterparts (Matt 26:2, 17; Mark 14:1, 12; Luke 22:1, 7). However, the content of his reference (13:1; cf. 19:14) actually contradicts the Synoptic chronology[25]! According to the Synoptic Gospels, the Last Supper happened on the night of the Passover, while John records that it took place prior to the Passover. Geldenhuys, along with others, has argued valiantly that πρὸ δὲ ἑορτῆς τοῦ πάσχα (13:1) should be read with εἰδώς only, and not as an introductory note defining the chronological setting for Jesus' supreme act of love[26]. More probable, however, is that the introductory clause complements the main verb (cf. 6:22; 13:3).

Three basic explanations for this conflict have been voiced: (1) John preserves the correct chronology; (2) the Synoptics are correct, but John

---

23 A helpful list of, and introduction to, these difficulties is provided by Schnackenburg, *John*, 3:7—15. Cf. also Richter, "Fusswaschung", 250—255.
24 Sabbe, "Footwashing", 287. Our analysis will interact with Sabbe's at several specific points, but here we can note a few more general problems with his approach. (A) Without exception, the points of convergence he notes prove to be at best ambiguous pointers to Johannine dependence on the Synoptics, and at worst irrelevant. (B) At some points, he tries to demonstrate Johannine dependence with reference to theological motifs that prove to be of special interest to the Fourth Evangelist regardless of the source-question, or to common themes not peculiar to the Synoptic accounts. The presence of ὥρα in John 13:1, which he regards as a reminiscence of Luke 22:14, is a case in point. (C) In fishing for verbal agreements he casts his net so wide that his results are open to question. For example, he supposes ὁ κύριος in 13:13—14 to have its origin in the Synoptic accounts of Jesus' entry into Jerusalem. (D) Some parallels are considered much too superficially, when a closer examination might have suggested some other theory of origins – such as where both Mark and John refer to Ps 41:9. (E) He completely fails to account for the continuing influence of oral tradition.
25 See "Table 4: The Chronology of the Last Supper", in Marshall, *Last Supper*, 184—185. On this problem, see Jeremias, *Eucharistic Words*, 16—26; Geldenhuys, *Luke*, 649—670; Marshall, *Last Supper*, 66—75; Brown, *John*, 2:555—556; Barrett, *John*, 48—51; Annie Jaubert, *The Date of the Last Supper* (Staten Island: Alba House, 1965).
26 Geldenhuys, *Luke*, 657—660. See also Jeremias, *Eucharistic Words*, 80.

has revised the Synoptic chronology for theological reasons; and (3) both are correct, but are based on different calendars. If either (1) or (3) is correct, there is no indicator here that John must have known the Synoptic form of the Supper traditon. As for (2), it could be argued that the Synoptics present the accurate record without the additional argument that John knew and deliberately revised the Synoptic chronology, for he could have gained his reference by means of an alternative tradition. Moreover, if John were familiar with the Synoptics, we can assume his "community"[27] shared his knowledge. With this in mind it is not easy to credit the evangelist with deliberately altering this important detail, knowingly introducing a contradiction into the tradition — an action which would have resulted in confusion among, and elicited hostile reaction from, his intended readers. Therefore, the chronological reference with which John's narrative of the Last Supper opens does not speak for dependence on the Synoptics, but may well be taken as evidence to the contrary.

The remainder of vv 1—3 is very much Johannine in style and content. Two points are worthy of note. First, ἦλθεν αὐτοῦ ἡ ὥρα may be reminiscent of Luke 22:14: ἐγένετο ἡ ὥρα[28], but as it picks up a major theme of the structure of the Johannine Gospel[29], there is no inherent reason for crediting the Synoptic parallel with providing the inspiration for its appearance here. Set in the midst of elements of Johannine interpretation, it too may be Johannine. A note about the reference to the devil (v 2) will come in our discussion of v 27. Second, δεῖπνον (v 2) is unparalleled in the Synoptic accounts of the Last Supper, but is read in the context of the Lord's Supper in 1 Cor 11:20, 21. This may be taken as a hint (but no more) that John's narrative is related to a non-Synoptic-like eucharistic tradition[30].

Following these introductory verses, John launches into a description of the footwashing itself. This is an appropriate place to point out three glaring discrepancies between the Synoptic and Johannine narratives: John records no preparation for the Passover and no eucharistic words, and the Synoptics make no mention of footwashing. These are divergences of monumental significance for they strike at the core of the respective narratives. Hence, it is necessary that we look at each in more detail.

---

27 With this reference to "community" we mean no more than that the author of the Fourth Gospel was a practicing Christian associated with more or less like-minded Christians in worship, fellowship, and mission.
28 So Sabbe, "Footwashing", 289.
29 Cf. 2:4; 7:6, 8, 30; 8:20; 12:23, 27; 17:1; Wilcox, "Composition", 144; Dunn, *Unity and Diversity*, 75.
30 So also Wilcox, "Composition", 144. Cf. C. H. Dodd, *Historical Tradition in the Fourth Gospel* (Cambridge: Cambridge University, 1963) 63.

Trocmé, whose particular interest is in demonstrating that John knew a pre-canonical passion story similar to that in the Synoptics, has argued that John knew the story of the preparation episode, but omitted it for editorial reasons[31]. He reasons that John, in his concern to portray Jesus as the Paschal Lamb, would have suppressed this, the only feature connecting the Last Supper with the Passover Feast. As is readily evident, this view is closely linked with that considered above in which John's chronology was alleged to reflect a purposeful departure from the Synoptic timetable. Thus, it must overcome the same obstacle noted there — namely, it can only account for John's redaction once dependence on the Synoptics is assumed; it cannot demonstrate that dependence. Moreover, Trocmé has overstated the evidence when he refers to the preparation scene as "the only feature in tradition that connected the Last Supper with the Passover Meal". In fact, even without a recounting of this episode in John's Gospel, Jeremias can point to six features identifying the Last Supper as a Passover Meal, and his list is not exhaustive. To be sure, not all of his points are equally convincing[32], but their cumulative weight raises doubts about Trocmé's thesis.

Sabbe, on the other hand, suggests that John has referred to the Synoptic account of the preparation for the Passover, though in a veiled way[33]. He recognizes the following allusions: (A) the Johannine meal, like that of the Synoptics, may be a Paschal Meal; (B) δεῖπνον (13:2, 4) may have its origin in Luke's μετὰ τὸ δειπνῆσαι (22:20); (C) ἀναπίπτω is employed by both John (13:25) and Luke (22:14); (D) Peter and the beloved disciple appear first in 13:23–24 — possibly inspired by the introduction of Peter

---

31 Trocmé, *Passion*, 40.
32 Jeremias, *Eucharistic Words*, 41–84. Of the 14 features listed by Jeremias pointing to the conclusion that the Last Supper was a Passover meal, 6 are found in John's account. (1) It took place in Jerusalem. (3) It happened at night. (5) Jesus and his disciples were reclining at the table. (6) The Supper was eaten in a state of levitical purity. (10) John 13:29 records that some thought Judas was to make last-minute purchases — a plausible action on the night of the Passover. (11) John 13:29 records that some thought Judas was to give something to the poor — a customary action on the night of the Passover. There is no reason to limit the sense of νύξ to a symbolic nature, as does Eduard Schweizer (*The Lord's Supper according to the New Testament* [Philadelphia: Fortress, 1967] 30). However, "reclining at the table" (5) loses its force in view of the many times the practice is mentioned in the Gospels, and in view of its wider usage in numerous festive occasions and not only at the Passover. Jeremias's exposition of 13:10 (6) is doubtful. As for (10) and (11), Schweizer's insistence that 13:29 is used as a literary device by the evangelist (*Lord's Supper*, 31; also, Schnackenburg, *John*, 3:36) is inconsequential. Even if it is a literary device and not historical, it still speaks against Trocmé's theory; moreover, Marshall (*Last Supper*, 60-61) has observed that even a literary device must be convincing to the readers. (See further Marshall's identification of the Last Supper as a Passover – *Last Supper*, 57–66). A feature not noted by Jeremias, but which may suggest a Passover setting for the Supper, is the reference to "dipping the morsel" into a common bowl (13:26).
33 Sabbe, "Footwashing", 287–289.

and John in Luke 22:8; (E) Jesus' foreknowledge in 13:1, 3 could reflect the foresight accorded him in Mark 14:16; Luke 22:13; and (F) the reference to "the hour" in 13:1 might recall Luke 22:14. So, "as in Lk 22, 14 when the time of his passion arrived, Jesus organized a farewell meal with his disciples"[34].

The speculative nature of these alleged points of contact is clearly evident. We have already mentioned (B) and (F) above; and, while it is possible that (D), (E), and (F) all stem from the Synoptic tradition, they all reflect special Johannine themes and this renders their use as evidence here rather dubious. Sabbe may well be correct in ascribing Passover features to the Johannine meal (A), but if John had known the Synoptics and had desired to portray this meal as a Passover, it is not clear why he would have omitted the two most obvious indications of the Paschal nature of the Last Supper — the preparation and the eucharistic words. With the weight of these objections, the common use of $ἀναπίπτω$ (C) cannot be said to be consequential, especially since (1) John is responsible for 5 of the 12 appearances of the verb in the NT (Matt — 1x; Mark — 2x; Luke — 4x), (2) John uses the verb to signify "to lean back" whereas in Luke it suggests the idea of "to recline at a meal", and (3) the two evangelists use the term in different contexts.

From these observations we may conclude that the Last Supper in John may have been intended as a celebration of the Passover, but we see no basis for claiming that this idea originates for the Fourth Evangelist with the Synoptic Gospels. Given John's redactional freedom, which far outdistances that of the Third Evangelist, the possibility that he knew the story of the preparation of the Passover cannot be ruled out completely. Yet, it must also be said that thus far there is no hard evidence for a conclusion favoring Johannine dependence on the Synoptic Gospels.

Had John known one or more of the Synoptic Gospels, why would he have neglected to report the eucharistic words of Jesus? This way of posing the question draws attention to John's omission of a piece of Synoptic tradition, but in fact the question is just as valid if he did not know any of the first three Gospels. On the basis of the early tradition recorded in 1 Cor 11:23—25, other allusions to the Supper in the NT, and the fragmentary and metaphorical allusions to the eucharistic words in John 6:48—58, there can be little doubt that the sayings were widespread in early Christianity and that John had some familiarity with them. As a number of scholars have recognized, the omission of an explicit mention of this tradition in John's passion narrative is likely due to the concern of the Fourth Evangel-

---

34 Sabbe, "Footwashing", 289.

ist against an excessive sacramentalism; thus, the deletion should be regarded as a manifestation of John's critical positon *vis-à-vis* the Lord's Supper[35]. In any case, that John's Gospel lacks a record of the Words of Institution cannot be regarded as proof that he did not know the Synoptics, nor can his implicit reference to the eucharistic tradition in John 6, in and of itself, be taken as proof that he had before him a Synoptic account. In both instances, the existence of a tradition apart from the testimony of the Synoptic Gospels complicates any attempt to reconstruct John's sources and redactional procedures.

Nevertheless, a closer look at John 6:48—58 is worthwhile. Obviously, this text includes fragments of eucharistic origin, as indicated by its accumulation of eucharistic terminology — e.g. ἄρτος, ἐσθίω, δίδωμι, ὑπέρ, πίνω, and αἷμα μου. Herein lie a few clues that steer us away from regarding the Synoptics as the basis for John's redaction, and point strongly to John's dependence on the sort of tradition employed by Paul.

First, John is capable of using σῶμα, the term used for "body" in Matt 26:26; Mark 14:22; Luke 22:19; 1 Cor 11:24, but here he has σάρξ. Interestingly, both Greek words could have been used in translations of an original Aramaic בשר (בשרא); instead of following the Synoptics here, then, John may be reproducing a parallel but variant translation of an earlier, Semitic original[36]. Second, except for the one Matthean usage of the word in 24:38, τρώγω is found in the NT only 5 times — all in John's Gospel. Moreover, the verb is read only here (6:54, 56, 57, 58) and in the setting of the Last Supper (13:18). This alone is enough to suggest the relation of the two texts and it is not implausible that for the Fourth Evangelist the word originated in the eucharistic tradition. This theory might explain the peculiar use of τρώγω in the quotation of Ps 41:9 in 13:18[37]. Third, like 1 Cor 10:16—17 and 11:27—29, so in John 6, eucharistic traditon has not been employed in the form of a set quotation, but as a common, generally recognized, experiential and theological basis from which to argue a point. That is, John must have been aware of the "homiletical"

---

35 Cf. Rudolf Bultmann, *Theology of the New Treatment*, 2 vols. (New York: Charles Scribner's Sons, 1951) 2:59 (It is often said that Bultmann viewed John's position as that of an antisacramentalist, but consider his own conclusion: "It is therefore permissible to say that though in John there is no direct polemic against the sacraments, his attitude toward them is nevertheless critical or at least reserved"); Barrett, *John*, 82—85; Dunn, *Unity and Diversity*, 168—171; Marshall, *Last Supper*, 133—139; R. Wade Paschal, "Sacramental Significance and Physical Imagery in the Gospel of John", *TynB* 32 (1981) 161—168. Contra Jeremias (*Eucharistic Words*, 136), who attributes this omission to John's desire to "protect the sacred text". Additional positions are listed and critiqued in Schnackenburg, *John*, 3:42—44.

36 Cf. Ign. *Rom*. 7.3: ἄρτον θεοῦ θέλω, ὅ ἐστιν σάρξ Ἰησοῦ χριστοῦ, τοῦ ἐκ σπέρματις Δαυείδ, καὶ πόμα θέλω τὸ αἷμα αὐτοῦ, ὅ ἐστιν ἀγάπη ἄφθαρτος. See also, *idem, Phld*. 4.1; *Smyrn*. 7.1.

37 See also Peder Borgen, *Bread from Heaven* (Leiden: E. J. Brill, 1965) 93.

use of the eucharistic tradition, witnessed in Paul and, later, in Ignatius (cf. *Trall.* 6.1–2; *Rom.* 7.3) — a use that goes beyond the kind of straightforward recording one finds in Matthew, Mark, and Luke.

Fourth, we read verbal and, more importantly, conceptual parallels between John 6 and 1 Cor 10:1–10. As for the verbal parallels, one may observe the following: οἱ πατέρες ἡμῶν (1 Cor 10:1; ὑμῶν in John 6:31, 49), ἔφαγον, and ἐν τῇ ἐφήμῳ. God's provision is described by Paul and John in analogous ways — πνευματικὸν βρῶμα in Paul, τὸ μάννα and ὁ ἄρτος ἐκ τοῦ οὐρανοῦ in John. Also, while Paul uses βρῶμα and πόμα, John employs βρῶσις and πόσις. Finally, in place of Paul's various descriptions of the death of "our ancestors" — "scattered in the desert" (10:5), "fell down dead" (10:8), "killed by snakes" (10:9), and "killed by the death angel" (10:10) — John has the more simple epitaph, "they died". Both Paul and John appear to be combating an exaggerated sacramentalism, and both make use of a midrash-type argument, the point of which is the ideal picture of God's provision at the Exodus as it came to be understood in contemporary speculation about the life-giving properties of the new manna in the Messianic Age[38]. Though in different ways, both Paul and John show that the source of divine provision is Christ (Paul: ἡ πέτρα δὲ ἦν ὁ χριστός; John: Jesus is ὁ ἄρτος [τῆς ζωῆς] [ὁ καταβὰς ἐκ τοῦ οὐρανοῦ] [ὁ ζῶν ἐκ τοῦ οὐρανοῦ καταβάς]), and both, again in different ways, assert that salvation-life is made secure not by participating in the sacraments as such, but *by continual participation in Christ and his death*[39].

There are, therefore, far-reaching similarities between the respective arguments provided by John and Paul. Both authors, without any cross-fertilization of Christian tradition, might have taken over this argument directly from Jewish haggadah[40]. In view of the correspondences we have noted, however, one should not rule out the perhaps more likely possibility that the tradition used by John and Paul had already been "baptized" into Christian usage and was circulating in Christian circles[41]. Alternatively, one might conjecture that Paul was the originator of this application of

---

38 Cf. *2 Apoc. Bar.* 29.8; R. Meyer, "Μάννα", in *TDNT*, 4:463–465; Wainwright, *Eucharist*, 22.

39 That is, John 6 is not about the Lord's Supper *per se*; rather, Lord's Supper language is employed by the evangelist to communicate his point about life through participation in Jesus' death. See James D. G. Dunn, "John VI – A Eucharistic Discourse?", *NTS* 17 (1970–71) 337; Caird, *Language*, 55–56; Marshall, *Last Supper*, 134–137; Paschal, "Sacramental Symbolism", 166.

40 Cf. Geza Vermes, "He Is the Bread: Targum Neofiti Exodus 16:15", in *Neotestamentica et Semitica*, 256–263; Vermes, asserts that a comparison of *Tg. Neof.* Exod 16:15 and the exegesis found in 1 Cor 10:4 and John 6 indicates how NT authors took over Jewish haggadah and made use of it in the creation of theology (263). He does not take up the possibility of cross-influence among Christian writers.

41 "As the exegesis in 1 Cor. 10.4 is not typically Pauline, and Paul does not otherwise draw positive connections with the time of Moses . . . we must assume that this exegesis comes from non-Pauline Greek-speaking Jewish Christianity" (Hengel, *Son of God*, 73).

Jewish interpretation to Christ, and that John was influenced by Paul's use of the tradition as it became more widely known. In any case, it is certain that John was influenced by a tradition more closely aligned with that found in Paul than that in the Synoptic Gospels.

As for the footwashing itself, the absence of this scene from the Synoptics has raised doubts about its historicity, and some have regarded it as a Johannine creation fashioned on the basis of Luke 22:27[42]. Both texts present a role reversal, casting Jesus in the part of a servant, and the Johannine scene is consonant with the evangelist's preference for symbolic acts[43]. Literary-critical analyses have largely dealt with the source problems presented by 13:1–3, 6–20; however, our special concern lies with the brief recounting of the footwashing itself, and not with the introduction to, or interpretation of, the narration. Did the Fourth Evangelist create the episode? In view of the correspondences mentioned above, one must allow for the possibility that John, inspired by the Lukan text, is responsible for the origination of this story. However, appeal to the testimony of four lines of evidence reveals the improbability of this hypothesis.

First, as Dodd has reminded us, the tradition of Jesus' servanthood is well-attested in the NT.

> We find it variously formulated, in aphorism, in dialogue, in extended passages of combined narrative and dialogue where the whole setting gives point to the particular saying, in catechetical maxims, and, finally, in the kind of credal hymn ... which we have in Phil. ii. To these manifold forms under which this fundamental *Lehrstück* might be presented we must now add what we may call the 'exemplary story,' as we have it in John xiii.4–17[44].

In stating his conclusion thus, Dodd has gone beyond his evidence, for the diversity and pervasiveness of the motif does not in itself disprove either Johannine creation of the text or John's dependence on Luke's Gospel. Nevertheless, Dodd has shown the absurdity of drawing a direct line from the Third Gospel to Johannine redaction simply on the basis of the use of a common theme.

Second, the key term in Luke's portrayal of Jesus as servant is διακονέω, a word conspicuously absent from the Johannine picture. In fact, if John were basing his story on Luke's Gospel, we might have expected him to have Jesus "wait on tables", for this is the sense of the term in Luke 22:27 (cf. 12:37; John 12:2). That John shows Jesus washing his disciples' feet is an indication that John has another, though not contradictory, idea of "service" in view[45].

---

42 See, e.g., Strauss, *Jesus*, 625; Barrett, *John*, 436.
43 On these arguments, see the remarks in Lindars, *John*, 447; Schnackenburg, *John*, 3:39–40.
44 Dodd, *Historical Tradition*, 62; cf. pp. 60–63.
45 Cf. Schnackenburg, *John*, 3:41; Dodd, *Historical Tradition*, 60 n.3.

Third: nevertheless, it is not inconceivable that the Lukan and Johannine portraits stem from a similar traditional basis, though we need not go so far as to follow Bailey's suggestion that Luke knew the very tradition taken over by John[46]. Special mention is due here of the logion in Luke 12:37b: "Truly I say to you that he (the master) will gird himself, cause them (the servants) to recline at the table, and coming to them, he will serve ($\delta\iota\alpha\kappa o\nu\epsilon\omega$) them". The saying is pre-Lukan and may well be authentic[47]; its focal point is the behavior of the $\kappa\upsilon\rho\iota o\varsigma$ at the messianic banquet. It, along with Jesus' self-reference in Luke 22:27, suggests an occasion when Jesus acted as a servant, and may reflect a tradition in which the image of Jesus' servanthood belonged to the Last Supper episode[48]. It is therefore likely that this motif surfaced independently, and in variant ways, in the Third and Fourth Gospels.

Fourth, the pre-Johannine character of the narrative of the footwashing is indicated by traces of Semitic influence in the account[49]. Worthy of special mention on this score is that 13:5 includes the only incidence of the auxiliary $\mathring{\alpha}\rho\chi o\mu\alpha\iota$ (reflecting Semitic usage) in the Gospel of John[50]. Taken together, these four factors render most improbable the thesis that in narrating the footwashing scene John was dependent on the Third Gospel.

As for the remainder of the story of the footwashing, the only other segment demanding our attention here is the citation of Ps 41:9 (41:10 MT; 40:10 LXX) in 13:18, a possible parallel to Mark 14:18. Considering first the quotation in John's Gospel, we may mention at the outset Freed's observation that the introductory formula — $\mathring{\iota}\nu\alpha\ \mathring{\eta}\ \gamma\rho\alpha\phi\mathring{\eta}\ \pi\lambda\eta\rho\omega\theta\mathring{\eta}$ — appears elsewhere in the NT only in John 17:12 and 19:24, and should be regarded as Johannine[51].

The quotation itself corresponds neither to the LXX or the MT, though it seems more closely related to the latter. For comparative purposes we may list the passages together, including also the relevant text from Qumran.

---

46 Bailey, *Traditions*, 36–37. Cf. Roloff, "Anfänge", 60.
47 Bultmann, (*History*, 118, 205) regards the saying as a community formulation due to its metaphorical shape. However, J. Ramsey Michaels (*Servant and Son: Jesus in Parable and Gospel* [Atlanta: John Knox, 1981] 83–84) suggests that such formulations lie at the root of Jesus' proclamation. The saying employs $\mathring{\alpha}\mu\mathring{\eta}\nu$, a term Luke is not likely to have introduced on his own (see above, chapter 3.V.C., on 22:17), and betrays signs of Semitic influence – cf. Black, *Aramaic Approach*, 59; Jeremias, *Parables*, 54 n.18; Marshall, *Gospel of Luke*, 536–537.
48 Cf. Lindars, *John*, 447; Schnackenburg, *John*, 3:41; Roloff, "Anfänge", 55–58; Temple, "Two Traditions", 80–81.
49 Cf. Bultmann, *John*, 466 n.4; Schnackenburg, *John*, 3:17–18; Black, *Aramaic Approach*, 125.
50 See MHT, 2:455.
51 Edwin D. Freed, *Old Testament Quotations in the Gospel of John* (Leiden: E. J. Brill, 1965) 89. Cf. Sabbe, "Footwashing", 290.

John 13:18: ὁ τρώγων μου τὸν ἄρτον ἐπῆρεν ἐπ' ἐμὲ τὴν πτέρναν αὐτοῦ.
Ps 40:10 (LXX): ὁ ἐσθίων ἄρτους μου, ἐμεγάλυνεν ἐπ' ἐμὲ πτερνισμόν.
Ps 41:10 (MT): אוכל לחמי הגדיל עלי עקב.
1QH5.23–24: א(ם או)כלי לחמי עלי הגדילו עקב.

Ὁ τρώγων recalls the earlier use of the verb in John 6 (see above) and parallels ὁ ἐσθίων (LXX) and אוכל (MT). We have mentioned hitherto the relative scarcity of the verb in the NT and we may now take note of the complete absence of the term in the Greek OT. Μετ' ἐμοῦ follows ὁ τρώγων in an impressive list of textual witnesses (p⁶⁶ א A D W Θ Ψ ƒ¹·¹³ M lat sy bo). It has been suggested that the Qumran text, which transposes the position of עלי, may witness to a variant Hebrew textual tradition that would have read "those who eat bread with me"[52], but this is highly speculative. Much more likely is that the longer Johannine text is a later assimilaton to the parallel in Mark 14:18[53], though the possibility of an original longer reading having been assimilated to the LXX text should not be overlooked.

Τὸν ἄρτον agrees in number with the MT (לחמי) against the LXX (ἄρτους). John's use of ἐπαίρω is a paraphrase of גדל, whereas the LXX rendering (μεγαλύνω) is more literal. Ἐπ' ἐμέ, read both in John and the LXX, is a faithful rendering of עלי. For "heel" (עקב), the LXX uses πτερνισμός — a word never found in the NT and only one other time in the LXX (4 Kgs 10:19), and John has πτέρνα — the usual word for "heel" in the NT (also found 11x in the NT). It is difficult to decide John's OT source, but it may be that he has given his own translation of the MT (or another Hebrew text), adapted to suit his own purpose[54].

The words ὁ ἐσθίων μετ' ἐμοῦ in Mark 14:18 have also been regarded as an allusion to the psalm[55]. Given the Markan context, these words may represent an OT reminiscence, in spite of the fact they find no strict parallel in either the MT or LXX. Nor does the absence of this allusion in the Matthean parallel speak decisively against the intention of an allusion by the Second Evangelist. Matthew may not have recognized the reference, or he may have considered it redundant in view of the similar wording in Mark

---

52 Moo, *OT – Passion*, 237.
53 Metzger, *Textual Commentary*, 240; Schnackenburg, *John*, 3:26.
54 Cf. Moo, *OT – Passion*, 239; Freed, *OT Quotations*, 92; Günter Reim, *Studien zur alttestamentlichen Hintergrund des Johannesevangeliums* (Cambridge: Cambridge University, 1974) 40.
55 So, e.g., Cranfield, *Mark*, 423; Taylor, *Mark*, 540; Moo, *OT – Passion*, 237 –238; Lohse, *Geschichte*, 45; Goppelt, *Typos*, 100; Reim, *Studien*, 41; Mohr, *Passion*, 171; Lothar Ruppert, *Jesus als der leidende Gerechte? Der Weg Jesu im Lichte eines alt- und zwischentestamentliche Motivs* (Stuttgart: Katholische, 1972) 50; Gnilka, *Mark*, 2:236–237; Pesch, *Mark*, 2:347–350; Lindars, *NT Apologetic*, 98; et al. Contra Schenke, *Stuiden*, 226.

14:20[56]. Nevertheless, it is worth asking (in view of Matthew's interest in drawing bridges from the OT to the passion narrative)[57] how it is that the Fourth Evangelist (if he were following the Markan narrative) but not the First (who certainly was following the Markan narrative) saw this passing reference and exploited it.

We may conclude that both John and Mark refer to Ps 41:9. In the light of this agreement the range of dissimilarities becomes all the more remarkable. There is, of course, first the obvious fact that whereas John quotes the psalm, Mark's text represents a mere allusion. This distinction is not particularly significant, however, for an implicit reference could easily have triggered an explicit one. Secondly, the reference is applied to two different sayings of Jesus. John's parallel to Mark 14:18 comes in 13:21, but there the text reads just as that in Matt 26:21. Third, Mark's terminology is closest to the LXX, while John's is nearer the MT. These points do not preclude the possibility that John received his inspiration from the Gospel of Mark, but they do weaken considerably the case for literary borrowing.

Finally, we must take note of the value of Ps 41:9 for primitive Christianity. Psalm 41 embraces a variety of language forms, and is best understood as a psalm of illness[58]. Our citation belongs to the central section of the psalm, wherein the lament of the sufferer is expanded. The peak of the lament comes in v 9: "Even my good friend, whom I trusted, who shared my bread, has lifted his heel against me". The greatest horror, then, is that one with whom the sufferer shared table fellowship now rejects or betrays[59] him[60]. Regarded as a "prophecy" by early Christians, this text explains the problem presented by Judas — the one chosen by Jesus, who shared table fellowship with Jesus, and yet became Jesus' betrayer. So valuable was this text that we would be naive to think that the Gospel of Mark was the only witness to it available at the time of John's writing. With the differences between the references of John and Mark aforementioned, this factor is a strong indication that the use of Ps 41:9 belongs to a fundamental tradition of interpretation of the events of Jesus' passion

---

56 In any case, this is no reason to regard the phrase in Mark as a gloss, as suggested in Taylor, *Mark*, 540; Cranfield, *Mark*, 423. For alternative explanations, see Gundry, *Matthew*, 526; Moo, *OT — Passion*, 238.

57 See above, chapter 2.II.F.

58 Cf. Sigmund Mowinckel, *The Psalms in Israel's Worship*, 2 vols. (Nashville: Abingdon, 1962) 2:1–9; followed by Peter C. Craigie, *Psalms 1–50* (Waco, Texas: Word, 1983) 319.

59 "To lift the heel" is a curious idiom, expressive of contempt and rejection. See the note in Craigie, *Psalms 1–50*, 319, 321; and the use of גדל in the psalms of lament (cf. R. Mosis, "גדל", *TDOT*, 2:405).

60 Cf. Magnus Ottosson, "אכל", in *TDOT*, 1:241; Moo, *OT — Passion*, 239.

whereby an explanation was provided for the Judas-problem. On this tradition, both the Second and Fourth Evangelists independently drew[61].

The second story found in our text from John 13 is the narration of the betrayal announcement and subsequent departure of Judas, embracing vv 21–30. Contact with the Synoptic tradition has been noted especially in John 13:21b (Matt 26:21b; Mark 14:18b) and 13:27 (Luke 22:3), and more generally in the shape and progression of the story line. Sabbe goes even further in asserting Johannine dependence. He thinks that *the whole passage* can be traced back to the Synoptics. By way of demonstrating the way in which he reaches this decision, it is worth quoting him at some length.

> The ἔβλεπον εἰς ἀλλήλους οἱ μαθηταὶ ἀπορούμενοι of v. 22a can perfectly be understood as a reminiscence of Lk 22,23a καὶ αὐτοὶ ἤρξαντο συζητεῖν πρὸς ἑαυτούς just as in Jn 13,22b ἀπορούμενοι περὶ τίνος λέγει ... reminds us of Lk 22,23b τὸ τίς ἄρα εἴη ἐξ αὐτῶν ὁ τοῦτο μέλλων πράσσειν. The last words are even recognizable in the prediction of Jn 6,71 οὗτος γὰρ ἔμελλεν παραδιδόναι αὐτόν, εἷς ἐκ τῶν δώδεκα. In the Synoptics the disciples in general begin to question one another whom Jesus meant; in John they do likewise, but some of them are identified as Peter and the Beloved Disciple and ask Jesus for information ... the repeated mention of Peter in Lk 22,8 (Peter and John!) and in the prediction of his denial of Lk 22,31 (and par. Mk 14,29; Mt 26,33) may have inspired Jn 13,24. The question can hardly be more clearly formulated than in Jn 13,25 κύριε, τίς ἐστιν, which is nothing but a paraphrase of Mk 14, 19; Mt 26,22 μήτι ἐγώ (εἰμε, κύριε)[62].

And this sort of reasoning continues for much of the narrative in question. Of course, this is not the only way to read the evidence, as demonstrated by Wilcox's essay on "The Composition of John 13:21–30"[63]. Wilcox is of the opinion that John and Mark reflect similar but not identical basic traditions. As we shall show, Wilcox has the better case.

The new section opens with two typically Johannine features: the linking formula ταῦτα εἰπών ('Ιησοῦς) (cf. 7:9; 9:6; 11:43; 13:21; 18:1; and the comparable use of τοῦτο εἰπών); and ἐταράχθη τῷ πνεύματι. The latter phrase is paralleled in 11:33 and 12:27 and, as in 12:27, is used here of Jesus' reaction when confronted with his painful fate. Barrett regards ταράσσω as a Johannine word[64]; however, it is likely that here, as in 12:27, the term is inspired by Ps 41:7 LXX. Μαρτυρέω (along with μαρτυρία) is also characteristic of John's interests. Verse 21b – ἀμὴν ἀμὴν λέγω ὑμῖν ὅτι εἷς ἐξ ὑμῶν παραδώσει με – is very close to Mark 14:18b (Mark has only one ἀμήν and adds ὁ ἐσθίων μετ' ἐμοῦ – on which, see above), but

---

61 See the similar remarks in Reim, *Studien*, 41; Wilcox, "Composition", 145; Moo, *OT – Passion*, 235–240; Lindars, *John*, 454; Brown, *John*, 2:571; Schnackenburg, *John*, 3:25–26. *Contra* Freed, *OT Quotations*, 92; Sabbe, "Footwashing", 290.
62 Sabbe, "Footwashing", 292; cf. pp. 292–293.
63 Wilcox, "Composition", 146–156.
64 Barrett, *John*, 425. Of the 17 times the verb appears in the NT, 6 are in the Gospel of John (5:7; 11:33; 12:27; 13:21; 14:1, 27). The term is absent from the other Johannine literature.

is even closer to Matt 26:21b (Matthew has only one ἀμήν, following Mark). The doubling of ἀμήν is characteristic of John (e.g. 1:51; 5:19, 24, 25; 6:26, 32, 47, 53; et al.); hence, we must conclude for the possibility that John is dependent on Mark or Matthew at this point, though the employment of Ps 41:9 in the betrayal scene independent of the Synoptics raises the alternative possibility of a separate, similar source for the whole betrayal-prediction scene.

The closest Synoptic parallel for v 22 is Luke 22:23. While each of the disciples in Matthew and Mark asks "Is it I?", in Luke and John the attention of each is turned on the others in the band of disciples. As Dodd has aptly remarked, "The sense is the same, the wording entirely different"[65].

With v 23 the Fourth Evangelist begins a sub-section of 3 verses (vv 23—25) with no real Synoptic parallel. This material introduces "the beloved disciple", unknown in the other Gospels, and carries further the move to identify explicitly the betrayer early on within the narrative, a tendency already manifest in Matt 26:15. Wilcox has argued that these verses may be of Johannine origin[66]; while this may be, they certainly reflect developing Christian tradition prior to John.

Verse 26 takes us back into the quadruple tradition (cf. Matt 26:23; Mark 14:20; Luke 22:21). Jesus' answer to the beloved disciple in John has its closest parallel in the comparable statements in Matthew and Mark, but the case for literary dependence is weak. The vocabulary is dissimilar and the actions described conflict with one another. Moreover, it is worth noting a peculiar construction in John's account: ἐκεῖνος ἐστιν ᾧ – that is, the resumptive pronoun following a relative pronoun. This phenomenon reflects Semitic influence and, while it is not unknown in Classical Greek, it may be of significance that it is found here in a saying of Jesus[67]. Caution should accompany the use of this evidence, however.

Verse 27 is another instance of agreement between Luke and John, in this case regarding the entry of Satan into Judas. This motif was anticipated in 13:2, but as it now stands it appears in divergent settings in the two Gospels. In Luke 22:3 we read εἰσῆλθεν δὲ σατανᾶς εἰς Ἰούδαν τὸν καλούμενον Ἰσκαριώτην within the report of Judas's arrangement with the chief priests. In John, τότε εἰσῆλθεν εἰς ἐκεῖνον ὁ σατανᾶς comes within the meal scene, following the betrayal prediction. In both, however, the "entry of Satan" is coupled with the treachery of Judas[68]. It is common to point out that σατανᾶς appears only here in the Fourth Gospel, where διάβολος

---

65 Dodd, *Historical Tradition*, 53.
66 Wilcox, "Compositon", 148–149, 156.
67 Black, *Aramaic Approach*, 100–101; BDF para. 297; MHT, 2:435; 3:46; 4:21.
68 Cf. Klein, "Die lukanische-johanneische Passionstradition", 164–165.

is the preferred designation. What is not so often emphasized in this context is that Luke, too, prefers διάβολος⁶⁹. This fact, together with Wilcox's observation that John's language and style are less polished than Luke's⁷⁰, must be seen as a strong argument in favor of a common source, probably written, utilized independently by the two. Most likely, the source placed the "entry of Satan" at the outset of the passion narrative, prior to the meal, as in Luke's account. John, then, took over the reference at a later point in order to emphasize the control and initiative of Jesus (only after Jesus identifies the betrayer is Satan "allowed" to enter into Judas), but preserved the point of the source by inserting τοῦ διαβόλου ἤδη βεβληκότος εἰς τὴν καρδίαν ἵνα παραδοῖ αὐτόν Ἰούδας Σίμωνος Ἰσκαριώτου in 13:2.

Verses 28–30 are peculiar to John. It is doubtful that νύξ has been taken over by John from Luke 22:53 because (A) the two scenes are distanced from one another both in the chronology of events and in the individual developments of the story by the two evangelists; (B) we have already argued that John was aware of a Supper-tradition akin to that in Paul — which included a reference to "the night he was betrayed" (1 Cor 11:23); and (C) John elsewhere shows his theological interest in the term (cf. 9:4; 11:10), so he would have needed no prompting from a Synoptic source to employ it here.

On the basis of the preceding considerations, we conclude that John's story of the prediction of the betrayal and ensuing departure of Judas has been constructed from material independent of the Synoptic Gospels. Recalling our earlier conclusion about the footwashing episode, we may now summarize for the whole of John 13:1–30 that the evidence through which we have sifted is best accounted for by a decision for John's independence from the Synoptic Gospels.

C. John 18:13–27 (Mark 14:53–72)

For this final "test case" for studying the relation of the Synoptics and John, we are not proposing a detailed literary-critical analysis of the relevant texts. Rather, we plan to inquire into the repercussions for our understanding of the literary relationship of John and Mark of the intercalation of Jesus' trial before the Jewish leaders and Peter's three-fold denial common to the two narratives. Not only have we to consider the general

---

69 The noun is used 5 times in the Third Gospel (10:18; 11:18; 13:16; 22:3, 31) and in every case comes from a pre-Lukan source. In his redaction of Mark, Luke omits Mark's reference to σατανᾶς in Mark 3:23 and 8:33, and changes it to διάβολος in 1:13 (Luke 4:2); 4:15 (8:12). Schramm (*Markus-Stoff*, 182–184) decides that the Lukan reference to Satan in 22:3 is drawn from "seiner Sondertradition". See above, chapter 3.III.
70 Wilcox, "Composition", 152.

phenomenon of the intercalation itself, but also the fact that the common use of this literary device has created an editorial seam in both accounts. That is, in both renditions, the story breaks off with Peter warming himself (Mark 14:54; John 18:18) in order to develop the scene of Jesus' trial (Mark 14:55–65; John 18:19–24), then resumes with Peter warming himself (Mark 14:66–67; John 18:25). A reasonable argument is that at one time in the history of the traditions, the story of Peter's denial and the account of Jesus' trial were not intertwined (cf. Luke), and their combination represents a desire to indicate simultaneity[71]. How is it that the respective accounts of Mark and John testify to the same phenomenon?

John R. Donahue has argued that the intercalation of the two stories is the product of Markan redaction, and that the parallel in the Fourth Gospel is due to John's direct dependence on the Markan narrative[72]. Of course, Donahue's case is strengthened by the general recognition of intercalation as a literary device characteristic of Markan redaction[73]. To facilitate a comparison, the two texts are juxtaposed in outline form below.

Mark 14	John 18
A. Jesus taken before the Sanhedrin (v 53).	A. Jesus taken before Annas (vv 13–14).
B. Peter follows Jesus into the courtyard of the high priest; he sits with the guards and warms himself at the fire (v 54),	B. Peter and "another disciple" follow Jesus into the courtyard of the high priest; they gain entry by the maid at the door; Peter denies Jesus for the first time; Peter stands with the guards and warms himself at the fire (vv 15–18).
A^1. Jesus questioned and condemned by, then mocked before the Sanhedrin (vv 55–56).	A^1. Jesus questioned by the high priest (vv 19–24).
B^1. Peter denies Jesus three times (vv 66–72).	B^1. Peter denies Jesus a second and third time (vv 25–27).

In both accounts, the "sandwich" pattern is A-B-A^1-B^1, and to this extent there is agreement. Any comparison of the two passages, however, will reveal a number of differences — not all of which consist in minor details[74]. We will mention only the more important. (A) In John, the party to whom Jesus is taken does not seem to include the whole assembly of the Sanhedrin, but only its convenor. (B) John apparently has access to a non-Markan tradition identifying Annas as the high priest[75]. Because of his

---

[71] See above, chapter 3.XIII; Brown, *John*, 2:837; Craig A. Evans, "'Peter Warming Himself': The Problem of an Editorial 'Seam'", *JBL* 101 (2, 1982) 245.
[72] John R. Donahue, *Are You the Christ? The Trial Narrative in the Gospel of Mark* (Missoula, Montana: Scholars, 1973) 58–63; idem, "Passion Traditions", 9–10. Cf. also Dewey, "Peter's Curse", 104–105; Norman Perrin, *The New Testament: An Introduction* (New York: Harcourt Brace Jovanovich, 1974) 229.
[73] See, e.g., 3:20–35; 5:21–43; (14:1–11?); Ernest Best, *Mark: The Gospel as Story* (Edinburgh: T. & T. Clark, 1983) 11; Kee, *Community*, 54–56.
[74] Cf. further, Dauer, *Passionsgeschichte*, 62–63, 66–99; Trocmé, *Passion*, 42; Bultmann, *John*, 641–643; Winter, *Trial*, 47–50.
[75] On which see below, chapter 8.VII.B.

attempt also to bring Caiaphas into the story, we may conclude that John believed his tradition to be historical. (C) John's narrative exhibits knowledge of a second disciple to whom hardly any significance is attached. (D) The interweaving of the two stories has left all three denials of Peter for the climactic finale in Mark, but John has the first separated from the others. (E) John's narrative mentions no false testimony against Jesus. (F) John's narrative presents a simplied version of the interrogation when compared with the Markan account (cf. John 10:22–39). (G) John appears to have possessed additional material which had it that Jesus was struck while demanding that valid testimony be brought by his accusers. (H) John's narrative records no verdict against Jesus. Appeal to John's theological agenda can hardly explain away all of these discrepencies.

Two additional factors strike at the root of Donahue's theory. First, while it is true that intercalation is a sign of Markan redaction, the present instance of this literary phenomenon is without parallel in Mark's Gospel. Elsewhere the pattern is not $A-B-A^1-B^1$, but simply $A-B-A^1$. Moreover, with reference to Greek romances, Evans has demonstrated the pattern of digression and resumption was relatively common in story-telling, both oral and written[76].

Second, in his examination of the comparable seams at John 18:18c/25a and Mark 14:54/67, Evans has drawn attention to the fact that the seam in John is very wooden and quite obvious, repeating key words with only a minimum of stylistic variation. By comparison, Mark's seam is less obvious and more polished, with only the barest repetition of words — and that in different cases. On the basis of his comparative analysis of these seams, he argues that one might justifiably assume Mark's use of John, improving the simplistic construction of the Johannine statements, rather than John's dependence on Mark[77].

Closely related to Evan's linguistic argument, we may draw further attention to the greater dramatic appeal of the Markan version, accomplished by placing the three denials in close sequence. It would seem more probable that a Markan-type sequence would develop from a Johannine-type than vice-versa.

For all these reasons, therefore, it seems best to support the hypothesis that for the two passages in question Mark and John independently drew on similar tradition, though we must allow that John, at least, was familiar with additional source material not found in the Markan parallel.

---

76 Evans, "Peter Warming Himself", 248–249.
77 Evans, "Peter Warming Himself", 246–247.

D. Conclusion

Thus we come to the close of our investigation of three "test cases" for a Johannine-Synoptic literary relationship in the passion narrative. We have examined three Johannine texts with their Synoptic counterparts — the anointing of Jesus, the Last Supper with the betrayal announcement, and the interwoven stories of Jesus' trial and Peter's denial. In each case we saw that the evidence did not support a direct literary relationship between the author of the Fourth Gospel and the other canonical Gospels. Our inquiry has underscored the complexity of developing Christian tradition and pointed to John's use of traditions sometimes more, sometimes less in common with, but never radically dissimilar to those reflected in the Synoptic narratives. In short, the passion narrative of the Gospel of John is related to, but not directly dependent on, the passion stories of the Gospels of Matthew, Mark, and Luke[78]. If John's account of Jesus' passion develops along similar lines as that found in the Synoptics, then there are data of enormous consequence for a pre-canonical passion account. It now remains to consider more broadly the shape and form of John's *Passionsgeschichte*.

III. The Shape of the Johannine Passion Narrative

We may commence our survey of the shape of John's passion narrative with a few remarks of a more general nature. First, of the four canonical accounts, John's is by far the longest, owing to John's extensive addition of the farewell discourse (14:1−16:33) and prayer of Jesus (17:1−26). Second, whereas the other canonical Gospels each have a clear point of beginning for their passion account, it is not easy to mark the onset of John's, for he disperses the first episodes of the narrative within chapters 11 and 12. Third, so extensively has the Fourth Evangelist wielded his redactional pen, and so pervasively has he reinterpreted certain events, that

---

78 See the monograph-length study by Dauer, *Passionsgeschichte*. Dauer holds that Matthew and Luke drew on the Gospel of Mark, thus the redactional features of the texts of Matthew and Luke serve as legitimate criteria for discerning a Johannine-Synoptic relationship. His conclusion is that direct literary dependence is highly unlikely, but that a good case exists for indirect dependence via post-Synoptic oral tradition. Of course, Dauer's methodology may be faulted in that it is unable to account for the possibility that John's only (or even primary) source was Mark's Gospel. Also, as we have shown, not all of the differences between Matthew and Mark, and Luke and Mark can be attributed to redaction of the Markan text by the other Synoptic Evangelists. Especially in the case of Luke's Gospel, and to a lesser extent with regard to Matthew's, one must allow for additional source material. Dauer's study is nevertheless an important one which can be cited in support of our own conclusions.

at times his story departs rather significantly from the Synoptic parallels and it is not always clear where we may discern in his narrative an underlying tradition. We must attend to these points as we attempt to determine whether the Fourth Evangelist has made use of a connected passion account as source material.

A. John 11:45–47

John's version of the plot to kill Jesus parallels Mark 14:1–2, though in relation to the Markan account John's is misplaced and greatly expanded. Also, whereas in Mark the chief priests and scribes appear to plot informally against Jesus, in John we read of a preliminary meeting of the Sanhedrin. In this, John is close to Matthew, who has the chief priests and elders gather in the palace of the high priest (26:3). Interestingly, both Matthew and John mention Caiaphas in this connection.

John's placing of this scene draws an obvious link between Jesus' raising of Lazarus and the plot against Jesus. In typical Johannine fashion[79], vv 45–46 relate how the miracle resulted both in faith in, and opposition toward, Jesus. Jesus' miraculous activity thus becomes that which provokes the Jewish conspiracy against him. A note of irony is sounded here, for in consequence of his giving life to the one whom he loved, Jesus' own life will now be required of him (cf. 15:13). There is good reason for agreeing with Trocmé, then, that had John known a connected narrative beginning with the plot against Jesus it is reasonable to believe he has repositioned this scene to serve his own theological purpose[80].

Verse 48 introduces a motif not found in the Synoptic parallels — namely, the threat from Rome. However, this idea is known to Luke, whose narrative brings out the political nature of Jesus' "offense" (23:1, 5; cf. John 19:12), and it is likely based on historical reminiscence[81].

Verses 49–52 set forth the significance of Jesus' death by developing Caiaphas's statement — "it is better for you that one man die for the people than that the whole nation perish" — as an unconscious prophecy. Again, these verses serve admirably John's theological purposes, but may have been taken from traditional or apologetic material[82]. Verses 55–57 provide a transitional link to the narrative of the events leading to the Passover.

---

79 Cf. Bultmann, *NT Theology*, 2:44–49; Barrett, *John*, 404.
80 Trocmé, *Passion*, 39.
81 See above, chapter 3.XVI; Brown, *John*, 1:442.
82 Cf. Lindars, *John*, 403; Brown, *John*, 1:442. Additional ways in which John's *Vorlage* exhibits a debt to pre-Johannine tradition are given in Walter Grundmann, "The Decision of the Supreme Court to Put Jesus to Death (John 11:47–57) in Its Context: Tradition and Redaction in the Gospel of John", in *Jesus and Politics*, 295–318.

B. John 12:1—11

As in the Markan account, the plot against Jesus leads into the story of Jesus' anointing at Bethany (14:3—9). The Johannine connection between the plot and the raising of Lazarus is thus maintained. John now adds that the conspiracy against Jesus has been extended to include plans to kill Lazarus as well. Of the many points raised earlier about the relationship of the four accounts of the anointing, the most important for our present discussion is that it is set in John chronologically prior to the entry into Jerusalem. It is doubtful that we should see this placement as a deliberate attempt to picture Jesus as the anointed king riding into Jerusalem[83], for the language of such an anointing is missing from the Johannine version and the perfume is poured not on his head but on his feet. John may have seen this pericope as a prophetic reference to Jesus' death (vv 7—8), but this would not in itself explain its placement before the entry, and it may be that its location is due simply to its traditional link with the conspiracy scene. This, then, would raise questions against the widely-held view that the anointing scene in Mark 14:3—9 appears in its Markan context in the passion narrative solely as a result of Mark's intercalation of it with the material about the plot against Jesus[84].

C. John 13:1—30

We have already discussed this extended passage in some detail, so our present comments may be held to a minimum. As with Luke's narrative, so with John's, the idea of Jesus' servanthood is integral to the scene of the Last Supper. As with the Synoptics, the announcement of the betrayal is related to the Supper scene; Luke and John place the prophecy after the meal, Matthew and Mark locate it in an anterior position. John has no "preparation for the Passover" as recorded by the other three evangelists, and earlier we questioned whether he knew such a story. In fact, as Matthew and Luke were each dependent on the Second Gospel for this episode, we have thus far found no reason to postulate a non-Markan pre-canonical tradition for it. Could it be that the story originated with Mark and that its absence in John is due to his ignorance of it? Earlier, we also noted points of agreement between 13:1—30 and a Supper tradition akin to that employed by Paul in 1 Cor 10—11.

D. John 13:31—38

These verses serve as a transition from the narrative of the Last Supper to the farewell discourse and, in some ways, anticipate the prominent

---

83 So Barrett, *John*, 409. Cf. below, chapter 8.II.B.
84 A view held by, e.g., Best, *Temptation and Passion*, 90; Bultmann, *History*, 263; Dibelius, *Tradition*, 181.

themes of that discourse — Jesus' departure and the love-motif[85]. Verses 31 and 32 introduce a typical Johannine emphasis on Jesus' departure and glory[86] and recall the language of 12:23, 27. Similarly, the language of v 33 is reminiscent of 7:33—34; 8:21, and these three verses, 31—33, may be drawn from those earlier texts. Verses 34—35 are closely related to 13:1, 15 — where Jesus' exhibition of his love in the taking up of the towel and basin is regarded as exemplary[87]. These verses prefigure the imperative of 15:12: "This is my commandment, that you love one another just as I have loved you". Within this pericope, v 36 serves a transitory function, introducing Peter, the center of attention in vv 37—38, while at the same time employing the thought of v 33.

Only in vv 37—38 do we come to a passage with parallels in the Synoptic passion narratives, though even here we find a noticeable degree of divergence[88]. All four stories have Peter declare his willingness to die and all agree in the formalized announcement of Peter's denial by Jesus. Otherwise, John's account is closest to that of the Third Gospel — for these two agree against Matthew and Mark in the setting of the dialogue in the meal-context, and in focusing more directly on Peter himself.

E. John 18:1—19:42

After the intervening chapters 14—17, John resumes his passion story with his account of Jesus' arrest. From this point forward his story line is very much like that of Mark's, as will be demonstrated shortly, so we may deal with the shape of his narrative more summarily. First, however, it is necessary to discuss in more detail 18:1—12, for John has omitted mention of the prayer of Jesus prior to his arrest.

While John does report that Jesus and his disciples crossed the Kidron Valley and entered the garden, he does not tell us the purpose of their presence in the garden. We can be certain, nevertheless, that he knew the tradition of Jesus' troubled, submissive prayer both from the allusion to it in 12:17 and from the cup-reference in 18:11[89]. John is alone in drawing a connection between the popularity of the place for Jesus and his followers and Judas's knowledge of his whereabouts on this particular night, though Luke also remarks that it was "according to custom" that Jesus went to the Mount of Olives (22:39). While Luke's reference is cast in his

---

85 Cf. Brown, *John*, 2:608—609; Barrett, *John*, 449.
86 Schnackenburg, *John*, 3:49—52.
87 So Victor Paul Furnish, *The Love Command in the New Testament* (Nashville: Abingdon, 1972) 136—137; cf. pp. 135—139.
88 On which, see Dodd, *Historical Tradition*, 55—56; Brown, *John*, 2:614—616 (see his chart on p. 615); Schnackenburg, *John*, 3:56. See also below, chapter 8.IV.C.
89 Cf. Jeremias, *Eucharistic Words*, 90; Lindars, *John*, 410, 426, 430—431; Trocmé, *Passion*, 41—42. See below, chapter 8.V.A.

own language, it may be that the Third and Fourth Evangelists thus witness to a common tradition[90]. As with the Synoptics, so here Judas is the head of the arresting party, but at this point the similarity ends as regards Judas's role. Not Judas, but Jesus takes the initiative in John's narrative of the arrest, and vv 4—9 clearly cast Jesus as the one in command of the events here.

> Just as earlier attempts to lay hands on Jesus went wrong because 'his hour had not yet come' (7:30; 8:20; cf. 7:44), so now that it has arrived, and Jesus gives himself to the envoys, his greatness, which they cannot touch, is again to be demonstrated[91].

Verses 4—9 are probably the fruit of John's own hand[92].

We may illustrate how the Johannine passion account follows a sequence of events much like that of Mark in the form of a chart.

John	Mark
(A) 18:1—12 — The Arrest and Departure of the Disciples.	(A) 14:43—52 — The Arrest and Departure of the Disciples.
(B) 18:13—27 — The Examination by Annas and Peter's Denial.	(B) 14:53—72 — The Trial before the Sanhedrin and Peter's Denial.
(C) 18:28—38a — Jesus before Pilate.	(C) 15:1—5 — Jesus before Pilate.
(D) 18:38b—40 — The Barabbas Episode.	(D) 15:6—15a — The Barabbas Episode.
(E) 19:1—16 — Jesus Flogged and Mocked, Questioned by Pilate, and Sentenced.	(E) 15:15b—20 — Jesus Flogged, Sentenced, and Mocked.
(F) 19:17 — The *Via Dolorosa*.	(F) 15:21—22 — The *Via Dolorosa*.
	(—) 15:23 — Jesus Offered Wine to Drink.
(G) 19:18a — The Crucifixion.	(G) 15:24a — The Crucifixion.
(H) 19:18b — Two Others Crucified.	(J) 15:24b — Jesus' Clothes Divided.
	(—) 15:25 — Time Reference.
(I) 19:19—22 — The Inscription on the Cross.	(I) 15:26 — The Inscription on the Cross.
(J) 19:23—24 — Jesus' Clothes Divided.	(H) 15:27 — Two Others Crucified with Jesus.
	(—) 15:29—34 — The Crucified Jesus Mocked, the Darkness over the Land, and the Cry of Dereliction.
(K) 19:25—27 — Women at the Cross.	(L) 15:36 — Jesus Given Wine to Drink.
(L) 19:28—30a — Jesus Given Wine to Drink.	(M) 15:37 — Jesus' Last Cry and Expiration.
	(—) 15:38—39 — The Temple-Curtain Torn and the Centurion's Confession.
(M) 19:30bc — Jesus' Last Words.	(K) 15:40—41 — The Women at the Cross.
(N) 19:31—37 — Assurance of Jesus' Death.	(O) 15:42—43, 46 — Jesus' Burial.
(O) 19:38—42 — Jesus' Burial.	(N) 15:44—45 — Assurance of Jesus' Death.

---

90 Cf. Schnackenburg, *John*, 3:222. Lindars (*John*, 539) argues that the wording of 18:2 is Johannine and so the reference must not be traditional; he overlooks the possibility that a tradition has been recast by the evangelist in his own *Vorzugsvokabeln*. See also, Dauer, *Passionsgeschichte*, 24—25.

91 Schnackenburg, *John*, 3:225. For details of this emphasis, see esp. Lindars, *John*, 540—542. On v 6 ("they drew back and fell to the ground"), see Dauer, *Passionsgeschichte*, 41—43; Schnackenburg, *John*, 3:224—225.

92 "Sprache, Kompositionstechnik und theologische Motive haben deutlich gemacht, dass Johannes für Zwischenstück 18, 4—9 keine Traditionen verarbeitet hat, sondern die Szene selbst erst entworfen und gestaltet hat" (Dauer, *Passionsgeschichte*, 43).

Our chart shows that with only minor transpositions the two stories follow the same order, providing much the same content. This observation does not detract from the obvious differences in the two narratives — seen most clearly at those points where John has no parallel for certain Markan episodes and in the abbreviation — e.g. (D) and (F) — or expansion — e.g. (I) and (J) — of certain episodes relative to Mark's narrative. Nevertheless, as we have already indicated reasons for denying that John made use of Mark's Gospel (or any other Synoptic Gospel), this high degree of convergence with respect to general content and sequence speaks rather emphatically for a pre-Johannine, non-canonical narrative of Jesus' passion built along similar lines to the Markan story. This narrative would have embraced at least the events beginning with the arrest of Jesus.

We have also noted the correspondence between Mark and John in relating the conspiracy against Jesus and his anointing; and between John and the Synoptics (esp. Luke) in relating the Last Supper, Jesus' service on behalf of his disciples, the betrayal-announcement, and the prophecy of Peter's denial. These agreements suggest John's use of a connected narrative tradition relating the sequence of passion events beginning at least with the Last Supper. Further, we have found that the Fourth Evangelist would have had legitimate reason to bring forward the two scenes in which we read of the plot against Jesus and the anointing in Bethany. Hence, the hypothesis that John had access to a tradition that narrated the plot against Jesus, the anointing, the Last Supper, and so on, up to and perhaps including the burial scene, enters the realm of probability.

IV. Conclusion

At the end of our discussion of the relationship between the Johannine passion story and its counterparts in the Synoptic Gospels we may briefly summarize our findings as follows. First, our investigation of three pericopae, all of which had been used by other scholars to demonstrate the debt of the Fourth Evangelist to the Synoptic Gospels, pointed to the likelihood that the Fourth Gospel shared no direct literary relationship with the other three canonical Gospels. Then, we saw that with relatively few exceptions the passion narrative of the Fourth Gospel is structurally very close to the Markan narrative of Jesus' suffering and death. The "exceptions" we noted are all of such a nature as can be explained in terms of Johannine theological interests, so that it is reasonable to believe that John's passion source was built along lines very similar to the Markan version. With a high degree of confidence we can speak of a Supper-tradition underlying John 13:1–38 and of a passion tradition behind John 18:1– 19:42. With less certainty, but still very much within the realm of good probability, we may think in terms of a *continuous narrative source* at the root of John 11:45–13:38; 18:1–19:42[93].

V. The Relationship between the Canonical Passion Narratives: Summary

Thus, we have reached the final stage of our study of the relationships among the four canonical passion narratives. Based on our conclusion that Mark's was the Earliest Gospel and that it was used independently by the First and Third Evangelists, we have sought to investigate whether Matthew and Luke made use of a connected source for their respective passion narratives other than that found in Mark's Gospel. Similarly, we queried whether the Fourth Evangelist knew the Synoptic passion narratives or some other connected narrative source(s). All that now remains for us is to briefly summarize our earlier conclusions and point out the significance of this portion of our study for the possibility of answering the two-fold question whether there existed a pre-canonical passion narrative, and if so what were its contents.

We have seen that the Gospel of Matthew offers no evidence independent of the Second Gospel for an early passion story. The passion account found in Matthew's Gospel does witness to the respect with which the First Evangelist treated his Markan source here, relative to earlier parts of his Gospel, but as a testimony for the pre-canonical stability of the tradition, this factor is dubious. Additionally, Matthew's passion narrative provides evidence of reflection on the suffering and death of Jesus in addition to that

---

[93] Trocmé (*Passion*, 45–46) goes further: "In short, the author of John's Gospel used as his source for chs. 11–20 a continuous Passion narrative that had exactly the same limits, the same narrative thread and the same stories as those used by Luke and by the redactor who appended a story of the sufferings and death of Christ to the original Gospel of Mark". He allows for the possibility that John borrowed that narrative from one or more Synoptic Gospels, but considers this most unlikely. It will be remembered that we have already found reason to question John's knowledge of an account of the preparation for the Passover and this, along with the divergences in describing the Last Supper, places serious questions against taking Trocmé too literally. Cf. Dauer, *Passionsgeschichte*. Jeremias (*Eucharistic Words*, 93–95) concludes from his comparison of the arrangement of the material in Mark and John that the arrest of Jesus marked a distinct break in the tradition, that at a very early stage of the tradition-history of the passion narrative there was a "short account" beginning with Jesus' arrest. In support of his theory, Jeremias appeals to the various "early summaries" of the passion kerygma in the NT. We shall have occasion to return to this line of thinking below (see esp. chapters 6–7), for a judgment of this kind can come only after all the evidence is in – and Jeremias has marshalled only a part of it. Mohr (*Passion*) concluded from his comparative study of the Markan and Johannine passion narratives that, ultimately, the two accounts could be traced back to the same source. We will summarize more fully and critique his study below (see chapter 8.1).

reported by Mark, some of which finds agreement with the Lukan and Johannine narratives. This fact suggests the existence of early, broad-based tradition. However, Matthew's Gospel provides no foundation upon which to raise any hypothesis of a pre-canonical passion account.

As for the passion narrative of the Third Gospel, our study has demonstrated that while Luke did make use of the Markan narrative of Jesus' suffering and death, this was not his only source. Indeed, at only two points — namely, the stories of the preparation of the Passover and of Jesus' burial — did we discover pericopae wherein Luke used Mark alone, without the testimony of additional source material. (In the burial scene we suggested that Luke had been influenced additionally by oral tradition in the make-up of one phrase.) Our redaction-critical inquiry was not sufficient to allow for "moral certainty" in our conclusions as to the extent of Luke's other source(s), but the evidence was adequate to support an hypothesis that, in addition to the Markan story, Luke employed much more than a string of isolated traditional fragments. That is, we are able to speak with confidence of a pre-Lukan, non-Markan *narrative* source, or combination of such extended sources, behind the Lukan passion narrative. Significantly, this source or these sources were built along comparable lines to that found in the Second Gospel, though our study has brought out differences in detail and emphasis.

Finally, in considering the Johannine testimony, we first set forth our case against regarding the Synoptic Gospels as sources for the Fourth Evangelist. Building from this conclusion we followed numerous earlier critics in noting the striking similarity in form and content of the Johannine passion narrative when compared with the Markan. While the two evangelists open their respective accounts in different ways, we were able to put forth satisfactory reasons against taking this observation as a necessary argument for denying John's use of a passion tradition built along the same lines as that found in the Gospel of Mark. As with our study of the Lukan narrative, additional evidence will be necessary before we will be able to speak with a high level of confidence about the *extent* of the narrative source or sources employed by the Fourth Evangelist, but we can already speak with virtual certainty about the *existence* of the same.

In order to gain that needed additional evidence we will turn in the following chapters to the Second Gospel and to form-critical considerations.

Chapter Five:

Mark and His Gospel:
Redactional Procedure and Literary Plan

I. Introduction

As our approach to a study of the Gospel of Mark differs markedly from our approach to the other canonical traditions, a brief note of explanation is due. In chapter 1 we outlined a long and full history of attempts at locating behind the Markan passion narrative a pre-Markan passion source. We saw that the more recent studies differed among themselves with regard to certain points of procedure, but all were in basic agreement in taking redaction criticism as their primary point of reference. As we observed, this methodology has yielded a diversity of conclusions, sometimes contradictory. Hence, our approach will be along another route. The central questions we will ask are whether we can properly speak of Mark as a "creative theologian" who was given to making broad and sweeping changes in his source material as opposed to his being a "conservative redactor", and what conclusions can be reached from a consideration of the relationship between chapters 1–13 and 14–16 in Mark.

It will readily be seen that our investigation will not take us directly into a point-for-point examination of Mark's passion account. This is quite intentional – though it is true that below, in chapter 8, we will deal in some detail with large portions of the Markan narrative. Our justification for following this route is simple: if Mark can be shown to be a conservative redactor (so Pesch), if we can determine on other grounds the high probability that a passion account was produced in early Christianity, and if we can demonstrate the probability that Mark's passion story closely modeled that more primitive narrative, then we will be well on our way to answering the larger question – i.e. What was the content of that narrative and how did it interpret Jesus' death? – without having to fall back on what have been shown to be rather dubious *redaktionsgeschichtliche* criteria. Thus, our thesis regarding an early passion story is built up in stair-step fashion, or as an edifice erected piece by piece with each section standing on its own and with each additional part providing a stabilizing effect for the whole.

Thus far we have seen two sections erected — the one representing the probable, non-Markan, pre-Lukan passion source employed along with the Markan narrative by Luke; the other representing the probable, non-Synoptic, pre-Johannine narrative passion source employed by John. In what follows we will see what additional sections can be added, and how they might interlock with those earlier components.

II. Mark the Evangelist — A Conservative Redactor?

Among modern-day champions of the thesis postulating the existence of an early-formulated, pre-canonical passion narrative, pride of place should be assigned to Rudolf Pesch. Both in his essay on "Die Ueberlieferung der Passion Jesu" and in his massive commentary on the Second Gospel Pesch sets forth his position, summarized in his own words as follows:

> Als *terminus ante quem* der Enstehung der vormk [vormarkinische] Passionsgeschichte ist folglich das Jahr 37 n.Chr. zu nennen ... Alters- und Herkunftsindizien sprechen zusammen eindeutig für eine frühe Enstehung der vormk Passionsgeschichte in der aramäisch sprechenden Urgemeinde in Jerusalem[1].

Though he draws on additional evidence in support of this conclusion, pivotal for Pesch's argument is his evaluation of Mark as a conservative redactor[2].

Pesch's attempt to cast Mark as a guardian of tradition may seem naive, a throwback to the heyday of form criticism — when the evangelists were described by Dibelius as "principally collectors, vehicles of tradition, editors"[3] — or even a return to the era before Wrede[4]. Two decades after the wide acceptance of the redaction-critical approach to Gospels studies, must not any attempt at minimizing the extent and effect of Mark's redactional activity be judged as un- or pre-critical? Certainly, recent work on the Second Gospel has often been guided by a concern to highlight the creativity of the evangelist and the uniqueness of his theology. As Hengel has observed:

> Fast könnte man meinen, dass sich beim ältesten Evangelium die Ansichten in eine ähnliche Richtung entwickeln, wie sie beim Johannesevangelium schon längst vorherrschend geworden sind: d.h., dass man allein nach der theologischen "Tendenz" des Autors und vielleicht noch nach den von ihm verarbeiteten Quellen fragt ... [5].

---

1 Pesch, *Mark*, 2:21; cf. 2:1–27. See also, *idem*, "Ueberlieferung"; *idem*, "Evangelium".
2 See Pesch, "Ueberlieferung", 150–151; *idem, Mark*, 1:15–32; 2:10.
3 Dibelius, *Tradition*, 3. Similarly, Bultmann, *History*, 350.
4 William Wrede's study, published in German in 1901 (ET: *The Messianic Secret* [Cambridge: James Clarke, 1971]), had a profound influence in turning the tide away from regarding the Gospels as records of "what really happened" to viewing them as intentional theological statements.
5 Martin Hengel, "Probleme des Markusevangeliums", in *Das Evangelium*, 223.

It may be countered, however, that this modern *Tendenz* has too quickly sundered redaction criticism from the sometimes valuable insights of form- and source-critical studies. What is more, this approach (and with it the newer literary criticism) may itself be working with faulty presuppositions about the generic character of the Markan enterprise[6]. Our question regarding the fidelity of Pesch's description of the Second Evangelist, then, cannot be answered merely by showing that the weight of scholarly opinion is against it. Rather, we must turn our attention to the evidence presented by the Second Gospel, but it is precisely here that we encounter a most "vexing problem" — namely, that of distinguishing the boundaries of pre-Markan tradition and Markan redaction[7].

We were introduced to this issue previously, for we noted that the work of such exegetes as Dormeyer and Schenke consisted especially in distinguishing Mark's editorial hand from the source material(s) available to him. The complexity of their studies and the variations in their conclusions may be taken as evidence of the difficulties inherent in their quest. Moving from the Markan passion account to the Gospel as a whole does not render the task any easier, for nowhere do we have direct access to Mark's sources. So ambiguous are the particulars involved in this detective work that widely divergent conclusions regarding Mark's editorial technique have been reached. For example, Trocmé denies that any redactional style exists in Mark, while Pryke offers evidence for some 14 syntactical features and is even so bold as to print a "Redactional Text of Mark"[8]. Moreover, while Neirynck's study of *Duality in Mark* suggests the stylistic unity of the whole Gospel[9], Reiser's investigation of *Syntax und Stil des Markusevangeliums* supports the conclusion that

> innerhalb des Evangeliums lassen sich stilistische Unterschiede zwischen der Passionsgeschichte Mk 14–15 und den Anfangskapiteln feststellen, die sich in der Wortstellung, im Gebrauch der Partikeln καί und δέ und in der Häufigkeit von Partizipialkonstruktionen, nicht zuletzt asyndetisch gereihter Partizipia coniunota äussern. Dies liegt zum Teil am Unterschied in der Komposition und Erzählstruktur, zum Teil aber sicher auch daran, dass die Passionsgeschichte eine grössere stilistische Sorgfalt erfahren hat[10].

---

6 As Hengel ("Probleme") goes on to argue.
7 Cf. Jack Dean Kingsbury, "The Gospel of Mark in Recent Research", *RelSRev* 5 (2, 1979) 104; Robert H. Stein, "The Proper Methodology for Ascertaining a Markan Redaction History", *NovT* 13 (1971) 181–182; Neirynck, "Redactional Text"; J. M. Robinson, "The Literary Composition of Mark", in *Évangile selon Marc*, 11–12.
8 Trocmé, *Passion*, 17; Pryke, *Redactional Style* ("Redactional Text of Mark" is appendix 2 in his book, pp. 149–176).
9 Frans Neirynck, *Duality in Mark: Contributions to the Study of the Markan Redaction* (Leuven: Leuven University, 1972); cf. *idem*, "Duplicate Expressions in the Gospel of Mark", in *Evangelica*, 83–142.
10 Reiser, *Syntax und Stil*, 167.

Mark the Evangelist – A Conservative Redactor? 139

Clearly, the extent of "Markan redaction" is open to diverse interpretations.

For determining Markan redaction two canons are frequently employed: alleged Markan style and characteristic Markan vocabulary – lists of which are collected from "known" or "generally agreed" verses exhibiting Mark's redactional handiwork. Lest this method seems to rest on a circular argument it is argued that Mark's Gospel contains obvious places wherein we would expect to encounter the evangelist's hand – most notably the connective seams and Markan summaries[11]. Nevertheless, even this approach fails to circumvent the realm of subjectivity. By way of illustration we have listed below the respective judgments on redactional verses in only the first chapter of Mark of six scholars – Gaston (G), Dormeyer (D), Pryke (R), Pesch (P), Schmithals (S), and Gnilka (N)[12]. (Initials are listed beside the verses each holds to be redactional; 1 asterisck [*] signifies only part of the verse is considered redactional, while 2 [**] signifies a minor redactional intrusion into a traditional verse.)

1	G	D	R	P	S	N	24				
2	G*	D	R		S		25				
3		D	R		S	N**	26		R		
4			R			N**	27	D*	R	P*	
5							28	G D	R	P**	N**
6			R				29	D	R*	P*	S*	N*
7						N*	30		R*		
8			R			N**	31		R*		N**
9		D*	R*	P**		N**	32	G	R	P*	N
10			R				33	G	R		N
11		D					34	G	R	P*	S*	N
12			R				35		R		N
13							36			S*	N
14	G	D	R			N	37		R		N
15		D	R			N*	38		R	P*	N
16			R*	P**	S	N*	39	G	R	P*	N
17					S		40		R*		
18			R		S		41		R*		
19					S		42				
20			R*	P**	S		43	D	R		
21	G	D*	R	P**		N*	44	D*	R*		
22	G	D	R	P		N	45	G D	R	P*	S*	N
23			R*	P**		N**					

Of these 45 verses, all but 5 are considered redactional by at least one of these six interpreters, but all 6 agree on the redactional character of only 1 verse (2, if we allow v 45). In short, a consensus of what in the Gospel

---

11 Cf. Best, *Temptation and Passion*, 63; idem, *Mark*, 10; Stein, "Proper Methodology", 183–185; Jeremias, *Parables*, 14.
12 Gaston, *Electronicae*, 6; Dormeyer, *Passion Jesu*, 59–65; Pryke, *Redactional Style*, 10–24; Pesch, *Mark*, 1:71–149; Schmithals, *Mark*, 1:73–147; Gnilka, Mark, 1:39–94.

of Mark is redactional continues to elude its students, and we may justifiably echo Neirynck's statement, "... it would be of great help for the discussion on Mark if we could reach an agreement concerning a redactional minimum"[13]. Yet, even if such an agreement could be reached, the question remains how far Mark was influenced by the vocabulary and style of his sources. Even Pryke must concede that "... any neat and tidy solution to the problem of redaction and linguistics in Mark must be ruled out of court"[14].

All of this comes by way of expressing a needed word of caution against speaking with unwarranted certainty of "Markan redaction" and "Markan tradition". This is not to deny the possibility or necessity of enquiring into how Mark has employed and added to his source materials[15], nor do these considerations rule out the necessity or possibility of testing Pesch's assertions about the limits of Markan redaction.

In what follows, our purpose is not to identify Markan redaction in the Second Gospel. Rather, ours is the somewhat less ambitious task of determining to what extent Mark was free to modify his sources. Early on in Christian history Eusebius reported Papias's words to the effect that "... Mark wrote down accurately, though not indeed in order, whatsoever he remembered of the things said or done by Christ"[16]. Can we discover evidence in the Second Gospel itself to corroborate this description of Mark's faithful preservation of the tradition? In fact, numerous texts in the Gospel of Mark suggest to us the evangelist's respect for his sources. Some of these have been cataloged by Pesch, others noted by Best — both of whom have explicitly taken up this question[17]. While we will not attempt to repeat their earlier work, our discussion of a representative sampling of relevant texts, gathered under four headings, will include passages already mentioned by these two scholars.

A. Texts with Ambiguity in Character Identification

At several points in the Markan narrative, pre-Markan material shows its head in the guise of inconsistency in the use of Jesus' titles, inconsistency

---

13 Neirynck, "Redactional Text", 619.
14 Pryke, *Redactional Style*, 31. Cf. Trocmé, *Passion*, 16–17. This ambivalence is further noted in Reiser, *Syntax und Stil*, 163–164.
15 See esp. Best, *Mark*, 9–11; Stein, "Proper Methodology".
16 Eusebius, *Hist. eccl.* 3.14.15 (ET in Arthur McGiffert, ed., "The Church History of Eusebius", in *A Select Library of Nicene and Post-Nicene Fathers of the Christian Church*, second series, vol. 1: *Eusebius: Church History, Life of Constantine, and Oration in Praise of Constantine*, ed. Philip Schaff and Henry Wace [Grand Rapids, Michigan: Wm. B. Eerdmans, n.d.]).
17 Pesch, "Ueberlieferung", 150–151; idem, *Mark*, 1:15–32, 2:10; Ernest Best, "Mark's Preservation of the Tradition", in *Évangile selon Marc*, 21–34.

in the ways people are introduced or described, and in the introduction of persons who serve no apparent purpose for the evangelist.

1:24. In the midst of an exorcism scene (1:21–28), the unclean spirit (i.e. ἄνθρωπος ἐν πνεύματι ἀκαθάρτῳ) recognized and named Jesus as ὁ ἅγιος τοῦ θεοῦ[18]. That Mark should use this title for Jesus in this context is puzzling — and that for three reasons. First, the title itself is rare, appearing only here in the Second Gospel, and elsewhere in the NT only in the Lukan parallel (4:34) and in John 6:69 (cf., however, Luke 1:35; Acts 3:14; 4:27, 30; 1 John 2:20; Rev 3:7). Second, not ὁ ἅγιος τοῦ θεοῦ, but ὁ υἱὸς τοῦ θεοῦ is the characteristic designation of Jesus by unclean spirits in Mark's Gospel (3:11). Third, as Martin has recognized,

> If one theme runs through [the Gospel of Mark] from its initial title (1:1) to the declaration of the Roman centurion (15:39), that theme is concerned to promote the majesty and power of Jesus Christ *the Son of God*[19].

Hence, in a confessional text such as this we would have expected the evangelist to bring the words of the unclean spirit into line with his christological agenda — particularly in this case where the change would have been made so easily. As the text now stands, the confession of the unclean spirit actually gets in the way of the Markan redaction[20]; this factor, along with the title's pre-Christian usage, renders highly probable its traditional quality[21]. In this very important instance, then, Mark shows himself to be a conservative redactor.

3:6; 12:13. Mark 2:1–3:5 records a series of scenes wherein Jesus' mission and message bring him into conflict with the religious authorities of his day. The culmination of this theme comes in 3:6: "Then the Pharisees went out and began to plot with the Herodians how they might kill Jesus". On the one hand, this climactic scene is not unusual for it is only one of a series of Markan texts that anticipate Jesus' passion[22]. Indeed, for this reason Dibelius regards 3:6 as a Markan compilation[23]. On the other hand, the statement is puzzling because of its mention of the Herodians.

---

18 On the interpretation of this scene, cf. esp. Best, *Temptation and Passion*, 16–18; Carl L. Kazmiersk, *Jesus, the Son of God: A Study of the Markan Tradition and Its Redaction by the Evangelist* (Würzburg: Echter, 1979) 100–101; Kingsbury, *Christology*, 86–88.
19 Ralph P. Martin, *Mark: Evangelist and Theologian* (Grand Rapids, Michigan: Zondervan, 1972) 126 (emphasis added); cf. pp. 104–105, 126–132. Similarly, Kazmiersk, *Jesus, Son of God*; Kingsbury, *Christology*.
20 This is true even if, as argued by Cullmann (*Christology*, 285), Cranfield (*Mark*, 76–77), and Schmithals (*Mark*, 1:124–125), the two titles are related, for Mark has not elsewhere drawn out this kinship or even so much as used the ἅγιος-title.
21 Cf. Best, "Mark's Preservation", 22–23; Kazmiersk, *Jesus, Son of God*, 100–101; Gnilka, *Mark*, 1:81; Schweizer, *Mark*, 52; Karl Georg Kuhn and Otto Procksch, "Ἅγιος", in *TDNT*, 1:101–102.
22 On which see below, chapter 5.III.
23 Dibelius, *Tradition*, 219, 223. Cf. Bultmann, *History*, 52.

The Herodians appear in only three texts in the NT — Mark 3:6; 12:13; and Matt 22:16 — and their identity has been the object of much speculation[24]. It is now generally agreed that in the Markan texts the Herodians are political figures, united against Jesus with the religious authorities[25]. In 3:6 they are partners in plotting against Jesus; in 12:13 they attempt to trap Jesus in a theological discussion. Both texts, then, may be regarded as pointing toward Jesus' arrest, trial, and execution. What is inexplicable is that *the Herodians have no part whatsoever in the narrative of Jesus' passion*! This enigma is underscored by the fact that with this exception only every detail of the pre-passion anticipations in Mark 1–13 finds its counterpart in Mark 14–16[26]. It might plausibly be conjectured that the Herodians have no role in the passion narrative because of the evangelist's tendency to downplay the political aspect of the story (manifest plainly in the Lukan and Johannine versions) while emphasizing the religious. As the text now stands, nevertheless, the Herodians are introduced for no apparent reason. Neither their role nor the political ramifications of their presence are developed. We can only conclude from this that Mark has thus preserved a tradition that actually runs against the grain of his own theological interests.

2:14; 3:16–19. The call of discipleship ("Follow me!") given to Levi (2:14) is an important one, for in calling a tax collector to be his disciple Jesus effectively demonstrates the breaking down of all barriers in his mission[27]. It is surely significant, then, that Levi is not listed among the chosen (or appointed) in 3:16–19 where, instead, Matthew's name appears (cf. Matt 9:9). Whether Matthew and Levi are two names for the same person or whether there was already at the time of the writing of the Gospel of Mark some confusion as to who were included in the "Twelve", the important point for our discussion is this: *Mark has not harmonized his sources.*

10:46. Mark records that while Jesus, along with his disciples and a large crowd, was leaving Jericho, a blind man was sitting by the road begging. His name is identified as ὁ υἱὸς Τιμαίου Βαρτιμαῖος. Had Mark found Βαρτιμαῖος in his tradition, we might have expected him to provide a Greek translation of the Aramaic name, for it is characteristic of Markan redaction

---

24 On their identity, see H. H. Rowley, "The Herodians in the Gospels", *JTS* 41 (1940) 14–27; Walter Otto, "Herodianoi", in *Real-Encyclopädia der classischen Altertumwissenschaft*, supplement vol. 2, ed. Wilhelm Kroll (Stuttgart: J. B. Metzler, 1913) 201–202; Norman Hillyer, " 'Ηρῳδιανοί", in *TDNT*, 4:441–443; Cranfield, *Mark*, 53–54; Josephus, *Ant.* 14.15.10.
25 Cf. Gnilka, *Mark*, 1:128–129.
26 See below, chapter 5.III.
27 Cf. Günther Bornkamm, *Jesus of Nazareth* (London: Hodder and Stoughton, 1960) 145–146; Eduard Schweizer, *Jesus* (London: SCM, 1971) 40; idem, *Lordship and Discipleship* (London: SCM, 1960) 13.

that translations of foreign words are provided in parenthetical clauses[28]. However, in doing so, Mark normally utilizes the formula ὅ ἐστιν or ὅ ἐστιν μεθερμηνευόμεν (cf. 3:17; 5:41; 7:11, 34; 12:42; 15:16, 34, 42). That he has not done so here implies that both name and translation are pre-Markan, and that Mark was content to use his tradition without even the minor revision entailed in bringing this translation into conformity with his own style[29].

3:21, 32, 34; 6:3. In regard to 6:3, Best draws attention to the fact that the names of Jesus' brothers would have been of little interest to Mark's readership and so were unnecessary[30]. In addition, we may note that in his earlier references to Jesus' family in chapter 3, Mark betrays no knowledge of Jesus' sisters (mentioned in 6:3), nor of the names of Jesus' brothers. That he has not harmonized his references to Jesus' family may be taken as an additional example of his preservation of the tradition.

We have considered five examples of ambiguity in character identification in which Mark's narrative demonstrates the evangelist's reluctance to deal freely with his traditions. It should be emphasized that these are only five such texts; more are mentioned by Pesch and Best (e.g. 9:33–37; 10:47–51; 15:40)[31]. What we have seen lends support to an evaluation of Mark as a conservative redactor.

B. Texts with Ambiguity in Geographical Notations

In his defense of "The Posteriority of Mark", Parker argues that the author of the Second Gospel is ignorant of Palestinian geography[32]. He asks: Where in the Palestinian wilderness would Jesus have encountered wild beasts (1:13)? How can one square Mark's statements about Capernaum with a map of Galilee? We can grant Parker's point that the Gospel of Mark contains a number of geographical ambiguities without following his conclusion that such oddities point to the relative posteriority of Mark. How, we may ask, could an author who used the Gospels of Matthew and Luke have introduced such inconsistencies? Indeed, speaking more generally, Pesch has turned this sort of argument on its head:

Der Vergleich des [Markusevangeliums] mit den Grossevangelien des Mattäus und Lukas lehrt, dass die späteren Evangelisten eine Reihe von Unausgeglichenheiten, stilistischen Nachlässigkeiten, Unklarheiten usw. zu beseitigen Anlass nahmen. Im Vergleich erscheint Markus als konservativer Redaktor[33].

---

28 See, e.g., Pryke, *Redactional Style*, 59–60.
29 See Best, "Mark's Preservation", 32; Schweizer, *Mark*, 224.
30 Best, "Mark's Preservation", 32.
31 Pesch, "Ueberlieferung", 150–151; *idem, Mark,* 1:15–32, 2:10; Best, "Mark's Preservation", 21–34.
32 Pierson Parker, "The Posteriority of Mark", in *New Synoptic Studies,* 68–70.
33 Pesch, "Ueberlieferung", 150–151.

In the following examples we see that the evidence favors an explanation that recognizes Mark's convervative use of his traditions.

3:9, 13. In v 9 Mark records that Jesus had his disciples prepare a small boat for him, so as to allow him refuge from the crowds. Yet, v 13 has him going not to the boat but up to the hills. Indeed, he returns to a (the same?) boat only in 4:1. Mark's intermingling of traditions has gotten in the way of his story line[34].

6:45, 53. In v 45 Jesus reportedly sends his disciples on to Bethsaida, across the lake. He later joins them en route to their destination, still on the lake (vv 47–52). Yet, when they cross over they land at Gennesaret (v 53), not Bethsaida. Again, the intrusion of a variant geographical note (which has nothing to do with Mark's familiarity with Palestinian geography!) confuses the story line.

Additional mention is made of 3:20; 4:1; 7:24, 31 by Pesch[35], but the examples we have given demonstrate that in constructing his Gospel Mark sometimes joined together stories with conflicting topographical or geographical notations without bringing them into harmony with the flow of his narrative.

C. Ambiguity in Particulars of Selected Pericopae

At some points, Mark has set a tradition within a context, or brought together traditions, in such a way that details or language in one part of the pericope do not agree with the details or language in another. In this way, too, Mark shows his tendency to preserve tradition.

1:16–17, 29; 10:28–30. In his study of Mark's use of his traditions, Best draws attention to the existence of just this sort of contradiction in 10:28–30[36]. There, as spokesperson for the disciples, Peter declares, "Look! We have left everything and followed you!" Jesus replies by giving a list of items abandoned by those who follow him – homes, fields, and kin. Yet, we are told in 1:16–17 that Peter left his vocation as a fisherman (not a farmer). Moreover, it might be questioned whether Peter left his family, for in 1:29 (cf. 1 Cor 9:5) Jesus and his followers go to the home of Simon and Andrew. Hence, Jesus' list has not been adapted to its Gospel context. Best concludes that Mark has taken over a traditional saying without adaptation. Admittedly, however, this example lacks decisive weight for our purposes, for it depends on what may be a rather wooden rendering of Jesus' words in 10:28–30 – which may better be read elliptically.

---

34 Even the recent monograph by Elizabeth Struthers Malbon, *Narrative Space and Mythic Meaning in Mark* (San Francisco; Harper & Row, 1986), which otherwise contributes much to our understanding of the "Markan geography", fails to resolve this narrative tension.
35 Pesch, "Ueberlieferung", 151.
36 Best, "Mark's Preservation", 25.

6:6b−13. In relating how Jesus sent out the Twelve two by two, Mark says that Jesus gave them authority over unclean spirits and instructed them concerning their mission (vv 7−11). Verses 12−13 summarize their mission: they went out and preached that people should repent; they cast out demons; and they anointed many sick people with oil and healed them. Interestingly, a lack of convergence exists between the sort of authority given (for exoricisms − v 7) and the type of ministry carried out (preaching, healing, and exorcism − vv 12−13). To be sure, it is widely held that vv 7, 12, and 13 have been constructed by the evangelist so as to provide a context for the instructions of Jesus in vv 8−11[37], but this theory does not do justice to the text. It is more likely that vv 12−13 have been taken over from the language of the early Christian mission and appended to the tradition of the disciples' being sent forth as a summary of their mission. In joining the statements, however, Mark has not harmonized the language.

9:14−29. In the Markan story of Jesus' healing a boy with an unclean spirit we read a number of inconsistencies that have not been ironed out by the evangelist. The crowd is *twice* introduced and in *both* instances they are said to have been running up to Jesus (vv 15, 25). Moreover, the boy is described twice. Further, the enumerated effects of his being possessed by the spirit differ in each case (vv 17−18, 20−22). Still further, the spirit itself is known as πνεῦμα ἄλαλον (v 17), πνεῦμα (v 20), πνεῦμα ἀκαθάρτον (v 25), and finally, as τὸ ἄλαλον καὶ κωφὸν πνεῦμα (v 25). The presence of these rather noticeable ambiguities demonstrates how little Mark has shaped his traditions to yield a consistent narrative with inner harmony.

These are but three illustrations from Mark's Gospel of the difficulties encountered even among the particulars of individual pericopae. Again, these examples lend support to the evaluation of the Second Evangelist as a conservative redactor.

D. Miscellaneous Instances of Unmodified Tradition

Under this heading we shall consider two points from one text − 8:31 (cf. 9:31; 10:33−34). This is an important text not only from its place and purpose in the Second Gospel, but also because it retains certain instances of traditional language, the modification of which would have been to the advantage of the evangelist. Many have debated the authenticity of this prediction of Jesus' passion and resurrection; likewise, it has often been denied that this text was present in the earliest tradition[38]. Here we

---

37 Cf. Bultmann, *History*, 331; Taylor, *Mark*, 303, 306; Gnilka, *Mark*, 1:236−237; Pryke, *Redactional Style*, 14.
38 Cf. Schmithals, *Mark*, 1:384; Bultmann, *History*, 152; Bornkamm, *Jesus*, 154; Werner Georg Kümmel, *The Theology of the New Testament* (London: SCM, 1974) 86; Dibelius, *Tradition*, 225−226.

will raise only two points concerning the language of 8:31 that militate against that critical position and lend weighty support to regarding the prediction as ancient tradition, at least.

First, for Jesus' death the text employs a passive form of ἀποκτείνω, not σταυρόω[39]. There are at least three reasons why σταυρόω would have been preferred by the evangelist. First, it more accurately describes the way of Jesus' death. Second, for Mark the death of Jesus is above all the death of a *crucified* Messiah. Throughout his narrative of Jesus' passion we read the verb σταυρόω 7 times (15:13, 14, 15, 20, 24, 25, 27), and 3 times we read of ὁ σταυρός (15:21, 30, 32). In 16:6 Jesus is referred to by the angel at the tomb as τὸν ἐσταυρωμένον. Third, in 8:34, would-be disciples are told of the necessity of taking up the cross (ἀράτω τὸν σταυρὸν αὐτοῦ). The close and deliberate identification of the fate of the Son of Man and of Jesus' disciples in the closing verses of Mark 8 would have been advanced even further had Mark simply substituted σταυρόω for ἀποκτείνω in 8:31. That he has not done so is an indication of the pre-Markan origin of the verse and of Mark's fidelity to his tradition.

A similar conclusion may be reached from a consideration of the phrase μετὰ τρεῖς ἡμέρας in 8:31[40]. "After three days" is clearly at variance with the Markan narratives of the passion and resurrection — unless we allow for a Jewish time-reckoning[41]. For this reason, Mark's language was recast to conform with Greek usage by Matthew and Luke (τῇ τρίτῃ ἡμέρᾳ — Matt 16:21; Luke 9:22). We would have expected a similar wording from Mark for his Gentile readership (cf. the language of 14:58; 15:29, which stands in tension with the passion- and resurrection-predictions). It is doubtful that the expression can be credited to Mark, and this is another sign of Mark's preservation of the tradition.

E. Conclusion

By tracing four lines of evidence we have sought to test the validity of Pesch's assertion that Mark the evangelist is a conservative redactor. Our study of the issue has hardly been exhaustive, but we have seen enough to suggest that a significant measure of truth exists in Pesch's evaluation. It

---

39 Cf. Georg Strecker, "The Passion- and Resurrection Predictions in Mark's Gospel", *Int* 22'(1968) 430; Best, "Mark's Preservation", 26–27; Gerald O'Collins, *Interpreting Jesus* (London: Geoffrey Chapman, 1983) 87; Hans F. Beyer, *Jesus' Predictions of Vindication and Resurrection: The Provenance, Meaning and Correlation of the Synoptic Predictions* (Tübingen: J. C. B. Mohr [Paul Siebeck], 1986) 160.

40 Cf. Jeremias, *NT Theology*, 285–286; Cranfield, *Mark*, 278; Best, "Mark's Preservation", 26–27; Strecker, "Predictions", 429; Taylor, *Jesus*, 86; Charles H. Talbert, ed., *Reimarus: Fragments* (Philadelphia: Fortress, 1970) 162–163; Bayer, *Jesus' Predictions*, 205–208.

41 Cf. Gerhard von Rad and Gerhard Delling, " Ἡμέρα", in *TDNT*, 2:949–950.

does appear that our evangelist operated with a positive respect for his tradition, and we may justifiably assent to Pryke's judgment concerning Mark: "When he is called a redactor it is not suggested that he seriously tampered with the traditions, for often the traditions can be seen to hamper his intentions"[42].

What are the implications of our judgment that Mark was restrained in his use of the traditions for our inquiry into the possibility of a pre-canonical passion narrative? First, it should be stated quite openly that the texts we have examined (and our study goes beyond the lists found in Pesch's essay) are not sufficient to support Pesch's assertion that Mark has virtually taken over without alteration a pre-Markan passion account. Likewise, that Mark was a conservative redactor does not prove *ipso facto* the existence of a pre-Markan passion story. However, if other evidence can be found that Mark made use of such a narrative account, our judgment about Mark's conservative stance *vis-à-vis* his tradition would suggest that the present form of Mark's account of Jesus' passion closely resembles that of his source. Finally, if it can be shown that chapters 14–15 depart from chapters 1–13 with regard to narrative style, progression, and cohesiveness, we would be justified in putting forth as a probable explanation of this phenomenon the hypothesis that Mark had access to a connected narrative of Jesus' suffering and death.

This third implication should not be passed over lightly, for here we recall the observations of the early form critics that first led them to speak of the uniqueness of the passion narratives in the Gospels – its relative self-sufficiency, its closed narrative sequence, its geographical and chronological cohesiveness, and its fullness of detail. Not only the early form critics, but more modern students of the Gospels – including Jeremias, Bornkamm, Nineham, Schneider, Schweizer, Pesch, and Gnilka – have concluded that its narrative style sets the passion account apart from the rest of the Gospel story[43]. Given Mark's status as a conservative redactor, this "consensus"[44] is a significant voice for the existence of a pre-Markan passion account to which the Second Evangelist had access. But here we enter the realm of form-critical disputes, a discussion of which properly follows a brief consideration of the relationship of the Markan passion narrative with the Gospel's earlier chapters.

---

42 Pryke, *Redactional Style*, 9; cf. pp. 29, 31. See also Taylor, *Mark*, 53; Hengel, "Probleme", 223–232; Best, "Mark's Preservation", 33; *idem*, *Mark*, 13–14.
43 Cf. Schmidt, *Rahmen*, 303–304; Dibelius, *Tradition*, 178–179; Bultmann, *History*, 275; Jeremias, *Eucharistic Words*, 62; Bornkamm, *Jesus*, 155; Nineham, *Mark*, 365; Schneider, "Probleme", 222; Schweizer, *Mark*, 284; Pesch, "Ueberlieferung", 151–152; Gnilka, *Mark*, 2:217.
44 Linnemann (*Studien*, esp. 54–68) has attempted to counter the form-critical arguments for a pre-canonical passion account, as has Kelber (*Gospel*, 187–199). On their arguments see below, chapter 6.

III. The Relationship between Mark 1−13 and 14−16

As will be recalled, form critics posited a radical distinction between the kinds of materials used in Mark 1−13 and 14−16. The resulting belief in a hiatus between these two sections persisted in Markan studies, helped along by Kähler's description of the Gospels as passion narratives with extended introductions, until 1967, when Schreiber's *Theologe des Vertrauens* developed the relationship of the Markan passion story to the rest of the Gospel[45]. Nevertheless, Trocmé has recently once again denied any stylistic or theological unity between the two sections − this in his attempt to support his argument that chapters 14−16 constitute an "appendix" added later to the original edition of Mark's Gospel, which reached its finale at 13:37[46]. His thesis rests on three points: (A) chapters 14−16 are more biographical than 1−13; (B) while chapters 1−13 contain allusions and prophecies to the *fact* of Jesus' passion and resurrection, they anticipate no *narrative* of Jesus' suffering, death, and resurrection; and (C) contradictions exist between chapters 1−13 and 14−16 in respect to attitude toward christological titles, Jesus' attitude toward the temple, and the time-lapse between the death and resurrection of Jesus.

In reply we may note the following. Assuming the validity of Trocmé's first observation, we may recognize that the stylistic variations to which he calls attention could be due simply to the original author's having taken over without radical revision a pre-Markan passion account. As for the third point, the contradictions listed, while sometimes overdrawn, are well accounted for by our earlier conclusion that Mark conserved his tradition. Unevenness in theology and style is to be expected from an evangelist like Mark who characteristically takes over traditional material without extensive alteration. As for Trocmé's second point, we have kept it for last because here he raises an issue deserving a more extensive treatment. Of course, on the one hand we could argue that the many forward-looking texts in Mark 1−13 certainly anticipate *something*, but under Trocmé's thesis all are left without a referent in the Markan narrative. On the other hand, a comparison of the texts anticipating Jesus' passion and resurrection with the narrative of those events will reveal how tightly these two sections are interwoven.

---

45 See now Norman R. Peterson, *Literary Criticism for New Testament Critics* (Philadelphia: Fortress: 1978) 49−80; Robert C. Tannehill, "The Gospel of Mark as Narrative Christology", in *Perspective − Mark's Gospel*, 57−95; Best, *Mark*; Hengel, "Probleme", 226−230; Martin, *Mark*; F. C. Lang, "Kompositionsanalyse des Markusevangeliums", *ZTK* 74 (1972) 1−24; Theodore J. Weeden, *Mark − Traditions in Conflict* (Philadelphia: Fortress, 1971); Malbon, *Narrative Space*.
46 Trocmé, *Passion*, 7−19; esp. pp. 9−12.

Of course, in anticipating the results of this comparison, we recognize that we are dealing with not one problem but two. It is true that Trocmé would have us drive a wedge between chapters 13 and 14, but, at the other end of the spectrum, numerous modern interpreters deny that any separation at all — whether literary or theological — is possible. This, they remark, is because chapters 1–16 are all the original, creative work of Mark, the redactor-evangelist who exercised a free hand in shaping the whole Gospel. That is, observeations *vis-à-vis* the relationship between Mark 1–13 and 14–16 lead one scholar to opt for the existence of a pre-canonical passion story, another to conclude against the existence of the same. As we will see, a choice between these options is not necessary, for a *via media* can be charted through the whole debate.

While Peterson has overstated his case in arguing that the chief plot device in Mark's narrative is temporal in orientation, he is nevertheless more broadly correct in his recognition that prediction and anticipatory allusion have a significant role in the Second Gospel[47]. In what follows we will outline only the various passion- and resurrection allusions and predictions in Mark 1–13, then indicate their fulfillment in the closing chapters of the Gospel.

2:19–20. These verses, which constitute the earliest reference to Jesus' death in the Gospel of Mark[48], are set in the context of a dispute over fasting. Assuming that true piety and regard for the anticipated kingdom find expression in fasting, some people have come to Jesus asking why his disciples do not so discipline themselves. His reply takes the form of an analogy: just as guests do not fast in the presence of the bridgegroom at the wedding celebration, so now, while Jesus is present, fasting is out of place. The surprising twist in this brief parable comes in v 20, when Jesus predicts a time when the bridegroom will be taken away (ἐλεύσονται δὲ ἡμέραι ὅταν ἀπαρθῇ ἀπ' αὐτῶν ὁ νυμφίος); when that time comes, fasting will be in order. For the interpretation of this analogy one need not retreat into speculation about the eschatological or messianic connotations of "bridegroom" in late Judaism[49]. Rather, one need only follow the simple correspondence Jesus draws from the bridegroom at a normal, if festive occasion, to himself. Thus, a time will come when *he* will be "taken away". (Compare this with the turn of events in 2 Esdr 9:38–10:4.)

---

47 Peterson, *Literary Criticism*, 49–80.
48 Best (*Mark*, 66) regards 1:9–11 as the earliest implicit reference to Jesus' impending death in Mark, since the revelatory word of God (1:11), whether based on Isa 42:1 or Gen 22:2, embraces the thought of death.
49 This is the approach taken by Joachim Jeremias, "Νύμφη, νυμφίος", in *TDNT*, 4:1099–1106. See also Kümmel, *NT Theology*, 87.

The intended nuance of ἀπαίρω in this passage is not readily apparent and little interpretative help is forthcoming from the use of the compound elsewhere in the Greek Bible. The verb is found some 130 times in the LXX, characteristically denoting the idea of "travel" (e.g. "to set out", "to move on", "to travel", et al.). In the NT the word appears only here and in the Synoptic parallels (Matt 9:15; Luke 5:35; cf. Acts 1:9 D [sa]). Some commentators have found here an allusion to Isa 53:8 (ὅτι αἴρεται ἀπὸ τῆς ἡ ζωὴ αὐτοῦ . . .) — a possibility flatly denied by Hooker[50]. For this and possibly other (unstated) reasons, some scholars regard Mark 2:20 as an intimation of Jesus' expectation of a violent death[51]. Aside from the rather minimal verbal correspondence, nothing suggests that the text is a throwback to the last Servant Song, nor does anything within the Markan text suggest a "violent" death. Jesus' analogy, however, does suggest "a startling departure from the norm"[52]; that is, in predicting his death in 2:20, Jesus intimates that it will come *unexpectedly*, perhaps *suddenly*, and that for his disciples his death would seem an *enigmatic* end to his mission.

3:6. Coming as it does at the close of a string of loosely-connected stories reflecting the controversy Jesus' ministry stirred up, stories in which one may chart a progressive growth of hostility towards Jesus, 3:6 stands as the fitting climax of the section 2:1—3:5. More than that, it may be regarded as a critical point in the Gospel of Mark. Already in the Markan narrative, Jesus' divine authority is manifest with respect to unclean spirits, teaching, sickness, sin, tradition, and the law, and his mission thus exhibited calls for persons to declare their response to him, either in allegiance or in opposition. The religious leaders in Galilee, the *Pharisees* and *Herodians*, sharply oppose him and begin to *plot* his death. Indeed, it is arguable that Jesus' actions as reported in these pericopae could be interpreted as infractions punishable by death[53]. From now on, "as a dark cloud the death of Jesus hangs over the further course of His ministry"[54].

6:4. In view of the unbelief of the people in his home town Jesus cites an apparently well-known aphorism: "A prophet is not without honor except in his own homeland, among his kin, and in his own home"[55]. Jesus does not thereby claim for himself the title "prophet", but does identify

---

50 Hooker, *Jesus*, 92.
51 See, e.g., Cranfield, *Mark*, 110—111; Taylor, *Mark*, 211; Delling, *Kreuzestod*, 58; George Barker Stevens, *The Theology of the New Testament*, 2d ed. (Edinburgh: T. & T. Clark, 1918) 123; Donald Guthrie, *New Testament Theology* (Downers Grove, Illinois: InterVarsity, 1981) 437.
52 See Michaels, *Servant and Son*, 144.
53 See Delling, *Kreuzestod*, 58; Jeremias, *NT Theology*, 278—279.
54 Taylor, *Mark*, 224.
55 For parallels, see *Pap. Oxy.* 1.5; *Gos. Thom.* 31; Gnilka, *Mark*, 1:232.

his own fate with that of the prophets. Implicit here, then, is a prediction of Jesus' *rejection, suffering,* and *death* — for in some strands of OT tradition and in late Judaism it was widely held that persecution was the lot of the prophet[56]. This identification is furthered by the fate of the "prophet" John the Baptist, subsequently reported (6:14—29).

6:14—29; 9:11—13. The passion of John the Baptist anticipates Jesus' own suffering and death. Not only do the two experience comparable fates (cf. 9:11—13), but the narratives of their respective stories exhibit important similarities. In both cases we find the Roman authority basically *sympathetic* toward his prisoner, whom he regards as *innocent* (6:20; 15:14), and in both instances he pronounces the *death sentence* only under duress from others (6:26; 15:15). Moreover, the story of John's death ends with his disciples *coming, taking his body,* and *laying it in a tomb* (6:29) — just as in 15:42—47 Joseph of Arimathea went to Pilate, *requested and was given Jesus' body,* and *laid it in a tomb.* In this surprisingly long account of John's death, then, we gain a preview of Jesus' passion[57].

8:31; 9:12, 31; 10:32—34. Following the confession of Peter at Caesarea Philippi (8:27—30), Jesus speaks frankly to his disciples about his suffering, death, and resurrection. Thus the suspense afforded by earlier anticipations of Jesus' passion is heightened as we become cognizant of many of the details of Jesus' death, as well as its *necessity.* He *must suffer;* he will be *betrayed;* he will be *rejected* and *condemned* by the *Jewish leaders;* he will be *handed over to the Gentiles* who will *mock* him, *spit* on him, *flog* him, and *kill* him. Then, after three days, he will *arise.* Again, the suspense is sharpened as we turn to the fourth of these more explicit, formal predictions: Jesus is leading the way to *Jerusalem* and it is *there* that the passion predictions will be fulfilled. Already the disciples are *puzzled* and *afraid,* as they are confronted with the prospect of Jesus' death (8:32—33; 9:6, 10, 32; 10:32).

10:38—39. Immediately following the most detailed prediction of Jesus' passion in Mark's Gospel (10:33—34), the sons of Zebedee request of Jesus that they be allowed seats of honor in his glory (10:35—40). The relation of this pericope to the preceding prediction underscores what is already clear in Jesus' reference to his resurrection in 10:34 — namely, *suffering* and *death* will give way to *glory.* Likewise, within vv 35—40 we discover an anticipation of Jesus' death together with an allusion to his expectation

---

56 Cf., e.g., Neh 9:26; Jer 2:30; Gerhard Friedrich, "Prophets and Prophecy in the New Testament", in *TDNT,* 6:834—835; David E. Aune, *Prophecy in Early Christianity and the Ancient Mediterranean World* (Grand Rapids, Michigan: Wm. B. Eerdmans, 1983) 157—159; Hill, *Prophecy,* 57; Dunn, *Unity and Diversity,* 210.

57 See Donald Senior, *The Passion of Jesus in the Gospel of Mark* (Wilmington, Delaware: Michael Glazier, 1984) 16—20; Hengel, "Probleme", 227.

of *vindication*. The latter point is exhibited in Jesus' implicit acceptance of James and John's reference to his future glory. The former lies in the metaphors Jesus employs in his reply to the brothers' request.

In 10:38–39 Jesus speaks of the *cup* he will drink and the *baptism* with which he will be baptized. In both instances the verbs used are in the present tense (πίνω, βαπτίζομαι), suggesting that the metaphors refer to the whole of Jesus' mission; however, as the climax of Jesus' mission is his death (10:45), we have good reason for regarding these metaphors in an anticipatory sense as well. As the two concepts occur in parallel it is likely that the one is analogous to, and confirmed by, the other. On the sense intended by the use of "the cup" in this passage (as in 14:36) there is wide agreement[58]. In the main, figurative references to "the cup" in the OT and intertestamental literature are restricted to two usages: to drink the cup is to participate in God's salvation (e.g. Pss 23:5; 116:13) or to undergo suffering in bearing divine *judgment* (e.g. Ps 75:8; Isa 51:17, 22; Jer 25:15–38; Ezek 23:31–34). In view of Jesus' request in 14:36 that the Father remove the cup, it is surely the latter sense that is intended here. Thus,

<small>mit dem Bildwort vom Becher spielt darum Jesus nicht nur auf seine Leiden und seinen Tod an, sondern deutet diese auch als göttliches Gericht, das er – dann für die Frevler – übernimmt[59].</small>

Likewise, the baptismal metaphor signifies calamity and judgment (cf. 2 Sam 22:5; Pss 42:7; 69:2–3; Isa 43:2; 1QH3:13–18)[60]. Set in figurative language, here is a further signpost in the Markan narrative, pointing forward to Jesus' passion, which must precede his glory.

10:45. Debates over the authenticity of the ransom-logion do not concern us here. What is of vital importance for an understanding of Mark's Gospel is the programmatic nature of this logion in the context of the Gospel. Here, Jesus identifies the purpose of his mission: to provide the ultimate service to others in giving up his own life for them (cf. John 15:13). Thus, the sum of Jesus' *mission* is focused narrowly on his death. If this is true, then, *contra* Trocmé, it would be unthinkable that the evangelist would have purposely brought his own work to a close in 13:37, having never related Jesus' death.

11:18. Mark 11:15–18 is somewhat reminiscent of 2:1–3:6, for in both sections Jesus' actions in fulfilling his mission bring him into sharp *opposition* with persons in authority. In the present text, in setting himself over against those who abuse the temple, he provides the occasion for a renewed

---

<small>58 See Taylor, *Jesus*, 97–99; Schweizer, *Mark*, 220; Best, *Temptation and Passion*, 152–153; *idem*, *Mark*, 69–70; Lane, *Mark*, 380; Gnilka, *Mark*, 2:101–102; Pesch, *Mark*, 2:156–157; Leonhard Goppelt, "Ποτήριον", in *TDNT*, 6:149–153.
59 Gnilka, *Mark*, 2:102.
60 Cf. Best, *Temptation and Passion*, 153–154; Gnilka, *Mark*, 2:102; Pesch, *Mark*, 2:157–158.</small>

plot against his life. This time, now in *Jerusalem,* it is the *chief priests* and *scribes* who seek to put him away. Jesus' safety is guaranteed only because the *crowds* are taken with him; should popular opinion be swayed, Jesus would be in grave danger.

12:1—12. In his monograph on Jesus, Michaels refers to this, the parable of the tenants, as "a kind of passion story in miniature"[61]. Regardless of its origin or *Traditionsgeschichte* the text certainly fulfills such a function for the Second Evangelist. Jesus is identified as God's beloved son (12:6; cf. 1:11), who would be killed by the Jewish leaders, just as they had killed the prophets before him. As indicated earlier in our discussion of 6:4, Jesus' end is the same as that of the *martyred prophets.*

As it now stands in the Markan narrative, 12:1—12 must be seen in connection with the question put to Jesus in 11:27. There the religious authorities *(chief priests, scribes,* and *elders)* question by what authority Jesus had cleared the temple. Though in 11:33 Jesus refuses to answer, according to the Markan story he reveals in this parable that he was sent by God himself. Oblique though this revelation may seem, the Jewish leaders recognize the point of the story (12:12). As a result, they look for a way to *arrest* him, and thus take steps to do to Jesus what the parabolic tenants did to the owner's son. Again, the favor of the *crowds* toward Jesus arrests any immediate plans to take Jesus into custody. Verse 10, citing Ps 118:22—23, anticipates the Lord's *vindication* of Jesus following his death.

While Mark 12 relates additional controversy between Jesus and the authorities (both religious and political), with v 12 we come to the last of the texts anticipating the events of Jesus' passion outside the passion account itself. Additional predictions and news of plots against Jesus are found in the passion story, but we have seen in chapters 1—13 that Jesus' mission is carried out in the shadow of the cross. At some points along the way we have had occasion to allude to the connection between the various predictions and anticipatory allusions in Mark 1—13 and the passion narrative itself. Such connections must now be developed more fully.

Opening the passion narrative in Mark's Gospel is a narrative statement regarding the *plot* to *arrest* and *kill* Jesus (14:1—2). The verses have a backward reference as well as a forward one, recalling similar statements in 3:6; 11:18; 12:12. Ἀπόλλυμι — used in 3:6 and 11:18, and κρατέω — used in 12:12, to describe the proposed action against Jesus, both appear in 14:1. Moreover, the problem presented by *public opinion,* witnessed in 11:18 and 12:12, reappears in 14:2. In 14:1—2 it is the *chief priests* and *scribes*

---

[61] Michaels, *Servant and Son,* 143.

who conspire against Jesus. This agrees with 11:18 and 12:12 (11:27), though the third person plural reference in 12:12 also includes the *elders*. Mark 3:6, set not in Jerusalem but in Galilee, mentions the *Pharisees* and *Herodians*.

In 14:8 Jesus reveals the significance of his anointing by the women at Bethany: in anointing Jesus she prepared his body beforehand for *burial*. While this recalls no particular prediction of the passion in chapters 1–13, it does heighten the anticipation of *death* brooding over the whole Gospel.

Mark 14:10–11 relates Judas's agreement with the *chief priests* to *betray* Jesus to them. In this way he plays into their hands by giving them an occasion to carry out their *plot* (cf. 11:18; 12:12; 14:1–2). Additionally, this agreement, and the prediction of Jesus in 14:18, recalls the earlier reference to Jesus' *betrayal* (9:31; 10:33–34).

The *divine "must"* ($\delta\epsilon\hat{\iota}$) of Jesus' passion, asserted in the passion predictions in 8:31; 9:12; 10:38–39, finds correspondence in the passion narrative in the first part of Jesus' saying in 14:21: "The Son of Man will go just as it is written about him . . ."; and the *betrayal* motif (9:31; 10:33–34; 14:10–11, 18) raises its head in the second half: "But woe to that man through whom the Son of Man is betrayed".

The significance of Jesus' death with respect to his *mission* is stated in 10:45, but is also present in the eucharistic words of Jesus in 14:22–24. Similarly, in 14:25 we find a reference to Jesus' *future in the kingdom*, implying that his death will not be the end (cf. 8:31; 9:9–13, 31; 10:33–34, 35–40; 12:10).

With respect to 2:19–20 and the formal predictions in chapters 8–10 we observed the *puzzlement* on the part of the disciples that would surround the passion of Jesus. At the prospect of Jesus' death they were *fearful* and *perplexed*. These ideas continue in the passion account, such as in 14:27 where Jesus predicts that they will all fall away, and in 14:50 where they all in fact flee at his arrest.

Mark 14:28, with its straightforward reference to Jesus' *resurrection*, refers backwards to the growing list of statements regarding Jesus' *vindication, glory*, and *resurrection* (8:31; 9:9–13, 31; 10:33–34, 35–40; 12:10; 14:25).

At Gethsemane (14:32–42), Jesus' prayer of submission employs the *cup*-image (10:38–39); this *judgment* theme is present as well in the cry of Jesus from the cross (15:34). The Gethsemane story also re-introduces the *divine necessity* of the cross (8:31; 9:12; 14:21). Mark 14:41–42 narrates the *betrayal* by Judas, drawing to completion this aspect of the passion predictions (9:31; 10:33–34; 14:10–11, 18, 21).

Jesus is then *arrested* in 14:43–49 (cf. 12:12; 14:1) by a party acting on behalf of the *chief priests, scribes,* and *elders* (cf. 11:18; 12:12; 14:1–2, 10–11). Again, the *necessity* of this fateful progression of events is accented by Jesus' words: "But let the Scriptures be fulfilled" (14:49; cf. 8:31; 9:12; 14:21, 32–42).

Having been *arrested*, Jesus is brought before the *chief priests, elders, and scribes* (14:53; cf. 8:31; 10:33–34) who *reject* his claim to messiahship and *condemn* him as worthy of death (14:61–64; cf. 8:31; 10:33–34). The *Sanhedrin delivers him over* to Pilate (15:1, 3; cf. 10:33–34). Though he is *sympathetic* toward Jesus and thinks him *innocent*, Pilate gives into the *crowds* (15:2–15; cf. 6:14–29) who have now turned against Jesus (cf. 11:18; 12:12; 14:2). Pilate hands Jesus over to be crucified. The *(Gentile)* soldiers *mock, flog,* and *spit* on Jesus (15:16–20; cf. 10:33–34), and finally lead him away to his *death*.

Afterwards, Joseph of Arimathea *claims his body* and *lays it in a tomb* (15:42–46; cf. 6:29). Later, the angel declares that Jesus has *risen from the dead* (16:6; cf. 8:31; 9:9–12, 31; 10:33–34, 35–40; 12:10; 14:25, 28).

By way of summary a few statements are in order. (A) The Herodians are the only figures in connection with Jesus' passion in chapters 1–13 who play no role whatsoever in the passion account. Earlier we saw reasons for this omission. The Pharisees, mentioned 12 (or 13) times in Mark 1–13 are never explicitly mentioned in Mark 14–16, though they would have been included in the Sanhedrin. (B) Otherwise, our review of the story indicates that without fail every detail of Jesus' passion anticipated in chapters 1–13 finds a corresponding referent in chapters 14–16. (C) The close interrelation of Mark 1–13 and 14–16 thus seems a reasonable — indeed, a necessary conclusion. That is, even though the Markan passion narrative begins in chapter 14, the reader has been conscious of how the story must end from early on.

> The cross is not a stunning surprise; its shadow falls across the entire span of Jesus' ministry. By weaving allusions to the passion into the body of his Gospel, Mark illustrates the inner connection between Jesus' ministry and his death on the cross ... The Jesus of Mark's Gospel is no mere victim, passively accepting an unjust death. He "takes up the cross," not by morbidly choosing death, but by choosing a way of life that would ultimately clash with those who could not see Jesus' way as God's way[62].

Hence, Trocmé's thesis will not stand.

In demonstrating the degree to which Jesus' death has welded together these two sections of Mark's Gospel, we bring to the fore an issue that moves beyond our initial agenda of testing Trocmé's argument. Given the relationship between chapters 1–13 and 14–16, how should this relationship be explained? Does the evidence demand that we regard Mark 1–16 as one redactional whole and dismiss the hypothesis that Mark made use of a pre-Markan passion story? Or, it is possible that "Mark's task was to fash-

---

62 Senior, *Passion: Mark*, 15.

ion these opening chapters [i.e. 1–13] in such a way that they would dovetail perfectly with his predetermined conclusion"[63]? In point of fact, neither alternative is proven by the evidence discussed thus far. Nor can comparisons such as we have undertaken — or more comprehensive redaction-critical studies tracing themes throughout the Gospel, such as that conducted by Matera — ever conclusively deny the latter alternative in favor of the former. To be sure, it is exactly this that Matera has tried to do as he begins drawing together the implications of his study of Jesus' kingship:

> The royal theme of chapter 15 complements earlier motifs in the gospel supporting our contention that Mark has not simply appropriated an older passion story. Rather, we believe that he has carefully redacted the gospel from start to finish[64].

In truth, however, on the basis of such investigations we can never be sure that Mark has not simply molded his early chapters on the model provided by a pre-Markan passion account. *That is, redactional study can never take the place of source- and form-criticism.*

Nevertheless, a decision as to whether Mark did make use of an early passion narrative is not forever out of reach. However, it is in the context of our long-awaited consideration of form-critical matters that the necessary, additional evidence rests. To such matters we now turn.

---

63 So Michael J. Cook, *Mark's Treatment of the Jewish Leaders* (Leiden: E. J. Brill, 1978) 52. Similarly, see Marxsen, *Mark*, 31.
64 Matera, *Kingship of Jesus*, 150. Of course, Matera's conclusion is supported, in the first instance, by his analysis of Mark 15 (pp. 7–55). Therein he argues on redaction-critical grounds that the Second Evangelist is responsible for the content and form of this section of the passion narrative. We find his work inadequate for two reasons. First, he too easily presumes to know what is "Markan redactional vocabulary and style" (on which, see above, chapter 5.II). Second, while redaction criticism can show the hand of the evangelist, editorial presence does not necessarily imply redactional creativity nor deny the use of source materials — a factor Matera overlooks all too often.

Chapter Six:

The Passion in the Early Church: Form-Criticism Revisited

I. Introduction

In an earlier day one might have "proven" the early existence of a narrative of Jesus' passion merely through a rehearsal of the standard form-critical arguments set forth in the first instance by Dibelius, Schmidt, and Bultmann. Thus, when in 1958 T. A. Burkill launched a discussion of Mark's understanding of the passion by asserting the probable existence of an account of its principal events from a very early date, he offered as supportive evidence the narrative's self-sufficiency and coherence, its indications of time and space, and the correspondence of narrative sequence in the four Gospels[1]. Following the explosion of redaction- and literary-critical studies of the passion narrative, however, a simple appeal to the form-critical arguments of fifty and sixty years ago will no longer convince. Perhaps no one is more responsible for this shift than Eta Linnemann, who first challenged the form-critical arguments *en masse*. After dealing one by one with the form-critical points raised by Bultmann, Schmidt, Jeremias, Lohse, Schille, Taylor, and Trocmé, Linnemann placed the form-critical hypothesis of a pre-canonical passion narrative in its sepulcher and sealed it off as a presupposition lacking any basis in the texts themselves[2].

Many of those entombed arguments will never be resurrected and remain little more than fossils from a bygone era of NT criticism. On the other hand, as we have already hinted, there is life in some of those dry bones, and it is our purpose to see what can be done to breathe into them new vitality. In particular, we will raise anew the issue of narrative coherence, the generic debate, and (in the next chapter) the problem of positing a plausible *Sitz im Leben* for a pre-canonical passion story. We will show that

---

[1] T. A. Burkill, "St. Mark's Philosophy of the Passion", *NovT* 2 (1958) 246–247. See also, *idem, Mysterious Revelation: An Examination of the Philosophy of St. Mark's Gospel* (Ithica, New York: Cornell University, 1963) 219–220.

[2] "Die Annahme eines vormarkinische Zusammenhangs in der Passionsgeschichte ist letzlich nicht durch die Ergebnisse der Textbeobachtung aufgenötigt worden, sondern war die Voraussetzung, mit der man bereits an die Texte herangig" (Linnemann, *Studien,* 173; cf. pp. 54–68, 173–174).

each of these arguments was consigned to the grave prematurely, that when considered in a different way or in the context of additional findings they still have much to offer.

Since Linnemann's study of the Markan passion narrative appeared in 1970 the most eloquent and forceful case against a pre-canonical narrative of Jesus' suffering and death has come from the pen of W. H. Kelber[3]. His thesis that the first passion narrative was formulated by the Second Evangelist rests to a large degree on his dismissal of form-critical arguments, and on his understanding of the tension between death and oral communication. For our purposes we may regard Kelber's handling of the form-critical issues as representative of a more general ambivalence toward the vitality of those older arguments. Hence, we may formulate our own case on these matters in response to his discussion — though it will be necessary to draw in at appropriate points other studies, particularly that of Linnemann. It will be seen that a form-critical argument, taken together with other evidence, issues a formidable response against Kelber's thesis concerning the impossibility of an early-formulated passion narrative. First, then, we will outline Kelber's argument.

II. W. H. Kelber and the Markan Passion Narrative

Kelber's discussion of the Markan passion narrative comes at the close of his study of *The Oral and the Written Gospel*. The book itself is cast as a challenge to those who view the written Gospel as having evolved smoothly from oral tradition. The written Gospel, Kelber says, is a counterform to, rather than an extension of, oral hermeneutics. In his final chapter, Kelber turns from the story of Jesus' life in Mark 1–13 to the story of Jesus' death, thus drawing to a close his inquiry into the ability of language to handle each. He wants to show that as orality was especially attentive to Jesus' words and deeds, it belongs to textuality to bring death to language.

Mark's passion narrative, he observes, is laden with death — narrating as it does the death of Jesus, the death of the temple, and the demise of the disciples. It is also a tightly-plotted story, where narrative compactness replaces orally discernible materials. Of course, it was this narrative coherence that led earlier critics to theorize about a primitive passion account; however, Kelber insists, narrative coherence is not an indication of early compilation, but of narrative competence. In setting forth their theories about a pre-canonical passion story, form critics failed to address the prior, linguistic questions:

---

3 Kelber, *Gospel*, 184–199.

How does one account for the oral tendency to seize upon the life of Jesus and the greater ability of textuality to appropriate death? Did one not speak about Jesus' death? What is the nexus between death and textuality[4]?

Further work — e.g. that of Schrenk and Dormeyer — has only demonstrated further the narrative compactness of the Markan passion account. Kelber summarizes:

> If the scholarship of the past half century teaches us anything, it is that the extraordinary dense textuality of the Markan passion narrative does not lend itself well to decompositioning[5].

Hence, Pesch was right to call for a reappraisal of the whole discussion, and to speak of the unified character of the whole passion narrative. Where Pesch went wrong, in Kelber's view, was in his failure to give Markan composition a fair hearing. That is, in crediting the passion story as a whole to early tradition Peash did not take seriously enough the redactional and theological agenda of the Second Evangelist.

Kelber goes on to lay aside the various arguments for the development of an early passion narrative, insisting that there is little foundation for suggesting the story's evolutionary growth. His real case against a written narrative from early Christian times, however, is that what we otherwise know of the development of the early Jesus-tradition suggests a climate not given to the composition of a passion story. The early source Q, for example, never mentions Jesus' death, nor is there any reflection on Jesus' death in the "didactic stories", "stories of Jesus' powerful deeds", or in the parabolic tradition (apart from the parable of the wicked tenants).

Moreover, literary-aesthetic and psychocultural considerations deny the possibility of an early, written passion narrative. A reluctance to deal with crucifixion and death in the written medium circumvents the composition of a passion narrative in earliest Christianity.

> In view of widespread reluctance to write about crucifixion, and of synoptic orality's reticence to speak about Jesus' execution, is it plausible that the first recollection early Christians committed to writing would become one of the most realistic passion narratives in antiquity? There can be no doubt whatsoever that Jesus' execution was a profoundly traumatic experience for his followers. Early christophanies promoted the living Christ and in part at least will have triggered oral remembering of words and deeds, but not of death. Is not *distance from the trauma* an essential psychocultural prerequisite for most mediations of death? Must we not assume geographical, chronological, and psychological distance before the cross could be assimilated into a developed narrative dramatization[6]?

Indeed, it was only through the eucharist that Jesus' death was assimilated by early Christians, though Kelber finds scarce evidence that the celebration of the Lord's Supper itself could have given rise to a passion narrative.

---

4 Kelber, *Gospel*, 188.
5 Kelber, *Gospel*, 189.
6 Kelber, *Gospel*, 193–194.

In other words, there was no oral passion narrative, nor an early, written passion story. Rather, Mark created the first passion narrative — accomplishing this task after 70 A.D. What, then, was its manner of composition? The passion narrative, argues Kelber, was built up from OT texts, and OT texts as they circulated in the oral medium.

We can appreciate Kelber's emphasis on the distinctiveness of orality over against textuality as a corrective to excessive assumptions about the development of the Gospel tradition circulated since Bultmann's seminal work[7]. There is much about his approach that rings true, even if it is also true that he seems to have overdrawn the line between the two media — orality and textuality. Even so, his case against a pre-canonical passion narrative will not hold up to close scrutiny, and it now remains for us to respond in some detail to his arguments.

III. The Implications of Narrative Coherence

In the main, we can readily agree with Kelber's evaluation of Mark 14—15 as a tightly-plotted story. As indicated earlier, a general consensus exists that the passion narrative displays an inner coherence not found elsewhere in the Gospel. This judgment takes into account the appearance this section of the Gospel gives of being a self-contained, self-sufficient story, with its own "introduction" and "conclusion". Likewise, it allows for the plotted time and topographical movement of the narrative, and it embraces the observation that there is little excess in the story line from beginning to end. Almost without exception, the various pericopae are integral to the progression of the story.

Moreover, this evaluation recognizes the improbability that more than a very small minority of the individual units that together form the passion narrative would have circulated independently[8]. To be sure, numerous interpreters have argued that the anointing scene (Mark 14:3—9) was brought to the narrative by the Second Evangelist, and the presence of a similar tradition outside the passion narrative in Luke 7:36—50 may support this judgment. On the other hand, as we have observed, the intersection of the Markan and Johannine narratives on the location of this scene together with the plot against Jesus by the Jewish leaders at the outset of

---

[7] See already, E. Earle Ellis, "New Directions in Form Criticism", in *Prophecy and Hermeneutic*, 242—247; *idem*, "Gospels Criticism: A Perspective on the State of the Art", in *Das Evangelium*, 41.

[8] See above, chapter 3.XXV; Trocmé, *Passion*, 49—51; Schweizer, *Mark*, 284; Pesch, "Ueberlieferung", 151—152; Dibelius, *Tradition*, 178; Lane, *Mark*, 486.

the passion story suggests that from an early time the episode of Jesus' anointing at Bethany was understood as an ingredient of the passion story.

Neither do references to events in the passion story outside the Gospels constitute evidence that from an early date a number of individual units received independent circulation. The sermons of Acts — especially 2:23—24; 3:13—15; 13:27—30 — retain reminders of some episodes in the passion account — including Jesus' being "handed over" to the Jews and to Pilate, his being found innocent by Pilate, the Barabbas incident, Jesus' crucifixion, and his burial. One might argue that these references are traditional, and thus point to an embryonic passion narrative already composed for the early Christian mission. Alternatively, one might argue that these references were inspired by the Lukan passion narrative. A discussion of the possibility of locating primitive material in the *Missionsreden* of Acts is outside the boundaries of this investigation; at present it is enough to conjecture that Luke was aware that the early mission incorporated the incidents of Jesus' passion and death in its apologetic, so, borrowing from traditional sources (at least some of which were non-Markan — cf. Acts 13:28), he represented what was originally proclaimed. In any case, these recollections do not support an hypothesis that individual stories circulated on their own. Conversely, the individual incidents are presented in their wider connections even in these sermons.

First Timothy 6:13 and 1 Pet 2:23 make passing references to Jesus' trial before Pilate and the abuse Jesus suffered in that context. In both texts Jesus' exemplary behavior is spotlighted with reference to a specific episode in the passion. However, in both instances the wider context of Jesus' example in suffering and death is implicit, and it is probable that such brief allusions as these actually assume some knowledge of the whole story on the reader's part. Similarly, Heb 5:7, regarded by many as a throwback to the prayer of Jesus at Gethsemane[9], does not witness to an independent account of that event, for it also embraces the fuller context of Jesus' suffering and vindication. Again, the larger story is assumed.

The Pauline citation of the tradition of the Last Supper (1 Cor 11:23—25), on the other hand, provides unequivocal evidence that this material enjoyed independent circulation. However, even this "exception" will

---

9 Much about Heb 5:7 can be explained in terms of the use of OT language (Martin Dibelius, "Gethsemane", in *Botschaft*, 1:261—262), "but even here the strength of the language overruns its Psalm allusions" (Dunn, *Jesus*, 364 n. 38). F. F. Bruce, *The Epistle to the Hebrews* (Grand Rapids, Michigan: Wm. B. Eerdmans, 1964) 99—102; James Moffat, *A Critical and Exegetical Commentary on the Epistle to the Hebrews* (Edinburgh: T. & T. Clark, 1924) 64—65; Dunn, *Jesus*, 18—19 — these interpreters see Gethsemane as the historical referent of this verse. Cf., however, Harold W. Attridge, "Heard Because of His Reverence (Heb 5:7)", *JBL* 98 (1979) 90—93. See below, 8.V.

later be shown to be less a departure from the norm than might at first seem. Even here it should not be overlooked that the tradition Paul quotes includes two phrases — "on the night he was betrayed" and "after supper" — that immediately place it within the larger context of the passion events.

In this discussion of various episodes in the passion narrative, we may recall the earlier notation we made of the possibility of a "Peter trajectory" that might have served some biographical interest or at least briefly circulated on its own on account of the prominence of Peter. Such reminiscences of the apostle as might have been collected may have included the prediction of Peter's denial and the fulfillment of that prediction apart from the greater context given them in the passion narrative. Nevertheless, even if such a Petrine tradition existed we should also remember that we have hitherto found evidence that from an early date the story of Peter's denial was connected to that of Jesus' trial before the Jewish leaders.

In short, for the most part, the pericopae in the passion account are mutually interdependent and so lose their meaning when divorced from their immediate context. We would be overstepping the evidence if we insisted that no single incident in the passion story originated or circulated autonomously prior to the formation of the passion narrative. Likewise, we must at this point allow for the possibility that an aggregate of incidents, such as those having to do with the Last Supper, circulated on its own apart from the fuller story. Yet, for the most part, each narrated episode makes sense only in the greater context.

The conclusion thus stated will be readily accepted by most scholars. The disputed question lies in the implications following from it. Linnemann recognizes the inner coherence of Mark 14—15, but credits this to the coherency of the events themselves[10]. Kelber argues that the coherence, vividness, and realism of the story prove narrative competence — i.e. the high level of literary ability possessed by the story's author[11]. Both attribute the original passion narrative to Mark. However, as our consideration of the evidence has shown, it is precisely this narrative coherence that indicates that Mark is not the account's originator. Our case for this position, worked out in this and previous chapters, can be outlined as follows: (A) We have found no basis for supposing that more than two or three of of the episodes narrated in the passion story circulated on their own, apart from their greater context in that story. (B) Therefore, no foundation exists for thinking (with, e.g., Linnemann) that the Second Evangelist had available a collection of unassociated episodes of what happened with regard to Jesus' suffering and death. (C) Further, if the coherency of this

---

10 Linnemann, *Studien*, 173—174.
11 Kelber, *Gospel*, 187—188.

narrative lies already in the coherency of the events, then there is no reason to believe (as does Linnemann) that it took a Mark, writing some three decades (or more) after the events themselves, to join them into a coherent narrative. Their chronological, topographical, and thematic coherence would have drawn them together in the period prior to the writing of the Second Gospel. (D) Mark's editorial agenda and redactional procedure exhibited in Mark 1–13 are restricted; thus we have no *a priori* reason to suspect he would operate differently in chapters 14–16.

(E) Thus, in crediting Mark with "narrative competence", Kelber has overrated Mark's redactional agenda and procedure. This is all the more true in that Kelber's thesis does not allow for the availability of "reports" or even fragmentary traditions of the episodes having to do with Jesus' passion. As such items were avoided in oral hermeneutics, Mark must be credited with constructing the whole narrative solely on the basis of OT texts understood to anticipate Jesus' suffering and death. Without even a skeletal outline of the events of Jesus' passion, therefore, Mark was to have created a tightly-woven, detailed passion narrative. Aside from the fact that Kelber has not shown how every detail of Mark 14–15 rests on OT texts, nor whether the hermeneutical climate of early Christianity embraced this sort of approach to the Jewish Scriptures[12], not only because of the editorial procedure Mark adopts in his earlier chapters, but not least for this reason, Kelber's hypothesis is untenable.

(F) Therefore, the balance of the evidence favors a coherent narrative of Jesus' passion as part of Mark's pre-canonical tradition. The extent of this narrative will be discussed below, but we have already found reason to believe that the main outline of the narrative as it now stands in Mark's Gospel approximates the shape of that earlier account.

Nevertheless, considerations such as we have just assembled would be subjected to serious and damaging counter-questions if Kelber is otherwise correct in his view of the literary-aesthetic and psychocultural climate of the period prior to the fall of Jerusalem. If it can be demonstrated that Jesus' death was not a topic for preaching and oral communication in the early Christian mission and community life, then this would certainly constitute an insurmountable obstacle for any theory of a pre-canonical passion narrative. In fact, a number of lines of evidence from the NT and the pre-Christian milieu converge to overturn Kelber's proposal *and* to corroborate the pre-canonical existence of an extended narrative of Jesus' suffering and death.

---

12 On this issue, see Moo, *OT – Passion; Gospel Perspectives,* vol. 3.

IV. Jesus' Death in Earliest Christianity

A. "Christ Cruficied"

Some twenty-five years after Jesus' crucifixion, Paul wrote of the scandal and folly of the cross of Christ (1 Cor 1:18, 23). Martin Hengel has devoted a monograph to a survey of the use of crucifixion in the Graeco-Roman world by way of filling in the background of the stigma associated with the cross in the first-century milieu in which Christianity was born. His study makes clear that

> when Paul talks of the 'folly' of the message of the crucified Jesus, he is ... not speaking in riddles or using an abstract cipher. He is expressing the harsh experience of his missionary preaching and the offense that it caused, in particular the experience of his preaching among non-Jews, with whom his apostolate was particularly concerned[13].

According to the evidence Hengel has assembled, the one crucified suffered the utmost humiliation and was understood not only by the courts, but also by the general populace, as having received the just deserts of a criminal. How could a man found guilty and thus humiliated among his people be God's "Anointed One"?

Yet, the scandal runs deeper. Already by the time of Jesus, Deut 21:22–23 – "anyone who is hung on a tree is under God's curse" – was being applied to the penalty of crucifixion[14]. That is, the crucified one – in this case, Jesus – was not only judged a criminal by his peers, but also was understood to bear the curse of God[15]. In referring to Jesus as the Messiah – a usage rooted in the period of Jesus' own lifetime[16] – early Christians involved themselves in what must have seemed a most unlikely oxymoron, for if the idea of a *suffering Messiah* runs counter to what we know of messianic expectation in first-century Judaism[17], how much more an antithesis the concept of a *crucified Messiah* must have been! Still further, we know that already in pre-Pauline Christianity the cross was accorded soteriological significance[18]. For all these reasons it would be unthinkable that those

---

13 Hengel, *Crucifixion*, 89; cf. p. 19.
14 See above, chapter 4, n. 327.
15 See Gal 3:13; Friedrich, *Verkündigung*, 122–130; Hans Weder, *Der Kreuz Jesu bei Paulus· Ein Versuch. über den Geschichtsbezug des christlichen Glaubens nachzudenken* (Göttingen: Vandenhoeck & Ruprecht, 1981) 186–193.
16 The most impressive evidence for this judgment is that Jesus was condemned as a messianic pretender – see Harvey, *Jesus*, 120–151; Dunn, *Unity and Diversity*, 41; I. Howard Marshall, *The Origins of New Testament Christology* (Downers Grove, Illinois: InterVarsity, 1976) 85–91.
17 See N. A. Dahl, "The Crucified Messiah", in *Crucified Messiah*, 23–24; Vermes, *Jesus*, 38; Hengel, *Crucifixion*, 10; Schürer, *History*, 2:547–549. However, Sam K. Williams (*Jesus' Death as Saving Event: The Background and Origin of a Concept* [Missoula, Montana: Scholars, 1975] 117) and F. F. Bruce ("The Background of the Son of Man Sayings", in *Christ the Lord*, 61) suggest that the Isaianic Servant may have been subjected to a messianic interpretation at Qumran.
18 Hengel (*Atonement*) insists that from the beginning, founding their belief on Jesus' own interpre-

earliest Christians were not forced to come to terms with Jesus' death on the cross. *Jesus' death had to be talked about and reflected upon in missionary apologetic and community life, for it was precisely this crucified-and-dead Jesus who was being proclaimed as Messiah.* Kelber's rhetoric about the psychocultural considerations opposing the development of a tradition regarding Jesus' crucifixion overlooks the cardinal importance of demonstrating early on that "Christ crucified" was not a contradiction in terms[19].

B. "Oral Hermeneutics" and Jesus' Death

A few comments are also in order regarding Kelber's judgment that oral hermeneutics was preoccupied with aspects of Jesus' life, but silent or reticent with respect to his death. Within the parabolic tradition the most significant exception to Kelber's datum is the parable of the wicked tenants (Mark 12:1—12), as Kelber admitted. A further exception, not noted in this context by Kelber, is the parable of the bridegroom (Mark 2:19—20). Earlier, we discussed both of these texts as anticipatory allusions to Jesus' death. Moreover, Michaels has argued that the parables of growth are susceptible to a passion interpretation[20]. This level of interpretation is fairly explicit in the Fourth Gospel according to Michaels, who finds in such texts as 12:23—24 a Synoptic-like parable of growth that has become a vehicle for proclaiming Jesus' death and resurrection. Of course, it is debatable when such an interpretation arose, so undue weight ought not be placed on this theory.

Apart from the parables, we read in Mark of other references to Jesus' death, particularly in 8:31; 9:31; 10:33—34, 38, and 45. Earlier, we saw that 8:31; 9:31; and 10:33—34 rest on pre-Markan tradition, at least in part. Kelber does not seem to question the traditional quality of 10:38, 45 either; the latter text has been the subject of a long debate with the result that there are now very strong arguments for supporting its fundamental authenticity[21]. As we have seen, both of these texts point unambiguously to Jesus' death.

---

tation of his death, Jesus' disciples understood the cross as the saving event *par excellence*. The objections to Hengel's approach voiced by Williams (see his review of *The Atonement* in *JBL* 102 [3, 1983] 491—493; and *idem, Jesus' Death,* 203—229) are not persuasive (see below, chapter 7.IV.B). Hence, reflection on the soteriological significance of Jesus' death was taking place long before the formation of the passion narrative, according to Kelber's thesis.

19 See Dunn, *Unity and Diversity,* 42; Lohse, *Geschichte,* 17—18; Dahl, "Crucified Messiah"; Lindars, *NT Apologetic,* 73—137; Hengel, *Atonement,* 39—75.
20 Michaels, *Servant and Son,* 145—150.
21 See now Page, "Authenticity"; Peter Stuhlmacher, "Existenzstellvertretung für die Vielen: Mk 10, 45 (Mt 20, 28)", in *Werden und Wirken,* 412—427; Kim, *Son of Man,* 38—43; Pesch, *Abendmahl,* 170—180.

Additonally, while Kelber restricts his discussion to the evidence of the Jesus-tradition, it would seem methodologically suspect to speak only of this aspect of the developing christological tradition when reflecting on the "hermeneutical climate" of the first decades following Jesus' death. The formulaic tradition, a tradition rich in its references to the fact and significance of Jesus' death[22], ought also to be considered. To be sure, the existence of a formulaic tradition dealing with the cross of Christ does not imply the existence of an early-formulated passion narrative. Yet, any approach to early christological development runs amiss when it completely sunders the two traditions – narrative and confessional. Early christology developed along both lines in the same period and in the same places, the one informing and influencing the other[23]. From the confessional tradition we have unequivocal evidence that early Christians did reflect on Jesus' death, and we may place this testimony alongside the materials in the Jesus-tradition as evidence against Kelber's judgment that the early church was controlled by a reticence to speak of Jesus' death.

It may be objected that it is one thing to demonstrate the capacity to speak of Jesus' death among early Christians, but quite another to credit the early church with a written narrative of that event. Of course, such an objection would be well-taken, but it must not be overlooked that we have in this way overcome Kelber's argument that a reluctance to come face to face with Jesus' death would have precluded the early formulaton of a literary account of Jesus' passion. In fact, the christological faith of those early Christians precluded any such reluctance. This we have demonstrated not only by indicating the theoretical necessity of overcoming the contradiction of the crucified Messiah, but also with reference to the Jesus-tradition and primitive christological confessional tradition which testify to Jesus' death. That is, "oral hermeneutics" would not have disallowed reflection on the event and interpretation of Jesus' death. Now we must face the question whether "literary-aesthetic" considerations tell against a written passion narrative in the early church.

---

22 See, e.g., Rom 3:25–26; 4:25; 8:32–34; 1 Cor 5:7; 15:3–5; 2 Cor 5:18–21; Gal 1:3–4; 2:20–21; 3:13–14; 1 Thess 5:9–10; 1 Tim 2:6; Lohse, *Märtyrer*, part two; Hengel, *Atonement*, chapter two; Ralph P. Martin, *Reconciliation: A Study of Paul's Theology* (London: Marshall, Morgan and Scott, 1981) 81–89, 93–97; Marshall, "Development of the Concept of Redemption"; Archibald M. Hunter, *Paul and His Predecessors*, rev. ed. (Grand Rapids, Michigan: Wm. B. Eerdmans, 1961); et al.

23 Cf. Goppelt, *NT Theology*, 2:26–30; Hengel, *Acts*, 43–44; idem, *Crucifixion*, 18; Richard B. Hays, *The Faith of Jesus Christ: An Investigation of the Narrative Substructure of Galatians 3: 1–4:11* (Chico, California: Scholars, 1983), esp. pp. 256–258.

C. Literary Conventions and Jesus' Death

Surveys of the ways in which "death" was handled in the literature of antiquity often draw attention to the reserve of the OT in such matters when compared with Greek writings of the classical era[24]. Speaking generally of OT thought, death as such signified little more than the end of life. For example, that David, Solomon, and Abijah "slept with their fathers" (1 Kgs 2:10; 11:43; 15:8) offers little evidence of attempts at explicating the meaning of death. Second Samuel 14:14 ("Like water spilled on the ground, which cannot be recovered, so we must die") and Gen 3:19c ("for dust you are and to dust you shall return") reflect the inevitability of death without raising the question, Why? Even the martyr-deaths of the prophets (e.g. Jer 26:20–23; 2 Chron 24:20–22; Neh 9:26) receive little more than matter-of-fact references. Though 1 Chron 10:13–14 asserts that Saul's death was the Lord's doing because of Saul's sins, the actual narrative of his death in 1 Sam 31:1–16 provides no interpretation of its significance. Faced with the prospect of falling into the hands of the Philistines, Saul commits suicide; yet, there is no hint that his was a heroic end. In the relatively lengthy account of Samson's death we learn that in vengeance "he killed more when he died than when he lived", but as to the meaning attached to his death as such, we have no clues (Jud 16:23–31).

As both Hengel and Williams have demonstrated[25], the situation among the Greeks was quite different. In Hellenistic literature death might be a way of achieving glorious fame or even deification. Frequently, one reads that individuals gave their lives for the benefit of their families, friends, cities, or for philosophical truth. Even brief accounts of death embellish the act of dying with statements of meaning or reward. For example, after Heracles had armed the people of Thebes for battle against Erginus an oracle promised them victory if the noblest-born citizen would take his life. Antipoenus, from the lineage of the "Sown Men", was reluctant to do so, but his daughters did so gladly in his stead – and were afterwards honored as heroines[26]. Here, the act of dying is completely subordinated to an explanation of its significance and reward, and to the willingness with which death was embraced by the two girls.

---

24 See esp. Hengel, *Atonement*, 1:32; Williams, *Jesus' Death*, 96-102, 137–163. On death in the OT, see also Walter Brueggemann, "Death, Theology of", in *IDBSup*, 219–221; Gerhard von Rad, *Old Testament Theology*, 2 vols. (New York: Harper & Row 1962/65) 1:387–391; D. S. Russell, *The Method and Message of Jewish Apocalyptic* (London: SCM, 1964) 353–357; Walter Schmithals, "Death, Kill, Sleep" in *NIDNTT*, 1:432–434; Elmer B. Smick, " מות " in *TWOT*, 1:496–497.
25 Hengel, *Atonement*, 1–32; Williams, *Jesus' Death*, 137–163.
26 See Pausanias, *Description of Greece*, 9.17.1.

While such reports are not infrequent in Greek mythology, one also reads of instances in which the *way* someone meets death is recounted by way of lavishing greater honor on the person. Thus, Heracles's own death is recounted at some length so as to underscore his courage and the noble way in which he faced death[27]. The history of ancient Israel has nothing with which to compare such a heroic portrayal of death and dying.

However, with the rise of apocalyptic and the influx of Hellenism as a cultural force in Palestine, long-held patterns of thought about death were transformed[28]. We may note three changes of special importance. First, the hope of resurrection was made explicit. Second, death became a heroic way in which to testify to the faith. Third, the deaths of martyrs were understood as effective — both as an act atoning for one's own sins or even the sins of the nation[29], and as a means by which evil forces were opposed. This conceptual metamorphosis is especially manifest in certain writings of the intertestamental period, in which the problem presented by the death of the faithful is treated in narrative fashion. See, for example, 1 Macc 2:27–38 (vv 29–41); 2 Macc 6:18–7:42 — texts in which the horror of persecution and death are paramount, together with explicit reflection on the meaning of death. Similarly, while the story of the persecuted righteous in Wis 2:12–20; 4:18–5:14 has little to say about the act of dying as such, it does testify to the capacity of the author to deal openly with death and its meaning.

From such texts as these we note a perceivable shift toward coming to terms with the significance of the suffering and death of the faithful. Moreover, in the Maccabean martyr-tale we observe what appears to have been a near fascination with the horrible details of torturous suffering and death.

---

27 See Apollodorus, *The Library*, 2.7.7.

28 See Martin Hengel, *Judaism and Hellenism*, rev. ed. (Philadelphia: Fortress, 1974) 97–98; idem, *Atonement*, 6–7; Williams, *Jesus' Death*; W. H. C. Frend, *Martyrdom and Persecution in the Early Church: A Study of a Conflict from the Maccabees to Donatus* (Oxford: Basil Blackwell, 1965; reprint ed., Grand Rapids, Michigan: Baker, 1981) 31–78; Schmithals, "Death, Kill, Sleep", 435; Russel, *Method and Message*, 357–390.

29 In his study of *Jesus' Death*, Williams severely downplays the atoning effect of the death of the martyrs, grudgingly allowing such an interpretation only in the case of 4 Macc 6:28–29 (on this text, see his pp. 176–179). Indeed, he concludes that this text "... does not intend to present a 'doctrine of expiatory death'" (178). As this text so explicitly raises the issue of redemption, if it does not intend to present such an idea, this is all the more reason to question the novelty of this idea in contemporary Judaism. On the other hand, Williams is virtually alone in denying the expiatory nature of the suffering and death in 2 Maccabees (see his pp. 76–90). This notion is clear, if undeveloped, in 7:37–38 — see John Downing, "Jesus and Martyrdom", *JTS* n.s. 14 (1963) 282–283; Hengel, *Judaism and Hellenism*, 2:68 n.326; Lohse, *Märtyrer*, 66–69; W. D. Davies, *Paul and Rabbinic Judaism*, 4th ed. (Philadelphia: Fortress, 1980) 272; H. J. Schoeps, *Paul: The Theology of the Apostle in the Light of Jewish Religious History* (Philadelphia: Westminster, 1961) 130; et al.

In view of these considerations it is difficult to avoid the conclusion that a concern to explicate in the form of a story the events and significance of Jesus' passion would not have been out of place in the milieu of infantile Christianity.

Seen against the background of this line of evidence, a literary account of Jesus' passion would not have been the novelty Kelber's discussion makes of it. There is even more to this line of evidence than we have noted, however, and we must now turn to show the close relationship of the narrative of Jesus' passion on the one hand, and a certain, well-attested strand of pre-Christian tradition on the other.

V. The "Suffering/Vindication" Genre and a Pre-Canonical Passion Narrative

In 1972 George W. E. Nickelsburg published his study of *Resurrection, Immortality, and Eternal Life in Intertestamental Judaism,* a major contribution of which consisted in his form-critical work identifying a traditional schema describing the vindication of the persecuted innocent. In a subsequent article he refined his analysis, which he has also worked into his textbook on intertestamental literature[30]. His investigation dealt with the stories of persecution and vindication in Gen 37–42, the *Story of Ahikar,* Esther, Dan 3 and 6, and Susanna. In addition, he discerned influence from this tradition in Wis 2, 4–5 – a story also bearing the imprint of a traditional apocalyptic interpretation of Isa 52:13–53:12. Third Maccabees and 2 Macc 7 both share affinities with the Isaianic tradition attested in Wis 2, 4–5, and are related in other ways to the stories thus listed.

Nickelsburg writes:

> All of the aforementioned stories are characterized by a common theme: the rescue and vindication of a persecuted innocent person or persons. This theme is emplotted by means of a limited number of narrative elements or components, most of them describing "actions," a few of them, motivations or emotions. The components perform specific functions in the flow and logic of the narrative[31].

The components about which Nickelsburg writes are basically of two kinds. On the one hand are those that are integral to the genre, that ordinarily appear in a fixed sequence from story to story. On occasion, however, a component may be employed in retrospect or prospect, and, as a result, appear out of order. On the other hand are the variable components. Their

---

30 Nickelsburg, *Resurrection,* 48–106. A revision of that original analysis appears in his "The Genre and Function of the Markan Passion Narrative", *HTR* 73 (1980) 156–163. This form-critical work is assumed in his *Jewish Literature.*
31 Nickelsburg, "Genre and Function", 156–157.

presence in a story is optional; when they do appear they follow no strict sequential pattern. Their function is to enrich the individual narratives and provide specific details needed for a particular story.

Nickelsburg outlines the components of this genre as follows: *introduction, provocation, conspiracy, decision, trust, obedience, accusation, trial* (into which *decision, trust,* and *obedience* may be incorporated), *condemnation, protest, prayer, assistance, ordeal, reactions,* and *rescue;* then, the following are plotted in variable sequence: *vindication, exaltation, investiture, acclamation, reactions,* and *punishment*[32].

One key point at which this form-critical reconstruction is open to criticism concerns the sequential relationship of *rescue* and *death*[33]. One cannot overlook the fact that in most, and especially in the earlier, of the stories Nickelsburg draws together, the protagonist(s) *do(es) not die*, whereas in 2 Macc 7 and Wis 2, 4–5, *death* does occur. In the former examples, the *rescue* is from death, while in the latter, *rescue* follows *death*. However, this is not the obstacle it might at first seem, for it is only indicative of a development in the way in which divine *rescue* was perceived. In the latter tales, *death* is acceptable since life with God persisted after the grave. Hence, there is evidence here of the flexibility of the literary genre to accommodate conceptual development.

Since first identifying the genre in intertestamental literature, Nickelsburg has begun to carry the results of his study into the NT, inquiring into the possibility that this literary form has influenced NT writings. In a recent article he claims to have recognized in major parts of the Markan passion narrative a reflection of this traditional pattern[34]. As he himself is aware, this identification is not without its problems. Nevertheless, two important points merge with regard to our investigation already. Most fundamental, one finds in Nickelsburg's work forceful evidence of the ability to deal with death in pre-Christian Judaism – and that in a stylized literary pattern. In addition, in documenting points of correspondence between the traditional story of the persecuted and vindicated righteous with the narrative of Jesus' passion, Nickelsburg has cast doubt on any attempt to deny the possibility of an early literary development of a passion narrative. What, then, of the problems of his analysis?

---

32 See the summary in Nickelsburg, "Genre and Function", 157–162.
33 See Robert Doran, "The Martyr: A Synoptic View of the Mother and Her Sons", in *Ideal Figures*, 189–190.
34 See Nickelsburg, "Genre and Function", 163–167. See also David R. Catchpole, "The Poor on Earth and the Son of Man in Heaven. A Re-Appraisal of Matthew xxv.31–46", *BJRL* 61 (1978–79) 355–397; here, Nickelsburg's generic insights are employed on another piece of the Gospel tradition.

From the perspective of our question concerning the possible existence and shape of a pre-canonical passion account, two difficulties are outstanding. First, Nickelsburg must introduce 11:15—18 (*provocation*) into the passion narrative. Second, his analysis finds no room for the following segments of the Markan story: 14:12—52, 65—72; 15:21—25, 27—28, 33, 35, 40—47. Nickelsburg attempts to set these points aside with reference to Mark's redactional interests. It is at least arguable, however, that his comparison of the Markan passion story with the traditional account of the persecution and vindication of the righteous has raised unnecessary problems. That is, the passion narrative in Mark's Gospel may conform more closely to the literary genre he has identified than his study allows. In what follows, we shall show that this is indeed the case.

If there was an early passion narrative containing an *introduction* and *provocation*, these two components have been excised from the passion story as it now stands in the Second Gospel. This is not surprising in that the whole of Mark 1—13 may be understood to serve these purposes. This is not to suggest that these earlier chapters are only introductory and preparatory for the passion story and thus have no purpose of their own[35]. Rather, it is a recognition of the point made earlier that Jesus' condemnation and death are prepared for, and anticipated in, the first 13 chapters of Mark's Gospel. It is perhaps worthy of mention that the lack of *provocation* in the passion narrative corresponds to the ambivalence in the narrative regarding the *reason* for Jesus' condemnation. By way of underscoring Jesus' innocence and the *heilsgeschichtliche* necessity of his death, any mention of *provocation* might have been purposely left out of the story, or excised from it at an early stage. That is, the requirements peculiar to narrating the story of *Jesus'* death may have resulted in slight modifications of the traditional literary pattern.

On the other hand, in a secondary sense, 14:3—9 may be regarded as *provocation*, for the anointing scene results in an indignant response on the part of Judas and leads to his involvement in the *conspiracy* (14:10—11)[36], which first appears in 14:1—2.

Nickelsburg finds no room in his analysis for 14:12—52, and locates the *decision, trust,* and *obedience* of Jesus in the story of Jesus' *trial.* It is true that 14:12—16 serve no recognizable function within the traditional genre identified in other literature, but a like decision for the other aspects of this large section would be overly hasty. Jesus' *acceptance* of his fate along with his certainty that this death is God's will (i.e. *trust* and *obedi*-

---

35 See Best, *Mark*, 140; Böttger, *König der Juden*, 93; Hengel, "Probleme", 226—230, 235—236.
36 So John Bowman, *The Gospel of Mark: The New Christian Passover Haggadah* (Leiden: E. J. Brill, 1965) 256.

ence) comes to the fore in 14:17—21 (the betrayal-announcement), in 14: 22—24 (the Supper-words), and in 14:27 (the quotation from Zech 13:7). Moreover, 14:25, with its forward-looking reference to drinking in the kingdom, is evidence of his *trust* in, and anticipation of, God's *rescue* and his own *vindication/exaltation*. Likewise, 14:28, with its anticipation of the resurrection, is a testimony to Jesus' *vindication/exaltation* beforehand. The episode in Gethsemane (14:32—42) has long been regarded as the critical point in the fateful progression of events leading to the cross[37]. Certainly, the motifs of *decision, trust,* and *obedience* are present here, in a scene in which the *prayer* occurs out of sequence, employed prospectively.

The arrest (14:43—49), too, is a time of *decision* as Jesus irreversibly *accepts* his fate. In addition, this episode is preparatory to the *trial* and has parallels in other examples of this literary model — e.g. Dan 3:13; 2 Macc 7:1. The narration of the *trial* (14:53, 55—65) embraces additional components: *accusation, reaction, condemnation,* and *ordeal.* Jesus' answer to the high priest anticipates his *rescue, vindication,* and *exaltation* (and, perhaps, *judgment*).

The story of Jesus before Pilate (15:1—5) likewise embraces a number of elements. Above all, it is a *trial* scene in which Jesus is *accused.* Jesus' silence before his *accusers* leads to Pilate's amazed *reaction* and his *protest* (on behalf of Jesus) of his *innocence*. He provides Jesus with *assistance*, attempting to have him released, but in the end announces his *condemnation.*

In an ironic way, the soldiers anticipate Jesus' *investiture* and *acclamation* (15:16—20). The element of *ordeal* is present as well, for the soldiers mock Jesus according to the question put to him at the *trial* (15:2). Carrying forward the irony of the story, the inscription on the cross (15:26) is an *acclamation* of Jesus' true status.

With reference back to the *trial* before the Sanhedrin, the mockery hurled at Jesus in 15:29—32 takes the form of an *ordeal.* Mark 15:33—36 is reminiscent of Wis 2:17—20 and thus carries forward the *ordeal,* as the lookers-on wait for Jesus to be *rescued* from the cross. Jesus' *death*, however, intervenes (15:37). Immediately following (15:38—39) are the elements of *vindication* and *judgment* in the form of the rending of the veil of the temple. The centurion's *reaction* takes the form of an *acclamation.*

Our comparison of the Markan passion story with the traditional literary genre identified by Nickelsburg demonstrates that the two correspond much more closely than Nickelsburg suspected. Nevertherless, additional comment is required on three points. First, the story of Jesus' passion is

---

37 See Barbour, "Gethsemane".

somewhat complicated by the presence of events — e.g. two *trials* rather than one — not evidenced in the earlier examples of the literary form. This not only reflects the ability of the generic pattern to absorb additional features without losing its basic shape, but also suggests that the early framers of the passion account felt bound to represent the historical events with faithfulness.

Second, unlike the other examples Nickelsburg cites, the Markan passion narrative offers no *rescue* and *exaltation/vindication per se,* though we have noted how at several points these components are anticipated. Thus, the Markan passion story corresponds more closely to "scene one" of the tradition, as found in Wis 2, without developing the content of "scene two", as found in Wis 4—5. The separation of the two scenes within the whole pattern is not unique, for in 1 Enoch 62—63 we see a comparable emphasis on scene two.

Finally, our analysis fails to account for the specific presence of 14:12—16, 54, 66—72; 15:21—24, 40—47. While the Supper scene (14:17—31) embraces elements of the traditional genre, it is arguable whether one may consider this scene as integral to it. In the context of these two points we may recall that Nickelsburg's analysis of the traditional pattern leaves room for "variable elements".

It is perhaps debatable how far a genre can be modified and still retain its identity. Certainly, one must allow for some variability — e.g. we continue to refer to Matthew and Luke as "Gospels" in spite of their addition of birth stories (and much more) to Mark. However, this is a question we need not address here, for whether or not one may legitimately refer to the Markan passion narrative as an *example* of the traditional genre of the persecuted and vindicated righteous, the probability is very high that it has at least been *influenced* by that literary pattern. This conclusion is even further substantiated by the Lukan passion narrative with its notable parallels to Wis 2, 4—5 — as Beck has demonstrated[38].

VI. Summary

In this chapter we have examined form-critical arguments, both old and new, regarding the existence of a pre-canonical passion narrative. While some interpreters had previously denounced such arguments as worthless, we have seen that some retain abiding significance. In particular, the phenomenon of narrative coherence, with all it entails, remains an important

---

38 Beck, "*Imitatio Christi*" 43—47.

witness to the traditional character of the Markan narrative *once it is combined with additional evidence* concerning (A) Mark's redactional procedure and (B) the very low probability that more than two or three passion episodes circulated independent of the passion account as a whole. Additionally, we demonstrated that Kelber's psychocultural and literary-aesthetic objections to the hypothesis of an early written passion account themselves contradicted the available evidence. Finally, we observed a large degree of congruence between the traditional "persecution/vindication" genre identified by Nickelsburg and the Markan passion narrative — a fact that forcefully suggests the strong, early influence of the traditional literary pattern on attempts to recount Jesus' death. Our comparison of the generic pattern with the Markan passion narrative leaves open the possibility that the following scenes were not original to that story: the preparation for Passover (and perhaps the whole Supper-sequence?), the narrative of Peter's denial, the way to the cross, and the burial scene. Of course, these scenes may only be examples of "optional components" of the genre, so their exclusion from the primitive passion account is hardly proven on the basis of the comparative analysis conducted above.

In this context it should not be forgotten that our earlier investigation of the Johannine passion narrative *vis-à-vis* the Markan yielded a strong affirmation of the earlier form-critical argument that coincidence in the passion account between the Johannine and Synoptic Gospels favors a strong, traditional basis. This finding should be added to the form-critical evidence of this chapter.

Chapter Seven:

The *Sitz im Leben* for the Early Passion Narrative

I. Introduction

In the previous chapter we demonstrated the existence in the dawning years of Christianity of the necessity of coming to terms with Jesus' death, with special attention to its significance in God's purpose. Moreover, we noted the existence of literary conventions for providing such a narrative in the form of a self-contained account. All that remains, then, is to answer the question whether primitive Christianity offers a plausible setting in which a narrative of Jesus' suffering and death could have taken shape.

The question of the *Sitz im Leben* of a pre-canonical passion story is especially complex[1]. In the past, three primary hypotheses have been championed: early Christian instruction, missionary preaching, and worship. While it has often been the case that scholars have emphatically argued on behalf of one or another of these "settings" so as to totally exclude the other two, this is a questionable approach. One facet of the church's ministry may have been of key importance in the development of an early passion narrative, but the business of the Christian community can never be categorized strictly, and activity in one area of ministry would certainly have affected the others[2]. Moreover, the centrality of the cross (along with the resurrection) to the Christian faith was such that reflection on, and communication about, its significance would have pervaded the whole of the church's existence. So, due to the nature of church life and because of the utmost importance of Jesus' passion for the Christian faith, the issue confronting us in this section is not easily resolved. Further clouding this whole question is the narrative itself, for, taken as a whole or in its various parts, it is capable of a number of plausible functions. At one point a biographical/historical interest comes to the fore; at another, a paraenetic; at another, an apologetic; at another, a cultic; and so on. In the face of such complexity we will nevertheless find it helpful to take up each of the three aforementioned contenders in turn.

---

1 See Pesch, "Ueberlieferung", 170: "*Sitz im Leben und Ueberlieferungsintention* der Passionsgeschichte sind nicht leicht bestimmbar".
2 See McDonald, *Kerygma*.

II. Early Christian Instruction

In an essay first published in 1952, and recently reprinted, C. F. D. Moule wrote of "a more or less definable body of teaching for catechumens underlying the New Testament writings". In doing so, he was attempting to take a step further the work of Philip Carrington and Edward Gordon Selwyn by inquiring into the possibility that early Christian catechesis made use of parables and sayings as illustrative material[3]. The point of departure for Moule's essay was the fact that the Lukan story of Mary and Martha (10:38—42) provides an apt pictorial illustration for the attitude suggested by Paul in 1 Cor 7:35, and is also close to that text in vocabulary. Moule writes:

> One cannot help wondering, therefore, whether this story, which St Luke was later to include in his gospel, was not already current, perhaps orally, and whether St Paul was not mentally drawing upon it to illustrate his ethical teaching[4].

He goes on to discuss further echoes of Gospel material in other epistolary texts on ethical matters, and finally suggests a classification of the ethical teaching of the NT according to the degree and manner of its illustrative material: (A) "The completely unadorned injunction"; (B) "An injunction supported by an Old Testament quotation"; (C) "An injunction supported by a gnomic saying, whether of Jesus or from general proverbial sources"; (D) "Instruction illustrated by a full-length parable, allegory, or anecdote"[5].

Similarly, though apparentlly independently, C. H. Dodd looked into the possible relation of the primitive catechesis and the sayings of Jesus[6]. Building on the work of Carrington and Selwyn, Dodd first set out in outline form a "pattern of teaching" which, he says, was traditional in the NT period. This schema was developed along the following lines:

A. The holiness of the Christian calling.
B. The repudiation of pagan vices, leading up to —
C. The assertion of the Christian law of charity ($\dot{\alpha}\gamma\dot{\alpha}\pi\eta$, including $\phi\iota\lambda\alpha\delta\epsilon\lambda\phi\acute{\iota}\alpha$).

---

[3] C. F. D. Moule, "The Use of Parables and Sayings as Illustrative Material in Early Christian Catechesis", in *Essays*, 50—53. See Philip Carrington, *The Primitive Christian Catechesis* (Cambridge: Cambridge University, 1940); Edward Gordon Selwyn, *The First Epistle of St. Peter: The Greek Text with Introduction, Notes, and Essays*, 2d ed. (London: Macmillan, 1948; reprint ed., Grand Rapids, Michigan: Baker, 1981) 363—466.
[4] Moule, "Use of Parables", 50.
[5] Moule, "Use of Parables", 52—53.
[6] C. H. Dodd, "The 'Primitive Catechesis' and the Sayings of Jesus", in *More Studies*, 11—29. Dodd's essay represents an expansion of his earlier article by the same name, published in *NT Essays*, 106—118. References here are to the later redaction.

D. Eschatological motives.
E. The order and discipline of the church . . . [7].

Dodd illustrates this pattern with reference to 1 Thessalonians, Rom 12–13, and the Didache, and he asserts that it can be traced in other NT epistles as well. But can it also be traced in the Gospels? Dodd answers in the affirmative, and as preliminary evidence he offers the observation that the Gospels, like his "pattern of teaching", include an eschatological discourse toward the close of their narratives. He further observes that traces of the catechetical schema are evident in the Sermon on the Mount in Matthew. In actuality, neither of these two examples are especially convincing.

More impressive is Dodd's attempt to show significant points of similarity in language or substance between the catechetical schema and material in the Gospels. He turns first to the eschatological section ([D], in his outline above), and notes that this section in the catechesis is particularly concerned with the existential demands on the Christian in view of the nearness of the end (cf. 1 Pet 4:7; Jas 5:8; Rom 13:11; et al.). When turning to the "eschatological discourse" in the Gospels one finds a similar paraenesis. In fact, the language of Luke 21:34–36 is strikingly similar to that of the eschatological sections of the epistles (cf. 1 Thess 5:3, 7; Eph 6:13, 18; 1 Pet 4:7). He suggests that the primitive catechesis, serving as a vehicle for transmitting Jesus' teaching, has helped mold the report of his sayings. After citing additional examples he concludes:

> The 'Primitive Christian Catechesis' . . . , itself largely based on pre-Christian models, provided a frame within which Christian teaching on a wide range of topics could conveniently be organized for paedagogic purposes. It appears that this framework was utilized by some of those who made it their business to hand down the Sayings of the Lord, as these appear in the gospels[8].

For our purposes, these two studies raise two points requiring further discussion. The first has to do with the use of the word "catechesis": What is meant by the term; and how prudent is it to speak of a "primitive Christian catechesis"?

We know that in post-apostolic times "catechesis" was used to denote the faith-instruction given to persons prior to their baptism. It appears with this sense already in 2 Clem 17:1: εἰ γὰρ ἐντολὰς ἔχομεν, ἵνα καὶ τοῦτο πράσσωμεν, ἀπὸ τῶν εἰδώλων ἀποσπᾶν καὶ κατηχεῖν, πόσῳ μᾶλλον ψυχὴν ἤδη γινώσκουσαν τὸν θεὸν οὐ δεῖ ἀπόλλυσθαι;. "Catechumens", as persons under instruction in preparation for baptism, appear in texts from the late second and early third centuries[9]. The NT evidence, however, is not so straightforward.

---

7 Dodd, "Primitive Catechesis", 13.
8 Dodd, "Primitive Catechesis", 28.
9 See Tertullian, *Praes. Haer.* 41; *idem, Adv. Marc.* 5.7.6.; Cyprian, *Letter* 73.22. While these

Κατήχησις is nowhere found in the NT, and κατηχέω occurs only 8 times, 4 each in Luke and Paul. These eight instances illustrate well both of the primary connotations of the verb — the general nuance "to inform", and the more specific "to instruct"[10]. In Rom 2:18 Paul uses the verb with the latter sense, declaring that it is through the instruction received from the law (κατηχούμενος ἐκ τοῦ νομοῦ)[11] that the Jew knows God's will and discerns what is decisive (or essential). "To instruct" is also the sense intended by Paul in 1 Cor 14:19, though, in contrast to the usage in Romans, here we have to do with the teaching activity suited to the Christian assembly. Likewise, the double use of the verb in Gal 6:6 has in mind Christian instruction. In this text Paul speaks of the one who receives instruction (κατηχούμενος) and the one who exercises the role of instructor (κατηχῶν), and he identifies the content of the instruction as ὁ λόγος. As Bruce has noted, the verb κατηχέω is thus treated like διδάσκω (cf. 2 Thess 2:15: τὰς παραδόσεις ἃς ἐδιδάχθητε)[12]. So, whereas in Paul the term is especially associated with the notion of "instructing in the faith", we find here no firm basis for thinking Paul had in mind catechumens as a group apart from others of the church, preparing for baptism, nor is there any straightforward evidence regarding the possibility that a formalized body of teaching is intended here.

Κατηχέω is found in Acts 21:21, 24 with the more general sense "to inform". Yet, in Acts 18:25 the idea of "being instructed in the faith" is definite (οὗτος ἦν κατηχημένος τὴν ὁδὸν τοῦ κυρίου). The intended sense of the verb in the prologue to Luke's Gospel (1:4: ἵνα ἐπιγνῷς περὶ ὧν κατηχήθης λόγων τὴν ἀσφάλειαν) is problematic and opinions with regard to it are diverse. For example, Schürmann, writes: "Vermutlich muss man hier besonders an die Taufunterweisung denken, die Theophilus — und die Leser, die Lukas im Auge hat — empfangen haben, wenn auch nicht nur an diese"[13]. Conversely, van Unnik favors a rendering along the lines of "to

---

texts indicate the meaning of "catechism" as instruction received prior to baptism, none provide much evidence as to the content of the instruction.
10 See BAG, 423–424; Hermann Wolfgang Beyer, "Κατηχέω", in *TDNT*, 3:638–640.
11 Ernst Käsemann (*Commentary on Romans* [London: SCM, 1980] 70) argues that the prepositional phrase should be rendered "in the law", and that Paul had in mind here "the fixed catechetical traditions of Judaism". This interpretation goes beyond the evidence offered by the text itself, where "law" should probably be understood in a more general sense.
12 Bruce, *Galatians*, 264. (Bruce's reference to 1 Thess 2:15 should read *2* Thess 2:15.)
13 Schürmann, *Untersuchungen*, 254. Similarly, idem, *Luke*, 1:15–16; Klaus Wegenast, "Κατηχέω", in *NIDNTT*, 3:771–772; Fitzmyer, *Luke*, 1:300–301; Schweizer, *Luke*, 13; Marshall, *Gospel of Luke*, 43; idem, "Luke and His 'Gospel'", 296; Ellis, *Luke*, 66. These latter scholars emphasize more the "instruction" Theophilus received than its "pre-baptismal" character. Marshall in particular underscores its informal nature.

have heard by rumor"[14]. As Luke's use of the verb elsewhere shows his familiarity with the range of ideas associated with this term, a decision here is not easy, and depends in part on whether we find evidence elsewhere in the NT for the sort of instruction presumed by Schürmann. At this point, it is well to be reminded that even if catechetical instruction of the nature found in post-apostolic times had not yet developed in Christianity's first decades, a case for some sort of "Christian education" is not thereby ruled out. Nevertheless, our consideration of the use of κατηχέω in the NT has enabled us, on the one hand, to affirm the existence of a faith-teaching for Christians early on, and, on the other, to deny that any case can be supported on the basis of the use of this language in the NT for a formalized, pre-baptismal catechesis such as was current in later Christian times.

In addition to the evidence provided by the appearance of the term κατηχέω, two other NT passages are of possible relevance. First, some have suggested that in Heb 6:1–2 the author was drawing from a catechetical outline as he lists the rudiments of the "elementary doctrine of Christ"[15]. This list, including repentance from dead works and faith toward God; and instruction (διδαχή) concerning washings (plural of βαπτισμός – cf. Mark 7:4; Heb 9:10), the laying on of hands, the resurrection of the dead (νεκρῶν, and eternal judgment – is surprisingly Jewish in character. Even though we may conjecture safely that when explicated among Christians these points would have been subjected to a christocentric hermeneutic (see 6:1: τῆς ἀρχῆς τοῦ Χριστοῦ), it is clear that we have to do with an outline of some kind current among Jewish Christians still operating very much within the Jewish community.

While the list shows some points of affinity with the evangelistic preaching in Acts, the latter mentions no "washings" or the "laying on of hands". Moreover, missionary sermons before Jewish audiences in Acts are careful to bring the death and resurrection *of Christ* into the foreground; Heb 6:1–2 lacks any hint of Jesus' death, nor does it specifically refer to his resurrection. Likewise, while there are come points of contact between this text and the preaching tradition Paul records in 1 Thess 1:9–10, the dissimilarities are also striking. Most conspicuous are the call to faith in *one* God in the Pauline text and the explicit mention of Jesus (the Son) and his resurrection, parousia, and role in judgment. For these reasons, it is very doubtful that we should read Heb 6:1–2 as a list of elements from mis-

---

[14] W. C. van Unnik, "Once More St. Luke's Prologue", *Neot* 7 (1973) 18. See also Beyer, "Κατηχέω", 639–640.

[15] See Otto Michael, *Der Brief an die Hebräer* (Göttingen: Vandenhoeck & Ruprecht, 1966) 237–240; Bruce, *Hebrews*, 112; Ulrich Wilckens, *Die Missionsreden der Apostelgeschichte: Form-und traditionsgeschichtliche Untersuchungen*, 3d ed. (Neukirchen-Vluyn: Neukirchener, 1974) 82–84.

sionary preaching[16], and so, for explaining the origin of this list, the catechism is the most likely candidate. But what sort of catechesis? All that can be said from the evidence at hand is that new Christians in this apparently Jewish-Christian community were to have received instruction on these fundamentals. No basis exists here, however, for regarding Heb 6:1–2 as testimony for a "baptismal catechesis".

A similar verdict must be pronounced in the case of 1 Cor 3:1–3 where, while a distinction in level of instruction is made, the distinction is based on spiritual maturity and not on whether or not one had been baptized. Moreover, the record of Acts indicates that the call to be baptized came as the climax of evangelistic preaching, as a final appeal or invitation – that is, preaching was not followed by a course of instruction leading up to baptism[17].

Finally, despite our comments on Heb 6:1–2 above, it is now generally agreed that no sharp line may be drawn between the content of kerygma and didache, though differences in emphases would be expected as a matter of course[18].

It would not be going beyond the evidence to conclude that the activity of those early Christians included basic instruction for new converts in the content of the faith. In fact, a number of texts seem to demand such a conclusion – e.g. Matt 28:19–20; Acts 2:42; 18:25; 1 Cor 3:6–8; 11:2; et al. At the same time, however, the case for a *pre-baptismal* catechesis is not firmly based, nor have we any foundation for suggesting that in apostolic Christianity there existed on any universal scale a codified, formalized course of instruction or pattern of teaching for Christians young or old. While certain emphases may well have been suited to new Christians, the NT provides no specific testimony for a normative catechesis[19]. So, when the term "catechesis" is used of activity in the NT era, it should not be vested with the nuances given it by usage in the post-apostolic age. "Catechesis" may be used to connote "instruction in the faith" – but in the apostolic era this "instruction" was neither formalized or (necessarily) pre-baptismal.

To return to the essays by Moule and Dodd, then, we should, on the one hand, resist their efforts to codify the "primitive catechesis" or otherwise

---

16 *Contra* Dunn, *Unity and Diversity*, 145. For an analysis of the differences between Heb 6:1–2 and 1 Thess 1:9–10, see Wilckens, *Missionsreden*, 82–86.
17 See Goppelt, *Apostolic and Post-Apostolic Times*, 41–42; Johannes Munck, *Paul and the Salvation of Mankind* (London: SCM, 1959) 18 n. 1; Dunn, *Unity and Diversity*, 144.
18 See, e.g., Robert H. Mounce, *The Essential Nature of New Testament Preaching* (Grand Rapids, Michigan: Wm. B. Eerdmans, 1960); McDonald, *Kerygma*; Victor Paul Furnish, *Theology and Ethics in Paul* (Nashville: Abingdon, 1968). *Contra* Dodd, *Apostolic Preaching*.
19 See J. Christiaan Beker, *Paul the Apostle: The Triumph of God in Life and Thought* (Edinburgh: T. & T. Clark, 1980) 320; McDonald, *Kerygma*, 99–100.

speak of a normative body of teaching for catechumens, in favor of a more fluid, flexible understanding of early Christian instruction. On the other hand, we may allow for the possibility that the insights offered by these two scholars with regard to the employment of Jesus-tradition in Christian instruction are essentially valid. In fact, as our investigation has already hinted, the thoughts of Moule on this subject are especially apropos. The second issue raised by their essays, therefore, has to do with the possible use of the Jesus-tradition — and to be more specific, the passion narrative — in early Christian instruction.

Initial mention must be made of three texts to which we have alluded earlier in our study — 1 Tim 6:13; Heb 5:7; and 1 Pet 2:23. In each of these cases an episode from the passion story is used to illustrate an ethical or theological point. And, as we earlier observed, in each text, while the reference is to a specific event, the wider context offered by the passion is assumed. As the allusions are much more conceptual than verbal, it is clear that such a story lies at the root of these paraenetic illustrations.

Similarly, the interweaving of Peter's denial with Jesus' trial before the Jewish leaders (in the accounts of Matthew, Mark, and John) has paraenetic value. By this measure Christians were encouraged to be faithful in their confession of their allegiance to their Lord. Luke has presumably preserved a form of the tradition unaffected by this paraenetic interest. On this basis, then, one could justifiably, if provisionally, hypothesize that paraenetic interests influenced the shape of the passion tradition, but do not lie at the passion story's origin.

This theory finds support in the Gethesmane story, where paraenetic concerns helped remodel the account of Jesus' prayer of submission to God's will. This shaping of the tradition is evident already in the Markan account, but even more so in the framing of the Lukan with the imperative to watch and pray. Here, Jesus' example points the way for subsequent believers faced with temptation and opposition.

One important segment of the Gospel passion narratives may owe much more to the teaching life of the primitive church, however — namely, the Supper-tradition and table-talk. In his study of paraenesis and catechesis, McDonald isolated the "farewell discourse" as an important aspect of paraenesis in the Graeco-Roman world and in Jewish tradition. To be sure, the farewell discourse is not exclusively paraenesis: it may intersect with other forms of communication — *viz.* the exhortatory address and the proclamation of divine revelation. In Jewish tradition, valedictory and farewell speeches occur frequently in the OT and in later tradition show a number of marked similarities to the "farewell discourses" in the Gospels, especially those of the Third and Fourth Evangelists. Included in this *Gattung* are, for example, a final meal, revelations and warnings about the future, exhortations of an ethical nature, prayer for those left behind, and the appointment of a "successor" — all of which find correspondence in the Gospel narratives. Form-critically, then, it is plausible that this segment of the passion narrative was shaped within the teaching life of the church, on the model of the old farewell-discourse *Gattung*.

We may conclude that the passion narrative was *used in,* and *influenced by,* Christian instruction in embroynic Christianity. The evidence points to the impact of early catechesis on the shape and format of the passion story; however, we have found nothing to suggest that early Christian instruction itself provided the *Sitz im Leben* for the whole narrative. By and large, the creative influence of the teaching life of the community *vis-à-vis* the passion account was secondary — helping to mold certain aspects of the developing story, and suggesting ways in which the story could be used to illustrate qualities important for maturing Christians.

III. Early Christian Missionary Preaching

As is well known, Dibelius believed that " . . . missionary purpose was the cause and preaching was the means of spreading abroad that which the disciples of Jesus possessed as recollections"[20]. In his form-critical investigation of the passion story, he consistently applied this programmatic principle, asserting that " . . . we must presuppose the early existence of a Passion narrative complete in itself since preaching, whether for the purpose of the mission or of worship, required some such a document"[21]. In this, Dibelius has been followed by an impressive list of interpreters — among them Dodd, Burkill, Lohse, Goppelt, Schweizer, and Senior[22]. However, no consensus exists on the *means* by which early preaching was to have given birth to a primitive passion story. The formation of a passion account from scriptural apologetic has at times been tied up with the view that early Christian preaching was the *Sitz im Leben*, but not necessarily so. By far the most prevalent way of supporting the hypothesis of preaching as the *Sitz im Leben* for a pre-canonical passion narrative has been cast in terms of an *evolutionary growth of the kerygma*[23].

---

20 Dibelius, *Tradition*, 13 (original in italics).
21 Dibelius, *Tradition*, 23.
22 C. H. Dodd, *History and the Gospel* (London: Nisbet, 1938) 82–83; Burkill, "Mark's Philosophy", 247–248; Lohse, *Geschichte*, 9–25; Goppelt, *NT Theology*, 1:224–225; Schweizer, *Mark*, 285–286; Senior, *Passion: Mark*, 11. Dodd, however, refers both to the mission and to the celebration of the eucharist; and Schweizer refers to the mission, early Christian instruction, and worship.
23 For this view, see Bultmann, *History*, 275–284; Jeremias, *Eucharistic Words*, 89–96; Lohse, *Geschichte*, 9–25; idem, *The Formation of the New Testament* (Nashville: Abingdon, 1981) 113–114; Taylor, *Mark*, 524–526, 653–664 (esp. p. 659).

According to this hypothesis, a kerygmatic formula (such as 1 Cor 15: 3—5), the prophecies of the passion and resurrection (such as Mark 8:31; 9:31; 10:33—34), or the kerygma upon which are based the *Actareden* gave rise to a brief continuous narrative, which in turn attracted a number of anecdotes which were then worked into the narrative sequence. Finally, several isolated units were attached to the narrative which, by this point in the process, was beginning to reflect the form of the story found in the Gospels. A number of points can be raised against this hypothesis.

(A) As we have hitherto observed, from start to finish the passion story gives the appearance of a tightly-woven unit, with a very small minority of "unattachable episodes".

(B) According to this hypothesis, one of the stories added last to the evolving narrative was the anointing at Bethany. Certainly, this episode can be detached from the overall story without greatly affecting the progress of the narrative, but earlier we have found reason to believe it was attached to the report of the plot against Jesus from an early date, and not relatively late in the evolutionary process. As the late joining of this episode to the passion story is one of the primary examples offered by proponents of the hypothesis for the evolutionary growth of the passion narrative, our judgment constitutes a serious counterargument.

(C) One of the presuppositions of this hypothesis is that since we know Luke and Matthew appended stories to the Markan account, we can assume that the earlier evangelist, operating in much the same way, made his own additions to the evolving narrative. However, we have argued that the Lukan "additions" are not additions to the Markan narrative, strictly speaking, but have come to Luke via his own non-Markan narrative tradition(s). As for the Matthean traditions, Trocmé has pointed out that the stories of Judas's suicide (27:3—10) and the guard at the tomb (27:62—66) are not integral to the developing story and so provide no strong evidence for the earlier evolutionary growth of the narrative[24]. In any case, a dubious presupposition lies behind any claim that the Matthean redactional approach is paradigmatic for the tendencies of the developing tradition.

(D) If the kerygmatic statement of 1 Cor 15:3—5 lies at the root of the passion story, why do we not find in the passion account a prominent emphasis on the interpretation of Jesus' death "for our sins"?

(E) A further point is made by Trocmé, this one striking at the very root of this whole theory by raising questions about its assumptions regarding an evolutionary model for the passion tradition.

Oral tradition has its laws, but these vary with the type of tradition and with the kind of transmitting agent. The synoptic tradition may to some extent be compared with rabbinic tradition,

---

24 Trocmé, *Passion*, 63.

but does not obey exactly the same rules. The sayings of Jesus are not handed on in exactly the same ways as his miracle stories, etc. Is the tradition of a lengthy, complex narrative like the story of the sufferings and death of Jesus a process of growth or one of reduction, as may have been the case for the miracle stories, if we are to judge from a comparison of Mark and Matthew? Or was it perhaps a transmission *ne varietur*, intended to be literal and unchanging, as was the case with some at least of the sayings of the Master, even if some changes occurred on the occasion of their being translated, collected, and written down? All I want to say at this point is that we do not know and that there is no reason to prefer the hypothesis of growth to those of reduction or stability[25].

There is therefore little basis for supporting the hypothesis that the passion narratives are the end result of an evolutionary process beginning with the kerygmatic tradition.

To be sure, it is one thing to deny the plausibility of this theory regarding the means by which the passion narrative was formulated, and another to dismiss the mission as a possible *Sitz im Leben* for the narrative. Is there any evidence supporting the validity of Dibelius' argument that the demands of the early mission would have required a demarcation of the events in question? By way of answering this question we can pursue a number of lines of evidence. First, as we argued earlier, the passion must have occupied a key position in the interaction between Christians and Jews, for Jesus' suffering and death would have been taken as a forceful denial of his messianic status. Thus, in the early Christian mission, it would have been important to establish, at least, Jesus' innocence and the integral relation of his passion to God's redemptive plan.

Second, if the sermons in Acts are to be trusted there is more specific evidence that the contents of missionary preaching embraced some form of a passion account, however skeletal. For example, consider the following texts:

> This man [Jesus], delivered up according to the set purpose and foreknowledge of God, you killed with the help of wicked men, nailing him to the cross (Acts 2:23).

> The God of Abraham, Isaac, and Jacob, the God of our fathers, glorified his servant Jesus, whom you delivered up and disowned before Pilate, after he had decided to release him. You disowned the Holy and Righteous One, and asked that a murderer be granted to you (Acts 3:13—14).

> The inhabitants of Jerusalem and their rulers did not recognize him [Jesus], yet in condemning him they fulfilled the utterances of the prophets read every Sabbath. Though they found no basis for the death penalty, they asked Pilate to have him executed. And when they had carried out all that was written about him, they took him down from the tree and laid him in a tomb (Acts 13:27—29).

Again, without jumping off into the deep waters of the dispute regarding the historical veracity of the *Actareden*, a few observations may be made concerning certain events and characters of the passion. (A) In 2:23 the use

---

25 Trocmé, *Passion*, 64. See also, Kelber, *Gospel*, 190—191.

of προσπήγνυμι – a word found nowhere else in the NT, nor in the LXX – rather than, say, σταυρόω (cf. Luke 23:21, 23, 33; 24:7, 20; Acts 2:36; 4:10) is puzzling. (B) Likewise in 2:23, ἄνομος, used for Romans (consistent with Jewish usage), is surprising given Luke's otherwise amply attested bias towards the Romans, especially evidenced in the passion story in Luke's attempt to exonerate the Romans from their part in Jesus' execution[26]. (C) In 13:29, we read that "they" – i.e. "the inhabitants of Jerusalem and their rulers" (v 27) – removed Jesus' body from the cross and buried it. In John 19:31 the Jews initiate the removal of the crucified ones from their crosses prior to the Sabbath, but there is no such tradition in Luke's passion account. Rather, Luke reports that Joseph of Arimathea – a good and upright man who did not consent to the action of the Sanhedrin against Jesus, and who was awaiting the kingdom of God – was responsible for taking Jesus' body from the cross (Luke 23:50–53)[27]. (D) Moreover, in 13:29 it is not from the "cross" (σταυρόω – cf. Luke 9:23; 14:27; 23:26), but from the "tree" (ξύλον) that Jesus' body is removed. This reflects ancient usage, and ξύλον is never found in Luke's passion narrative with this nuance.

While these considerations hardly demonstrate the traditional character of the speeches in question *in toto*, they do provide persuasive evidence against taking the references to passion events in the speeches simply as Lukan formulations based on his own passion account. To assert such an hypothesis would introduce into Lukan creativity inconsistencies in theology, linguistic usage, and detail. It seems much more reasonable to assume that Luke had access to additional source material. Hence, the testimony of the missionary speeches in Acts provides support for Dibelius's claim.

Depending on how one perceives Paul's intending meaning of προγράφω in Gal 3:1, this text may be taken as additional evidence for the use of a passion account in missionary proclamation. The full verse reads: ὦ ἀνόητοι Γαλάται, τίς ὑμᾶς ἐβάσκανεν, οἷς κατ' ὀφθαλμοὺς Ἰησοῦς Χριστὸς προεγράφη ἐσταυρωμένος;. With this statement, Paul comes to the central theological argument of his letter to the Galatians, calling to their remembrance the content of the "gospel of Christ" (1:7) first proclaimed to, and received by, them[28]. By the emotive tone of this text, it is clear how incredible it must

---

[26] F. F. Bruce, (*The Acts of the Apostles: The Greek Text with Introduction and Commentary* [Grand Rapids, Michigan: Wm B. Eerdmans, 1951] 92) writes: "Luke would never have designated the Romans thus".

[27] Haenchen (*Acts*, 410) suggests that in the Acts account Luke has only shortened the story as much as possible; however, this really does not overcome the difficulty here, raised by the repeated use of the third-person plural in vv 27–29, the antecedent of which can only be "the Jews".

[28] See Hans Dieter Betz, *Galatians* (Philadelphai: Fortress, 1979) 131; David John Lull, *The Spirit in Galatia: Paul's Interpretation of Pneuma as Divine Power* (Chico, California: Scholars, 1980) 55; Hays, *Faith of Jesus*, 196–198.

have seemed to the apostle that the Galatians, having received so lucid a presentation of that Gospel, should have failed to comprehend its ramifications with regard to the validity of the law as a means of justification (see 2:21). Elsewhere in the NT (Rom 15:4; Eph 3:3; Jude 4), προγράφω is used with its more common sense of "to write in advance". Here, however, we must understand the prefix προ- locatively, not temporally. The verb is used thus in classical literature to connote something like "to proclaim publicly" or "to publish publicly"[29]. Numerous commentators have adopted this rendering as the intended sense in Gal 3:1[30].

However, three factors indicate that the rendering "to proclaim publicly" is perhaps too weak here. In the first place, οἷς κατ' ὀφθάλμους . . . προεγράφη suggests the graphic quality of Paul's missionary proclamation. Second, and closely related, Betz has observed that "one of the goals of the ancient orator was to deliver his speech so vividly and impressively that his listeners imagined the matter to have happened right before their eyes"[31]. Finally, "Jesus Christ portrayed as crucified" could serve nicely as a catch-phrase recalling Paul's initial recounting of Jesus' passion in his evangelist preaching[32]. We cannot regard our case as certain, but given these three considerations, an interpretation of Paul's language in Gal 3:1 as referring to a passion story in his missionary preaching is at least as probable as, and perhaps even preferable to, that which sees here a colorless reference to "public promulgation". An hypothesis that early missionary preaching made use of a passion story could not rest on Gal 3:1, but this text is suggestive of the validity of that theory.

Thus, we have been able to suggest three lines of evidence that support the thesis of Dibelius that missionary preaching would have required a passion account, though it is arguable how extensive such an account would

---

29 See LSJ, 1473; Gottlob Schrenk, "Προγράφω", in *TDNT*, 1:771.
30 See, e.g., J. B. Lightfoot, *Saint Paul's Epistle to the Galatians*, 10th ed. (London: Macmillan, 1890) 134; Ernest de Witt Burton, *A Critical and Exegetical Commentary on the Epistle to the Galatians* (Edinburgh: T. & T. Clark, 1921) 143; Hermann W. Ridderbos, *The Epistle of Paul to the Churches at Galatia* (Grand Rapids, Michigan: Wm. B. Eerdmans, 1953) 112; Heinrich Schlier, *Der Brief an die Galater* (Göttingen: Vandenhoeck & Ruprecht, 1962) 119–120; Franz Mussner, *Der Galaterbrief* (Freiburg: Herder, 1974) 207; Bruce, *Galatians*, 148; Weder, *Kreuz Jesu*, 182 (but: "Allerdings verbeitet schon das betonte ἐσταυρωμένος eine völlige Ausschaltung geschichtlicher Dimensionen" [182]]; Günther Bornkamm, *Paul* (New York: Harper and Row, 1971) 159.
31 Betz, *Galatians*, 131.
32 See A. Goffinet, "La prédication de l'Evangile et de la croix dans l'Epitre aux Galates", *ETL* 41 (1965) 429 (Paul's preaching must have included a narrative of the event of the cross); Bruce, *Paul*, 101 ("Not only from its repetition at celebrations of the Lord's Supper did the passion story acquire firm outlines, but also from its repetition in the proclamation of the gospel. According to Paul, 'Jesus Christ was publicly portrayed as crucified' [Galatians 3:1] when the gospel was peached . . ."). Hays sees here an allusion to the whole Jesus-story (*Faith of Jesus*, 197).

have been necessary. This need further corroborates the existence of a passion narrative early on. Yet, we cannot regard the early Christian mission as the *Sitz im Leben* for the creation of the passion story on the scanty evidence available to us.

IV. Early Christian Worship

Since 1922, when the notion that the formulation of the passion narrative was somehow directly related to the worship of the *Urgemeinde* was heralded with the publication of Georg Bertram's *Die Leidensgeschichte und der Christuskult*, many have argued that the *Sitz im Leben* of the passion story is to be found in some aspect of Christian worship. As Kelber has rightly judged, the most plausible of these theories focuses on the Lord's Supper — and among these, the most plausible formulation to date is that by Etienne Trocmé[33].

A. The Hypothesis of Trocmé

Trocmé's argument is three-tiered. First, he notes the liturgical coloring of the whole passion narrative, as well as its chronological framework reflecting Jewish liturgical custom. These factors already point to a *Sitz im Leben* in the worshipping life of the Jewish-Christian community. He goes on to note that in the case of at least three Jewish festivals current at the beginning of the Christian era (Pentecost, Purim, and Passover), the reading of a lengthy narrative telling the story of the relevant events, or at least a kind of midrash of that story, was included in the celebration. This fact opens the way for an analogous recounting of the passion events within the Christian community. Finally, we are reminded that the anniversary of the death of Jesus coincides with Passover and that, in all probability, early Christians would have celebrated Passover by commemorating both the Exodus and the suffering and death of Jesus. Trocmé concludes: "The *Sitz im Leben* of the original passion narrative thus was doubtless the liturgical commemoration of Christ' death by Christians during the Jewish Passover celebration"[34]. Trocmé's thesis is open to question on at least two important fronts: (1) Did early Christians celebrate Passover[35]? (2) Do liturgical features pervade the passion narrative to the extent he would have us believe?

---

33 Kelber, *Gospel*, 194. For Trocmé's thesis, see his *Passion*, 77–89.
34 Trocmé, *Passion*, 82. In this he is indebted to the work of Philip Carrington, *The Primitive Christian Calendar* (Cambridge: Cambridge University, 1952). Carrington's thesis has fallen on hard times (see the summary in Martin, *Mark*, 85–87), but Trocmé believes that Carrington's suggestion that the Markan passion story was the *megillah* to be read at early Christian celebrations of Jesus' passion held on the occasion of the Jewish Passover can be salvaged.
35 The broader question regarding the degree to which early Christian worship mirrored that of the

(1) Testimony concerning the celebration of Passover by early Christians may be assembled under five headings. a. Testimony from Luke-Acts[36]. The Passover flavor of *Luke 22:15–18* is obvious and these verses, reflecting liturgical use in the primitive church, are indicative of the close relation of the Supper and the Passover, at least on the interpretive level. The Synoptics exhibit additional evidence for this connection, but this text is the most explicit. These verses do not demonstrate that early Christians celebrated the Passover, however, but do indicate the importance for them of the theological motifs the festival embraced. The formulation of these verses could be due to the celebraton of the Lord's Supper in association with the range of ideas suggested by the identification of the Last Supper with the Passover whether that identification was first made historically by Jesus himself or not. *Acts 20:6* is part of a travelogue, reporting that Paul and his companions sailed from Philippi after the Feast of Unleavened Bread. (The Feast of Unleavened Bread and Passover were separable in fact, but not in current practice – see Luke 22:1.) This reference has often been taken as an indication that Passover was thus celebrated by Paul and his companions at the church at Philippi. It may be only a time-reference based on the Jewish calendar, such as one finds in 27:9[37] – or, as seems more probable, a reference to the celebration of Easter with the Philippian Christians. *Acts 12:3–4* mentions Passover, but only by way of reporting when Peter was seized by Herod and why his trial was delayed. Thus, there is no direct evidence here for a Christian celebration of the Jewish Passover.

b. Testimony from John's Gospel[38]. When John refers to Passover, he sometimes adds the phrase τῶν Ἰουδαίων (2:13; 6:4; 11:55), and this has suggested to some that he thus distinguishes between a Jewish Passover and

---

Jews need not detain us here, for it is generally agreed that with regard to daily and weekly worship there was a large measure of continuity – see Roger T. Beckwith, "The Daily and Weekly Worship of the Primitive Church", *EvQ* 56 (1984) 65–80, 139–158; C. F. D. Moule, *The Birth of the New Testament*, 3d. ed. (San Francisco: Harper & Row, 1982) 20–33; Hans Lietzmann, *The Beginnings of the Christian Church* (London: Lutterworth, 1949) 63; Dunn, *Unity and Diversity*, 63; Ralph P. Martin, *Worship in the Early Church* (Grand Rapids, Michigan: Wm. B. Eerdmans, 1964) 11–12, 18–27; et al.

36 Among those who find in Luke-Acts evidence for the early celebration of Passover among Christians, see Jocahim Jeremias, "Πάσχα", in *TDNT*, 5:900–901; Reinhold Mayer and Bernd Schaller, "Feast, Passover", in *NIDNTT*, 1:634; Beckwith, "Daily and Weekly Worship", 69 n.9. For a discussion of the evidence in Acts that the oldest church followed the Jewish festival-calendar, see Bernard Lohse, *Das Passafest der Quartadecimaner* (Gütersloh: C. Bertelsmann, 1953) 98–101. Lohse's case rests heavily on the festival of Pentecost and he can only infer the observance of Passover.

37 So Haenchen, *Acts*, 582. Lohse (*Passafest*, 100) asserts that there is "mehr als eine blosse Datumsangabe" here, but offers neither hard evidence nor convincing argumentation that Paul actually celebrated the Jewish feast at Philippi.

38 For the opinion that John offers testimony for a Christian Passover, see Jeremias, "Πάσχα", 901; Mayer and Schaller, "Feast, Passover", 634.

a Christian Passover. Such verses as John 2:6 (τὸν καθαρισμὸν τῶν Ἰουδαίων); 5:1 (ἑορτὴ τῶν Ἰουδαίων); and 7:2 (ἡ ἑορτὴ τῶν Ἰουδαίων ἡ σκηνοπηγία) should be added to the list, however, and these texts taken together suggest John is doing no more than setting Judaism in general over against Jesus and his followers. These texts provide no evidence that John knew a Christian celebration of the Passover[39].

c. Testimony from Paul. Christ is analogously identified with the Passover lamb (τὸ πάσχα) in 1 Cor 5:7, and Jeremias has suggested that this idea stems from a primitive Christian Passover liturgy[40]. A connection with the Jewish Passover is obvious, but an appeal to an early Christian Passover Haggadah takes us beyond the evidence. Indeed, the metaphor is more likely firmly embedded directly in the identification of the Last Supper with the Passover Meal, such as is found in the Synoptic Gospels. It is not necessary, then, to appeal to the continuing celebration of Passover by Christians in order to account for this motif. Moreover, elsewhere Paul speaks of Christ's sacrificial death with reference to another Jewish festival, Yom Kippur (Rom 3:25), but no one suggests on this basis that early Christians observed their own "Day of Atonement". Both texts evidence the importance of the Jewish background for early reflection on Jesus' death, and both indicate how the practice of, and reflection on, the Lord's Supper fostered early Christian thought. First Corinthians 5:7, then, may be regarded as a "neutral" text for our present purposes, though elsewhere the Pauline corpus provides evidence of another sort.

At a number of points, Paul's letters betray his generally unsympathetic orientation *vis-à-vis* Christian involvement in the Jewish liturgical year[41]. Romans 14:5–12; Gal 4:10–11; and Col 2:16–17 are of signal importance in this respect. However, this evidence is difficult to evaluate. While it is obvious that Paul himself considered these customs either superfluous or out-of-bounds for Christians, the very fact that he had to raise the issue in his correspondence is itself implicit evidence that others held a contrary opinion. In addition, as important as the Pauline epistles may be for an understanding of the worship habits of the early church, it is certainly arguable how representative they are of the worship of the church in Palestine. Nevertheless, we learn from Paul that certain Jewish Christians probably included selected elements from the Jewish liturgical year in their worship routine as Christians, but nowhere in Paul do we encounter hard evidence that Passover was observed in primitive Christianity.

---

39 See Klaus Wengst, *Bedrängte Gemeinde und verherrlichter Christus* (Neukirchener-Vluyn: Neukirchener, 1981) 47; Barrett, *John*, 197; Lindars, *John*, 137.
40 Jeremias, "Πάσχα", 901 n.41. See also Lohse, *Passafest*, 101ff.
41 See Leon Morris, "The Gospels and the Jewish Lectionaries", in *Gospel Perspectives*, 3:141; Dunn, *Unity and Diversity*, 147.

d. Testimony from Eusebius. In his *Historia Ecclesiastica*, Eusebius reports the existence of a dispute in second-century Christianity regarding the proper day for celebrating τῆς τοῦ σωτηρίου πάσχα ἑορτῆς (5.23.1). His record (5.23—25) includes citations from earlier documents related to the controversy; from these we learn that the apostles Philip and John, as well as other first-century Christians, were remembered to have celebrated "the day" — variously described as τὴν ἡμέραν (5.24.2, 12), τὴν ἡμέραν τῆς τεσσαρεσκαιδεκάτης τοῦ πάσχα (5.24.6), and τὴν ἡμέραν . . . ὅταν ὁ λαὸς ἤρνυεν τὴν ζύμην (5.24.6). The most extensive treatment of this controversy is Lohse's *Das Passafest der Quartedecimaner*[42]. His study goes so far as to work out four essential aspects of the Passover celebration of the Quartodecimans.

1. Ihr Passa wird durch Fasten begangen, und zwar fasten sue für die Juden, damit Gott ihnen ihre Schuld vergeben möge.
2. Ex. 12 wird vorgelesen und ausgelegt.
3. Sie erwarten die Wiederkunft des Herrn am Passa.
4. Gegen 3 Uhr morgens werden die Agape und die Eucharistie gefeiert, vermutlich als christliches Passamahl in dem Sinne von "Marana tha"[43].

Apart from the fact that the available evidence for such a reconstruction is minimal, the real question for us concerns the possibility that this kind of observance can be projected back into earliest Christian times. What we can say from the report of Eusebius is that some Christians in Asia Minor, supporting their custom with an appeal to early Christian practice, followed the Jewish celebration of the date of Passover as they celebrated "the day". However, the term "Passover" is clearly used in this dispute to mean "Easter"[44], and it does not necessarily follow that this celebration would have embraced the Jewish Passover. Unambiguous evidence for the Christian celebration of the Jewish Passover, then, is lacking here.

e. Liturgical Continuity. There appears to have been a remarkable degree of continuity from Jewish to Christian worship, along with a persistent loyalty among those first Christians towards (at least some aspects of) the Jewish temple. Texts such as Acts 2:46 and 3:1 suggest those earliest believers took part in the daily worship of the temple. Similarly, recent studies on the observance of the Sabbath among early Christians indicate the degree to which early Christian weekly worship practices remained within the general boundaries of Jewish practice[45], even if it is also true

---

42 See also Jeremias, *Eucharistic Words*, 122—125; idem, "Πάσχα", 901—902.
43 Lohse, *Passafest*, 89.
44 For τὸ πάσχα as "the Easter celebration", see *Diog.* 12.9; BAG, 663; Jeremias, "Πάσχα", 901.
45 See, e.g., Willy Rordorff, *Sunday* (London: SCM, 1968) e.g., pp. 118—119; and among the essays in *Sabbath*, esp. Max M. B. Turner, "The Sabbath, Sunday, and the Law in Luke/Acts", 124—126. See also Goppelt, *NT Theology*, 1:96.

that from the beginning Christians kept their own special meetings as well[46]. To be sure, evidence for continuity in terms of *daily and weekly worship* constitutes no solid testimony for the taking over by early Christians of the *annual Jewish liturgical calendar*; however, an openness toward Jewish custom in the one area may imply openness in the other, and from this a *prima facie* case might be constructed for the observance of Passover among early Jewish Christians.

Our question is this: Did early Christians celebrate Passover, as Trocmé's hypothesis concerning a *Sitz im Leben* for a pre-canonical passion narrative demands? In the final analysis, we cannot completely rule out the possibility that, in the first years of Christianity, Jewish Christians joined in the annual observance of Passover. In fact, our instincts may tell us that there is a high probability that they did so, for, as Trocmé is quick to point out, the cross-event coincided with the Passover festival. Nevertheless, the NT nowhere specifically supports this idea — and what implicit evidence may be taken in its favor is not only scarce but, due to its ambivalent character, should be regarded with caution. In other words, Trocmé's hypothesis itself rests at this point on another hypothesis for which there is very little foundation.

(2) The second point at which Trocmé's thesis is open to suspicion regards his attempt to find liturgical coloring throughout the passion narrative. The anointing at Bethany, the Last Supper, the preparation for Passover, the burial, the empty tomb, and so on — these emphasize the story's liturgical element, according to his theory. Against this reading of the material in question, Kelber's comments are well-aimed:

> Not all the observed liturgical features are equally convincing, however. It is difficult to see why the threefold division of the Gethsemane prayer should give the impression of "an incantation or a sacred dance," or why the triple denial of Peter must be located in a cultic drama. Not even the three-hour schematization of Jesus' death . . . must necessarily have originated in Jewish-Christian worship[47].

To these examples may be added others: What is particularly liturgical about the preparation for the Passover? The plot against Jesus? The arrest?

What is of special interest about this aspect of Trocmé's reconstruction is its superfluity. It really is not necessary to account for the liturgical origin of every individual section of the narrative in order to theorize that the whole was recounted in a liturgical setting. Each pericope need not fit into a "cultic drama" in order for the whole to have been birthed in a context of worship. This is obviously true with respect to the canonical passion narratives — since we have already seen how the needs of the mission and community instruction would have helped mold the developing

---

46 See, e.g., Acts 2:46b; Martin, *Worship*; Beckwith, "Daily and Weekly Worship", 140–142; et al.
47 Kelber, *Gospel*, 195.

story — but also with respect to a pre-canonical passion story, depending on what sort of "context of worship" is envisioned.

B. The Lord's Supper as Sitz im Leben

We propose that the *Sitz im Leben* of the passion narrative was the celebration of the Lord's Supper within the context of the life of the Christian community[48]. This proposal makes good on several advantages, rendering it not only plausible, but greatly to be preferred over the others we have hitherto reviewed. These points, to be explicated in greater detail below, can be outlined as follows. First, since the focal point of the Supper is Jesus' death along with its significance and divine implications on behalf of humanity, the Supper provides a ready context for remembering the events and working out the significance of Jesus' death. Second, in instituting the Supper, Jesus himself purposed that the Supper be repeated and that it be an occasion for "remembering" his suffering and death. Within the process of this regular and repeated anamnesis, there was ample room for reflection on the relevant events, application of lessons suggested by Jesus' behavior and attitudes, and modification of the form taken by the various episodes. Third, from early on, the Supper was integral to the life of the Christian community — that is, from the beginnings of Christianity, there existed this context for assimilating, recounting, and reflecting upon Jesus' death. While additional points will be enlisted to support and flesh-out this skeletal proposal, these three are the mainstays, and the following discussion will take them as points of departure.

(1) Not without good reason do we refer to Jesus' *Last* Supper, for this was indeed a farewell meal — a meal at which Jesus interpreted his death, predicting and explaining its significance for his table companions. Likewise, the Lord's Supper looks back to Jesus' death and recalls its significance. An inseparable bond links the passion of Jesus and the Supper as an aspect of community life[49]. Hence, there is nothing artificial about our argument for a vital connection between the Supper and the development of a narrative of Jesus' suffering and death.

---

[48] No claim for originality can be made for this proposal, though it is true that this theory has not hitherto been worked out in adequate detail. It has been asserted by a number of scholars — e.g. Weber, *Cross*, 46–48; Martin, *Worship*, 127; Schweizer, *Mark*, 285–286; Dodd, *History and the Gospel*, 82–83; Lane, *Mark*, 486; Bruce, *Paul*, 100–101; et al. It is hoped that the following discussion will place this hypothesis on a more firm standing.

[49] On this general point, see, e.g., Jeremias, *NT Theology*, 290–291; Schweizer, *Lord's Supper*, 1–2; Marshall, *Last Supper*, 147–148; Willi Marxsen, *The Beginnings of Christology together with The Lord's Supper as a Christological Problem* (Philadelphia: Fortress, 1979) 71, 96–97; Bernard Cooke, "Synoptic Presentation of the Eucharistic as Covenant Sacrifice", *TS* 21 (1960) 15; Daly, *Sacrifice*, 56.

Of course, within this context, our thoughts turn immediately to the *Deuteworte* recorded in the Supper-accounts. In recent years, these interpretive sayings have been subjected to a multitude of studies[50], but our present purpose will not require a full rehearsal of all the points raised and issues argued. On the contrary, at this juncture it is enough merely to point to two aspects of the eucharistic words by way of undergirding out statement regarding the inseparability of the Supper and the cross.

First, one finds in the Supper-words *an open and unmistakably obvious prediction of Jesus' death*. Some interpreters have read a prophecy of Jesus' death into his "breaking of the bread" (Matt 26:26; Mark 14:22; Luke 22: 19; 1 Cor 11:24)[51]; however, inasmuch as κλάω is used only to describe what is done to the bread prior to its consumption and is thus only introductory to the meal, it should not be accorded any further, symbolic reference. Apart from this, nevertheless, one reads in these texts other, certain anticipations of Jesus' imminent death. The bread-word — "this is my body given for you" — is a prophecy concerning Jesus' approaching death and probably also suggests his self-surrender[52]. Likewise, the phrase about "blood poured out", found in the cup-word (Matt 26:28; Mark 14: 24; Luke 22:20), signifies death, especially sacrificial death[53]. A further, forward-looking allusion to Jesus' death is found in the eschatological sayings in Matt 26:29; Mark 14:25; and, especially, Luke 22:15–18.

Second, one observes in the Supper-words *the centrality of Jesus' death to God's redemptive plan*. Numerous OT motifs and bits of OT language — including that having to do with the covenant, the Servant of Yahweh,

---

50 See, e.g., Lohse, *Märtyrer*, 123–129; Cooke, "Synoptic Presentation"; Marxsen, *Beginnings*, 69–76, 92–102; Daly, *Sacrifice*, 56–58; Taylor, *Jesus*, 114–142; France, *Jesus*, 121–123; Moo, *OT – Passion*, 130–132, 301–311; Marshall, *Last Supper*, 43–51, 85–93; Norman A. Beck, "The Last Supper as an Efficacious Symbolic Act", *JBL* 89 (1970) 192–198; Günther Bornkamm, "Lord's Supper and Church in Paul", in *Experience* (London: SCM, 1969) 138–146; Alexander Gerken, *Theologie der Eucharistie* (München: Kösel, 1973) 17–60; Karl Hermann, "Das Herrenmahl", in *Rechtfertigung*, 385–402; Enrst Kutsch, "Von der Aktualität alttestamentlicher Aussagen für das Verständnis des Neuen Testaments", *ZTK* 74 (1977) 286–289; Joachim Gnilka, "Wie urtiele Jesus über seinen Tod?", in *Tod Jesu*, 31–41; Schürmann, *Einsetzungsbericht*; Lietzmann, *Mass*; Jeremias, *Eucharistic Words*; Kilpatrick, *Eucharist*; Kim, *Son of Man*, 38–73; A. J. B. Higgins, *The Lord's Supper in the New Testament* (London: SCM, 1952) 45–55; Bertold Klappert, "Lord's Supper", in *NIDNTT*, 2:522–526; Markus Barth, *Was Christ's Death a Sacrifice?* (Edinburgh: Oliver and Boyd, 1961) 42–44; Pesch, *Abendmahl*; Patsch, *Abendmahl*.
51 So Taylor, *Jesus*, 118–119; Beck, "Last Supper", 194; Lietzmann, *Mass*, 180–181; Jeremias, *Eucharistic Words*, 223–224. Against this view, see Johannes Behm, "Κλάω", in *TDNT*, 7:729; Marshall, *Last Supper*, 86; Williams, *Jesus' Death*, 205–207.
52 See Klappert, "Lord's Supper", 532; Marshall, *Last Supper*, 87–89.
53 See Klappert, "Lord's Supper", 525; Marshall, *Last Supper*, 91; Moo, *OT – Passion*, 308–309; Morris, *Apostolic Preaching*, 121–128; Barth, *Jesus' Death*, 44; Gnilka, "Wie urteilte Jesus über seinen Tod?", 33; Pesch, *Abendmahl*, 93–94.

martyrdom, atonement, and forgiveness of sins — are drawn together to emphatically make this point[54]. By this means, the eucharistic words assert that "[Jesus'] outpoured life would be the medium of a renewed fellowship with God"[55].

The covenant-theme is present in all four renditions of the Supper-words, with Matthew and Mark preserving one common form — τοῦτο (γάρ) ἐστίν τὸ αἷμά μου τῆς διαθήκης, and Luke and Paul another — τοῦτο τὸ ποτήριον ἡ καινὴ διαθήκη (ἐστίν) ἐν τῷ (αἵματί μου) (ἐμῷ αἵματι). The debate regarding which of these two represents the more original form has yielded no decisive results[56]. However, there is an important sense in which this issue is superfluous, for since "blood" and "covenant" are closely related in either case[57], that to which the statements refer is not substantially altered either way. It is true that καινὴ διαθήκη explicitly refers to Jer 31: 31—34, but the additional mention of "blood" draws Exod 24:8 into view as well. Similarly, while αἷμά μου τῆς διαθήκης points directly to Exod 24:8, we may not rule out the possibility of an additional allusion here to the Jeremiah prophecy. This is true for two reasons. On the one hand, inasmuch as Jesus instituted a covenant at the Last Supper there is no escaping the conclusion that he had in mind an other, different (=new) covenant. On the other, "covenant", in this context, may easily and naturally be understood as an ellipsis for "new covenant"[58]. This latter possibility is not only theoretical, but is amply attested in the Dead Sea Scrolls, where "covenant" and "new covenant" are virtually interchangeable[59]. The concept of a *new* or *renewed* covenant was important at Qumran, as exemplified in these texts[60]:

---

54 In addition to the studies cited above, see Goppelt, *Typos*, 116; Adrian Schenker, *Das Abendmahl Jesu als Brennpunkt des Alten Testaments* (Fribourg: Schweizerisches Katholisches Bibelwerk, 1977).
55 Taylor, *Atonement*, 14.
56 See, e.g., Hengel, *Atonement*, 53; Goppelt, *Typos*, 112; Kilpatrick, *Eucharist*, 27; Moo, *OT — Passion*, 305; Marshall, *Last Supper*, 92; Cooke, "Synoptic Presentation", 34; Kim, *Son of Man*, 72.
57 Against Kutsch ("Von der Aktualität alttestamentlicher Aussagen für das Verständnis des Neuen Testaments", 286—288), Pesch (*Abendmahl*, 74—76) has shown the authenticity of the association of these two elements.
58 On this semantic innovation, see Moisés Silva, *Biblical Words and Their Meanings: An Introduction to Lexical Semantics* (Grand Rapids, Michigan: Zondervan, 1983) 82—83.
59 On the idea of "covenant" at Qumran, see J. G. Harris, "The Covenant Concept among the Qumran Sectaries", *EvQ* 39 (1967) 86—92; G. R. Driver, *The Judaean Scrolls* (New York: Schocken, 1965) esp. pp. 72—74, 305—310; Delbert R. Hillers, *Covenant: The History of a Biblical Idea* (Baltimore: John Hopkins University, 1969) 169—178; Geza Vermes, *The Dead Sea Scrolls in English*, 2d ed. (New York: Penguin, 1975) 25—26, 35, 38—39; idem, *The Dead Sea Scrolls: Qumran in Perspective* (Philadelphia: Fortress, 1977) 164—165.
60 The following translations are my own. For the respective primary texts, see: 1QpHab 2, 1—4: Maurya P. Horgan, *Pesharim: Qumran Interpretations of Biblical Books* (Washington, D.C.:

The interpretation of the word concerns the treacherous ones with the man of deception, since they did not believe the words of the teacher of righteousness from the mouth of God. And it concerns the treacherous ones to the new covenant (בברית החדשה), since they were not faithful to the covenant of God (בברית אל) and profaned his holy name (1QpHab 2, 1–4).

But you chose for yourself a people in the time of your favor, for you remembered your covenant (בריתך). You . . . them, separating them unto yourself as holy among all the peoples and you renewed your covenant (ותחדש בריתך) for them in a vision of glory (1Q34 3 ii 5–6).

May the Lord bless you from his holy dwelling and designate you a thing made perfect for glory among the holy ones. A covenant of eternal priesthood may he renew (וברית כהונת עולם יחדש) for you and give you your place in a holy dwelling (1Q28b 3, 25–26).

And the covenant of the union (community) may he renew (וברית היחד יחדש) for him, to establish the kingdom of his people forever to judge in righteousness the needy and to reprove in uprightness the poor of the land . . . (1Q28b 5, 21–22).

Yet, without citing all of the relevant texts here, we can note that Karl Georg Kuhn lists some 104 incidences of the word "covenant" without the modifier "new" in the Qumran texts[61]. Clearly, then, even as important as "new covenant" was at Qumran, the modifier "new" was not always made explicit. Similarly, the Matthean/Markan covenant-reference may be understood as an allusion to Jeremiah's "new covenant".

Nevertheless, even if one remains unconvinced that the Matthean/Markan form of the cup-word embraces the Jeremiah-passage, the idea of forgiveness of sins in association with the new covenant, made plain by the allusion to Jeremiah, is still present. This is obviously true in the case of Matthew, where εἰς ἄφεσιν ἁμαρτιῶν has actually been added to the Markan text. Even without this addition, however, the image of covenant-blood refers back to Exod 24:8, and Jewish interpretation of this passage stressed the atoning effect of the blood sprinkled on the altar by Moses. Whereas this notion is lacking in both the MT and LXX, it is quite apparent in the Aramaic versions[62]:

Catholic Biblical Association of America, 1979) 1:1; 1 Q34 ii 5–6: *Discoveries in the Judean Desert*, vol. 1: *Qumran Cave 1*, ed. D. Barthélemey and J. T. Milik (Oxford: Clarendon, 1955) 154; 1Q28b 3, 25–26; 5, 21–22: *Discoveries*, 1:124, 127. See also 1QH 13, 12: CD 6, 19; 8, 21; 19, 34: 20, 12.

61 Karl Georg Kuhn, *Kondordanz zu den Qumrantexten* (Göttingen: Vandenhoeck & Ruprecht, 1960).

62 The following translations are my own. For the respective primary texts, see Alexander Sperber, *The Bible in Aramaic*, vol. 1: *The Pentateuch according to Targum Onkelos* (Leiden: E. J. Brill, 1959) 130; M. Ginsburger, *Pseudo-Jonathan. (Thargum Jonaathen ben Usiël zum Pentateuch)* (Berlin: C. Calvary, 1903) 142. Both *Tg. Onk.* and *Tg. Ps.-J.* employ the construction לכפרא, rendered here as "to atone". J. W. Etheridge (*The Targums of Onkelos and Jonathan ben Uzziel on the Pentateuch; with the Fragments of the Jerusalem Targum: From the Chaldee, Genesis and Exodus* [London: Longman, Green, Longman, and Roberts, 1862] 399, 525) offers the translations "to propitiate" and "to expiate", respectively.

And Moses took the blood and sprinkled it on the altar to atone for the people, and he said, "Behold, this (is) the blood of the covenant which the Lord has decreed with you according to all these words (*Tg. Onk.*).

And Moses took half of the blood which was in the bowls and sprinkled it on the altar to atone for the people and said, "Behold, this is the blood of the covenant which the Lord has decreed with you according to all these words" (*Tg. Ps. -J.*).

In other words, the sacrifices offered by Moses atoned for the sins of the people, and thus they were brought into covenant with God. The cup-word draws a typological relationship between the sacrifice of Exod 24:8 and the death of Jesus[63]. By analogy Jesus' death atones for the sins of the people and enables them to enter the (new, eschatological) covenant with God. That is, "his death inaugurates the eschatological order or covenant of salvation"[64].

The importance of Jesus' death in God's salvific plan is further demonstrated by the Servant-imagery employed in the Supper-words. In particular, allusions to Isa 52:13–53:12 have been observed in the presence of ἐκχυννόμενον and in the phrase ὑπέρ/περὶ πολλῶν/ὑμῶν[65]. This measure of correspondence has not proven convincing to all critics, however. Williams comments:

> The widespread use of the phrase "to pour out blood" in the OT (especially in connection with sacrificial rites), the frequent occurrence of "many" in the OT, and the fact that the phrase "poured out for many" has no parallel in Isaiah 53 makes untenable the claim that the words of Mark 14:24 par. echo Isaiah 53:12 in particular[66].

Against this skeptical approach to the evidence we may offer the following points. First, while it is true that "many" is frequently employed in the OT, Moo has observed that *as an inclusive reference* (i.e. to denote "all"), the term is not so common in the OT; yet, as an inclusive term it is a key word in the Isaianic text[67]. Second, a further key concept for the Isaianic text is ὑπέρ, and its linkage with πολλοί in the cup-word suggests a derivation from the Servant-passage[68]. Third, ἐκχυννόμενον is a literal translation of הערה in Isa 53:12, and fourth, both in the Isaianic text and in the cup-word it is closely linked with πολλοί. Thus, as Moo has observed, "...

---

63 See, e.g., Pesch, *Abendmahl*, 95; Klappert, "Lord's Supper", 533; Goppelt, *Typos*, 112; Moo, *OT – Passion*, 302; Bornkamm, "Lord's Supper", 39–40. On the theory that "blood of the covenant" refers instead to Zech 9:11, see now Moo, *OT – Passion*, 302.
64 Klappert, "Lord's Supper", 533 (with reference to Lohse, *Geschichte*, 56); Marshall, *Last Supper*, 92–93.
65 See, e.g., Lohse, *Märtyrer*, 124; Hengel, *Atonement*, 72; Daly, *Sacrifice*, 56–57; Marshall, *Last Supper*, 89; France, *Jesus*, 122–123; Moo, *OT – Passion*, 130–132; Jeremias, *Eucharistic Words*, 226–228; Pesch, *Abendmahl*, 95–101; Jeremias and Zimmerli, "Παῖς θεοῦ", 711–713, 716.
66 Williams, *Jesus' Death*, 224.
67 Moo, *OT – Passion*, 131.
68 See Jeremias and Zimmerli, "Παῖς θεοῦ", 710.

while the individual components of the expression would not certainly need to be dependent on Is. 53, the phrase taken as a whole demonstrates undeniable verbal and conceptual affinities to Is. 53:12"[69]. In this way, the Supper-words affirm a theological understanding of Jesus' death and its necessity: in dying, Jesus fulfills the role of the Servant of Yahweh who gives himself on behalf of others, effecting redemption for "the many".

On the basis of these points there can be no question as to the signal importance given the passion of Jesus in God's redemptive plan by the Supper-words. In addition, we may note in passing the intimate relation accorded the fulfillment of the kingdom of God and Jesus' death in the context of the Supper. The covenant established by Jesus' death has as its teleological end the consummation of the kingdom. That this theme is in view in the celebration of the Supper is manifest in the eschatological references in Matt 26:29; Mark 14:25; Luke 22:15–18; and 1 Cor 11:26[70]. Again, we see that Jesus' death is thus represented as the eschatological saving event — instituting the new covenant and rendering present the reconciliation-life of God's reign while anticipating its final fulfillment.

Thus, it is clear that the focus of the Supper is Jesus' death, together with its divine effects on behalf of humanity. The continual celebration of the Supper would keep the death of Jesus ever at the fore of Christian thought and experience. Persons would thereby be motivated and enabled to reflect on Jesus' passion and the significance in God's program of his final days. Having demonstrated the inseparable link between Jesus' death and the Supper, it remains to be shown whether anything more specific can be said regarding the Supper as an occasion for recounting the passion narrative, and whether the Supper was in fact a significant aspect of the life of the earliest Christian church.

(2) In outlining our proposal earlier we asserted that, in instituting the Supper, Jesus himself purposed that the Supper be repeated, and that it be an occasion for "remembering" his passion. On this we have to do directly with the authenticity and meaning of the anamnesis-formula, and here we wade into troubled waters indeed. In his early inquiry into the problem of the Lord's Supper, Albert Schweitzer listed among the pressing relevant questions the following two: "Did [Jesus] command the disciples to repeat the celebration"? "Assuming that the command of repetition is not historical, how do we explain the fact that the disciples nevertheless come to repeat the celebration"[71]?

---

69 Moo, *OT – Passion*, 132.
70 See further, Wainwright, *Eucharist*, esp. 41–42.
71 Albert Schweitzer, *The Problem of the Lord's Supper according to the Scholarly Research of the Nineteenth Century and the Historical Accounts*, vol. 1: *The Lord's Supper in Relationship to the Life of Jesus and the History of the Early Church* (Macon, Georgia: Mercer University, 1982)

The command is altogether missing in Matthew and Mark, but is found in conjunction with the bread-word in Luke 22:19. The phrase — τοῦτο ποιεῖτε εἰς τὴν ἐμὴν ἀνάμνησιν — along with other aspects of the Supper-tradition recorded in Luke, does not conform to Lukan style; yet, earlier we found reason to believe that the phrase was original to the Lukan text[72]. We may surmise on this basis that the anamnesis-formula in Luke belongs to Luke's tradition and has not been added or created by Luke. In the Pauline form of the paradosis, the expression is repeated twice, once each with the bread- and cup-words. The apparent difference between Luke and Paul here is minimized by Schürmann's observation that Luke's ὡσαύτως implies the existence of the double command in the earlier tradition[73]. Nevertheless, the absence of the phrase in the Matthean/Markan form of the tradition has convinced a number of exegetes that the command is a later addition to the tradition, for it is easier to account for its addition than for its omission[74]. In evaluating the force of this argument, it should be remembered that we are not dealing with a *text-critical problem* at this point, as if Luke and Paul deliberately altered the Markan tradition, or as if Mark willfully changed the Pauline/Lukan form of the text. Rather, we are dealing with a living tradition employed in more or less diverse forms in early community life. Thus the differences between the text-forms should not be judged too harshly by text-critical canons.

Nor will it do to argue, with Patsch, that since the effect of the liturgical usage of the tradition tended toward conserving and not deleting the words of Jesus the Markan form represents the more primitive[75]. We already see in the case of the tradition cited by Paul that the eschatological saying of Jesus has been replaced by Paul's own statement about Jesus' parousia (1 Cor 11:26). Moreover, the eucharistic tradition could have been reported in slightly divergent forms from the very outset, just as other aspects of the Jesus-tradition were remembered in variant forms.

On the other hand, there are a few positive considerations which, when taken together, present a reasonable case for holding to the authenticity of

---

59–60. Following Friedrich Schleiermacher (*The Christian Faith* [Edinburgh: T. & T. Clark, 1948] para. 139.3), Schweizer assumed the inauthenticity of the command.

72 See above, chapter 3.V.D. On the phrase in question, see esp. Kilpatrick, *Eucharist*, 31; Jeremias, *Sprache*, 287–288.

73 See Schürmann, *Einsetzungsbericht*, 123–126. Pesch (*Abendmahl*, 49) argues that the doubling of the expression is not a secondary development.

74 See, e.g., Kilpatrick, *Eucharist*, 24–25; Jeremias, *Eucharist Words*, 168, 172; Bornkamm, "Lord's Supper", 140. *Contra* Taylor, *Jesus*, 206; Marshall, *Last Supper*, 53. The earlier argument, that the formula represented a borrowing from ancient commemorative meals, and was thus secondary, has been effectively countered — see Jeremias, *Eucharist Words*, 238–243; Schürmann, *Einsetzungsbericht*, 125–126; Taylor, *Jesus*, 207.

75 See Patsch, *Abendmahl*, 79.

the anamnesis-command. There is, first, the fact itself that the early church did feel compelled to celebrate the Supper on a continuing and frequent basis. This was recognized early on by Schürmann, and his case has been strengthened by Marshall, who adds two related points.

> First, if the Last Supper was a Passover meal, it is hard to see how the Lord's Supper came to be held not annually but much more frequently in the early church without some indication from Jesus himself. Second, if the decisive events that established the church were the resurrection appearances and the outpouring of the Spirit, it is all the more remarkable that the early church celebrated his death in the Lord's Supper and made no explicit reference to his resurrection; could they have done so without a very firm conviction that Jesus had commanded them to remember his death in this way [76]?

On this basis, then, we may argue at the very least that the command was implicitly purposed by Jesus[77].

Further, the language of the expression belongs to a Palestinian provenance. This point, discussed at length by Jeremias, has recently been taken up anew by David W. A. Gregg[78]. Gregg has found in the Hebrew of Ben Sira impressive, possible antecedents to the anamnesis-formula. His investigation strengthens the case in favor of the authenticity of the expression to the original ordinance of Jesus.

Finally, recalling our earlier note about evaluating the significance of the absence of the expression from Mark with what amounts to a text-critical argument, we may now mention more matter-of-factly the overall conclusion reached by the various attempts at reconstructing the one original report of the Last Supper. In the words of Joachim Gnilka:

> Ein weitgehend übereinstimmendes Resultat besteht darin, dass keine der überlieferten Formen, weder die markinische-matthäische noch die lukanische oder paulinische, als die älteste oder ursprüngliche angesehen weder darf, sondern dass ältere Elemente sich da und dort aufbewahrt haben[79].

As a result, all due caution must be exercised when weighing the absence of the command in one form of the tradition with its presence in the other.

At the very least, then, the command to repeat the Supper in "remembrance" of Jesus was implicitly purposed by Jesus himself. Beyond that, it is not unreasonable to believe that the command itself can be traced back to Jesus' own verbal expression of his intention that the Supper be contin-

---

76 Marshall, *Last Supper*, 52. See Schürmann, *Einsetzungsbericht*, 123–126; Gerken, *Theologie der Eucharistie*, 38.
77 See Kilpatrick, *Eucharist*, 24; Goppelt, *NT Theology*, 1:222; Davies, *Paul*, 251–252 – all of whom deny the authenticity of the saying but allow that it is consistent with Jesus' unexpressed purpose.
78 For Jeremias's discussion, see his *Eucharist Words*, 238–243. See now, David W. A. Gregg, "Hebrew Antecedents to the Eucharistic ΑΝΑΜΝΗΣΙΣ Formula", *TynB* 30 (1979) 165–168.
79 Gnilka, "Wie urteilte Jesus über seinen Tod?", 31.

uously celebrated by his followers. It remains to be seen, however, what sort of "remembrance" is intended by the command.

In the second of his 1975 Moorehouse Lectures, Kilpatrick outlined three primary ways in which this ἀνάμνησις has been understood[80]. First, he lists the normal nuance given it: "memory", "rememberance", or "memorial". The difficulty with this interpretation is three-fold, he says: (1) it ignores Paul's own explanation, "You proclaim the Lord's death until he comes"; (2) the idea of memory plays little part in the Supper; and (3) this interpretation does not rest on a discussion of any of the nuances given the term in the dictionaries[81]. Second, Kilpatrick mentions the interpretation of ἀνάμνησις as a "re-calling" or "re-presenting". He regards this as a modern idea without any real foundation in the ancient texts. However, as we shall see, his complete dismissal of this option is premature[82]. A third interpretation of ἀνάμνησις is that of Jeremias: "remember and help" – that is, "Do this in order that God may remember me [Jesus] and act"[83]. In Kilpatrick's view, this rendering founders on three points: (1) it, too, ignores the Pauline remark in 1 Cor 11:26; (2) Jeremias's interpretation is tied up with his view that, while the phrase in question does not belong to the earliest liturgical tradition, it is original to Jesus – a judgment Kilpatrick finds untenable; and (3) the remainder of the tradition emphasizes the past, not a future hope.

Thus, with each of the interpretations of ἀνάμνησις found wanting, Kilpatrick is ready to present a fourth. The point of departure for his understanding is Paul's use of καταγγέλλω in close association with ἀνάμνησις. Additionally, upon noting that the Greek verb corresponding to the noun ἀνάμνησις is ἀναμιμνήσκω, he notes a handful of instances in the Greek Bible where the verb has the sense "to proclaim" (Exod 23:13; Amos 6:10; Ps 45:17 [44:18] [for the latter two examples from the OT,

---

80 Kilpatrick, *Eucharist*, 12–13. See also Gerken, *Theologie der Eucharist*, 39–42.
81 The rendering "for the sake of memory itself" in this context is also denied by McDonald, *Kerygma*, 121; Schweizer, *Luke*, 335–336; Goppelt, *Typos*, 112; Gregg, "Hebrew Antecedents", 168.
82 This idea of "re-presenting" may be tied to the "remembrance" enacted in the celebration of Passover. In any case, we will note instances where the related verb can signify something like "let the past be effective for the present". Among the exegetes who support an interpretation akin to that which Kilpatrick here dismisses, see Schweizer, *Luke*, 335–336; Martin, *Worship*, 126–128; Johannes Behm, "'Ανάμνησις, ὑπόμνησις", in *TDNT*, 1:348–349.
83 See Jeremias, *Eucharistic Words*, 237–255. Against this view, see A. R. Millard, "Covenant and Communion in 1 Corinthians", in *Apostolic History*, 245–247; Marshall, *Last Supper*, 90; Alan M. Stibbs, *Sacrament, Sacrifice, and Eucharist* (London: Tyndale, 1961) 44; Karl-Heinz Bartels and Colin Brown, "Remember, Remembrance", in *NIDNTT*, 3:244–245; Douglas Jones, "'Ανάμνησις in the LXX and the Interpretation of 1 Cor XI.25", *JTS* n.s. 6 (1955) 183–191; Conzelmann, *A Commentary on the First Epistle to the Corinthians* (Philadelphia: Fortress, 1975) 198–199.

the textual tradition cited is that of Theodotion, Acquila, and Symmachus] ; 2 Cor 7:14–15; 2 Tim 1:6). He then comments:

> I have argued that in some passages of the Greek Bible the corresponding verb seems to mean 'tell, proclaim', and in others may have this meaning. We may go on to infer the corresponding meaning 'proclamation' for the noun. This agrees with what the apostle wrote: ' "Do this as often as you drink it to proclaim me". For as often as you eat this bread and drink this cup you proclaim the Lord's death until he comes.' On this showing, the *Anamnesis* or proclamation of Jesus is interpreted as the proclaiming of his death and the stress is not on remembrance but on this proclaiming[84].

To be sure, this line of reasoning is not completely original to Kilpatrick. Others have capitalized on the close relation of καταγγέλλω and ἀνάμνησις in Paul, and others have noted this use of ἀνάμνησις in the OT[85]. It is true, nonetheless, that Kilpatrick's presentation is the fullest defense of this position offered to date.

Yet, even he has not overcome the obstacles to this interpretation. First, we must ask if it is methodologically sound to take Paul's "commentary" on the practice of the Lord's Supper (1 Cor 11:26) as the key to understanding this one term in the pre-Pauline tradition. The force of this question is heightened when it is remembered that we have hitherto shown Kilpatrick's reasoning against the originality of Luke 22:19–20 to be wide of the mark[86]. Given that the anamnesis-formula is witnessed both in Paul and Luke, and that the tradition pre-dates Paul's writing, why should Paul's καταγγέλλω be regarded as the hermeneutical key for determining the sense of ἀνάμνησις as intended by Jesus, or even by the earliest church?

Second, we can affirm Kilpatrick's methodological move away from viewing ἀνάμνησις in isolation from other related terms, but we may also legitimately ask whether his discussion deals adequately with the additional material thus brought onto stage. A brief survey of the evidence is enlightening[87].

The noun ἀνάμνησις appears 5 times in the LXX, 4 in the NT. Of the latter, 3 are found in reports of the Last Supper. More frequent are the occurrences of the verbal form ἀναμιμνήσκω: 24 times in the LXX (plus

---

84 Kilpatrick, *Eucharist*, 16.
85 See, e.g., Käsemann, "Pauline Doctrine", 120–121; Goppelt, *NT Theology*, 1:222; Bornkamm, "Lord's Supper", 140–141; K. J. Scaria, "Eucharistic Celebration in the Early Church", *Biblebhashyam* 4 (1978) 54. See also the similar ideas expressed in McDonald, *Kerygma*, 121; Schweizer, *Lord's Supper*, 1; Bultmann, *NT Theology*, 1:313.
86 See above, chapter 3.V.D.
87 See H. Eising, "זכר", in *TDOT*, 4:64–82; Bartels and Brown, "Remember, Remembrance"; Behm, "'Ἀνάμνησις, ὑπόμνησις"; O. Michel, "Μιμνῄσκομαι, μνεία, μνήμη, μνῆμα, μνημεῖον, μνημονεύω", in *TDNT*, 4:675–683; G. B. Caird, "Towards a Lexicon of the Septuagint. I", *JTS* n.s. 19 (1968) 458; Jones, "'Ἀνάμνησις"; Brevard S. Childs, *Memory and Traditon in Israel* (London: SCM, 1962).

an additional incidence in the B text of 1 Kgs 3:1) and 6 in the NT. The nuances intended by the words may be cataloged as follows.

1. On 4 occasions – 2 Sam 20:24; 1 Kgs 4:3; 2 Kgs 18:18, 37 – ἀναμιμνήσκω translates the nominalized hiphil participle of the Hebrew root זכר (מזכיר). The term is employed thus as a title for a court official, a "recorder".

2. At two points the verb has the sense "to speak", "to invoke", or "to proclaim". Verbal speech is certainly the intended sense in Exod 23:13, where οὐκ ἀναμνησθήσεσθε appears in apposition to μὴ ἀκουσθῇ ἐκ τοῦ στόματος ὑμῶν[88]. Likewise, in Jer 4:16, where ἀναμνήσατε is juxtaposed with ἀναγγείλατε, verbal communication, with the sense of "to announce" or "to proclaim", is at the fore.

3. "God remembers and helps" is the apparent sense of the verb in Gen 8:1 ("But God remembered Noah . . . , and he sent a wind over the earth and the waters receded") and in Num 10:9 ("Then you will be remembered before the Lord your God and rescued from your enemies"). Jeremias finds this nuance in the titles to Pss 38 (37:1 LXX; 38:1 MT), and 70 (69:1 LXX; 70:1 MT)[89]. In these texts the hiphil infinitive construct of זכר (להזכיר) has been rendered as εἰς ἀνάμνησιν. Given the content of the psalms in question, one might expect that with this phrase the psalms were identified for use by a worshipper bringing his or her suffering to God's remembrance. However, the context does not allow us to ascertain with any certainty the intended meaning of the phrase[90].

Leviticus 24:7 and Num 10:10 should also be mentioned here. Both verses place ἀνάμνησις in a cultic context, but it has been pointed out that in both instances the "memorial portion" has to do with a reminder of the covenant – a reminder with both a God-ward and a human-ward reference, though the former is obviously primary[91].

4. The verb ἀναμιμνήσκω may also be used of human remembering, of recollection as a mere mental exercise – see Gen 41:9; Job 24:20; Mark 11:21; (14:72).

5. However, contextual considerations demonstrate that sense "4" is quite rare. More frequently, human "remembering" (as with divine – see "3", above), often triggered by verbal communication for that purpose, provides the impetus for some response or action. That is, "remembering"

---

[88] Nevertheless, there is little to support Kilpatrick's assertion (*Eucharist*, 15) that this reference is to "proclaiming other gods" in the sense suggested by καταγγέλλω.
[89] Jeremias, *Eucharistic Words*, 246–247.
[90] See Craigie, *Psalms 1–50*, 303; Mowinckel, *Psalms*, 2:212; Jones, "'Ἀνάμνησις", 187; Bartels and Brown, "Remember, Remembrance", 239.
[91] See Jones, "'Ἀνάμνησις", 183–187; Bartels and Brown, "Remember, Remembrance", 239.

is quite often either a three-stage process (outside stimuli + mental process + response) or a two-stage process (mental process + response), and not a mental process only. Thus, for example, presumably by verbal communication, Timothy will call to memory Paul's Christ-like lifestyle, with the effect that the Corinthians will be more Christ-like in their own behavior (1 Cor 4:16—17). Similarly, according to Wis 16:6—7, God's people were troubled, and thus reminded of the command of God's law, that they might turn toward it and be saved. For other examples of this use of ἀνάμνησις/ἀναμιμνήσκω see Neh 9:17; Ezek 29:16; 4 Macc 16:18; (Mark 14:72); 2 Cor 7:15; 2 Tim 1:6; Heb 10:32.

6. Finally, these terms are frequently employed with the sense of "recollection or memory of past action as effectual for present or future benefit". This nuance is illustrated in Ezek 33:13—16:

> If I tell the righteous man that he will surely live, but then he trusts in his own righteousness and does evil, none of the righteous things he has gone will be remembered; he will die for the evil he has done. And if I say to the wicked man, 'You will surely die,' but then he turns away from his sin, and does what is just and right . . . , he will surely live; he will not die. None of the sins he has committed will be remembered against him.

On this usage see also Num 5:15; 1 Kgs 17:18; Ps 109:14 (108:14 LXX); Ezek 21:23, 24 (vv 28, 29 LXX); Sir 3:15; Heb 10:3[92].

From this sketchy survey we can see, *contra* Kilpatrick, that no sharp line need be drawn between ἀνάμνησις as mental process and as verbal activity. "To tell" and "to remember" are often interrelated aspects of the same process. Moreover, we have seen that in ἀνάμνησις a direct line is often drawn from past to present (or future) experience. While we would not want to understanding too woodenly an idea such as "re-presentation" in this regard, it is nevertheless true that in ἀνάμνησις the past has present (or future) impact or effect. Past events become effectual and place demands on present existence.

How, then, are we to understand the anamnesis-formula of the Supper? We propose that this Jesus-saying ("Do this in remembrance of me") can be interpretively paraphrased thus: *Celebrate the Supper again and again, for thus you continually remind yourselves that my passion must be as central to your faith as it is to God's redemptive purpose — a purpose moving toward its consummation.* In defense of this interpretation we offer the following observations. First, it is reasonable to suggest that the sense intended by the terse anamnesis-formula is greatly determined by the other Supper-words. Our paraphrase embraces the heavy emphasis Jesus himself placed on his death, its place in God's salvific plan, and its effects for the people. Second, and similarly, our proposal embraces the eschatological

---

92 See Jones, "'Ἀνάμνησις'", 185—186.

emphasis found in the Supper. Third, our proposal does not rest on a speculative or dubious rendering of ἀνάμνησις, but goes right to the heart of the term's otherwise amply-attested meaning.

Fourth, here anamnesis is not understood as meditative retrospection, but is the sort of dynamic recollection affected by actions and words calling forth appropriate response. Thus, the idea of "proclamation" championed by Kilpatrick is at the same time included and broadened in scope. Fifth, our investigation is consistent with the interpretations of the Supper offered by John and Paul. As we have shown, these writers use motifs and terminology from the Supper to redirect the thoughts of their respective audiences to the centrality of Jesus' death. Additionally, the very reason motivating Paul's inclusion of the Supper-tradition in his epistle was to show how Jesus' passion had practical consequences as regards the lives of believers: in remembering the self-giving quality of Jesus' death, Christians are reminded of the ramifications of the cross for community life (1 Cor 11:17—34).

Finally, whether one holds that the Supper was originally a Passover — as seems most likely — or merely admits that the Supper had some associations with Passover, apparently ample reason existed to regard it as such from early on, and the interpretation of the anamnesis-formula proposed here dovetails well with the idea of "remembrance" associated with the Passover[93]. With the repetition of the Supper, as with Passover (see Exod 12:1—20), the memory of the divine act of salvation was kept alive. In analogy with the Passover, moreover, the significance of the cross and its claims on human lives is made real for each successive generation by the repetition of the Supper.

Summarizing from our discussion of the anamnesis-formula, we have argued that Jesus himself purposed that the Supper be repeated, and that its perpetual celebration be an occasion for remembering his passion. This anamnesis entails mental process, but also the active declaration of Jesus' passion and its significance in God's redemptive plan, and the response of those who participate in the Supper whereby they allow the cross to lay its claim on their lives and they appropriate for themselves its benefits. Thus, with the celebration of the Supper, believers were to focus on the passion of Jesus as a historical event with ever-present ramifications.

(3) Finally, our proposal that the celebration of the Lord's Supper in the primitive church provided the *Sitz im Leben* for the formation of the passion narrative takes note of the fact that from the birth of Christianity

---

93 On this association, see Higgins, *Lord's Supper*, 35—36; Davies, *Paul*, 251—252; Stibbs, *Sacrament*, 44—45; Jones, "'Ἀνάμνησις'", 188—189; Martin, *Worship*, 126—128; Goppelt, *Typos*, 112; Marshall, *Last Supper*, 90—91.

the Supper was integral to the church's life. That is, from the very outset, already in the observance of the Supper, there was both the occasion and the context for assimilating, recounting, and reflecting upon Jesus' passion. Because our statement regarding the celebration of the Supper *from earliest times* is not universally acknowledged, a brief consideration of the evidence will be necessary.

a. Some scholars insists that the "Institution of the Lord's Supper" is only a reading back of the Lord's Supper into the last meal of Jesus since, it is alleged, the Supper has the character of a sacrament in the sense intended in the mystery religions. The name of Bultmann is especially associated with this view, though it can be traced as well in other scholars, including Lietzmann and Marxsen. The contrast of pagan meals with the table of the Lord (1 Cor 10:20–21), the Supper as an acting out of the Lord's death (11:26), the tracing of the founding cause of the Supper to the fate of the Lord (11:23), the so-called magical effects of unworthy participation (11: 30), and the identification of the elements of the Supper as vehicles of Christ's presence – these are among the more prominent pointers to the character of the Supper as a cultic meal of the mystery religions[94]. If this reading of the evidence is correct, then our earlier statements about the Supper would be valid only insofar as they could be projected onto "later Christianity" as it developed around Paul, and not for Jesus' own understanding or that of the most primitive church.

That as the church moved into the pagan world, and as its membership included many former pagans, there arose interpretations of the Supper analogous to those of the celebration-meals of the mysteries is a defensible position. Indeed, it is only on this basis that Paul can argue as he does in 1 Cor 10. However, to draw these parallels into an identification intrinsic to the Supper and thus to argue for the origin of the Supper under the influence of the mysteries is to push the evidence too far. Some Christians may have celebrated the Supper as a mystery guaranteeing immortality (φάρμακον ἀθανασίας – e.g. Ign., *Eph.* 20.2), but this does not demonstrate that the Supper's origin or intended purpose was somehow necessarily tied to the mystery religions.

Comparisons between the Supper and sacramental meals of the mystery religions must first overcome the wide disparity over what constitutes a "mystery religion" and the diversity of sacramental celebrations observed in each of the congregations of the mysteries[95].

---

[94] See Bultmann, *NT Theology*, 1:148–149, 313; *idem, History,* 265–266; Lietzmann, *Mass,* 182; Marxsen, *Beginnings,* esp. pp. 73–74, 106.

[95] See A. D. Nock, *Early Gentile Christianity and Its Hellenistic Background* (New York: Harper & Row, 1964) 72–76; Koester, *NT Introduction,* 1:196–203; Hans-Josef Klauck, *Herrenmahl und hellenistischer Kult* (Münster: Aschendorff, 1982).

Even if one chooses to speak in generalities, however, a number of observations tell against this thesis. (a) Paul, in 1 Cor 10:1–13, argues *against* viewing the Supper as "the medicine of immortality". (b) Paul's overall emphasis is not on what is eaten, but on the sharing of the one loaf and cup. (c) The sin with the so-called magical effects was against the "body", not against the elements themselves (1 Cor 11:29–30). (d) The Supper was repeated for the purpose of anamnesis, not to honor a god. (e) In the Supper one ate in the presence of the Lord; one did not eat the god or share a meal with a god. (f) The Supper entails no literal sacrifice: Jesus' death is not re-enacted, but remembered and proclaimed[96].

The most exhaustive study of this problem is Han-Josef Klauck's recent monograph, *Herrenmahl und hellenistischer Kult*. The hiatus between his discussion of Hellenistic religion and his analysis of the meal in 1 Corinthians speaks for the significant gap between the two categories of meal in question. It would appear that Bultmann's hypothesis should be laid to rest, permanently.

b. From a literary pont of view, the Supper-tradition cited by Paul is the earliest. Paul introduces the tradition with a statement concerning its origin with the Lord and Paul's own role in the traditioning process. In doing so, he employs the technical terms παραλαμβάνω and παραδίδωμι to denote links in the chain of Christian tradition[97]. That is, the tradition did not originate with Paul, nor does it rest on his own authority. According to Paul, the eucharistic words go back to Jesus himself and so the church is responsible to recognize the Supper's significance and perpetuate its celebration. We know from 1 Cor 11:23, then, that (1) the Supper-tradition was received from an established Christian community, and (2) Paul had passed it on to the Corinthians, presumably during his evangelistic mission to Corinth (cf. 11:2; 15:3), *circa* A.D. 49/50–51/52[98]. That is, within two decades of Jesus' death the tradition Paul cites was in existence as a fixed, authoritative formula.

But from whence did Paul receive this tradition? On this, certainty can not be reached, though the primary candidates would be Jerusalem (see Gal 1:18; 2:1), Damascus (see Acts 9:19; Gal 1:17), and Antioch (see Acts 11:

---

96 On arguments against Bultmann's view, see Dunn, *Unity and Diversity*, 164–165; Robert Banks, *Paul's Idea of Community* (Grand Rapids, Michigan: Wm. B. Eerdmans, 1980) 87; Käsemann, "Pauline Doctrine", 108–109; Lohse, *Märtyrer*, 123; Marshall, *Last Supper*, 27–31; Goppelt, *NT Theology*, 1:214–215; Patsch, *Abendmahl*, 18–21; Bornkamm, "Lord's Supper", 132.

97 See 1 Cor 11:2; 15:3; Gerhard Delling, "Παραλαμβάνω", in *TDNT*, 4:13; Friedrich Büchsel, "παραδίδωμι", in *TDNT*, 2:171; Conzelmann, *1 Corinthians*, 195–196; Klauck, *Herrenmahl*, 300–301.

98 See, e.g., Conzelmann, *1 Corinthians*, 12–13; Robert Jewett, *Dating Paul's Life* (London: SCM, 1979) 38–40.

25—26; Gal 2:11). Even if it was not at Jerusalem that Paul received this tradition, it is yet possible that Jerusalem could have been the ultimate source of the tradition, for the churches at Damascus and Antioch were founded by Jerusalam Christians. Thus, Marshall's conclusion is well-founded:

> The probabilities are that Paul's formula goes back to Greek-speaking Christians in Jerusalem, who had translated it out of the story of the Last Supper used by Hebrew- or Aramaic-speaking Christians. We are, then, on strong ground in tracing Paul's formula about the Last Supper right back to the very early days of the church ... [99].

c. Jeremias has argued in some detail that the eucharistic words of Jesus recorded in the NT ultimately derive from a Semitic *Urtext*[100]. His treatment of the evidence has been criticized by Williams, however[101]. Prior to taking up Williams's counterpoints, it will be helpful to outline Jeremias's evidence. Because Williams concerns himself only with the words of institution themselves, and not with the subsequent eschatological saying, we will likewise restrict our discussion. For Mark 14:22—24 Jeremias lists the following Semitisms:

(a) Καί at the beginning of a pericope.
(b) Καί-parataxis.
(c) Λαβὼν ἄρτον εὐλογήσας — a Semitic idiom, with the superfluous λαμβάνω.
(d) Εὐλογήσας used absolutely — a Semitic idiom.
(e) Ἔκλασεν καὶ ἔδωκεν — a Semitic idiom.
(f) Ἔκλασεν for "breaking break" — a technical term of Semitic origin.
(g) Καὶ ἔδωκεν αὐτοῖς — a Semitic idiom.
(h) Λαβὼν ποτήριον εὐχαριστήσας — a phrase of Semitic origin.
(i) Εὐχαριστήσας with no direct object.
(j) Εὐχαριστήσας ἔδωκεν αὐτοῖς — a phrase of Semitic origin.
(k) Τὸ σῶμά μου — a Semitic word order; the variant with σάρξ in John 6:51c suggest a Semitic *Urtext*; the pairing of σῶμα/σάρχ — αἷμα is a Semitism.
(l) Τὸ αἷμα μου — see (k) above.
(m) Ἐκχυννόμενον — a literal rendering of העלה in Isa 53:12 (MT, not LXX); present tense reflects Semitism.
(n) Ὑπέρ — a rendering of a Semitic equivalent since ὑπέρ + genitive is lacking in the LXX of Isa 53; ἀντὶ πολλῶν in Mark 10:45 represents a translation variant of the Semitic *Urtext*.
(o) Πολλῶν in the inclusive sense.

---

99 Marshall, *Last Supper*, 33; Goppelt, *NT Theology*, 1:214. Cf. Kilpatrick, *Eucharist*, 22—24.
100 Jeremias, *Eucharist Words*, 173—186. Also, Black, *Aramaic Approach*, 238—239.
101 Williams, *Jesus' Death*, 217—220.

(p) Τὸ ἐκχυννόμενον ὑπὲρ πολλῶν — reflects Semitic word order, with the prepositional phrase at the end.

To these observations we may add the following.

(q) In Mark's tradition the genitive always follows the corresponding noun, reflecting Semitic word order.

(r) In Mark's tradition, the verbs are always situated at the beginning of their clauses, reflecting Semitic word order.

(s) As earlier noted, the anamnesis-formula (in Luke and Paul) reflects Semitic usage[102].

Williams makes the following observations. First, he grants (d) and (f), but asserts that Acts 27:35 demonstrates how apparently neutral (f), "to break bread", was for a Greek-speaking Christian. What Williams fails to notice here is that the language of Acts 27:35 reflects that of the other religious meals in Acts, which itself models that of the Supper, the feeding of the multitudes, and the Emmaus episode (see further, below). Hence, Acts 27:35 should not be considered in isolation from these other texts, all of which reflect Semitic usage.

Second, he debates the significance of the word order in (k), (l), and (p) — and so, presumably, also in (q) and (r). Here Williams is right to argue that the fact that the Greek text corresponds to Semitic word order is not proof *ipso facto* that the Greek rests on a Semitic *Urtext*; after all, the order of words in Greek is itself relatively flexible. What is remarkable, nonetheless, is the piling of incidences in this short pericope wherein Semitic word order is paralleled. The accumulative case here is strong, if not decisive.

Third, Williams gives little weight to Jeremias's appeal to the use of καί — (a) and (b) — for, he says, parataxis is a feature of Markan style. Williams thus too easily sets aside the fact that the excessive use of this conjunction may indeed result from Semitic influence[103]. Still, he is correct in pointing to the inconclusiveness of this evidence[104].

Fourth, he takes issue with Jeremias's assertion that "having taken bread and blessed" (c) corresponds to a typically Semitic idiom: "took and did". Here, Williams has apparently confused two points Jeremias is trying to make about the one phrase. On the one hand, Jeremias wants to urge that "take and bless" is a Semitic idiom. On the other, he insists that λαμβάνω

---

[102] See Gregg, "Hebrew Antecedents"; Jeremias, *Eucharistic Words*, 238–243; Kilpatrick, *Eucharist*, 21.

[103] See, in addition to Jeremias (*Eucharistic Words*, 173–186), Black, *Aramaic Approach*, 69; MHT, 2:420–423.

[104] See Reiser, *Syntax und Stil*, 99–137; David Barrett Peabody, *The Redactional Features of the Author of Mark* (Ann Arbor, Michigan: University Microfilms, 1983); BDF, para. 458.

is often used in a cumbersome and superfluous way in Semitic idiom. While Williams is right to deny that the superfluous use of λαμβάνω should be taken as an indicator of Semitic influence, he fails to deal with the first, and primary, aspect of Jeremias's point.

Fifth, (g) would have been familiar to readers of the LXX — a valid point. Sixth, (h) corresponds to Jewish practice but does not necessarily rest on a Semitic original — again a valid point. Seventh, as regards (k), the pair "body/blood" is not confined to Semitic usage, but is also found in the LXX and in Philo — a point Jeremias himself acknowledges[105]. Eighth, Williams asserts that (m) and (n) can be quickly dismissed, but we have already demonstrated their validity[106]. With this, Williams rests his case.

After Williams's attempt at demolishing Jeremias's argument for the Semitic origin of the eucharistic words, what remains? We may summarize as follows. Points (d), (f), and, presumably, (i) are granted by Williams. Points (k), (l), (p), (q), and (r) — all having to do with word order — present an accumulative case in favor of a Semitic original. Points (a), (b), (g), (h), and the linguistic aspect of (k) are shown to be inconclusive in themselves though, again, in view of the remaining evidence, they should not be completely discarded. Williams has failed to adequately counter points (c), (e), (j), (m), (n), and (o). Point (s) was not taken up in William's study. In conclusion, therefore, the balance of the evidence still favors the thesis that behind the eucharistic words of Jesus as recorded in the NT there lies a Semitic original — and this suggests that the Supper was celebrated from early on in an Aramaic-speaking Christian community.

d. Returning to 1 Corinthians, it has often been observed that here we have the earliest evidence of how the Supper was celebrated in the life of the church. It is clear from 1 Cor 11:17—34 that the Supper was held in the context of a fellowship meal, but just how often the meal was celebrated is difficult to say. The impression one gains is that the Corinthians frequently gathered for the common meal and eucharist as a part of their worship (compare 1 Cor 11:18; 14:26). How frequently? If we assume that 16:2 ("On the first day of the week") denotes a regular weekly meeting of the Christian community we might take the next step and suggest that when the Corinthians met for worship it was customary to partake of the common meal and celebrate the Supper[107]. This can only be conjectural, however.

e. When turning to the testimony provided by the Acts of the Apostles, one is immediately struck by the apparent diversity between the commun-

---

105 Jeremias, *Eucharistic Words*, 222.
106 See above, chapter 7.IV.B (1).
107 See Klauck, *Herrenmahl*, 295.

ity meal in Acts and the Supper as we know it from Paul. Before we allow the testimony of Acts any weight for our present argument we must first ask whether Acts really does speak of a "Lord's Supper", complete with the words related to Jesus' death.

At the outset we may note several important variations between the meals as reported by Paul and Luke. (a) Luke records no connection between the community meal and the Last Supper, as does Paul. (b) Luke does not report the repetition of any interpretive words in the context of the church meal, as does Paul. (c) Unlike Paul, Luke makes no reference in the church meal to the death of Jesus. (d) Neither does Luke, as opposed to Paul, mention the use of wine in the meal. As for common elements, one may refer to the basic fact that both were community meals, and to the shared eschatological outlook – signified in the Lukan reference to "joy" (Acts 2:47)[108], and in the Pauline phrase "until he comes" (1 Cor 11:26).

These kinds of differences led Lietzmann to conclude some years ago that there were two kinds of church meal in early Christianity. One type had its roots in the daily fellowship-meals of the disciples of Jesus. It was a meal associated with the ancient Jerusalem community, a meal in which there was a consecration of the bread as in the Jewish *haburah*, a meal celebrated in the context of eschatological joy. On the other hand was a meal modelled after the Last Supper, a memorial to Jesus' death. Paul himself was responsible for drawing the line from this meal back to the Last Supper and its related death metaphor, for he had received this schema in a private revelation from the Lord[109].

Subsequent scholars have not been slow to question Lietzmann's reconstruction, their critiques focusing on three main points[110]. First, he attributed too much to Pauline originality. Second, the variations between the two forms of community meal are more apparent than real. The absence of the mention of wine is no warrant for regarding the Lukan meal as a *communio sub una*, but rather corresponds to the unavailability of wine in some areas. "The breaking of the bread" could have been an alternative expression for the Lord's Supper – as in 1 Cor 10:16. Moreover, that the words of interpretation are missing may be explained easily enough when it is remembered that Luke never describes what happened at the meals, but only relates that the meals took place. Third, it is a false antithesis which sets the one

---

108 See Rudolf Bultmann, "'Αγαλλιάομαι, ἀγαλλίασις", in *TDNT*, 1:21.
109 Lietzmann, *Mass*, 204–215. Cf. the related views of Marxsen (*Beginnings*, 108–113) and Bultmann (*NT Theology*, 1:58).
110 See esp. Higgins, *Lord's Supper*, 57–61. Also Marshall, *Last Supper*, 131–133; Oscar Cullmann, *Early Christian Worship* (London: SCM, 1953) 17; Gerhard Delling, *Worship in the New Testament* (London: Darton, Longman, and Todd, 1962) 145.

meal as a joyful celebration over against the other as a death-memorial, for both meals exhibited joyful anticipation.

Speaking summarily, as regards points one and three, the evidence against Lietzmann is quite convincing. However, one can admit the validity of these two arguments and still not have overcome the substantial diversity of form and content as outlined above. In fact, attempts at harmonization have not been successful. Certainly, 1 Cor 10:16 cannot be used as evidence that "the breaking of the bread" was a shorthand designation for the Pauline-type Supper, for this text also uses the parallel phrase "the cup of thanksgiving". In conjunction with the variations listed above, it should be underscored that while the "Pauline" Supper is filled with theological content, the "Lukan" is practically devoid of the same.

Indeed, "the breaking of the bread" is very much like an ordinary meal, distinguished by only two factors. First, there is the religious character of these meals, made plain by the contexts of the meals in Luke's narrative. This is observed easily enough in the case of the first two references – Acts 2:42, 46 – where "the breaking of the bread" is set in the midst of other characteristic activities of the early community. In Acts 20:7, Luke reports that the church at Troas gathered on the first day of the week to break bread together. While Paul is named as "guest speaker", it is quite probable that this was a regular, weekly meeting – a constitutive part of which was "the breaking of the bread". Probably, the "first day of the week" corresponded with resurrection day, the day of the first meal with the resurrected Jesus.

The religious sense of the meal in 27:35 is not so clear and might even be denied on the grounds that it was a meal shared not only by Christians but also, we may assume, by the pagans aboard the Rome-bound vessel. Nevertheless, the language employed models that of the miraculous feeding of the multitude (Luke 9:16), the Last Supper (22:19), and the Emmaus episode (24:30), so it is difficult to avoid the conclusion that the scene should be interpreted as a religious, "communal" meal. The logical alternative would be to deny every "breaking of the bread" in Luke-Acts any special, religious sense[111]. It is not unlikely that at this early stage of the church's life the common meal could have been extended in such circumstances. Indeed this is precisely what we might have expected in this second half of Luke's two-volume "Gospel", for in the first half Jesus is characteristically portrayed as engaging in a profoundly *inclusive* table fellowship. His table intimates are not limited to his chosen disciples, but rather include "tax collectors and 'sinners'" – as the summary text in Luke 15:1–2 has it.

---

111 As Giles rightly concludes ("Is Luke an Exponent of 'Early Protestantism'?", 203–204).

Given this pattern in the Gospel of Luke should we be surprised by a sign of open fellowship at the table in the Acts of the Apostles?

The second factor setting "the breaking of the bread" apart from ordinary meals is that they are characterized by joy — stemming from a renewed anticipation of the kingdom based on the post-resurrection appearances with the exalted Lord and the present experience of salvation[112].

Therefore, it is too much to say regarding "the breaking of the bread" that "here in Acts, the phrase has become a fixed designation in the Church's language for a sacramental meal"[113], but not enough to designate it "simply as the *sharing of food*"[114].

The evidence points to a distinction between "the breaking of the bread" represented in Acts and the Supper as related in 1 Corinthians. The former should be seen as directly related to the post-resurrection meals with Jesus. However, given the terminology used to describe the post-resurrection meals, their link with the Lord's Supper should not be totally denied. Rather, the Supper as related by Paul is directly linked to the Last Supper through the post-resurrection meals. Eventually, the community meal inclusive of the interpretive words eclipsed the more simple form, though both were present from early on. It is likely, then, that Luke belonged to a community in which "the breaking of the bread" was the normal communal meal, the focus of which was the resurrected Lord, and not his salvific death.

Of course, it might be countered that the writer of Luke-Acts would not have included the command to repeat the Supper (Luke 22:19) without indicating how this imperative was somehow fulfilled in the life of the primitive church. In response, we might draw attention to the continuity that does exist between the meals in Acts and the Last Supper as a religiously-charged fellowship meal. After all, whatever else the Last Supper was, it was certainly one more in a series of meals shared between Jesus, his disciples, and others — events which were of special significance for the Third Evangelist[115]. "Fellowship meals", then, were continued, and to this degree early Christians as portrayed in Acts did carry out Jesus' wish.

---

112 See further, Cullmann, *Worship,* 15–16; Giles, "Is Luke an Exponent of 'Early Protestantism'?", 204.
113 Goppelt, *Apostolic and Post-Apostolic Times,* 45.
114 Dunn, *Jesus,* 185; cf. pp. 184–185. Robinson ("Emmaus Story", 491–493) stresses the religious character of these meals.
115 See, e.g., Otfried Hofius, *Jesu Tischgemeinschaft mit den Sündern* (Stuttgart: Calwer, 1967) — where the bulk of evidence for the subject stems from Luke's Gospel; Willibald Bösen, *Jesusmahl, Eucharistisches Mahl, Endzeitmahl: Ein Beitrag zur Theologie des Lukas* (Stuttgart: Katholisches, 1980); Robert J. Karris, *Luke: Artist and Theologian. Luke's Passion Account as Literature* (New York: Paulist, 1985) 47–78; Joachim Wanke, *Beobachtungen zum Eucharistieverständnis des Lukas auf Grund der lukanischen Mahlberichte* (Leipzig: St. Benno, 1973).

At the same time we must sound a cautionary note against bringing to Luke-Acts an expectation for a narrative free of rough spots and inconsistencies. In our analysis of the Lukan passion narrative (chapter 3) we encountered instances wherein the traditional material employed by Luke actually works against his own thought. For example, in our discussion of the trial scene we saw problems of consistency arise with respect to Luke's christology and we noted how his basically positive attitude toward the temple is at times seemingly contradicted by the traditional elements he takes over. Again, the role of Herod in Luke 23 fails to dovetail with that in Acts 4, and the removal of Jesus from the cross in Luke 23 is inconsistent with the report in Acts 13. The lack of precise, literary continuity from Jesus' words at the Last Supper (borrowed from pre-Lukan material!) to the meals in Acts would not be altogether novel, and probably reflects Luke's overarching portrayal of fellowship meals in his two-volume work.

From the Acts account it is plain that the community meal was a central aspect of Christian experience. Interpolating from this, we might argue for a similar frequency for the Lord's Supper among other Christians.

f. Finally, we return to the observation made earlier regarding how widespread in early Christianity the Supper-words were. We have argued that in the Synoptics and Paul we have three accounts of the Supper that share no direct literary relationship, and John 6:48—58 exhibits a fourth. Moreover, Kilpatrick has found that in 1 Cor 10:16; 11:27 Paul makes use of traditional language from a Supper-formula independent of that in 1 Cor 11:23—25, but more akin to the Markan formula[116]. This suggests a fifth form of the tradition. This evidence, taken together with our earlier, sketchy observations about the extent to which the Supper has influenced the theology of the developing church, is *prima facie* testimony favoring the early and broad-based celebration of the Supper.

Thus, we have found several lines of testimony to support our statement that the Lord's Supper was an important aspect of the life of the primitive Christian community. As such, it was well-suited to provide the focal point for communication about Jesus' death — communication which would have entailed discussion of the events of the passion as well as their significance. Our proposal for a *Sitz im Leben* for the passion narrative demands that the Supper was celebrated from early on; this requirement is met with virtual certainty.

---

116 Kilpatrick, *Eucharist*, 23.

V. Concluding Remarks

We have proposed that the *Sitz im Leben* of the passion narrative was the celebration of the Lord's Supper in the context of early church life. We have argued that this proposal fits well with what we know of the practice of the Lord's Supper in the early church, and we have seen that a constitutive part of the Supper, the anamnesis, provided a ready context for remembering and recounting Jesus' death. Here we may also refer back to Trocmé's work, which indicated antecedents for this kind of recounting in Jewish worship, especially at the Passover. In concluding this portion of our inquiry, a few additional remarks, focusing more directly on the passion narrative in the Supper-context, are in order.

First, our proposal leaves room for influence on the developing passion story from other aspects of the church's life and mission. We noted earlier the problem of trying to segregate the various ingredients of community life — evangelistic preaching, community life, and so on, and we have already indicated how the mission and the teaching ministry of the early church left their marks on the passion account. An advantage of our proposal is that it does not require that the whole narrative be the product of the same formative process, as though the Supper was somehow separate from the currents of thought in the goings-on of the church apart from divine worship. Nor does our proposal require that each episode in the passion narrative be directed at meeting the same purpose, but takes account of the fact that other aspects of the church's ministry influenced the form of certain pericopae. Our proposal envisions a dynamic process wherein the total, integrated life of the Christian community is focused at the anamnesis of the Supper on Christ's death — so that reflection on, and lessons from, the passion of Jesus could be welded together in one continuous narrative. The Supper, then, acted as the crucible for the creation of the passion narrative.

Second, this proposal does not specify that the one, original, magisterial passion narrative took shape in Jerusalem, Antioch, or some other center of developing Christianity. We have already demonstrated that the canonical Gospels represent at least three forms of the narrative of the passion of Jesus. While our investigation below will provide strong evidence for a large measure of cross-fertilization between the various traditions and for a fairly firm, extensive, literary and theological outline underlying the canonical accounts, and while the possibility of an "archetypal passion narrative" (Trocmé) should not be ruled out, our proposal leaves room for the influence of different Christian communities on the developing passion tradition.

Finally, while our analysis has taken up a number of possible, important objections to our proposal, we may anticipate one further protest. If the

Supper emphasized so emphatically the salvific character of Jesus' death, and if the Supper was the *Sitz im Leben* for the passion narrative, then why is this interpretation of Jesus' death not more prominent in the passion account? Here, of course, we can only raise this issue, for we have yet to deal in any intensive way with the interpretation of Jesus' death offered by the passion story.

In positing the celebration of the Lord's Supper as the *Sitz im Leben* for the early passion narrative, then, we recognize that in its focus on Jesus' death as central to God's redemptive plan and in its anamnesis of Jesus' passion the Supper provided a ready occasion and impetus for remembering, recounting, and reflecting upon the events and significance of the cross of Christ.

Part One

Summary

New Testament scholarship of this century has been unable to reach a consensus of opinion on the question whether there existed from earliest Christian times a narrative outlining the events and explicating the significance of Jesus' suffering and death. Our *Forschungsbericht* demonstrated the diversity of methodologies and conclusions of a large number of interpreters — from the Continent, Great Britain, and North America. Recent studies have largely rejected the older approaches, but have not been able to erect convincing methodological alternatives in their place, with the result that study on our subject has reached something of an impasse. In this section of our study we have attempted to indicate the usefulness and limitations of new methodologies, especially redaction criticism, while at the same time arguing that certain of the older tools, especially those related to form criticism, were discarded unnecessarily. Our basic approach to the problem of a pre-canonical passion narrative has taken its point of departure from the conviction that any convincing thesis regarding the existence of such an account will never survive the ebb and flow of critical tides by depending on a monolithic base of support. We have therefore argued from a variety of vantage points and set forth a number of distinct *testimonia* — each of which has the ability to stand on its own, while also interlocking with the others in order to yield a more stable edifice. Along the way we have set aside numerous counter-arguments which, if allowed to go unchallenged, might have eaten away at our columns of support.

Thus we have argued that both Luke and John had access to non-Markan traditions of Jesus' passion — traditions that may have shared close affinities with the fullness of outline exhibited by the Markan passion account. Moreover, we demonstrated that the coherence of the Markan narrative, when viewed in relation to Mark's conservative treatment of his material and the high improbability that more than two or three episodes of the passion story were recounted independent of the greater whole, favored the existence of a narrative of Jesus' passion at the base of Mark 14—15. Further, we saw that there were (1) the theoretical imperative for coming to grips with the significance and events of Jesus' death in earliest Christianity, (2) evidence that primitive Christianity did deal with these issues, both orally and literarily, (3) literary convention(s) (*Gattung* or *Gattungen*) for dealing with the events described by the Gospel passion narratives which (4) were closely followed by the Gospel accounts. That is, the "Suffering/Vindication" genre and, perhaps, that of the "farewell discourse", has influenced the construction of the narrative of Jesus' passion. Finally, we have seen that the practice of the Lord's Supper within the early Christian community life provided both a setting and the impetus for the development of the passion story. While the various others aspects of the church's life would have influenced the development of the passion account, it was the Supper — with its focus on, and anamnesis of, Jesus' death — that provided the ready occasion and motivation for the construction of the passion narrative. The combination and intersection of these distinct yet related conclusions adds up to a formidable argument favoring the existence of a pre-canonical passion narrative.

To be sure, our treatment of the Markan passion narrative has been surprisingly indirect — surprising, that is, since previous studies of this nature have focused almost exclusively on the Markan account. Quite reasonably it may be asked, What is the relation of the Markan passion narrative to the pre-canonical passion narrative? A tentative answer has already been supplied: in view of the character of Markan redaction we would expect Mark to have followed closely his passion source in constructing his chapters 14—15. A more comprehensive answer can be worked out only in the context of a fuller discussion of the extent and content of the pre-canonical passion narrative — to be treated along with an explication of the theology of that narrative in part two.

Part Two

The Significance of Jesus' Death in the Passion Narrative

Chapter Eight:

Jesus' Suffering and Death in the Passion Narrative

I. Introduction

That we have only later abridgements of the earliest passion story and not the "original" itself presents a major methodological hurdle for our interpretive agenda. In our consideration of the Lukan passion narrative we already recognized the futility of any quest for the original wording of the Lukan *Sondergut*. Can we, then, with any confidence, hope to uncover the important themes by which Jesus' death was interpreted in the narrative?

The investigation of the first part of our thesis has demonstrated that Mark, Luke, and John each made use of pre-canonical passion traditions. Luke, of course, also made use of Mark and, in all probability, Matthew's only narrative source for his passion account was Mark. We might expect, therefore, that by a careful comparison of Mark, John, and those parts of Luke which are independent of Mark, we will be able to point out where the more original form of the tradition has been preserved at each juncture of the passion narrative. From this, we will be able to recover the general outline, content, and theological themes important in that narrative.

Such a comparison as we propose was foreshadowed by the recent analysis of the Markan and Johannine narratives by Till Arend Mohr. On the basis of his pericope-by-pericope investigation Mohr reached the rather novel thesis that Mark

> hatte einen umfangreichen, schriftlichen Passionsbericht zur Verfügung, der bereits eine vormkn. Ueberarbeitung (B) aufweis und in seiner [ursprungliche] Gestalt (P) mit der von den Synoptikern unabhängigen vor joh. Leidensgeschichte im wesentlichen übereinstimmt[1].

Mohr's methodology, however, does not lead us readily to adopt his hypothesis. Primarily, Mohr's is an investigation of the possible existence of, and tradition-history behind, the pre-Markan passion story, utilizing above all the previous linguistic work on Mark's Gospel by Schenke[2]. We have already found reason to view with suspicion attempts at "getting behind" the Markan passion story by means of linguistic data[3], so, at the very out-

---

[1] Mohr, *Passion*, 404.
[2] See Schenke, *Studien; idem, Christus*.
[3] See above, chapters 1 and 5.

set, there is cause to question the validity of Mohr's procedure. In addition, Mohr has really not investigated in any great depth the Johannine passion story for he is apparently more concerned to show that the redactional features present in Mark are absent in John. Without a more convincing argument regarding Mohr's ability to get behind the Markan narrative to an early narrative source and a pre-Markan redactor this line of reasoning can indicate nothing more than the literary independence of the Second and Fourth Evangelists. Moreover, Mohr's approach fails to deal with the Lukan-Johannine parallels, and the possibility of an early narrative source behind the passion accounts of the Third and Fourth Gospels. That is, Mohr's methodology is too narrowly focused. Our own investigation will avoid these pitfalls as it draws on the form-, redaction-, tradition-, and literary-critical judgments made earlier in part one of our study.

One significant contribution of Mohr's study that must not be overlooked is its pointed reminder that the Fourth Gospel need not necessarily witness to a relatively late form of the passion tradition.

Because our interpretive agenda necessarily embraces a tradition-historical element, we will make use of a pericope-by-pericope investigation. While this "vertical approach" to the evidence (whereby we analyze the theological content of each story) will be beneficial in pushing the focus of our inquiry beyond the redactional elements of the evangelists to the more primitive material, the results thus gained may appear disjointed, lacking in continuity. That is, by looking at the theology of Jesus' death in each part of the passion account we may fail to gain an overall view of the theology of Jesus' death. This is not to say that the passion narrative will necessarily exhibit throughout only one, uniform understanding of Jesus' passion; rather, it is to call attention to the fact that our methodology may result in our seeing the trees when what we are really after is a bird-eye's view of the whole forest. For this reason, the inquiry of this chapter must be supplemented (or complemented) by a further one, which seeks to sketch the individual themes of the various pericopae as they appear throughout the narrative. In other words, the vertical-oriented approach must prepare for a "horizontal approach" which takes as its point of reference the findings of our study of the individual pericopae. The purpose of this chapter, then, is to pursue the former agenda — looking into the theology of Jesus' death in each segment of the passion story.

In addition to the methodological comments made previously, we should make explicit at the outset of this interpretive venture one further point. We have already identified the point of departure for our inquiry as a comparison of the independent accounts, so it is worth asking, What conclusions are possible when, say, Mark stands alone against the other versions on particular details? By way of dealing with such problems, we propose to ask at such points (1) whether the Markan text can be explained in terms of

Markan redactional interests, (2) whether the Johannine and/or Lukan "omissions" can be explained in terms of their redactional interests, and (3) whether observations of a *traditionsgeschichtliche* nature best account for the omission in one or addition in another of the material in question at the pre-Gospel stage. Unfortunately, at times this approach will not provide absolute certainty for our conclusion, but it is worthy of note that, regarding the significant theological themes of the passion story, our case need never rest on these more speculative judgments.

II. Conspiracy and Anointing

A. Mark 14:1–2; Matt 26:1–5; Luke 22:1–2; John 11:47–57

Earlier, we saw that in these introductory verses Luke has only reworked his Markan source[4]. Likewise, Mark was Matthew's only written source here. Thus, Mark and John present the only two independent accounts of the Jewish plot against Jesus, though the Matthean-Johannine agreements in these verses should not be overlooked. To be sure, the Second and Fourth Evangelists differ markedly in their versions of this report, but they are united on the central point: not long before Passover, the Jewish authorities (i.e. Jesus' enemies) reached a decision to do away with Jesus and therefore were looking for an opportune time for carrying out their plan.

The precise identity of the Jewish leaders is not decisive for our purposes; nevertheless, John's rendition appears to have a good claim to being the more original of the two in this respect[5]. Other aspects of the Johannine version are in all likelihood traditional — e.g. the reference to οἱ 'Ρωμαῖοι (only here in John); the use of ὁ τόπος for the temple (rather than ἱερόν — 10x, or ναός — 3x)[6]; the theme of temple-destruction (cf. Mark 13:2; 15:29); and the political motif (cf. Luke 23:2, 5, 14; John 19:12). To designate these points as traditional, however, does not imply that John found all of them at *this* point in his passion source. In the same way that he brought this whole scene forward in order to associate it directly with the Lazarus-episode[7], so he was perfectly capable of relocating these

---

4 See above, chapter 3.II.
5 Mark: οἱ ἀρχιερεῖς καὶ οἱ γραμματεῖς; John: οἱ ἀρχιερεῖς καὶ οἱ φαρισαῖοι, who gathered τὸ συνέδριον. From his investigation of the groups of Jewish leaders in Mark's Gospel, Dormeyer (*Passion Jesu*, 69–71) concludes that in the oldest tradition Jesus' enemies were designated as οἱ ἀρχιερεῖς καὶ ὅλον τὸ συνέδριον. This is supported by John 11:47a (regarded as traditional in Klein, "Die lukanische-johanneische Passionstradition", 164; Mohr, *Passion*, 125–126) – which itself finds implicit support from Matt 26:3–4. Senior's declaration (*Passion*, 25) that Matthew has only expanded Mark's account here ignores the Johannine parallels.
6 See the linguistic evidence in Mohr, *Passion*, 126.
7 See above, chapter 4.

individual references. The statement of Caiaphas in John 11:49—50 may also be pre-Johannine[8], even if the editorial quality of 11:51—52 (cf. 18: 14) is manifest. "For this man performs many signs" (11:47b) obviously reflects John's redactional interests (cf. 3:2; 4:48; 7:31—32[!]; 9:16; 12: 37; et al.), though in drawing a direct line from Jesus' ministry to Jewish opposition he is treading a well-worn path.

At the most basic level, these verses serve to introduce the passion narrative proper. In each of the four canonical Gospels, the opposition against Jesus by the Jewish authorities reaches a high point as the malicious intent of the Jewish leaders against Jesus is narrated. In each version, the crowd (i.e. "the people") are understood to be friendly toward Jesus, though this idea is presented by John in a distinctive way when compared with the Synoptics. Matthew in particular has drawn out the anticipatory character of this introduction; in his version, Jesus' words give a preview of the events to follow and, in an important sense, initiate the progress of events that will culminate at Golgotha[9]. The Matthean redaction of Mark thus develops further what was present only in embryonic form in the earliest passion story — the somber foreboding of Jesus' imminent death at the hands of his enemies.

According to a number of interpreters the language of Matt 26:3—4 has been influenced by Ps 31:13 (30:14 LXX)[10]. This psalm speaks of those who scheme together to do away with the Suffering Righteous — a theme well-suited to the present context in Matthew. Might the earliest passion story have incorporated already in its introductory section a view of Jesus mirroring the psalmic Suffering Righteous[11], and so have anticipated the more noticeable allusions in Matthew's version? A number of psalms communicating the same fundamental message as Ps 31 paint a picture very much akin to that found in this initial segment of the passion narrative.

---

8 So Lindars, *John*, 403; Mohr, *Passion*, 126. Noting that "on behalf of the people" implies a redemptive theology that seems strange on the lips of Caiaphas, Brown (*John*, 1:440) regards this phrase as a gloss. The textual witnesses to which he alludes, however, provide no adequate foundation for his decision. Moreover, the language reappears in 18:14 — a verse that Brown does not regard as a gloss.
9 See Dahl, "Passion", 49; Senior, *Passion*, 19. The cause-effect relationship is signified above all by Matthew's τότε (26:3) — see Gundry, *Matthew*, 518; Schweizer, *Matthew*, 486.
10 See, e.g., Robert Horton Gundry, *The Use of the Old Testament in St. Matthew's Gospel: With Special Reference to the Messianic Hope* (Leiden: E. J. Brill, 1967) 56; idem, *Matthew*, 518; Lindars, *NT Apologetic*, 94—95; Dibelius, *Tradition*, 187 n.1; Senior, *Passion*, 24 n.1; Dahl, "Passion", 44 n.20; Moo, *OT — Passion*, 234—235.
11 See Pesch, *Mark*, 2:320, 322.

> They conspire against me
> and plot to take my life (31:13).
> The wicked lie in wait for the righteous
> and seek to kill them (37:32).
> He lies in ambush in the villages;
> from ambush he murders the innocent,
> watching in secret for his victims (10:8).
> For my enemies speak against me;
> those who wait to kill me conspire together (71:10).
> The arrogant are attacking me, O God;
> a band of ruthless men seeks my life –
> men without regard for you (86:14).

Of course, verbal agreement between these texts and the introduction to the passion narrative (as witnessed in Mark and John) is not very significant, so direct influence from these psalmic texts to the passion story is not easily argued. One important hint in this direction, however, is the unambiguous borrowing from the psalms that lament the suffering of the righteous found in other parts of the passion account. Moreover, the degree of conceptual agreement between the psalms and the Markan and Johannine accounts – especially with regard to the ideas of secretly conspiring, stealth, seeking to kill, and well-defined opposing parties – is striking. We may infer from this that already in the opening of the passion story Jesus' fate was being viewed in the light of the psalmic representation of the suffering of the righteous. Matthew recognized these conceptual allusions and made them more explicit.

B. Mark 14:3–9; Matt 26:6–13; John 12:1–8

In our earlier comparison of the four canonical versions of the anointing story we concluded that whereas Matthew drew on Mark's account, John was dependent on a source which itself reflected cross-fertilization between the traditions represented in the Second and Third Gospels[12]. Because Luke's anointing scene (7:36–50) appears outside of the passion narrative and is not inherently bound to the passion by allusion or subject matter our present analysis may pass it by. Hence, we are left with the Markan and Johannine renditions of the anointing episode.

Inasmuch as they are peripheral to our concern with the interpretation of the death of Jesus in the passion narrative, a number of discrepancies between the two accounts merit only brief mention. First, there is the matter of the chronology of the event. Because Mark 14:3–9 is an intercalation, separating 14:1–2 and 14:10–11 (which were joined in the pre-Markan tradition), the Johannine dating of the event is the original – or so

---

12 See above, chapter 4.

it has been argued[13]. For two reasons, however, this reasoning fails to convince. First, we have already indicated the high probability that John's positioning of the scene in his passion narrative is the result of his own editorial preferences. Second, with the publication of Pesch's essay on "Die Salbung Jesu in Bethanien (Mark 14:3—9)", it is no longer possible simply to assume with Bultmann and Dibelius that the shape of Mark's narrative is the result of his inserting the anointing scene into the introduction to the passion story[14]. Here, Pesch queries the oft-assumed direct sequential relationship between vv 1—2 and 10—11, while observing that neither the use of the genitive absolute nor "die Erzähltechnik der Schachtelung" are stylistic featues peculiar to Markan redaction. It must be admitted, nevertheless, that Pesch's arguments rest in part on his view of the pre-canonical passion narrative — which allows him to designate as "traditional" what other scholars refer to as "redactional". Recognition of this presupposition blunts Pesch's presentation somewhat. Still, even if Pesch is correct and Mark did find his 14:1—11 in the present arrangement in a pre-Markan passion story, we cannot be confident that the chronological note of 14:1 governs the timing of the anointing at Bethany, though the discrepancy between Mark and John as regards the placing of the scene *vis-à-vis* that of the entry into Jerusalem remains. Historically, the precise dating of the event is now beyond our grasp though, for reasons to be given shortly, we should conclude that the anointing scene would have been placed at some time shortly before the passion itself. Literarily, we can restate our former conclusion that the early passion narrative held in close sequential association the introductory note regarding the Jewish conspiracy against Jesus and his anointing at Bethany.

Second, the fact that Mark and John do not agree on the precise identity of the host, the woman, and the one(s) who reacted negatively to the woman's deed is likely due to (1) John's having brought the story forward in his chapter 11, and (2) further development in the oral tradition (evidenced already in John 6:70—71) regarding the Judas-problem. The extended parenthetical remark concerning Judas's motive for his statement against the woman can be explained in the same way.

Third, the variance in the way the anointing is carried out, while seemingly of great consequence, is actually unimportant for our inquiry[15], and

---

13 See, e.g., Hunter, *Work and Words*, 143; Cranfield, *Mark*, 415; Mohr, *Passion*, 146; Swete, *Mark*, 320.
14 Rudolph Pesch, "Die Salbung Jesu im Bethanien (Mk 14,3—9). Eine Studie zur Passionsgeschichte", in *Orientierung*, 267—271. See, *idem*, *Mark*, 2:328.
15 For the opposite view, see J. K. Elliott, "The Anointing of Jesus", *ExpTim* 85 (1973—74) 107. The significance accorded this shift is directly determined by the meaning given the anointing in each instance. We will argue (*contra* Elliott) that, head or feet, the anointing retains the same interpretation — a non-messianic interpretation.

is to be explained with reference to influence from the Lukan tradition of the anointing at the pre-Johannine level of development.

Fourth, the additional statement of Jesus in defense of the woman as read in Mark (καλὸν ἔργον ἠργάσατο ἐν ἐμοί) is in any case implicit in Jesus' rebuke of Judas in the Johannine account.

Turning to more substantial matters, Mark 14:7b (καὶ ὅταν θέλητε δύνασθε αὐτοῖς εὖ ποιῆσαι) has been regarded as an insertion into the traditional text, artificially breaking the antithesis between 14:7a (πάντοτε γὰρ τοὺς πτωχούς and 14:7c (ἐμὲ δὲ οὐ πάντοτε ἔχετε)[16]. This judgment, however, fails to account for the parallelism between 14:7b and 14:8a (ὃ ἔσχεν ἐποίησεν), and overlooks the train of thought inherent in the passage as it now stands — namely, the full contrast between the presence of the poor (always) and of Jesus (temporary), *and* between doing deeds for the poor (whenever you wish) and for Jesus (now!). Likewise, *contra* Bultmann and Dibelius, 14:8 is integral to the story as a whole[17]. This has been convincingly demonstrated by Jeremias, who notes that 14:8 presupposes a (Rabbinic) distinction between the *gift* of love and the *work* of love[18]. That is, whereas the disciples criticize the woman's action because the value of the unguent would have been better spent on alms (i.e. "a gift of love"), Jesus, in 14:8, defends the woman's action by noting the greater value of the "work of love", the work of anointing his body for burial. The traditional character of 14:8 is further underscored by the similar phraseology in John 12:7, despite the latter's problematic construction[19].

Before taking up 14:9, a few words are in order regarding the possibility that Mark has nevertheless created vv 8—9 *ex nihilo* in order to relate Jesus' messiahship to his death. Had he been guided by such an interest we would have expected him to use the verb χρίω in referring to Jesus' anointing, for this verb translates משח in the LXX. Instead, he uses the obscure

---

16 See, e.g., Schweizer, *Mark,* 289; Gnilka, *Mark,* 2:222.
17 Bultmann, *History,* 263; Dibelius, *Tradition,* 56. For linguistic reasons, Dormeyer (*Passion Jesu,* 78—82) and Schenke (*Studien,* 76—78) include 14:8 in the pre-Markan tradition.
18 Joachim Jeremias, "Die Salbungsgeschichte Mk 14,3—9", in *Abba,* 107—115; *idem, NT Theology,* 284. See also, Martin, *Mark,* 202.
19 Robert Holst ("The One Anointing of Jesus: Another Application of the Form-Critical Method", *JBL* 95 [3, 1976] 444) argues that the explanation of Mark 14:8/John 12:7 is an early addition to the story by the early church, noting that it is unlikely that Luke would have ignored this explanation. Against this reasoning we may note the following: (1) Luke has, in fact, ignored this tradition, for he had before him Mark's Gospel; and (2) Holst fails adequately to account for the wide divergence between the Lukan and Markan anointing stories which suggests, at least, a more complex tradition-history than that for which he allows. In any case, that both locate the anointing scene in the passion account is evidence enough that from early on the event was located chronologically in conjunction with Jesus' last days. This observation also speaks against Holst's implicit conclusion (439) that the most primitive tradition did not know when the anointing took place.

μυρίζω — found only here in the NT and never in the LXX. To be sure, the related noun, μύρον, translates שמן from time to time in the LXX, and שמן is often associated with משח. However, when שמן and משח are found in tandem in the MT, שמן is most frequently rendered in the LXX as ἔλαιον. In Exod 30:25 and Amos 6:6, שמן is translated as μύρον, signifying "anointing oil", but in neither text is any messianic idea present. Only in Ps 132:2 (LXX) do we find anything approaching a "messianic" motif — and that only in a reference to Aaron's anointing (ὡς μύρον ἐπὶ κεφαλῆς). Apart from this linguistic consideration, it may be further questioned whether an anointing by a woman (and that of no apparent status or reputation) would be given messianic overtones. Hence, there is no unambiguous pointer to a *messianic* anointing here, and we must therefore (1) question attempts to regard Mark 14:8—9 as a Markan attempt to show that Jesus' death was the death of God's Messiah, and (2) look more closely to the texts themselves for our understanding of the significance accorded Jesus' pre-passion anointing.

Mark 14:9 has often been regarded as a Markan creation on linguistic grounds. In this respect special attention may be drawn to the following: ὅπου + ἐὰν + aorist subjunctive; the absolute use of εὐαγγέλιον; the employment of κηρύσσω; the combination κηρύσσω + εὐαγγέλιον; and the remarkable parallels in 13:10; 16:14 (cf. 8:36)[20]. Of course, it may be countered that the presence of Markan *Vorzugsvokabeln* demonstrates Markan redaction without proving Markan creation. On the other hand, it is surely significant that the whole of v 9b (i.e. the ὅπου-phrase) is cast in language repeatedly found in Mark's Gospel. Worthy of note, too, is the striking parallelism of v 9b and v 9c:

ὅπου ἐὰν κυρυχθῇ τὸ εὐαγγέλιον εἰς ὅλον τὸν κόσμον
καὶ ὃ ἐποίησεν αὕτη λαληθήσεται εἰς μνημόσυνον αὐτῆς.

In view of this parallelism, it seems doubtful that 14:9b is a Markan insertion into a traditional v 9ac, and we may therefore be favorably disposed toward the view that the whole of this verse is Markan. This conclusion finds support in the absence of the saying in John's version.

In what way does this early anointing scene contribute to our understanding of the interpretation of Jesus' passion in the passion story? As has been hinted earlier, many exegetes see in the anointing scene a messianic interpretation of Jesus' passion. This is especially true with respect to the

---

20 On these points, see Gnilka, *Mark*, 2:222; Peabody, *Redactional Features*, 67, 70, 310; Jeremias, "Markus 14,9", in *Abba*, 115—120; idem, *NT Theology*, 134; Dormeyer, *Passion Jesu*, 78—79; Schenke, *Studien*, 84—86.

Markan text, for here the head is anointed[21]; however, Barrett has argued that Jesus is presented as the anointed king in John's narrative, too[22]. Barrett's suggestion lacks any real foundation, not least because John has it that Jesus' *feet* are anointed and not his head. In fact, apart from the act of anointing itself in the Markan version, neither John nor Mark provide any hint that this is a royal anointing. Moreover, we have seen that Mark has not employed the terminology of messianic anointing, so the potential messianic significance of the woman's act, even in Mark, is greatly curtailed. Still further, in the Luken story of Jesus' anointing, in which Jesus' *feet* are anointed, Jesus speaks of anointing the guest's *head* as an act of hospitality (7:44–46) – i.e. an act with no messianic significance. Whether or not this was a widely practiced custom[23], it is nonetheless evident that an anointing of the head did not point unambiguously to a royal anointing.

For coming to terms with the significance accorded Jesus' death in this scene, the following three points are potentially more helpful. First, it might be argued that the real point of the story scarcely moves beyond that of predicting Jesus' imminent death[24]. Jesus' words, ἐμὲ δὲ οὐ πάντοτε ἔχετε (Mark 14:7; John 12:7), call to mind the earlier logion regarding the "time of the bridegroom" in Mark 2:19–20, which we have interpreted as a prophetic foretelling[25]. Likewise, the phrase about "anointing my body in anticipation of my burial" (Mark 14:8; John 12:7) clearly looks forward to an impending death. This is more than a simple prediction, however, for inasmuch as the saying is credited to *Jesus* we have here the explicit motif of Jesus' prophetic foreknowledge and the implicit motif of Jesus' acceptance of his death. Moreover, the placement of this scene in the traditional passion account indicates that Jesus is himself an active, causal agent in his own passion. In effect, his anticipation, prophecy, and acceptance of his impending passion set in motion the relentless chain of events leading ultimately to his death. In narrative form here is a parallel to the credal-type

---

21 See Elliot, "Anointing", 105; John Bowman, *The Gospel of Mark: The New Christian Jewish Passover Haggadah* (Leiden: E. J. Brill, 1965) 255; Best, *Temptation and Passion*, 90; Cranfield, *Mark*, 415; Nineham, *Mark*, 372–373; Dibelius, *Jesus*, 96. Contra Swete, *Mark*, 322; Lindars, *John*, 414.
22 Barrett, *John*, 409. Contra Brown, *John*, 1:454.
23 The closest parallels appear in Str.-B., 1:427–428, but this evidence is not particularly impressive as a means of authenticating Jesus' remark. On the other hand, the Lukan text appears to predate the Third Gospel (see, e.g., Jeremias, *Sprache*, 172), so the custom would seem to have some traditional basis.
24 On this theme, see Gnilka, *Mark*, 2:224–226; Pesch, "Salbung Jesu", 281; Böttger, *König der Juden*, 83; Jeremias, *NT Theology*, 284; Schweizer, *Mark*, 290; Lane, *Mark*, 494; Brown, *John*, 1:454; Senior, *Passion*, 36–38; Elliott, "Anointing", 106.
25 See above, chapter 5.

formulae which assert that Christ "gave himself up"[26]. This interpretation has the advantage of resting on (1) the close association of the central act of this story and Jesus' own interpretation of it, and (2) the probable narrative sequence of the introduction to the passion narrative.

Less certain is a second approach which holds that in explaining the women's deed as a death-anointing (Mark 14:8; John 12:7), Jesus anticipated his death as that of a common criminal who would otherwise have received no burial preparation. In this way, so the theory goes, Jesus identified his fate with that of the Suffering Servant, alluding to Isa 53:9[27]. We may allow the possible validity of this hypothesis. At the same time, however, we must urge that nothing in the Gospel texts necessarily points to the influence of the Isaianic passage — or, indeed, to any but the most general anticipation of his own death by Jesus. In any case, it must be questioned how central this motif could have been to the original story.

Third, F. W. Danker has set forth the thesis — adopted *in toto* by Lane and apparently developed independently by Pesch — that the anointing scene (and with it the whole of Mark 14:1–25) should be understood in the light of Ps 41 (40 LXX)[28]. Of course, it is futile to argue that Mark 14:1–25 was wholly constructed from this psalm, for such a theory does not explain the presence of all the significant material (e.g. the preparation for the Passover in vv 12–16). From the perspective of tradition-history we might also query Danker's thesis with respect to the Johannine parallels to the section of Mark he has studied. Nevertheless, the possibility that Ps 41 stands in the background of the anointing scene renders necessary a more extensive consideration of Danker's thesis.

Danker observes three principal themes in Mark 14:1–25: the question of attitudes toward the poor, the fate of Jesus, and the expectation of Jesus' ultimate triumph — each of which has its counterpart in Ps 41. In addition, he notes that according to the psalms the "poor man" ($\pi\tau\omega\chi\acute{o}\varsigma$) often appears in the garb of the Suffering Righteous. Arguing that the contrast in Mark 14:7 is between πάντοτε and οὐ πάντοτε, and not between πτωχούς and ἐμέ, he goes on to suggest that the story identifies Jesus as the "poor sufferer". He is recognized as such by the woman, whose deed thus becomes an act of piety towards the poor (cf. Ps 40:2–3 LXX). Jesus

---

[26] Of course, these formulae include the important proviso "for us" — a qualification lacking in the anointing story. See Gal 1:4; 2:20; Eph 5:2, 25; Titus 2:14; 1 Tim 2:6.

[27] See esp. Jeremias, "Salbungsgeschichte"; *idem, NT Theology,* 287; Zimmerli and Jeremias, "Παῖς θεοῦ", 712. Also, Martin, *Mark,* 202; Lane, *Mark,* 494; David Daube, *The New Testament and Rabbinic Judaism* (London: Athlone, 1956) 313–314; Hunter, *Work and Words,* 143. *Contra* Moo, *OT – Passion,* 159 – whose arguments are overdrawn.

[28] Frederick W. Danker, "The Literary Unity of Mark 14:1–25", *JBL* 85 (1966) 467–472; Lane, *Mark,* 493–494; Pesch, "Salbung Jesu", 281–282; *idem, Mark,* 2:334–335.

commends the woman for recognizing the superior claim that *"this* πτω-
χός*"* (i.e. the "poor man" *par excellence*?) has over against the more general obligation to assist the poor (Deut 15:11) who will always be present. In this view, Mark 14:9 is understood in terms of Ps 40:2–3 (LXX), wherein is promised a special blessing for the one who considers the needs of the poor.

This thesis has much to commend it, and one might be tempted to adopt it without further comment. However, obstacles are encountered at two obvious points. First, we find here no attempt to explain how Mark 14:8 – surely an integral part of the story – fits into this interpretation. Second, we have already seen the probability that v 9 was not original to the story[29]. If these two points of concern raise doubts, we may add further that Jesus is not identified in the anointing scene as a "poor man" – nor is he at this point described as "suffering", nor is there any correspondence in detail between the situation of the "poor man" in Ps 41 and Jesus in Mark 14:3–9. Moreover, we may observe that Jesus' commendation for the woman is explained quite naturally by the gift/deed-of-love contrast discussed earlier by Jeremias, and that the poor-saying most certainly derives from Deut 15:11. One might reply by recalling that Mark 14:1–25 *as a whole* (in Danker's view) makes clear that the psalm stands behind this πτωχός-saying. However, this rejoinder only introduces a circular argument, for the poor-theme in vv 4–7 is one of only three pillars upon which is based the thesis that Ps 41 stands behind vv 1–25[30].

Like the thesis encountered earlier that in Mark 14:8 we may discern the influence of Isa 53, so in this instance it is difficult to assert the impossibility of conceptual borrowing. Be that as it may, we have found reason to dismiss the notion that the interpretation of the anointing scene is governed by recognition of the influence of Ps 41. Neither the concept of the Isaianic Servant nor that of the Poor (Righteous) Sufferer has played a major role in the telling of this story.

C. *Mark 14:10–11; Matt 26:14–16; Luke 22:3–6; John 6:70–71; 13:2, 27; 18:3*

The primary source for both the Matthean and Lukan accounts of the betrayal of Judas was Mark 14:10–11. Where the later accounts diverge

---

29 It could be countered that Danker's theory treats the story at the level of the Markan redaction, and so this second obstacle is more apparent than real. But then one is forced to contend as well with the presence of the poor-saying in the Johannine version of the story – a version in which the overall influence of Ps 41 is lacking.

30 It is worth noting, further, that there is no strict correspondence between the "fate of Jesus" in Mark 14:1–25 and the "problem of the sufferer in relation to his enemies" in Ps 41:5–10. Hence, a second pillar of this whole argument must be called into question. In fact, the entire argument must rest, finally, on the allusion to Ps 41:9 in Mark 14:18.

most from the earlier, the occasion seems to be the addition of supplementary material having to do with the motive or impetus behind Judas's treachery. Even Mark's rather bald narrative hints at the scandalous character of the betrayal (by "one of the Twelve") — a point which speaks strongly for the historicity of the betrayal[31] — and it is apparent from the other three Gospels that early Christians felt compelled to somehow indicate the reason for Judas's act. Thus, Matthew indicates that it was for money that Judas behaved as he did (cf. 26:16: καὶ ἀπὸ τότε)[32], and goes on to associate the act with OT prophecy (Zech 11:12)[33]. In John's version of the anointing scene we find evidence that Judas was motivated by monetary concerns (see 12:6), but with respect to the act of treachery John and Luke are in agreement in ascribing responsibility to the devil (John 6:70−71; 13:2) — that is, to Satan (Luke 22:3, John 13:27).

Earlier, we observed with respect to this Lukan-Johannine agreement a clear "connection between the two texts within the history of traditions"[34]. While John has nothing that corresponds strictly with Mark 14: 10−11, he does know that Judas had made a treacherous pact of some sort with the Jewish authorities prior to the arrest (18:2−3), and he agrees with Luke (and so with Mark) in locating the initial note regarding Judas's decision to betray Jesus just prior to the account of the Last Supper (13:2). Hence, his editorial procedure has left traces of evidence supporting the conclusion that his passion source included a brief report roughly corresponding to Mark's apart from the detail about the cause of treachery. On this point, he is closer to Luke who, as we have observed, may have also known an alternative, non-Markan (though very similar to Mark) version of the story. We conclude, therefore, that the earliest passion story included a skeletal account of the betrayal of Jesus by Judas, resembling most that of Mark. It is likely that this account mentioned the exchange (or promise?) of money, and that this initial reference has been expanded in the oral tradition taken over by Matthew.

The "entry" of Satan into Judas's heart has a close parallel in *Mart. Isa.* 3.11; 5.1[35]. In this apocryphal text, Beliar (=Belial) dwells in the hearts of Manasseh and his court, and as a consequence, the king has Isaiah seized and sawn asunder with a tree saw. We should not suppose thereby

---

31 See, e.g., Cranfield, *Mark*, 418; Gnilka, *Mark*, 2:230.
32 On which, see Schweizer, *Matthew*, 487−488; Georg Strecker, "The Concept of History in Matthew", in *Interpretation of Matthew*, 71; Gundry, *Matthew*, 522−523. Taylor (*Mark*, 535) regards this elaboration of Mark as "legendary".
33 On this issue in Matthew, see Senior, *Passion*, 46; Moo, *OT − Passion*, 187−189, 199; F. F. Bruce, "The Book of Zechariah and the Passion Narrative", *BJRL* 43 (1960−61) 340−341.
34 Thus Schnackenburg, *John*, 3:31. See above, chapters 3.III and 4.
35 This has been observed by Marshall, *Gospel of Luke*, 788; Schneider, *Luke*, 2:440; Schweizer, *Luke*, 330. Cf. Schnackenburg, *John*, 3:31; 404 n.93.

that the tradition lying behind Luke and John was necessarily influenced by a martyrological concern. Rather, the view of reality expressed in the *Martyrdom of Isaiah* may be symptomatic of the more general spirit-theology present in the Qumran Community[36]. The language employed by John and Luke (εἰσέρχομαι + εἰς) is used elsewhere in the Gospels for the entering of demons and evil spirits into persons (e.g. Matt 12:45; Mark 9: 25; Luke 8:30; cf. Mark 5:13; Luke 8:32—33). The most that can be made of the introduction of direct satanic influence here is that the developing tradition thereby intended to narrate the passion in greater-than-human terms, making clear early on that Jesus' passion was a struggle of cosmic proportions.

As for the more primitive account, the thought of this text follows closely that of the scheme of the Jewish leaders. They were looking for a means by which to take Jesus unawares, and Judas provides them with the answer to their need. An obvious contrast is thus established between the woman who anointed Jesus and Judas — the one served Jesus in love, the other dealt him a malicious deed[37]. The identification of Judas as (1) one of the inner circle of disciples and (2) the betrayer sets up the reader for the use of Ps 41:9 in the Supper scene. The analogy of the Suffering Righteous more explicit later is therefore certainly at the fringe here. Indeed, Pesch is confident that the betrayal by Judas has been narrated "im Licht der *passio iusti*"; Judas, then, is revealed as the δόλιος of Pss 43:2; 52: 3—6; 109:2—5[38]. As before (II.A), the direct influence of these OT texts on the present account is doubtful. Certainly, the language employed would not lead anyone to argue for direct borrowing. It is nonetheless probable, given the scandal of Jesus' having been betrayed by his close associate and the reference to Ps 41:9 in the Supper scene, that Judas's role was seen in typological relationship to the insidious man of the texts Pesch has listed. In support of the presence of the *passio iusti* theme here, we may also refer to Pss 55:12—14, 20—21; Jer 12:6; 20:10.

D. Summary

From our investigation of the stories of the conspiracy and anointing, we may outline the following observations.

(1) The probability is very high that the primitive passion narrative closely associated the accounts of the Jewish plot and the anointing at

---

36 See, e.g., 1 QS 3.13—4.26; Nickelsburg, *Jewish Literature*, 144; Millar Burrows, *Burrows on the Dead Sea Scrolls, An Omnibus of Two Famous Volumes: The Dead Sea Scrolls and More Light on the Dead Sea Scrolls* (Grand Rapids, Michigan: Baker, 1978) 2:280—283.
37 On this motif, see Dormeyer, *Passion Jesu*, 85; Pesch, *Mark*, 2:339; Mohr, *Passion*, 184—185.
38 Pesch, *Mark*, 2:338—339. See also, Goppelt, *Typos*, 100.

Bethany in its introduction. The probability is high that the introduction to the passion story closed with a terse account of Judas's betrayal.

(2) Most fundamentally, this introductory section introduces the active agents of the passion account: the Jewish leaders, the now-friendly crowds, Judas the Betrayer, and Jesus. The active role of Jesus in his own passion should not be slighted, for he not only knows his future but willingly accepts it and sets in motion the fateful wheels that will come to rest finally at the Place of the Skull.

(3) Apart from the role played by these verses as introductory, anticipating the general course of the passion events, no one theme stands out above the rest to bind together the three units of this one section. To be sure, we are already encountering the prominence of the motif represented by the Suffering Righteous, but even it is not sufficient to embrace the various strands of meaning in this section. The influence of the Suffering Servant may raise its head here, but if so only barely. This should warn us against presuming that any one theme, figure, or background will be adequate to guide our understanding of the significance attributed to Jesus' passion in this narrative of his suffering and death.

III. The Supper Scene

A. Mark 14:12–16; Matt 26:17–19; Luke 22:7–13; John 13:1

The preparation for the Passover is narrated independently only by Mark. Neither Matthew nor Luke give any indication of being aware of a further source[39]. While one might suggest a parallel between Jesus' remark in Matt 26:18 (ὁ καιρός μου ἐγγύς ἐστιν) and the editorial phrase in John 13:1 (εἰδὼς ὁ Ἰησοῦς ὅτι ἦλθεν αὐτοῦ ἡ ὥρα), this is hardly an adequate basis for arguing in the absence of other supportive evidence that the Fourth Evangelist was cognizant of this story[40]. Even before looking more closely at the Markan account, then, there is occasion for doubting the inclusion of this narrative in the primitive passion story. Such misgivings are largely confirmed by evidence of a source-critical nature. To be sure, as a number of critics have shown, the basis of these verses is pre-Markan[41];

---

39 On the Lukan version, see above, chapter 3.IV.
40 See above, chapter 4.
41 See Dormeyer, *Passion Jesu*, 88–94; Mohr, *Passion*, 150–163; Schenk, *Passionsbericht*, 182–184; Pesch, *Mark*, 2:340–345; Cranfield, *Mark*, 419–420; Taylor, *Mark*, 535–536, 658. Exegetes who insist that the addition or even composition of vv 12–16 by Mark is *Mark's* way of indicating that the meal to follow was a Passover fail to explain why, if this motif was so important to Mark, he has not explicated this symbolism elsewhere in the Supper-scene, in the passion narrative, or in his Gospel.

moreover, in all probability, the passion source employed by Mark already associated the introductory account with the Supper scene[42]. Yet, there are telltale signs that this story is not indigenous to the earlier narrative. Most obviously, Jesus' followers are described 4 times in this brief narrative as "disciples" (vv 12, 13, 14, 16), whereas before and after this pericope they are designated as "the Twelve" (vv 10, 17, 20). In addition, an inconsistency exists between the sending of the two in v 13 and the coming of the Twelve in v 17. We conclude that this episode was lacking in the primitive passion narrative.

B. Mark 14:17–21; Matt 26:20–25; Luke 22:14, 21–23; John 13:18–30

Discussions of this pericope in Mark often make much of the double reference to eating in v 18 (καὶ ἀνακειμένων αὐτῶν καὶ ἐσθιόντων) and in the following section of the Supper-scene, in v 22 (καὶ ἐσθιόντων αὐτῶν)[43]. From this observation some have gone on to argue that the announcement of the betrayal has been introduced at this point by the Second Evangelist. We should note to the contrary the close affinity between the present section and 14:10–11 — both dealing with the betrayer who is "one of the Twelve". Moreover, it is of obvious significance that with v 22 we encounter the beginning of a set tradition regarding the Last Supper. Some interpreters regard the genitive absolute in v 22a as integral to the eucharistic tradition[44], but it seems more likely that καὶ ἐσθιόντων αὐτῶν was prefixed to the tradition by way of tying it to the immediate context[45]. That this is so is suggested by the absence of a comparable formula from the independent parallels in Luke and Paul. It would appear, then, that the doublet in question should not be evaluated as the end-result of Markan editorial work, but rather regarded as the product of an early joining of an earlier, set tradition of the eucharistic words (14:22–25) to the primitive passion account as it took shape. Two further lines of evidence — the one direct, the other indirect — confirm the presence of this story in the early narrative.

---

42 See Lohse, *Geschichte*, 42; Nineham, *Mark*, 376; Schweizer, *Mark*, 294–297; and, perhaps, Bultmann, *History*, 264; Dibelius, *Tradition*, 182, 189.
43 Cf., e.g., Pierre Benoit, "The Holy Eucharist", in *Jesus*, 97; Bultmann, *History*, 265–266; Best, *Temptation and Passion*, 91–92; Nineham, *Mark*, 378; Schenke, *Studien*, 199–203; Gnilka, *Mark*, 2:235. Keith Hein ("Judas Iscariot: Key to the Last Supper Narratives", *NTS* 17 [1970–71] 227–232) asserts that ". . . all [investigators] agree that Mark xiv.17–21 cannot be attributed to the same source as the following verses (22–25)" (227).
44 See Dormeyer, *Passion Jesu*, 101; Schmithals, *Mark*, 2:614; Mohr, *Passion*, 188.
45 See Schenke, *Studien*, 286–290; Schenk, *Passionsbericht*, 190; Jeremias, *Eucharistic Words*, 113; Gnilka, *Mark*, 2:240. Gnilka regards the genitive absolute as an amendment to the tradition at the pre-Markan stage.

As for direct testimony to the inclusion of a betrayal-announcement in the Supper-scene of the primitive passion narrative, without delving at this point into a detailed analysis of the points of contact and difference between the canonical narratives, we may at this stage recall our earlier finding that both Luke and John independently support the Markan account on this matter. In our analysis of the accounts we concluded that Luke knew an alternative tradition with which he conflated the Markan tradition, that John had before him yet another version of the episode, and that, at some early tradition-historical crossroads, the traditions used by Luke and John intersected[46]. The criterion of "multiple attestation", then, supports the thesis that the primitive passion account itself already included the announcement of the betrayal in the context of the Last Supper.

As for indirect testimony, here we take our point of departure from our earlier discussion of the *Sitz im Leben* of the early passion narrative[47]. At that earlier point, we argued that the narrative in question had its origin in the celebration of the Lord's Supper. Two corollaries follow from this viewpoint. First, it suggests that prior to the development of the passion story the Lord's Supper had become a formalized aspect of community life among Christians, with its own set liturgical tradition regarding the Words of Institution. Hence, a eucharistic tradition would have been available for insertion into the passion narrative. Second, in that the early passion narrative had its beginning and development within the early confines of the celebration of the Lord's Supper — and was thus held in the closest possible relation to the Lord's Supper with its interpretative words, one may reasonably question whether the need for actually incorporating the eucharistic words into the passion narrative would have been felt at first — that is, until the narrative began to take on a life of its own, as it were. Because the passion account was given birth in the celebration of the Lord's Supper — a celebration in which the interpretive words of the Last Supper were central, it is doubtful that these same words would have been *explicitly and formally recounted again in the same and immediate context* as a part of the telling of the passion story. This theory is supported by a further observation: the announcement of betrayal appears in two difference chronological positions within the Last Supper narratives of the canonical accounts. In Luke (see John), the announcement occurs after the meal proper, whereas in Mark (followed by Matthew) the announcement precedes the meal. If, as we have argued, the betrayal-announcement was set in the Supper scene in the earliest tradition and was not a later

---

46 On Luke, see above, chapter 3.V–VI; on John; chapter 4.
47 See above, chapter 7.

addition, then it would appear that the eucharistic words were inserted into an already developing account, but in slightly different positions in the different traditions. This hypothesis takes account of the doublet in Mark already mentioned, and also explains the rather abrupt shift in Luke's account from Luke 22:20 to 22:21.

On these bases we submit that the primitive story of Jesus' suffering and death included an announcement of betrayal, though its original position in the Supper-sequence is no longer known. With this decision in hand we are now prepared to look more intensively at the reports themselves in order to determine what about them was original to the primitive account and how Jesus' death was understood in it.

The introduction to the betrayal announcement in Mark 14:17–18a is not strictly paralleled in Luke or John (cf., however, Luke 22:14) since the latter evangelists differ from Mark in their placement of the episode. The absence of this transitional element is inconsequential for our interpretive enterprise, and we may move directly to the core of the story.

The prediction in Mark 14:18bc and John 13:21 is less straightforward in Luke 22:20, though the same idea is communicated: one of Jesus' table companions will betray Jesus. The introductory comment in John 13:21a ("Having said these things, Jesus was troubled in spirit and testified . . .") has been inserted by John under the influence of Ps 42:6. Even Luke's version recalls the fate of the Suffering Righteous in Ps 41:9, whose table companion betrays his friendship, but for verbal reminiscences of this psalm we must look to Mark (v 18) and John (vv 18, 21b)[48]. Surely, something of the depth of this tragedy and its justification in terms of the psalm were already in view in the account of the prediction of the betrayal from the beginning. Mark 14:19–20 and John 13:22–30 betray a tendency – also present in the peculiar aspects of Matthew's version *vis-à-vis* his Markan source – to identify beyond doubt the disciple-*cum*-betrayer. In Matthew's v 23 one may discern a move toward a more direct reference to the betrayer[49], and in v 25 his identity becomes unmistakable. Indeed, not only is Judas named as ὁ παραδιδοὺς αὐτόν, but, in that Judas addresses Jesus as ῥαββί and not κύριε (cf. v 22), Judas is actually portrayed as an unbeliever[50]. Mark's narrative is less advanced in this respect, though v 20 does suggest how Jesus pointed the finger at the person in question. John's narrative not only identifies Judas (and makes certain the reader knows

---

[48] See above, chapter 4.
[49] Cf. Schweizer, *Matthew*, 489; Senior, *Passion*, 72.
[50] Cf. Jack Dean Kingsbury, *Matthew: Structure, Christology, Kingdom* (Philadelphia : Fortress, 1975) 92, 112 ; Schweizer, *Matthew*, 489; Senior, *Passion*, 70-71 ; Gundry, *Matthew*, 527 ; Brevard S. Childs, *The New Testament as Canon: An Introduction* (London : SCM, 1984) 68. On the development toward a more direct reference to Judas, see Taylor, *Jesus*, 112.

which "Judas" is the culprit — v 26: Judas, son of Simon Iscariot), but has him depart to accomplish his dastardly deed. Contrariwise, Luke has it only that the disciples question among themselves who would betray Jesus (v 23; cf. John 13:22) and there is no attempt to name the betrayer. On this point, then, Luke would appear to represent the more primitive form of the tradition[51].

Luke 22:22 corresponds closely to Mark 14:21a. Strictly speaking, John offers no parallel, but his vv 18–19 testify to the same general motif, indicating the necessity of Jesus' passion. The parallel logion in Luke 17:1 is proof that Mark did not originate the present saying[52], and we argued earlier that for his version of the logion Luke may not have depended on Mark. Hence, it is quite probable that Mark 14:21a and Luke 22:22 represent the primitive passion story. As for Mark 14:21b, here one finds a sentence of judgment with apocalyptic overtones, implying the exaltation of the Son of Man (cf. 1 Enoch 38). While Mark is alone in reporting this phrase here, we read parallels to this cycle in Mark 9:42; Matt 18:6–7; Luke 17:1–2. Additionally, in Mark 14:22–25 a pointer to Jesus' death is followed by an implicit reference to his exaltation; this, too, is a parallel instance in which death and resurrection appear (thematically) in tandem. There is therefore good basis for arguing for the inclusion of this part of the saying in the primitive passion narrative as well.

In short, apart from the developed character of v 20b, at which point the Lukan parallel is the more original, the Markan account of the announcement of the betrayal approximates closely the form of the story in the primitive passion narrative. What portrait of Jesus' death is sketched in this story? The presence of four themes, of unequal importance, calls for discussion.

(1) The first theme has enjoyed wide acclaim in recent discussion of the theology of the passion narrative: the portrayal of Jesus as the Righteous Sufferer. Speaking of the correspondence between the announcement of betrayal and Ps 41:9, Ruppert rightly notes "die *Analogie der Situation*" — not only in the "Ausgestaltung der Verratsansage", but also in "ihrer Lokalisierung während eines Mahls"[53]. In the same way that the Righteous Sufferer is betrayed by one with whom he has shared table fellowship, so one of Jesus' table-intimates has become Jesus' betrayer. The presence of this motif in the recollection of Ps 41:9 has been previously discussed[54]; are there additional, less obvious testimonies to this idea? According to Pesch,

---

51 See above, chapter 3.VI.
52 In addition, Morna Hooker (*The Son of Man in Mark* [London: S.P.C.K., 1967] 159–161) argues that the vocabulary of the saying suggests an early origin. Cf. Lindars, *Jesus*, 60.
53 Ruppert, *Jesus*, 50 (emphasis his).
54 See above, chapter 4.

the *Wehe-Spruch* is related to the theme of the Suffering Righteous, but his commentary does not make very clear the justification for this assertion[55], so we may fill out his discussion.

Death-laments constitute the well-spring for expressions of woe (הוי, אוי), taken over by the prophets by way of italicizing their proclamations of judgment. While in the NT οὐαί is employed especially to connote sorrow and sadness, it would be wrong to completely divest the expression of its judgmental overtones: if sorrow is expressed, it is in light of the condemnation lying at the end of the road of reproachful attitudes and behavior. Certainly this is true in the present case, where the woe-pronouncement is both an expression of sorrow and a general prophecy regarding the betrayer's fate. Described as ὁ ἄνθρωπος ἐκεῖνος, Judas is regarded as already having been sundered from relationship with Jesus[56]. Form-critically, then, there seems to be no justification for tying the woe-pronouncement as such to the *passio-iusti* idea. Yet, there is a general correspondence between Judas and the opponent(s) of the Suffering Righteous — whose recompense is anticipated or even predicted[57]. Moreover, inasmuch as Mark 14:21b reflects the expectation of Jesus' ultimate triumph over his opposition, here, too, the format of this pericope is linked to the interpretive model of the Suffering Righteous who is ultimately vindicated or exalted. With respect to this point, it is well to be reminded that the roots of the suffering-exaltation scheme run deep into the subsoil of Isa 52:13—53:12[58].

(2) Second, this passage indicates further the responsible agents in Jesus' passion, introducing "a profound, dialectical relationship between human and divine causation"[59]. Jesus' passion must take place — i.e. it is a divine necessity; nevertheless, Judas is responsible for his own actions which lead to Jesus' arrest and the culmination of the many forward-looking texts regarding Jesus' being killed by his opponents.

---

55 Pesch, *Mark*, 2:351—352.
56 On the background of the woe-pronouncement, see H.-J. Zobel, "הוֹי", in *TDOT*, 3:359—364. Norman Hillyer ("Woe", in *NIDNTT*, 3:1051—1054) is generally unwilling to see any expression of condemnation in the NT use of "woe", though he admits the idea of divine wrath is present in Mark 14:21 and parallels. Taylor (*Mark*, 542) and Swete (*Mark*, 333) consider this woe-pronouncement an expression of sadness, not a curse. However, the two — expression of sadness and statement of judgment — are not mutually exclusive.
57 Cf., e.g., Pss 10:15; 31:17—18; 37:35—36; 71:12—13. This idea is more apparent in Acts 1:20, where Ps 69:25 is cited.
58 Cf., e.g., Pss 31:14—17; 37:33—34; 41:10; Wis 5:1—8; 1 Enoch 94—104; Nickelsburg, *Resurrection*.
59 Childs, *NT Introduction*, 91. See also D. A. Carson, *Divine Sovereignty and Human Responsibility* (London: Marshall, Morgan and Scott, 1981) 130—132; Roloff, "Anfänge", 39—42; Senior, *Passion: Mark*, 53.

(3) Introduced thereby is a further point meriting separate elucidation — namely, the interpretation of Jesus' death as central to God's redemptive plan. Using different but roughly equivalent phrases, Mark (καθὼς γέγραπται) and Luke (κατὰ τὸ ὡρισμένον) both testify to the reality that the passion of Jesus stands as the fulfillment of God's redemptive plan[60]. As for which OT text(s) was(were) in view here, certainty can never really be reached. Some have suggested in view of the immediate context that this is an allusion to Ps 41[61], but the nuance of "death" given ὑπάγει in Mark argues strongly against this view, for this psalm contains no reference to the necessity of death. With good reason, Best has stated, "It is natural to think of Isa. liii and difficult to think of any other suitable passage"[62]. The divine necessity of suffering is certainly present in the Isaianic prophecy, and there is further, verbal correspondence with the Gospel texts signaled by the appearance of παραδίδωμι. The closely related fact that the present narrative refuses to disallow the active role of God in Jesus' passion also intimates a relation to Isa 52:13—53:12. It must be admitted that the case for verbal dependence is very weak, however. Even though παραδίδωμι is a key word in both texts, the verb is employed with the acceptable nuance of "to betray" in Mark, whereas in Isaiah the intended sense is more along the lines of "to give up to death". It is nonetheless arguable that the obvious conceptual affinity was deliberate, though the possibility of an intentionally vague reference to "the Scriptures" cannot be dismissed.

(4) Finally, in this pericope we discover that "Jesus geht freiwillig mit prophetischen Wissen in den Tod"[63]. Neither his death nor even his betrayal by a close companion came as a surprise to Jesus, for he possessed anticipatory (prophetic) knowledge of these happenings. In thus picturing him as a prophet, the primitive passion account not only underscores Jesus' control over the passion events (pre-knowledge gives opportunity for preventive action), but also places him in the ranks of a long line of God's spokespersons who died as martyrs.

---

60 Lindars (*Jesus*, 75) argues that the meaning of Luke's version is at variance with Mark's, and he is surely right to assert that "the predetermined plan of God" (for Luke) includes, but may transcend, the forward-looking witness of the OT — cf. Marshall, *Luke*, 111; Conzelmann, *Luke*, 158. Both statements, however, witness to one point — namely, the divine necessity (δεῖ) of the coming events. On this theme in the present section, see Dunn, *Christology*, 234—235; Marshall, *Gospel of Luke*, 809; Best, *Mark*, 68; Nineham, *Mark*, 379; Dormeyer, *Passion Jesu*, 97—99.
61 E.g. France, *Jesus*, 57 ;Pesch, *Mark*, 2:351; Gnilka, *Mark*, 2:238.
62 Best, *Temptation and Passion*, 150. Similarly, see Taylor, *Mark*, 542; idem, *Jesus*, 113; Moo, *OT — Passion*, 106—109; Lindars, *NT Apologetic*, 80—81. *Contra* France, *Jesus*, 125—126; Lindars, *Jesus*, 184. Best himself admits that attempts to specify exactly what text(s) is(are) in view here are only speculative; he concludes that this reference is traditional and Mark left it vague because he himself did not know the precise reference.

C. *Mark 14:22–25; Matt 26:26–29; Luke 22:14–20, 24–30; John 13:2–17; 14:17–26*

Given that both Mark and Luke independently witness to the inclusion of the eucharistic tradition in the passion narrative, and the probable knowledge but deliberate suppression of that tradition by John[64], there can be little question that the Last Supper was joined to the primitive passion story from a very early point. Equally obvious, however, is the observable tension noted earlier both in Mark and Luke between the eucharistic material and the surrounding narrative. For this and other reasons we theorized that the most primitive passion story had not yet incorporated the Words of Institution into its story line in a direct way. Nevertheless, because of its *Sitz im Leben*, the passion account would always have shared the closest possible relationship with the recitation of the interpretive words. From the beginning, the eucharistic words would have been integral to the sphere in which the passion account took shape and moved toward its relatively fixed form. As these points have already been argued, only three issues need to be discussed here – namely, the place of the "table talk" (Luke and John) in the passion tradition, the possibility of declaring the Markan-type account or the Lukan more original to the passion story, and the significance of this section for our understanding of Jesus' death. These questions are of the utmost significance not only in view of the complexity of the tradition-history of the Supper tradition apparent from the canonical sources, but also because it was a worshipful context, the focal point of which was the interpretive words of the Last Supper, that the passion narrative as a whole was conceived, given birth, and nursed.

(1) The common ground between Luke and John extends beyond the bare fact that both evangelists portray Jesus in a pedagogical role following the Supper, for there is a noticeable intersection as to the content of the instruction. In Luke's version, Jesus first underscores the servant-role for his disciples – a motif expressed in no uncertain terms in John 13:1–17. Then, in vv 28–30, Luke records how Jesus promised his followers a share in his own divine inheritance – a theme paralleled in John 14:2–3. Finally, there is the common theological orientation – recognized by Schnackenburg[65], whereby Jesus' instruction is couched between a symbolic anticipation of his death (Luke: eucharist; John: footwashing) and the pivotal time at which Jesus accepts his own passion as God's will (Luke: at the Mount

---

63 Dormeyer, *Passion Jesu*, 99. Cf. Pesch, *Mark*, 2:349; Nineham, *Mark*, 379; Schweizer, *Mark*, 298; Jeremias, *NT Theology*, 278; Best, *Temptation and Passion*, 91, Senior, *Passion: Mark*, 52–53.
64 On Luke, see above, chapter 3.V; on John, chapter 4.
65 Schnackenburg, *John*, 3:39.

of Olives; John: across the Kidron valley, in a garden). Taken together with earlier evidence[66], these considerations indicate that the traditions utilized by Luke and John share a common ancestry[67]. The absence of this portion of the tradition from Mark and Matthew suggests the table-talk was added to the developing passion account relatively late, according to the needs of community instruction[68]. The tradition has been most developed in the case of the Johannine narrative, but the germ cell for this discourse would have pre-dated the writing of the Third and Fourth Gospels.

(2) When asking which is the more primitive — the shorter, Markan-type Supper or the longer, Lukan — we are primarily concerned with the relative antiquity of Luke's vv 15–18 *as an integral part of the passion narrative*. Hence, we are not simply looking for some canon by which to measure which tradition, Mark 14:22–25 or Luke 22:15–18, pre-dates the other — and in any case we have already shown how both have a claim to early use in Palestinian Christianity[69]. Two considerations are decisive for our question. First, both Mark and Luke witness to the inclusion of the Words of Institution. Second, if Mark was interested in underlining the Passion-overtones of the Supper, it is inexplicable that he knew a tradition similar to that recorded in Luke's vv 15–18 and yet failed to include it in his narrative. For our purposes, then, the eucharistic tradition with the interpretive logia is of central importance. Even so, it should not be overlooked that the emphases of Luke 22:15–18 are largely present in Mark 14:25, and so these interests may be included in our explication of the meaning of Jesus' death by this portion of the passion tradition.

(3) As we have demonstrated, the important themes of the Supper-tradition influence the total interpretive view of the passion narrative — even though, in all probability, the Supper-words were not explicitly recounted as a part of that narrative at first. This is so because of the

---

66 See above, chapter 4.
67 See the remarks in Pierson Parker, "Luke and the Fourth Evangelist", *NTS* 9 (1962–63) 335–336; F. Lamar Cribbs, "The Agreements That Exist Between John and Acts", in *Perspectives – Luke-Acts,* 61; Maddox, *Luke-Acts,* 175; Schnackenburg, *John,* 3:41. In his essay on "Die lukanische-johannineische Passionstradition", Klein speculates that Luke's passion narrative and John's can be traced back to a common source "G" which, itself, derives from the Markan *Vorlage.* This reconstruction appears too simple when viewed against the totality of the evidence.
68 Glöckner (*Verkündigung,* 177–182) is followed by Büchele (*Tod Jesu,* 168–169) in asserting that Luke is responsible for the placement of vv 24–27, that this placement was done in order to allow this pericope to interpret the surrounding material, and that this redaction gives us Luke's special emphasis on Jesus' death. However, Jesus' death was being used as a lesson for humility and sacrificial service long before Luke wrote his Gospel (cf. Paul's use of the eucharistic tradition in 1 Cor 11). Further, this hypothesis turns a blind eye to the Lukan-Johannine parallels.
69 See above, chapters 3.V; 7.

closest degree of contact between the Supper and the narrative while the former was being celebrated in the life of the *Urgemeinde*. Moreover, we have seen that regardless of which form is taken as the initial point of reference — whether Luke's eucharistic words or Mark's — the understanding of Jesus' death thereby presented is not altered substantively. Hence, rather than repeat our earlier inquiry, we may simply outline the two relevant conclusions[70].

a. In the Supper-words, one finds an open and obvious prediction of Jesus' death. The presence of this theme is yet another illustration of Jesus' foreknowledge and implicit acceptance of his fate.

b. According to the Supper-words, Jesus' death is central to God's plan. In making this significance known a number of motifs are brought into play: the covenant, the Servant of Yahweh, martyrdom, atonement, and the forgiveness of sins.

In addition to these two points, there is one further theme of importance — namely, Jesus' anticipation of vindication in God's kingdom (i.e. beyond death) as witnessed in Mark 14:25 and Luke 22:16, 18. As before, here is an important testimony for the influence of the Isaianic Servant and the Suffering Righteous on the interpretation of Jesus' suffering and death.

D. Summary

From our investigation of the recounting of the supper scene, we may outline the following conclusions.

(1) The probability is high that the primitive passion account reported no preparation for the Passover as is found in Mark 14:12—16, nor did it include an after-Supper discourse as is found in Luke and John. The betrayal scene, on the other hand, was most probably already present in the primitive passion story, though we can no longer recover the precise chronological relationship for the announcement *vis-à-vis* the meal itself. Finally, it is probable that the primitive passion narrative did not include an explicit recitation of the eucharistic words — though these words would have been incorporated into the narrative early on in its development.

(2) No one theme dominates the interpretation of Jesus' death in this section of the passion story. With the reference to Ps 41:9 in the betrayal-announcement, the *passio-iusti* motif raises its head rather sharply. Influence of this idea on the interpretation of Jesus' death is not confined to word-choice, however, for traces of this motif are seen as well in Jesus' anticipation of vindication. There may be cause for finding this idea in the background of the recompense promised Judas, but we will have cause to raise serious questions regarding this possibility below.

---

70 See above, chapter 7.

(3) The Isaianic Suffering Servant is recognizable at two distinct points in this section — at the roots of the expectation of vindication after suffering and in the eucharistic words in which Jesus' death is cast in a role central to God's redemptive plan. Through this latter text, we discover that Jesus' death, like the suffering of the Servant, is to be the basis for others to receive the salvation of God.

(4) That Jesus' death was central to the divine economy takes on other nuances besides that given it by the Servant-metaphor. Other background themes — e.g. the covenant — are employed. Similarly, by way of communicating this motif, one can merely write "as it is written" (Mark) or "as it has been determined" (Luke). There is, further, the paradoxical measure by which the question of causal agency is handled in this section: God remains in sovereign control of Jesus' passion while Judas is fully responsible for his betrayal. By this means, it is shown that the events of Jesus' passion — even that of Judas's treachery — constituted no surprise to God, nor do they nullify his salvific plan. Jesus' passion was central to God's plan for bringing redemption.

(5) Finally, Jesus' foreknowledge is evident here — not only in his prediction of Judas's treachery, but also in the eucharistic words. Jesus both anticipated his death and embraced it (if only implicitly at this point).

IV. Three Prophecies

A. Mark 14:26; Matt 26:30; Luke 22:39; John 18:1

In Mark, v 26 has a transitional functon, moving the narrative *topically* from the eucharistic words of the Last Supper to the predictions of the flight of the disciples, Jesus' resurrection, and Peter's denial; and *topographically* from the "upper room" (14:15) to Gethsemane (14:32). Matthew has both reproduced Mark's wording verbatim and preserved his ordering of events. Luke and John, however, record the departure from the Supper later, following the completion of their respective accounts of Jesus' table-talk, which includes the prophecy of Peter's denial. In this correspondence, these two evangelists may betray the influence of a common source. On the other hand, Luke's version of the prediction of Peter's denial (22:31—34) is easily extracted from its immediate context, and John's (13:36—38) shows signs of having been fashioned by the Fourth Evangelist[71]. Hence, the Markan sequence is to be preferred as the more original.

---

71 "There can be no doubt that the evangelist himself composed this scene [from 'special tradition']. His literary style and freedom in employing tradition are both unmistakeable" (Schnackenburg, *John*, 3:55).

What, then, of Mark 14:26? Is it traditional[72]? It should not be overlooked that the construction of the verse — καί + aorist of ἔρχομαι or its compounds + εἰς + place name + καί (v 27) — is found frequently in Mark (cf. 1:35; 2:1; 3:1; 5:1; 6:32, 46, 53; 7:31; 8:10, 13, 27; 9:33; 11:11; 14:16, 68). In addition, εἰς τὸ ὄρος τῶν ἐλαιῶν appears elsewhere in 13:3 and is closely paralleled in 11:1: πρὸς τὸ ὄρος τῶν ἐλαιῶν. On the basis of linguistic evidence one might favor regarding this sentence as the product of Markan redaction.

What our linguistic survey has failed to indicate, however, is why Mark, had he been working up this verse from nothing, included a reference to hymn-singing (ὑμνήσαντες; apart from the Matthean parallel in 26:30, ὑμνέω appears in the NT only in Acts 16:25 and Heb 2:12 [citing Ps 22:23]). Why would so insignificant a detail have been added in a transitional sentence? A number of interpreters have found in ὑμνέω an allusion to the Passover-character of the Last Supper — the reference being to the singing of the hallel[73], and some go so far as to designate ὑμνέω as a *terminus technicus* for the singing of the hallel at the Passover[74]. Building from this, some have proposed the Markan origin of this reference, by which Mark further portrayed the Last Supper as a Passover[75]. While this meaning is possible[76], it is certainly outstripping the lexical evidence to regard ὑμνέω as a *terminus technicus* for the singing of the hallel[77]. That is, whereas a reference to the hallel would likely have employed this verb, its use here does not prove *ipso facto* a reference to the hallel[78]. In association with other Passover-allusions it may be prudent to regard the intended nuance of ὑμνέω in this instance as "to sing the hallel", but, as we have seen, Mark cannot be attributed with introducing all of the Passover imagery into the Last Supper scene, and so it does not follow

---

72 Mark 14:26 is regarded as pre-Markan by Cranfield, *Mark*, 428; Nineham, *Mark*, 387; Mohr, *Passion*, 213–225 (who credits this verse to a pre-Markan redactor). It is reckoned to be Markan by Linnemann, *Studien*, 86–87; Lohse, *Geschichte*, 57; Best, *Temptation and Passion*, 92, 173; Schenke, *Studien*, 348–354; Schenk, *Passionsbericht*, 224.
73 Thus Cranfield, *Mark*, 428; Strauss, *Jesus*, 635; Jeremias, *Eucharistic Words*, 55 n.1, 87, 255, 261; Schweizer, *Mark*, 307; Nineham, *Mark*, 387; Lane, *Mark*, 509; Pesch, *Mark*, 2:379; Schmithals, *Mark*, 2:626; Gundry, *Matthew*, 529; Gerhard Delling, "Ὕμνος, ὑμνέω, ψάλλω, ψαλμός", in *TDNT*, 8:499; Senior, *Passion: Mark*, 62; Swete, *Mark*, 337; Gnilka, *Mark*, 2:247 (who also notes its suitability for the close of the Lord's Supper).
74 So Schenke, *Studien*, 348; Dormeyer, *Passion Jesu*, 111.
75 E.g., Schenk, *Passionsbericht*, 224; Schenke, *Studien*, 348–354.
76 Philo (*Spec. Leg.*, 2.148) associates "thanksgivings and hymns" with the Passover banquet. See also Str.-B., 4:72–73, 75–76.
77 Cf. BAG, 836; Delling, "Ὕμνος".
78 Taylor (*Mark*, 548) recognizes the ambiguous nature of this reference, and Linnemann (*Studien*, 87; see pp. 86–87) concludes: "Die Erwähnung ὑμνήσαντες in Mk. 14,26 ist keine Anspielung auf das Passafest".

necessarily that he has inserted this one. Hence, we suggest that the reference to hymn-singing, and with it some transitional statement, has come to Mark from his source — which contains here an historical reminiscence.

It is doubtful whether we should credit this hymn-singing with any theological significance, despite the attempts of Jeremias and Lane to read into the text the content of Ps 118, thus arguing that Jesus is here anticipating his final triumph[79]. One cannot help but think that if an important theological idea had been intended here, then the content of the song would have been spelled out. Indeed, it is a sign of the reserve on the part of the tradition and the evangelist that no words were added by way of filling in further the interpretive significance of Jesus' passion — a reserve lacking in the apocryphal *Acts of John* (94—96). Therein, speaking of Jesus, "John" relates:

> But before he was arrested by the lawless Jews, whose lawgiver is the lawless serpent, he assembled us all and said, 'Before I am delivered to them, let us sing a hymn to the Father, and so go to meet what lies before (us)'. So he told us to form a circle, holding one another's hands, and himself stood in the middle and said, 'Answer Amen to me'. So he began to sing the hymn . . .[80].

There follows in the apocryphal account an extended "Hymn to Christ" incorporating the author's own theological position. In contradistinction to this development, apparently neither Mark nor his tradition had any theological interest in the hymn-singing, and passed it on only as a part of the transitional statement in which it was found.

B. *Mark 14:27—28; Matt 26:31—32; John 16:1, 32—33*

Apart from a few subtle changes that heighten the drama of the narrative and further develop the relation of Jesus to the disciples, Matthew's version of the predictions of the flight of the disciples and Jesus' resurrection follows closely that of Mark[81]. Similarly, the First Evangelist follows the Second in closely associating the prophecy of the *Jüngerflucht* with that of Peter's denial. Luke, following another source here[82], reports the announcement of Peter's denial on its own, offering no parallel to the Markan text now in view. This does not necessarily rule out the possibility that his *Sonderquelle* contained a prediction of the flight of the disciples. Its absence from Luke may be deliberate, the tradition having been suppressed by the Third Evangelist who is at pains in the passion narrative to show the continuing close relationship between Jesus and the disciples. The parallel in John's Gospel is found in a context which differs significantly from Mark's — *before* the departure from the Supper, but *after* (and *far removed*

---

79 Jeremias, *Eucharistic Words*, 261; Lane, *Mark*, 509.
80 K. Schäferdiek, "The Acts of John", in *NT Apocrypha*, 2:227; see pp. 227—232.
81 On the Matthean redaction, see esp. Senior, *Passion*, 89—94; Gundry, *Matthew*, 529—530.
82 See above, chapter 3.IX.

from) the announcement of Peter's denial (13:36–38). Apparently, then, the tradition-history of the accounts of the *Jüngerflucht* — especially as related to that of Peter's denial — is not straightforward; however, as we shall see, there is sufficient reason for affirming the appearance of both in the primitive passion account. The same may be said for the associated motif of Jesus' triumph found in Mark 14:28; again, however, the *traditionsgeschichtliche* puzzle presented by this verse is not easily solved.

Turning first to the Markan account, we immediately encounter a consequential literary-critical issue. While vv 27–31 must be defined as a single unit, grammatically bound by the repeated reference to "all" in vv 27 and 31[83], it is widely held that vv 27b–28 — or at least v 28 — represents a redactional intrusion into the story of the prophecy of Peter's denial[84]. Three primary reasons are given for this judgment. First, speaking of the quotation of Zech 13:7 in v 27b, Suhl remarks:

> Dieser gewichtige Hinweis auf die Schrift stört den Gang der Perikope. Ohne V.27b und V.28 is sie klar und einheitlich aufgebaut und als Einleitung für eine ursprünglich selbständige Erzählung über die Verleugnung des Petrus durchaus verständlich[85].

Mohr goes even further, declaring, "Ja, V.28 widerspricht der ganzen Tendenz der Perikope V.26–31"[86]. In this regard, one may observe the continuity between vv 27a and 29 effected by the use of σκανδαλισθήσεσθε by Jesus in v 27a and Peter's use of σκανδαλισθήσονται in v 29. Following on this observation is a second point. Whereas Peter, in v 29, explicitly refers back to Jesus' words in v 27a, he betrays no knowledge of the OT citation in v 27b or of the triumphal claim of Jesus in v 28. This suggests that vv 27b–28 were inserted into an already-fixed traditional account. Third, inasmuch as v 28 corresponds so closely to 16:8, the two related as prophecy and fulfillment, this statement must have been a free-floating logion. To these points we may add a fourth — namely, the close syntactical correspondence between v 28 and the summary statement in 1:14: adversative particle + εἰς τὴν Γαλιλαίον. This agreement suggests common (i.e. Markan) authorship[87].

---

83 Cf. Gnilka, *Mark*, 2:251.
84 Cf., e.g., Bultmann, *History*, 267; Max Wilcox, "The Denial Sequence in Mark XIV.26–31, 66–72", *NTS* 17 (1970–71) 429–431; Kee, *Community*, 203, n.19; Alfred Suhl, *Die Funktion der alttestamentlichen Zitate und Anspielungen im Markusevangelium* (Gütersloh: Gerd Mohn, 1965) 62–63; Best, *Temptation and Passion*, 92, 157 n.3; idem, *Mark*, 55; Taylor, *Mark*, 549; Schweizer, *Mark*, 306; Schmithals, *Mark*, 2:626; Gnilka, *Mark*, 2:252; Schenk, *Passionsbericht*, 226–227; Klein, "Verleugnung", 296–297; Mohr, *Passion*, 213–218; Dormeyer, *Passion Jesu*, 111–113; Lindars, *NT Apologetic*, 129–130; Schenke, *Studien*, 354–460; Linnemann, *Studien*, 87–93.
85 Suhl, *Funktion*, 62.
86 Mohr, *Passion*, 217.
87 As is well known, the Fayyum Fragment omits 14:28, but this is inconsequential, given the fact that this fragment is not a full copy of the Greek text.

On the other hand, the original position of vv 27b—28 within the pericope has not gone undefended. Thus, France asserts:

> However, the form of Jesus' saying (warning, with its scriptural confirmation, balanced by encouragement) is not in itself improbable, and the fact that Peter's reply does not interrupt proves nothing. . . Moreover, the quotation agrees with many uses by Jesus of the shepherd motif from the OT . . . , and also with his frequent use of Zc. 9—14 during the passion[88].

Cranfield is also unimpressed with the argument that Peter apparently does not "know" vv 27b—28: ". . . it would be natural for him to be too taken up with the implied slur on his loyalty to pay much attention to anything else"[89]. As for the shepherd-motif, this is of particular importance for it represents one way of demonstrating the close relationship between vv 27b—28. The sense of προγράφω should be understood temporally — "to go before", but even so the verb holds an implicit reference to Jesus' position as leader following his being raised[90]. Hence, the sequence of events prophesied in vv 27b—28 demonstrates in parallel fashion the close relationship between Jesus (the shepherd) and his disciples (the sheep): the shepherd is struck, with the result that the sheep are scattered; the shepherd is raised up, enabling the regathering of the sheep[91].

Before making any final comments about the literary unity of vv 27—31, an additional remark regarding the unity of vv 27b—28 (and thus the incorrectness of the view that v 28 is easily sundered from its context) is due. Verse 28 is an obvious vindication-reference, overturning what then must be a death-reference (πατάξω)[92] in v 27b. What we have here, then, is the death and resurrection of Jesus held in tandem — as in the earlier "passion predictions" (8:31; 9:31; 10:33—34) and in Paul (e.g. Rom 4:25; 1 Cor 15: 3—5; 2 Cor 5:14—15)[93]. The parallel in John 16:32—33 should not be overlooked either. There the cross-reference is transparent in the phrase "the hour is coming" (v 32) and the idea of vindication is present in v 33, where Jesus proclaims his victory over the world. We conclude that the connection of vv 27b—28 is not artificial.

Nevertheless, in the final analysis, all that can be said is that vv 27b—28 are appropriate to their present context, but that the tension stemming from their placement here has not been entirely removed by the counterarguments noted above. We propose, then, that vv 27b—28, while Markan

---

88 France, *Jesus*, 107 n.87.
89 Cranfield, *Mark*, 429.
90 Attempts to read in 14:28 a reference to the parousia have not met with success; see the comments against this reading in Best, *Mark*, 76—78 ; Gnilka, *Mark*, 2:253; Gundry, *Matthew*, 530.
91 Cf. Joachim Jeremias, *The Central Message of the New Testament* (London: SCM, 1965) 47—48; idem, *NT Theology*, 297; Moo, *OT — Passion*, 216—217; Kingsbury, *Christology*, 136.
92 Cf. Heinrich Seesemann, "Πατάσσω", in *TDNT*, 5:939—940; Pesch, *Mark*, 2:380.
93 Cf. the remarks in Swete, *Mark*, 339; Burkill, "Mark's Philosophy", 259; Gnilka, *Mark*, 2:253; Pesch, *Mark*, 2:381.

in their present redaction, were already present in Mark's source, which itself combined the citation and promise with the material dealing with Peter's denial. We have already seen the high probability of an early, independent tradition having to do with Peter's role in the passion events[94]. Due to thematic commonality, it was only natural that the passion-vindication prediction having to do with the *Jüngerflucht* (including that of Peter) should be joined at some early point to the prediction of Peter's denial in the development of the tradition. At what point? It is difficult to determine whether the tradition represented by Matthew and Mark (which joins the two) or by Luke and John (which narrates the denial prediction on its own) is the more original. We have already seen why Luke may have failed to follow his source point-for-point here; and, given the preponderance of motifs in the context of the prophecy in 16:32 and the relative freedom with which John otherwise organizes his material, the evidence of the Johannine account should not be regarded as decisive either. There is one consideration, however, which strongly intimates that Mark preserves the more original placement and that is the fact that the primitive passion narrative lacked any extensive table-talk, and it is precisely the material of this discourse which separates the two predictions in John. That both Mark and John testify to the prediction of a "falling away" related to a promise of ultimate triumph is reason enough to hold that this material is primitive, but as to its exact relation to the prophecy of Peter's denial in the early passion story we must remain agnostic.

Mark 14:27 includes a citation of Zech 13:7. John's version contains no explicit quotation, but it is nevertheless probable that the prediction in John 16:32 is to be traced back to a tradition like Mark's which drew on the Zechariah text[95]. John uses $\sigma\kappa o\rho\pi i\zeta\omega$ in 16:32 (Mark: $\delta\iota\alpha\sigma\kappa o\rho\pi i\zeta\omega$; LXX[A]: $\delta\iota\alpha\sigma\kappa o\rho\pi i\zeta\omega$; LXX[B]: $\dot{\epsilon}\kappa\sigma\pi\acute{\alpha}\omega$; MT: פוץ; Mark, John, and LXX[A] thus more accurately represent the MT than does the LXX[B]) and $\sigma\kappa\alpha\nu\delta\alpha\lambda i\zeta\omega$ in 16:1 (as in Mark 14:27, 29). That John has made use of old tradition is further demonstrated by the incongruity of the prophecy of 16:32 with his account of Jesus' arrest[96]. There, John mentions no flight of the disciples as they desert their leader at his arrest, as does Mark; rather, Jesus procures for them their safe departure (18:8). To be sure, a number of exegetes regard the use of this OT passage as traceable not to Jesus but to the early church, who wanted to take the sting out of the flight of the disciples[97]. Even if this reference is not authentic — though it must be

---

94 See above, chapter 3.IX.
95 So Bruce, *John*, 325; Reim, *Studien*, 45, 187; Dodd, *Historical Tradition*, 56–57; Lindars, *John*, 514; Barrett, *John*, 497; Schnackenburg, *John*, 3:165.
96 As noted by Dodd, *Historical Tradition*, 57; Brown, *John*, 2:736–737.
97 E.g., Bertram, *Leidensgeschichte*, 42; Schweizer, *Mark*, 307; Lindars, *John*, 514.

admitted that it accords well with Jesus' use of the image of the shepherd[98] — there is nonetheless no reason why it may not be traced as far back as the primitive passion account. If the present use of Zech 13:7 stems from the primitive passion narrative, what does this mean for our understanding of Jesus' death?

The first point to be developed is the identification of Jesus as the shepherd. In the OT[99], "shepherd" most often appears as a designation for God, though others are given "shepherding" tasks (e.g. David in 2 Sam 5:2). In the later prophets, "shepherd" becomes a nomenclature for God's agent of salvation — i.e. a messianic term, broadly speaking. In Mic 5:4, the promised ruler from Bethlehem will "stand and shepherd his flock in the strength of the Lord", and in Ezek 34:23 God promises to place over his flock "one shepherd, my servant David, [who] will tend them" (cf. Ezek 37:22, 24; Jer 3:15; 23:1—6). The messianic role of the "shepherd" is further evidenced in *Ps. Sol.* 17:40: ἰσχυρὸς ἐν ἔργοις αὐτοῦ καὶ κραταιὸς ἐν φόβῳ θεοῦ ποιμαίνων τὸ ποίμνιον κυρίου ἐν πίστει καὶ δικαιοσύνῃ. In Zech 13:7, the shepherd is presumably God's agent, a royal figure, "the one who stands next to me", and it is difficult not to discern messianic overtones here (cf. CD 19:5—9, where Zech 13:7 is interpreted eschatologically). In this OT context the shepherd's death, a result of God's judgment, is decisive as a turning point in salvific history. As the shepherd, Jesus bears the judgment of God (cf. Mark 10:38)[100], and his death is of eschatological significance as the turning point in redemptive history (though how it functions thus is not made clear).

Second, in employing this image and citing this verse in a self-identification, Jesus is again portrayed as one who was cognizant of his death and its divine importance prior to the fateful events themselves.

Moreover, this citation gives God the role of primary actor in Jesus' passion. With the use of the first person singular future tense of πατάσσω, the hand of God becomes directly involved in Jesus' death, though it would be a mistake to regard this idea as missing in the MT and LXX of Zech 13:7, where the imperative is employed, addressed to the "sword"[101].

---

98 Cf. France, *Jesus*, 107 n.87; Taylor, *Jesus*, 146—147; Longenecker, *Christology*, 49; Bruce, "Book of Zechariah", 343.
99 See Moo, *OT — Passion*, 173—178; F. F. Bruce, *The New Testament Development of Old Testament Themes* (Grand Rapids, Michigan: Wm. B. Eerdmans, 1968) 100—114; Longenecker, *Christology*, 48—49; Joachim Jeremias, "Ποιμήν, ἀρχιποίμην, ποιμαίνω", in *TDNT*, 6:487—490; Erich Beyreuther, "Shepherd", in *NIDNTT*, 3:562—566.
100 This is the meaning of "to strike" in the context of Zech 13:7, and more generally — see Seesemann, "Πατάσσω", 940. On this motif, see Best, *Temptation and Passion*, 158; Jeremias, "Ποιμήν", 493.
101 Jeremias ("Ποιμήν", 493 n.78) has attempted to explain this change in verb form with appeal to the influence of Isa 53:6, which allows him to incorporate the redemptive theology of the

The significance of Mark 14:28 and John 16:33 as references to triumph has already been mentioned. It is perhaps worthy of further mention, however, that the sequence of events prophesied in Mark 14:27–28; John 16:1, 32–33 follows thematically that of Zech 13:7–9. In view of the explicit use of this OT text in Mark and its implicit use in John, one may reasonably conjecture that Zech 13:7–9 lies in the background of the promise of triumph in the tradition[102]. This thematic development parallels, but is not necessarily dependent on, the fates of the Righteous Sufferer and the Suffering Servant.

C. Mark 14:29–31; Matt 26:33–35; Luke 22:31–34; John 13:36–38

With these verses we come to the prediction by Jesus of Peter's denial. Matthew's version is dependent solely on Mark, though his editorial modifications indicate a tendency to make Peter less an exception to, and more a representative of, the other disciples[103]. Luke 22:31–33 originates in Luke's *Sonderquelle*, but v 34 may come from Mark[104]. Verse 31, though addressed to Simon, is apparently a warning to all of the disciples (ὑμᾶς), and in this limited respect this verse is associated more with the Markan prophecy of the *Jüngerflucht*. The introduction of Satan and with him the cosmic setting of this testing, Jesus' role on behalf of Peter (σοῦ – v 32), and the anticipated pastoral role Peter is to have among the others – all of these points are unique to Luke in this setting, though John narrates the third idea in 21:15–17. In the Lukan narrative, Peter understands this warning as implying his lack of readiness to follow Jesus to the end, so in 22:33 he asserts his readiness to do just that – whether in prison or death. As observed earlier, Luke and John place this section in the context of the meal, whereas Mark places it on the way to Gethsemane. In John's version, the prediction of Peter's denial follows a dialogue between Peter and Jesus concerning "where Jesus is going".

Hence, Mark, Luke, and John all differ in how they introduce the prophecy of Peter's denial, and this is additional evidence that this "Petrine material" at first enjoyed independent status. As to the content of the account itself, however, there are two points of unanimity. First, all agree

---

Suffering Servant into this citation. There is really no basis for this theory, however, and it seems much more probable that the modification is due to the citation of only part of the OT text, making necessary the introduction of another definite subject. On the theme of divine agency announced thereby, see Kee, *Community*, 203 n.18 ; Best, *Temptation and Passion*, 157 ; Matera, *Kingship of Jesus*, 118; Schmithals, *Mark*, 2:631–632; Taylor, *Jesus*, 147.

102 Jeremias, ("Ποιμήν", 493) states that Mark 14:28 " . . . is a free rendering of the contents of Zech 13:8f.". Cf. Goppelt, *Typos*, 88.
103 On this *Tendenz* in the First Gospel, see Eduard Schweizer, "Matthew's Church", in *Interpretation of Matthew*, 135–136.
104 See above, chapter 3.IX.

in reporting Peter's willingness to die. The additional statement in Mark — ὡσαύτως δὲ καὶ πάντες ἔλεγον — is not found in the other independent versions. It may be Markan, for the Second Evangelist frequently adds such clauses to his traditions[105]; in any case, we cannot trace it back to the primitive passion narrative. Second, the relative stability of the Jesus-logion addressed to Peter and anticipating his denial before the cockcrow suggests its very primitive character. The verbose chronological reference in Mark — σήμερον ταύτῃ τῇ νυκτί — has been abbreviated in different ways by Matthew (ἐν ταύτῃ τῇ νυκτί) and Luke (σήμερον). While the reference may stem from tradition (cf. 1 Cor 11:23), as it now stands in Mark it apparently reflects Mark's tendency to employ adverbs with additional modifiers (cf. 1:28, 35, 45; 2:20; 5:11; 6:3, 25; 7:21; 8:4; 9:2; 10:30; 11:4)[106].

This aspect of the primitive passion account was passed along for biographical and paraenetic reasons and suggests almost nothing about how Jesus' death was understood in the early passion account. At most, we can see here another indication that the events of Jesus' passion came as no surprise to him, for he possessed prophetic foreknowledge.

D. Luke 22:35–38

This pericope, incorporating the so-called sword-saying, is witnessed in the Gospel tradition only by the Third Evangelist. Its relation to the passion is evident not only from the sword incident at Jesus' arrest, but, even more importantly, from Jesus' instruction that the present time (νῦν) marks a change of strategy, a remark well-suited to this critical stage in Jesus' life and in salvation-history. The Isaianic quotation in 22:37 (Isa 53:12) also suggests a passion context while encouraging, at the same time, an identification of Jesus with the Suffering Servant of Yahweh. The tradition is certainly pre-Lukan[107]; yet, in view of its absence from the other canonical passion stories, we have no substantial basis for arguing for its inclusion in the primitive passion narrative.

E. Conclusion

From our investigation of the three prophecies we may outline the following observations.

(1) As to the literary context of this section, there is disagreement

---

105 Best, *Mark*, 11, 27–28.
106 Peabody, *Redactional Features*, 92–93. Dormeyer (*Passion Jesu*, 113–115) and Mohr (*Passion*, 220–225) allow only vv 29 and 30 as pre-Markan, while Schenke (*Studien*, 389–400) argues for the Markan creation of the whole pericope. These opinions fail to deal seriously with the independent testimony to the respective traditions found in Luke and John.
107 See above, chapter 3.X.

among our versions, but we have found that the Markan sequence has a good claim to being the more original. While a precise determination of the content of this section in the primitive passion narrative is beyond our grasp, we have argued that a transitional statement, a prediction of the flight of the disciples together with a note of triumph, and a prediction of Peter's denial before the cockcrow, together with Peter's assertion of his readiness to die with Jesus, all stem from the primitive passion narrative.

(2) The most pervasive theme in this section concerns Jesus' prophetic foreknowledge. He is not surprised by the events of his own passion, not even by the desertion of his friends at the crucial moment.

(3) Additionally, with the quotation of Zech 13:7, the emphasis on God's active and direct role in the passion of Jesus again lifts its head.

(4) Finally, in this section Jesus is said to have identified himself with the shepherd of Zech 13. Hence, in his death he is seen to bear the judgment of God, but his death is regarded as the decisive eschatological event which gives way to triumph and the reconstitution of his scattered "flock".

V. Prayer in Gethsemane

A. *Mark 14:32–42; Matt 26:36–46; Luke 22:39–46; John 12:27–28; 14:31b; 18:1–2, 11b*

In presenting his rendition of Jesus' prayer at Gethsemane, Matthew " ... effects extensive although not substantial development of the scene offered by Mark"[108]. The First Evangelist knew no additional *Gethsemane-source*, but, as we shall see, in his construction of Jesus' prayer he has been influenced by language from the "Lord's Prayer". The Third Evangelist possessed a *Sonderquelle* for this scene which he has conflated with the Markan narrative. The effect of his redaction is again to bring to the fore his interest in portraying Jesus as the Servant of the Lord and, to a lesser extent, to accent a martyrological theme in the interpretation of Jesus' death[109]. It is true that John narrates no Gethsemane-like scene as such, but his knowledge of the same is evident, as many scholars agree[110].

---

108 Senior, *Passion*, 100.
109 See above, chapter 3.XI. On the effect of Luke's redaction, see Green, "Mount of Olives", where the oft-emphasized martyrological theme is downplayed in favor of a primary accent on the Servant idea.
110 So, e.g., Pierre Benoit, *The Passion and Resurrection of Jesus Christ* (London: Darton, Longman and Todd, 1969) 19; Schnackenburg, *John*, 3:221; Bruce, *John*, 265, 342; Barrett, *John*, 516 (Barrett admits a non-Synoptic source for John here – 517–518); Lindars, *John*, 430–431, 543; Brown, *John*, 1:474; Dodd, *Historical Tradition*, 68-69; Lohse, *Geschichte*, 65–66; Mohr, *Passion*, 245–247; Ernst Haenchen, "History and Interpretation in the Johannine Passion Narrative", *Int* 24 (1970) 199.

Along with Mark's account, then, there are two additional, independent narratives of the Gethsemane-incident. Hebrews 5:7, while not a Gethsemane *narrative,* likely constitutes a further, independent witness to the one event and should not be overlooked in this context.

As for the pre-history of the Markan text itself, some seven decades of literary criticism have failed to achieve anything approaching a consensus opinion. Following the early hypothesis of Bultmann, a large number of exegetes have agreed in regarding the Gethsemane narrative as an amplification of an original primitive, simple tradition[111]. Beyond this common denominator, however, the measure of coincidence among this band of scholars is short-lived, for there is little unity among them in identifying the precise perimeters of that traditional account, nor even in designating the redactional influence of the Second Evangelist on the "final form" of that tradition. A second group of scholars argues that the present form of the Markan story is actually the result of combining two pre-Markan narrative units[112]. Within this group, the hypothesis of Kuhn is particularly noteworthy for its identification of two primitive sources – the one christological and eschatological, the other paraenetic. Finally, Pesch and Lohmeyer regard the entire scene as a traditional unit[113], while Dibelius and Kelber insist that, apart from the most minute tiaditional core, the whole is a Markan creation[114]. Not without good reason does Schmithals observe:

> Die Disparatheit dieser formgeschichtlichen Analysen lässt erkennen, dass die literarische Verfassung der Getsemani-Erzählung eine einigermassen deutliche literar- oder formkritische Analyse nicht erlaubt[115].

---

[111] Butlmann, *History,* 267–268. See, e.g., Linnemann, *Studien,* 27–32; Dormeyer, *Passion Jesu,* 124–137; Schenke, *Studien,* 461–540; Gnilka, *Mark,* 2:257–258; Werner Mohn, "Gethsemane (Mk 14:32–42)", *ZNW* 64 (1973) 195–202; Mohr, *Passion,* 226–248; Lohse, *Geschichte,* 63–64.

[112] The work of Kuhn ("Gethsemane") and that of Best (*Temptation and Passion,* 92–94) are apparently independent. Schenk (*Passionsbericht,* 193–206) refines Kuhn's thesis, and both Benoit (*Passion,* 21) and Barbour ("Gethsemane", 232–234) adopt his reconstruction. See also Schweizer, *Mark,* 310.

[113] Ernst Lohmeyer, *Das Evangelium des Markus,* 16th ed. (Göttingen: Vandenhoeck & Ruprecht, 1963) 313; Pesch, *Mark,* 2:386.

[114] Dibelius (*Tradition,* 182; *idem,* "Gethsemane", 258–271) argues that the Gethsemane story arose from the early church's reading of the psalms regarding the suffering of the righteous as prophecies of Jesus' suffering. Nevertheless, he admits that "eine historische Beurteilung ist erst möglich" ("Gethesemane", 270). For his part, Kelber ("Gethsemane", 176, see pp. 169–176) concludes: "Mark is not merely the redactor, but to a high degree the creator and composer of the Gethsemane story". In his opinion, the location of the incident in Gethsemane is pre-Marken (174), the lament and prayer may be traditional (174–175), and the γρηγορεῖν-logion is pre-Markan (175–176).

[115] Schmithals, *Mark,* 2:634. Limited surveys and critiques of literary analyses on this pericope are found in Linnemann, *Studien,* 13–27; Kelber, "Gethsemane", 166–169.

While we cannot altogether escape a treatment of the issues debated here, it will not be necessary for our purposes to engage in an exhaustive discussion of the pre-history of the Markan text. Rather, our primary interest must rest, as before, on what can be gleaned about a pre-canonical account from a comparison of the available sources[116]. Our task will be accomplished by considering in turn the various ingredients of the story.

(1) Mark situates the episode in Gethsemane, Luke at the Mount of Olives, and John in a garden across the Kidron valley. "Gethsemane" has been deliberately omitted by Luke, however, and there is no real tension between the designation of Mark and John. Nor should one push the apparent discrepancy between "Mount of Olives" and "Gethesemane" in Mark 14:26, 32: Pesch may be right in his suggestion that "die knappe *Situationsangabe* (V32a) knüpft an 14, 26–31; der Gang zum Oelberg (V26) endet in einem landgut namens Getsemani"[117]. That Mark's "Gethsemane" is traditional is suggested by its specificity, Mark's apparent lack of theological interest in the designation, and by the fact that Mark has provided no translation for this Aramaism[118].

(2) Luke 22:39 and John 18:2 agree against Mark in suggesting why Jesus went to this particular locale and how Judas knew to meet him there. Luke's phrase is undoubtedly given in his own wording, but this should not blind us to the possibility that Luke and John are again drawing on similar tradition[119]. The phrase may witness to an historical reminiscene (cf. Luke 21:37), but its location in the early passion narrative is suspect since it is missing in Mark and because it answers the question raised by Judas's knowledge of Jesus' whereabouts on the night in question — a factor more likely to have been added than deleted in the history of tradition.

(3) The separation of the three disciples by Jesus in Mark's account (14: 33a) has been thought to reflect Markan interests (cf. 5:37; 9:2; 13:3) and thus regarded by some as a Markan embellishment of the tradition[120]. Even though this issue is not central to our concerns, we may observe that the absence of the detail in the Lukan parallel — compared with the inclusion of such a segregation in 9:28 — may support this judgment. On the other hand, there is nothing inherently unlikely about the mention of this

---

116 The very existence of other sources — i.e. in Luke and John — is a severe blow to Kelber's thesis, for it proves that Gethsemane-material like that found in Mark existed apart from Markan creation.
117 Pesch, *Mark*, 2:388.
118 See Schweizer, *Mark*, 311; Lohse, *Geschichte*, 57; Kelber, "Gethsemane", 174.
119 So Barbour, "Gethsemane", 235; Schnackenburg, *John*, 3:222. *Contra* Dauer, *Passionsgeschichte*, 55-56.
120 See, e.g., Lohse, *Geschichte*, 63; Gnilka, *Mark*, 2:257; Bultmann, *History*, 268; Kelber, "Gethsemane", 174–175.

action in the pre-Markan tradition — nor, indeed, about the historical genuineness of this aspect of the story.

(4) As for the report of, and saying about, Jesus' anguish in Mark 14: 33b and 34a, respectively, Kelber has maintained that the former is redactional, the latter traditional. In support of the Markan origin of v 33b, he alludes to its Markan style (ἄρχεσθαι + infinitive) and vocabulary (ἐκθαμ-βεῖσθαι)[121]. We would not deny the presence of Mark's hand in this verse, but we must assert that redaction and creation are not synonymous enterprises. In this case, Luke 22:43–44 and Heb 5:7 testify to the presence of this kind of report independent of the Markan version. Whichever judgment is adopted vis-à-vis v 33b, the lament-saying, witnessed independently in Mark 14:34 and John 12:27, is a positive indicator of the antiquity of this *theme* in the Gethsemane-material. In both cases — i.e. with the report and the logion — an OT background is important. Of course, Matt 26:37 shows how the anguish-report could be borrowed from Mark and recast in OT terminology (Ps 42:5), but even without this revision one may discern conceptual, if not always verbal, affinity with certain psalmic laments: Pss 60:3 LXX; 101:1 LXX; 142:4 LXX — all of which use ἀκηδιᾶν; 54:5–6 LXX; 115:1 LXX. As for the logion in Mark 14:34a, from the combination περίλυπος + ψυχή, the general scarceness of the term περίλυπος, and the obvious conceptual affinity, one may discern here an allusion to Pss 42:5, 6, 11; 43:5. Likewise, John 12:27 alludes to Ps 6:3–4 LXX; 42:5 (cf. 6:4; 41:6 LXX — ψυχή + (συν)ταράσσω; 6:5 LXX — σῶσόν με; 41:6 LXX — σωτήριον τοῦ προσώπου μου ὁ θεός μου)[122] Thus, "... the Psalms have been quarried to provide the words which express Jesus' emotions"[123] — and it is worthy of note that with the use of these texts we are brought back into the realm of the *passio-iusti* motif. To speak of Jesus' anguish is also to draw attention to his humanity[124].

---

121 Kelber, "Gethsemane", 174–175.
122 On the Markan allusion in 14:34a, see Pesch, *Mark*, 2:389; Taylor, *Mark*, 552–553; Swete, *Mark*, 342; Senior, *Passion*, 104; Moo, *OT – Passion*, 240–242 ; Suhl, *Funktion*, 49–50; Lohse, *Geschichte*, 58. Contra Linnemann, *Studien*, 30–31 n.48; Kelber, "Gethsemane", 175. On the Johannine allusion, see Lindars, *John*, 430–431; Dodd, *Historical Tradition*, 69; Moo, *OT – Passion*, 241; Barrett, *John*, 425; Mohr, *Passion*, 246.
123 Lindars, *John*, 431. Lindars compares this use of "psalm-tags" in the Gospel material with that used by the writer of the Qumran *Thanksgiving Hymns*. See esp. 1QH8.32, where Ps 42 is employed in a comparable way. When properly nuanced this comparison seems well-founded inasmuch as in both cases we find biblical expressions or terminology borrowed in order to draw out a theological motif or in order to give a ring of authority to a later writing. See Bonnie Pedrotti Kittel, *The Hymns of Qumran: Translation and Commentary* (Chico, California: Scholars, 1981) 48–52.
124 See *Gos. Nic.* 20, where Jesus' anguish is regarded by the devil as proof of his less-than-divine status.

Prayer in Gethsemane

The distinctive motif of the angelic presence in Luke 22:43—44, if it were present at all in the primitive passion narrative, probably existed only in the form of an assurance that Jesus' prayer had not fallen on deaf ears — a theme picked up independently in John 12:27—29 ("Then a voice came from heaven") and Heb 5:7 ("He offered up prayers . . . and was heard"). Here may be a reminiscence of Ps 22:24:

> For [the Lord] has not despised or disdained
> the suffering of the afflicted one;
> he has not hidden his face from him
> but has listened to his cry for help.

Beyond that, the reference to an angel in John 12:29 ("others said an angel had spoken to him") is remarkable and is yet one more indication that the traditons used by John and Luke intersected at some early point. This probability stands irrespective of the fact that a closer parallel to John's "voice from heaven" itself is found in the synoptic baptismal scene (cf. Mark 1:9—11).

(5) The need for prayer and/or spiritual alertness is stressed both in Mark:

14:34: μείνατε ὧδε καὶ γρηγορεῖτε;
14:37: οὐκ ἴσχυσας μίαν ὥραν γρηγορῆσαι;; and
14:38: γρηγορεῖτε καὶ προσεύχεσθε, ἵνα μὴ ἔλθητε εἰς πειρασμόν;;

and in Luke:

22:40: προσεύχεσθε μὴ εἰσελθεῖν εἰς πειρασμόν; and
22:46: ἀναστάντες προσεύχεσθε, ἵνα μὴ εἰσέλθητε εἰς πειρασμόν.

Earlier, we set forth our reasons for suggesting that on this matter Luke was not wholly dependent on Mark[125]. Admittedly, however, our case was not a strong one and, in view of the number of exegetes who regard the presence of this motif (or at least 14:38) as an amplification of the Second Evangelist[126], we must treat this matter more fully here before accepting its presence in the primitive passion narrative. By way of initiating our discussion it will be helpful to catalog the primary objections to the originality of this motif in the pre-Markan account. a. Mark 14:38a was originally a free-floating logion which has been inserted in this context by Mark. b. Originally, the story focused only on Jesus; this motif would have been added later for paraenetic purposes. Hence, the theme has no integral role here. c. The saying refers to a great eschatological trial of the disciples and

---

125 See above, chapter 3.IX.
126 So Nineham, *Mark*, 390, 392; Benoit, *Passion*, 21—22; Best, *Mark*, 90; Bultmann, *History*, 268; Kelber, "Gethsemane", 170—171; Dibelius, "Gethsemane", 263; Lohse, *Geschichte*, 59; Schenke, *Studien*, 512—515; Dormeyer, *Passion Jesu*, 129; Linnemann, *Studien*, 31.

has no place in this context; their "watching" and "praying" would not have kept Jesus from being arrested. d. Γρηγορέω is a key word for Mark. e. Singling out Peter as the representative disciple, as in 14:37–38, is characteristic of Markan interests.

Of these points, three are of little consequence. Thus, Mark was certainly not alone among early Christians in giving Peter a prominent place among the disciples (e.); if in fact 14:38a was a free-floating logion, this is no evidence that it was not attached to this context prior to the formulation of Mark's Gospel (a.); and, as we shall see, Mark does not have exclusive rights on the use of γρδγορέω (d.). With a fuller discussion of (d.), we must also deal with (b.) and (c.), for all have to do with the theme of "watching" and its significance and appropriateness for this context and for early Christian instruction.

Γρδγορέω occurs 16 times in the NT apart from the Synoptic accounts of Jesus' prayer at Gethsemane. "Eschatological readiness" is the general sense given the term in most texts. First Thessalonians 5:10 may be an exception for here, in a play of the words γρηγορέω and καθεύδω, it should be rendered "alive" (as opposed to "dead"). On the other hand, the eschatological context of this text (4:13–5:11), along with the specific admonitions to maintain alertness (5:1–11), are likely responsible for the choice of γρηγορέω here. If present at all, the eschatological accent on γρηγορέω has certainly receded into the background in Acts 20:21 – where the emphasis falls on general moral and doctrinal wakefulness; and in Col 4:2 – where the command to "be devoted to prayer, being watchful and thankful" is set in the midst of a series of instructions for Christian living. In view of Col 3:4, 6, 24; 4:5, however, one may not wish to completely disregard the eschatological nuance given the term in 4:2[127]. The case is similar with respect to 1 Cor 16:13 where the immediate context suggests alertness with regard to faith and in practicing Christian love, but, when viewed with 1 Cor 15 (see esp. 15:52), an eschatological coloring may be discerned.

The remaining instances of the verb are decidedly eschatological in their reference – though, in saying so, we are using the word "eschatological" rather loosely. On the one hand, a number of texts seem to refer exclusively to alertness in view of the imminent parousia – as in Rev 16:15:

> Behold, I come like a thief! Blessed is he who stays awake and keeps his clothes with him, so that he may not go naked and be shamefully exposed.

---

127 Peter T. O'Brien (*Colossians, Philemon* [Waco, Texas: Word, 1982] 237–238) argues for the eschatological character of the term, stating that Paul is encouraging his readers to be on the alert for the parousia. However, his argument is based almost solely on the sense of the term in other contexts, even if he does draw attention to the notion of "redeeming the time" in 4:5.

On this nuance, see also Matt 25:13; Luke 12:37; 1 Thess 5:6; Rev 3:2, 3. On the other hand, other passages, while at times also speaking of the parousia, speak of alertness *vis-à-vis* the presence and activity of hostile powers[128]. The occurrences of γηγορέω in Mark 13:34, 35, 37 fall into this category once they are viewed in their larger context, which includes 13:9–13 (see v 9, where βλέπετε δὲ ὑμεῖς ἑαυτούς occurs as a parallel to the imperatives of 13:33, 37; cf. also Matt 24:9–12, 42–43). In the light of 1 Pet 4:7; 5:9, 10, the use of γρηγορέω in 1 Pet 5:8 should also be listed here. This sense of γρηγορέω is closely matched by the intended nuance of its close relative, ἀγρυπνέω, in Mark 13:33; Luke 21:36; and Eph 6:18[129].

We may conclude from this that the concept of watchfulness or alertness was of signal importance in early Christian instruction (i.e. in the paraenetic appeal) and that the concept was apparently well-suited to contexts dealing with trials or opposition from hostile powers. As such, the idea is particularly suited to the Gethsemane incident, at which time Jesus demonstrated by his actions and made explicit by his command how one might overcome πειρασμός. One should note further that at Gethsemane, Jesus was not the only one being "tried", nor is the πειρασμός only a reference to the upcoming "trial" of the disciples at Jesus' arrest. Without denying the timeless, paraenetic value of the imperative to watch and pray, we should not, at the other extreme, miss the appropriateness of this motif *on this night in particular* – an "hour" characterized most comprehensively by the onslaught, trial, and apparent victory of hostile powers.

One may yet object that the three-fold reference to "watching" in Mark and the parallel commands that frame the Lukan account appear artificial and should not be credited to an early passion account. After all, we may be reminded, this articulated paraenetic emphasis detracts from the real point of the story – namely, Jesus' struggle and response to God. This point is well-taken, but should not be exaggerated. As Schenke insists, the failure of the disciples serves to highlight Jesus' responsible behavior all the more[130]. The interests of Christian instruction were an important influence in bringing closer to the fore the command of Jesus to watch and pray; however, the probability is very high that this theme was already present in the primitive passion story[131].

---

128 See G. R. Beasley-Murray, "Second Thoughts on the Composition of Mark 13", *NTS* 29 (3, 1983) 417–418. Of course, in view of the appearance of πειρασμός, the uses of γρηγορέω in the Gethsemane account must be listed under this heading – *contra* Eduard Schweizer, "Eschatology in Mark's Gospel", in *Neotestamentica et Semitica*, 117–118.
129 The only other use of ἀγρυπνέω in the NT is in Heb 13:17, where it has the sense of "to guard someone" or "to keep watch over".
130 Schenke, *Studien*, 548; cf. Gnilka, *Mark*, 2:257.
131 The sole witness to the saying contrasting the willing spirit and weak flesh is Mark 14:34b. While

(6) At first sight, there seems to be a large measure of diversity among the reports of Jesus' prayer. Mark recounts the content of Jesus' prayer first in indirect speech, then direct, followed by a report that Jesus repeated the same prayer, and finally, by implication, that the prayer was said a third time. Matthew omits the indirect report, but records two in direct discourse, followed by a statement that the same words were used a third time. Luke records only one prayer, and that in direct speech. John narrates a short prayer in 12:27, but also uses Synoptic-prayer-like language in the arrest scene (18:11b). Interestingly, despite the above-noted diversity in form and method of narration, there is a remarkable degree of commonality among the traditions as to the *content* of Jesus' prayer.

Before noting the motifs that are constant in the tradition, we may suggest the influence of the "Lord's Prayer" on the development of the material at an early stage, probably for paraenetic reasons (i.e. to show Jesus as a living example of his own teaching)[132]. Earlier, we noted the parallelism between Matt 6:10 and 26:42 and, in turn, Luke 22:42[133]. This is the most obvious of the points in which the influence of the "Lord's Prayer" is evident, but there are others[134]. In Matt 26:39, 42, Matthew's πάτηρ + *personal pronoun* may be due to influence from a similar combination in 6:9. Likewise, Matthew's redundant preposition (εἰσέρχομαι + εἰς) may reflect comparable usage in 6:13. Finally, in John 12:28, Jesus' exclamation, "Father, glorify your name!", not only agrees thematically with the opening of the "Lord's Prayer" — both asking God to bring to fruition his divine plan, but also the phraseology itself is somewhat parallel (cf. Lev 10:3).

There are primarily four points at which the traditions in question intersect with regard to the content of Jesus' prayer. First, all are agreed that, in some way, Jesus contemplated the possibility that his death would not be necessary (Mark 14:35–36; Luke 22:42a; John 12:27a; Heb 5:7). Second, Jesus' prayer ultimately focuses on God's will, on his purpose (Mark 14:36; Luke 22:42; John 12:27; 18:11). In this way, Jesus' prayer is cast as a prayer of submission to God (cf. Heb 5:7). Third, Mark and John both use the hour-metaphor to designate the time appointed by God for Jesus'

---

this logion shows signs of being pre-Markan (Kelber, "Gethsemane", 175-176), there is no good reason for including it in the primitive account and good basis for imagining that it was added to the account as paraenetic interests were heightened.

132 See Senior, *Passion*, 112, 118.
133 See above, chapter 3.XI.
134 See esp. Senior, *Passion*, 107, 110, 112; Birger Gerhardsson, "The Matthean Version of the Lord's Prayer (Matt 6:9b–13): Some Observations", in *NT Age*, 213, 216. Anthony Kenny ("The Transfiguration and the Agony in the Garden", *CBQ* 19 [1957] 450–452), however, goes too far in drawing out possible parallels between the Lukan version of the prayer on the Mount of Olives and the "Lord's Prayer".

passion (Mark 14:35; John 12:27). To be sure, the metaphorical use of "hour" is well attested in John (cf. 2:4; 7:30; 8:20; 12:23, 27; 13:1; 17:1), so one may be tempted to discount the force of this correspondence. The significance of its appearance here in both Gospels in parallel contexts should not be set aside too easily, however. Fourth, there is agreement on the use of the cup-metaphor (Mark 14:36; Luke 22:42; John 18:11) — which speaks of Jesus' bearing the judgment of God. Unlike ὥρα, ποτήριον is far removed from Johannine redactional interests, appearing in the Fourth Gospel only here; this is an important indicator of its traditional quality.

(7) As for the three-fold pattern whereby Jesus returns to find his disciples sleeping (Mark), whether or not this scheme existed as a part of the primitive passion narrative is irrelevant to our interpretive agenda. Hence, we may note only the previously-mentioned observation by Schenke that a simplified presentation of this motif (perhaps as is found in Luke?) would have served well to spotlight the main feature of this narrative, focused especially on Jesus' behavior[135].

(8) The problem presented by Mark 14:41—42 is not easily resolved. The question (statement?) to the disciples in 14:41a, unparalleled in Luke and John, is of little consequence to us here. In contrast, the Son of Man saying in v 41 is of great import, but it is also unparalleled; moreover, it closely models the passion prediction in Mark 9:31a. In fact, Luke omits all this material, and John evidences only a few scattered but comparable fragments. What, then, stems from the primitive passion account? In spite of the absence of strict parallels in the non-Markan material, a few constructive remarks are possible. First, Jesus' statement, "The hour has come" (v 41), obviously refers back to v 35, where Jesus asks if the hour might pass from him. Here, then, is an indicator that God's will for Jesus is that Jesus embrace this "hour". The same thought is introduced by the Son of Man logion, for the παραδίδωμι of v 41 points not simply to the impending act of ὁ παραδιδούς (v 42; cf. 14:18, 21), but also to divine agency[136]. Hence, in the process of praying at Gethsemane, Jesus discerns the certainty of the divine necessity of his passion and he resolves to follow the path marked out for him by God. In his own way, John testifies to this same idea — first, in 12:27, then in 18:11b. In 12:27 we are informed

---

135 Numerous interpreters regard this three-fold schema as a Markan development — e.g. Kelber, "Gethsemane", 170—172, 179, 186; idem, "The Hour of the Son of Man and the Temptation of the Disciples (Mark 14:32—42)", in Passion in Mark, 44, 47; Dibelius, Tradition, 182, 212—213; Lohse, Geschichte, 64. Mark has a fondness for the construction ἦσαν/ἦν + γάρ + parenthetical remark (cf. v 40b: "for their eyes were heavy") — e.g. 1:16, 22; 2:15; 5:42; 6:31, 48; 10:22; 14:40; 16:4. See Margaret E. Thrall, Greek Particles in the New Testament (Leiden: E. J. Brill, 1962) 41—50.

136 See, e.g., Hooker, Son of Man, 161—163.

that whereas Jesus contemplates a prayer for deliverance from "this hour", he quickly withdraws that request for he realizes that "this hour" is key to the redemptive purpose of God for which he was sent. Jesus acknowledges and submits to this purpose. Then, in 18:11 he again acknowledges that it was the Father who gave him this cup to drink. Additionally, through his words to Peter, he declares himself ready to drink that cup — i.e. to obey God by willingly entering the final road to Golgotha. Moreover, Mark 14:42 and John 14:31 both attest to Jesus' words to his disciples: ἐγείρεσθε, ἄγωμεν. If John has torn these words from an original context at the close of the Gethsemane-material, where they appear in Mark, this is further evidence from an early passion story of Jesus' willingness, even initiative, in following through in his submission to the will of God.

B. Conclusion

From our investigation of the narrative of Jesus' prayer at Gethsemane, we may outline the following observations.

(1) The early passion narrative contained an account of Jesus' prayer struggle, but in a form less developed than is read in the Synoptics and more extensive than is found in the Fourth Gospel. The episode was probably located at Gethsemane, and in all likelihood the account already provided a simple paraenetic comparison of Jesus' behavior with that of his disciples in which the motif of alertness/prayer was prominent. There is a high probability that the narrative spoke of Jesus' anguish and included Jesus' spoken testimony regarding his agony. A note to the effect that Jesus was heard by God may have been included. As for the content of Jesus' prayer, we have found reason to believe the primitive story recorded Jesus' contemplation of the possibility of deliverance from death, his subsequent focus on God's will over his own, and the hour- and cup-metaphors. Finally, the early account somehow indicated that Jesus left his prayer struggle convinced that God's will for him embraced his death and committed to a response of submission and obedience to God's will.

(2) Above all, this episode is cast as the crisis point in the passion story, the point at which Jesus irrevocably commits himself to a behavior marked by an acceptance of the necessity of his death as he submits to God's will.

(3) This does not mean, however, that Jesus is not affected by the prospect of his impending passion. Like the Righteous Sufferer, he is overwhelmed with anguish.

(4) God himself is active in bringing about Jesus' passion. "For this reason" Jesus was sent (John) and now God delivers him over to those who will have responsibility (humanly speaking) for Jesus' death (Mark).

(5) In employing the cup-metaphor here, the early story also gave expression to the notion that in his death Jesus would come under the judgment of God.

(6) Inasmuch as πειρασμός and γρηγορέω are used, there is evidence that the passion is the setting for a conflict of cosmic proportions, having eschatological significance, and involving supernatural forces.

(7) Before departing from this scene, we must inquire into the possibility that either a martyrological motif or an emphasis on the Isaianic Servant has been directly incorporated here, for the presence of both has been championed[137]. A number of points that might be marshalled in support of a martyrological interpretation of the passage — e.g. the emphasis on supernatural conflict or the presence of the cup-motif — are too general and too well-attested outside of martyrological contexts to be of any value here[138]. The most decisive argument against viewing this scene within a martyrological matrix is that, contrary to the boldness and unquestioned willingness to die characteristic of martyrs, Jesus actually puts forth a request for deliverance from death! Moreover, the presence of statements regarding Jesus' anguish in this pericope is diametrically opposed to the courage of the martyrs. The peaceful serenity that stands as the hallmark of martyr-tales is altogether lacking here.

Taylor, noting the degree of Jesus' anguish, suggests that Jesus was not simply shrinking from death, but rather from death *as he interpreted it*. That is, Jesus saw his passion as vicarious, along the model of the Suffering Servant. This interpretation, however, must be read into the text and so provides no justification for discerning the presence of the Servant-motif in this text. This does not mean the Servant-imagery is totally lacking, however. Even though there are no explicit references to the Servant (though see παραδίδωμι in Mark 14:41; Isa 52:13–53:12), there are some notable parallels between Jesus and the Servant in this context. The necessity of Jesus' suffering by way of fulfilling God's purpose and the willing obedience of Jesus — these are the two most prominent themes pointing to the figure of the Servant of Yahweh in Isa 49:4; 50:4–7; 52:13–53:12.

VI. The Arrest

A. Introduction

Like the narratives that frame it, the account of Jesus' arrest has served as the focal point of an active history of critical inquiry — and not only as a part of endeavors to exorcise the theological content from the historical. A number of formidable scholars — among them Bultmann, Jeremias,

---

137 On the idea of martyrdom, see Dibelius, "Gethsemane", 265–266. On the Servant-theme, see Taylor, *Jesus*, 149–150.
138 See, e.g., Green, "Mount of Olives".

Lohse, and Schneider — have argued that the oldest passion narrative began with a story of Jesus' arrest[139]. Others, pointing to the interrelationship of this scene with the Gethsemane episode, have overturned this widespread hypothesis, however[140]. The chief concern among students of this scene in its Markan form seems to have been with decomposing and explaining what appears to be a loose-fitting, hodgepodge account[141]. (In what follows, we will note some of the irregularities of the account in Mark[142].) With the notable exception of Linnemann's examination of this story, the consensus opinion has it that "Mk 14,43—52 wurde nie selbständig überliefert"[143].

B. *Mark 14:43—46; Matt 26:47—50; Luke 22:47—48, 52a, 54a; John 18: 2—6, 12*

For the most part, Matthew and Luke are dependent only on Mark in this first section of the arrest-scene. We have already observed the independence of both Matthew and Luke from Mark in the response to Judas's kiss (Matt 26:50a; Luke 22:48). In addition, Luke shows his reliance on a non-Markan account in 22:52a (the identification of the posse responsible for Jesus' arrest) and, possibly, in 22:54a (the narration of the actual event of Jesus' capture). These parallel traditions must be considered alongside the independent stories of Jesus' arrest in Mark and John.

All are agreed that a large group of persons, together with Judas, came to the place of Jesus' prayer seeking Jesus, but there is disparity as to the exact make-up of the group, the identity of the leaders responsible for the arresting party, and the precise role played by Judas. Our understanding of the theological significance of Jesus' death in the passion narrative does not turn on a determination of the precise identity of the arresting party. It seems most probable, however, that the primary actors here were Jewish[144]. More important is the stated role of Judas, and here the differences

---

139 Bultmann, *History*, 275, 277—279; Jeremias, *Eucharistic Words*, 89—96; Lohse, *Geschichte*, 23; Gerhard Schneider, "Die Verhaftung Jesu: Traditionsgeschichte von Mk 14:43—52", *ZNW* 63 (1972) 207.
140 Above all, see Schenke, *Christus*, 111—134. See also, Gnilka, *Mark*, 2:266. Mohr, *Passion*, 249—251.
141 Cf., e.g., Best, *Temptation and Passion*, 94; Lohse, *Geschichte*, 68; Taylor, *Mark*, 557, 656, 658; Gnilka, *Mark*, 2:266—268; Schenke, *Christus*, 114—124; Linnemann, *Studien*, 44—52; Schneider, "Verhaftung Jesu"; Mohr, *Passion*, 249—251; Dormeyer, *Passion Jesu*, 138—145; Schenk, *Passionsbericht*, 206—215. Surveys of attempts to explain the prehistory of the Markan text are given in Linnemann, *Studien*, 42—44; Schneider, "Verhaftung Jesu", 189—191.
142 For lists of the same, see esp. Schenke, *Christus*, 112—114; Linnemann, *Studien*, 41—42.
143 Mohr, *Passion*, 250. Similarly, Pesch, *Mark*, 2:397; Gnilka, *Mark*, 2:266; Schmithals, *Mark*, 2:645. Contra Linnemann, *Studien*, 41—69; esp. p. 46.
144 Catchpole (*Trial*, 149—151) argues that John's σπεῖρα and χιλίαρχος are Jewish, not Roman personages. If this interpretation is correct, then there is even more agreement between John and

among the evangelists are more apparent than real. John places Judas in the crowd (18:5 – μεθ' αὐτῶν), suggesting that Judas was only one among the many who stood over against Jesus. However, a theological *programme* is at work here, for John wants his readers to know that Judas, too, was overwhelmed by Jesus' presence and divine stature. In naming Judas as ὁ παραδιδοὺς αὐτόν (18:2, 5), and in recording that Judas obtained (λαβών) the soldiers, John's version accords well with the Synoptic picture of Judas as the instigator of the arrest process and as the guide (cf. 18:2: Judas knew where Jesus was) for the posse (cf. Acts 1:16). Thus, whereas Mark (followed by Matthew) is alone in recording the premeditation of a sign between Judas and the arresting party, it is not unreasonable to believe that John was aware of a parallel report. John does not record Judas's kiss of greeting and it might be urged on this account that Mark is the sole independent witness to this tradition. However, the convergence between Matthew and Luke on the narration of Jesus' response to the kiss suggests the antiquity of the report of the act itself. Moreover, in John 18: 4–6, John has allowed his redactional pen to rest especially heavy on the narrative by way of emphasizing Jesus' majesty, his foreknowledge, his initiative, his control over the passion events, and his willingness to give himself over to his enemies – so there was no room (theologically speaking) for Judas's kiss of greeting. (Similar ideas are suggested by the use of τότε in Matt 26:50: Jesus' words set the arrest into motion.) Hence, Judas's deceitful kiss should be traced back to the primitive passion story. It is here, in Judas's greeting and premeditation with the posse, that we may discern again the pattern of the Suffering Righteous – the opposing parties of whom are characterized by falsehood and deceit (cf. Pss 38:12; 41:6))[145].

Even though Luke omits the explanation found in Mark that the kiss was a sign, it is no less clear that the kiss was the means of betrayal, for Jesus himself says as much in 22:48. Matthew's ἑταῖρε, ἐφ' ὃ πάρει parallels Jesus' response in Luke, though it is obviously independent. The meaning of Jesus' statement in Matthew is widely debated[146], though a rendering along the lines of "What you are here for, let it take place" seems most

---

Luke on this point. It must be admitted, however, that Catchpole really has not done away with the most serious objection to his view arising from the apparent distinction between σπεῖρα and χιλίαρχος on the one side and οἱ ὑπηρέται τῶν Ἰουδαίων on the other in 18:12. Dauer (*Passionsgeschichte*, 27; cf. Schnackenburg, *John*, 3:222) decides that σπεῖρα and χιλίαρχος stem from John's source, but whereas they are understood as Romans by John, in the source they had some other significance.

145 See Lothar Ruppert, *Der leidende Gerechte und seine Feinde: Eine Wortfelduntersuchung* (Würzburg: Echter, 1973) 47–48; 132–139.
146 See the survey of possibilities in Stählin, "Φιλέω", 140 n.241; BDF, para. 300.2; Senior, *Passion*, 125–127.

probable¹⁴⁷. In any case, "... its difficulty suggests that it is not a Matthean creation"¹⁴⁸. Hence, though in different ways, both Matthew and Luke stress Jesus' prophetic insight (cf. Luke 7:39) and it may be that here is an element from the early tradition not preserved by Mark.

It almost goes without saying that here we have a fulfillment of Jesus' prophecy of Judas's betrayal.

Mark's narrative proceeds immediately to the actual arrest of Jesus while both Luke and John hold this event back for the finale of their respective accounts. The simplicity with which the actual arrest is reported underscores Jesus' resolve, stemming from his prayer-struggle at Gethsemane, to submit to God's will and thus now to the hands of his enemies. This motif will show itself even more clearly in the sword-incident that follows.

C. Mark 14:47; Matt 26:51–54; Luke 22:49–51; John 18:10–11

Schneider insists that the original arrest-account recounted no reaction of the disciples(s) to Jesus' arrest¹⁴⁹. Setting aside momentarily the fact that the Markan narrative Schneider has before him is not clear as to the identity of the aggressor in question, we may observe two points in the Markan text which support his contention. First, the introductory εἷς δέ τίς¹⁵⁰ τῶν. παρεστηκότων (14:47a) conforms to syntactical patterns found elsewhere in Mark. General parallels occur in the use of τινές/τίς + partitive genitive (cf. 2:6; 7:1, 2; 8:3; 9:1; 11:5; 12:13; 15:35) and of εἷς + partitive genitive (cf. 5:22; 6:15; 8:28; 9:37, 42; 10:37; 12:28; 13:1; 14:10, 20, 43, 66; 16:2). More specifically, one may refer to the instance of τινές/τίς + τῶν (παρ)εστηκότων in 9:1; 11:5; 15:35¹⁵¹. Second, even with the connecting δέ suggesting that the action in v 47 is a reaction to the arrest in v 46, a certain incongruity exists in the narrative sequence from vv 46–49. Thus, the sword-incident goes completely unnoticed by Jesus and the "αὐτοῖς" to whom he speaks in v 48 must refer back to the arresting party (οἱ) in v 46. Moreover, this incident introduces for the first time a representative of the high priest (cf. v 44).

On the other hand, it is surely remarkable that the other three evangelists knew a sword-incident apart from the Markan report. With this assertion

---

147 Matthew himself seems to have understood the saying thus – cf. his τότε in 26:51. Moreover, there are parallels for this idiom – cf. BDF, para. 300.2; Stählin, "Φιλέω", 140 n.241 ; Benoit, *Passion*, 40–41 n.1. This is the rendering adopted by, e.g., Senior, *Passion*, 127; Schweizer, *Matthew*, 495; Benoit, *Passion*, 40–41 ; BDF para. 300.2; Gundry, *Matthew*, 537.
148 Marshall, *Gospel of Luke*, 836.
149 Schneider, "Verhaftung Jesu", 201–202.
150 This reading is found in B C Θ Ψ f^{13} M a l vg sy^h, and the inclusion of τίς is further supported by D (it) W (f^1). In addition to the textual evidence, see the Markan texts listed below.
151 Cf. Schenke, *Christus*, 119; Dormeyer, *Passion Jesu*, 141.

we are not suggesting that Matthew has not taken his description of the episode from Mark, for Markan influence is apparent. Luke, too, has borrowed from the Markan account. However, the four areas of convergence between two or three of the other evangelists against Mark strongly intimate the existence of parallel, non-Markan tradition.

(1) Matt 26:51; Luke 22:49; John 18:10 — the designation of the sword-bearer as a disciple. The diversity with which this identification is made (Matthew — εἷς τῶν μετὰ Ἰησοῦ; Luke — ἰδόντες δὲ οἱ περὶ αὐτὸν τὸ ἐσόμενον εἶπαν κύριε ... ; John — Σίμων ... Πέτρος) speaks against any direct literary relationship between the three.

(2) Luke 22:50; John 18:10 — the *right* ear. The judgment that this detail is an embellishment of the earliest tradition[152], if true, still does not detract from the significance of this agreement as a testimony to Luke's and John's awareness of a parallel, non-Markan traditon.

(3) Matt 26:52—54; Luke 22:51; John 18:11 — all three agree against Mark that Jesus responded to the wielding of the sword with a negative command. Though in strikingly different ways, in each case it is stressed that Jesus will offer no resistance for all is proceeding according to the plan of God. Whatever attempts are made to counter the divine plan must be firmly rejected.

(4) Matt 26:52; John 18:11 — the command to re-sheath the sword: Matthew: ἀπόστρεψον τὴν μάχαιράν σου εἰς τὸν τόπον αὐτῆς; John: βάλε τὴν μάχαιραν εἰς τὴν θήκην[153].

With these considerations in view, we should not be swayed so much by the problems of the Markan text that we opt for the unoriginality of this aspect of the narrative in the primitive account. Most probably, at the root of an apparently complex *traditionsgeschichtliche* entanglement lies an arrest-scene inclusive of the sword-incident and a simple command of Jesus to the disciples against any form of resistance[154].

D. Mark 14:48—49; Matt 26:55—56a; Luke 22:52—53; John 18:20

Matthew and Luke[155] do not seem to have been influenced by a non-Markan source at this juncture. However, John knows a parallel, which he locates in the narrative of Jesus' trial before the high priest. The similarity between the Markan and Johannine versions extends beyond the bare mention of Jesus' teaching to emphasize its public character; in addition, as Dodd has maintained, the ethos of the two scenes is similar[156]. This suggests the traditional character of the motif in the early passion story[157]. Again, though, there are problems regarding the possibility that these

---

152 So, e.g., Taylor, *Mark*, 560; Marshall, *Gospel of Luke*, 837.
153 Efforts to find Matthean creation in 26:52a (e.g. Senior, *Passion*, 132—133) must not overlook this point of correspondence.
154 Cf. the view of Rehkopt (*Sonderquelle*, 65—71) that an older source lies behind both Mark 14:47 and Luke 22:50.
155 See above, chapter 3.XII.
156 Dodd, *Historical Tradition*, 92—93.
157 So Lindars, *John*, 550; Dodd, *Historical Tradition*, 92—93. Barrett (*John*, 528) sees the connection, but ascribes it to John's dependence on Mark. Noting the proliferation of Johannine editorial features here, Dauer (*Passionsgeschichte*, 80—81) and Schnackenburg (*John*, 3:237) regard 18:20 as a free invention by the Fourth Evangelist.

verses are indigenous to the pre-Markan tradition. Most importantly, as a number of commentators have noticed[158], Jesus' words are best understood as directed to the Jewish leaders — but in Mark's narrative there are no Jewish leaders at hand, but only their representatives. Lest this obstacle seem insurmountable, it is well to recall that the Lukan narrative has it that the Jewish leaders were present at the arrest. If the Lukan narrative is the more primitive on this point, then Jesus' words make good sense in this context. If not, it is still possible (and the Markan-Johannine parallel speaks in favor of this possibility) that the logion of Mark 14:49 was included in the early passion account, perhaps in the Jewish trial-scene, and has been relocated in the tradition witnessed by Mark. In this latter case, 14:48 may well have been a Markan construction (cf. conjunction + ἀποκριθείς + a form of λέγω + dative — 3:33; 6:37; 8:29; 9:5, 19; 10:3, 24, 51; 11:14, 22, 33; 12:35; 15:2, 12; ἀποκριθείς to introduce an "answer" to an event — 9:5; 10:51; 11:14[159]; and the similar vocabulary in 14:43)[160]. In any case, the use of λῃστής in 14:48 should not tempt us to interpret Jesus' death as that of a revolutionary, given the tone of admonishment characterizing Jesus' words here.

Mark 14:49b (ἀλλ' ἵνα πληρωθῶσιν αἱ γραφαί) is paralleled in Matthew and Luke, though these two evangelists recast the idea of divine necessity in their own ways. A similar theme has already appeared in the response of Jesus to the attempt to free him by means of swordplay in Matthew, Luke, and John. Hence, in some way, all of the evangelists witness to the notion that the arrest of Jesus happened as a part of God's plan, and that Jesus allowed his arrest as a corollary to his submission to God's will.

E. Mark 14:50–52; Matt 26:56b; John 18:7–9

Luke omits the flight of the disciples for theological reasons, and John has removed the scandal from their apparent cowardice by showing how Jesus arranged for their release. While the thought of substitutionary death may not be far from view here (cf. John 11:50), John himself interprets Jesus' action as the fulfillment of an earlier Jesus-logion (18:9; cf. 6:39; 17:12). Hence, we are left with only one independent witness to the flight of the disciples — Mark 14:50, and it fits well into the narrative sequence as the reaction of the disciples to Jesus' arrest. There is every possibility that this brief notice stems from earliest tradition[161]; indeed, it is difficult

---

158 E.g., Taylor, *Mark*, 560; Nineham, *Mark*, 396; Schweizer, *Mark*, 318; et al.
159 See Schneider, "Verhaftung Jesu", 202.
160 Schneider, "Verhaftung Jesu", 202–204; Schenke, *Christus*, 120; Dormeyer, *Passion Jesu*, 141–143; Schenk, *Passionsbericht*, 213–215 — all regard 14:48–49 as Markan.
161 So, e.g., Dormeyer, *Passion Jesu*, 143–144; Schenke, *Christus*, 121–122; Schenk, *Passionsbericht*, 215; Mohr, *Passion*, 250. *Contra* Best, *Mark*, 11; Schneider, "Verhaftung Jesu", 204–205.

to imagine the early church inventing such a slanderous episode. Like the Suffering Righteous, Jesus is forsaken by his friends (cf. Pss 31:11–12; 38:11; 69:9; 88:8)[162]. In addition, this act fulfills the Scriptures and Jesus' own prophecy (Zech 13:7; Mark 14:27).

As for the flight of the young man recorded in Mark 14:51–52, this report has the appearance of having been appended to the generalizing statement in 14:50[163]. Neither of the two Synoptic writers borrowed this note from Mark, nor do they present any alternative parallel. Before dismissing this report as an addition to the pre-canonical story by Mark, however, one should not fail to notice the presence of the "other disciple" in John 18:15–16. Mark's "young man" and John's "other disciple" appear in the narrative sequence at approximately the same time, and though their roles are different in each case, neither has any significant function. Indeed, in both instances – the Markan and Johannine – the mention of an unnamed disciple seems enigmatic, and this has resulted in a plethora of speculation regarding the redactional significance of each[164]. Is it perhaps too simplistic to suggest that the most obvious route out of this labyrinth is the correct one? Could it not be that the early passion account knew of a person who was present here as an eyewitness[165], and that this record has been preserved in variant ways by Mark and John? Like Mark 15:21 (the drafting of Simon of Cyrene to carry the cross), then, this note would contain an historical reminiscence.

In any case, the presence (or absence) of this report (i.e. Mark 14:51–

---

162 See Ruppert, *Feinde*, 145–149; Pesch, *Mark*, 2:402; Schenke, *Christus*, 133; Schneider, "Verhaftung Jesu", 206.
163 Many exegetes speak of the awkwardness of the literary connection between vv 50 and 51 – e.g. Dibelius, *Tradition*, 182; Schenke, *Christus*, 122; Taylor, *Mark*, 561; Nineham, *Mark*, 396; Schenk, *Passionbericht*, 212; Dormeyer, *Passion Jesu*, 144–145; Lane, *Mark*, 526–527.
164 For the history of interpretation of the Markan text, see Frans Neirynck, "La fuite du jeune homme en Mc 14,51–52", in *Evangelica*, 215–238. The brief account has especially been exposed to symbolic interpretations – cf. Albert Vanhoye, "La fuite du jeune homme nu (Mc 14, 51–52)", *Bib* 52 (1971) 401–406 (an enigmatic prefiguration of Jesus' death); Robin Scroggs and Kent I. Groff, "Baptism in Mark: Dying and Rising with Christ", *JBL* 92 (1973) 531–548; esp. pp. 541–542 (baptism); Harry Fleddermann, "The Flight of the Naked Young Man (Mark 14:51–52)", *CBQ* 41 (1979) 412–418 (a dramatization and concretization of the flight of the disciples that signifies the disciples in contrast with Jesus). The symbolic approach to the exegesis of this text has been called into question by Michel Gourgues, "A propos du symbolisme christologique et baptismal de Marc 16,5", *NTS* 27 (1980–81) 672–678. It is surprising that no more has been made of the obvious parallels centering on the common ideas of watching and nakedness in this context and in a text like Rev 16:15.
For the history of interpretation of the Johannine text, see Frans Neirynck, "The 'Other' Disciple in Jn 18:15–16", in *Evangelica*, 335–364. Scholars are divided on whether this expression was introduced into a Synoptic-like account by the Fourth Evangelist (e.g. Haenchen, "History and Interpretation", 204; Lindars, *John*, 548) or was already present in his source (e.g. Dauer, *Passionsgeschichte*, 73–75; Schnackenburg, *John*, 3:235).

52) in the primitive passion account does not alter our understanding of the interpretation of the death of Jesus in the early account.

F. Conclusion

From our investigation of the accounts of the arrest of Jesus, we may outline the following observations.

(1) Tradition-critical problems with the accounts of this episode are legend. Nevertheless, we can speak with virtual certainty of the presence of an arrest-scene located in the proximity of Gethsemane in the primitive passion account. In this scene, Judas plays out his role as betrayer — both as organizer of the means by which Jesus would be taken into custody and as the one who located and identified Jesus with a kiss of greeting. There is a good probability that the story recounted the sword-incident — the purpose of which was to free Jesus from the arresting party. Equally probable is the report of Jesus' refusal to be a part of such an escape attempt and his admonishment to the swordbearer. Though in a simplified form when compared with the Gospel accounts, the early narrative likely included Jesus' mention of his public ministry by way of admonishing his captors for their stealth — though this part of the tradition may have originally stood in the Jewish trial scene. In some fashion, during his arrest, it is probable that Jesus is said to have given notice that this event was part of God's plan. A brief report of the flight of the disciples was also included in this narrative.

(2) The most pervasive motif given expression in this pericope is the realization that Jesus' passion — and thus his arrest — was integral to God's plan. Because Jesus had already resolved to submit to the divine will, he now submits to his captors. Any attempts to resist arrest are therefore attempts to resist God's will and must be halted.

(3) Also of theological importance here is the typological correspondence between Jesus and the Suffering Righteous: he is the victim of falsehood and deceit; his friends forsake him; he is alone in his suffering.

(4) There is the further, general motif of fulfillment of Scripture — either generally (Mark 14:49; cf. 1 Cor 15:3—5) or specifically (Mark 14:60; cf. 14:27; Zech 13:7), and of Jesus' own prophecy (Mark 14:27, 50; cf. John 18:9). Jesus is shown to be a true prophet both by the fact that his predictions come true and by the prophetic insight with which he is able to perceive the deceit behind Judas's kiss of greeting.

---

165 Trocmé (*Passion*, 70—71) and Dormeyer (*Passion Jesu*, 144—145) both regard vv 51—52 as stemming from the earliest passion account. Noting the significance of the young man and of Simon of Cyrene as eyewitnesses, Dibelius (*Tradition*, 183; cf. pp. 182—183, 204) writes: "It follows that these two references are older than the Gospel".

VII. Peter's Denial and Jesus before the Sanhedrin

A. The Petrine Tradition

Despite the magnitude of scholarly attention paid it in recent years, the narrative of Peter's denial continues to raise haunting historical (*historische*) and tradition-critical questions for modern exegetes[166]. Our observations regarding what this pericope has to offer *as regards an interpretation of Jesus' death in the passion account* do not rest on the outcome of these exegetical complexities, so it will suffice to bring forward a few earlier remarks concerning the inclusion of this scene in the primitive passion account before moving on to a more detailed consideration of Jesus' hearing before the Jewish leadership. First, we have already demonstrated that in the Gospels of Mark, Luke, and John we have access to three parallel but independent accounts[167]. Second, against the general consensus on this issue[168], we indicated that the intercalation of the denial-sequence with the trial-scene in Mark and John did not orginate with the Second Evangelist, but should be traced back to a very early (though not to the earliest) stage in the developing tradition. As we suggested[169], the intertwining (*not* "sandwiching") of these two narratives served a paraenetic purpose, for the result of the employment of this literary device in this context is the achievement of the starkest contrast between Jesus' brave and exemplary confession before the Sanhedrin and Peter's traumatic and cowardly denial of any relationship with Jesus while in the courtyard.

Before leaving this scene, one note of interpretive significance should be sounded. In "following from afar" (Mark 14:54; Luke 22:54) and in denying Jesus, Peter appears in the dress of the friend (the companion, the neighbor) of the Suffering Righteous. Special attention may be directed to the correspondence between Mark 14:54 (ὁ Πέτρος ἀπὸ μακρόθεν ἠκολούθησεν) and Ps 38:11 (37:12 LXX: οἱ ἔγγιστά μου ἀπὸ μακρόθεν

---

[166] Among the pertinent studies, see Klein, "Verleugnung"; Rudolf Pesch, "Die Verleugnung des Petrus: Eine Studien zu Mk 14,54.66–72 (und Mk 14,26–31)", in *NT und Kirche*, 42–62; Schneider, *Verleugnung*, 73–96; Linnemann, *Studien*, 70–108; Wilcox, "Denial Sequence", 433–436; Schenke, *Christus*, 15–23; Schenk, *Passionsbericht*, 215–223; Dormeyer, *Passion Jesu*, 150–155; Dewey, "Peter's Curse"; Mohr, *Passion*, 276–281.

[167] See chapters 3.XIII and 4.

[168] As represented by, e.g., Lohse, *Geschichte*, 69; Schenke, *Christus*, 15–16; Best, *Temptation and Passion*, 94; Gnilka, *Mark*, 2:275; Schweizer, *Mark*, 321; Winter, *Trial*, 33; Schenk, *Passionsbericht*, 215; Dormeyer, *Passion Jesu*, 150. Neirynck ("Other Disciple", 352–354) cites this general unanimity and suggests that " . . . the Fourth Evangelist was not unaware of the Markan model of sandwiching the Peter story" (354).

[169] See above, chapter 4. Cf. also Birger Gerhardsson, "Confession and Denial before Men: Observations on Matt 26:57–27:2", *JSNT* 13 (1981) 46–66; Senior, *Passion: Mark*, 86–88. Winter (*Trial*, 33) speaks of an "hortatory interest" at work here.

ἔστησαν). Even if this phrase is redactional in Mark[170], the motif of the faithless friend is certainly pre-Markan, and it belongs within the sphere of ideas associated with the *passio-iusti* theme[171].

B. Mark 14:53; Matt 26:57; Luke 22:54b, 66ab; John 18:13–14, 24

As with the report of the trial itself, so here in this introductory verse Matthew has followed his Markan source. He and John name the high priest as Caiaphas, but this is no reason to argue in favor of a second source for Matthew (cf. Matt 26:3)[172]. For his part, Luke has adopted material from his *Sonderquelle* in 22:66[173]. Thus, alternative group-names are used in Luke when compared with Mark, but on the *dramatic personae* involved, the two evangelists are still in substantial harmony. Nevertheless, the two accounts differ as to the timing of the "trial" (Mark – immediately after the arrest; Luke – the following morning) and the nature of the event (Mark writes of a more formal hearing than does Luke). As for John's account, here we encounter what Pierre Benoit has rightly described as "a celebrated problem"[174], for John's narrative bristles with difficulties, both with respect to internal consistency and with regard to attempts at harmonization with the Synoptics.

Concerning internal problems with John's account we may observe the following. (1) Much is made of Caiaphas's identity (18:13, 14, 24); yet,

---

170 So, e.g., Schenke, *Christus*, 16. Contra Schenk, *Passionsbericht*, 218; Dormeyer, *Passion Jesu*, 149–150 (who concludes that 14:54c is the handiwork of R's, the pre-Markan redactor). The combination ἀπό + μακρόθεν appears in the Second Gospel in 5:6; 8:3; 11:13; 14:54; 15:40. Luke uses it in 16:23. Apart from the Synoptic texts borrowing the expression from Mark (Matt 26:58; 27:55; Luke 23:49), it occurs elsewhere in the NT only in Rev 18:10, 15, 17.
171 Ruppert, *Feinde*, 85–96.
172 Pesch (*Mark*, 2:21) thinks it highly significant that whereas Matthew (26:3, 57), Luke (3:2; Acts 4:6), and John (11:49; 18:13, 14, 24, 28) all identify the high priest as Caiaphas, Mark does not. "Deiser Sachverhalt, welcher Voraussetzung lokaler Kenntnisse bei den Hörern der Passionsgeschichte entspricht legt den Schluss (nahezu zwingend) nahe, dass Kajafas als Hohenpriester noch amtierte, als die [vormarkinische] Passionsgeschichte zunächst gebildet und erzählt wurde. Kajafas amtierte von 18–37 n.Chr. Als *terminus ante quem* der Entstehung der [vormarkinische] Passionsgeschichte ist folglich das Jahr 37 n.Chr. zu nennen". (Whether Caiaphas served as high priest to the year 37 – see Jeremias, *Jerusalem*, 155, or 36 – see Schürer, *History*, 2:230, is not the main point at issue here.) One might wish to dismiss this viewpoint with an appeal to the Gospel of Mark's Gentile origins (see Brown, *John*, 2:821) or the evangelist's lack of interest in a denial of this kind. Elsewhere in his Gospel, however, Mark is willing enough to include material from his sources that are Jewish in orientation. Moreover, in view of what was said earlier about the character of Mark as a conservative redactor (see above, chapter 5), it is doubtful that he would have deleted this detail if he had found it in his tradition. Indeed, no theological purpose motivated his retention of the name of Simon of Cyrene (and of his two sons!) in 15:21. Even so, the absence of Caiaphas's name at this juncture in the Lukan version should teach us to regard with caution Pesch's argument from silence.
173 See above, chapter 3.XV.
174 Pierre Benoit, "Jesus before the Sanhedrin", in *Jesus*, 1:154.

when Jesus is taken to Caiaphas in 18:24, we hear nothing of what transpired. (2) Before Jesus is transferred to Caiaphas, he is questioned by the "high priest" (18:19—23), but this person is never named and we only assume from 18:24 that it was in fact *Annas* who conducted this hearing. (3) Yet it was Caiaphas and the Sanhedrin who plotted against Jesus (11: 47—53) and who were responsible for sending out a segment of the arresting party (18:3, 12). One might therefore have anticipated their playing an important role in the subsequent trial process. (4) Indeed, John apparently was aware that Caiaphas and the Jewish leaders were involved. Not only does he relate that Jesus was taken to Caiaphas (18:24), but we also discover in 18:28 that "the Jews" led Jesus from Caiaphas to Pilate. Where is the "missing" account?

What are the salient points at which the accounts of the Synoptics and John diverge? (1) Most obviously, the Synoptics say nothing of an Annas-Jesus dialogue, but (2) do speak of a trial of some kind before the Jewish Council. On both points their accounts are to be distinguished from John's. (3) Mark narrates a formal trial, John an informal hearing — and in this the Third and Fourth Evangelists are in general harmony[175]. (4) In John the high priest questions Jesus "about his disciples and his teaching", whereas in the Synoptics the interest falls more directly on the issue of Messiahship.

Attempts at resolving these issues are legend, if not altogether satisfactory. They have been surveyed briefly in Schnackenburg's commentary, and we need not repeat his work[176]. Instead, we shall attempt to outline a solution, borrowing insight from Schnackenburg and from Dauer[177]. (1) "Annas" appears in the NT only 4 times — Luke 3:2; John 18:13, 24; Acts 4:6. John is much more interested in Caiaphas than Annas, and in fact presents the latter in the most unadorned way. Why mention him at all? Apparently without theological or literary provocation, Annas is introduced as a competing figure in the passion drama. We must assume therefore that John is here dependent on earlier tradition. (2) The content of the Johannine hearing (regarding Jesus' public ministry) is not peculiar to John, even if it does differ markedly from what is reported of the Sanhedrin hearing in Mark and Luke. Earlier[178], we determined the good probability that it was present already in the primitive passion account.

---

175 David Rensberger's assertion ("The Politics of John: The Trial of Jesus in the Fourth Gospel", *JBL* 103 [1984] 400) — "... in contrast to the Synoptic narrative, no Jewish court ever formally charges or condemns Jesus ..." — assumes a false unanimity among the Synoptic account. In fact, a formal sentence against Jesus is lacking in Luke, too.
176 Schnackenburg, *John*, 3:230—232.
177 Dauer, *Passionsgeschichte*, 62—99; Schnackenburg, *John*, 3:232—233. See also Dodd, *Historical Tradition*, 88—96; Lindars, *John*, 548.
178 See above, chapter 8.VI.D.

Again, then, here is reason for rejecting any view that identifies this hearing as a Johannine creation. (3) John was certainly cognizant of Synoptic-like material regarding Jesus' Jewish trial. He has used such material in his Gospel, distributing it widely (cf. 2:9; 10:24–26, 33, 36; 18:24, 28). This suggests that either John had access to two competing traditions he has chosen to harmonize, or his narrative source recorded both the hearing before the Sanhedrin and the Annas-trial, and he has retained only the latter in his passion narrative. In either case, he could easily have been motivated by his apparent interest in sharpening the role of the Romans in the whole arrest-trial process[179]. (4) Nevertheless, the Fourth Evangelist's editorial activity with respect to his tradition(s) was not as aggressive as it could have been, so outcroppings of a tradition regarding the second hearing/trial remain, complicating his story.

(5) Can anything more definite be said about the tradition inherited by John? In our discussion of Luke's passion narrative we observed both that Luke's account of the hearing before the Sanhedrin pictured a less formal event than the Markan parallel and that Luke includes no formal sentence pronounced by the Jewish body[180]. It is certainly striking that with respect to these two points John's version is closer to Luke's than to Mark's. One may observe further parallels between Luke 22:67–68 and John 10:24. That Luke and John were not making independent use of the same source is guaranteed in view of the explicit charge of blasphemy and the slippery mention of the second hearing in John (10:33; 18:24). These two points notwithstanding, the pre-Johannine tradition and that employed by Luke most probably came into contact with one another early on. We may conjecture that the source used by John narrated both the hearing before Annas and the hearing before the Sanhedrin, and that John was unwilling completely to sunder the latter from his own account or to allow it to stand in its passion context as a unit. This was due to his focus in the passion narrative on the agency of the Romans and his desire to preserve the less formal character of the hearing taken from his passion source. Thus, our solution is not slavishly harmonistic, but recognizes a complex interaction between the traditions in the pre-Gospel period.

What can be said about the section of the primitive passion account now under review? First, how Annas was introduced into the developing tradition must remain the subject of speculation; his scarcity in the pages of the NT and his absence from the passion stories of the Synoptic Gospels speak overwhelmingly against his having been mentioned in the earliest account. According to that original narrative, Jesus was most probably

---

179 On this emphasis, see Rensberger, "Politics".
180 See above, chapter 3.XV.

led before the Sanhedrin. We have already noted the likelihood that the less formal hearing is the more historical[181]; moreover, it has long been noted that the Luke chronology of the trial before the Jews is the most probable from an historical viewpoint[182]. One might therefore expect that the Lukan witness to the *character* of the hearing (which receives some confirmation from John) and its *timing* represents the more original.

Of course, it might be objected that one cannot simply draw the general equation, the most historical equals the earliest tradition (or vice versa). However, two additional considerations serve to support just such a conclusion in this instance. First, as the Lukan narrative stands, a whole night stands "empty" with the respect to the criminal process. It is not unreasonable to imagine that in the developing tradition this intervening period of inaction was dropped as the whole scene came to be viewed, as it were, through a telescopic lens. The interweaving of the accounts of the trial and the denial as observed in Mark and John would have helped this process along, filling in the hours not otherwise used in the story line. Indeed, Linnemann has rightly observed that the Markan trial, when considered entirely on its own, has no *Zeitangabe*[183]. Second, with increased tensions between Christians and Jews, the desire to accentuate the role played by the Jews in the trial process, along with the desire to draw even more attention to the travesty of justice represented by the proceedings, could have been added to the cauldron in which the developing passion story was brewing, with the result that certain phrases were transformed and nuances added to render the hearing more formal, the condemnation by the Jews more explicit.

C. Mark 14:55−64; Matt 26:59−66; Luke 22:66−71; John 10:22−39

The history of the interpretation of Mark 14:55−64, "Jesus before the Sanhedrin", could easily prove the focal point of a fascinating case study in the complex interaction of *historische, überlieferungsgeschichtliche, traditionsgeschichtliche, redaktionsgeschichtliche,* and *dogmatische* concerns in the exegetical task. This scene has been the subject of a virtual

---

181 In addition to our discussion in chapter 3.XV, see Tyson, "Lucan Version", 253.
182 See, e.g., Benoit, "Jesus before the Sanhedrin", 153−154; Marshall, *Gospel of Luke,* 847; Catchpole, *Trial*; Tyson, "Lucan Version", 253.
183 Linnemann, *Studien,* 109 n.1. A. N. Sherwin-White (*Roman Society and Roman Law in the New Testament* [Oxford: Oxford University, 1963; reprint ed., Grand Rapids, Michigan: Baker, 1978] 45) regards the Markan time-table as the correct one, pointing to the "quite unessential detail of the fire": "Why light a fire − an act of some extravagance − if everyone was sleeping through the night?" Similarly, F. F. Bruce, "The Trial of Jesus in the Fourth Gospel", in *Gospel Perspectives,* 1:11. Sherwin-White thus takes the interpretation of Jesus' trial and Peter's denial as representative of historical timing and not as a literary phenomenon. His reasoning is hardly compelling, however: Luke does not have everyone "sleeping through the night"!

flood of articles and monographs witnessing to a wide diversity of conclusions on every major issue[184]. While our investigation cannot totally circumvent this larger debate, it is nevertheless true that our real concern dictates that we enter the discussion only at those points having to do with the primitive form of this scene and its interpretation of Jesus' death.

With the possible exception of 26:61 and the command to "tell us" in 26:62, Matthew has merely rewritten his Markan source here[185]. As for Luke's account, we have already determined its largely non-Markan character[186]. In his trial-scene, John has no strict parallel to this episode, but his awareness of this tradition is manifest earlier in his Gospel (10:22–39). Here, John's material shows points of contact with the Lukan narrative.

Among the three independent renditions, Mark's is alone in recording that the council was seeking testimony against Jesus, that false witnesses did speak against Jesus, that the temple-saying was used against Jesus, and that Jesus was silent before his accusers (14:55–61a). That the testimony was *false* emphasizes Jesus' innocence; his silence recalls that of the Suffering Servant[187]; and the whole narration of this sub-pericope is reminiscent of the action taken against the Suffering Righteous[188]. The crucial question,

---

184 Recent literature on the Markan text and parallels includes David Flusser, "A Literary Approach to the Trial of Jesus", *Judaism* 20 (1971) 32–36; Josef Blinzler, "The Trial of Jesus in the Light of History", *Judaism* 20 (1971) 49–55; idem, *Der Prozess Jesu* (Regensburg: Friedrich Pustet, 1969); Gerard S. Sloyan, "The Last Days of Jesus", *Judaism* 20 (1971) 56–68; idem, *Jesus on Trial: The Development of the Passion Narratives and Their Historical and Ecumenical Implications* (Philadelphia: Fortress, 1973); Haim Cohn, "Reflections on the Trial of Jesus", *Judaism* 20 (1971) 10–23; idem, *The Trial and Death of Jesus* (London: Weidenfeld and Nicolson, 1972); Benoit, "Jesus before the Sanhedrin"; Linnemann, *Studien*, 109–135; Schenke, *Christus*, 23–46; Schneider, *Verleugnung*; Donahue, "Temple"; Norman Perrin, "The High Priest's Question and Jesus' Answer (Mark 14:61–62)", in *Passion in Mark*, 80–95; Mohr, *Passion*, 252–275; Winter, *Trial*; Dormeyer, *Passion Jesu*, 157–174; Schenk, *Passionsbericht*, 229–243; Dieter Lührmann, "Markus 14,55–64: Christologie und Zerstörung des Tempels im Markusevangelium", *NTS* 27 (1981) 457–474; Sanders, *Jesus*, 294–318; August Strobel, *Die Stunde der Wahrheit: Untersuchungen zum Strafverfahren gegen Jesus* (Tübingen: J. C. B. Mohr [Paul Siebeck], 1980); William Riley Wilson, *The Execution of Jesus: A Judicial, Literary and Historical Investigaton* (New York: Charles Scribner's Sons, 1968); William Horbury, "The Trial of Jesus in Jewish Tradition", in *Trial of Jesus*, 103–121; J. C. O'Neill, "The Charge of Blasphemy at Jesus' Trial before the Sanhedrin", in *Trial of Jesus*, 72–77; D. R. Catchpole, "The Problem of the Historicity of the Sanhedrin Trial", in *Trial of Jesus*, 47–65; idem, *Trial*; Harvey, *Jesus*, 11–35; K. Schubert, "Biblical Criticism Criticised: With Reference to the Markan Report of Jesus' Examination before the Sanhdrein", in *Jesus and Politics*, 385–402.
185 On the possible antiquity of 26:61 when compared with Mark 14:58, see Sanders, *Tendencies*, 292; Schweizer, *Matthew*, 499.
186 See above, chapter 3.XV.
187 See, e.g., Isa 53:7; Acts 8:32–33; 1 Pet 2:23; Strauss, *Jesus*, 657; Swete, *Mark*, 358; Goppelt, *Typos*, 101; Pesch, *Mark*, 2:436; Moo, *OT – Passion*, 149, 248–249; Senior, *Passion: Mark*, 94. Contra Best, *Temptation and Passion*, 151.
188 See, e.g., Pss 27:12; 31:18; 35:11, 20; 37:32; Wis 2:20; Ruppert, *Jesus*, 52; Goppelt, *Typos*, 101; Pesch, *Mark*, 2:431–432; Gnilka, *Mark*, 279–280; Donahue, "Temple", 67; Taylor, *Mark*, 566.

then, is whether this material existed in the primitive passion story, and we may initiate our discussion of this issue by directing our attention to the temple-saying.

While the authenticity of the Jesus-logion upon which this charge is based should not be denied[189], its originality to the present context may be questioned. One aspect of the saying in particular, the χειροποίητος-ἀχειροποίητος contrast, is regarded as secondary by many scholars who see in it the influence of Hellenism or who note its absence from the parallels[190]. Indeed, one might argue against the genuineness of the whole saying in this context due to the variety of contexts in which it is found in the Gospels and Acts[191]. By far the most significant argument in favor of viewing the temple-charge as a later amendment is set forth by Donahue: its apparent artificiality – i.e. the charge plays no role in the trial[192].

The kingpin in Donahue's argument is his rejection of the messianic significance of the temple-charge. Noting the number of scholars who hold that Mark 14:58 reflects a current Jewish expectation that the Messiah would build a new temple, he counters that "... this 'expectation' is more a creation of contemporary scholarship than a motif of first century Jewish thought". After listing the variety of expectations concerning the temple, he concludes: "What is lacking prior to Mk is the definite conjunction of destruction and rebuilding of the Temple which is attributed to a person other than Yahweh". In thus denying the messianic connotations of the temple-charge, Donahue finds himself in company with other scholars – including Linnemann and Lührmann[193].

---

189 See, e.g., Mark 15:29: οὐὰ ὁ καταλύων τὸν ναὸν καὶ οἰκοδομῶν ἐν τρισὶν ἡμέραις; Matt 26:61: δύναμαι καταλῦσαι τὸν ναὸν τοῦ θεοῦ καὶ διὰ τριῶν ἡμερῶν οἰκοδομῆσαι; John 2:19: λύσατε τὸν ναὸν τοῦτον καὶ ἐν τρισὶν ἡμέραις ἐγερῶ αὐτόν; Acts 6:14: Ἰησοῦς ὁ αζωραῖος οὗτος καταλύσει τὸν τόπον τοῦτον; Gos. Thom. 71: ⲡⲉⲝⲉ ⲓ̅ⲥ̅ ϫⲉ ϯⲛⲁϣⲟⲣϣ̅ⲣ̅ ⲙⲡⲉⲉⲓⲏⲉⲓ ⲁⲩⲱ ⲙⲛ̅ ⲗⲁⲁⲩ ⲛⲁϣ ⲕⲟⲧϥ︥ⲟⲛ ⲛⲕⲉⲥⲟⲡ Bultmann, History, 120; Bornkamm, Jesus, 163; Cranfield, Mark, 441–442; Hengel, "Between Jesus and Paul", 22; Meyer, Aims, 180–185; Sanders, Jesus, 71–75.
190 See, e.g., Lindars, NT Apologetic, 68–69; Cranfield, Mark, 442; Catchpole, Trial, 129; James D. G. Dunn, "The Messianic Secret in Mark", in Messianic Secret, 125; Pesch, Mark, 2:434; Hengel, Jesus and Paul, 151–152 n.138.
191 Cf. Lohse, Geschichte, 82–93; Linnemann, Studien, 116–127.
192 John R. Donahue, "Temple, Trial and Royal Christology (Mark 14:53–65)", in Passion in Mark, 62, 66–71; cf. the similar comment in Sanders, Jesus, 72. Schenke (Christus, 33–37), Dormeyer (Passion Jesu, 159–162) and Mohr (Passion, 102–104) – none of these interpreters regard the temple-charge as original to the passion story.
193 Donahue, "Temple", 68; Linnemann, Studien, 125–127; Lührmann, "Markus 14,55–64", 465. Scholars affirming the messianic significance of the temple-charge include Otto Betz, What Do We Know about Jesus? (London: SCM, 1968) 88–91; Kim, Son of Man, 79–80, 83–84; Senior, Passion: Mark, 93; Dunn, "Messianic Secret", 125–126; Taylor, Mark, 566–567; Meyer, Aims, 179–180; Pesch, Mark, 2:434–435; Dormeyer, Passion Jesu, 160. Supporting the more general view that the temple-saying is well-suited to contemporary Jewish eschatological expectation are Sanders, Jesus, 77–90; Jeremias, Eucharistic Words, 217.

The obvious response to Donahue is to draw attention to the fact that the temple-charge *is* located in this scene. If Donahue is correct, then how can our account move directly from temple-charge to the messianic question? If the temple-charge has no function here, why would Mark have introduced it here? Donahue's thesis that the temple-statement has been introduced in order that the evangelist might in this way bring to culmination the anti-Jerusalem and anti-temple polemic traced throughout his Gospel is not an adequate solution for two reasons. First, Mark's (alleged) purpose would have been far better served if this statement had been placed on *Jesus'* lips and not on those of *false witnesses*. Second, Donahue has still not reckoned with the issue raised by the presence of the logion *here*, in this context. Why here, and not elsewhere — say, in 12:15—18 or 13:2?

On a more fundamental level, we must inquire whether Donahue is correct in ascribing the current expectation that the Messiah would build the temple to scholarly imagination. In fact, Donahue's opinion rests on the foundation built by Lloyd Gaston in a major study of the temple in Judaism, *No Stone on Another*. Gaston's treatment of the evidence led him to conclude that a statement predicting the destruction and rebuilding of the temple would have had no context in Judaism prior to 70 A.D., and that eschatological expectation focused especially on the "New Jerusalem" or "New Zion", but not on the "new temple"[194]. At approximately the same time that Gaston's monograph appeared, R. J. McKelvey published his book on *The New Temple* which demonstrated that biblical texts regarding "Zion" embrace the temple, and that hope centering on the New Zion presupposed a new temple[195]. More recently, concluding an historical prologue to his study of post-biblical Jewish literature, Nickelsburg writes in a similar vein:

> The destruction of Jerusalem and the Exile meant the disruption of life and the breaking up of institutions whose original form was never fully restored. Much of post-biblical Jewish theology and literature was influenced and sometimes governed by a hope for such a restoration: a return of the dispersed; the appearance of a Davidic heir to throw off the shackles of foreign domination and restore Israel's sovereignty; the gathering of one people around a new and glorified Temple[196].

Now Sanders has underscored and further developed McKelvey's work by dealing with Gaston's arguments in the context of a new survey of key passages that suggest the framework of Jewish eschatological expectation in the first century. His argumentation overturns Gaston's thesis. He is able

---

194 Gaston, *No Stone*, chapter 3.
195 R. J. McKelvey, *The New Temple: The Church in the New Testament* (London: Oxford University, 1968).
196 Nickelsburg, *Jewish Literature*, 18.

to show most convincingly that the expectation of a new temple is entirely comprehensible. While the evidence for the prediction of destruction is less well-attested[197], more generally " . . . the connection between disaster, God's chastisement, and the subsequent redemption of a remnant was so firmly fixed in Judaism that we should assume that even a bare statement of destruction would not be altogether misunderstood"[198]. While the direct association of new temple and eschaton in current Jewish hope is thus established, the question remains what possible role the Messiah would play vis-à-vis the temple. An overview of the pertinent evidence is in order.

2 Sam 7:13: "He is the one who will build a house for my name (הוא יבנה־בית לשמי), and I will establish the throne of his kingdom forever". Distinguishing between "the general Messianic *expectation* of Palestinian Jewry, and the peculiar Messianic *speculations* characteristic of certain learned and/or esoteric minorities", Vermes indicates the centrality of the Davidic redeemer in intertestamental hope and thus underscores the significance of 2 Sam 7:5–16[199]. For our purpose it is worth noting that in this section we find a play on the word בית – which should be rendered "temple" in vv 5 and 13, and as "dynasty" in vv 11 and 16. Hence, whereas *God* establishes the dynasty, *David's offspring* builds the temple. To be sure, this prophecy by Nathan was linked historically with Solomon[200], but it cannot be denied that here is the raw material for relating the eschatological work of God's Messiah to the construction of the temple.

Zech 6:12–13: "Behold the man whose name is Branch (צמח). He will branch out from his place and build the temple of Yahweh (ובנה את־היכל יהוה). It is he who will build the temple of Yahweh (והוא יבנה את־היכל יהוה) and he will 'assume royal dignity'[201] and will sit and rule on his throne". The messianic sense of the use of the noun form of צמח here may be traced back to 2 Sam 23:5, where David's "last words" (23:1) are said to have included the question, "Will not (God) cause all my salvation and all my desire to sprout (יצמיח)?" (cf. Ps 132:17; Isa 4:2; Jer 23:5–6; 33:15–16; 19:26; Zech 3 :8)[202]. The parallel between this text and 2 Sam 7:13 regarding the building of the temple is obvious. Additionally, we may draw attention to *Tg. Neb.* Zech 6 :12–13. "Behold the man whose name is Messiah, destined to be revealed, installed in office, and to build the temple of Yahweh(ויבני ית היכלא דיני). It is he who will build the temple of Yahweh (הוא יבני ית היכלא דיני) and 'assume royal dignity'[203] and will sit and rule on his throne". The Aramaic paraphrase leaves no doubt as to the identity of the builder of the temple: he is the Messiah – and in this the targum makes explicit what was likely already present in the MT. Of course, with respect to the references to the targumim here and below, we must acknowledge the current ambivalence with regard to the dating of these texts. At the very least, however, it must be granted that the written targumim incorporate earlier tradition[204].

Tg. Neb. Isa 53:5: "And he (i.e. משיחא), will build a house of holiness (והוא יבני בית מקדשא), which was profaned on account of our sin". Whereas there is some basis in the

---

197 Sanders (*Jesus*, 88) mentions 1 Enoch 90:28–30. We will briefly discuss this and other relevent texts below.
198 Sanders, *Jesus*, 88; cf. pp. 77–90.
199 Vermes, *Jesus*, 130–134, 197. Cf. Bruce, *NT Development*, 68–78.
200 See Joachim Becker, *Messianic Expectation in the Old Testament* (Edinburgh: T. & T. Clark, 1980) 25–31.
201 So the NEB renders והוא־ישא הוד.
202 See Walter C. Kaiser, "צמח", in *TWOT*, 2:769–770; France, *Jesus*, 100.
203 The Aramaic והוא יטול זיו is comparable to the MT (above).
204 See Martin McNamara, *Targum and Testament. Aramaic Paraphrases of the Hebrew Bible: A Light on the New Testament* (Shannon: Irish University, 1972).

MT for the change from "he was pierced" to "it was profaned"[205], the opening clause represents an unexpected and quite novel addition to the MT. Interestingly, the targum provides further evidence for the expectation that the Messiah would build the temple, but also implies the need for a new temple after the destruction of the old because of Israel's sin[206].

I Enoch 90:28–29:
> Then I stood still, looking at that ancient house being transformed: All the pillars and all the columns were pulled out; and the ornaments of that house were packed and taken out together with them and abandoned in a certain place in the South of the Land. I went on seeing until the Lord of the sheep brought about a new house, greater and loftier than the first one, and set it up in the first location which had been covered up – all its pillars were new, the columns new; and the ornaments new as well as greater than those of the first, (that is) the old (house) which was gone. All the sheep were within it.

These verses come from the last, future-looking section of the apocalypse (164–160 B.C.)[207] and tell of God removing the old Jerusalem and setting up the new one. Gaston, noting that "all the sheep were within it", insists that this can be no reference to a new temple[208]. His reading fails to do justice to the apocalyptic imagery, for the concluding sentence quoted above should be understood in a symbolic sense. Moreover, the "house", pillars, columns, and ornaments all naturally point to the temple. Still further, that the temple is in view is suggested by the pollution of the same in 89:73, which gave rise to the futuristic vision in chapter 90. The real point at issue here in the light of our own investigation is that it is "the Lord of the sheep" and not the Messiah (cf. 90:37?) who is associated with the destruction and building of the temple. This distinction must not be stressed overmuch, however, for in eschatological expectation it is often the case that a personal mediator or agent of salvation is only given the role(s) previously reserved for the Lord whose direct intervention was expected. In Dormeyer's words, " . . . die Unterscheidung zwischen dem Tun Gottes und dem seines Messias ist in der Apokalyptik nicht so gravierend, dass ein Aufgabenbereich Gottes nicht auf seinen Messais übergehen kann . . ."[209].

4 Ezra 10:27 (see 9:38–10:28): "And I looked, and behold, the woman was no longer visible to me, but there was an established city, and a place of huge foundations showed itself". For the sake of brevity, we have not quoted at length the relevant material, but we may refer in addition to 10:19–22, where it is intimated in no uncertain terms that the writer has in mind in this larger section the fate of the temple (e.g. "our sanctuary has been laid waste, our altar thrown down, our temple destroyed"). Of course, inasmuch as this passage was written post-70 A.D.[210], here is no evidence for an earlier, eschatological expectation of the temple's demise. The anticipation of a newly-built temple, however, is present here, and should be viewed in continuity with other, earlier evidence. According to 4 Ezra, who is responsible for the construction of the temple? Is it the Messiah? On the one hand, our text does not credit the Messiah with this task, and in the light of the imagery employed, one should probably identify the builder as the Most High. On the other, it would be unwise to press too far any functional distinction between the Most High and "my Son the Messiah" (7:28). Both are said to deliver the inhabitants of the earth (13:26, 29), judge at the end of time (13:37–38; 7:33–34), and perform miracles (13:44, 50). In addition to fulfilling these roles, the Messiah will lead those who have been delivered (13:26, 39, 49).

On the basis of this survey[211], we may conclude that the temple-charge did raise the messianic question. Hence, Donahue's objection against the

---

205 The Hebrew חלל may be rendered "to pierce" or "to profane" (BDB, 319–320). The Aramaic paraphrase plays on this dual sense of the verb.
206 So Pesch, *Mark*, 2:435.
207 Nickelsburg, *Jewish Literature*, 93.
208 Gaston, *No Stone*, 114. *Contra* Sanders, *Jesus*, 81–82.
209 Dormeyer, *Passion Jesu*, 160.
210 Nickelsburg (*Jewish Literature*, 287–294) dates 4 Ezra at the end of the first century A.D.
211 In addition to the evidence we have cited, some draw attention to 4QFlor 1.1–13, for there the promise to David in 2 Sam 7 is referred to in certain eschatological terms. (For the text, see

genuineness of the saying — i.e. that the indictment has no function here — falls to the ground, for the charge sets the scene for the subsequent, more explicit christological question of the high priest. Moreover, in view of the growing consensus that the basis for Jesus' condemnation was sedition[212], the probability that the issue of temple-destruction was raised at the trial is significantly advanced. We therefore urge that the earliest passion narrative included the temple-charge, and that even at this early stage the christological implications of the statement partially eclipsed its political ramifications. This resulted from a twin desire to underscore Jesus' innocence and to demonstrate his christological identity. As the narrative developed, the temple-charge was deleted in favor of a greater emphasis on the christiological question.

If some sort of temple-question was included in the early passion account, can the same be said of the remaining material in Mark 14:55—61a? We have already seen the likelihood that with respect to the nature of the hearing Luke has preserved the earlier account, so we may set aside as later developments the more formalized aspects of the trial as recorded in Mark (i.e. the heavy accent on gaining testimony against Jesus, the emphasis on the inability of the witnesses to agree, Jesus' silence, and, later, the explicit condemnation of Jesus as a blasphemer in 14:64). Behind this literary metamorphosis we may discern such concerns as (1) the need to demonstrate more fully the travesty of justice as represented by these events — e.g. by showing how the Jews overran their own proscriptions for a fair trial (cf. Deut. 19:15—20); (2) the desire to show more fully the involvement of the Jewish leaders in Jesus' passion; and (3) the effort to fill out more completely the picture of Jesus' passion along the lines of OT "prophecy". Concerning this latter interest, we may recall the bridge between this trial and the Servant of Yahweh built by the employment of the silence-motif. Additionally, the hearing as developed by Mark reflects more fully the pattern of the Suffering Righteous as set forth in Ps 35:20—21:

> They do not speak peaceably,
>   but devise false accusations
>   against those who live quietly in the land.
> They gape at me and say, "Aha! Aha!
>   With our own eyes we have seen it!"

J. M. Allegro, "Fragments of a Qumran Scroll of Eschatological Midrasim", *JBL* 77 [1958] 350—354.) While, when viewed as a whole, the passage may be understood to link the new temple with the Davidic Messiah (see Bertil Gärtner, *The Temple and Community in Qumran and the New Testament: A Comprehensive Study in the Temple Symbolism of the Qumran Texts and the New Testament* [Cambridge: Cambridge Unversity, 1965] 30—42), the crucial statement, 2 Sam 7:13a, is not cited, nor is any direct link drawn between Messiah and temple.

212 Cf., e.g., Harvey, *Jesus*, 11—35; Sanders, *Jesus*, 294—318; Meyer, *Aims*, 178.

The second half of the citation is reminiscent of a phrase quite likely present in the early passion narrative, recorded in variant forms in Mark 14:63 and Luke 22:71, to the effect that Jesus' confession is so incredible that no additional testimony is required:. "We ourselves have witnessed his wrongdoing!" With the increased accent on false witnesses in Mark 14:55–56, 59, the narrative more fully intersects with the first half of the above-cited text, increasing the similarity between the Suffering Righteous and Jesus.

Moving then to the question asked of Jesus by the Sanhedrin, we may recall our earlier decision that as regards the form of that question, the Lukan version is the more primitive. Thus, in the primitive passion story, Jesus was probably asked two questions, the one as to his messiahship, the other as to his sonship. (In John 10:24–39, Jesus is only requested to speak plainly about his being the Christ, but his status as God's Son is also brought forward in the ensuing confrontation.) Likewise, we saw the good possibility that Jesus' vague answers in Luke (cf. John 10:25–26) were more primitive than the straightforward reply in Mark. Finally, given the correlation of the sources there can be no doubt that the Son of Man reference, tied to the allusion to Ps 110:1, was present in the primitive account[213]. As regards our understanding of Jesus' death, this text is most important for its clear testimony to Jesus' expectation of his enthronement and exaltation.

D. Mark 14:65; Matt 26:67–68; Luke 22:63–65

Both Mark and Luke independently report Jesus' mockery in the context of the Jewish hearing, though the circumstances vary. This is enough to suggest strongly the presence of such a scene — a scene in which Jesus was abused and mocked — in the early passion account[214]. Inasmuch as $ῥάπισμα$ and $ἐμπτύω$, recalling Isa 50:6, appear in the Markan story but not in the Lukan, we may be assured that this allusion to the Isaianic Servant was added to the developing story through the simple substitution of descriptive words. Of course, the general theme of abuse is reminiscent of the lot of the Suffering Righteous[215], but the central role of the command for Jesus to prophesy also demands that we see here a reference to the rejection of Jesus as a false prophet[216].

E. Conclusion

From our investigation of the accounts of Peter's denial and Jesus' hearing before the Sanhedrin, we may outline the following observations.

---

213 See above, chapter 3.XV. At that earlier point we also discussed the titles employed here.
214 See above, chapter 3.XIV.
215 Cf., e.g., Pesch, *Mark*, 2:441–442.
216 See Jeremias, *NT Theology*, 78; Dunn, *Jesus*, 82–84.

(1) The early passion story narrated a denial scene apart from the trial scene, although paraenetic interests soon related the two events more intimately. In the trial-account itself, Jesus was probably led before the Sanhedrin on the morning after the arrest for an informal, "preliminary" hearing. It is most likely that the issue of temple destruction/building raised its head in the early story, and that this matter was already related christologically to the three titles — Christ, Son of Man, and Son of God — which appeared in this context. Whether Jesus was Christ or whether he was Son of God — these two issues were probably presented as two separate but related questions in the early narrative. At some point in this process, perhaps in the night prior to the hearing (so Luke), Jesus was abused and mocked as a false prophet in the early account.

(2) There can be no doubt that, according to the earliest passion story, Jesus was presented as a messianic pretender. His passion was that of the Christ. This is clear not only from the explicit question about his messiahship, but also from the temple-issue which played an important role in the early narrative.

(3) In a number of ways, the *passio-iusti* theme is raised in this section, filling in the typological mural drawing out the many parallels between Jesus and the Suffering Righteous. Peter's behavior recalls the theme at the outset, but the actions taken against Jesus — the abuse and mockery, and the conclusion by the Sanhedrin regarding his alleged wrong-doing — also bring to mind the psalmic representation of this figure. The emphasis on Jesus' enthronement and vindication points to the Isaianic Servant (e.g. Isa 53:11−12) as well as to the Suffering Righteous. Later amendments to the trial narrative emphasized even more the *passio-iusti* idea.

(4) Finally, one again encounters the identification of Jesus with the martyr-prophet, suggesting his forthcoming identification with the prophets in violent death.

VIII. Jesus before Pilate

In his dissertation on *The Kingship of Jesus*, Matera has set forth his views on the composition and theology of Mark 15. We will have occasion to return to his study in the sections that follow, but here we may briefly outline his thesis regarding the Markan story of the hearing before Pilate and the mockery by the Roman soldiers[217]. Noting the parallels between the hearing before Pilate and the preceding, Jewish trial, Matera argues that the Second Evangelist has molded the two accounts simultaneously, thus

---

217 Matera, *Kingship of Jesus*, 7−24.

producing two scenes, similar in nature and structure, if not perfectly parallel — as in the feeding stories (6:34—44; 8:1—9), the healing stories (7:32—37; 8:22—26), and the stories of Jesus' prophetic knowledge (11:1—6; 14:12—16). He regards 15:1 as a Markan creation designed not to speak of a morning trial but to recall the Jewish trial held during the night. Verse 2, Pilate's question, is also the handiwork of the evangelist, who drew material for this query from the inscription on the cross (15:26). With vv 3—5, however, we enter the realm of material available to Mark in an earlier form. This existing tradition related Jesus' silence before his accusers. Matera undergirds his conclusions on vv 1—2 with reference to linguistic data, yet offers no reason for his supposition regarding vv 3—5.

As for the Barabbas-episode, according to Matera the evangelist has inherited a story embracing vv 6, 9, 11—15a. (Again, no apparent justification is given for this judgment.) To this core, Mark has added vv 7—8 by way of filling out the introduction, v 10 by way of lessening the guilt of the crowd, and v 15b by way of forming a loose bracket with v 1 ($\pi\alpha\rho\alpha\delta\iota\delta\omega\mu\iota$). Mark's editorial work has resulted in an increased accent on the guilt of the priests.

Finally, capitalizing on the presence of mockery scenes at various points in other Gospels, Matera argues for the free-floating character of the material found in 15:16—20a. This pericope is said to be a reworking of an earlier tradition, inserted into its present sequence in the passion narrative by the evangelist himself. Mark's "clumsy" arrangement of the elements making up this scene emphasizes its irony.

The obvious obstacle facing Matera's reconstruction of the process by which Mark "created" a trial-scene before Pilate is his apparent reluctance to compare the four canonical narratives at this point. If the accounts of Luke and/or John are independent of Mark here (as we have argued), then Matera is hard-pressed to explain the degree to which their narratives coincide with this "Markan creation". Our own comments will carry this point further.

As for the thesis that v 1 takes the reader back to the Jewish trial held during the night, we must ask whether the syntax of the verse will carry the weight of this interpretation. Matera insists that $\pi\rho\omega\ddot{\iota}$ does not refer to the time of the consultation but only to the time when Jesus was delivered to Pilate. Surely the more natural reading would see the phrase $\kappa\alpha\grave{\iota}$ $\epsilon\dot{\upsilon}\theta\grave{\upsilon}\varsigma$ $\pi\rho\omega\ddot{\iota}$ — which, after all, heads this verse — as a *Zeitangabe* for all four actions credited to the Jewish leaders here: $\sigma\upsilon\mu\beta\upsilon\acute{\upsilon}\lambda\iota\upsilon\nu$ $\pi\upsilon\iota\acute{\eta}\sigma\alpha\nu\tau\epsilon\varsigma$, $\delta\acute{\eta}\sigma\alpha\nu\tau\epsilon\varsigma$, $\dot{\alpha}\pi\acute{\eta}\nu\epsilon\gamma\kappa\alpha\nu$, and $\pi\alpha\rho\acute{\epsilon}\delta\omega\kappa\alpha\nu$.

More generally, as we have insisted, caution must be exercised when basing source-critical judgments on the alleged presence of Markan redactional features in a given text, for the presence of Mark's hand does not necessarily imply his literary creativity. Matera himself is apparently cognizant of this: following his observations concerning alleged Markan features in 15:16–20a he ventures to conclude only that "these stylistic traits suggest that *in some way* the redactor has been at work"[218]. In spite of this awareness, however, Matera's work falls prey to a tendency to confuse "redaction" and "creation" in descriptions of the evangelist's literary activity.

One last comment: by focusing exclusively on theological concerns, Matera has circumvented the possibility that historical probabilities might have served his reconstructional enterprise. From an historical point of view, the sequential positions of the scourging and the mockery may be more likely at one point than another. The possibility that Mark's "inherited tradition" preserved the correct historical sequence should not be overlooked.

With these introductory comments behind us, we may turn to a more detailed look at the various parts of this major section of the passion narrative.

A. *Mark 15:1; Matt 27:1–2; Luke 23:1; John 18:28*

Luke 23:1 may be a Lukan redaction of Mark 15:1 or of a non-Markan *Quelle*[219]. Hence, we are left with only two certain independent traditions — those of Mark and John. The verse is transitional, and all accounts agree that the Jewish leaders were responsible for handing Jesus over to Pilate (cf. also Mark 10:33; Acts 2:23; 3:13; 13:28). John is alone in his mention of τὸ πραιτώριον at this point in the narrative, but the location of these events is supported by the subsequent reference in Mark 15:16 (Matt 27:27). On παραδίδωμι, see below on Mark 15:15 and parallels[220].

B. *Mark 15:2–5; Matt 27:11–14; Luke 23:2–5, (6–12), 13–16; John 18: 29–38; 19:4–15*

Apart from 23:3, which has the appearance of having been borrowed from Mark, the Lukan story of Jesus' hearing before Pilate (and Herod) is based on Luke's *Sonderquelle*[221]. Both Luke and John split the hearing

---

218 Matera, *Kingship of Jesus*, 23 (emphasis added).
219 See above, chapter 3.XVI.
220 Many exegetes regard Matt 27:3–10 (cf. Acts 1:18–19) as having been based on traditional material with a long pre-history – e.g. Dahl, "Passion", 39; Hill, *Matthew*, 348–349; Gundry, *Matthew*, 552–558; Schweizer, *Matthew*, 502–504; Moo, "Tradition", 157–175. *Contra* Senior, *Passion*, 343–397. In any case, its absence from the other canonical passion accounts speaks against its inclusion in the primitive narrative.
221 See above, chapter 3.XVI. The material concerning Jesus' hearing before Antipas is unparalleled in the other canonical Gospels, so its existence in the original passion story is improbable. A number of scholars argue in favor of its fundamental historicity – e.g. Blinzler, *Prozess*, 284–293; Benoit, *Passion*, 144–145; Marshall, *Gospel of Luke*, 854–855. Its narration here, how-

before Pilate into two parts, though not in the same way, and both introduce material for which Mark has no parallel. Our treatment of the material in this sub-section is therefore best handled by focusing on the broad strokes whereby this scene is painted by these three independent witnesses.

Both Luke and John open this episode with references to the accusations made against Jesus by the Jewish leaders. Beyond this, the similarity between the two breaks down. Luke recounts the accusations brought against Jesus, preparing for Pilate's question concerning Jesus' kingship, but John details no such indictments. Luke's account is the most logical among the canonical Gospels at this point, for it alone gives Pilate a reason for framing his question as he does. There can be no doubt that the primitive passion narrative saw the political character of the trial of Jesus, for this is evidenced here in Luke; it underlies John 18:36—37; it is understood in the question put to Jesus by Pilate (Mark 15:2; John 18:33); and it is apparent in the inscription on the cross (Mark 15:26; Luke 23:38; John 19:19—22).

The content of the question of Pilate is identical in all four canonical Gospels: σὺ εἶ ὁ βασιλεὺς τῶν Ἰουδαίων;. The title, "King of the Jews", is central to this Roman trial, even as "Messiah" was central to the "religious" hearing — and the two titles are obviously linked, the former exposing the political side of the latter[222]. Again, it is certain that we are to understand that it is as the Messiah of God that Jesus undergoes his passion. Jesus' answer to Pilate — σὺ λέγεις — is also found in all four Gospels (Matt 27:11; Mark 15:2; Luke 23:2; John 18:37). The meaning of this answer has been the subject of some controversy and one should probably allow that it is intentionally ambiguous. "Die Ambivalenz des Titels berücksichtigt die Antwort Jesu. 'Du sagst es' is keine glatte Bejahung wie 'Ich bin es', aber auch keine Zurückweisung"[223]. What is the purpose of this ambiguity? It is apparent that in these accounts Jesus is unwilling to accept the full, political content of the title as used by Pilate and so is not free to adopt the title without reservation[224]. A similar circumlocution appears in the Jewish hearing where Jesus reserves the right to "define his terms"; this is the purpose behind the Johannine elaboration of Jesus' answer in

---

ever, seems to have been influenced by the more generally known trial before Pilate. Luke's apparent familiarity with information or tradition about Herod (cf. 8:3; 9:7—9; 12:31—33; Acts 13:1) may explain his knowledge of this material and his incorporation of the same into his Gospel.

222 Cf. Dahl, "Crucified Messiah", 27; Dunn, "Messianic Secret", 125; Kingsbury, *Christology*, xi, 118—128; Dibelius, *Tradition*, 213; Best, *Temptation and Passion*, 95—96; Schnackenburg, *John*, 3:247—248; cf. Matt 27:17, 22, where "King of the Jews" in Mark has been rendered as "Christ" — in spite of the fact that in 27:11 Matthew retains the title "King of the Jews".
223 Gnilka, *Mark*, 2:300.
224 See Kingsbury, *Christology*, 125—126, 151—152; Dormeyer, *Passion Jesu*, 176; Matera, *Kingship of Jesus*, 63—64; Lane, *Mark*, 579.

18:34—38. Only after Jesus has made his reply do the Jewish leaders in Mark begin to set forth their accusations against Jesus. This, along with the fact that in all the versions the trial is allowed to continue, suggests that Pilate either took Jesus' answer to be negative or did not take his claim to kingship seriously.

To these accusations in Mark, Jesus answers only with silence (15:5). Since they give the hearing in a different order, Luke and John do not witness to the silence-motif here; however, this theme is not absent from their accounts. In 23:9 Luke records Jesus' silence before Herod, and in 19:9 John relates Jesus' refusal to speak. Jesus' silence is heavily accented in the Matthean account (cf. 27:12, 14). Matera is therefore justified in regarding this motif as traditional, and we may justifiably urge that the primitive passion account made mention of this theme in the setting of the Roman trial. Jesus' silence before his (false) accusers points to his readiness to undertake suffering; his assumption of so passive a role highlights his self-giving. Additionally, his silence before his accusers calls to mind Jesus' identification with both the Suffering Servant (who "did not open his mouth" — Isa 53:7[225]) and the Suffering Righteous (Ps 38:13—14). The typological identification with the Suffering Righteous is furthered by the vehemence with which Jesus' enemies set forth their accusations (cf. Pss 38:19; 109:3)[226].

In every Gospel, Pilate proclaims Jesus' innocence. This is least evident in Mark, but is nonetheless present (15:5, 14). Matthew even records how Pilate's wife referred to Jesus as τῷ δικαίῳ ἐκείνῳ (27:19). Luke has both Herod and Pilate assert Jesus' innocence — and that in no uncertain terms (23:4, 14—15, 22). Likewise, John's account reports Pilate declaring Jesus' innocence no less than three times (18:38; 19:4, 6; cf. 19:12).

While it is obvious that Mark, Luke, and John are relating the same basic story, their accounts diverge from one another on a number of significant details. This fact notwithstanding, we have observed a large measure of agreement on certain key actions and themes which may be traced back to the interests witnessed by the primitive passion narrative.

C. Mark 15:6—15; Matt 27:15—26; Luke 23:18—25; John 18:39—19:1, 16

We have already determined Luke's use of a similar but non-Markan tradition for his description of the Barabbas-episode[227]. Matthew has included non-Markan material in his version (27:19), and has made much

---

225 See Moo, *OT – Passion*, 148—151; Senior, *Passion: Mark*, 110; Taylor, *Mark*, 580; Dodd, *Historical Tradition*, 104.
226 See Ruppert, *Feinde*, 132—142; Gnilka, *Mark*, 2:300; Pesch, *Mark*, 2:458.
227 See above, chapter 3.XVIII.

more explicit the contrast between Jesus and Barabbas, but there is no room to suggest he made use of any other narrative report. Hence, we are left with three independent accounts of the Barabbas-episode, and this is enough to put away any serious doubts as to the inclusion of such an account in the earliest passion story[228].

Historical problems aside, the detail that the release of a prisoner at Passover was customary was probably contained in the primitive account, as it is witnessed both in Mark 15:6 and John 18:39. Mark goes on to introduce Barabbas in some detail (v 7), especially when compared with John's brief, almost parenthetical remark (v 40). Luke holds back this description until after the release of Barabbas as requested by the crowds (23:19), but then his version is comparable to Mark's in content. The historical veracity of the description in Mark and Luke is quite probable given the political climate of the time; this characterization would have found a place in the earliest passion narrative as a counterfoil, a way of underscoring Jesus' innocence. Matera insists that no such contrast is intended by the Markan version[229], but surely to depict Barabbas as one who committed murder in the uprising (v 7) and Jesus as one who has done no evil (v 14) is to introduce just such a contrast.

Though in different ways, all the independent accounts introduce a choice given the crowds between Jesus and Barabbas. Clearly, the one deserving death is Barabbas, but it is he whom the crowds chose to have released. It is true that the formulaic, confessional language of "dying in one's stead" is nowhere to be found here; nevertheless, given the clarity with which the two prisoners are delineated and contrasted, there could hardly be a more realistic picture than this of vicarious death. Barabbas deserved to die because of his crime. Jesus, on the other hand, was innocent: no crime was found in him that was worthy of capital punishment (Luke 23:22). Yet, the sentenced criminal is released and the innocent one dies instead.

In the end, all accounts agree that Jesus was handed over to be crucified. According to the Markan version, Jesus is first scourged as a prelude to the cross (15:15). Luke records no such action taken against Jesus, but instead relates that Pilate offered to "chastise" Jesus as an alternative to crucifixion (23:16, 22). John's record is different still, for he relates that Jesus was whipped in the course of the trial itself (19:1). The bare convergence of these accounts on the mention of some form of "whipping" is indicative

---

228 *Contra*, e.g., Schenke, *Christus*, 47–51. Most exegetes allow the presence of the story at least in outline form in the pre-Markan account – e.g. Dormeyer, *Passion Jesu*, 179–185; Matera, *Kingship of Jesus*, 16–20; Gnilka, *Mark*, 2:296–298; Schmithals, *Mark*, 2:669–676.
229 Matera, *Kingship of Jesus*, 19.

that some mention of the same was found in the earliest passion story. Inasmuch as scourging is known to have accompanied crucifixion[230], Mark's account is probably of greater historical value here; perhaps, therefore, it should be given the benefit of the doubt as the more accurate representation of the early account.

In passing, it is worth observing the reserve with which this "whipping" is related. While modern commentators seem to revel in portraying for the reader the horror of this punishment, no such details are forthcoming from the text itself. Reserve of this nature is in diametric opposition to the dramatic, almost nauseatingly detailed narratives of torture and punishment included in the martyrological tales of this approximate period. This antithesis speaks sternly against (1) too close an identification of the passion account with the martyr-tale, and (2) positing too direct or significant an influence from the martyr-tale to the passion narrative.

In relating that Pilate handed Jesus over to crucifixion, all four evangelists employ the aorist active form of παραδίδωμι. It has been argued that the use of this term is strictly juridical — that even as a technical term for Jesus' passion it would have been devoid of any theological content[231]. Of course, it cannot be denied that the verb is often used in the NT in this more limited way, as a term of imprisonment (e.g. Matt 4:12; 5:25; 10:17; Luke 12:58; 21:12; Acts 8:3; 12:4; 21:11; 22:4; 27:1; 28:17). Be that as it may, we may still ask whether the juridical and theological shades of the words are mutually exclusive in the immediate context. Already in the passion predictions in Mark 9:31 and 10:33 the word appears in theologically-charged contexts. Moreover, the term is used elsewhere in the passion narrative in ways which cannot simply be laid aside as theologically valueless (Mark 14:21, 41; cf. 1 Cor 11:23). Still further, in Acts 3:13 παραδίδωμι is used in a context in which historical and theological interests intertwine[232]. The influence of Isa 52:13 on Acts 3:13a is widely acknowledged[233]; in addition, a strong case can be made for a more pervasive influence of Isa 52:13–53:12 on this *Missionsrede*.

Acts 3	Isa 52:13–53:12 (LXX)
v 13: ὁ θεός . . . ἐδόξασεν τὸν παῖδα αὐτοῦ	52:13: ὁ παῖς μου . . . δοξασθήσεται
v 13: ὃν ὑμεῖς μὲν παρεδώκατε	53:6: παρέδωκεν αὐτόν
	53:12: ἀνθ' ὧν παρεδόθη εἰς θάνατον ἡ ψυχὴ αὐτοῦ

---

230 Cf., e.g., Swete, *Mark*, 374; Taylor, *Mark*, 584; Dodd, *Historical Tradition*, 102.
231 See Norman Perrin, "The Use of (παρα)διδόναι in Connection with the Passion of Jesus in the New Testament", in *Ruf Jesu*, 204–212; Moo, *OT – Passion*, 92 n.3.
232 Jürgen Roloff, *Die Apostelgeschichte: Uebersetzt und erklärt* (Göttingen: Vandenhoeck & Ruprecht, 1981) 74–75.
233 E.g. Wilckens, *Missionsreden*, 37–39.

v 14: τόν ... δίκαιον   53:11 : δίκαιον
v 18: παθεῖν τὸν Χριστὸν αὐτοῦ   53: The suffering of the Servant
                                    pervades this whole chapter.

Of course, the correspondence is not precise in every case, but we are not arguing for any literal or "midrashic" citation of the Fourth Servant Song in Acts 3. We are only drawing attention to the certainty that this Isaianic text lies in the immediate background of the Petrine address. Importantly, we have here an instance of the use of a form of παραδίδωμι employed in a decidedly juridical way, yet also rooted in the image of the Suffering Servant. It is interesting that all four points of correspondence outlined above are likewise very much at home in the trial scene: Jesus' (anticipation of his) glorification, his innocence, his suffering, and, naturally, his "being delivered up". We conclude, therefore, that in all probability the theological content of παραδίδωμι, based on the Fourth Servant Song, would not have been lost on those who were involved in the shaping of the primitive passion narrative[234].

D. Mark 15:16–20a; Matt 27:27–31a; (Luke 23:11); John 19:2–3

Luke neglects to narrate the Roman mockery of Jesus because he wants to downplay Roman involvement in Jesus' passion. This *Tendenz* aside, his story of the hearing before Herod includes a mockery scene, albeit in the barest skeletal form (23:11). This independent testimony[235] may be taken with the accounts of Mark and John to indicate the likelihood that the early passion narrative contained a scene in which Jesus was mocked by Roman soldiers as a pretender to the throne. Therein, the soldiers hailed him as a king and paid him homage, thus ironically identifying him correctly as the King of the Jews, Unwittingly, they make themselves confessors of Jesus' true identity[236]. In this they find themselves in company with Pilate who, unknowingly but repeatedly, correctly refers to Jesus as the King of the Jews.

Additionally, one observes in this scene a typological identification of Jesus with the Isaianic Servant through the influence of Isa 50:6 on the vocabulary of the scene[237].

---

234 Some commentators allow the influence of Isa 53:6, 12 here – see Taylor, *Mark*, 578; Nineham, *Mark*, 415–417; Lane, *Mark*, 557; Gnilka, *Mark*, 2:303.
235 See above, chapter 3.XVII.
236 On Jesus' being mocked as a pretender to the throne, see the comments in Lane, *Mark*, 546, 559–560; Senior, *Passion: Mark*, 112–113; Kee, *Community*, 55; Schnackenburg, *John*, 3:254; Pesch, *Mark*, 2:470. For historical parallels, see Philo, *Flacc.* 6.36–39; Schweizer, *Mark*, 340; Pesch, *Mark*, 2:470. Cf. *Gos. Pet.* 3.6–9. On the irony here, see Donald Juel, *Messiah and Temple: The Trial of Jesus in the Gospel of Mark* (Missoula, Montana: Scholars, 1977) esp. pp. 49–50; Matera, *Kingship of Jesus*, 24.
237 See Goppelt, *Typos*, 101; Ruppert, *Jesus*, 52; Nineham, *Mark*, 418; Moo, *OT – Passion*, 139–140, 143–144.

Isa 50:6: τὸν νῶτόν μου δέδωκα εἰς μάστιγας, τὰς δὲ σιαγόνας μου εἰς ῥαπίσματα, τὸ δὲ πρόσωπόν μου οὐκ ἀπέστρεψα ἀπὸ αἰσχύνης ἐμπτυσμάτων.
Mark 15:19: καὶ ἐνέπτυον αὐτῷ
Matt 27:30: καὶ ἐμπτύσαντες εἰς αὐτόν
John 19:1: καὶ ἐμαστίγωσεν
John 19:3: καὶ ἐδίδοσαν αὐτῷ ῥαπίσματα.

Given the rarity with which ἐμπτύω and ῥάπισμα occur in the Greek Bible[238], the similarity in context between the Isaianic text and this scene, and the association of words from this text in John 19:1, 3, we are justified in seeing here an attempt to bring into view an identification of Jesus' fate with that of the Servant[239]. The variety of ways in which Isa 50:6 has influenced these Gospels texts suggests that this OT passage was associated with Jesus' passion in general and this scene in particular from very early times.

Of course, abuse of this nature is also the lot of the Suffering Righteous, but here the correspondence is not verbal but conceptual (cf. Pss 22:7; 35:15–16; 102:8).

E. Conclusion

From our investigation of the accounts of the hearing before Pilate, we may outline the following observations.

(1) The primitive passion narrative contained a trial of Jesus before Pilate, in the vicinity of the Praetorium, an account which began with a statement to the effect that Jesus was handed over to Pilate by the Jewish leaders. There Jesus was questioned by Pilate, most probably using the very words unanimously attested by the canonical accounts. Jesus' answer to Pilate's question regarding his kingship was probably ambiguous, as all the evangelists report. This was a political trial, according to the earliest narrative. In all probability, Jesus' silence and innocence would have been significant themes in this primitive account. Moreover, there is a high probability that this scene would have contained a Barabbas-episode, even if in an abbreviated form when compared with the Markan or Lukan renditions. The narration of this event would have drawn out the contrast between Jesus and Barabbas, and mentioned that it was customary for a prisoner to be released at the Passover. Other material may have been present here, but we cannot reconstruct the content of the hearing with any degree of certainty beyond this. After Jesus' condemnation and Barabbas's release, this

---

238 The evidence is set forth in Moo, *OT – Passion*, 88–89, 139.
239 On the use of Isa 50:6 in the Johannine text, see Reim, *Studien*, 163, 222; Dauer, *Passionsgeschichte*, 126; Schnackenburg, *John*, 3:254; Dodd, *Historical Tradition*, 102.

early story would have related that Jesus was, in some way, whipped prior to the crucifixion – perhaps as recorded in the Second Gospel. Jesus was then handed over to be crucified and mocked. In this final scene, language from Isa 50:6 would already have found a prominent place. Neither the narration of Judas's death (Matthew) or the hearing before Herod (Luke) has much claim to having been integral to the primitive passion story.

(2) The narration of this scene is pregnant with irony, as we have seen. Through the use of this device and the accusations and titles employed, we are to understand that it is as the Christ that Jesus goes to his death.

(3) Death is accepted willingly, passively by Jesus, as is evident from his refusal to defend himself against those who falsely accuse him.

(4) In this section, Jesus is portrayed as the Isaianic Servant of the Lord – who is innocent yet condemned, silent before his accusers, mocked, and delivered up to death. Closely related, we have found here a symbolic hint that Jesus' death is vicarious.

(5) Similarly, Jesus is pictured as the Suffering Righteous – who is innocent, angrily accused, yet silent, and who is mocked. Here we see the degree to which the figures of the Suffering Servant and the Suffering Righteous overlap as models for understanding Jesus' death.

(6) Finally, we have found a further reason to cast doubt on hypotheses that draw too direct a line from the martyr-tales to the narrative of Jesus' suffering and death.

IX. Jesus' Crucifixion and Death

With their numerous attemptes to lay bare the earliest traditional stratum (or strata) of the Markan *Kreuzigungspericope* by means of meticulous excavation, NT scholars have proven themselves tireless. Prolific though they may be, students of the passion have nevertheless continually fallen short of setting forth a literary-critical analysis capable of winning consensus-level support. Below, we have charted the conclusions of a selection of scholars on what material in the Markan crucifixion narrative would have belonged to a pre-Markan source(s)[240].

---

240 Bultmann, *History*, 279; Taylor, *Mark*, 587; Schreiber, *Theologie*, 22–49 (on which, see Linnemann, *Studien*, 139–146; Schenke, *Christus*, 87–88; Dormeyer, *Passion Jesu*, 210–211); Best, *Temptation and Passion*, 97; Schweizer, *Mark*, 342–343, 347–349, 351–352; Linnemann, *Studien*, 146–170 (on which, see Schenke, *Christus*, 88–90; Dormeyer, *Passion Jesu*, 209–210); Schenk, *Passionsbericht*, 13–25; Schenke, *Christus*, 90–102; Dormeyer, *Passion Jesu*, 191–215; Gnilka, *Mark*, 2:310–314; Schmithals, *Mark*, 2:680–701; Hans-Jürg Steichele, *Der leidende Sohn Gottes: Eine Untersuchung einiger alttestamentlicher Motive in der Christologie des Markusevangeliums* (Regensburg: Friedrich Pustet, 1980) 201–238; Mohr, *Passion*, 313–350.

Bids for a convincing reconstruction of the pre-history of the Markan narrative, it would seem, have been victimized by the employment of critical tools too blunt for the precise surgery attempted by some — that of excising tradition from redaction and tradition from tradition. Amazingly, after surveying previous attempts at isolating pre-Markan material and remarking about the wide disparity among the results of those analyses, Matera goes on to outline the criteria common to those earlier endeavors in order that he might put these same criteria to work in his own attempt at determining the nature of the material at hand[241]. That is, he adopts the very methods that had led his predecessors into a cul-de-sac of irreconcilable conclusions on almost every verse. Perhaps here more than at any other point in the passion story we must take seriously Pesch's call for "eine methodische Neubesinnung und ein methodenpluralistischer Neuansatz"[242]. While this is not to urge that the literary-critical tools wielded by such exegetes as Dormeyer and Mohr must be retired, we must insist that they have proven themselves to be largely inconclusive and in need of supplementation on a significant scale.

As in our investigation of previous pericopae, in what follows we shall take as our first landmark a comparison of the independent traditions witnessed in the canonical Gospels. Beyond this, we must take our bearings from other kinds of observations — be they source-, tradition-, or redaction-critical.

A. Mark 15:20b–21; Matt 27:31b–32; Luke 23:26–31; John 19:17a

There can be little question that an early passion story would have required some mention of the *Via Dolorosa* by way of making the topographical transition from the location of the Roman trial and mockery to the scene of the crucifixion. This argument from storytelling convention is supported by the existence of three independent accounts of the one event in the four canonical Gospels. To be sure, Luke 23:26 represents only a simple revision of Mark 15:20b–21, but, as we have seen, the independent, pre-Lukan character of 23:27–31 is evidence that comparable transitional material was present in Luke's *Sonderquelle*[243]. The brevity of John's parallel does not detract from its value as evidence here.

Apparently, the tradition gave special interest to the role of Simon of Cyrene — most probably as an eyewitness. His being mentioned here by name (Mark 15:21) serves no theological purpose, even if the manner in which he is said to have carried out the task for which he was drafted may

---

241 Matera, *Kingship of Jesus*, 35–39.
242 Pesch, *Mark*, 2:10.
243 See above, chapter 3.XIX.

Selected Literary-Critical Views on the Crucifixion Narrative

	20b	21	22	23	24	25	26	27	28	29	30	31	32	33	34	35	36	37	38	39	40	41
Bultmann	X	X	X	X	X*			?										?				
Taylor		X	X		X		X			X	X					X	X	X		X		
Schreiber-A		X		X		X	X			X*			X*X		X*X	X	X	X	X	X*		
Schreiber-B	X	X	X*		X			X														
Best	X		X	X	X		X	X	X	X	X											
Schweizer	X		X	X	X*	X	X	X		X*			X*		?*	X	X*	X			X*	
Linnemann			X*	X*	X*	X*								X	X X*			X				
Schenk-S		X	X*	?*	X		X	?*														
Schenk-A						X	X			X*	X			X	X*	X		X	X	X*		
Schenke	X		X*X	X		X	X		X	X*		X* X	X* X	X* X	X*	X	X* X	X* X	X	X		
Dormeyer-T		X	X* X	X	X*		X	X	X	X*		X* X	X* X		X*	X	X	X	X		X	
Dormeyer-Rs												X* X	X*									
Gnilka	X*	X	X	X	X	X	X	X	X	X	X	X* X*	X* X*	X	X	X	X	X	X		X*	
Schmithals		X	X	X	X		X		X	X*		X*	X*		X	X	X	X	X		X	X
Steichele		X	X	X	X		X		X	X*			X*	X*	X*			X	X			
Mohr-P	X	X	X*		X			X						X*	X*		X* X*	X		X		
Mohr-B				X				X	X	X	X	?*	X						X	X	X	

Schreiber believed Mark had access to two traditions, here designated "A" and "B". Best was unable to distinguish tradition and redaction in vv 33–41. Like Schreiber, Schenk uncovered two traditions: a "Simon-Tradition" ("S") and an "apokalyptisch gestalte Tradition" ("A"). Dormeyer's "T" refers to the oldest tradition, "Rs" to the pre-Markan redactor. Mohr thinks in terms of "der unbearbeitete vormarkinische Passionsbericht" ("P") and "der vormarkinisch Bearbeiter" ("B"). An "X" indicates a verse is regarded as traditional. An asterisk (*) indicates that only part of a verse is regarded as traditional. A question mark (?) signifies the uncertainty of the exegete on the traditional quality of a verse.

be intended to recall Jesus' words about discipleship in Mark 8:34 (ἀράτω/ ἄρη τὸν σταυρὸν αὐτοῦ). Not a few scholars have seen in Mark 15:21 an indication that the evangelist or his readership (or both) had a personal acquaintance with Simon of Cyrene — or perhaps with his sons, Alexander and Rufus[244], but this need not be the case. So conservative a redactor as we have found Mark to be could easily have contented himself with a mere reproduction of this traditional material here. In any case, it seems doubtful that Matthew, Mark, and Luke would all have known Simon personally, yet all recount his presence in this episode. Undoubtedly, the name of Simon of Cyrene was deeply embedded in the passion tradition.

One may counter that this hypothesis runs aground in view of the absence (and indeed contradiction!) of the Simon-tradition in the Johannine narrative[245]. On the contrary, that the Fourth Evangelist goes to the trouble of narrating that Jesus bore his *own* cross (καὶ βαστάζων ἑαυτῷ τὸν σταυρόν) is suggestive that he is at least aware of the Simon-tradition, and that he has redacted his material to make a theological point. It will be important to pursue this idea further, for if we can indicate why John would have edited this tradition out of his account, this will corroborate our suggestion that the Simon-material was integral to the earliest passion account despite the fact that it is independently attested only in Mark. What theological point might have guided John's redaction? Four theories have been argued.

(1) Some have seen here an allusion to the Akedah — and in particular to Gen 22:6, wherein we read that the wood for the burnt offering was placed on Isaac by his father[246]. Speculation regarding the "binding of Isaac" was prominent in current Jewish literature and Christian thought[247], and later Christian typology did see a connection between Gen 22:6 and John 19:17a. In his *Homilies on the Gospel of St. John* (85.1), Chrysostom, having observed that " . . . they laid the cross upon Him as a malefactor", concluded, "This was also the case in the type; for Isaac bare [sic]

---

244 E.g. Dibelius, *Jesus*, 132; Hunter, *Work and Words*, 152; Senior, *Passion: Mark*, 116; Lohse, *Geschichte*, 92; Benoit, *Passion*, 163; Dodd, *Historical Tradition*, 125; Nineham, *Mark*, 421–422; Cranfield, *Mark*, 454; Lane, *Mark*, 563; Schweizer, *Mark*, 343; Swete, *Mark*, 378; Taylor, *Mark*, 588.
245 See Strauss, *Jesus*, 677; Dodd, *Historical Tradition*, 125.
246 E.g. Brown, *John*, 2:917–918; Grant R. Osborne, "Redactional Trajectories in the Crucifixion Narrative", *EvQ* 51 (1979) 93. *Contra* Barrett, *John*, 548; Bruce, *John*, 366; Lindars, *John*, 574; Schnackenburg, *John*, 3:270.
247 Among the relevant literature, see Schoeps, *Paul*, 141–149; Geza Vermes, *Scripture and Tradition in Judaism: Haggadic Studies*, 2d ed. (Leiden: E. J. Brill, 1973) 193–227; N.A. Dahl, "The Atonement — An Adequate Reward for the Akedah (Ro 8:32)?", in *Neotestamentica et Semitica*, 15–29.

the wood"[248]. Even more explicit is the parallel drawn between Isaac and Christ by Tertullian:

> And so Isaac, to begin with, when delivered up by his father for a sacrifice, himself carried the wood for himself, and did at that early date set forth the death of Christ, who when surrendered as a victim by his Father carried the wood of his own passion (*Adv. Marc.* 3.18.2)[249].

In view of the possibility that elsewhere the Fourth Gospel may be seen to employ an Issac-typology[250], one may not completely rule out the possibility that our evangelist intended a further reference here. However, had he been led by such a motive, would he not have drawn out the parallel more clearly?

(2) A second suggested *Tendenz* at work here is John's attempt to counter a Docetic interpretation of the Synoptic parallels to the effect that, in the end, Simon actually took Jesus' place on the cross (cf. Irenaeus, *Adv. Haer.* 1.19.2)[251]. The Achilles' heel of this theory is that it assumes that a Gnostic interpretation of this kind was already circulating by the time of the writing of the Fourth Gospel and that John was aware of it. Both assumptions lack solid foundation.

(3) Dodd, followed by Lindars, has urged that John's text must be understood in the light of the cross-saying in Luke 14:27 which emphasizes that each must carry his or her *own* cross[252]. However, Dodd does not tell us why we should need to look in the Third Gospel for an explanation of a statement in the Fourth. This is all the more perplexing since he argues that John did not know the Synoptics. To insist that John must have known a tradition like Luke 14:27 takes us nowhere either, for we encounter no parallel logion in John's Gospel. Had John wanted to communicate Jesus' "moral example" by the wording of this account, surely he would have provided some means by which to interpret it as such in his own Gospel.

(4) The most satisfying solution to this dilemma is also the most obvious. We have already seen various ways in which our evangelist tells us that throughout his passion Jesus is master of his own fate — never losing control of his circumstances (see, e.g., the arrest and trial). That Jesus carried his

---

248 Chrysostom, "Homilies on the Gospel of St. John" ed. Philip Schaff, in *A Select Library of the Nicene and Post-Nicene Fathers of the Christian Church*, first series, vol. 14: *Saint Chrysostom: Homilies on the Gospel of St. John and the Epistle to the Hebrews*, ed. Philip Schaff (Grand Rapids, Michigan: Wm. B. Eerdmans, n.d.) 317.
249 Translation in *Adversus Marcionem*, 1:255. See *Barn*, 7.3.
250 As many scholars agree; but cf. Schnackenburg, *John*, 3:455–456 n.8.
251 So Benoit, *Passion*, 165. *Contra* Brown, *John*, 2:917; Lindars, *John*, 574.
252 Dodd, *Historical Tradition*, 125; Lindars, *John*, 574. *Contra* Brown, *John*, 2:918.

own cross dovetails well with this more pervasive theme[253], so there is really no need to have recourse to more speculative possibilities.

We conclude that the earliest passion narrative included a brief narrative of the *Via Dolorosa* that served primarily as a topographical transition-statement. This account already mentioned the role of Simon of Cyrene, though not for any theological purpose. The "warning to Jerusalem" read in Luke 23:27–31 is without parallel in the other Gospels (at this stage in their respective narratives), and must be regarded as secondary. Originally, this material may have belonged in a collection of Jesus' apocalyptic sayings; it would have been added here by way of accenting the theme of God's judgment as related to the cross.

B. *Mark 15:22–25; Matt 27:33–36; Luke 23:33–34; John 19:17b, 23–25a*

In our analysis of the Lukan passion narrative, we determined that in this sub-section, apart from Jesus' prayer of intercession in 23:24a, Luke was merely redacting Mark[254]. Given the intersection of Luke 23:33c and John 19:18b (Jesus crucified with two others, not mentioned in Mark until v 27), however, one cannot overlook the possibility that Luke knew a tradition that was very close to the Markan material but that also had interacted with pre-Johannine material. In any case, with the Johannine account we have evidence of a second tradition with very close points of contact with the Markan.

In narrating that Jesus was brought to Golgotha Mark may have been using his own editorial style; however, comparison with John's narrative clearly demonstrates Mark's debt to earlier tradition for the substance of his report. Both agree in telling how Jesus came to Golgotha (Γολγοθα – do both evangelists thus evidence an early mistranslation of the Aramaic גלגלתא, or was the formation גלגתא in current use?), and in translating the word with Κρανίου Τόπος. As with the mention of Simon in the previous section, this information must be traced back to the primitive narrative and its inclusion is not theologically motivated.

All accounts agree on the amazing brevity with which the actual act of crucifixion is recounted, employing only the barest statement: And/There they crucified him. Matthew's participial clause only highlights the matter-of-fact approach to recounting the event. Commentators are quick to point out that the details regarding how a crucifixion was carried out would have been well known in the Roman world at the time the Gospels were written.

---

253 So Trocmé, *Passion*, 74; Schweizer, *Mark*, 343; Brown, *John*, 2:917; Bruce, *John*, 366; Schnackenburg, *John*, 3:270; Osborne, "Trajectories", 73.
254 See above, chapter 3.XX.

Recognition of this likelihood should not blind us, however, to the obvious reserve of this statement. Indeed, we have only peripheral and scattered evidence that Jesus was affixed to the cross with nails (cf. Luke 24:39; John 20:25; Acts 2:23; Col 2:14; *Gos. Pet.* 6.21). Such brevity stands in stark contrast to the gory details offered by the martyr-tales current at this time.

Luke is alone in reporting Jesus' prayer of intercession for those humanly responsible for his death. Neither of the other canonical Gospels appear to have known this tradition, so there is little basis for asserting that it was a component of the primitive narrative.

Mark, followed by Matthew, includes the detail that Jesus was offered a beverage prior to the crucifixion, but that he declined to accept. This occurrence is missing in both Luke and John, and this may be further evidence that their traditional sources encountered and influenced one another at some early period. If the primitive passion narrative is best represented at this juncture by the Second Evangelist, Jesus' rejection of the beverage — an indication of his desire to endure the appointed sufferings fully conscious — would be added to the list of ways in which Jesus' acceptance of his fate is demonstrated. However, a firm judgment on the presence of this matter in the early account is not possible.

The evangelists agree in recounting the division of Jesus' garments among the soldiers; Ps 22:18 has influenced the way this event has been worded. The elaboration of this scene found in John 19:23—25a is clearly secondary in its attempt to show how the OT was precisely "fulfilled". In the narrative of this event, which would have been a part of the early passion narrative, we see a general concern to indicate that Jesus' passion was willed by God, as evidenced by OT prescription. More specially, here is one further point at which Jesus' passion is interpreted against the background of the *passio-iusti* motif.

Only Mark fixes the time of Jesus' crucifixion (15:25), though earlier (19:14) John designates the hour of Pilate's judgment. As John has it that Jesus was condemned at the sixth hour whereas Mark reports the crucifixion as having taken place at the third[255], clearly both cannot be historically correct nor reproduce with any precision the primitive passion narrative. Blinzler has made a valiant attempt to dismiss Mark 15:25 as a later gloss, despite the lack of textual support for this theory[256]. Nevertheless, his theory really does not do away with the problem at hand

---

[255] Some witnesses substitute τρίτη for ἕκτη in John, while others read ἕκτη for τρίτη in Mark. The manuscript evidence is overwhelming, and these variants must be dismissed as attempts at harmonization. See Metzger, *Textual Commentary*, 118, 252—253.
[256] Blinzler, *Prozess*, 416—421; followed by Lane, *Mark*, 566—567.

since Mark 15:33 has Jesus already on the cross and darkness over the land at the sixth hour. To add to the problem, Dauer has produced evidence that

> die theologischen Ueberlegungen des Johannes lassen sich viel eher verstehen, wenn schon sein überlieferter Bericht davon sprach, dass Jesus am 14. Nisan, an dem Tag, da die Passalämmer geschlachtet wurden, ans Kreuz geschlagen wurde[257].

Is there a way out of this dilemma?

The starting point for a solution is the recognition that while the use of ὥρα is a convenient way to add to the dramatic progression of the narrative, it is also a theologically-packed term in the passion narrative — embracing the interconnected themes of judgment, divine appointment, and apocalyptic-eschatological struggle. Even the modifier "third" cannot mask the theological significance of the term, as suggested by (1) the designation of the third hour *as the moment of the crucifixion*, and (2) by analogy, the use of the term "sixth" in 15:33, where apocalyptic-eschatological connotations are drawn from Amos 8:9. Thus, as Schweizer has hinted, ὥρα does not refer simply to "the hour of the day", but rather to the "time" designated by God for the decisive eschatological event[258]. The attempt to show that Jesus dies at the hour when the Passover sacrifices were made, witnessed in John, is a parallel attempt to demonstrate the eschatological decisiveness of Jesus' death in God's redemptive economy. Hence, even though the idea has taken on different trappings in the separate traditions, it nevertheless seems to have been present early on. Exactly what shape it took in the primitive passion narrative is now beyond our ability to discern. This uncertainty notwithstanding, we may conjecture that the Johannine-type tradition was amended through liturgical requirements in circles where the theme "Christ, our Passover" (1 Cor 5:7) had special importance, so that the tradition attested by Mark may be the more primitive.

C. *Mark 15:26; Matt 27:37; Luke 23:38; John 19:19—22*

At this point in the passion narrative, both Mark and John relate the inscription on the cross, a matter Luke intentionally holds back. It is not

---

257 Dauer, *Passionsgeschichte*, 142 (original in italics); cf. pp. 133—136, 140—142; also Schnackenburg, *John*, 3:264—265. Similarly, Taylor (*Mark*, 590) suggests that John and Mark are only utilizing different traditions. On the other hand, a number of scholars assert that John has been influenced by a desire to represent Jesus as the true Paschal lamb, and this has resulted in the time-reference of 19:14 — e.g. Cranfield, *Mark*, 456; Benoit, *Passion*, 175; Schweizer, *Jesus*, 10; Reim, *Studien*, 177; Barrett, *John*, 545.

258 Schweizer, (*Jesus*, 10) writes: "With this chronology, Mark is therefore trying to say that this day marks the fulfillment of time, that on this day, hour by hour, God's will was done". According to Pesch (*Mark*, 2:483—484), no symbolic sense is intended by this or other time designations in Mark 15; instead, they are integral to the progression of the story. Why they cannot serve in both ways is not clear.

clear whether Luke drew his form of the title from Mark or from his *Sonderquelle*²⁵⁹, but it nevertheless seems certain that ὁ βασιλεύς τῶν Ἰουδαίων was firmly fixed in the original tradition.

The ironical and proclamatory value inherent in the report of the inscription on the cross is further emphasized in the Johannine version, which adds that the inscription was trilingual and that the Jews insisted that Pilate alter the notice to read ὅτι ἐκεῖνος εἶπεν· βασιλεύς εἰμι τῶν Ἰουδαίων. These additions are secondary²⁶⁰.

D. Mark 15:27–32; Matt 27:38–44; Luke 23:32, 33b, 35, 37, 39–43; John 19:18

Having introduced with minimal wording the two criminals who were crucified with Jesus, Mark goes on to narrate how Jesus was mocked on the cross. Luke has been led by his Markan source in reporting the crucifixion of the two criminals in vv 32, 33b²⁶¹; however, in that Luke and John agree against Mark in positioning this report before the account of the inscription on the cross, and that Luke includes additional material regarding the criminals in vv 39–43, we have proof that Luke's *Sonderquelle* somewhat paralleled Mark's version on this detail. As for the mockery itself, Luke has drawn on his non-Markan source for his rendition²⁶². There is no comparable mockery scene in the Johannine account, but this does not mean John was ignorant of such a tradition. Quite the contrary, there is every reason to believe that John has intentionally neglected to mention this sort of degradation in order not to detract from his portrait of Jesus as a noble figure even in death²⁶³. We conclude that the early passion source spoke of both the crucifixion of the criminals with Jesus and his being mocked on the cross. It now remains for us to see how much more precisely we can reconstruct that primitive scene and determine its theological position *vis-à-vis* Jesus' death.

Using different language, John and Mark both record that Jesus was crucified between two others. This detail, which probably stems from the earliest passion tradition, has given rise to a number of interpretations²⁶⁴. One may argue for its essential historicity, but this would not detract from the possibility that this seemingly insignificant point was remembered and included in the passion account *because of its interpretive value*. Perhaps

---

259 See above, chapter 3.XX.
260 Cf. Lindars, *John*, 573; Schnackenburg, *John*, 3:272; Brown, *John*, 2:919.
261 See above, chapter 3.XIX–XX.
262 See above, chapter 3.XX.
263 Trocmé, *Passion*, 74; Dodd, *Historical Tradition*, 129; Weber, *Cross*, 131; Schnackenburg, *John*, 3:271.
264 See the brief survey in Moo, *OT –Passion*, 154–155.

the oldest explicit attempt to interpret this episode is found in the textual tradition which has it that this event fulfills Isa 53:12, read by a minority of witnesses in Mark 15:28. It is doubtful that this citation of the Isaianic text is original to the Markan Gospel, not only because it is weakly attested but also because it is probably an assimilation to Luke 22:37. There are good reasons, nonetheless, for believing that this gloss has only made explicit in the later textual tradition what was already implicit in the minds of those early Christians. Luke's redaction of Mark underscores Jesus' identification with the two others who were crucified, thus pointing more directly to a typological correspondence from Isa 53:12 to this narrative. The description of Jesus as an innocent victim in contrast to the others as criminals is reminiscent of the contract in Isa 53:11–12. Moreover, the overall importance of the Suffering Servant for understanding the passion of Jesus, heretofore documented, hastens a similar identification here. We are not insisting that the early church saw in this event a "fulfillment" of Isa 53:12 as much as we are urging that this relationship between the OT text and this passion event would not have escaped the notice of a people accustomed to viewing Jesus' death through a lens constructed in part from Suffering Servant texts[265].

Turning now to the mockery of Jesus, one is initially impressed with the absence of Mark's first scene — the mockery of the passers-by (15:29–30) — from the Lukan account. In its place, Luke reports only that "the people stood by, watching" (v 35). As we have previously intimated, this deficiency is hardly surprising for it matches well Luke's general tendency to portray "the people" in essentially benign terms. For this reason there is no basis for doubting that an episode of this nature was an ingredient of the early passion account and, perhaps, was present in Luke's other source, but was intentionally excised from the story through Lukan redaction. The fact that both Mark and Luke nevertheless independently witness to the use of Ps 22:7 at this point only confirms this opinion, while also adding yet another brushstroke to the portrait of Jesus in the guise of the Suffering Righteous. The interjection, "Aha!", in 15:29b, is reminiscent of similar taunts in Pss 35:21; 40:15; 70:3, even though the LXX (34:21; 39:16; 69:4) reads εὖγε rather than οὐά; again, Jesus appears as the Suffering Righteous.

Mark and Luke agree that the Jewish leaders derided Jesus on the cross. Additionally, Luke records a mockery of Jesus by the soldiers (23:36–37),

---

[265] Cf. the similarly positive conclusions regarding the significance of Isa 53:12 here in Christian Maurer, "Knecht Gottes und Sohn Gottes im Passionsbericht des Markusevangeliums", in *Redaktion und Theologie*, 118–119; Benoit, *Passion*, 172; Goppelt, *Typos*, 102; Lohse, *Geschichte*, 93.

but the statement credited to the soldiers is so close to that spoken by Mark's Jewish leaders that we need not treat the two scenes separately. As for the content of the mockeries thrown up to Jesus in Mark, there is little agreement among literary critics as to what was pre-Markan, as we have hitherto noted. A comparison with the Third Gospel reveals some common themes which, then, may justifiably be traced back to the early account. Running through the words of the mockers is a notable thread of paradoxical irony, for they insist that if Jesus was who he claimed to be, he would certainly not be in his present predicament[266]. Perhaps here is an echo of a Jesus-Logion like that in Mark 8:32: "For whoever wants to save his life will lose it, but whoever loses his life . . . will save it". The stance taken by the mockers, though, is more along the lines of that taken by the enemies of the Suffering Righteous: If he has some special relationship with God, he will be rescued from death (cf. Matt 27:43; Ps 22:7–8; Wis 2:18, 20). In their ironic way, the Jewish leaders witness to Jesus' role as savior (cf. *Gos. Pet.* 4.13); could it not be that the intended message is that precisely in *not* saving himself (i.e. in submitting to an undeserved death), Jesus saves others? Even though the Jewish leaders will presumably have been referring to Jesus' healing miracles, the Christian will certainly have understood σῴζω in its deeper sense. Again, Jesus is named as Christ, furthering the impression we are undoubtedly intended to take away from our reading of the passion story that this is indeed the passion of God's Messiah.

Finally, Mark adds, even those crucified with Jesus verbally abused him. Following a different tradition, Luke has it that only one of the criminals derided Jesus, but this measure of correspondence is enough to certify the existence of this brief report in the early passion account. Luke's more extensive report, recording how one of the criminals spoke on Jesus' behalf, was likely added in the interest of furthering the apologetic character of the narrative: even a criminal could recognize Jesus' innocence and impending vindication. Even without this dialogue, the inclusion of a report along the lines reported in Mark is of theological consequence. This mockery from a new source continues the effort to cast Jesus as the Suffering Rightoues who is taunted by his foes (e.g. Ps 42:10).

E. Mark 15:33–39; Matt 27:45–54; Luke 23:36, 44–48; John 19:28–30

A comparison of the literary analyses conducted within the German scholarly community over the last two decades reveals a marked inability for exegetes to agree on the contribution of old tradition to Mark 15:33–39. If one takes into account the studies of Schreiber, Linnemann, Schenk,

---

266 Cf. Osborne, "Trajectories", 83, 87; Best, *Mark*, 81, 132; Senior, *Passion*, 291; idem, *Passion: Mark*, 121; Böttger, *König der Juden*, 89; Bornkamm, *Jesus*, 166; Taylor, *Mark*, 591.

Schenke, Dormeyer, Schmithals, Gnilka, Steichele, and Mohr, one discovers a consensus only on the traditional character of the citation of Ps 22:1 in v 34 and of v 37b, while at least one analyst credits each of these nine verses to the pre-Markan narrative! Unfortunately, comparison with the Lukan narrative is of little assistance in the endeavor to peel back redaction to uncover the traditional core, for Luke's story is largely dependent on Mark's[267]. The sparseness of John's account is troubling in that it raises the question whether it closely models the primitive report or whether material parallel to that read by Mark has been stripped away. We may initiate our investigation by focusing on the independent material held in common by the evangelists.

The offer of ὄξος to Jesus is narrated in Mark 15:36; Luke 22:36; and John 19:29. Mark and John locate the offer just prior to Jesus' expiration, whereas in Luke it has been moved forward to become one more form of mockery. Commentators have been at a loss to explain the function of this scene in the narrative progression of Mark, but in John it is placed quite naturally as a response to Jesus' declaration of thirst. The prominence of this episode in the crucifixion story was assured in earliest times inasmuch as it provided a point of contact with OT "prophecy" — in this case, Ps 69:21. With this allusion, the *passio-iusti* theme comes to the fore as the passion narrative rushes toward its climax. Moreover, this allusion forbids our regarding this episode as a doublet with the similar event in Mark 15:23 — which originally contained no psalmic reference (see now, however, Matt 27:34).

The other point at which the independent traditions intersect is in reporting the moment of death. Matthew and John agree in wording their accounts so as to suggest that even at the point of death Jesus remained the master of his own destiny (cf. John 10:18)[268]. Mark, followed by Luke, employs the more straightforward term, ἐξέπνευσεν.

Of course, Mark, Luke, and John each record Jesus' "last word(s)", but beyond this bare fact there is no further coincidence: each records a different saying. According to John's version, Jesus, having received a drink, said, τετέλεσται. Had John known the Markan "cry of dereliction" it is most probable that he would have omitted it, substituting in its place a logion more suited to his passion theology — as Lindars remarks:

---

267 See above, chapter 3.XXII–XXIII.
268 Thus, Dibelius, *Tradition*, 197–198; Osborne, "Trajectories", 86; Senior, *Passion*, 305–307; Lindars, *John*, 582; Dauer, *Passionsgeschichte*, 214–215. Brown (*John*, 2:931) leaves open the possibility that John intends to communicate with these words that the time of the outpouring of the Spirit (John 7:37–39) had come, but this does not seem likely in view of John 20:21–22. Against this view, see further, Dauer, *Passionsgeschichte*, 215–216; Barrett, *John*, 554 (who is hesitant to venture a straightforward opinion); Schnackenburg, *John*, 3:285.

> For John at any rate it would have spoilt [sic] the calm triumph of his presentation of the Passion ... John does not mention the loud cry, but *tetelestai* is presumably his idea of what the cry was. It makes a most appropriate ending to his account of the crucifixion, combining the awful finality of that moment and the triumphal note of completion[269].

If, then, John's tradition had included the citation of Ps 22:1 on Jesus' lips, there is good reason for concluding that he has deliberately set it aside as contradictory to his theological purposes. Luke knew the tradition which had it that Jesus quoted Ps 22:1 from the cross, for he had Mark's Gospel before him. He found it offensive, however, and refused to include it in his narrative. In its place he substituted a citation from Ps 31:5 — borrowing from his *Sonderquelle*[270]. The language of the citation, combining elements from Greek and Hebrew versions of the psalm, the popularity of this verse as an evening benediction in Jewish circles, and the coincidence of this citation with the final clause in John 19:30 argue in favor of the antiquity of Luke's tradition. Is it original to the primitive narrative? What of Ps 22:1?

In both the First and Second Gospels (cf. *Gos. Pet.* 5.19), Jesus, on the cross, is represented as identifying his suffering and death with that of the Righteous Sufferer by quoting Ps 22:1. The appropriateness of this correspondence has provided the impetus for some to regard this cry as artificial, a secondary addition to the crucifixion narrative. According to a now widely-held hypothesis, the quotation of Ps 22:1 in Mark 15:34 is simply a way of providing the content of the wordless cry in 15:37. According to this theory, then, there should be read only one cry, not two[271]. Despite its large number of adherents, this view is not compelling. First, no article or demonstrative pronoun identifies the "great cry" of v 37 with that of v 34. Second, the common use of φωνή + μεγάλη does not necessarily point to the simple identification of the two cries, for this combination may be due merely to the evangelist's redactional preferences[272]. Third, nor must we assume with Domeyer that "ἀφείς [in v 37] greift auf V 34 züruck"[273], for ἀφείς is quite naturally read with ἐξέπνευσεν (v 37). Fourth, if the quotation in v 34 is intended to provide the content of the cry in v 37 — i.e. if the two cries are really one — then we must presume that the writer wants us to imagine that already at v 34 Jesus has

---

269 Lindars, *John*, 582. See also Barrett, *John*, 547; Schnackenburg, *John*, 3:284. Dauer, (*Passionsgeschichte*, 209–213) regards this a Johannine formulation.
270 See above, chapter 3.XXII.
271 For this view, see Bultmann, *History*, 313; Dormeyer, *Passion Jesu*, 200–201, 204; Linnemann, *Studien*, 148–153; Matera, *Kingship of Jesus*, 30, 125–127; Nineham, *Mark*, 428–429; Schenk, *Passionsbericht*, 43–45; Schenke, *Christus*, 96–97; Schweizer, *Mark*, 353; Winter, *Trial*, 156–157.
272 See 1:26; 5:7; 15:34, 37.
273 Dormeyer, *Passion Jesu*, 204. Similarly, Schenke, *Christus*, 97.

died; so, the vinegar is offered to a "dead Jesus" (v 36) and "a certain one" remarks about Elijah's coming to rescue an already-dead Jesus. Finally, this view presupposes that Ps 22:1 was not offensive to the *Urgemeinde*, for it allegedly placed the psalmic citation on Jesus' lips. We have already seen, however, that the Third Evangelist found it offensive, and the substitution from ἐγκατέλιπές με in v 34 (which duplicates the LXX) to ὠνείδισάς με in D (witnessed also in certain Old Latin mss.) is further testimony that the quotation was at least subject to further, offensive interpretation. Of course, Ps 22 records the suffering and anticipates the vindication of the Righteous One, so it could be argued that the quotation of the opening of the psalm, intended to recall the whole, lacks the accentuated note of despair on Jesus' lips that would have been offensive to primitive Christianity[274]. Aside from the fact that Rabbinic sources testifying that a psalm could be referred to in this way are late, Moo has reminded us that this usage is confined to liturgical settings in which the opening phrases might serve as titles. "Furthermore", he adds, "while OT quotations were often made with the context in mind, there is little evidence that a verse could point to its context, while its own meaning was ignored"[275].

It is reasonable to expect, then, that the quotation of Ps 22:1 itself was directly related to the experience of Jesus on the cross. Hence, the old argument that "the saying is certainly original, for it was offensive to the church"[276] is still relevant.

The certainty of its relative antiquity in the passion tradition is certified by this offensiveness, but is also supported by the fact that the logion could have given rise to the Elijah-mockery (15:35—36) only if the cry was known in its Hebrew form[277]. Not without good reason do the many exegetes listed earlier all agree on the inclusion of the cry, at least in its Semitic form, in the primitive passion narrative.

In all likelihood, the citation of Ps 22:1 by Jesus was present in the early account. This judgment does not in and of itself throw out the possibility that Ps 31:5 was also cited in this context in the passion story, but it does render it rather unlikely. It is far easier to account for the disappearance of the former than of the latter; in addition, we must recall the arguments set forth by Lindars — which do not prove, but raise the possibility — that Ps 31:5 was introduced from early Christian usage[278].

---

274 So, e.g., Nineham, *Mark*, 428—429; Ruppert, *Jesus*, 51; Matera, *Kingship of Jesus*, 132—135.
275 Moo, *OT — Passion*, 272; cf. pp. 271—272.
276 Goppelt, *Typos*, 104. See also, Taylor, *Jesus*, 157—159; *idem, Mark*, 594; Cranfield, *Mark*, 458.
277 See Schweizer, *Mark*, 351—352; Taylor, *Mark*, 593; Gustof Dalman, *The Words of Jesus* (Edinburgh: T. & T. Clark, 1902; reprint ed., Grand Rapids, Michigan: Klock & Klock, 1981) 53—54. Hence, the Matthean version (27:46) may represent older tradition — cf. Pesch, *Mark*, 2:495.
278 Lindars, *NT Apologetic*, 93—95; *idem, John*, 582.

With the use of Ps 22:1, the primitive passion account pictures Jesus as the Suffering Righteous *par excellence*.

In arguing for the traditional character of Mark 15:34a, we introduced through the back door an argument in favor of a similar judgment regarding the Elijah-material in vv 35—36b. The close relation of the cry from Ps 22 and the Elijah-material is confirmed by the fact that John and Luke refuse to narrate the cry, and also fail to implement the reference to Elijah. This is obviously another taunt from those standing by, capitalizing on Jewish speculation that Elijah would provide divine help in times of great distress[279]. While in new garb, this mockery does not advance much beyond that already discussed, though it does make explicit that the source of Jesus' "expected" rescue is heaven. Like the enemies of the righteous man in Wis 2—5, these onlookers (wrongly) anticipate the deliverance of the just from, rather than through, death.

The primary motive for rejecting the traditional character of Mark 15: 38—39 — the rending of the temple veil and the centurion's confession — would appear to be that both statements reflect Markan theological concerns. As Chronis has observed, "In Mark 15:37—39, Mark has creatively woven together the central themes of his gospel to bring the drama to a powerful climax"[280]. Of course, inasmuch as Chronis's essay focuses only on how this passage functions in the whole Gospel, it does not concern itself with distinguishing between pre-Markan tradition and Markan redaction of that tradition. Steichele, on the other hand, wants to know how v 39 functions in the context of the whole Gospel, but first sets out to determine the boundaries of the pre-Markan story. Concerning v 39 he writes:

> Zweierlei spricht für die mk Herkunft dieses Verses: Zuallererst das Bekenntnis zu Jesus als dem "Sohn Gottes"! Der Gottessohntitel kommt sonst im Kreuzigungsbericht, ja im ganzen Kap. 15 nicht vor: er ist jedoch ein bevorzugter christologischer Hoheitstitel des Redaktors Mk[281].

The second matter to which Steichele (and others) refers is the lack of any apparent continuity between vv 38—39[282]. Interestingly, Steichele regards this *Spannung* as an argument for the secondary character of v 39 when it seems far better suited for use in constructing a similar case against v 38. This is true since v 37 leads directly into v 39, and since vv 37 and 39 are

---

279 See Schweizer, *Mark*, 353; Pesch, *Mark*, 2:496; Swete, *Mark*, 385—386; Joachim Jeremias, "Ἠλ(ε)ίας", in *TDNT*, 2:930, 935.
280 Harry L. Chronis, "The Torn Veil: Cultus and Christology in Mark 15:37—39", *JBL* 101 (1, 1982) 114.
281 Steichele, *Leidende Sohn Gottes*, 209. Similarly on v 39, see Schweizer, *Mark*, 352; Dormeyer, *Passion Jesu*, 206. On v 38, see, e.g., Schenke, *Christus*, 100; Matera, *Kingship of Jesus*, 137.
282 Steichele, *Leidende Sohn Gottes*, 210. This tension has been noted by, e.g., Kee, *Community*, 32; Bultmann, *History*, 273—274; Linnemann, *Studien*, 138; Schenke, *Christus*, 86; Martin, *Mark*, 183.

joined by the double-reference to Jesus' expiration — just the sort of repetition we might expect if v 38 is an intrusion into an originally unified story.

We propose that the alleged tension between vv 38 and 39 is more apparent than real, that modern exegetes have too hastily credited these verses to Markan redaction, and (therefore) that there is good reason to regard both verses as having been drawn essentially from early tradition. In order to substantiate these claims we will examine v 38 first, then the centurion's confession in v 39.

The parataxical use of καί to introduce v 38 is meant to introduce a result, and should be rendered "and so" or "and then"[283]. That is, we are intended to see the activity of v 38 in a cause-effect relationship with v 37. Early Christians were not content to announce the death of Jesus without already including here a pointer to its significance.

In view of the earlier references to the temple in the passion narrative — at the Jewish hearing and at the mockery scene, at which time Jesus was ironically proclaimed as the one (the Messiah) who would destroy and rebuild the temple — there can be no doubt that v 38 is intended to declare the truth of that announcement, but also to explain in what sense it is true. Jesus' vindication is the overarching theme of this verse, a vindication which turns a tragic end and cry of lament into a song of victory. Jesus' vindication is pictured thus: in his death his kinship with God is revealed. The rending of the temple veil from top to bottom symbolizes the end of the temple: God's glory is no longer hidden from view but is manifest in Jesus' death[284]. Temple worship is finished; it is no longer necessary, for the time of the temple — and with it, that of the old covenant — has passed. The judgment of God has fallen on the old epoch. Jesus' death marks the turning point in history as the old aeon is dismissed and the new era introduced. The death of Jesus marks the fall of the temple, but in his death the new covenant is established. The temple is "destroyed", for its salvation-historical purpose is ended. But there can be no destruction of the temple without a rebuilding — and so we encounter a veiled anticipation of Jesus' new status. "Im Kreuzestod Jesu wird Gottes Majestät offenbar"[285] — and thus we recognize that he who would destroy the temple is actually he who replaces the temple[286].

Was this statement Mark's own addition to the passion story; or did he find it already in his tradition? Two points suggest Mark's hand here —

---

283 For this usage, see BAG, 392.
284 Linnemann, *Studien*, 162–163.
285 Linnemann, *Studien*, 163.
286 See Böttger, *König der Juden*, 90–91; Best, *Mark*, 71; Senior, *Passion: Mark*, 126, 128–129; Lohse, *Geschichte*, 95–96; Bornkamm, *Jesus*, 167; Hengel, *Atonement*, 53; Schenke, *Christus*, 100; Matera, *Kingship of Jesus*, 139.

the first of lesser importance: the use of ἀπό + adverb in -θεν (cf. 5:6; 8:3; 11:13; 14:54; 15:40). The second is of more consequence. Σχίζω is used only twice in the Second Gospel — in 1:10 and 15:38. In that early point in the Gospel, the heavens are rent and Jesus is proclaimed as ὁ υἱός μου. Now, in v 38, the veil is rent and, in v 39, Jesus is proclaimed as υἱὸς θεοῦ. Mark may well have introduced this formal schematization whereby his Gospel is framed by the declaration of Jesus as God's Son, but there are significant reasons for concluding that the substance of v 38 belonged to the early account. First, Jesus' attitude toward the temple as portrayed by Mark may be idealized, but in its essentials it is not likely to be fictitious. While arguments may continue regarding the authenticity of certain details in the material about the temple, "the conflict over the temple seems deeply implanted in the tradition, and that there was such a conflict would seem to be indisputable"[287]. Moreover, the problem of the temple would have been a vexing one for early Christians prior to the writing of the Second Gospel — as suggested by Acts 6—7[288]. Hence, it would be flying in the face of the historical data to suggest that only Mark could be responsible for the less sympathetic view of the temple attested in this material. Second, v 38 forms a fitting climax for the temple-material that did come to the evangelist from the primitive passion story: indeed, the charges and mockery narrated earlier almost demand a finale such as v 38 provides. A case for the antiquity of the temple-material in the passion story is strongest with the charge found in the Jewish hearing, but its almost certain presence there speaks authoritatively for the inclusion of related material in the mockery scene: " . . . the mockery of the condemned travesties the charge of which he [sic] has been accused . . ."[289]. Third, we have argued that the early passion narrative would have been modelled somewhat on the "Suffering/Vindication" genre. Though we must not put too much weight on what may be perceived as a circular argument, the other, quite extensive number of affinities between the passion story and this genre favors the presence of some sort of note of vindication at this very point in the narrative.

What, then, of v 39 — the centurion's confession? This, too must be seen as a testimony to Jesus' vindication at his death. The clause ὅτι οὕτως ἐξέπνευσεν is designed to indicate not only the cause-effect relationship of Jesus' death and the centurion's confession (i.e. between vv 37 and 39), but also that vv 38 and 39 narrate "events" that took place simultaneously,

---

[287] Sanders, *Jesus*, 61. See further, Sanders, *Jesus*, esp. pp. 61—76, 296—306; Harvey, *Jesus*, 129—135; William R. Farmer, *Jesus and the Gospel: Tradition, Scripture, and Canon* (Philadelphia: Fortress, 1982) 29, 42.
[288] On which, see Hengel, "Between Jesus and Paul".
[289] Jeremias, *Eucharistic Words*, 79.

the one independent of the other. Both events, occurring at one and the same time, happen as a result of Jesus' death, which becomes in both instances a divine revelation. Interestingly, whereas in v 38 we are within the unmistakeable perimeters of Jewish religion, in v 39 we encounter a Gentile witnessing this manifestation of Jesus' relation to God. (Luke records the rending of the temple veil prior to the crucifixion; however, like Mark, Luke has a Gentile [23:47] and a Jewish [23:48] response to Jesus' death.)

There is nothing artificial about the presence of this confession in v 39. Steichele's observation that "Son of God" appears nowhere else in the crucifixion report or even in Mark 15 is useless, for it draws the boundaries too narrowly. In the Jewish hearing, Jesus is asked about his Sonship, and he replies with a reference to his vindication. Not coincidently, here we read of Jesus' acclamation as God's Son in conjunction with his death. Moreover, the parallels — both linguistic and conceptual — in Isa 52:13– 53:12 and Wis 2, 4–5 demonstrate what a natural niche this confession (even the title, "Son of God") fills in this narrative. Paraphrasing, in Wis 5:2, 4–5, the enemies of the righteous man see (ἰδόντες) the one they put to death and speak (ἐροῦσιν) to one another, asking (ἐροῦσιν) how it is that this man (οὗτος ἦν) has been numbered among the sons of God (υἱοῖς θεοῦ; cf. 2:18 – υἱὸς θεοῦ; 2:13, 16). Likewise, with the Suffering Servant, vindication after maltreatment is an important motif (cf. Isa 52: 13–15; 53:10–12). While the fact that a centurion made this confession may be a secondary development in the tradition under the influence of an interest in showing the universal significance of the cross, the confession itself appears to belong to the primitive account[290].

All that remains now are the time-references in Mark 15:33–34a. Earlier, we alluded to the apocalyptic nuance of "darkness at the sixth hour", the eschatological significance of "hour", and the importance of the repeated hour-references for the drama of the account. Presumably, if the note about the third hour in 15:25 belongs to the early account, so would these references. We have cautiously suggested the likelihood that v 25 belongs to the primitive narrative, and the earlier emphasis on the term in the passion narrative supports this suggestion. Greater certitude eludes us, however.

F. Mark 15:40–41; Matt 27:55–56; Luke 23:49; John 19:25b-27

Luke's version of the witnesses at the cross is modelled on Mark's[291]; hence, John and Mark are our only independent witnesses. Comparison of

---

290 See the similar conclusion in Kazmierski, *Jesus, Son of God*, 193–200. Kazmierski, however, deals very little with the arguments of those who deny the pre-Markan nature of this text.
291 See above, chapter 3.XXIII.

these accounts renders almost certain that the primitive passion story knew of women at the cross. Moreover, as others have observed, it seems likely that John's tradition located the mention of the women after Jesus' death rather than before, and that John has brought this material forward in order to draw a sharp contrast between the women and the soldiers and in order to record the dialogue between Jesus and his mother[292]. On the phrase ἀπὸ μακρόθεν (15:40) and its relation to the *passio-iusti* theme, see above on 14:54; as this report is cast in a more sympathetic mood and since it follows the positive notes about Jesus' vindication, an intentional allusion to the "aloof friends" of the Suffering Righteous is less likely here.

G. Conclusions

From our investigation of the crucifixion accounts we may outline the following observations.

(1) The primitive passion narrative apparently recounted the story of Jesus' crucifixion and death very much along the lines of the report we read in Mark's Gospel. This story would have begun with a brief account of the *Via Dolorosa*, followed by a colorless report of Jesus' crucifixion. Perhaps the narrative included at this point the offer and Jesus' refusal of a drink. It is virtually certain that the passion narrative recounted the division of the garments and described the inscription on the cross. However, when speaking of the hour-scheme found in Mark's Gospel we must be less dogmatic; the chance of its having been found in the early account we judge to be somewhere between "perhaps" and "probably". There is, on the other hand, every probability that the primitive passion account spoke of two criminals crucified on either side of Jesus, and of his being mocked by the passers-by and the Jewish leaders. The offer of a beverage just before his death, the cry of dereliction, and a straightforward report of his "dying breath" also belonged to the early report. We are still very much within the realm of good probability when we speak of the inclusion of the Elijah-mockery, the rending of the temple veil, and the centurion's confession in the old account. Finally, there can be no doubt that this narrative reported the presence of women at the crucifixion site.

(2) This is not the first time we have encountered such details, but it is worthy of note that three significant aspects of this narrative seem to have been recounted for no christological reason — namely, the mention of Simon of Cyrene by name, the location of the crucifixion as Golgotha, and the presence of witnesses at the cross.

(3) As in earlier sections, too, both with the inscription on the cross and the words of the mockers we have inescapable, ironic, evidence that the

---

292 See, e.g., Dauer, *Passionsgeschichte*, 193; Schnackenburg, *John*, 3:276.

early passion story intended to show that Jesus' death was the death of the Messiah of God.

(4) Jesus is also portrayed in this section as the Suffering Servant — who is "numbered with transgressors" and vindicated.

(5) Likewise, Jesus appears in the dress of the Suffering Righteous — whose clothes are divided, who is mocked, who is offered a drink, who feels himself forsaken by God, who is expected to have been delivered from death, and who is ultimately vindicated.

(6) While no theoretical undergirding is provided, in an ironic way Jesus' death is presented as having salvific significance.

(7) Through the use of the eschatological "hour" and through the description of the rending of the temple veil, Jesus' death is portrayed as the decisive eschatological event, the turning point in history.

(8) Jesus' death is presented as divine revelation — the moment at which he is revealed as the Son of God.

(9) Finally, one may add to the list of reasons for doubting the direct or consequential influence of martyr-tales on the narration of Jesus' passion the brevity with which the act of crucifixion is described.

X. Final Matters

A. *The Ending of the Primitive Passion Narrative*

With an examination of the crucifixion and death of Jesus we conclude our investigation of the passion narrative. Before summarizing our findings, however, we must deal with a potential objection: Have we not drawn the boundaries of the passion narrative too narrowly? Does not the narrative of Jesus' burial belong to the passion story? At least two students of the pre-canonical passion account — Schenke and Pesch — would no doubt insist that these questions must be answered in the affirmative. Schenke devoted a brief section of his book, *Der gekreuzigte Christus*, to an examination of "Der Abschluss der Passionsgeschichte in 15,42–47"; Pesch's contribution to a symposium on *L'Évangile selon Marc* consists of a lengthy essay on "Der Schluss der vormarkinische Passionsgeschichte und des Markusevangeliums: Mk 15,42–16,8"[293]. Taken together, these studies set forth two fundamental arguments to support the inclusion of the burial account in the early passion story: (1) the pre-Markan character of Mark 15:42–47 (Schenke, not Pesch, regards v 42 as secondary); and (2) the continuation from the passion story into the burial account of a com-

---

[293] Schenke, *Christus*, 77–83; Rudolf Pesch, "Der Schluss der vormarkinische Passionsgeschichte und des Markusevangeliums: Mk 15,42–16,8", in *Évangile selon Marc*, 365–409.

mon story line, common characters, and common style. We not only regard these arguments as ambiguous at best, but also insist that other considerations demonstrate that the primitive passion narrative contained no burial account. We may outline our points as follows.

(1) There does indeed appear to be a good case for regarding Mark's burial scene as consisting of a substantially pre-Markan account; however, as we have observed in the preceding inquiry, pre-Markan material need not have existed already as a component of the early passion story (e.g. the story of the preparation for Passover).

(2) Certain examples of stylistic continuity, which Pesch regards as evidence that the burial scene was originally of a piece with the passion story, most exegetes would rightly regard as evidence of Mark's editorial pen (e.g. ὅ ἐστιν in 15:42). In any case, common style is an ambiguous canon; it may easily be evaluated as a sign that one redactor was responsible for bringing the burial story into the passion account, and that redactor could have been pre-Markan without having been the constructor(s) of the primitive passion story.

(3) Similarly, the ties between the burial account and the passion story (e.g. the repeated references to the centurion and Pilate) are ambiguous as evidence. They could stem from historical roots and/or they may be signs of attempts at dovetailing the one account into the other. That is, Pesch's "erzähl(psycho)logische Beobachtungen" may demonstrate only that the author or redactor of the burial account had the passion story in hand.

(4) At the very least, it is difficult to imagine how the passion narrative may be seen to prepare for or anticipate the burial scene. Rather, the passion story has its climax in Jesus' death and immediate vindication. Mention of the request to obtain the corpse and the details of the burial would only detract from the story line.

(5) With the introduction of Joseph of Arimathea as "a prominent member of the Council, who was himself awaiting the kingdom of God", we encounter a narrative with a radically different climate with respect to the Jewish leadership. One gains the impression from the passion account that the Jewish leaders are incapable of giving Jesus an objective hearing, much less a sympathetic one. Would the primitive passion narrative have thus changed course in mid-stream?

(6) Also, why use βουλευτής when, by this time in the passion narrative, even Gentile readers would have been familiar enough with the Sanhedrin?

(7) Apart from the story of the preparation of the Passover, the narrative of the burial scene is the only section where Luke's *Sonderquelle* is completely lacking. (We saw the possibility that Luke was influenced to a small degree by oral tradition in his redaction of the Markan account here.) If the primitive passion story included a burial scene, why is it lacking in Luke's passion source?

(8) If, as we have argued, the primitive passion narrative was given birth in the context of the celebration of the Supper, what purpose would have been served in this context by a recounting of the burial?

(9) Assuming a passion narrative did circulate on its own, one could understand how a burial scene was appended to it in order to serve a transitional function when the passion- and resurrection stories were joined. Of course, this proposal assumes a "burial narrative" circulated independently — and this is not easily imagined except for possible biographical interests. Might mention of Jesus' burial be regarded as a necessary prelude to the resurrection account? Such a prologue would be important by way of indicating not only that Jesus had in fact died (cf. Acts 13:29; 1 Cor 15:4; Mark 15:44), but would also set the topographical and chronological stage for the resurrection account.

(10) Finally, when considering the general outline of the "Suffering/Vindication" genre as identified by Nickelsburg — even when taking the genre rather loosely, as we have suggested one must do — there is no room for the inclusion of a burial account.

For these reasons, we conclude that the early passion narrative would have reached its finale at the point of reporting Jesus' death and vindication.

B. Conclusion

We set out in this chapter with two objectives: to ascertain as far as possible the shape and content of the primitive passion narrative and to determine what theological significance that story gave to Jesus' death. We have fulfilled our objectives, and the task of summarizing our findings will constitute the bulk of the next chapter.

Chapter Nine

Jesus' Death in the Passion Narrative: Thematic Overview

I. Jesus' Death Interpreted in the Passion Narrative

The narrative of Jesus' suffering and death presents no monolithic interpretive picture. While a minority of motifs come in for major development there is no one point or theme to which the recounting of the whole series of events is subjected. Indeed, we have found instances in which no interpretive agenda at all seems to have been at work in the inclusion and recounting of certain details. Pluralism of this nature has not caught us unawares, however, given our earlier observations regarding the variety of factors at work in the process by which the passion narrative received its shape in the primitive church. Early Christianity itself was multi-chromic, so we would naturally anticipate the prismatic character of this archaic story.

Our interest in the passion account has focused first on whether there existed from earliest Christian days a primitive passion story; answering this question in the affirmative, we went on to consider its boundaries and contours, and its basic outline and perspective on Jesus' death. In the preceding chapter we pursued this latter agenda, and here we shall endeavor to see what can be done to summarize those earlier findings. Then, we looked at the interpretation of Jesus' passion "from above" – that is, by treating each narrated episode in isolation. Now, we propose to view the evidence from a different perspective – horizontally, in order to see what theme or themes are embraced by the passion narrative as a whole. Our plan will be to focus initially on the more general motifs that pervade the entire story, turning then to suggest what pre-Christian "models" or "figures" were of significance for understanding Jesus' death, and finally treating in quick succession a number of lesser themes present, if not pervasive, in the narrative.

A. Jesus' Death and God's Redemptive Plan

While the presence of other interests in the passion narrative justifies our opening declaration that no one theme completely dominates the recounting of the whole story, it is nevertheless true that with respect to the interpretation of Jesus' death in the passion account there is one, overarching, organizing theme — namely, the centrality of Jesus' death in God's redemptive plan. For this reason, one might justifiably comment that every theme to be summarized below constitutes only a sub-category under this one heading. The "stumbling block" of the cross made it imperative that those very first Christians come to terms with Jesus' passion in light of God's *heilsgeschichtliche* purpose. This point never really leaves center stage throughout the primitive account of Jesus' suffering and death.

Perhaps nowhere in the passion narrative is this motif more transparent than in the general allusions to the fulfillment of "the Scriptures" in the narration of the betrayal-announcement and of Jesus' arrest. More generally, every reference to the OT — whether by slightest allusion or most explicit citation — must be regarded as serving this more general theme. Thus, the account whereby Jesus' clothes were divided among the guards is quite likely included in the narrative only because it provided a means by which to indicate the fulfillment of "prophecy" — in this case, Ps 22:18. In this way we are taught that, far from being a contradiction of God's purpose or an inexplicable enigma in view of salvation-history, Jesus' passion was actually foreordained by the Holy Scriptures, predetermined by God. Likewise, the relatively lengthy account of Jesus' prayer at Gethsemane has as one of its focal points the certainty that God's will is "the cup" — i.e. Jesus' death. The Supper-words employ a conglomeration of images to portray Jesus' death as the fulfillment of salvation-history. Even the time-references at the arrest and the crucifixion should not be understood in the first instance as temporally determined, for their primary purpose is to indicate the fulfillment of the divine plan in handing Jesus over to death.

Additional illustrations could easily swell this sampling of the evidence, but the central point is already well-established. According to the passion account, why did Jesus die? Because God willed it! It was necessary in God's salvific plan. This is the most significant theme around which all others are related and from which they draw their significance.

B. Jesus' Death: A Self-Giving

We would never suggest that the passion narrative constitutes raw data for a psychological profile of Jesus, but it is true that this account stresses Jesus' own attitude toward his death. First, from the initial appearance of Jesus in the story the reader has no doubt that Jesus knows what is about to happen, for he interprets his anointing as a pre-burial act. He predicts his betrayal by Judas, his denial by Peter, and his being forsaken by his followers. He anticipates his death at the Last Supper. Nothing regarding his passion comes as a surprise to him. Second, it is clear that Jesus accepts his fate. He embraces his death in the Supper-words. He submits to his fate at Gethsemane. He makes no attempt to resist arrest. He makes no defense for himself at his trial. He even refuses the mildly anesthetic drink at the crucifixion. Third, underlying all of these examples, but perhaps most evident in the literary placement of the anointing scene and in the context of Jesus' arrest, Jesus' own actions, together with his acceptance of this, God's will, set in motion the subsequent events which end only at Golgotha. Here in the form of a story we find poignant witness to the reality of the credal formulae: Christ gave himself up.

C. Human and Divine Causation

In view of the above comments, it comes as no surprise that Jesus' death is the result of "divine causation", according to the passion narrative. The cross is God's will. Indeed, God himself "strikes the shepherd". Yet, a long chain of events indicates the responsibility of humanity in Jesus' death. The Jewish leaders plot against Jesus; Judas conspires to betray him; Judas hands him over to the Jews; the Jews hand him over to Pilate; Pilate hands him over to the executioners; the executioners crucify him. All share in the guilt. This paradoxical motif is plainest in the betrayal announcement and in the arrest. In the former, God remains in sovereign control while Judas remains fully responsible. In the latter, God himself brings about Jesus' passion, yet he is handed over to those people who will carry out the sentencing and execution.

D. Suffering Righteous

The significance of the Suffering Righteous for portraying the passion of Jesus was anticipated much earlier, when we traced the large degree of generic correspondence between the passion story and the "Suffering/ Vindication" genre. It was subsequently demonstrated that throughout the passion account — from its opening to its finale — by means of conceptual allusions, linguistic agreements, and explicit OT citations, the Suffering Righteous stands in the background of this portrayal of Jesus' death. Like the Suffering Righteous, Jesus

> (1) had enemies that plotted against him, abused him, accused him, divided his clothes, offered him a drink, and anticipated his rescue prior to death;
> (2) is betrayed by a table-intimate — an insidious, deceitful one, whose recompense is anticipated;
> (3) experiences anguish and abandonment by God;
> (4) is forsaken by his friends — one of whom denies him and follows him from a distance — so that he must suffer alone;
> (5) is innocent;
> (6) maintains his silence;
> (7) anticipates his exaltation/vindication; and
> (8) is vindicated at his death and called "Son of God".

Without a doubt, the model of the Suffering Righteous played an important role in the portrayal of Jesus' passion.

We should note, however, that the correspondence between Jesus and the pre-Christian personality of the Righteous Suffer is not complete, for Jesus does not altogether fit the pattern. First, Jesus died in physical *and spiritual* anguish — and in this his death is unique when viewed against the background of this model as it was expressed in the period before (and after) Jesus. Comparable literature (where an actual death is portrayed) depicts dying persons as impervious to pain and torment, praising God to the last breath[1]. Second, the passion story's uniqueness *vis-à-vis* comparable literature may be seen in the way the political authorities are whitewashed.

Third, and much more significant, throughout the history of the Suffering Righteous in the psalms and intertestamental literature, suffering persons call for their tormentors or enemies to be damned. For them, "vindication" entails not only "show them that we are right", but also "let our opponents be damned!" (e.g. Ps 35:22–26; 2 Macc 7:9, 14, 17, 19, 31, 34–36). Jesus makes no such threats and prays no such prayers against his Jewish or Roman accusers and executioners. Even the woe-pronouncement at the Supper retains a decided note of sorrow. The witness of 1 Pet 2:23 aptly summarizes this portrayal of Jesus in the passion story: "When they hurled insults at him, he did not retaliate; when he suffered, he made no threats". Certainly it is not accidental that the addition of Jesus' intercessory prayer for his enemies (Luke 23:34a) into the developing story has resulted in no incongruity in the spirit of the story.

Fourth, our investigation has indicated the close relationship between the Suffering Righteous and the Servant of Yahweh, for at many points evidence favoring an identification of Jesus with the one also speaks for an identification with the other. To this second figure we now turn.

E. The Servant of Yahweh

As with the former pattern, traces of influence from the Isaianic Servant may be found at numerous points in the passion narrative. Like the Servant, Jesus

(1) is God's chosen one who will complete his mission through suffering;
(2) willingly submits to his divine mission;
(3) is innocent;
(4) maintains his silence;
(5) dies "for many";
(6) is "handed over";
(7) is abused;

---

1 This point has already been made by Schweizer, *Jesus*, 17–18.

(8) is "numbered with transgressors";
(9) anticipates his vindication; and
(10) is vindicated after maltreatment.

In addition to these points, we may also refer to the discussion below regarding Jesus' death "for us" — where the concept of the Servant's salvific death is at least paralleled, and perhaps embraced.

F. The Crucified Messiah

Understandably, the early passion account described the death of Jesus as the death of the crucified Messiah. Jesus' messiahship is often presented through the use of irony — such as in the trial before Pilate, the account of his being mocked by the Roman soldiers, and the abuse experienced at the crucifixion. Additionally, his messiahship is at issue in his hearing before the Jews — raised first in the guise of the temple-charge, and then most explicitly in the question, "Are you the Christ?" While stated in terms less familiar to Jewish messianic speculation, the inscription on the cross also proclaims the crucified one as the Messiah of God.

Hence, from early on we find no attempt to remove the offensive character of Jesus' death. There was no denying the scandalous method of Jesus' death, which itself constituted an obvious means by which to refute any claim to his messiahship. Yet, in proclaiming this crucified one as God's Anointed One, the passion narrative witnessed to the understanding of the centrality of Jesus' death to his divine mission.

G. The Martyr-Prophet

Jesus is cast in the role of a prophet in two less conspicuous ways in the passion story, but most openly in the mockery scene related to the Jewish hearing. There, he is commanded, "Prophesy!" From this it is arguable that Jesus was tried as a false prophet, though it must be admitted that little else in the passion story supports this view. Otherwise, we read that Jesus possessed prophetic *foresight*, for he predicted his betrayal, denial, and the flight of his disciples — all of which came to pass, and that he had prophetic *insight* (into Judas's motives at the arrest).

Hence, while evidence is not completely lacking, there is little to suggest that the passion narrative was written especially from the perspective that Jesus was one of a long line of prophets whose lot was rejection and martyrdom.

H. Jesus' Death: A Cosmic Event

Secondary developments increasingly incorporated into the passion story testify to its cosmic context, but already in its initial redaction this motif had arisen. Inasmuch as reference is made to "trial", "watching", and, perhaps, to "darkness" — especially in the Gethsemane account — the passion is set within the context of a conflict of cosmic proportions.

I. Jesus' Death: Eschatological Turning Point

Closely related, there is direct evidence in the passion account that Jesus' suffering and death marked the decisive watershed in salvation-history, when God's eschatological age of salvation would be inaugurated. This is evident in the use of Zech 13 in the announcement of the flight of the disciples, for in identifying Jesus with the shepherd, the passion story also brought into view the idea that the shepherd's demise gives way to triumph and the reconstitution of his "flock". The Supper-words, too, present Jesus' death as the turning point of salvation-history, making use of the "new convenant" idea. Hour-references at the arrest and crucifixion testify to this same theme: in Jesus' death God is bringing his redemptive plan to fruition. Finally, the temple-material indicates the decisiveness of Jesus' death. The rending of the temple veil — symbolizing at once the destruction of the temple and its replacement in the person of the crucified Christ — marks the death of Jesus as the decisive eschatological event.

J. Jesus' Death "For Us"

The atoning significance of Jesus' death is explicit in the passion story only in the Supper words, but we have suggested its conceptual presence in the Barabbas-episode and words of mockery at the crucifixion as well. In the first scene, a variety of images — the new covenant, covenant-in-blood, the Servant of Yahweh, martyrdom, and the forgiveness of sins — appear in conjunction with Jesus' death. In the Barabbas-episode, Jesus dies in another's stead, whereas in the words of mockery, Jesus' death is ironically presented as having soteriological effect.

K. Jesus' Death: God's Judgment

With the use of two OT images the notion that in his death Jesus bore the judgment of God is present. The first instance is found in Jesus' prediction of the flight of the disciples. Like the fall of the shepherd in Zech 13, Jesus' death is portrayed as divine judgment. Similarly, the cup-metaphor used in Jesus' Gethsemane-prayer is associated with the idea of "bearing the judgment of God".

L. Jesus' Death: Martyrdom?

Some interpreters have tried to draw a direct line of influence from the martyr-tales of contemporary Judaism to the passion narrative[2], but we

---

2 See the programmatic list in Frend, *Martyrdom,* 83—84.

have found reason to cast serious doubt on such an enterprise. Two outstanding points speak against viewing Jesus' death in this way. First, the passion story has Jesus shrinking away from the prospect of death in Gethsemane. Contrast this with the open willingness with which the martyrs embrace death! Second, we have drawn attention to the great reserve in the passion account when compared with the martyr-tales. Precisely at those points where a martyr-tale would relish in providing picturesque details – i.e. the whipping episode and the act of crucifixion – the passion story allows only the most abbreviated, colorless, matter-of-fact report. Theories favoring direct or substantial influence from the martyr-tales to the story of Jesus' passion founder on these significant discrepancies.

M. Conclusion

In summary, we might say that the passion narrative seems most interested in demonstrating that Jesus' passion was fully explicable in terms of God's will. His passion was prophesied in the OT Scriptures, preordained by God himself. His passion was not a contradiction of his claims or of the claims being made on his behalf – but instead demonstrated the validity of those claims.

Yet, it is also true that the passion story has very little to say about the significance of Jesus' death in salvation-historical terms, apart from the obvious point regarding its place of primacy in God's redemptive plan. We are told that Jesus' death was central to his mission, but we hear very little about why or how it so functions. We are told that Jesus' death was central to God's salvific purpose, but how it so functions is relatively unimportant in the passion account. In short, the passion account emphasizes much more the *that* of this connection than the *why* or *how* behind it.

II. The Passion Narrative and Atonement-Theology

With this tradition-historical and theological investigation of the passion narrative, we find ourselves at the threshold of what could easily become a full-scale study of the understanding of the death of Jesus in the passion story within the context of earliest Christian theology. That is, the bulk of the second part of our thesis might be considered as prolegomena to an all-embracing discussion of the theology of Jesus' death in the passion account – one that deals more exhaustively with the story's presentation of the death of Jesus as a unified whole, that points to the distinctive flavor of its characterization of Jesus' passion, that assesses the relationship of this narrative and other, more or less contemporary and later, christological and soteriological developments. Moreover, we now have before us the raw materials for an investigation of how the passion story itself was developed theologically, especially by each of the four evangelists as they incorporated this early connected material into their respective works. Before throwing open the door to this new area of study, however, it is well to remember our rather limited point of entry into this whole matter of the existence and theology of the passion narrative. Our original question had to do with the problem of the history of the idea of Jesus' substitutionary death, and our interest in what the passion account might teach us about that history. Concomitant with that original concern, then, we may allow ourselves to raise only one issue for final consideration: Why does atonement-theology scarcely raise its head in the primitive passion narrative?

Hengel, in his study of *The Atonement*, traced the development of early atonement-theology from the early church to those first disciples, who took as their point of reference the eucharistic words of Jesus at the Last Supper. Indeed, Hengel could find no room in primitive Christianity for a lengthy development at the base of which was a non-soterilogical interpretation of Jesus' death. Yet, by means of a more comprehensive interplay of methodological approaches and wide-ranging testimonies than has heretofore been deployed, our investigation has led to a two-pronged conclusion that at least appears to contradict Hengel's hypothesis: *(1) there existed in earliest Christianity a narrative of Jesus' suffering and death which (2) interpreted Jesus' passion as central to God's redemptive plan* without *a promiment or pervasive emphasis on the soteriological implications of the cross.* On the basis of our investigation, we may claim that primitive Christianity *did* know non-soteriological interpretations of Jesus' death; what is more, the early narrative of Jesus' suffering and death — which was from the beginning theologically-interpreted historical narrative — told the story in such a way that the soteriological implications of the cross appear to have played very much a minor role. Hengel denies the adequacy of the "suffering righteous" category for coming to terms with Jesus' death, and our analysis has shown that in this Hengel is justified, for even the framers of the early passion narrative were not content with this one image; moreover, even this theme is subordinated to the more general purpose of showing how Jesus' death was carried out in accordance with the divine plan. Even with the parallel preponderance of the Servant-motif in the passion story, however, we are still outside the immediate realm of an explicit, pervasive atonement-theology, for reference to the Servant's vicarious death is almost completely missing in the passion story. How is this tension to be explained?

It is, of course, arguable that even though early Christians universally recognized the cruciality of Jesus' death, not all recognized its foremost significance as a substitutionary act. Indeed, one finds in the NT old formulae that suggest salvation was not always and everywhere tied to the cross. In this case, the passion narrative would represent the emphasis of the primitive church on the centrality of the suffering and death of Jesus in God's plan, without making explicit that the cross was, in fact, *the* salvific event. While further study would be necessary to support this, a comparison thus seems possible between the understanding of Jesus' death in the passion account and Luke's primary emphasis on the cross as a divine necessity ($\delta\epsilon\hat{\iota}$) apart from significant reflection on *how* it functions in terms of the divine plan. New Testament study must at all times resist the temptation to presuppose or too quickly assume a unified theology or monochromic view of Jesus' death in the primitive church, and this is a warning against too easily dismissing this hypothesis for coming to terms with the theology of Jesus' passion in the early passion narrative within the context of early Christian thought.

On the other hand, our discussion has suggested an alternative, perhaps more obvious answer for the phenomenon under scrutiny here. We have argued that the primitive passion narrative had its *Sitz im Leben* in the context of the celebration of the Lord's Supper, and that the eucharistic words of Jesus set the stage and determined the climate for this whole community experience. The truth of this latter judgment is further evidenced by the negative example of Corinth. Because the Corinthian Christians were not allowing the eucharistic words of Jesus to set their stamp on the meal-celebration in particular and on community life in general, they were not, according to Paul, celebrating the *Lord's* Supper. We have put forward a body of evidence encouraging the thesis that the testimony of the eucharistic words, with their straightforward emphasis on Jesus' redemptive death, so pervaded the Christian celebration of the Lord's Supper, that no additional, explicit testimony to its soteriological significance was required in the passion narrative. Indeed, it is only in such a context that the Barabbas-incident and the ironic statement of mockery at the crucifixion, both found in the passion story, could be taken as implicit *testimonia* to an understanding of Jesus' death as having soteriological implications. Simply put, the passion narrative assumes the eucharistic emphasis on the soteriological effects of the death of Jesus.

We have therefore set forth two ways of explaining the apparent lack of any significant emphasis on atonement-theology in the early passion narrative. Inasmuch as both explanations stem directly from our earlier discussion, it is not necessary to support each in detail; rather, we have already seen how each is plausible in its own way. What must be asked is whether one is to be preferred over the other — i.e. which more closely fits the evidence we have assimilated? Alternatively, it is legitimate to ask whether we are in fact necessarily faced with the prospect of tendering an either-or verdict between these two alternatives, for it is certainly possible to recognize that the passion narrative assumes atonement-theology while at the same time recognizing that the narrative's more prominent theological emphasis is not so carefully nuanced. On the basis of the total evidence, no one can deny that in any case atonement-theology is not the central motif to which all others lead — and this is true not only for the passion narrative but also for the eucharistic words themselves. As we saw, the Supper-words gather together numerous OT motifs and bits of OT language to emphatically make the point, first, that Jesus' death is central to God's redemptive plan. Apparently, for earliest Christianity, the highest priority was on proving that Jesus' death was no surprise to God and constituted no contradiction of the christological claims that had been and were being advanced. The idea that Jesus died "for us" evidently constituted one very early and important means of making this point clear — as is evidenced in the repetition of the Supper words. In the early celebration of the Supper — the context in which the passion narrative was given birth, the christological and soteriological interpretations of Jesus' death flowed together. However, if the passion narrative is one trustworthy guide for understanding earliest Christian thought — as we have claimed — this salvific interpretation was only one among several by which Jesus' death was viewed in terms of God's redemptive purpose. The use of additional OT texts, themes, and figures — by allusion and citation — served a similar function.

Hence, we have seen that primitive Christianity could never have contented itself with mere factual statements concerning the death of Jesus. Rather, the cross-event cried out for interpretation, with the result that an interpretive story of Jesus' suffering and death soon took shape. This narrative not only allowed but indeed purposed the blending together of historical events and theological reflection. Jesus' passion was thus recognized and proclaimed for its cruciality in God's salvific plan, an awareness that to a large degree arose from the eucharistic words of Jesus as they were remembered at the Lord's Supper.

Appendix
Sources in Luke's Passion Narrative

The text printed below is that of Nestle, et al., *Novum Testamentum Grace*, 26th ed. The key to the markings is as follows:

————————— = Lukan redaction of Mark probable.
---------- = Lukan redaction of Mark possible.
.... = Lukan redaction of *Sonderquelle* probable.
. . . . = Lukan redaction of *Sonderquelle* possible.
.-.-.-.-.-.-.-. = Lukan conflation of Mark and *Sonderquelle*.
No special marking = "Free" Lukan creation.

22 ⌜Ἤγγιζεν δὲ ἡ ἑορτὴ τῶν ἀζύμων ἡ λεγομένη πάσχα. 2 καὶ ἐζήτουν οἱ ἀρχιερεῖς καὶ οἱ γραμματεῖς °τὸ πῶς ⌜ἀνέλωσιν αὐτόν, ἐφοβοῦντο γὰρ τὸν λαόν. 3 Εἰσῆλθεν δὲ σατανᾶς εἰς Ἰούδαν τὸν ⌜καλούμενον Ἰσκαριώτην, ὄντα ἐκ τοῦ ἀριθμοῦ τῶν δώδεκα· 4 καὶ ἀπελθὼν συνελάλησεν τοῖς ἀρχιερεῦσιν ᵀ ⌜καὶ στρατηγοῖς⌝ °τὸ πῶς αὐτοῖς παραδῷ αὐτόν. 5 καὶ ἐχάρησαν καὶ συνέθεντο αὐτῷ ἀργύριον δοῦναι. 6 ⸋καὶ ἐξωμολόγησεν,⸌ καὶ ἐζήτει εὐκαιρίαν τοῦ παραδοῦναι αὐτὸν ⌜ἄτερ ὄχλου αὐτοῖς⌝.
7 Ἦλθεν δὲ ἡ ἡμέρα ⌜τῶν ἀζύμων⌝, °[ἐν] ᾗ ἔδει θύεσθαι τὸ πάσχα· 8 καὶ ἀπέστειλεν Πέτρον καὶ Ἰωάννην εἰπών· πορευθέντες ἑτοιμάσατε ἡμῖν τὸ πάσχα ἵνα φάγωμεν. 9 οἱ δὲ εἶπαν αὐτῷ· ποῦ θέλεις ἑτοιμάσωμεν ᵀ; 10 ὁ δὲ εἶπεν αὐτοῖς· ἰδοὺ εἰσελθόντων ὑμῶν εἰς τὴν πόλιν ⌜συναντήσει ὑμῖν ἄνθρωπος κεράμιον ὕδατος βαστάζων· ἀκολουθήσατε αὐτῷ εἰς τὴν οἰκίαν ⌜εἰς ἣν⌝ εἰσπορεύεται, 11 καὶ ἐρεῖτε τῷ οἰκοδεσπότῃ τῆς οἰκίας ᵀ· λέγει °σοι ὁ διδάσκαλος· ποῦ ἐστιν τὸ κατάλυμα ὅπου τὸ πάσχα μετὰ τῶν μαθητῶν μου φάγω; 12 κἀκεῖνος ὑμῖν δείξει ἀνάγαιον ⌜μέγα ἐστρωμένον· ἐκεῖ ἑτοιμάσατε. 13 ἀπελθόντες δὲ εὗρον καθὼς εἰρήκει αὐτοῖς καὶ ἡτοίμασαν τὸ πάσχα.
14 Καὶ ὅτε ἐγένετο ἡ ὥρα, ἀνέπεσεν καὶ οἱ ⌜ἀπόστολοι σὺν αὐτῷ. 15 καὶ εἶπεν πρὸς αὐτούς· ἐπιθυμίᾳ ἐπεθύμησα τοῦτο τὸ πάσχα φαγεῖν μεθ' ὑμῶν πρὸ τοῦ με παθεῖν·

16 λέγω γὰρ ὑμῖν °ὅτι ⸀οὐ μὴ φάγω⸀ ⌜αὐτὸ ἕως ὅτου ⌐πληρωθῇ ἐν τῇ βασιλείᾳ τοῦ θεοῦ. 17 ⸀καὶ δεξάμενος ⸆ ποτήριον εὐχαριστήσας εἶπεν· λάβετε τοῦτο °καὶ διαμερίσατε ⸀εἰς ἑαυτούς⸃· 18 λέγω γὰρ ὑμῖν, °¹[ὅτι] οὐ μὴ πίω ⸂¹ἀπὸ τοῦ νῦν¹⸃ ἀπὸ τοῦ γενήματος τῆς ἀμπέλου ἕως ⌜οὗ ἡ βασιλεία τοῦ θεοῦ ἔλθῃ. 19 καὶ λαβὼν ἄρτον εὐχαριστήσας ἔκλασεν καὶ ἔδωκεν αὐτοῖς λέγων· τοῦτό ἐστιν τὸ σῶμά μου □τὸ ὑπὲρ ὑμῶν διδόμενον· τοῦτο ποιεῖτε εἰς τὴν ἐμὴν ἀνάμνησιν. 20 ˢκαὶ τὸ ποτήριον ὡσαύτως˨ μετὰ τὸ δειπνῆσαι, λέγων· τοῦτο τὸ ποτήριον ἡ °²καινὴ διαθήκη ἐν τῷ αἵματί μου τὸ ὑπὲρ ὑμῶν ἐκχυννόμενον.\⸃

21 Πλὴν ἰδοὺ ἡ χεὶρ τοῦ παραδιδόντος με μετ' ἐμοῦ ἐπὶ τῆς τραπέζης. 22 ⸀ὅτι ὁ υἱὸς μὲν⸃ τοῦ ἀνθρώπου ˢκατὰ τὸ ὡρισμένον πορεύεται˨, πλὴν οὐαὶ □τῷ ἀνθρώπῳ\ ἐκείνῳ δι' οὗ παραδίδοται. 23 καὶ αὐτοὶ ἤρξαντο συζητεῖν πρὸς ἑαυτοὺς τὸ τίς ἄρα εἴη ἐξ αὐτῶν ὁ τοῦτο μέλλων πράσσειν.

24 Ἐγένετο ⸀δὲ καὶ⸃ φιλονεικία ἐν αὐτοῖς, τὸ τίς ⸀αὐτῶν δοκεῖ εἶναι⸃ μείζων. 25 ὁ δὲ εἶπεν αὐτοῖς· οἱ βασιλεῖς τῶν ἐθνῶν κυριεύουσιν αὐτῶν καὶ οἱ ἐξουσιάζοντες αὐτῶν εὐεργέται καλοῦνται. 26 ὑμεῖς δὲ οὐχ οὕτως, ἀλλ' ὁ μείζων ἐν ὑμῖν γινέσθω ὡς ⸀ὁ νεώτερος⸃ καὶ ὁ ἡγούμενος ὡς ὁ διακονῶν⸀. 27 τίς γὰρ μείζων, ὁ ἀνακείμενος ἢ ὁ διακονῶν; οὐχὶ⸃ ὁ ἀνακείμενος; ἐγὼ ⸂¹δὲ ἐν μέσῳ ὑμῶν εἰμι⸃ ὡς ὁ διακονῶν.

28 ⸀Ὑμεῖς δέ ἐστε⸃ οἱ διαμεμενηκότες μετ' ἐμοῦ ἐν τοῖς πειρασμοῖς μου· 29 κἀγὼ διατίθεμαι ὑμῖν ⸆ καθὼς διέθετό μοι ὁ πατήρ μου ⌜βασιλείαν, 30 ἵνα ἔσθητε καὶ πίνητε ἐπὶ τῆς τραπέζης μου ἐν τῇ βασιλείᾳ μου, * καὶ ⌜καθήσεσθε ἐπὶ ⸆ θρόνων ˢτὰς δώδεκα φυλὰς κρίνοντες˨ τοῦ Ἰσραήλ.

31 ⸆ Σίμων Σίμων, ἰδοὺ ὁ σατανᾶς ἐξῃτήσατο ὑμᾶς τοῦ σινιάσαι ὡς τὸν σῖτον· 32 ἐγὼ δὲ ἐδεήθην περὶ σοῦ ἵνα μὴ ἐκλίπῃ ἡ πίστις σου· ⸀καὶ σύ ποτε ἐπιστρέψας⸃ στήρισον τοὺς ⌜ἀδελφούς σου. 33 ὁ δὲ εἶπεν αὐτῷ· κύριε, μετὰ σοῦ ἕτοιμός εἰμι καὶ εἰς φυλακὴν καὶ εἰς θάνατον πορεύεσθαι. 34 ὁ δὲ εἶπεν· λέγω σοι, Πέτρε, οὐ φωνήσει σήμερον ἀλέκτωρ ⌜ἕως τρίς ⸀με ἀπαρνήσῃ εἰδέναι⸃.

35 Καὶ εἶπεν αὐτοῖς· ὅτε ἀπέστειλα ὑμᾶς ἄτερ βαλλαντίου καὶ πήρας □καὶ ὑποδημάτων\, μή τινος ὑστερήσατε; οἱ δὲ εἶπαν· οὐθενός. 36 ⸀εἶπεν δὲ⸃ αὐτοῖς· ἀλλὰ νῦν ὁ ἔχων βαλλάντιον ἀράτω, ὁμοίως καὶ πήραν, καὶ ὁ μὴ

ἔχων πωλησάτω τὸ ἱμάτιον αὐτοῦ καὶ ἀγορασάτω μάχαιραν. 37 λέγω γὰρ ὑμῖν ὅτι ⊤ τοῦτο τὸ γεγραμμένον δεῖ τελεσθῆναι ἐν ἐμοί, τό· ⌜καὶ μετὰ ἀνόμων ἐλογίσθη⌝· καὶ ὁ γὰρ ⌜τὸ περὶ ἐμοῦ τέλος ἔχει. 38 οἱ δὲ εἶπαν· κύριε, ἰδοὺ μάχαιραι ὧδε δύο. ὁ δὲ εἶπεν αὐτοῖς· ⌜ἱκανόν ἐστιν⌝.

39 Καὶ ἐξελθὼν ἐπορεύθη κατὰ τὸ ἔθος εἰς τὸ ὄρος τῶν ἐλαιῶν, ἠκολούθησαν δὲ αὐτῷ ⸋καὶ οἱ μαθηταί. 40 γενόμενος δὲ ἐπὶ τοῦ τόπου εἶπεν αὐτοῖς· προσεύχεσθε μὴ ⌜εἰσελθεῖν εἰς πειρασμόν. 41 καὶ αὐτὸς ἀπεσπάσθη ἀπ' αὐτῶν ὡσεὶ λίθου βολὴν καὶ θεὶς τὰ γόνατα ⌜προσηύχετο 42 λέγων· πάτερ, ⌜εἰ βούλει ⌜παρένεγκε τοῦτο τὸ ποτήριον ἀπ' ἐμοῦ· πλὴν μὴ τὸ θέλημά μου ἀλλὰ τὸ σὸν γινέσθω⌝. ⟦43 ὤφθη δὲ αὐτῷ ἄγγελος ἀπ' ⊤ οὐρανοῦ ἐνισχύων αὐτόν. 44 καὶ γενόμενος ἐν ἀγωνίᾳ ἐκτενέστερον προσηύχετο· ⌜καὶ ἐγένετο⌝ ὁ ἱδρὼς αὐτοῦ ὡσεὶ θρόμβοι αἵματος ⌜καταβαίνοντες ἐπὶ τὴν γῆν.⟧ 45 καὶ ἀναστὰς ἀπὸ τῆς προσευχῆς ⊤ ἐλθὼν πρὸς τοὺς μαθητὰς εὗρεν κοιμωμένους αὐτοὺς ἀπὸ τῆς λύπης, 46 καὶ εἶπεν αὐτοῖς· ⸋τί καθεύδετε; ἀναστάντες προσεύχεσθε, ἵνα μὴ εἰσέλθητε εἰς πειρασμόν.

47 Ἔτι ⊤ αὐτοῦ λαλοῦντος ἰδοὺ ὄχλος ⊤, καὶ ὁ ⌜λεγόμενος Ἰούδας⌝ εἷς τῶν δώδεκα ⌜προήρχετο αὐτοὺς ⁎ καὶ ἤγγισεν τῷ Ἰησοῦ φιλῆσαι αὐτόν⊤¹. 48 ⌜Ἰησοῦς δὲ⌝ εἶπεν ⌜αὐτῷ· Ἰούδα,⌝ φιλήματι τὸν υἱὸν τοῦ ἀνθρώπου παραδίδως; 49 ἰδόντες δὲ οἱ περὶ αὐτὸν τὸ ⌜ἐσόμενον εἶπαν⌝· κύριε, εἰ πατάξομεν ἐν μαχαίρῃ; 50 καὶ ἐπάταξεν εἷς τις ἐξ αὐτῶν ⸌τοῦ ἀρχιερέως τὸν δοῦλον⸍ καὶ ἀφεῖλεν ⌜τὸ οὖς αὐτοῦ⌝ τὸ δεξιόν. 51 ἀποκριθεὶς δὲ ⸋ὁ Ἰησοῦς εἶπεν· ἐᾶτε ἕως τούτου· καὶ ⌜ἁψάμενος τοῦ ὠτίου ἰάσατο αὐτόν⌝.

52 Εἶπεν δὲ ⌜Ἰησοῦς πρὸς τοὺς παραγενομένους ⌜ἐπ' αὐτὸν ἀρχιερεῖς καὶ στρατηγοὺς ⌜τοῦ ἱεροῦ⌝ καὶ πρεσβυτέρους· ὡς ἐπὶ λῃστὴν ⌜¹ἐξήλθατε μετὰ μαχαιρῶν καὶ ξύλων⌝; 53 ⊤καθ' ἡμέραν ὄντος μου μεθ' ὑμῶν ἐν τῷ ἱερῷ οὐκ ἐξετείνατε τὰς χεῖρας ἐπ' ἐμέ, ἀλλ' αὕτη ἐστὶν ὑμῶν ἡ ὥρα καὶ ⸋ἡ ἐξουσία ⌜τοῦ σκότους⌝.

54 Συλλαβόντες δὲ αὐτὸν ἤγαγον ⸀καὶ εἰσήγαγον⸍ εἰς τὴν οἰκίαν τοῦ ἀρχιερέως· ὁ δὲ Πέτρος ἠκολούθει ⊤ μακρόθεν. 55 ⌜περιαψάντων δὲ πῦρ ἐν μέσῳ τῆς αὐλῆς καὶ συγκαθισάντων⌝ ἐκάθητο ⌜ὁ Πέτρος ⌜μέσος αὐτῶν⊤. 56 ἰδοῦσα δὲ αὐτὸν παιδίσκη τις καθήμενον πρὸς τὸ φῶς

καὶ ἀτενίσασα αὐτῷ εἶπεν· καὶ οὗτος σὺν αὐτῷ ἦν. 57 ὁ δὲ ἠρνήσατο ⊤ λέγων· ⌜οὐκ οἶδα αὐτόν, γύναι⌝. 58 καὶ μετὰ βραχὺ ἕτερος ἰδὼν αὐτὸν ⌜ἔφη· καὶ σὺ ἐξ αὐτῶν εἶ⌝. ὁ δὲ ⌜Πέτρος ἔφη⌝· ἄνθρωπε, οὐκ εἰμί. 59 καὶ διαστάσης ὡσεὶ ὥρας μιᾶς ἄλλος τις διϊσχυρίζετο ⌜λέγων· ἐπ' ἀληθείας⌝ καὶ οὗτος μετ' αὐτοῦ ἦν, καὶ γὰρ Γαλιλαῖός ἐστιν. 60 εἶπεν δὲ ὁ Πέτρος· ἄνθρωπε, οὐκ οἶδα ⌜ὃ λέγεις. καὶ παραχρῆμα ἔτι λαλοῦντος αὐτοῦ ἐφώνησεν ἀλέκτωρ. 61 καὶ στραφεὶς ὁ ⌜κύριος ἐνέβλεψεν ⌜τῷ Πέτρῳ⌝, * ⌜καὶ ὑπεμνήσθη ⌐ὁ Πέτρος⌝ τοῦ ⌜ῥήματος τοῦ κυρίου ὡς εἶπεν αὐτῷ ὅτι πρὶν ⊤ ἀλέκτορα φωνῆσαι ᵒσήμερον ⌜ἀπαρνήσῃ με τρίς⌝. 62 ⌐καὶ ἐξελθὼν ἔξω ἔκλαυσεν πικρῶς.⌝

63 Καὶ οἱ ἄνδρες οἱ συνέχοντες αὐτὸν ἐνέπαιζον αὐτῷ ᵒδέροντες, 64 καὶ περικαλύψαντες ⌜αὐτὸν ⌜ἐπηρώτων λέγοντες⌝· προφήτευσον, τίς ἐστιν ὁ παίσας σε; 65 καὶ ἕτερα πολλὰ βλασφημοῦντες ἔλεγον εἰς αὐτόν.

66 Καὶ ὡς ἐγένετο ἡμέρα, συνήχθη τὸ πρεσβυτέριον τοῦ λαοῦ, ἀρχιερεῖς τε καὶ γραμματεῖς, καὶ ⌜ἀπήγαγον αὐτὸν εἰς τὸ συνέδριον αὐτῶν 67 λέγοντες· εἰ σὺ εἶ ὁ χριστός⌜, εἰπὸν ἡμῖν. εἶπεν δὲ αὐτοῖς· ἐὰν ὑμῖν εἴπω, οὐ μὴ πιστεύσητε· 68 ⌐¹ ἐὰν δὲ⌝ ἐρωτήσω, οὐ μὴ ἀποκριθῆτε ⊤.⌝ 69 ἀπὸ τοῦ νῦν δὲ ἔσται ὁ υἱὸς τοῦ ἀνθρώπου καθήμενος ἐκ δεξιῶν τῆς δυνάμεως τοῦ θεοῦ. 70 εἶπαν δὲ πάντες· σὺ οὖν εἶ ὁ υἱὸς τοῦ θεοῦ·; ὁ δὲ πρὸς αὐτοὺς ἔφη· ὑμεῖς λέγετε ὅτι ἐγώ εἰμι·¹. 71 οἱ δὲ εἶπαν· τί ἔτι ⌜ἔχομεν μαρτυρίας χρείαν⌝; αὐτοὶ γὰρ ἠκούσαμεν ἀπὸ τοῦ στόματος αὐτοῦ.

23 Καὶ ⌜ἀναστὰν ⌐ἅπαν τὸ πλῆθος αὐτῶν⌝ ἤγαγον αὐτὸν ἐπὶ τὸν Πιλᾶτον.

2 Ἤρξαντο δὲ κατηγορεῖν αὐτοῦ λέγοντες· τοῦτον εὕραμεν διαστρέφοντα τὸ ἔθνος ᵒἡμῶν ⊤ καὶ κωλύοντα ⌜φόρους Καίσαρι διδόναι⌝ ⊤ καὶ λέγοντα ἑαυτὸν χριστὸν βασιλέα εἶναι. 3 ὁ δὲ Πιλᾶτος ⌜ἠρώτησεν αὐτὸν λέγων· σὺ εἶ ὁ βασιλεὺς τῶν Ἰουδαίων; ⌜ὁ δὲ ἀποκριθεὶς αὐτῷ ἔφη⌝· σὺ λέγεις·. 4 ὁ δὲ Πιλᾶτος εἶπεν πρὸς τοὺς ἀρχιερεῖς καὶ τοὺς ὄχλους· οὐδὲν εὑρίσκω αἴτιον ἐν τῷ ἀνθρώπῳ τούτῳ. 5 οἱ δὲ ἐπίσχυον λέγοντες ὅτι ἀνασείει τὸν λαὸν ᵒδιδάσκων καθ' ὅλης τῆς ⌜Ἰουδαίας, ᵒ¹καὶ ἀρξάμενος ἀπὸ τῆς Γαλιλαίας ἕως ὧδε⊤.

6 Πιλᾶτος δὲ ἀκούσας ⊤ ἐπηρώτησεν εἰ ⌜ὁ ἄνθρωπος Γαλιλαῖός⌝ ἐστιν, 7 καὶ ἐπιγνοὺς ὅτι ἐκ τῆς ἐξουσίας Ἡρῴδου ἐστὶν ἀνέπεμψεν αὐτὸν πρὸς ⊤ Ἡρῴδην, ὄντα καὶ αὐτὸν ἐν Ἱεροσολύμοις ἐν ταύταις ταῖς ἡμέραις.

8 Ὁ δὲ Ἡρῴδης ἰδὼν τὸν Ἰησοῦν ἐχάρη λίαν, ἦν γὰρ ἐξ ⸂ἱκανῶν χρόνων⸃ θέλων ἰδεῖν αὐτὸν διὰ τὸ ἀκούειν ⸀περὶ αὐτοῦ καὶ ἤλπιζέν τι σημεῖον ἰδεῖν ὑπ' αὐτοῦ γινόμενον. 9 ἐπηρώτα δὲ αὐτὸν ἐν λόγοις ἱκανοῖς, αὐτὸς δὲ ⸀οὐδὲν ἀπεκρίνατο αὐτῷ⸀. 10 ⸆εἱστήκεισαν δὲ οἱ ἀρχιερεῖς καὶ οἱ γραμματεῖς εὐτόνως κατηγοροῦντες αὐτοῦ. 11 ἐξουθενήσας δὲ αὐτὸν ⸂[καὶ] ὁ⸃ Ἡρῴδης σὺν τοῖς στρατεύμασιν αὐτοῦ καὶ ἐμπαίξας περιβαλὼν ἐσθῆτα λαμπρὰν ⸀ἀνέπεμψεν αὐτὸν τῷ Πιλάτῳ. 12 ⸀ἐγένοντο δὲ φίλοι ὅ τε Ἡρῴδης καὶ ὁ Πιλᾶτος ἐν ⸀αὐτῇ τῇ ἡμέρᾳ μετ' ἀλλήλων· προϋπῆρχον γὰρ ἐν ἔχθρᾳ ὄντες πρὸς ⸂αὐτούς.⸃ ⸃ ⸆

13 Πιλᾶτος δὲ συγκαλεσάμενος τοὺς ἀρχιερεῖς καὶ τοὺς ἄρχοντας καὶ τὸν λαὸν 14 εἶπεν πρὸς αὐτούς· ⸀προσηνέγκατέ μοι τὸν ἄνθρωπον τοῦτον ὡς ἀποστρέφοντα τὸν λαόν, καὶ ἰδοὺ ἐγὼ ἐνώπιον ὑμῶν ἀνακρίνας ⸀οὐθὲν εὗρον ἐν τῷ ἀνθρώπῳ τούτῳ αἴτιον ὧν κατηγορεῖτε ⸉κατ' αὐτοῦ. 15 ἀλλ' οὐδὲ Ἡρῴδης, ⸂ἀνέπεμψεν γὰρ αὐτὸν πρὸς ἡμᾶς⸃, καὶ ἰδοὺ οὐδὲν ἄξιον θανάτου ἐστὶν πεπραγμένον ⸆ αὐτῷ· 16 παιδεύσας οὖν αὐτὸν ἀπολύσω. ⸆

18 ⸀Ἀνέκραγον δὲ παμπληθεὶ λέγοντες· αἶρε τοῦτον, ἀπόλυσον δὲ ἡμῖν ⸉τὸν Βαραββᾶν· 19 ὅστις ἦν διὰ στάσιν τινὰ γενομένην ἐν τῇ πόλει καὶ φόνον ⸀βληθεὶς ἐν τῇ φυλακῇ. 20 πάλιν δὲ ὁ Πιλᾶτος προσεφώνησεν ⸀αὐτοῖς θέλων ἀπολῦσαι τὸν Ἰησοῦν. 21 οἱ δὲ ⸂ἐπεφώνουν λέγοντες⸃· ⸀σταύρου σταύρου⸃ αὐτόν. 22 ὁ δὲ τρίτον εἶπεν πρὸς αὐτούς· τί γὰρ κακὸν ἐποίησεν οὗτος; ⸂οὐδὲν αἴτιον⸃ θανάτου εὗρον ἐν αὐτῷ· παιδεύσας οὖν αὐτὸν ἀπολύσω. 23 οἱ δὲ ἐπέκειντο φωναῖς μεγάλαις αἰτούμενοι αὐτὸν ⸀σταυρωθῆναι, καὶ κατίσχυον αἱ φωναὶ αὐτῶν⸆.

24 Καὶ Πιλᾶτος ἐπέκρινεν γενέσθαι τὸ αἴτημα αὐτῶν· 25 ἀπέλυσεν δὲ τὸν ⸂διὰ στάσιν καὶ φόνον⸃ βεβλημένον ⸀εἰς φυλακὴν⸃ ὃν ᾐτοῦντο, τὸν δὲ Ἰησοῦν παρέδωκεν τῷ θελήματι αὐτῶν.

26 Καὶ ὡς ⸀ἀπήγαγον αὐτόν, ἐπιλαβόμενοι ⸂Σίμωνά τινα Κυρηναῖον ἐρχόμενον⸃ ἀπ' ἀγροῦ ἐπέθηκαν αὐτῷ τὸν σταυρὸν φέρειν ὄπισθεν τοῦ Ἰησοῦ.

27 Ἠκολούθει δὲ αὐτῷ πολὺ πλῆθος τοῦ λαοῦ καὶ ⸀γυναικῶν αἳ ἐκόπτοντο καὶ ἐθρήνουν αὐτόν. 28 στραφεὶς δὲ ⸂πρὸς αὐτὰς [ὁ] Ἰησοῦς⸃ εἶπεν· θυγατέρες Ἰερου-

Appendix

σαλήμ, μὴ κλαίετε ᵒἐπ' ἐμέ ᵀ· πλὴν ᵒἐφ' ἑαυτὰς κλαίετε καὶ ᵒἐπὶ τὰ τέκνα ὑμῶν, 29 ὅτι ᵒἰδοὺ ⌜ἔρχονται ἡμέραι⌝ ἐν αἷς ἐροῦσιν· μακάριαι αἱ στεῖραι καὶ αἱ κοιλίαι αἳ οὐκ ἐγέννησαν καὶ μαστοὶ οἳ οὐκ ⌜ἔθρεψαν. 30 τότε ἄρξονται λέγειν τοῖς ὄρεσιν· πέσετε ἐφ' ἡμᾶς, καὶ τοῖς βουνοῖς· καλύψατε ἡμᾶς· 31 ὅτι εἰ ἐν ᵒτῷ ὑγρῷ ξύλῳ ταῦτα ποιοῦσιν, ἐν τῷ ξηρῷ τί ⌜γένηται;
32 Ἤγοντο δὲ καὶ ἕτεροι ⌐κακοῦργοι δύο⌐ σὺν αὐτῷ ᵀ ἀναιρεθῆναι.
33 <u>Καὶ ὅτε ⌜ἦλθον ἐπὶ τὸν τόπον τὸν καλούμενον Κρανίον, ἐκεῖ ἐσταύρωσαν αὐτὸν</u> * <u>καὶ τοὺς κακούργους</u> ᵀ, <u>ὃν μὲν ἐκ δεξιῶν ὃν δὲ ἐξ ἀριστερῶν</u>. 34 ⬜〚ὁ δὲ Ἰησοῦς ἔλεγεν· πάτερ, ἄφες αὐτοῖς, οὐ γὰρ οἴδασιν τί ποιοῦσιν.〛⌐
⌜<u>διαμεριζόμενοι δὲ τὰ ἱμάτια αὐτοῦ</u> ⌜ἔβαλον ⌜¹κλήρους.
35 Καὶ εἱστήκει ὁ λαὸς θεωρῶν. * ἐξεμυκτήριζον δὲ ⌜καὶ οἱ ἄρχοντες⌝ λέγοντες· ἄλλους ⌜ἔσωσεν, σωσάτω ἑαυτόν, εἰ οὗτός ἐστιν ὁ χριστὸς τοῦ θεοῦ⌝ ὁ ἐκλεκτός. 36 ⌜ἐνέπαιξαν δὲ αὐτῷ καὶ οἱ στρατιῶται προσερχόμενοι, ⌜ὄξος προσφέροντες αὐτῷ⌝ 37 ⌜καὶ λέγοντες· εἰ σὺ εἶ⌝ ὁ βασιλεὺς τῶν Ἰουδαίων, ⌜σῶσον σεαυτόν⌝. 38 ἦν δὲ καὶ ἐπιγραφὴ ⌜ἐπ' αὐτῷ⌝·
⌜ὁ βασιλεὺς τῶν Ἰουδαίων οὗτος⌝.
39 Εἷς δὲ τῶν ᵒκρεμασθέντων κακούργων ἐβλασφήμει αὐτὸν ᵒ¹λέγων· ᵒγοὐχὶ σὺ εἶ ὁ χριστός; σῶσον σεαυτὸν καὶ ἡμᾶς.⌝ 40 ἀποκριθεὶς δὲ ὁ ἕτερος ἐπιτιμῶν αὐτῷ ἔφη· οὐδὲ φοβῇ σὺ τὸν θεόν, ὅτι ἐν τῷ αὐτῷ κρίματι ⌜εἶ; 41 καὶ ἡμεῖς μὲν δικαίως, ἄξια γὰρ ὧν ἐπράξαμεν ἀπολαμβάνομεν· οὗτος δὲ οὐδὲν ⌜ἄτοπον ἔπραξεν. 42 καὶ ⌜ἔλεγεν· Ἰησοῦ, μνήσθητί μου ὅταν ἔλθῃς εἰς τὴν βασιλείαν σου. 43 καὶ εἶπεν αὐτῷ· ἀμήν σοι λέγω⌝, σήμερον μετ' ἐμοῦ ἔσῃ ἐν τῷ παραδείσῳ.
44 ⌜Καὶ ἦν⌝ ᵒἤδη ὡσεὶ ὥρα ἕκτη καὶ σκότος ἐγένετο ἐφ' ὅλην τὴν γῆν ἕως ὥρας ἐνάτης 45 ⌜τοῦ ἡλίου ἐκλιπόντος⌝, * ⬜ἐσχίσθη δὲ τὸ καταπέτασμα τοῦ ναοῦ μέσον.⌝ 46 <u>καὶ φωνήσας φωνῇ μεγάλῃ ὁ Ἰησοῦς εἶπεν</u>· πάτερ, εἰς χεῖράς σου ⌜παρατίθεμαι τὸ πνεῦμά μου. τοῦτο <u>δὲ εἰπὼν ἐξέπνευσεν.</u> ᵀ
47 ⌜Ἰδὼν <u>δὲ ὁ ἑκατοντάρχης τὸ γενόμενον⌝</u> ⌜ἐδόξαζεν τὸν θεὸν λέγων· ὄντως ὁ ἄνθρωπος οὗτος δίκαιος ἦν. 48 καὶ πάντες οἱ συμπαραγενόμενοι ὄχλοι ἐπὶ τὴν θεωρίαν ταύτην, θεωρήσαντες τὰ γενόμενα, τύπτοντες τὰ στήθη ᵀ ὑπέστρεφον ᵀ.

49 Είστήκεισαν δὲ πάντες οἱ γνωστοὶ ⌜αὐτῷ ᵒἀπὸ μακρόθεν καὶ ᵀ γυναῖκες ᵒ¹αἱ συνακολουθοῦσαι αὐτῷ ἀπὸ τῆς Γαλιλαίας ὁρῶσαι ταῦτα.

50 Καὶ ἰδοὺ ἀνὴρ ὀνόματι Ἰωσὴφ βουλευτὴς ὑπάρχων ⌜[καὶ] ἀνὴρ⌝ ἀγαθὸς ᵒκαὶ δίκαιος 51 – οὗτος οὐκ ἦν ⌜συγκατατεθειμένος τῇ βουλῇ καὶ τῇ πράξει αὐτῶν – ἀπὸ ꜰἈριμαθαίας πόλεως τῶν Ἰουδαίων, ὃς ⌜¹προσεδέχετο τὴν βασιλείαν τοῦ θεοῦ, 52 οὗτος προσελθὼν τῷ Πιλάτῳ ᾐτήσατο τὸ σῶμα τοῦ Ἰησοῦ ᵀ 53 καὶ καθελὼν ⌜ἐνετύλιξεν αὐτὸ⌝ σινδόνι καὶ ἔθηκεν ⌜αὐτὸν ἐν ⌜μνήματι λαξευτῷ⌝ οὗ οὐκ ἦν οὐδεὶς ꜰοὔπω κείμενος ᵀ. 54 ⌜καὶ ἡμέρα ἦν παρασκευῆς καὶ σάββατον ἐπέφωσκεν⌝.

55 Κατακολουθήσασαι δὲ ⌜αἱ γυναῖκες, αἵτινες ἦσαν συνεληλυθυῖαι ἐκ τῆς Γαλιλαίας ⌐αὐτῷ, ἐθεάσαντο τὸ ⌜μνημεῖον καὶ ὡς ἐτέθη τὸ σῶμα⌝ αὐτοῦ, 56 ὑποστρέψασαι δὲ ἡτοίμασαν ἀρώματα καὶ μύρα. καὶ τὸ μὲν σάββατον ἡσύχασαν ▫κατὰ τὴν ἐντολήν⌝.

Index of Passages

1. Old Testament

Genesis
3:19	167
8:1	202
19:15	57
22:2	149
3	57
6	295
23:7	57
24:10	57
31:30	32
37–42	169
41:9	202
47:29–50:14	52

Exodus
5:4	78
12	190
12:1–10	204
21	69
23:13	200, 202
15	25
24:8	194, 195, 196
30:25	228
34:18	25

Leviticus
10:3	260
24:7	202

Numbers
5:15	203
10:9	202
10	202
11:4	32

Deuteronomy
15:11	231
16:16	25
19:15–20	281
21:22–23	95, 164

Joshua
23:1–24:32	52

Judges
16:23–31	167

Ruth
3:3	111

1 Samuel
12	52
31:1–16	167

2 Samuel
5:2	250
7	280
7:5–16	279
5	279
11	279
13	279, 281
16	279
14:14	167
22:5	152
20:24	202
23:1	279
5	279

1 Kings
2:1–9	52
10	167
3:1	202
4:3	202
11:43	167
14:27	98
15:8	167
17:18	203

2 Kings
12:20	111
18:18	202
37	202

1 Chronicles
10:13–14	167
28:1–29:28	52

2 Chronicles
5:6	50
8:13	25
10:19	121
12:10	98
24:20–22	167
30:13	25
21	25
22	25
35:17	25

Index of Passages

Nehemiah
9:17 — 203
26 — 151, 167

Esther — 169

Job
24:20 — 202

Psalms
2:1–2 — 81
2 — 93
6:3–4 — 256
4 — 256
5 — 256
10:8 — 225
15 — 239
22 — 305
22:1 — 97–98, 303, 304, 305, 306
7–8 — 302
7 — 90, 92, 291, 301
8 — 22
18 — 92, 298, 315
23 — 245
24 — 257
23:5 — 152
27:12 — 276
31:5 — 97–99, 304, 305
11–12 — 269
13 — 224–225
14–17 — 239
17–18 — 239
18 — 276
35:11 — 276
15–16 — 291
20–21 — 281–282
20 — 276
21 — 301
22–26 — 317
37:32 — 225, 276
33–34 — 239
35–36 — 239
38:1 — 202
11 — 269, 271
12 — 265
13–14 — 287
19 — 287
40:15 — 301
41 — 122, 230, 240
41:2–3 — 230, 231
5–10 — 231
6 — 256, 265
7 — 123
9 — 113, 117, 120–122, 124, 231, 233, 237, 238–239, 243
10 — 239
42 — 256
42:5 — 22, 256
6 — 237, 256
7 — 152
10 — 302
11 — 256
43:2 — 233
5 — 256
45:17 — 200
52:3–6 — 233
54:5–6 — 256
55:12–14 — 233
20–21 — 233
60:3 — 256
69:2–3 — 152
9 — 269
21 — 22, 94, 303
25 — 239
70:1 — 202
3 — 301
71:10 — 225
12–13 — 239
75:8 — 151
86:14 — 225
88:8 — 269
89:13 — 98
92:4 — 98
101:1 — 256
102:8 — 291
25 — 98
105:14 — 32
109:2–5 — 233
3 — 289
14 — 203
110:1 — 75, 282
111:17 — 98
115:1 — 256
116:13 — 152
118 — 246
118:22–23 — 153
119:73 — 98
132:2 — 228
17 — 279
142:4 — 256

Proverbs
31:6 — 91

Song of Songs
2:7 — 88
3:5 — 88
10 — 88
5:8 — 88
9 — 88
16 — 88
17 — 88
8:4 — 88

Isaiah
4:2 — 279
13–14 — 93
25:6–9 — 33
32:12 — 33
35:10 — 55
40:29 — 55

42:1	93, 149	33:13–16	203
43:2	152	34:23	250
49:4	263	37:22	250
50:4–7	263	24	250
6	66, 68, 282, 290–291, 292	*Daniel*	
51:1	55	3	169
17	152	3:13	172
22	152	6	169
52:13–53:12	93, 169, 196, 239, 240, 263, 289–290, 309	7:13	73, 74
13–15	309	*Hosea*	
13	289	10:8	88, 89
53	196, 197, 207, 231, 240		
53:5	279–280	*Joel*	
6	250, 289, 290	1:14	57
7	71, 79, 276, 287		
8	84, 150	*Amos*	
9	230	5:25–27	83
10–12	309	6:6	228
11	290	10	200
11–12	283, 301	8:9	299
12	50–52, 91, 196, 197, 207, 252, 289, 290, 301	*Jonah*	
		3:8	57
65:13	33	*Micah*	
		4:8	88
Jeremiah		5:4	250
2:30	151		
3:15	250	*Zephaniah*	
4:16	202	3:14	88
12:6	233		
20:10	233	*Zechariah*	
23:1–6	250	3:8	279
5–6	279	6:12–13	279
25:15–38	152	9–14	248
26:20–23	167	9:9	88
31:31–34	194	11	196
33:15–16	279	11:12	232
52:1	88	12:10–14	88
		13	253, 319
Ezekiel		13:7–9	251
21:23	203	7	247, 249, 250, 253, 269, 270
24	203		
23:31–34	152	8–9	251
29:16	203		

2. New Testament

Matthew		28	32
3:17	33	41	87
4:12	289	6:9	260
24	67	10	34, 56, 260
25	30	13	260
5:1	30	17	111
12	80	26	65
25	289	7:28	21

32	87	15	22, 124
8:3	60	16	21, 232
15	60	17–20	22
9:9	142	17–19	234–235
15	150	17	113
20	60	18	234
21	60	20–25	235–240
22	64	21	122, 123
29	60	22	44, 123, 237
10:16	62	23	44, 124, 237
17	289	24–25	23
32	47	25	22, 44, 237
33	47	26–29	241–243
34–36	52	26	117, 193
38	89	27	21
11:1	21	28	22, 193
17	89	29	47, 193, 197
26	85	30	244–246
27	47	31–35	23
12:25–26	34	31–32	246–251
45	233	31	22
50	47	33–35	251–252
13:21	47	33	123
53	21	36–46	253–263
14:13	53	37	22, 256
16:17–19	48–49	38	22
18	85	39	47, 260
21	146	42	21, 56, 260
23	64	47–50	264–266
17:7	78	47	59
18:6–7	238	50	59, 264, 265
7	44	51–54	266–267
13	80	51	21, 55, 59, 266, 267
19:1	21	52–54	22, 60, 267
26	65	52	60, 267
27	47	55–56	267–268
28	46–48	55	22
20:18	76	56	268–270
28	165	57–27:2	271
34	60	57	272–275
21:5	89	58	272
22:4	49	59–68	20
8	49	59–66	275–282
16	142	61	276, 277
24:3	96	62	276
9–12	259	63	72
34	34	64	34, 73
38	117	65	22
42–43	259	66	21
44	49	67–68	282
25:13	259	67	67
31–46	170	68	68
26–27	24	69–75	21, 23
26:1–5	223–225	71	63
1	21, 106	75	65
2	20, 113	27:1–2	285
3–4	223, 224	1	20, 22
3	22, 129, 272	3–10	22, 23, 102, 183, 285
6–13	106–111, 225–231	3	76
14–35	111–125	11–14	285–287
14–16	231–233	11	22, 286
14–15	21	12	287

2. New Testament

14	287	30	139
15–26	287–290	31	60, 139
19	22, 287	32	139
21	22, 84	33	139
24–25	22	34	139
27–31	290–291	35	69, 139, 245, 252
27	285	36	139
30	291	37	87, 139
31–32	293–297	38	91, 139
33–36	297–299	39	139
34	22, 303	40	73, 139
36	22	41	60, 139
37	22, 299–300	42	139
38–44	300–302	43	139
43	22, 302	44	83, 139
45–54	302–309	45	139, 252
45	97	2:1–3:6	152
46	305	2:1–3:5	141, 150
50	97	1	245
51–53	22, 97	3	87
55–56	309–310	4	83
55	272	6	91, 266
60	101	14	142
62–66	22, 183	15	53, 261
28:19–20	180	19–20	149–150, 154, 165, 229
		20	149, 150, 252
Mark		3	30
1–13	11, 15, 16, 23, 136, 142, 147, 148–156, 158, 163, 171	3:1	91, 245
		6	141–142, 150, 153, 154
1:1	72, 139, 141	7	53
2	139	7ff.	30
3	139	9	67, 144
4	139	10	60
5	139	11	85, 141
6	139	13	85, 144
7	139	16–19	142
8	139	17	143
9–11	149, 257	20–35	126
9	139	20	144
10	139, 308	21	143
11	139, 149, 153	23	125
12	139	24–25	73
13	125, 139, 143	25–26	34
14	139, 247	28	73
15	139	32	143
16–17	144	33	268
16	139, 261	34	143
17	139	4:1	144
18	53, 139	7	62
19	139	8	87
20	139	15	125
21–28	141	17	47
21	139	5:1	245
22	139, 261	6–7	84
23	84, 139	6	272, 308
24	139, 141	7	304
25	139	11	91, 252
26	139, 304	13	233
27	139	21–43	126
28	139, 252	22	266
29	139, 144		

24	53	27–30	151
27	60, 87	27	245
28	60, 73	28	266
30	60	29	268
31	60	31–33	49
37	101, 255	31	60, 145–146, 151, 154, 155, 165, 183, 248
41	143		
42	261		
6:1	53	32–33	151
3	143, 252	32	302
4	150–151, 153	33	125
5	91	34	53, 89, 146, 295
6–13	145	35	73
7–11	145	36	228
7	83, 145	38	73
8–11	145	9:1	74, 266
10	73, 91	2–13	13
12–13	145	2	252, 255
12	145	5	268
13	145	6	151
14–29	151, 155	9–13	154
15	266	9–12	155
17	60	10	151
20	151	11–13	151
22–23	73	12–15	154, 155
25	252	14–29	145
26	151	15	145
27–28	87	17–18	145
29	151, 155	17	87, 145
31	261	18	73
32	245	19	87, 268
33	91	20–22	145
34–44	284	20	87, 145
37	268	25	145, 233
45	144	27	60
46	245	30–35	13
47–52	144	31	145, 151, 154, 155, 165, 183, 248, 261, 289
48	261		
53	144, 245		
56	60	32	151
7:1	266	33–37	143
2	266	33	245
4	179	37	266
11	73, 143	38–39	78
21	252	42	238, 266
24	144	43	73
31	144, 245	45	73
32–37	284	47	73
32	87, 89	50	73
33	60	10:1	13
34	143	3	268
8–10	154	4	78
8	146	12	73
8:1–9	284	13	83
3	73, 266, 272, 308	21	65
4	252	22	261
10	245	24	268
13	245	27	65
22–26	284	28–30	144
22	60, 87	30	252
25	65	32–34	13, 151
27–33	13	32	53, 151

2. New Testament

33–34	145, 151, 154, 155, 165, 183, 248, 289	4	96
33	76, 285	9–13	259
34	67, 151	9	259
35–40	151, 154, 155	10	228
37	266	11	73
38–39	151–152, 154	13	52
38	165, 250	21	73, 91
41–45	36, 44–46	30	34
45	3, 37, 45, 152, 154, 165, 207	33	259
		34	259
46–52	13	35	259
46	142–143	37	54, 148, 152, 259
47–51	143	14–16	11, 12, 13, 14, 15, 16, 23, 136, 142, 148–156, 163
48	85		
51	268	14–15	5, 15, 24, 138, 147, 160, 162, 163, 216, 217
11–13	14		
11:1–23	13		
1–6	284	14	37, 149, 155
1	245	14:1–42	12
2	87	1–25	230–231
3	73	1–11	126, 226
4	252	1–2	25–26, 129, 153, 154, 171, 223–225, 226
5	91, 266		
7	87	1	20, 60, 106, 113, 153, 154, 226
9	53, 81		
11–17	71	2	27, 153, 155
11	245	3–9	26, 106–111, 130, 161, 171, 225–231
13	272, 308		
14	268	4–7	231
15–18	152, 171	7	227, 229, 230
17	43, 89	8–9	227–228
18	152–153, 154, 155	8	154, 227, 229, 230, 231
21	65, 202		
22	268	9	73, 110, 227, 228, 231
27–33	13		
27	153, 154	10–31	111–125
31	73	10–11	21, 26–27, 154, 171, 225, 226, 231–233, 235
33	153, 268		
12	153	10	235, 266
12:1–17	13	11	21, 80, 113
1–12	153, 165	12–52	171
3	67	12–16	27–28, 35, 171, 173, 230, 234–235, 243, 284
5	67		
6	153		
10	65, 153, 154, 155	12	31, 235
12	60, 153, 154, 155	13–16	13
13	141–142, 266	13	235
15–18	278	14	31, 73, 235
15	87	15	49, 81, 244
16	87	16	116, 235, 248
19	73	17–31	173
28	266	17–21	172, 235–240
34–37	13	17–18	28, 237
35	268	17	28–42, 235
41–44	13	18–25	43
42	143	18–21	43–44
13	149, 259	18	120–122, 123, 154, 231, 235, 237, 261
13:1–2	13		
1	266	19–20	44, 237
2	223, 278	19	123
3	245, 255		

Index of Passages

20	122, 124, 235, 237, 238, 266	51	101, 269
21	43, 154, 155, 238, 239, 261, 289	53–72	125–127, 132
		53–64	61–66
22–25	13, 28–42, 235, 238, 241–243	53–54	60
		53	13, 68–76, 126, 155, 172, 272–275
22–24	36, 38, 41, 154, 172, 207–209	54	13, 126, 127, 173, 271, 272, 308, 310
22	117, 193, 235	55–65	126, 172
23	21, 31, 34	55–64	68–76, 275–282
24	3, 36, 41, 193, 196	55–61	276, 281
25	31, 33, 42, 154, 155, 172, 193, 242, 243	55–56	126, 282
		58	146, 276, 277
26–31	48–50, 247, 255, 271	59	282
26–27	13	60	270
26	53–58, 244–246, 255	61–64	155
27–31	247, 248	61–62	276
27–28	246–251	63	282
27	48, 154, 172, 245, 247, 248, 249, 269, 270	64	21, 281
		65–72	171
28	48, 154, 155, 172, 247, 248, 251	65	66–68, 282
		66–72	13, 61–66, 126, 173, 271
29–31	13, 251–252	66–67	126
29	48, 123, 247, 249, 252	66	266
30	48, 252	67	65, 127
31	48, 73, 247	68	245
32–16:8	13	72	202, 203
32–42	53–58, 154, 155, 172, 253–263	15	12, 156, 283, 309
		15:1–5	77–79, 132, 172
32	13, 244, 255	1–2	284
33	22, 255, 256	1	13, 68–76, 155, 284, 285
34–36	13		
34	256, 257, 259	2–15	155
35–36	260	2–5	285–287
35	59, 261	2	172, 268, 284, 286
36	152, 260, 261	3–11	13
37–38	258	3–5	77, 284
37	13, 257	3	155
38–40	13	5	287
38	257, 258	6–15	82–86, 132, 287–290
39	21	6	284, 288
40	261	7–8	284
41–42	154, 261–262	7	288
41	13, 56, 261, 263, 289	9	284
42	43, 261, 262	10	284
43–53	58–61	11–15	284
43–52	132, 264	11	79
43–49	154	12	268
43–46	264–266	13	146
43	13, 266, 268	14	146, 151, 287, 288
44	266	15–20	132
46–49	266	15	13, 87, 146, 151, 284, 285, 288
46	13, 266		
47	266–267	16–20	68, 87, 155, 172, 284, 285, 290–291
48–50	13		
48–49	267–268	16	83, 143, 285
48	89, 266, 268	19	291
49	155, 268, 270	20–21	86–90, 293–297
50–52	268–270	20	146, 294
50	57–58, 154, 268, 269, 270	21–25	171
51–52	22, 269–270	21–24	173

2. New Testament

21–22	132	16:2	266
21	146, 269, 272, 293, 294, 295	4	261
		6	146, 155
22–32	90–94	7	91
22–25	297–299	8	247
22–24	13	14	228
22	87, 294		
23	132, 294, 303	*Luke*	
24	132, 146, 294	1–2	71
25	132, 146, 294, 298, 309	1:2	101
		4	178
26	132, 172, 284, 286, 294, 299–300	5	89
		9	53
		11	57
27–32	300–302	13	32
27–28	171	14	81
27	13, 89, 132, 146, 294, 297	18	32
		20	57
28	294, 301	22	47
29–34	132	26	57
29–32	172	28	81
29–30	301	31–32	72
29	13, 146, 223, 277, 294, 301	34	32
		35	141
30	94, 146, 294	48	34
31	13, 67, 294	50	94
32	13, 94–95, 146, 294	57	81
33–39	96, 302–309	63	85
33–38	95–99	68	57
33–36	172	77	92
33–34	309	2:6	91
33	171, 294, 299	9	57
34–37	13	13	57
34	143, 154, 294, 303, 304, 305, 306	15	57
		17	59
35–36	305, 306	20	99
35	171, 266, 294	21	32
36	90–94, 132, 294, 303, 305	23	43
		25	101
37–39	306	42	53
37	99, 132, 172, 294, 303, 304, 306, 307, 308	49	47
		3:2	272, 273
38–39	132, 172, 306–309	4	43
38	294, 306, 307, 308, 309	8	33
		13	83
39–41	99–101	14	46
39	141, 294, 306, 307, 308, 309	17	69
		18	68
40–47	171, 173	19–20	60
40–41	13, 132, 309–310	22	57
40	143, 272, 294, 308, 310	4:2	125
		3	46
41	53, 294	4	32, 43
42–16:8	311	5	81
42–16:1	101–102	8	43
42–47	151, 311	13	47, 54
42–46	155	21	32
42–43	132	23	93
42	13, 101, 143, 311, 312	33	84
43–47	13	34	141
44–45	132	36	32
44	313	38	67
46	132		

39	60	8	87
40	87	11	74
41	72, 85	12	125
42	43, 68	13	47, 54, 99
43	63, 74	19–21	29
5:1	85	21	47
8	59, 63	25	46
10	34, 39	27	81
11	53	28	59, 84
12	59	29	81
13	60	30	233
14	83	31	91
18	87	32–33	233
19	83	34	59
22	32	37	67, 77
24	43	39	74
25–26	99	44	60, 64, 87
25	64	45	32, 60, 67
26	74	46	60
27	46, 53	47	59, 60
28	53	48	43, 46
33	39	52	89
35	150	55	64
6:6	63, 91	9:1	83
8	57	3	32
10	46	4	91
12–19	30	7–9	286
12–16	29	11	53
12	74	12	43
13	69, 85	16	211
16	27	20	46, 74, 93
17ff.	30	22	60, 69, 146
17–21	29	23	53, 87, 89, 185
17	29	27	33, 74
19	60	28	54, 255
23	80	29	63
29	78	35	93
30	85	38–40	87
35	43	41	78, 87
39	46	42	60, 87
7:5	78	44	77
6	43, 96	46	46
9	53, 64	48	46
13	46	49–50	78
14	60	49	53
16	99	51	43
22	43, 46	54	57, 59
30	34	55	64
32	85	57	53
36–50	26, 106–111, 160, 225	59	53
38	59, 111	61	53
39	59, 68, 266	10:3	62
44–46	229	9	34
44	64	11	34, 43
45	59	18	57, 125
47–50	92	20	81, 98
8:1–3	29–30	22	47
1	30	23	64
2–3	101	24	33
3	68, 286	26	91
6	63	32	39
7	62, 63	38–42	176

2. New Testament

11:2	34, 98	17	34
4	47	18	57
5	32	20	57
9	85	21	57
10	85	32	81
11	85	16:18	63
12	85	23	272
13	85	17:1−2	44, 238
17−18	34	1	44, 238
18	125	5	32
20	34	8	34
23	69	15	99
26	43, 91	20	34
38	32	21	91
41	43	22	32
44	57	23	91
49−51	87	29	57
51	33	34	63
52	78	35	63
12:8	47, 57	37	91
9	47, 57	18:2	94
11	57	4	81
17−18	69	15	59, 83
18	91	16	78
20	85	22	53, 65
31−33	286	23	55
31	43	27	65
34	91	28	53
37	119, 120, 259	32	67, 76, 77
40	49	39	85
47−48	67, 92	43	53, 64, 74, 99
48	85	19:3	57
50	34, 67	6	81
51−53	52	7	81
52	34	9	100
58	77, 289	11	34
13:1−5	87, 88	20	63
8	34	23	83
12	59, 85	27	43
13	99	30	87
16	89, 125	35	87
17	81	37	77, 96
22	43	41−44	74, 87
34−35	87	41	88
34	88	43	67
35	71	44	88
14:1	83	45−46	71
17	49, 96	46	43, 89
18	79	47	69
24	33	20:1−8	73
25	64	1	69
27	87, 89, 185, 296	9	81
29	67	10−11	67
15:1−2	211	11	63
4	43	17	65
5	80	19	60
6	83	20−26	73
9	83	20	77
10	57	22	78
11−32	92	24	87
13	69, 91	27−40	73
15	87	31	39

Index of Passages

34	32	23	45, 83, 123, 124, 238
21:2	91	24–30	241–243
5–7	96	24–27	36, 37, 44–46, 242
8	87, 89	24	45
11	57	25	54
12	60, 67, 77, 289	26	77
16	77	27	45, 112, 119, 120
20–24	87	28–30	46–48, 52, 241
23	88	28	54, 55, 58
26	57	29–30	47
27	74	29	32
30	96	30	48
32	34	31–34	48–50, 52, 244, 251–252
34–36	177		
36	54, 85, 259	31–33	251
37–38	68	31–32	48, 49
37	53, 255	31	54, 57, 58, 123, 125, 251
22–23	24, 102		
22:1–2	25–26, 223–225	32	251
1	59, 91, 113, 188	33	43, 48, 49, 65, 251
2	27, 44, 60	34	48, 50, 64, 65, 251
3–30	111–125	35–38	50–52, 252
3–6	26–27, 231–233	35	27
3	26, 27, 43, 54, 58, 59, 123, 124, 125, 232	37	33, 50, 51, 52, 89, 95, 252, 301
4	27, 60, 77	39–46	53–58, 103, 253–263
5	80	39	48, 53, 89, 91, 131, 244, 255
6	77		
7–13	18, 27–28, 45, 103, 234–235	40–44	58
		40	47, 58, 257
7	113	41	59
8	43, 116, 123	42	47, 53, 98, 260, 261
10	53	43–44	53, 103, 256, 257
12	49, 91	45	58
13	116	46	47, 53, 58, 257
14–24:53	29	47–54	58–61
14–30	48	47–48	264–266
14–20	28–42, 241–243	47	25
14	28, 42, 104, 114, 115, 116, 235–240	48	77, 264, 265
		49–51	266–267
15–30	47	49	60, 267
15–20	28, 47	50	18, 58, 267
15–18	28, 30–35, 42, 188, 193, 197, 242	51	267
		52–53	267–268
15	31–32, 38, 42, 60, 75, 79, 83, 85	52	18, 27, 58, 69, 89, 264–266
16	31–34, 38, 42, 47, 49, 243	53	56, 58, 125
		54–62	61–66
17	31–35, 36, 37, 38, 42, 95, 120	54	53, 58, 77, 264–266, 271, 272–275
18	31–34, 38, 42, 47, 243	56	65
19–20	28, 30, 35–42, 201	57	49
19	37, 38, 39, 41, 42, 117, 193, 198, 211, 212	58	84, 85
		59	64, 99
20	37, 38, 39, 41, 42, 115, 193, 237	60–62	67
		61	49, 61, 64, 67, 89
21–34	52	63–65	66–68, 282
21–23	43–44, 235–240	63–64	68
21–22	77	64	68
21	37, 89, 124, 237	65	68, 79
22	43, 53, 238	66–71	68–76, 275–282
		66	76, 87, 272–275

2. New Testament

67–68	274	43	95
69	34	44–48	96, 302–309
71	282	44–46	95–99
23	78, 81, 213	44–45	18
23:1–25	77	44	92
1–5	77–79	45	71
1	79, 129, 285	46	98
2–5	285–287	47–49	99–101
2	77, 79, 83, 223, 286	47	101, 309
3	18, 77, 79, 285	48	26, 88, 92, 101, 309
4–5	84	49	99, 101, 102, 272, 309–310
4	77, 79, 82, 85, 100, 287	50–56	101–102
5	77, 79, 83, 129, 223	50–55	103
6–16	82, 85	50–54	101, 102
6–12	80–82, 285–287	50–53	185
7	81, 83, 88	50–51	101
8	81	52	85
9	71, 287	53	101
11	67, 68, 81, 83, 290–291	54	101
13–25	82–86	55–56	101, 102
13–16	82, 86, 285–287	56	102
13	26, 93	24:7	77, 185
14–15	82, 287	13–53	48
14	79, 94, 100, 223	20	77, 83
15	81, 82, 95	27	79
16	288	30	211
17–25	82	34	99
17	86	36	62
18–25	287–290	39	298
18	26	41	57
19	288	46	32
21	26, 185	47	79
22	79, 100, 287, 288	49	47
23	26, 185	51	64
24	297		
25	87	*John*	
26–32	86–90	1:41	110
26–31	293–297	51	124
26	90, 91, 185, 293	2:4	114, 261
27–32	90	6	189
27–31	87, 90, 293, 297	9	274
27	53	13	188
28	64, 85	19	277
32–33	95	3:2	224
32	87, 90, 91, 95, 300–302	4:25–26	110
		48	224
33–38	90–94	5:1	189
33–34	297–299	7	123
33	54, 87, 89, 185, 297, 300–302	19	124
		24	124
		25	124
34	34, 317	6	117, 118, 121
35–39	72	6:2	53
35	67, 83, 101, 300–302	4	188
36–37	301	22	113
36	67, 83, 302–309	26	124
37	300–302	31	118
38	286, 299–300	32	124
39–43	94–95, 300–302	39	268
39	89, 94	47	124
41	83	48–58	116–119, 213

49	118	6	111, 232
51	207	7–8	130
53	124	7	227, 229, 230
54	117	8	111
56	117	15	89
57	117	17	131
58	117	23–26	113
69	141	23–24	165
70–71	226, 231–233	23	114, 131, 261
71	123	27–29	257
7:2	189	27–28	253–263
3	132	27	114, 123, 131, 256, 260, 261
6	114	28	260
8	114	29	257
9	123	37	224
30	114, 261	13	110, 111, 123
31–32	224	13:1–38	133
33–34	131	1–30	30, 111–125, 130
37–39	303	1–20	112–123
44	132	1–17	42, 43, 45, 241
8:20	114, 132, 261	1–3	114, 119
21	131	1	113, 116, 131, 234–235, 261
9:4	125	2–17	241–243
6	123	2	27, 111, 112, 114, 115, 124, 125, 231–233
16	224	3	113, 116
22	110	4–17	119
10:18	303	4	111, 115
22–39	127, 275–282	5	111, 120
24–39	282	6–20	119
24–26	274	6	111
24	72, 274	8	111
25–26	282	10–11	112
25	73	10	111
33	274	12	111
36	274	14	111
11–20	134	15	131
11	128, 226	18–30	43, 235–240
11:2	111	18–20	112
10	125	18–19	238
27	110	18	117, 120–122, 237
33	123	20	237
43	123	21–30	112, 123–125
45–13:38	134	21	122, 123, 237
45–47	129	22–30	237
45–46	129	22	123, 124, 238
47–57	223–225	23–30	44
47–53	273	23–25	124
47	223, 224	23–24	115
48	129	23	112, 124
49–52	129	24	123
49–50	224	25	115, 123
49	272	26	27, 112, 124, 238
50	268	27	27, 114, 123, 124, 231–232
51–52	224	28–30	125
55–57	129	29	111
55	188	31–38	130–131
12	111, 128	31–33	131
12:1–11	130		
1–8	106–111, 225–231		
2	111, 119		
3	111		
5	111		

2. New Testament

31	131	25–27	126
32	131	25	63, 64, 126, 127
33	131	27	65
34–35	131	28–38	132
36–38	48, 244, 247, 251–	28	272, 273, 274, 285
	252	29–38	285–287
36	131	33	286
37–38	131	34–38	287
37	49	36–37	286
38	49	37	286
14–17	131	38–40	132
14:1–16:32	128	38	79, 100, 287
1	123	39–19:1	287–290
2–3	241	39	288
17–26	241–243	40	84, 288
27	123	19:1–16	132
31	253–263	1–12	84
15:12–13	113	1	288, 291
12	131	2–3	290–291
13	129, 152	3	291
18–21	52	4–15	285–287
16:1–4	52	4	79, 100, 287
1	246–251	6	79, 85, 100, 287
32–33	246–251	9	287
32	248, 249	12–15	77
33	52, 248, 251	12	129, 233, 287
17	112	14	113, 298, 299
17:1–26	128	15	84
1	114, 261	16	287–290
12	120, 268	17	132, 293–299
18:1–19:42	131–133, 134	18	91, 132, 297, 300–302
1–12	131–132	19–22	132, 286, 299–300
1–2	253–263	23–25	297–299
1	123, 244	23–24	132
2–6	264–266	24	92, 120
2–3	232	25–27	132, 309–310
2	53, 131, 132, 255, 265	28–30	132, 302–309
3	231–233, 273	29	303
4–9	132	30	97, 132, 304
4–6	265	31–37	132
4	83	31	185
5	83	38–42	109, 132
6	132	41	101
7–9	268–270	20:21–22	303
8	249	25	298
9	268, 270	31	110
10–11	266–267	21:15–19	49
10	60, 267	15–17	251
11	60, 131, 253–263, 267		
12	60, 264–266, 273	*Acts*	
13–27	125–127, 132	1–5	71
13–14	126, 272–275	1:3	32
13	272, 273	9	150
14	224, 272	13	30
15–18	126	16–20	102
15–16	269	16	265
18	62, 126, 127	18–19	285
19–24	126	20	239
19–23	273	22	79
20	267–268	2:2–3	57
24	272–275	23–24	161
		23	43, 184–185, 285, 299

34–36	75	26	57
36	185	32–33	276
37	63	33	84
38	92, 100	35	79
40	68	39	81
42	180, 211	52	57
46	190, 191, 211	9:7	67
47	210	18	57
3	213	19	57, 206
3:1	190	20–22	72
2	25	31	79
13–26	100	36	25
13–15	161	40	57
13–14	184	10:2	94, 101
13	77, 100, 285, 289–290	3	57
14	141, 290	22	78
17	83, 92	24	83
18	32, 290	37	79
19	92, 100	38	46
25	47	39	95
26	100	42	43
4:5	70, 83	43	92
6	272, 273	11:16	65
8	83	18	99
9	46	21	27
10	185	23	81
15	70	24	101
17	32	25–26	206–207
21	99	12:3–4	188
24–28	81–82, 86	4	289
25–27	81	5	57
27	81, 141	6	57
30	141	7	57
5:19	57	15	64
21	69, 70, 83	18	69
27	70, 72	23	57
30–31	100	13	213
30	95	13:1	286
31	92	8	78
34	70	10	78
41	70, 81	13–14	99
6–7	308	26	94
6:3	101	27–30	161
5	101	27–29	184–185
7	27	27–28	76
8	101	27	76, 83, 92, 185
9	25	28	161, 285
11–14	71	29	76, 95, 185, 313
12	70	36	57
14	277	38	92
15	70	48	81, 99
7:17	32	14:3	81
22	83	16	92
30	57	15:10	87
42	83	23	81
44–50	71	28	87
57	67	31	81
59	98	35	68
60	56, 57, 92	16:5	27
8:3	289	25	245
11	81	28	96
18	83	35	69

2. New Testament

17:3	32	35	208, 211
6–7	77–78	39	69
30	92, 100	28:8	67
31	43	17	77, 83, 289
18:5	67	19	78
6	34		
25	178, 180	*Romans*	
19:17	67	2:18	178
20:6	188	3:25–26	166
7	211	25	189
17–38	52	4:25	3, 166, 248
21	100, 258	5:6	3
28	37, 40	8	3
30	55, 78, 87, 89	8:32–34	166
33	32	32	3, 295
36	56	9:2	55
21:1	55	12–13	177
5	56	13:11	177
11	77, 289	14:5–12	189
20	99	15:4	186
21	178		
24	178	*1 Corinthians*	
26	83	1:18	164
28	77	23	164
36	84	3:1–3	180
22:3	83	6–8	180
4	289	4:16–17	203
5	69	5:6–8	42
11	65	7	35, 166, 189, 299
22	84	7:35	176
30	70	9:5	144
46	57	10–11	130
23:1	70	10	40, 205
6	70	10:1–13	206
7	77	1–10	118
12	69	1	118
14	32	5	118
15	70	9	118
20	70	10	118
26	81	16–17	117
28	70	16	210, 211, 213
24:2–5	77	20–21	205
2	78	11	37, 40, 242
10	78	11:2	180, 206
20	70	17–34	204, 209
25–26	77	18	209
25:24	77	20–21	114
25	76	23–25	38–42, 103, 116, 161, 213
26	82		
26:4	78	23	125, 205, 206, 252, 289
7	57, 63		
9	92	24	36, 117, 193
18	58, 92	26	42, 197, 198, 200, 201, 205, 210
30	62		
27:1	289	27–29	117, 213
9	81, 188	29–30	206
11	77	30	205
20	85	14:19	179
23	57	26	209
28	64	15	258
29	69	15:3–5	10, 166, 183, 248, 270
33	69		

Index of Passages

3	3, 206
4	313
52	258
16:2	209
13	258

2 Corinthians

2:1	55
3	55
5:14–15	248
14	67
18–21	166
7:14–15	201
15	203

Galatians

1:3–4	166
4	3, 230
7	185
17	206
18	206
2:1	206
11	207
20–21	166
20	3, 230
21	3, 186
3:1	185–186
13–14	166
13	95, 164
4:10–11	189
6:6	178

Ephesians

2:6	62
3:3	186
5:2	230
25	230
6:13	177
18	177, 259

Philippians

2	119
2:15	78
27	55
4:6	86

Colossians

1:13	58
2:14	298
16–17	189
3:4	258
6	258
24	258
4:2	258
5	258

1 Thessalonians

1:9–10	177
	179–180
2:15	178
4:13–5:11	258
5:1–11	258
3	177
6	259
7	177
9–10	3, 166
10	258

2 Thessalonians

2:15	178

1 Timothy

1:12–17	52
2:6	166, 230
4:14	69
6:13	161, 181
20	52

2 Timothy

1:6	201, 203
2:9	89
3:1–9	52

Titus

2:14	230

Philemon

11	81

Hebrews

2:12	245
5:7	161, 181, 254, 256, 257, 260
6:1–2	179–180
1	179
9:10	179
10:3	203
32	203
12:11	55
13:17	259

James

5:8	177

1 Peter

1:13–19	42
22	57
2:19	55
23	161, 181, 276, 317
24	95
4:7	177, 259
19	98
5:8	259
9	259
10	259

2 Peter

1:12–15	52
3:3–12	52

1 John

2:20	141
5:15	86

Jude			6:16	88
4	186		16:15	258, 269
			18:10	272
Revelation			15	272
3:2	259		17	272
3	259		19:17	33
7	141			

3. Jewish Texts

a. Apocrypha and Pseudepigrapha

Apocalypse of Abraham			*2 Maccabees*	
30–31	93		4:47	86
			6:18–7:42	168
Assumption of Moses	52		7	169, 170
			7:1	172
2 Baruch			9	317
29:5–8	33		14	317
8	118		17	317
			19	317
1 Enoch			31	317
38	238		34–36	317
39:6–8	93		37–38	168
45	93		12:15	27
48:6–10	93			
49	93		*3 Maccabees*	169
51:52	93		4:2	86
62–63	93, 173			
62:14	33		*4 Maccabees*	
71:14	93		6:18	203
89:73	280		28–29	168
90:28–30	279			
28–29	280		*Martyrdom of Isaiah*	
37	280		3:11	232
94–104	239		5:1	232
2 Esdras/4 Ezra			*Psalms of Solomon*	
7:28	280		17:40	250
33–34	280			
9:38–10:28	280		*Sirach*	
38–10:4	149		3:15	203
10:19–22	280			
27	280		*Susanna*	169
13:26	280			
29	280		*Testaments of the*	
37–38	280		*Twelve Patriarchs*	52
39	280			
44	280		*Tobit*	
49	280		2:5	55
50	280		7:18	55
Jubilees	52		*Wisdom*	
			2–5	306
1 Maccabees			2	93, 169, 170, 173, 309
2:27–38	168		2:12–20	168
29–41	168		13	309
6:4	55		16	309
			17–20	172

18	302, 309	*1QS*	
20	276, 302	3.13–4.26	233
4–5	93, 169, 170, 173, 309		
4:18–5:14	168	*4QpNah*	
5:1–8	239	3–4.1.7–8	95
2	309		
4–5	309	*4QFlor*	
16:6–7	203	1.1–13	280

b. Targums

Targum of the Prophets
Isa 53:5   279–280
Zech 6:12–13   279

Targum Neofiti
Exod 16:15   118

Targum Onkelos
Exod 24:8   196

Targum Pseudo-Jonathan
Exod 24:8   196

11QTemple
64.6–13   95

d. Josephus

Antiquitates Judaicae
14.15.10   142
18.64   1
117–118   76

Bellum Judaicum
6.300–305   76

c. Dead Sea Scrolls

CD
19.5–9   250

1Q28b
3.25–26   195
5.21–22   195

1Q34
3.iii.5–6   195

1QapGen
20.10–11   32

1QH
3.13–18   152
5.23–24   121
8.32   256

1QHab
2.1–4   194–195

e. Philo

In Flaccum
6.36–39   290

De Posteritate Caini
61   95

De Somniis
2.213   95

De Specialibus Legibus
2.148   245
3.152   95

f. Rabbinic Literature

Sanhedrin
6.5   76
43   91

4. Early Christian Texts

Acts of John
94–96   246

Acts of Peter
2.3.7   65

Barnabas
7.3   296

Clement of Rome

1 Clement
16:13   50

2 Clement
17:1   177

4. Early Christian Texts

Didache	177

Diognetus
12.9   190

Eusebius

Historia Ecclesiastica
3.14.15   140
5.23–25   190
5.23.1   190
5.24.2   190
5.24.6   190
5.24.12   190
5.24.20   190

Gospel of Thomas
31   150
71   277

Gospel of Peter   17
1:1   81
3:6–9   290
4:13   302
5:19   304
6:21   298
7:25   100

Ignatius

Ephesians
20.2   205

Philadephians
4.1   117

Romans
7.3   117, 118

Smyrnaeans
7.1   117

Trallians
6.1–2   118

Tertullian

Adversus Marcionem
3.18.2   296
4.42.2   81
5.7.6   177

De Praescriptione Haereticorum
41   177

www.ingramcontent.com/pod-product-compliance
Lightning Source LLC
Chambersburg PA
CBHW070554300426
44113CB00011B/1910